HUMANITY @ WORK & LIFE

Global Diffusion of the Mondragon Cooperative Ecosystem Experience

Edited by

Christina A. Clamp & Michael A. Peck

Published by OAK TREE PRESS, Cork T12 XY2N
www.oaktreepress.com / www.SuccessStore.com

A catalogue record of this book is available from the British Library.

ISBN 978 1 78119 570 3 (Paperback)
ISBN 978 1 78119 543 7 (PDF)
ISBN 978 1 78119 544 4 (ePub)
ISBN 978 1 78119 545 1 (Kindle)

Cover design: Kevin O'Brien, Worx Printing Cooperative.
Cover image: Co-op Cincy and the Justseeds Artists' Cooperative.

Contents

Part 3: Mondragon's Global Influence

Mondragon has earned an outsized mission and values-based influence far beyond its regional home in Spain. Today, the group annually hosts between three and four million industrial tourism visitors (returning to pre-Covid levels) from all parts of the world through Otalora, Mondragon's Center for Management & Cooperative Development, housed in a rural mid-14th century manor. This section examines how Mondragon continues to inspire and catalyze local stakeholder ownership, creating and preserving good worker cooperative and union jobs in Preston, UK, Germany and in South Korea.

Part 4: Worker Ownership in America

The focus in this section is telling the stories of efforts around the USA generating new worker cooperative development influenced by global models for which Mondragon is baseline.

Part 5: Resource Challenges for New Worker Cooperative Development

In the United States, the infrastructure for developing new worker cooperatives has lagged behind large scale European Union social economy (reaching 10% of GNP in some countries) and solidarity taxonomy progress. Here, we have asked leaders in the US cooperative movement to reflect on what it will take to grow similar movement scale throughout the US.

Dedication

HUMANITY @ WORK & LIFE is dedicated to its founding 36 contributors from six countries on three continents inspired by decades of the Mondragon Cooperative Ecosystem Experience (MCE[2]); to those who will write tomorrow's living transformation chapters, reflections, and sidebars in a never-ending series of "ordinary people together accomplishing extraordinary things"; and to honor the cooperative legacy of Chuck Snyder, former US National Cooperative Bank President and CEO, who first introduced the two of us in the hope that we might embark on such a mission.

Chris & Michael

Contributors

Ahalbidetu

Ahalbidetu is a mentoring initiative (programs, culture and methodology) born out of the 2008-2009 economic crisis to help new college graduates fill in the gaps of traditional professional development and education. Its tools include strengthening each participant's ability to succeed in the workplace through learning by doing, sharing heartfelt success and compelling stories, and building a significant learning journey for all involved. Ahalbidetu was developed by Basque serial entrepreneurs and executives with extensive mentoring experience who were also managers of Iberdrola Diversification, in its day the leading utility diversification company in Europe and the platform that launched some of Spain's current domestic and global renewable energy champions. The Ahalbidetu mission and team emerged from lessons learned during an earlier UDES (University of Deusto, Enterprise & Society) one-to-one mentoring experience helping professionals throughout the Bilbao metropolitan region to become executives of the companies they worked for. The chapter (**Chapter 9**) authors:

- **José Miguel Martínez Urquijo** is an industrial engineer with a PhD from the University of Pais Vasco. He served as founding CEO of Iberdrola Diversification and was an Iberdrola Executive Committee member as well as Director of Iberdrola Industrial Group, Director of the Basque Government's (Ministry of Industry) Center for Energy & Mining Conservation & Development, and founded ICR Consultants. He was a developer and board member of numerous enterprises in multiple sectors and developed and served as mentor for the UDES Project and collaborated with Lan Ekintza to form both mentors and mentoring culture and methodology. He also served as a mentor for various non-profit executives.

- **José Arturo Villanueva Barriocanal** is an industrial engineer, University of Pais Vasco, with courses in economic and entrepreneurial sciences. He served as Director of Strategy, Planning &

Corporate Services as well as Director for Knowledge Management, and was member of the Executive Committee for Iberdrola Diversification and as a member of Iberdrola's Integration Committee. Previously he held posts as Director of Research & Planning for the EVE Group – the Basque Energy Agency, as an energy consultant and water treatment engineer. He served as founding member and mentor of the UDES Project to mentor executives.

- **José Antonio López Egaña** is an industrial engineer, Graduate School of Industrial Engineers and Telecommunications Engineers of Bilbao, with a diploma in Culture & Sustainability from the University of Deusto in Bilbao. He held positions in the Basque energy sector as Director General for Technology in the Industrial & Energy Ministry of the Basque Government and served as Director General for the Basque Technology Center, ROBOTIKER. He developed and served as a board member of Tecnalia Corporation, as well as serving on boards of multiple private and public advanced technology enterprises. He is a professor of post-graduate courses dedicated to managing technology innovation and author of articles on innovation practice and the book, *Conversations from the Hill*.

Ana Aguirre

She is co-founder and worker owner at TAZEBAEZ S. Coop, an innovation group that focuses its activity on the creation of learning and training ecosystems for companies and education institutions (Travelling U.); visual communication (MakeItVisual); and participates in various companies in emerging sectors. In TAZEBAEZ Ana leads the Cooperative Development line and is a member of the innovation consultancy team. Since 2020 she is COO of Platform Cooperatives NOW! (Mondragon University and New School) and she was one of 12 participants at the Harvard Research Sprint on Data Cooperatives. Ana serves as Global President of the Youth Network and Youth Representative on the Board of the International Cooperative Alliance, where she also represents youth on the Cooperative Identity Advisory Group.

Kristen Barker

Kristen Barker is a social entrepreneur and the President and co-founder of Co-op Cincy and is a co-founder of 1worker1vote. She designs and leads participatory education events with English- and Spanish-speaking co-op workers, and helps worker-owners make their businesses more successful. Kristen also helps our design team determine the feasibility of potential co-op businesses, helps retiring business owners determine whether they can sell their business to their employees, and helps viable co-ops access the capital they need to leverage their ideas. Kristen has done groundbreaking work in adopting the Mondragon model to the US context, and hosts delegations from around the country, including the participants in Co-op Cincy's biennial Union Co-op Symposium. Kristen is a 2016-2018 Business Alliance for Local and Living Economies (BALLE) Fellow. Before becoming Co-op Cincy's Executive Director, she worked for 12 years fostering partnerships between people of faith, union members, and community members of diverse backgrounds. Kristen is a graduate of Xavier University and a lifelong Cincinnati resident – except for two years in El Salvador! Kristen is a single mother of a resilient daughter with special needs.

Charles Chawalko

Charles Chawalko likes to assemble and disassemble puzzles, especially ones that involve elements of history, politics, theory, and design. After receiving his Bachelor's in History and Master's in Design & Urban Ecologies, he worked for 596 Acres on the digital mapping of New York City's urban renewal plans, the Morris Justice Project in participatory action research on issues of policing and gentrification in the South Bronx, and, most recently, designing the WE, where his skills in design, mapping, and research helped accentuate the firm's work of developing new methodologies to promote more equitable systems. He is now a socio-spatial researcher for Designing for Democracy, a research and design agency that investigates the spatial infractions of democracy in the built environment.

Christina Clamp

Christina Clamp has over 40 years of teaching at Southern New Hampshire University (SNHU), as a professor of sociology and is the director of the Center for Co-operatives & Community Economic Development. She is consulting researcher on a national study of catalyzing community wealth with the American Sustainable Business Network. She is nationally and internationally recognized for her work in the study and promotion of cooperative ownership of businesses. She has been actively involved in promoting the study of cooperatives since her dissertation, which was a study of management in the Mondragon cooperatives. In 2019, Professor Clamp published *Shared Service: A Qualitative Analysis* with co-authors Eklou Amendah and Carol Coren (Cork: Oak Tree Press). Professor Clamp has served as a consultant to various clients, including the National Cooperative Bank (Washington, DC) and US Department of Agriculture Rural Development. She completed an interdisciplinary Bachelor's degree at Friends World College (now Global College of Long Island University) and her Master's and Doctoral degrees in sociology at Boston College. In her spare time, she volunteers on the boards of the Local Enterprise Assistance Fund, the ICA Group, and the Fund for Jobs Worth Owning.

Brian Corbin

Brian Corbin holds a Bachelor of Philosophy degree from the Pontifical School of Philosophy, and a Bachelor of Arts in Politics from the Catholic University of America, Washington, D.C. He completed his doctorate in Organizational Leadership in Health & Human Services at Youngstown State University (YSU) and continues his Ph.D. work at The Massachusetts Institute of Technology (MIT). Brian is the Executive Vice President of Catholic Charities USA and served as the Executive Director of Catholic Charities & Health Affairs in Youngstown, Ohio. He has published several academic and popular articles on Catholic social doctrine and political economy.

April de Simone

April de Simone is a transdisciplinary designer working at the intersection of design, planning, and systems thinking. In 2015, April co-founded Designing the WE where she co-curated Undesign the Redline, a nationally recognized exhibition exploring the historical and contemporary impacts of unjust policies and practices like residential racial ordinances, redlining, and urban renewal. More recently, she transitioned from her role as a Principal at Trahan Architects to co-launch We Arch. (We Architect) in the Fall of 2023.

She is also the curator of *The Practice of Democracy: We Hold These Truths*, a traveling exhibition and program which launched on the High Line in the summer of 2022. Her work is inspired by her experiences growing up in a Bronx, New York, neighborhood, steeped in the collateral consequences of intentionally designed systems of inequity. In partnership with diverse stakeholders, she seeks to cultivate reframed opportunities within spatial practice, advancing equitable, humane, and just frameworks and projects shaping the conditions of our society.

Julio Gallastegui

Julio Gallastegui is the retired general manager of Laboral Kutxa. He spent practically his entire professional life in Caja Laboral (from June 1981 to April 2019), initially in its Entrepreneurial Division, and then in its Banking Division, with an interval of two years (2008-2009) in Lagun Aro EPSV as its General Manager. He also participated in the Governing Council of Caja Laboral as vice president for two years and served on the Board of Directors of Lagun Aro Insurance for many years.

Caitlin Gianniny

Caitlin Gianniny is a writer, artist and co-founder of a majority women-owned worker cooperative, Samara Collective. Samara partners with values-based organizations to develop long-term creative pathways to progress using strategic communications and capacity building. Caitlin Gianniny brings a background in design, education and neuropsychology to building effective branding and messaging strategy. Prior to co-founding Samara, she worked with progressive organizations on issues ranging from education, healthcare, transportation and the environment, to racial and economic justice, including 1199SEIU Massachusetts, Community Labor United, and the Harvard Art Museums. At Samara, she leads on narrative and content strategy, graphic design, front-end web development, and systems design. Caitlin earned a Bachelor of Fine Arts from the Cooper Union School of Art and a Master of Education (Ed.M.) in Mind, Brain & Education from Harvard Graduate School of Education.

Damien Goodmon

27-year Leimert Park resident Damien Goodmon has been labeled a "visionary" by the *LA Times*, recognized as one of the LA's "100 Most Influential African Americans" by the *LA Wave Newspapers*, chosen beside former LA Mayor Richard Riordan and actress Drew Barrymore for the 2009 "LA People" issue of *LA Weekly*, and is a lead subject of the award-winning documentary *Beyond the Echo of the Drum*, which premiered at the prestigious Cannes Film Festival. As a nonprofit executive director, he has led some of the Crenshaw and Black Los Angeles' most impactful community advocacy campaigns. As a political operative, he has managed, led departments and advised electoral campaigns from the school board level up to the presidential. As an executive management consultant and systems thinker, he has built, reconstructed and managed multiple large companies and departments, including some with over 400 employees, and successfully guided complex projects and partnerships, featuring actors with divergent interests. In the public sector, Mr. Goodmon served as a policy assistant for Board District 1 of Los Angeles Unified School District, America's second largest school district. In that capacity he was directly responsible for overseeing the largest school expansion project in the country on behalf of the Board Member, and reviewing hundreds of contracts and bids in the LAUSD's multi-billion dollar procurement process. Mr. Goodmon has worked to secure public funding for large real estate projects, and advocate for additional investment in public infrastructure projects. In his most recent capacity, he served as a senior advisor and an initial thought leader for the creation of the affordable housing program of a global nonprofit. Mr. Goodmon is a fifth-generation Angelino and descendant of Charles and L.M. Blodgett, who were successful Black builders and the founders of the first Black-owned bank on the West Coast, Liberty Savings & Loan. The Blodgetts built the first FHA financed housing for Black people in America, Blodgett Tract. He is also a relative of Colonel Allen Allensworth, the founder of Allensworth, California, the only town in the state to be founded, financed and governed by Black people. A graduate of LA Loyola High School, he has studied at the University of Washington and Harvard University programs.

Roger Green

Roger Green currently serves as a Senior Fellow at the City University School of Law, Community Economic Development Clinic (CEDC). Building on his legacy as professor, legislator, social justice leader and policy entrepreneur, Roger recently co-founded Citizen Share Brooklyn (CSB), the Society for Effective Economic Democracy (SEED) and Brooklyn Community Collaborative (BCC), inspired by a grassroots effort that observed how structural racial and economic inequality contributes to health care disparities within poor and working poor Communities of Color (COC). He previously represented New York's 57th district from 1981 to 2006 as an elected member of the New York State Assembly in the roles of Chairperson of the Committee on Science & Technology, Chairperson of the Standing Committee on Children & Families, Chairperson of the Joint Budget Conference Committee on Health & Human Services, and Chairperson of the New York State Black, Hispanic & Asian Legislative Caucus with the distinction of being the longest serving Chairperson of this important legislative caucus. During his legislative tenure, Roger authored and sponsored more than 160 bills that were enacted into law. He considers his authorship of legislation supporting higher education, children and families, and human rights as being a defining characteristic of his public service. Retiring from the State legislature in 2014, Roger assumed a co-chairmanship of the Coalition to Transform Interfaith Medical Center (aka Coalition to Save Interfaith). This health justice organization which includes 1199SEIU Healthcare Workers East, New York State Nurses Association, health justice advocates, faith leaders and scholar activists successfully united with Assembly woman Annette Robinson and others to save Interfaith Medical Center (a Safety-Net hospital), by securing an $83 million annual appropriation for this institution. The coalition currently works with Citizen Share Brooklyn to ensure that Interfaith Medical Center and the larger New York healthcare sector's $40 billion supply chain is redirected and aligned with the needs of communities impacted by structural racial and economic inequality. Roger is married to Coraminita Mahr, a human rights advocate and labor leader, and is the father of Khalid, Imani and Corlita and the proud grandfather of Cora Belle and Asayah.

Rebecca Henderson

Rebecca Henderson is one of 25 University Professors at Harvard, a research fellow at the National Bureau of Economic Research and a fellow of both the British Academy and the American Academy of Arts & Sciences. She also has more than 25 years of major public board experience. Rebecca's research explores the degree to which the private sector can play a major role in building a more sustainable economy. Her publications include *Accelerating Energy Innovation: Insights from Multiple Sectors* (University of Chicago Press), *Leading Sustainable Change: An Organizational Perspective* (Oxford University Press) and *Political Economy & Justice* (University of Chicago Press). She is also the author of *Reimagining Capitalism in a World on Fire*, which was shortlisted for the FT/McKinsey 2020 Business Book of the Year Award.

Jesús María Herrasti

Jesús María Herrasti is the retired President of Mondragon International & Innovation. He is an engineer and worked for more than 47 years in the Mondragon co-operatives. He was the research and development Director and Chairman of the Board in Copreci S. Coop, He served as chairman of Lagun Aro Mútua, General Manager of Fagor Arrasate S. Coop, Chairman of Fagor Group, and Chairman of the Congress of MCC. In addition, he was the Mayor of the town of Aretxabaleta for eight years.

John Holdsclaw IV

John Holdsclaw IV serves as president and CEO of Rochdale Capital, an emerging national non-profit community development loan fund that promotes community ownership and cooperative principles. In a dual role, John also serves as executive vice president of strategic initiatives at the National Cooperative Bank (NCB). NCB is the founding and strategic partner of Rochdale Capital. Mr. Holdsclaw currently serves on numerous boards and holds degrees from NC Agricultural & Technical State University and Southern New Hampshire University, a Stonier Graduate School of Banking Diploma, Wharton Leadership Certificate and Certificate in Diversity & Inclusion from Cornell University. In 2019, John received NCB's Stanley W. Dreyer Spirit of Cooperation Award. In addition, John is an active member of Phi Beta Sigma Fraternity, Incorporated.

Mary Hoyer

Mary Hoyer is a founder and Executive Committee member of the Union Co-ops Council of the US Federation of Worker Co-ops. She chairs the Finance and Labor Co-op Committees of the Wellspring Co-op Corporation, and is an advisor to the Co-op Fund of New England. She has worked with the Cooperative Development Institute, the Eastern Conference for Workplace Democracy, Citizens Research Education Network, Asylum Hill Economic Development Committee, the Hartford Public Schools, the Hartford Federation of Teachers AFL-CIO Local 1018, and the Connecticut Anti-Apartheid Committee. She holds degrees from Occidental College, University of Kentucky, and University of Massachusetts Amherst. She lives in Amherst, Massachusetts.

Carmen Huertas-Noble

Professor Carmen Huertas-Noble is a Tenured Professor of Law and Senior Associate Dean for Clinical Programs at CUNY Law. She is the founding director of the Community & Economic Development Clinic (CEDC). CUNY Law School's Clinical Program ranks first in the nation and CUNY Law is consistently ranked as one of the top US public service law schools. Professor Huertas-Noble earned her J.D. from Fordham University Law School, where she was a Stein Scholar in Public Interest Law & Ethics. Prior to joining the CUNY faculty, Professor Huertas-Noble was an Adjunct Professor at Fordham Law School where she supervised students in its CED Clinic and worked with nonprofits creating immigrant-led worker-owned cooperatives providing childcare and house cleaning services. She also served as a senior staff attorney in the Community Development Project (CDP) of the Urban Justice Center, where she counseled cooperatives in navigating their legal entity formation options and on creating democratic governance structures. As part of CDP, she worked with ROC-NY in creating COLORS, a worker-owned restaurant in Manhattan. Since then, Professor Huertas-Noble and the CEDC have played a leading role in providing transactional legal and policy support to some of the most innovative and grassroots organizations creating and supporting worker-owned cooperatives, including co-founding and incorporating 1Worker1Vote, a global worker ownership movement-building non-profit, the American Sustainable Business Council's "Ownership4All" campaign, The Coalition to Transform Interfaith, Green Worker Cooperatives and the New York City Worker-Owned Cooperative Network (NYC NoWC). In addition, CEDC was instrumental in securing financial investment from the New York City Council in 2015 for the Worker Cooperative Budget Initiative that developed a city-wide ecosystem to grow and support the worker cooperative movement and has grown substantially since 2015. NYC's investment in the Initiative represents the largest, formal US city investment in worker cooperatives in North America. She is a member of the Cooperative Hall of Fame.

Sara Horowitz

Sara Horowitz is the founder of the Freelancers Union and the Freelancers Insurance Company. Formerly chair of the board of the Federal Reserve Bank of New York, Horowitz is a recipient of the MacArthur Fellowship and has been featured on NPR and in the *New York Times*, *Wall Street Journal*, and *The Atlantic*, among other publications. In her recently released book *Mutualism: Building the Next Economy from the Ground Up*, Sara takes a profound look at the crisis of work and the collapse of the safety net, and gives a vision for a better way forward, rooted in America's cooperative spirit. In 2021 she founded the Mutualist Society to begin to gather mutualists across the union, cooperative, faith, social enterprise, mutual aid and alternative currency communities together as a sectoral strategy.

Esteban Kelly

Esteban Kelly works to expand economic democracy through forms of multi-racial solidarity and collective ownership. He is the Executive Director for the US Federation of Worker Cooperatives (USFWC), founding President of the freelancer co-op Guilded, and a worker-owner and co-founder of AORTA (Anti-Oppression Resource & Training Alliance), a worker co-op that has built capacity for hundreds of social justice projects through intersectional training and consulting. He foregrounds political education, systemic thinking, and abolitionist principles into visionary organizing. He was a co-founder and first board President of the cross-sector Philadelphia Area Cooperative Alliance (PACA) and has served on numerous boards including the Democracy At Work Institute, the US Solidarity Economy Network, and the Cooperative Development Foundation. Esteban currently serves on the boards of NCBA–CLUSA, the Cooperative Innovation Lab, the Platform Co-ops Consortium, and the international worker co-op association known as CICOPA. Esteban is a Ford Global Fellow, an Executive Fellow at the Institute for the Study of Employee Ownership & Profit Sharing at Rutgers University, and a Futures4Good Fellow in the Equitable Enterprise Initiative at the Institute for the Future.

Garam Lee

Garam Lee is currently doing research and teaching in the Forestry Sociology Lab, Department of Forestry of Konkuk University, Republic of Korea. Her background is sociology and she obtained her PhD in sociology from Yonsei University, where she investigated how the meaning of "the social" is constructed and communicated in the social economy activities in Korea and its potential for social change, from the perspective of cultural economic sociology. Her current research interests include the social impact of the Social and Solidarity Economy (SSE) and SSE's contributions to the sustainable development goals (SDGs) and social changes. She has actively engaged in various research projects on SSE with Korean government research institutes and civil society organizations. She also authored "Role of social and solidarity economy for people-oriented inclusive growth: focusing on decent work, social inclusion and empowerment," a draft paper contributed to the UN Inter-Agency Task Force on Social and Solidarity Economy (UN TFSSE) SSE Knowledge Hub for the SDGs.

Sang-Youn Lee

Dr. Sang-Youn Lee works at the Division of Business Administration and Graduate School of Social & Solidarity Economy at Sungkonghoe University in South Korea. Before joining the university, he worked as an assistant professor in the State University of New York New Paltz School of Business. His interests include social entrepreneurship, governance, and new firm financing. His research has been published in *Long Range Planning*, *Corporate Governance*, *Annals of Public & Cooperative Economics*, *Journal of International Entrepreneurship*, *Journal of Entrepreneurial & Organizational Diversity*, and *Academy of Management Best Paper Proceedings*. In the real business area, he worked at Korea Telecom for 10 years and was the CEO's advisor and in charge of corporate strategy. He collaborated with UNRISD for the project on Policy Systems & Measures for the Social Economy in Seoul where he is a co-chair of 9th CIRIEC Research Conference on Social Economy on 4~6 July 2023.

Terry Lewis

Terry Lewis is the CFO of the Center for Community-Based Enterprises (C2BE) and Principal of LIA Advisors, LLC. By Presidential Appointment (Barack Obama), she served as a Director of the Overseas Private Investment Corporation (OPIC), the US government's development finance institution, from 2011 until the agency sunset to be replaced by the US Development Finance Corporation in 2019. Formerly, she was Vice President of Cooperative Development for the National Cooperative Bank (NCB) and President and CEO of NCB Community Works, its cooperative development subsidiary. She served as a Director, Treasurer, and eight years as Chair of the Cooperative Development Foundation (CDF). She is a member of the Cooperative Hall of Fame.

Rebecca Lurie

Rebecca Lurie is currently on faculty with the Urban Studies Department and is the founder of the Community & Worker Ownership Project at the City University of NY School for Labor & Urban Studies. She was a founding member of the worker-owned cooperative, New Deal Home Improvement Company & City Roots Contractors Guild. She began her working career as a union carpenter and transitioned into worker education through the union's apprenticeship program and the construction industry. Using a sector approach for understanding industries and businesses and their employment needs, she has remained dedicated to inclusive community economic development. Rebecca has collaborated on numerous initiatives in NYC, including pre-apprenticeship programs, a Bronx green jobs network, a kitchen business incubator and the design of Best for NYC. She was a founding member of the board of the Bronx Cooperative Development Initiative, is on the board of the Democracy at Work Institute and serves on the executive committee of the Union Coop Council/US Federation of Worker Coops. She is Trustee Emerita with the Brooklyn Society for Ethical Culture. She holds a Master's in Organizational Change Management from The New School, a certificate in Adult Occupational Education from CUNY and is certified in Permaculture Urban Design. She is a native New Yorker, raised by a fervent activist with the DNA and tireless passion for social justice.

Julian Manley

Julian Manley is Professor of Social Innovation at the University of Central Lancashire, Preston, UK. He was a founder member and was the first Chair of the Preston Cooperative Development Network, and is founder member and Director of the Preston Cooperative Education Centre and NewsSocial Coop. He is the co-editor of *The Preston Model and Community Wealth Building* (Routledge, 2021) and co-editor of the forthcoming *Cooperation and Cooperatives in 21st Century Europe* (Bristol University Press).

Agustín Markaide Soraluce

Agustín Markaide Soraluce is the retired president of Eroski (2011-2022) and Fundación Eroski (2011-2022) and was a member of the cooperative for over 27 years. He served for six years as president of the Permanent Commission of the Mondragon Congress. Prior to joining Eroski, Agustín was a member of the Erein Agri-food Group for six years. He was also president of AgeCore SA from 2020-2021.

Sandra McCardell

Sandra McCardell has broad experience as a business owner, faculty member, non-profit Director, and team member engaged in a variety of initiatives focused on sustainability through the company she started in 1989, Current-C Energy Systems, Inc. Sandra formed the New Mexico Green Collaborative in 2009 to focus on Green Jobs, and has worked with UNM Valencia, UNM Gallup, San Juan College and Northern New Mexico College on contract or teaching green energy, green building, and sustainability. In 2019, she co-founded the nonprofit Cooperative Catalyst of NM, a cooperative development center. She has served as an advisor to the Ministry of Energy & Water in Afghanistan, and worked with SmartGrid Asia in Thailand, as well as with many communities and Tribes in the West on similar initiatives. Sandra has degrees in Cultural Change / Adaptation from Princeton University, a Master's in International Administration from the School for International Training, and an MBA from the University of Chicago.

Oscar Muguerza

Oscar Muguerza serves as director of business development on behalf of Laboral Kutxa bank, part of the Mondragon cooperative ecosystem. In this capacity Oscar manages strategic alliances and agreements with entrepreneurial and social economy sectors, as well as banking relationships such as the European Investment Fund. As a recent graduate upon obtaining degrees in economics and business sciences from the University of Deusto (Bilbao), Oscar worked briefly for a well-known consulting firm and then has spent his entire professional career at Laboral Kutxa leading new business development ventures with entrepreneurs, freelancers, companies, social enterprises and corporations across all sectors. Oscar also serves as the coordinator and vice president of the Gaztenpresa Foundation, and is currently a member of the Youth Business Spain board of trustees and the Seed capital Bizkaia board of directors.

Elroy Natuchu, Jr. & Kandis Quam
Elroy Natuchu, Jr. and Kandis Quam are cousins from Zuni Pueblo. They are working artists and business partners in Natuchu Ink (natuchuink.com), a company they co-founded. Both have been instrumental in the development of the Ancestral Rich Treasures of Zuni cooperative (ARTZ, zunipuebloart.com), the only Zuni company owned and operated by Zuni artists and the only known Native-owned artist cooperative in New Mexico. Kandis and Elroy are creating an art apprenticeship program for the Zuni Youth Enrichment Project (ZYEP.org) where they work to transform the Zuni arts economy by encouraging thriving businesses to be able to charge prices that reflect the real value of the work, strengthening the community and empowering the next generation of Zuni artists. For Elroy and Kandis, as with many people from Zuni, art is an intergenerational calling to which each of the cousins returned after college. Kandis, first in her family to graduate from college, studied biology and has a degree in Cultural Anthropology; she is also a digital creator and worked for the Cooperative Catalyst of New Mexico. Kandis serves on the Board of ARTZ, and Elroy is Secretary for the organization. When Elroy was in college, he planned to work as a radiology technician, then received his degree in studio art and Native American studies. Both returned to Zuni and became artists with a focus on community. Elroy notes that "my passion is re-educating multiple generations of Zuni people, using art as the base for cultural teachings and the visual representation of our oral history."

Doug O'Brien
Doug O'Brien is the President and CEO of the National Cooperative Business Association CLUSA and works with the cooperative community, both domestically and internationally, to deepen its impact on families and communities. NCBA CLUSA is the primary voice for cooperatives in the US for using the cooperative business model to build a more inclusive economy. Before coming to NCBA CLUSA, he led the work of the White House Rural Council and served in top positions at the US Department of Agriculture, including leading the Rural Development Agency, a community economic development agency with over 40 programs and 5,000 employees that annually finances more than $30 billion.

Kevin O'Brien
Kevin O'Brien is the Founder and Managing Member of the Worx Printing Cooperative in Worcester, Massachusetts. He is an anti-sweatshop activist turned reluctant entrepreneur. For the past 25 years he has sought to better understand supply chains and work within them to improve the human and environmental experience and impact. He has worked with merchandising, design, manufacturing, imprinting, fulfillment, distribution, as well as finance and e-commerce. The foundation of his experience

comes out of the New York City and Los Angeles Garment Centers and from manufacturing facilities throughout the country. His experiences have brought him in contact with the creative and technical genius, as well as the shortcomings, of ethical manufacturing practices. He uses his experience to help chart a more progressive future that is of greater benefit to workers and the natural environment.

David O'Connell

David O'Connell is a trade unionist from the UK, currently writing his doctoral thesis in Germany. With a background in workplace organizing in both countries, he completed his Master's degree in Labor Policies & Globalization in 2016. His current research, funded by the Hans Boeckler Foundation, focuses on the role of unions in buying out and converting existing firms to employee ownership.

Imanol Olaskoaga

Imanol Olaskoaga is a specialist in prospecting and development of new businesses. He has extensive experience as director of large international projects in various industries. Presently, Olaskoaga is the founder of Powerfultree and CEO of Agrivoltaics, a startup. He was a new business promoter for the Mondragon Group in 2021 and the new projects manager for the ERREKA Group from 2020-2021. Previously, he was the business manager of Batz Automotive Group from 2018-2020 where he had management of 1,500 people and eight plants internationally. He was managing director for Erreka Fastening Solutions from 2011-2018, during its transition from a traditional business, very mature and in crisis, to what Erreka Fastening Solutions is today. His academic career includes an Executive MBA from Mondragon Unibertsitatea, and degrees from the University of Technology of Compiègne (UTC) in mechanical engineering and University of Navarra in industrial mechanical engineering.

Michael Alden Peck

Michael Alden Peck serves as executive director and cofounder of the non-profit worker ownership movement, 1worker1vote; co-founder and managing director of a second for-profit start-up, the Virtuous Cycle Collaboratory (tvc2) – a worker cooperative and social enterprise whose mission is to "flatten unequal socioeconomic curves into shared prosperity virtuous cycles"; board member of the American Sustainable Business Network (ASBN – includes the American Sustainable Business Council and Investors Circle), where Michael serves on the executive and governance committees (and was a 2019 recipient of ASBC's Sustainable Leaders Award); Blue Green Alliance corporate advisory board member; Worx Printing union coop board chair; member, Preston, UK, NewsSocial board; Coop Cincy volunteer staff member; former International Delegate (1999-2019) representing USA and Canada for MONDRAGON; and MAPA Group Inc. founder & president during its 25-year run (1994-2019). Prior to founding his first company in 1994, Michael served as a naval officer on active duty overseas from 1976 -1983, winning the competitive Commander-in-Chief, US Naval Forces Europe Leadership award in 1981 while posted as the US Navy's representative at France's Naval Academy, completing 20 years of service as a Commander in the Naval Reserves in 1996. Michael served as defense and economic development legislative assistant (1984-1986) to the US Senate Majority Leader; as executive assistant (1986-1988) to the President of the BDM Corporation (who held concurrent positions as Virginia's Council of Higher Education chair and cochaired the national Democratic Party Business and Finance Councils up through the 1992 presidential elections); and as a senior vice president for corporate business development at SAIC (1988-1994), then the nation's largest employee-owned, applied R&D company with its own internal stock market. Michael holds degrees from Rice University (1976), where he received the 1976 English Department senior honors thesis award and active-duty commission in the US Navy, and from the John Hopkins University Paul H. Nitze School of Advanced International Studies (SAIS 1985). Michael studied as a Rice University Schlumberger Foundation award recipient at the Sorbonne and the Institute of Political Science in Paris, France (1974-1975).

Jason Spicer

Jason Spicer is an Assistant Professor at the University of Toronto, where he directs the Community Economies Lab and primarily teaches in the graduate urban planning program. His research and his practice-based work focus on alternative ownership and governance models in the economy, including cooperatives. He has published on cooperatives and related solidarity economy models in a wide range of international scholarly and popular outlets.

Dan Swinney

Dan began his organizing career as a volunteer for SNCC in Georgia in the summer of 1965. He graduated from the University of Wisconsin in Madison with a BA in History in 1967. In 1970, he moved to Chicago and entered the world of manufacturing, where worked for 13 years as a machinist. He organized Steelworker Local 8787 at G+W Taylor Forge in Cicero. Taylor Forge closed in 1983. Dan then founded Manufacturing Renaissance (MR) in response to the massive plant closings in the Chicago area. MR is a not-for-profit that develops innovative approaches to community development, believing that manufacturing is the essential foundation of a modern society. As such, the development of our manufacturing sector must be profoundly tied to social inclusion. Dan writes and speaks regularly for organizations interested in promoting advanced manufacturing and its intersection with public interests.

Ellen Vera

Ellen Vera has organized people from diverse backgrounds to improve their workplaces for more than a decade, and became a co-founder of Co-op Cincy and of 1worker1vote in 2011 to develop a more sustainable model of organizing, economic democracy and wealth-building with marginalized communities. Ellen oversees new co-op organizing projects, the launch of Co-op Cincy's education arm, Co-op U, and makes sure we have the resources we need to be successful. Ellen's experience as part of a family with mixed immigration status deepens her perspective and her passion for organizing with immigrant worker-owners and worker-owners of color. Prior to accepting a position with Co-op Cincy, she helped people organize and strengthen their labor unions, as the National Organizing Coordinator for the manufacturing arm of the Communication Workers of America, and for United Food & Commercial Workers Local 75. Ellen earned a Master's in Business Administration (MBA) from Northern Kentucky University, which she uses to oversee our design team's work producing feasibility studies, business plans, capitalization campaigns and the initial management of cooperative enterprises.

Ibon Zugasti

Ibon Zugasti is the Managing Partner/Director of Prospektiker (http://www.prospektiker.es/), a foresight and strategy institute that is part of LKS (www.LKSNext.com), Mondragon's management and social transformation consultancy cooperative where he serves as Manager of International Projects. Mondragon (www.mondragon-corporation.com) is a member of Social Economy Europe (SEE - www.socialeconomy.eu.org).

Acknowledgements

This project began on a quiet Saturday morning when Michael Peck emailed me with a suggestion that we work on a book that would update the story of the Mondragon cooperatives and their influence in the world. Little did I know at the time that it would lead us on a shared journey to bring forth this book with all our wonderful contributors. We owe each of them our thanks for being part of this project. In particular, I want to thank our colleagues from Mondragon for their contributions to the book, as well as their insights on the current changes in the cooperative group.

My own involvement with the cooperative community in the US includes many individuals and institutions that have inspired and influenced the development of my ideas about the importance of worker cooperatives and labor unions to bring about a meaningful reset of our economy and society. Among those who have been important to that process are Steve Dawson, Rand Wilson, Chuck Turner, David Ellerman, Severyn Bruyn, Jim Megson, Howard Brodsky, Terry Lewis, Jessica Gordon Nembhard and Gerardo Espinoza. Over the past four decades, my involvement on the boards of the ICA Group, Local Enterprise Assistance Fund, the National Cooperative Business Association, the Allston Brighton Community Development Corporation, Childspace Development Training Institute, Cooperative Development Institute and the Food Cooperative Initiative have given me a unique opportunity to see the connections across co-operative sectors to catalyze community wealth building.

Michael observed that this has been a family enterprise for me. My daughter, Caitlin Gianniny, contributed a chapter about her journey in creating Samara Collective, a worker cooperative. Her sister, Megan Gianniny, provided editorial assistance. Lastly my thanks to my husband, Don, for his patience, love and support. I am very grateful to each of them.

Michael and I thank our copy editors, Megan Gianniny and Josh Wilson, for their thoughtful suggestions for improving the writing and for addressing our inconsistencies and gremlins in the quality of the manuscript. We especially want to acknowledge Kevin O'Brien for his brilliant work on the design of the book cover. He taught us so much in the process about the marketing side of this project. We also thank our publisher, Oak Tree Press, and in particular, Brian O'Kane, for his good humor and patience as we struggled to meet our deadlines.

Lastly, I want to thank Michael for his vision and passion for this project. In the course of this work, I have gotten to know Michael well and am amazed at his ability to juggle multiple projects and the depth and breadth of his knowledge.

We apologies for any errors or omissions here.

Christina
March 2023

We are launching *Odes to Joy* via <u>The 1worker1vote/NewsSocial Bridge</u> where we hope every inspired **HUMANITY @ WORK & LIFE** reader, present and future contributor will share your Acknowledgements voice.

Michael
March 2023

Foreword

Rebecca Henderson

How shall we realize economic justice? In the United States, the pandemic has turbocharged inequality, further dividing those with wealth and control from those who live paycheck to paycheck. Globally, Covid has destabilized developing nations across the world, eating through resources, devastating populations, and undoing years of work in health care and education. At the same time, we remain enormously wealthy. In my lifetime global GDP has increased more than sixfold (in real terms!). We have more than enough resources to provide everyone on the planet with enough to eat, somewhere to sleep and some sense of physical security.

How can we structure economic activity so that this wealth is more broadly distributed? One possibility is to double down on redistribution – to pair significant taxes on wealth with something like a universal basic income. The other is to broaden employment and to increase employee power. Redistribution undoubtedly has its place, but to my mind our priority must be the creation of "good jobs" – well paying, meaningful jobs in which everyone is treated with dignity and respect and employees are empowered to shape their own work. Satisfying work is one of the great joys of a life well lived – and the knowledge that one can take care of oneself and one's family is a bedrock of self-respect, of thriving communities and of engaged citizenship.

Where are these jobs to come from? The State can help, of course. Strong, effective educational systems, a decent minimum wage policy, the protection of the right to organize and the provision of some mechanism for employee voice – these and other policies like them can make an enormous difference in rebalancing power in the workplace. But the most fundamental solution is direct employee ownership – the creation of firms in which there is no conflict between labor and capital because the employees are in charge.

Why might a largescale move to employee ownership be a powerful step on the way to building a good jobs economy? Most obviously, making employees the residual claimants to the profits of the firm is likely to significantly increase employee wealth. Employee-owned firms – as you might expect – prioritize employment over profits and pay their employees above the going wage. Employee-owners have on average more than twice the amount in their defined contribution accounts as participants in comparable nonemployee-owned companies, and 20% more assets overall.

When employee ownership comes with greater job security and the ability to participate in decision-making it increases employee loyalty and motivation, lowers staff turnover, and drives higher levels of innovation and productivity. Freed from the short termism of modern capital markets, employee-owned firms find it much easier to make the investments that are essential to building and maintaining a highly engaged workforce—not only to provide training, decent wages, and benefits, but also to invest the time and energy required to ensure that information is widely shared, that sustaining the culture is a priority, and that everyone is engaged. It is not surprising that employee-owned firms also grow faster and are vastly overrepresented in the "Best Companies to Work For" rankings.

The big question, then, is how to form, fund and grow employee-owned firms at scale. We know that they are feasible. The Publix supermarket chain is the largest employee-controlled firm in the US, with more than 1,000 locations throughout the southeast and 200,000 employees. In the UK, the employee-owned retail giant, the John Lewis Partnership, which was founded in 1864, had revenues of more than £10bn ($12.3bn) and more than 80,000 employees. And then, of course, there is Mondragon, which in 2020 was one of the largest firms in Spain, coordinating more than 260 separate cooperatives, generating more than €13bn ($15bn) in revenues and employing more than 81,000 people.

Can we make employee-owned firms mainstream? It will not be easy, but it is eminently possible, as this important collection of path-breaking essays suggests. Most importantly, it is an idea whose time has come.

On July 4, 1927, Owen Young, then the CEO of the General Electric Corporation, was the guest speaker for the opening of the Baker Library at the Harvard Business School. As he spoke the "Roaring Twenties" were in full flight, and the US was experiencing levels of inequality that were not reached again until our own times. He dared to think that American capitalism might have the strength and the flexibility to embrace a quite different model:

> Perhaps someday we may be able to organize human beings engaged in a particular undertaking so that they truly will be the employer buying capital as a commodity in the market at the lowest price.... I hope the day may come when these great business organizations will truly belong to the men who are giving their lives and their efforts to them, I care not in what capacity.... Then we shall dispose once and for all, of the charge that in industry organizations are autocratic and not democratic.... Then, in a word, men will be as free in cooperative undertakings and subject only to the same limitations and chances as men in individual businesses. Then we shall have no hired men. That objective may be a long way off, but it is worthy to engage the research and efforts of the Harvard School of Business.[1]

In 2022, nearly 100 years later, HBS set up a Business & Society Initiative – an effort devoted to thinking about how firms can best contribute to building a just and sustainable society. My hope is that we'll take

Owen Young's advice. But we are merely a pebble in what must be an avalanche of change. We must reimagine capitalism. This book shows us how.

End-note

[1]   Mackin, C. (2020). Towards an economic democracy, *New Republic* (March 25, p.392) quoting Owen Young, Dedication address, *Harvard Business Review*, V.4 July (1927): 385–394.

Introduction

An Overview of the Book, Audience & Intended Impact

Christina Clamp & Michael Peck

Capitalism is a broken model, but it remains the dominant global economic order. The world has seen its flaws in light of the Covid-19 pandemic of 2020. As of the time of this writing, we are still challenged by the breakdown in the global supply chain for many types of imported manufactured goods, and disruptions in the workforce. A recurrent theme is that the pandemic has disproportionately affected women, Black communities, ethnic minorities, and precariat geographies and populations, mainly from the Global South, who are frontline workers, climate refugees, and those fleeing authoritarianism and warmongering.

Caregivers are essential to society, but are among the lowest-compensated workers, and many were already struggling financially before the pandemic. Meanwhile, school closures and the risks of exposure to the virus have meant that unemployment was often the only option for parents who had no one to help take care of their young children. Others who were close to retirement decided that it was time to retire. Research on the impact of Covid found that frontline workers in the United States and United Kingdom were often disproportionately affected by the virus. Low-wage workers had to choose between exposure to Covid and the ability to pay their rent while professional workers could work remotely (Moore *et al.*, 2022).

Others found that the "pandemic pause" led them to rethink what is important to them in a job — to be able to do worthy work, to be valued for one's contribution both financially and socially. Far too many in this world did not have those benefits.

Too often, people believe that there are no viable alternatives to this economic order. Political discourse traditionally focuses on the problem of either democratic liberalism or state-controlled socialism. Change need not be premised on those two extremes. A focus on the nature of work and business institutions can secure middle ground through systems of economic democracy that build accountability, equity, and democratic governance into the workplace (Restakis, 2010). Worker cooperatives give their workers a path to equity and security in their workplace. In worker cooperatives, people are able to work towards membership that gives them long-term stability in their employment, equitable participation in the profits of the firm, and an ability to participate in governance. This principled form of work ensures that economic benefits are distributed to all rather than the privileged few. Worker cooperatives work in an open market just as other businesses do.

Capitalism is characterized by competitive markets and the return of profits to investors. In the globalized economy, it is a race to the bottom as firms look for the best opportunities to find cheap labor and little to no regulation of their practices. Global inequality leaves the majority of workers living and working in substandard and often unsafe conditions. In advanced economies, it is a model of diabolical design to use working-class assets in the form of pension funds as an engine for capital markets, while keeping it invisible to the workers who own the pensions. In this way, it buys the complicity of workers in preserving the system in the hope that they will be left something to live on in their retirement. How much better the economy could be if we provided workers clear, transparent, and meaningful ownership of the firms in which they work!

These ideas are not new. Matthews (1999) in his study of the Mondragon Group,[1] a cooperative group of worker-owned firms, wrote of "distributism" — a political philosophy that first emerged in response to an earlier period of severe social inequality. Distributism is based on a belief of broadened ownership of property and a "society of owners" rather than the concentration of wealth in the hands of a few. It emphasizes socializing the ownership of the means of production, distribution, and exchange. Worker cooperatives are a well-tested vehicle for that broadened ownership. Surely this approach is superior to today's "shareholder primacy" model, which privatizes profits, socializes losses, and misinforms intentionally and mightily through "purpose washing" and virtue signaling.

An updated but related discussion of worker cooperatives can be found in the work of Horowitz (2021), who advocates for a return to the values of working together (see **Chapter 30**). Mutual aid — or *mutualism* — is key to her analysis of what it takes to create a virtuous cycle in our economy. Mutualist organizations, according to Horowitz, are created to solve a social problem and to serve their members. They are economic institutions guided by principles of sustainability and independence from outside third parties. Lastly, they have a long-term focus to serve future generations as well as the present members.

Just as an earlier generation turned to neighbors for barn raisings, and in later generations to the unionization of labor, and cooperatives in housing and banking, it is time for us to reclaim those values and promote these new approaches to address society's failings. There is a role for government in this work — but not in solving this challenge. Instead, government can create enabling legislation and provide seed funding to support the rebirth of this virtuous cycle. The rest is up to us.

The Case for Union Co-ops

Workers are dissatisfied and want to see changes. There is renewed interest in unionization in light of the pandemic and loose labor markets. Union drives are experiencing mixed results and much has focused recently on retail and service employment such as in Amazon's and Starbucks' US locations. The combination of slow wage growth, inflation, the Covid pandemic's "Great Resignation," and disparities in how workers were treated during the pandemic, have fueled this renewed interest in trade unions.

Unionized workers benefit from higher wages and better benefits, which benefits not only union members, but all workers. Unionized workplaces also see improvements for women and people of color. Union representation addresses issues of labor inequities such as occupational segregation, and discrimination due to structural racism and sexism (Economic Policy Institute, 2021).

Union density in the US as of 2018 has returned to pre-New Deal lows. Union membership is 10.8% of all wage and salary workers, and 6.4% in the private sector. Public sector membership has held steady since the 1970s but may be negatively affected by the US Supreme Court's *Janus* ruling (Milkman, 2020), that prevents unions from collecting mandatory "fair share" fees from non-members. These were partial fees charged to non-union members. Three of the unions (Teamsters, United Food & Commercial Workers, United Steelworkers) have seen about a 5% reduction in membership, but overall, the unions have not seen the loss of public sector memberships and fees (Bloomberg, 2020).

US unions have lost power and leverage, but there are encouraging signs. Milkman (2020) sees optimistic trends for the future of labor, citing the successful efforts of worker centers, the "Fight for $15" led by the SEIU in the fast-food industry, and the favorable view of unions by the millennial, Z and Alpha generations who were particularly impacted by the Great Recession. Also noteworthy was the successful 2018 teachers' strike in West Virginia that catalyzed similar walkouts in Oklahoma, Arizona, Kentucky, North Carolina, and Colorado (Milkman, 2020).

According to Peck, a cultural transformation is afoot:

> A crossover electoral majority is demanding a new culture of honorable work. As a result, in a melting-pot nation experiencing meltdown, hybrid labor-organizing opportunities abound. This process includes a democratic, cooperative, and marketplace-competitive approach to new work prospects, technologies, and structures reflecting the values of self-reliance, bootstrapped entrepreneurialism, and civic and workplace equity, combined with wage solidarity, democratic inclusion, inter-cooperation, and social transformation. Cooperatives that offer competitive marketplace examples of workplace democracy and represent significant scale are already uniting with unions who bring solidarity culture and journeyman training, including safety, back to the American productivity table (Peck, 2021).

Trade unionism has remained strong in some OECD countries. Iceland is the most unionized country with 90.4% of its workforce represented. Scandinavia has strong unionization: Denmark (67%), Sweden (65.2%), Finland (58.8%), and Norway (50.4%) (OECD, 2022). German trade-union memberships have been steadily declining; IG Metall is Germany's largest union and has had tremendous influence in speaking not only for its members, but also for much of the German workforce (Groll, 2013). As we will see in **Chapter 15**, this decline is leading some to rethink the nature of trade unionism and IG Metall's approach.

Trade unionism in the UK, while stronger than in the US, has also seen declining membership — from a high of 13 million in 1979 to a current level of 6.44 million (Roper, 2020). Yet, since the start of the pandemic, Trade Union Congress-affiliated unions are seeing an increase in memberships in both the public and private sectors. Union membership accounts for 23.5% of all UK workers (Roper, 2020). Membership increases have been noticeable amongst frontline workers and women.

Labor activism has traditionally focused on wages and benefits. The pandemic has shed light on another key area of union activity — the health and safety of workers. A study of UK and US workers found that health and safety committees are able to serve as a collective voice in advocating for the health and safety of all workers (Moore *et al.*, 2022). While unions walk a fine line on issues of vaccination and Covid, union health and safety committees are able to advocate for employer resources to educate and protect workers equitably. "To some extent, unions educate workers about the nature of their legal rights, facilitate exercise of these rights, and work to ensure such rights are protected by encouraging vigorous enforcement against violations" (Sojourner & Yang, 2022). In the US, given the limited effectiveness of the Federal Occupational Health & Safety Administration, union health and safety committees have a significant role to play in the workplace.

There is also a case for linking cooperatives and unions (Bird *et al.*, 2021), which could reinvigorate their memberships and strengthen their movements, given their mutual concern with social and economic equity. Through the joint efforts of unions and worker cooperatives in the form of union co-ops, workers are able to realize the benefits of ownership and are assured that the voice of all workers are heard. The growing, global, social-enterprise-economy movement includes both labor and worker cooperatives together with many other mission-aligned constituencies.

An Introduction to the Mondragon Cooperatives

For men and women to be owners of their own destiny they must have an inner "music." If the melody is that of money and the desire to live with unlimited comforts, it will not be possible to transform the structures. — Alfonso Gorroñogoitia (Altuna Garibilondo, 2008)

Those are words to live by as we seek to create a more ethical approach to our economic activities. Worker members in the Mondragon co-operatives understand the challenge of how to advance their business activities, while ensuring that individually their involvement is about transforming their communities, and not simply about their own personal gains. We, the editors of this book, share those values. One of our intentions here is to foster a focus on union cooperatives and other, similarly mission-aligned, hybrid worker-ownership structures that have both a commitment to place and to the people in those places.

The inspiration for this approach lies in successful examples of people who came together to improve their lives, such as the Mondragon Cooperative Corporation in the Basque region of Spain. Today it employs over 80,000 people in 96 cooperatives and 14 research and development centers in four sectors: finance, industry, retail, and knowledge. Yet as we go to press, the members of Orona, a cooperative manufacturer of elevators, and the Ulma Group (focusing on greenhouse, architecture and construction-related sectors), have voted to leave the Mondragon Group. This will reduce the scale of the industrial group by 50%. The significance of this change is addressed by Michael Peck in **Chapter 1**.

Mondragon has been built on a strong cooperative set of principles that place labor at the center, while recognizing that its success is based on its ability to engage in a free market system. It has served as a global touchstone for people seeking alternatives to the anti-union corporate model that prioritizes profits over labor, communities, and the environment. Much has been learned from their experience, and still more can be learned. This book examines how we can reimagine capitalism on principles of shared ownership, unionized worker ownership, and a commitment to the people and places where these firms are established. One of our goals here is to establish a theoretical framework for examining the problems of corporate capitalism, and how worker ownership and worker cooperatives address issues of equity and inequality in a free-market system.

Mondragon has been the muse for many who have pursued new worker-cooperative development, and explored the question of how to adapt the "Mondragon Experience" to other places in the world. These experiences are part of this book.

Among them is Chris's 1982 journey to Mondragón to conduct doctoral field work on the management of the cooperatives.[2] At that time, the director of public relations at the Caja Laboral Popular (Mondragon's affiliated bank) was Iñaki Aguirre Zabala, the son of the first Basque president. Her first meeting with Iñaki led to an invitation to conduct doctoral field work with access to the bank's library, and support from Iñaki's staff to organize interviews with managers (Clamp, 1986). Chris was eventually able to connect with three Mondragon founders who at the time were still with the cooperative: Jesús Larrañaga, José María Ormaetxea, and Alfonso Gorroñogoitia. As her field work progressed, she had the chance to become part of the community of Mondragón itself — the municipality in the Basque Country that the cooperative group is named after. There, she deepened her relationships with the Mondragon cooperative's founders and members. She worked with marketing staff on English-language translations, assisted visitors, got involved with the agricultural cooperative group, and joined a *cuadrilla* — a group of close friends who are core to Basque social life. During her stay, Chris interviewed 50 cooperative managers; most were mid-career; some joined the cooperatives for their potential to build and strengthen the local economy of the Basque Country. Inspired by the leadership of Mondragon's spiritual, moral, visionary, and practical founder, the Catholic village priest José María Arizmendiarrieta, they were able to create the first co-ops and contribute significantly to the redevelopment of the Basque region. Another contributor to this book, Mondragon's first international president, Jésus María Herrasti, writes in the context of a personal relationship with Father Arizmendiarrieta (see **Chapter 7**).

In 1980, the BBC produced a film about the Mondragon cooperatives that served to inspire others. Visitors came from trade unions in the UK and other parts of Europe, and from as far away as China. The Chinese wanted to study how this form of cooperation functioned in a free-market system. Thousands of people from all parts of the globe still visit Mondragón annually to see this exceptional example of social innovation and workplace democracy. In **Chapter 17**, Dan Swinney reflects on how influential that film was for him and many others.

Initially, the challenge was how we could replicate the Mondragon model. For others, it was to adapt those lessons that were relevant to a new setting. In the US, we wondered whether the Mondragon experience could be replicated, citing questions as to whether it was idiosyncratic to Basque culture and historical circumstances. Replication has rarely if ever worked in development. Still, there are many aspects that could be adopted, such as the structure of capital accounts, the role of social councils, and the labor indices that created a flatter compensation structure.

Innovation in the Mondragon Experience

Mondragon has undergone many changes since its first cooperatives were established in the 1950s. Another aim of this book is to examine Mondragon in its current form, and its continued value as a touchstone for us to learn from and to gain inspiration. Throughout its history, Mondragon has demonstrated an amazing ability to innovate. This can be seen in its recognition of the need to create a linked system of cooperatives with their own bank, research and development centers, and social insurance. Another important innovation is the capital structure of using internal capital accounts for each worker-member, and the allocation of a share of profits to support the local communities in the form of schools, hospitals, and strengthening the Basque culture.

Another goal of this book is to examine how important innovation has been to the sustainability of the Mondragon cooperative experience. First, we consider the role Caja Laboral Popular played as a development bank in the early years of the group. We then consider recent examples of innovation in banking in the case of Gaztenpresa; in mentoring a new generation of entrepreneurial leaders in Ahalbidetu (not a Mondragon entity, but situated in Bilbao in the Basque Country);[3] in product and service development at the Erreka Group; and lastly the creation of new cooperatives through Team Academy.

Mondragon's story is not just one of successful worker ownership but also of successful community economic development. This is evident in the 10% that is returned to social investments from the cooperatives. It is evident in the growth of the *ikastolas* — cooperative primary and secondary schools established in the 1960s and 1970s in the Basque Country. Today, there are 120 ikastolas in the region, with 6,000 teachers serving 60,000 students and 40,000 families. This represents 15% to 18% of the educational system in the region (Ikastolen Elkartea, 2022).

One can also see this in the growth of Mondragon University, with its three schools and its involvement internationally in the network of universities and incubators fostering the next generation of entrepreneurs and intrapreneurs. Mondragon, in the past, was criticized for not promoting its cooperative-group membership internationally. One of the managers that Chris interviewed in 1982 pointed out that they were not missionaries of cooperation; rather, they focused on how to improve their own region.

Today, Mondragon does have foundations — Mundukide (mundukide.org/es/) and the Eroski Foundation (https://corporativo.eroski.es/quienes-somos/fundacion-eroski/). Eroski is supported by the 10% social contribution from the Eroski Cooperative's annual profits. Mundukide receives both individual as well as corporate contributions from cooperative and noncooperative firms. Mundukide is currently engaged in development work in Ethiopia, Colombia, Ecuador, Brazil, and Mozambique, as well as the Basque Country.

Key to Mondragon's cohesion as a group are its clearly articulated cooperative principles. Mondragon continues to foster a principled approach committed to workers through cooperative ownership, and adheres to the following 10 principles:

1. **Free adherence** — Mondragon is open to anyone who accepts our Principles. There needs to be respect for diversity in who may be a member of the co-op, *i.e.*, no restrictions on the basis of religion, partisan politics, or ethnicity.

2. **Democratic organization** — a one-person, one-vote system for election of the cooperative's governing bodies and for deciding on the most important issues.

3. **Sovereignty of labor** — profit is allocated on the basis of the work contributed by each member in order to achieve this profit.

4. **Instrumental and subordinated nature of capital** — capital is a necessary resource, but it does not confer the right to vote and its stake in the profit is limited and subordinated to labor.

5. **Participation in management** -- workers participate in governance of their firms.

6. **Wage solidarity** — in accordance with the cooperative's real possibilities, and equitable at an internal and external level and for Mondragon.

7. **Inter-cooperation** — as a mechanism for solidarity between cooperatives and for business efficiency.

8. **Social transformation** — commitment to the supportive, sustainable development of our local area.

9. **Universality** — in solidarity with the promoters of economic democracy within the context of the social economy, fully embracing the goals of the international cooperative movement.

10. **Education** — promoting people and the cooperative culture, allocating human and financial resources to the cooperative, and professional education of the members and to young people in general. (Altuna Garibilondo, 2008.)

Figure 0.1: Basic Cooperative Principles

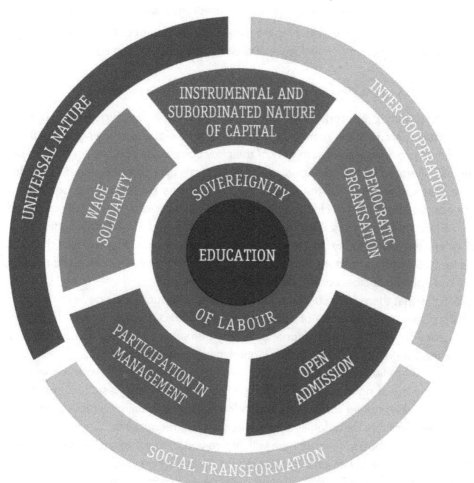

Source: MONDRAGON CORPORATION.

In this book we also examine Mondragon's influence in similar movements, first in the Catholic Church, then in England, Germany, the Republic of Korea (South Korea), and the US. The case examples explore how Mondragon has been a source of inspiration, and a resource to many. In the concluding section, our contributors discuss the resource challenges we face in new worker-cooperative development.

This book is intended to provide hope and inspiration by serving as a resource for those interested in developing worker cooperatives, as well as an introduction for those interested in the virtuous cycle/"solidarity dividend" alternatives to shareholder-primacy capitalism. It is also intended to peer over horizons and around corners, "showing, not telling" how Mondragon-inspired virtuous cycles transform "humanity at work" globally and locally. Virtuous cycle characteristics include self-reliance, the DIY (do-it-yourself) ethos, equal and inclusive opportunities and practices, shared wealth-creation with democratic governance, climate healing, and aspirational work with shared purpose and values.

The book was conceived in the middle of four lethal pandemics simultaneously threatening "humanity at work and life": embedded racism, withering economic-class inequalities, Covid's terrible death toll, and a global assault on democracy. Through the various chapters in this collection, our goal is to inform and inspire the efforts of a new generation of cooperative entrepreneurs. Its two-fold mission:

- First, to be a resource for those developing hybrid-model worker cooperatives and social enterprises as framework for an inclusive, and climate-respecting "stakeholders-as-shareholders" global economy.

- Second, to uplift and amplify critical new voices of those doing the work.

We encourage you to turn to the conclusion at the end of this book *first* to gain an appreciation of what this collection contains. Many of the contributors joined us for a virtual convening where they introduced themselves and then provided a short summary of their key points. The concluding chapter pulls together the main themes generated by the contributors and shows how they come together as a cohesive whole.

We believe that today's "war of the worlds" in Ukraine has presented a moment of urgency to reimagine our economic institutions. Neoliberal globalization has proven gratuitously cruel and ineffective in response to these multiple crises. The global pandemic has shone a harsher light on inequalities in society and offers the opportunity to develop hybrid worker-ownership models that seed virtuous economic cycles that no longer commoditize human and social capital. This book lifts the lid on building high-purpose and uplifting socioeconomics that work equally for all.

Our core belief is that there is no sustaining worker voice without worker power that is demonstrated through solidarity, democracy, equality of opportunity, and shared equity and wealth. Its premise is that an ineluctable policy for a fair and aspirational economy demands inclusive, broadened, and deepened stakeholder/worker ownership, undergirded by workplace democracy practices.

Like Mondragon, we believe single-class equity governance is synonymous with solidarity. Every equity share guarantees the equal right to vote for change, and provides the basis for a paradigm-changing culture that combines stakeholder community and individual civic mutualism, stability, and self-reliance to innovate, defend and facilitate more fulfilled lives and dignified retirements.

We hope that the contributions shared here will inspire you to look forward and see these testimonies as a means to look beyond what has already been done. We challenge you, and ourselves, to use the lens of these shared narratives to see, individually and collectively, just over the horizon, around corners and in the urgent present — and then act, wherever we are, to build the better world we know is possible.

There is always another step to take.

Father José María Arizmendiarrieta

Photo source: Wikipedia.

End-notes

[1] "Mondragon" is the current branding of the Mondragon co-operatives. Where we refer to the co-operative group, we have used the spelling Mondragon as in Mondragon Cooperative Corporation (MCC). Reference to the town is presented here in Spanish as Mondragón.

[2] Published information on the early years of Mondragon can be found in the following article: *The Evolution of Management in the Mondragon Cooperatives*, https://community-wealth.org/sites/clone.community-wealth.org/files/downloads/paper-clamp.pdf.

[3] Ahalbidetu is not a Mondragon entity, but a Bilbao entity resulting from Bilbao's singular industrial leadership in the Basque and Spanish experience… we are also framing the Basque region as well as that of Mondragón.

References

Altuna Garibilondo, L. (2008). *La Experiencia cooperativa de MONDRAGON*. Eskoriatza: Lanki-Huhezi, Mondragon University.

Bird, A., Conaty, P., Mangan, A., McKeown, M., Ross, C. & Taylor, S. (2021). Together we will stand. In J. Manley & P.B. Whyman, *The Preston Model & Community Wealth Building* (pp.93-110). London: Routledge.

Bloomberg Law (June 26, 2020): *Unions Fend Off Membership Exodus in 2 Years Since Janus Ruling*. Available at https://news.bloomberglaw.com/daily-labor-report/unions-fend-off-membership-exodus-in-2-years-since-janus-ruling.

Clamp, C. (2March 20, 1986). Managing Cooperation at Mondragon. *Unpublished doctoral dissertation*. Chestnut Hill, MA: Boston College.

Clamp, C.A. (1985). History and structure of Mondragon Cooperatives. in E.M. Bennett, *Social Intervention: Theory and Practice* (pp.349-370). Lewiston, NY: The Edwin Mellen Press.

Economic Policy Institute (April 23, 2021). *Unions help reduce disparities and strengthen our democracy*. Available at https://files.epi.org/uploads/226030.pdf.

Groll, E. (September 2, 2013). The world's most powerful labor unions. *Foreign Policy*. https://foreignpolicy.com/2013/09/02/the-worlds-most-powerful-labor-unions/.

Horowitz, S. (2021). *Mutualism*. New York: Random House.

Ikastolen Elkartea (2022). *Euskal Herriko ikastolak Europear Kooperatiba eta Ikastola mugimendua*. Donostia: Ikastolen Elkartea.

Matthews, R. (1999). *Jobs of Our Own*. Annandale: Pluto Press Australia.

Milkman, R. (2020). Union decline & labor revival in the 21st century United States. *Chicago-Kent Law Review, 95*(1), 273-298.

Mondragon Corporation (May 4, 2022). *About Us*. https://www.Mondragon-corporation.com/en/about-us/.

Moore, S., Burns, C., Carter, N., Clamp, C., Amendah, E. & Martin, W. (May 2022). *Understanding Vaccine Hesitancy Amongst Frontline Workers - the Influence of Trade Union & Community Representatives*. The British Academy: https://www.thebritishacademy.ac.uk/documents/3752/Understanding-Vaccine-Hesitancy-Amongst-Frontline-Workers.pdf.

OECD (May 22, 2022). *Trade Union Dataset*. https://stats.oecd.org/Index.aspx?DataSetCode=TUD.

Peck, M.A. (2021). The pandemic changes everything. In J. Manley & P.B. Whyman, *The Preston Model & Community Wealth Building*. London: Routledge.

Restakis, J. (2010). *Humanizing the Economy*. Gabriola Island, BC: New Society Publishers.

Roper, C. (May 7, 2020). *Union membership rises for third year running to 6.4 million*. TUC: https://www.tuc.org.uk/blogs/union-membership-rises-third-year-running-64-million#:~:text=Female%20membership%20now%20highest%20since%201995.&text=Over%20the%20last%20year%20union,by%20over%20200%2C000%20since%202017.

Sojourner, A.J. & Yang, J. (March, 2022). Effects of unionization on workplace-safety enforcement: Regression-discontinuity evidence. *ILR Review, 75*(2), 373–401.

Reimagining Capitalism

This section sets a theoretical framework for examining the problems of corporate capitalism, and how worker ownership and worker cooperatives address issues of equity and inequality in a free market system.

CHAPTER 1

Cooperative Capitalism at the Coalface

Michael Peck

Part 1: The Coalface

Humanity at Work and Life: Global diffusion of the Mondragon Cooperative ecosystem experience (MCE²)

Before automation replaced hand cutting in the darkest, most cramped, dirty and hazardous conditions, the coalface miner — a collier — was paid by the mine operator-owner to identify and select the best seams and veins. Masters of depth and density, coalface miners directed their teams to extract energy and wealth out of rock. Running in the deep undergrounds of globalized corporations, extractive commerce started in the mining sectors, where boom-bust local economies and job-site health risks — explosions, avalanches, closures, unheralded deaths lost to black lung darkness — provoked labor confrontations with owners and operators.

Financially compensated in direct proportion to meeting quality and quantity performance metrics, the original "coalface" — the mining-industry skill descriptor — evolved to signify workers' "hands-on" involvement and frontline leadership by example. Fairly distributed financial rewards for work, however relatively dignified on site, never kept up with sector production expertise and shared risks. Shared equity and democratic governance commensurate with productivity and earned profits also remain unrealized for subsequent coalface generations living with strip-mined mountaintops and hometown ecological toxicity after the easy pickings departed with the operating capital.

Today's world hypocritically decries coal, while demanding ever-more quantities "to electrify everything." Coal-producing regions face Hobbesian choices, trading coal's spoil tips, slag heaps, and dustbin detritus in exchange for hard-scrabble survival. Unchecked lethal pulmonary diseases are traced directly to vicious-cycle mastectomy removal of mountaintops and dumping of surface and strip-mined earth into adjacent valleys and streams, leaving no clean and healthy way out for local coalface stakeholders.

Each new industrial wave of extractive energy adoption demands more local earth, air, noise, heat, freshwater and precariat human sacrifice. Environmental safety threats fall through outdated and unrepaired safety nets, from mining to oil drilling and gas fracking, to megawatt wind-turbine towers dominating local mountain ridges whooshing through valley flatlands and graded ridges, and solar panels radiating across every available, flat-enough terrain.

These are the lands of no more body parts to barter.

Rising local and national resistance to right-of-way permitting follows a well-hewed path, pulling scabs off generational wounds earned from preparing hometown terrain for exported profits that strip regions of legacy environmental balance in exchange for regional economic lifeblood. Without credible, sustaining, inclusive economic formulas, these places written off by exterritorial economic elites as beyond cultural and stakeholder redemption, increasingly and reflexively vote in defiance and accumulated grievance. Monetizing Murdochian media monsters egg them on, selling proven lies for shareholder profit, whipping the faithful into partisan frenzy to then leave victims to rot in the trash folder aftermath of discounted anonymity when the trials and funerals begin.

This is the gospel of creative destruction without any faith in equally creative local reconstruction.

It takes a Basque village with topography similar to North-Central Appalachia, substituting a seagoing coastline for the five-state Ohio Valley River region, mastering the forging of iron and steel while confronting multiple incoming pandemics such as state-sponsored socio-economic devastation without pause after a Civil War, World War II and 40 years of dictatorship, to offer more equal and sustaining, generationally prosperous, sociocultural pathways forward.

It takes extended, networked village ecosystems — reeling worldwide from trickle-down misery, while dying of transformation thirst — to consider what alternatives creative and just reconstruction might offer to stakeholders and their communities treated as living, renewing, sacred human and social resources.

Forgotten people and places, not only in America's mountain ranges, their valleys, flatlands, townships, but also in suburbs, coastlines, and cities where Covid-19 "seamlessly" followed evilly marketed corporate fentanyl takeovers of unsuspecting local populations whose already degrading healthcare infrastructure was unable to cope with increased biological toxicity. This double gut punch, a coalface misery index avalanche in the making, added the moral injury of agony without hope to the civic insult of more solitary, disrespected deaths in unmarked graves.

Salvation at the coalface happens by joining climate- and energy-security subsets together with better social- and human-capital asset metrics, guiding impact investments in virtuous instead of vicious cycles. Applying purpose-driven common-ground solutions to intersecting common-good formulas rebuilds local existential resiliency. This is where the salvaging whole can greatly exceed the extracted parts.

Fixing planetary precarity starts at the coalface ground zero for unevenly broken places, keeping the carpetbaggers and plunderers at bay by empowering local stakeholders with agency, equity, and self-governance, recharging aspiration and fulfilment into a blue-green topography where demographics and natural resources can still forge regenerative destiny.

This book's practice origin flows from its globally diverse but values-aligned contributors, each bringing their own rationale and purpose in localizing 70 years of witnessed and shared Mondragon cooperative-ecosystem experiences "across borders, markets and societal silos."

Its individual chapters testify to Mondragon as an eclectically replicable model that endures and re-girds to meet incoming tests of time (Bamburg, 2018; Duda, 2016; Gilbert, 2015; Goodman, 2020; Hadfield, 2019; Mondragon, 2012; Neumann, 2022; Peck, 2014; Romeo, 2022; Tremlett, 2013; Tulankide, 2022a, 2022c), a living model experiencing its structural and mission trials as instructive towards future tribulations benefitting successive generations.

Starting with the Mondragon Cooperative Ecosystem Experience (MCE²), the book showcases civil-social compacts where all stakeholders equally and democratically exercise power, enabling for-profit platforms that prioritize place and occupation-based equity and prosperity. Local and regional inter-cooperating ecosystems practice purpose-driven and values-energized independence to alleviate and deliver freedom from want, fear, exploitation, and subjugation, by structuring solidarity and sovereignty in local workplaces and communities.

HUMANITY @ WORK & LIFE endeavors to reimagine and reconstitute a world where individual fulfilment and the common good do not line up as opposing, zero-sum choices, but prove themselves synergistic interdependencies. In this living and liberating context, the market's "visible hands" fulfil locally aligned cultural and commercial goals. The practice of creating broadened, deepened, higher-impact, dignified lives perfects the art of "doing well by first doing good" and equitably distributing both.

As demonstrated by Mondragon, profitability allows practitioners to afford chosen values.

HUMANITY @ WORK & LIFE offers recipes, testimonies, and reflections toward such results. Intentionally designed virtuous cycles self-actuate when good actions or events produce mutually good results, concurrently and sequentially for more recipients, in sustaining, benchmarked ways (Grover & John, 2015; Macmillan Dictionary, n.d.; Merriam-Webster, n.d.; A. Price, 2021).

Evidence shows these leaps of faith to "pay it forward" lead to more effective standard practice levels impacting greater common good. Commonplace, marketplace miracles baptized in solidarity, innovation, and transparent practice seed, cultivate and harvest themselves becoming everyday occurrences. No longer a miracle of grace but grace itself to feed, shelter, clothe, self-govern and employ those aspiring to the fullest dignity and mission potential of purpose-driven work.

ESG-SDG, Human & social capital seams reconfiguring capitalism's culturally disfigured coalface

Eighty-two years ago, after the first World War, Great Depression, and rising global fascism that ignited World War II, the lyrical American author Thomas Wolfe's posthumously published novel *You Can't Go Home Again* (Wolfe, 1940) lent a crescendoing voice to the prescient understanding in 1940 that humanity "cannot devour the Earth," that it "must know and accept its limitations":

> But it is not only at these outward forms that we must look to find the evidence of a nation's hurt. We must look as well at the heart of guilt that beats in each of us, for there the cause lies. We must look, and with our own eyes see, the central core of defeat and shame and failure which we have wrought in the lives of even the least of these, our brothers. (p.284)

And, let us hasten to add, our sisters, children, families, neighbors, colleagues, classmates, strangers, enemies and friends.

In the waning days of August 2022, and in a verbal shot heard round the world, US President Biden declared the United States faces rising, reoccurring 21st-century domestic "semi fascism" (Cadelago & Olander, 2022; Shabad, 2022; Tharoor, 2022b).

We can add justice, power, socioeconomic class, health, wealth, actuarial table longevity and even happiness to the right-wing pundit Andrew Breitbart's attributed quote that "politics is downstream from culture" ("Andrew Breitbart," 2023) with a bipartisan, academic definition of fascism by historian Robert Paxton (2004):

> Fascism in power is a compound, a powerful amalgam of different but marriageable conservative, national socialist, and radical right ingredients, bonded together by common enemies and common passions for a regenerated, energized and purified nation, whatever the cost to free institutions and the rule of law. (p.207)

We can feel the burn of at least one-third of sociopolitical America voting for the losing side in the 2020 presidential elections, agitating and glaring back at the nation, and a purposefully convened subset of this polity insurrecting on January 6, 2021, against the results and traditional peaceful handover of executive power (Montanaro, 2022).

Forty-one years ago, the iconic American political intellectual Susan Sontag dared to be the first to equate communism with fascism (*New York Times*, 1982), bravely and accurately predicting that the commonality between the two is marked by comparable repression where "democratic government and worker self-rule are clearly intolerable and will not be tolerated."

Events echo Sontag's realization, proving how and why Ukraine's continued resistance in the face of Putin's military aggression remains so vital to ongoing, bipartisan US foreign policy credibility (including how best to contain China's imperial designs on Taiwan), and securing domestic environmental and energy consensus (E.A. Cohen, 2022; Packer, 2022; Tharoor, 2022a). Ukraine is the climate-precarity Rorschach test (2023) where Planet Earth's climate resiliency hangs in the balance, starting with the interplay between zero-emission climate security, and fossil fuel hegemony that already incites so many 21st-century conflicts.

David Brooks (2022) in *The Triumph of the Ukrainian Idea* observes:

> The war in Ukraine is not only a military event; it's an intellectual event. The Ukrainians are winning not only because of the superiority of their troops. They are winning because they are fighting for a superior idea — an idea that inspires Ukrainians to fight so doggedly, an idea that inspires people across the West to stand behind Ukraine and back it to the hilt.

Ideas backed by values and performance can move markets, battlefields, vaccines, elections, hearts, and minds. Heather Cox Richardson (2022) defines a superior idea's globally motivating mission, rights, and responsibilities:

Τhe foundational principles of self-determination, territorial integrity, and political independence must be respected, international institutions must be strengthened, countries must be free to determine their own foreign policy choices, information must be allowed to flow freely, universal human rights must be upheld, and the global economy must operate on a level playing field and provide opportunity for all.

The proxy war in Ukraine — with climate security *vs* Russian and Chinese imperial ambition in the balance — influences politicized regulatory battles in the US over whether ESG (environmental, social, governance) and UN SDGs (sustainable development goals; sdgs.un.org) are financially true, helpful, and profitable, or just partisan-polluted greenwashing (Power, 2022; Wilson, 2021). In this context, the term "net zero" refers more to an aspirational accounting function than any documentation of actual reduction in carbon emissions.

Such intersectionality both terrifies and electrifies. It pushes us to reach for socio-economic justice and a climate-resilient planet. Securing "climate peace" seeded by capital allocation and enhanced performance restructuring will be just as critical as winning military wars to sustain these outcomes.

Foreseeing the last century's sociopolitical agonies and ecstasies, Thomas Wolfe (1940) observed:

Τhere had to be a larger world than this glittering fragment of a world with all its wealth and privilege … But tonight, in a hundred separate moments of intense reality, it had revealed to him its very core. He had seen it naked, with its guards down. He had sensed how the hollow pyramid of a false social structure had been erected and sustained upon a base of common mankind's blood and sweat and agony … Privilege and truth could not lie down together. (p.275)

HUMANITY @ WORK & LIFE confronts the same moral and civic struggle against unchecked privilege, rapacious power, and disinformation. In this bravest new world, social economies will run on self-energizing virtuous cycles. Those who can deliver metrics that generate scale will earn performance-driven leadership roles for their enterprises, regional ecosystems, and nations. Social-investments strategies will continue to outperform because they anticipate sunsetting industries, accompanied by inclusive, compassionate, and productive "just transition" exit strategies (Boffo & Patalano, 2020; EY Global, 2021; Junkus & Berry, 2015; Kempf & Osthoff, 2007). With corporations increasingly viewing workers as their most important asset (Brandenburg *et al.*, 2022), the art of impact funding depends on defining standards for measuring mutualist results, aligning mission values and purpose, seeding and nurturing inclusive practitioner and stakeholder as shareholder beneficiary ecosystems, and establishing replicable methodology and structuring templates.

"Evidence suggests that democracy does cause growth, and its effect is significant and sizable … a country that transitions from nondemocracy to democracy achieves about 20% higher GDP *per capita* in the next 25 years than a country that remains a nondemocracy' (Acemoglu *et al.*, 2019). Increasingly, investors and business sectors value the profit-generating upside of reliable, predictable, regulation-fostering, prosperous, safe, and stable communities that exhibit peaceful conflict resolution, respect for human dignity, basic freedoms, and equality before the law in safe and secure communities.

Pushing and pulling in less productive directions, America's civic, cultural and economic diseases continue to register as the world's entangling, pre-existing conditions. Untamed inflation prices out pandemics that mutate faster than cures, outstripping survival wages despite more empowered, rising labor mobility. Gig-economy platforms that misclassify labor become an "Uber for X" (Madrigal, 2019) tax on the working souls of the nations they infest.

In *The Matrix*, Agent Smith says to Neo: "We're not here because we're free. We're here because we're not free. There's no escaping reason. No denying purpose. Because as we both know without purpose, we would not exist" (The Matrix Wiki, *n.d.*).

Abandoned by the barbarians inside the tipping point gates, a blue-ocean planet struggles to breathe through "an estimated 171 trillion plastic particles that if gathered would weigh around 2.3 million tons" (Christensen, 2019) clogging its watery lungs. In response, triple bottom line (People, Planet, Profit) graduates into quadruple bottom line (People, Planet, Purpose, Profit) with *purpose* combating predatory, exterritorial, shareholder-primacy insanity that refuses to adequately invest in stakeholder cures.

Hope persists in spite of daily Ukraine civilian bombardments by an imperial antagonist intent on cultural obliteration. Hope becomes a pilgrimage, reshapes trade routes, inspires spiritual enlightenment, changes migratory patterns, and deepens civic engagement.

Hope appears in Spain's recent executive decision (aided by the example of Mondragon's advocacy and cooperative ecosystem) to devote €880 million last June to inclusively "just" socioeconomics transitioning a pandemic-challenged national economy (ranked 14th-largest by nominal GDP and the fifth-largest in Europe), and declaring worker cooperatives as the preferred enterprise conversion structure (*Economy of Spain*, 2023; *List of Countries by GDP (Nominal)*, 2023; *List of Sovereign States in Europe by GDP (Nominal)*, 2023; NationMaster, *n.d.*).

Better standards lead to better leadership. "To secure the future of the planet and humanity, we need to create innovative business models that drive shareholder returns by addressing the very challenges that threaten us" (Galston & Kamarck, 2022). We need both individual *servant leadership* by example and community "steward leadership, which is the genuine desire and persistence to create a collective better future" (O'Connor, 2022; Peshawaria, 2020, 2022), proven through mutualist performance metrics where those being measured have a say in defining the metrics.

ESG stands for environmental, social, and governance. ESG Investing (also known as — and sometimes confused with — "socially responsible investing," "impact investing," and "sustainable investing") refers to allocation of capital incorporating environmental, social, and governance (ESG) factors or outcomes with other standard financial reporting information. ESG juxtaposes four capital allocation areas (human, social, climate or natural, and financial) with some ESG investor practitioners, analysts and standards setters-placing, environmental and social factors on a more even scale to financial while many do not. Climate or natural capital allocation is further advanced through a plethora of announced funds and metrics than human and social capital investments. Many big asset managers made net zero commitments at Glasgow, Scotland (COP 26 — November 2021), and agreed to establish a fund to compensate vulnerable nations for "loss and damage" from climate-induced disasters at Sharm el-Sheikh, Egypt (COP 27 — November 2022) with governments rushing to catch up to create regulatory systemic solutions.

Both summits reveal performative intent outpacing execution as Planet Earth's cumulative ecological debts exponentially and regressively accumulate. Post-pandemic inflation and climate precarity are increasing, reveal embedded inequalities that accelerate global polarization, and lead to widening "trust gaps between businesses and governments," growing market instability, uncertainty, and "cratered economic optimism." Only respondents in China believe that they and their families will be better off in five years. That puts more pressure on CEOs to establish the trust among consumers that governments have failed to win (Allen, 2023).

The 17 interlinked sustainable development goals (SDGs) established in 2015 by the United Nations General Assembly are designed to be a "blueprint to achieve a better and more sustainable future for all" by 2030 (sdgs.un.org).

The rules of engagement for ESG metrics and SDG goals (if taken seriously and transparently pursued to envisioned investment horizons and beyond) hold the potential to change everything by deploying an implied, virtuous cycle strategy to "get more bees with honey." ESG/SDG impact investor practitioners begin to learn that human, social and natural capital can make or break financial-capital margins. This stakeholder-centric process of "flattening the curves" starts with building shared solidarity and mutualist culture, which drive shared profitable returns on balance sheets, and uplift workers, their families, and communities. This in turn can equalize labor and capital returns on investments, and end the feudalist-plantation practice of privatizing profits while socializing losses (IEA *et al.*, 2022; Larsen *et al.*, 2021; von Czechowski, 2020).

Flattening shareholder-primacy curves — like vaccines flattened the terrible, spiking mortality curves of the Covid-19 pandemic — enable stakeholders to become shareholders in their own, local, living economies. This elevates the "S" both in the "social" part of ESGs and the "sustainable" mandate for SDGs.

For capital providers, the "S" in ESG's formulations dominates and increasingly is based on resiliency algorithms. Resiliency and stakeholder ownership are inseparable; one provides the roots and rationale for the other. ESG provides the investor metrics tool chest (with the UNRISD's Sustainable Development Performance Indicators [SDPIs] manual as recent example; unrisd.org) for what Deloitte (Philip *et al.*, 2022) calls "an economic growth imperative," claiming:

> Rapidly achieving net zero emissions by mid-century could increase the size of the world economy by $43 trillion in net present value terms from 2021-2070. We have the technologies, business models, and policy approaches today to deliver rapid decarbonization and limit global warming to as close to 1.5°C by century's end.

ESG and impact investing are first cousins, not identical twins (Rose-Smith, 2022). The former analytically measures environmental, social, and governance key performance indicators (KPIs) to make decisions and assess risk to inspire and guide the latter — which is broadly mission defined and outcomes driven.

Democracy doesn't automatically sell itself abroad or domestically when the deciding, evaluating world is eyewitness to a global pandemic killing 15 million people ("excess deaths") in 2020-2021, according to the World Health Organization (2022). Individual and collective freedoms, opportunity costs, and common-good values eschew easy definitions in a domestic, continental, majority-consumer-generated market economy where "the three wealthiest Americans have more money than the bottom half of all Americans" (Molloy, 2019).

New stakeholder externalities should center on the "macroeconomics of the many" (Pothering, 2022), because that is where the greatest growth potential and competitive differentials reside. If pandemic economics teaches anything, it is that the most exposed precariat populations are the most essential to our common survival. Treating others as we would treat ourselves is just good business — in addition to being morally honest. Feed the village, and inspiring individuals will rise — as they are doing right here and now — to nourish the multitudes, heal the sick, flatten the curves, and protect the planet.

Shared prosperity is no miracle; it can be funded and measured by purpose-driven, righteously deployed human- and social-capital assets, replicated, and multiplied through innumerable social-economy virtuous cycles. This is a cause for rejoicing, not fear. Those who perfect practice will find it's true that "in giving by investing they will receive more profitable, inclusive" and sustaining outcomes (Boffo & Patalano, 2020; Polman & Winston, 2021).

Pandemics become resurrected as portals only when societies purposefully embrace something larger than themselves. Bridging opposing social, economic and political enclaves back into an intersecting Venn diagram center demands that we upgrade and enlarge our socioeconomic vision and commit to better practice.

The case for developing human- and social-assets capital portfolios with performance metrics designed and delivered by social-economy practitioners is presented in Zugasti & Peck (2021) and **Chapter 5.** The goal is for virtuous cycle, public benefit, social economy enterprises and ecosystems to transform social- and human-capital markets into solidarity-dividends the world can cash.

Similar to the UN-inspired 1992 Kyoto Protocol and 2015 Paris Accords, ESG is still a largely European phenomenon at the moment and an entire generation ahead of current practice in the US. Mostly large European pension funds and insurance companies provided the roughly "$40 trillion" (Kishan, 2022) invested globally in ESG funds in 2021, a figure that has declined somewhat in 2022. When the post-conflict Ukraine global Marshall reconstruction plan begins, it will dwarf all previous outlays in scope, vision, and impact bearing that name and purpose.

Instead of the last century's professional classes rushing to business schools and private equity firms when private funding for technology-driven startups began to outstrip and outpace public markets, 21st century "zoomers" (Generation Z), followed by Generation Alpha, want to focus on developing, sharing, and recruiting climate-science talent (Cortese, 2021a). "Talent is the X-factor in limiting warming to 1.5 degrees Celsius. Young people everywhere are trying to work in climate and that type of talent is undefeated" (Padilla, 2022). "Up to 95% of millennials are interested in investing sustainably," according to Morgan Stanley (2019).

Arundhati Roy's prescient, repeatedly quoted "pandemic as portal" serves as a just-in-time metaphor for today's resurging precariat aspiration to break decisively with yesterday's plantation *status quo*. Roy (2020) warns we can choose between:

> ... dragging the carcasses of our prejudice and hatred, our avarice, our data banks and dead ideas, our dead rivers, and smoky skies behind us. Or we can walk through lightly, with little luggage, ready to imagine another world. And ready to fight for it.

Global markets increasingly price this reality into corporate earnings projections and quarterly reports. It's no longer possible to lose a battle and win the war when both converge into unrecoverable ecological defeats that no reinsurance-industry actor is willing to underwrite.

Capital follows opportunities, which is why the anti-ESG-SDG campaigns — however viciously recycled, performatively popularized, and ideologically polarizing in the moment — will not inspire enduring conviction.

The pushback against naysayers has already begun. ImpactAlpha (Cortese & Price, 2022) describes how:

> ... [a] riskwashing crusade against ESG is hurting businesses, taxpayers, and retirees ... Firms engage in "greenwashing" when they deceive customers or investors about their environmental impact. Now come politicians who neglect their fiduciary and governing duties by substituting ideological agendas for attention to material risks to their cities and states ... Most stewards of other people's money want more, not less, information about investment risks.

Reinsurance actuarial tables tell the story to red state budgeteers: "The United States endured 18 separate disasters in 2022 whose damages exceeded $1 billion, with the total coming to $165 billion, according to a new report from the National Oceanic and Atmospheric Administration (NOAA)" (Morford, 2023; Rott, 2023). And that is before reaching climate tipping points.

Optimizing 2023 as the "Year of the S" — for social and human capital assets — compels us to consider purposeful, worker-owned, democratically governed, mutualist, social-economy businesses and ecosystems with equal regulatory and tax consideration to ensure transparent practice. Aspiring worker-owners and their host communities deserve the regulatory right to freely choose the structure locally and culturally best suited for them. Otherwise, already-outdated externalities will continue to drive the future of work instead of the reverse.

Part 2: Reinventing Cooperative Capitalism at the Coalface

First there is purpose. Professor Rebecca Henderson in *Reimagining Capitalism in a World on Fire* (2020) observes:

> This interplay between self-interest and a shared sense of the right thing is the energy that is propelling so many firms to explore the first four pieces of a reimagined capitalism — shared value, purpose-driven, rewired finance, and self-regulation — and is the reason I believe that they will increasingly support the fifth — the building of inclusive societies. Purpose-driven firms searching for shared value discover new business models that point the way toward making money, while simultaneously reducing pollution and inequality. They build firms authentically committed to doing the right thing, and tell the world — and their employees — that they are committed to making a difference in the world. They then discover that they need government if they are to meet their commitment. (p.244)

Then there is the law of "unintended consequences" (Norton, *n.d.*), defined by Robert K. Merton in 1936 as five sources, where the fifth, "self-defeating prediction," describes righting moments "when the public prediction of a social development proves false precisely because the prediction changes the course of history." Investing in this level of social-development transformation — from vicious to virtuous cycles — is foundational in structuring a stakeholder-centric economy, where the unintended consequences of first doing good for others increases the possibility of doing well for the originating doer (again, in Mondragon's worker-cooperative ecosystem, profitability is essential to be able to afford one's own values).

In rapid succession, the rejection and recalibrated adaptation, global development, and diffusion of vaccines, while far from perfect, indicate new global well-being collaboration formulas. Thomas Friedman (2022) observes that in Ukraine, "on the first day of the war, we saw invading Russian tank units unexpectedly being exposed by Google Maps, because Google wanted to alert drivers that the Russian armor was causing traffic jams."

Note the unintended positive consequence: Google mapping the invading and murdering Russian tank units, live, in real time. In a geopolitical context, Putin's red fascist invasion of Ukraine paves the way for a revitalized, stronger, and larger NATO, and motivates Europe to accelerate sunsetting Russia's continental energy influence through its geographically contiguous, fossil-fuel sourcing dependencies (P. Cohen, 2022; Cortese, 2022; Mathiesen *et al.*, 2022; Meredith, 2022; Reed, 2022).

Doing good by protecting and transforming individual human lives, advancing the civic health of nations, or saving a dying species, happens too often by fortuitous chance in a world of declining sustainability margins. Instead, an emerging, deliberate art of more profitable regenerating, and renewing circular economy deal-flow, aligns local stakeholder, community-based values with "profit as purpose" businesses in ways that interconnect, innovate, and inspire virtuous instead of vicious cycle practice.

Intentional transformation begins with the ever-more clear reality that breaking wealth downwards, instead of accumulating it upwards, creates a much larger, productive, and more equally shared global and local return on all capital and asset investments (financial, natural or climate, human and social). Interacting through interlocking, aligned values and purpose leads to the scaling of virtuous cycles as self-fulfilling prophecies. Henderson (2020) warns:

> Profit maximization only increases prosperity and freedom when markets are genuinely free and fair. Modern capitalism is neither. If massive externalities go unpriced or uncontrolled, if true freedom of opportunity is more dream than reality, and if firms can change the rules of the game to suit themselves at the expense of the public good, maximizing shareholder value leads to ruin. (pp.25-26)

The story of shareholder-primacy capitalism wildcatting "Coalface America" until every seam is stripped, drained, and discarded is one of "massive environmental degradation, economic inequality, and institutional collapse" (Henderson, 2020, p.8). But the emerging global moment places a premium on operating in hybrid, mosaic cultures of high purpose and impact, and delivering recurring, inclusive societal dividends. As precedent to respect and renew, American revolutionary solidarity during the 18th century married self-reliance, bootstrapping, and DIY (do it yourself) culture, leading to newly shared civic ethics and a mutualist social compact that inspired "ordinary people together achieving extraordinary things" (Sleigh, 2021).[1]

This is how today's coalface socioeconomic disunity transitions to the higher, cleaner, common ground of "*E Pluribus Unum*." To those able to see around corners and over immediate horizons, "risk washing" is far more dangerous and expensive to contain than greenwashing and virtue signaling.

But what if "the future is already here — it's just not evenly distributed, yet" according to William Gibson, author of the 1984 science fiction novel *Neuromancer*, presaging the iconic cinematic Matrix quadrilogy (Gibson, 1984; Ritholtz, 2017; Seth, 2021; *The Matrix*, 2023; *The Matrix Resurrections*, 2023)?

Today's highest-profile technology companies, such as Elon Musk's SpaceX and Twitter, continue to demonstrate how even employees from innovative sectors are consistently reduced to "my way or the highway" leadership (Bogage & Davenport, 2022; Knight, 2022; Lowenstein, 2022; Malik, 2022; Peck, 2022; Scheiber & Mac, 2022; Singletary, 2022). Paycheck-dependent workers — whether in the US, Russia, or China — are marginally disparaged, commoditized, arbitraged, disenfranchised, and demobilized because their labor is owned or rented by others — and not self-owned and self-determined.

The Great Resignation represents a reactive start, but it is symptomatic of shareholder-primacy capitalism's embedded failures, and not inherently proscriptive towards a more enlightened, productive, socially just and clean-climate future (Pandey, 2022).

Diehard judicial originalists might want to consider French humanist Jean-Jacques Rousseau (Deneys-Tunney, 2012), who understood back in the 18th century that humanity is born free but everywhere finds itself in chains of its own making. Today those chains are digital, perhaps even Web3 blockchains, forged by financial power and communicated through robots, or artificially intelligent bots and algorithms. In environments and geographies where inequalities are structurally locked and loaded, only renewing human-centric structures can break digital locks keeping societal liberation feudally in deteriorating place.

Professor Christina Clamp, who co-edited this book, relates:

> Menachem Rosner, an Israeli social scientist, pointed this out to me years ago. He said that workers in the former Yugoslavia had democracy upon entering the factory gates. Americans had democracy leaving the factory gates. Isn't the challenge to create the lived experience of democracy in all aspects of our lives which then becomes reinforcing of the political system? I found this to be very much the case when I went to Mondragon.

At every coalface juncture and toehold, vested vicious-cycle structures will resist, oppose, impose, and depose. Martin Luther King Jr.'s warning remains prescient: "Freedom is never given voluntarily by the oppressor; it must be demanded by the oppressed" (King, 1963). And yet, uplifting "ordinary people together achieving extraordinary things" can flatten socio-economic and geopolitical, hegemonic, and civic-infection curves that exploit existing, embedded inequalities (Peck, 2020).

In surfing terms, some will opt for the "bombs" or "grinders," the big and breaking waves commanding public attention; others will "backdoor a wave" by taking off "behind the peak of a hollow wave and surf through the barrel to the other side of the peak" (Cornwalls, 2016; Surfing Waves, *n.d.*).

Changing externalities starts with insisting on better workplace values:

> ... the ability to work in teams; to sacrifice for the common good; to be honest, kind, and trustworthy; to be creative and self-motivated. A sensible society would reward such traits by conferring status on them. A sensible society would not celebrate the skills of a corporate consultant while slighting the skills of a home nurse (Brooks, 2021).

Excerpts from a January 2023 Axios report (Allen, 2023) on the latest Edelman Trust Barometer released to coincide with the annual Davos World Economic Forum reveals: "Business continues to gain trust around the world ... Among respondents, 'my employer' is 25 points more trusted than government or elected officials." CEOs are now under pressure to take the lead on a wide range of societal issues that governments are no longer trusted to manage. Business holds a 54-point lead over government in competence — and 30 points in ethics. Societal leadership, Edelman argues, is now a core function of business:

> CEOs are expected to use resources to hold divisive forces accountable ... with 85% expected to play a role in strengthening our social fabric ... 72% want business to defend facts and expose questionable science being used to justify bad social policy ... 64% want companies to support politicians and media outlets that build consensus and cooperation ... Globally, 68% say "brands celebrating what brings us together and emphasizing our common interest would help increase civility and strengthen the social fabric" ... Individual companies are the best platform because they have a high level of trust. (Allen, 2023)

What better brand of social trust than one that leads on social-economy issues, starting with its own operating structure? Seventy years of the Mondragon cooperative ecosystem experience (MCE²) reaffirms a new breed of enterprise values and structures:

"Companies that disclosed the highest level of workforce diversity data saw 2.4% higher returns last year than those that did not" (Bonta & Patni, 2022; Vaghul, 2022). That's a virtuous cycle, social-capital asset metric to "rinse and repeat," and emulate.

Confirming the social economy strength of the MCE2 brand, the *Guardian* reports from Davos 2023: "Almost two in five of the bosses of global companies fear their businesses will be unviable within a decade because of the struggle to find talented workers and the need to adapt to technological change" (Elliott & Wearden, 2023). Those pursuing sustaining societal and market greatness understand the overriding imperative to reintegrate, rebuild, and restructure all stakeholders into the middle of every common good. This occurs when values combine with mission, and operational competitiveness delivers profit as purpose. "Measuring human, social, natural capital is not a trade-off but risk mitigation and predictability, just as doing good is not a trade-off but a moral, profitable discipline to build better and more resilient, valuable businesses" (EY Reporting, 2018; Thorn, 2019).

ESG metrics accompanying SDG goals inspire financial engineering innovations for global markets that never sleep. As an example, Intrinsic Exchange Group (IEG; intrinsicexchange.com), which developed the concept for "natural asset companies" (with grant funding from the Rockefeller Foundation [rockefellerfoundation.org], IDB Lab [bidlab.org], and Inter-American Development Bank [iadb.org]) claims:

> Natural Asset Companies (NACs) are a potential game-changer on a global scale. NACs will be newly formed, sustainable enterprises that hold the rights to the productivity and health of natural assets like land or marine areas. They are a new asset class on the New York Stock Exchange enabling owners to convert nature's value into financial capital, using that capital to re-invest in the natural assets to protect them or improve their sustainable use. (Cortese, 2021b; Stead, 2022)

The New York Stock Exchange NAC site (NYSE, *n.d.*) announced:

> To address the large and complex challenges of climate change and the transition to a more sustainable economy, NYSE and Intrinsic Exchange Group (IEG) are pioneering a new class of listed company based on nature and the benefits that nature provides (termed ecosystem services). NACs will capture the intrinsic and productive value of nature and provide a store of value based on the vital assets that underpin our entire economy and make life on earth possible. Examples of natural assets that could benefit from the NAC structure include natural landscapes such as forests, wetlands and coral reefs, as well as working lands such as farms.

So far on global exchanges, credible human and social capital metrics are missing in action and will need a trading-platform designation similar to NACs to be taken seriously, and driven by the most exacting investment criteria. Industrial ecosystems placing human capital front and center — such as Mondragon — could benefit by converting reimagined HACs (human asset companies) and SACS (social asset corporations) into measured, tradable assets that would help motivate better stakeholder ownership structures, missions, and projects, and attract better and fairer social impact lenders and investors worldwide.

NACs, HACs, and SACs can join an incoming deluge of creative worker-ownership and work-culture enfranchisement solutions, and models that offer choice, competition, and clarity to workers as "stakeholder clients." The challenge is not to water down ownership culture to meet financing, but to find better reasons for taking financing upwards to produce a more enlightened, effective, inclusive, competitive, and sustaining ownership culture.

A workforce that ends up owning its equity *self-governs* — and in that process earns the right to choose which values-driven supply chains to engage. It can reinvest its capital in a renewing, inclusive "solidarity dividend" where the whole is progressively more valuable than the sum of its headquarters, factories, distribution, and distributed office parts. In a growing, hybrid working world, the right to buy time to act — as opposed to facing forced reactions ceding to exterritorial decisionmakers — is a vital condition to survival, regional prosperity, and "the right to repair."

High-impact democratic workplace participation produces multiple, positive, *intentional* consequences — such as worker-owners exhibiting higher business financial literacy. Trusting fellow workers to follow clear, mutualist, values-infused "enterprise signals" represents a "pay it forward" leap of faith. It offers infinitely shareable returns, with shared risks balanced by shared rewards in the form of equity, salary remuneration including benefits, and democratic governance. Flexibility and remote work as part of this mission can help to dislodge and unseat

> … the true wellspring of populist anger: a scarcely understood phenomenon called economic unfairness … distinct from what we typically think of as economic inequality… characterized by low social mobility rather than inequalities of income or wealth. It's not that the rich have too much, it's that success depends on family wealth and status, when it should depend on good ideas, effort, and merit. It's anger at this rigged system, rather than anger at inequality, that drives contemporary populist movements. (Protzer & Summerville, 2022)

The antidote to this basic unfairness enshrines universal human rights, uproots legacy inequalities, and supports Earth's regenerative and restorative comeback from the brink.

To achieve this requires what may seem like Sisyphean labor by "ordinary people together achieving extraordinary things" to escape the precariat "servant economy," and its contemporary indentured servitude due to socioeconomic class origin and postal ZIP code address. These acts of personal and collective courage, according to Aristotle, represent the first of all virtues, followed by justice and practical wisdom (Fowers *et al.*, 2021).

Part 3: One Basque Province's "Coopexit"

The Kingdom of Spain, "a social representative democratic constitutional (or parliamentary) monarchy," consists of 17 autonomous communities, 52 provinces, and two autonomous cities in North Africa's Maghreb across the Mediterranean Sea's Atlantic entrance from the Rock of Gibraltar (contested by the UK).

Of these autonomous communities, *El Pais Vasco* (the Basque Country) is globally recognized as a leading, regional, social-economy ecosystem that confronted the ravages of the Spanish civil war, World

War II's genocidal Axis, and the subsequent economic deprivation of 40 years of Spain's fascist dictatorship, with solidarity, mutualism, industrial revolution, intellectual property, and multi-sector cooperativism.

There are three Basque Provinces within the Pais Vasco Autonomous Community: Álava, the capital of which is the mediaeval city Vitoria-Gasteiz, famed for its gothic architecture, one of Europe's greenest cities, and host of the Basque central government; Vizcaya, with its reindustrializing and circular-economy powerhouse of a capital, Bilbao, a city that has reinvented itself through culture, and was recognized as the top EU sustainable metropolis in 2017; and Gipuzkoa, with its 2023 EU Sustainable Capital of Donostia-San Sebastián, which ranks as one of the top global tourist destinations for seashore beauty (La Concha beach on Biscay Bay), and is known for its innovative cuisine (as the birthplace of tapas or "pintxos"), and for its first-tier international film and jazz festivals.

Today's Euskadi (Basque) region (Basque Country (Autonomous Community), 2023) fields over 1,300 local cooperatives, showcasing a dedication to democratic socioeconomic values unmatched anywhere except for Italy's Emilia Romagna (Duda, 2016). Significantly, Spain's Basque Region scores just as low (less is more) on the global GINI Index (Rich, 2020) measuring income inequality as do Scandinavian countries, but, in contrast to its northern neighbors, concurrently maintaining a more balanced tax structure similar to US coastal blue state levels.

As Spain's seventh-largest regional economy, Euskadi delivers 10.5% of the country's manufacturing industrial output and the second highest GDP *per capita* in Spain with less than 5% of the total population (CaixaBank, 2021). It's an inspiring example for other regions around the world that aspire to lower societal inequalities, and elevate community and municipal wealth, and individual and collective well-being.

In 2022, the MONDRAGON Corporation (mondragon-corporation.com), the region's flagship cooperative-ecosystem model headquartered in the central and most rural Basque province, Gipuzkoa, represented 95 separate, Tier I/II/III, self-governing cooperatives employing 80,000 people, with worker-owners benefitting from shared equity and democratic governance. The Mondragon cooperative ecosystem includes a nationally competitive bank, university, and insurance mutual, accompanied by 14 cooperative R&D centers, ranking first among Basque-origin businesses and 10th in Spain.

On December 16, 2022, Gipuzkoa, which hosts the majority of Basque cooperativism, witnessed two industrial cooperative general assemblies vote to withdraw from the formal MONDRAGON Corporation Tier I industrial structure — Orona (72% in favor) and Ulma Group (80% in favor). This departure, effective immediately, represents 13% of employment and 15% of turnover of MONDRAGON Corporation's industrial results, for a projected loss of "10,700 workers with the departure of both companies, as well as €1,700 million of billing" (*USANews*, 2022).

These latest departures are not without related precedents. Previously Ulma (ulma.com), founded in 1961, had voted in 1993 to separate from Mondragon until voting to return to the cooperative ecosystem fold in 2002. Equally important industrial cooperatives such as Irizar and Ampo — which manufacture commercial buses and valves, respectively — voted to leave Mondragon in 2008, at the height of the global Great Recession. One year earlier, the Barcelona-based cooperative wind-turbine manufacturer and installer, Ecotècnia, which joined Mondragon in 1999, voted to demutualize from the corporation in 2007, to be acquired by Alstom and rebranded as Alstom Wind in 2010.

Mondragon's first industrial cooperative, ULGOR in 1956, initially manufactured kerosene stoves, rebranded as Fagor Electrodoméstico in 1986, and became "the world's biggest industrial-worker cooperative for decades, the flagship of the MONDRAGON Corporation" (Fagor, 2023). It was Spain's leading, and Europe's fifth-largest, home appliance provider and electro-domestic supplier when it declared bankruptcy in October 2013.

The 2015 Harvard Business School case study by Professor Rebecca Henderson, *1worker1vote and Mondragon in the USA* (Henderson & Norris, 2015), outlines how the Fagor case is instructive not only for why the bankruptcy occurred — sparking an ongoing internal debate over "more or less centralized Mondragon" — but also in showing how the cooperative ecosystem's robust solidarity provisions, governance model, and operating values rallied to financially support, cross-train and re-employ over 1,500 Fagor Electrodoméstico workers within six months, leaving the industrial-plant equipment in place to retool for another day.

Nothing remotely comparable to this occurs in the US, where financialized, deindustrialized factory plant closings see tens of thousands of jobs outsourced and offshored for pennies on the domestic labor dollar, all to the cheers and jeers of "creative destruction" advocates.

It is in this context (assuming public declarations in December 2022 match deeds starting in 2023 and going forward) that Orona (orona-group.com) and Ulma, both representing successful cooperative businesses, can also represent *devolution without demutualization* departures from Mondragon's industrial group. This distinction and difference hold the potential to create a new, cohesive relationship-approach towards Mondragon's vibrant Tier II cooperative-support infrastructure (starting with the bank Laboral Kutxa [laboralkutxa.com], the insurance mutual Lagun Aro [lagunaro.es], and Mondragon University [mondragon.edu]). As in the high art of unpacking and demystifying politics anywhere and everywhere, truth follows money in pursuit of influence, wealth, and power, so we shall see what evolves and whether rhetoric matches practice.

Paraphrasing local news reports and interviews, Ulma Group announced its intent to replace its outgoing Mondragón Corporación Cooperativa relationship with a new civil-society model promoting future collaboration "for the development of the cooperative movement," as well as to "promote the necessary regulatory development so that the contributions made up to now in the funds managed by the Mondragón Foundation can continue to be used for the development of the cooperative movement;" its leadership further declaring that "we are part of the success model that the Basque cooperative model represents and we will always defend and support its values." This new "cooperative agreement model," shared also by Orona according to public declarations, proposes to maintain constructive, collaborative relationships with the MONDRAGON Corporation, but without being formally part of it, an approach not yet endorsed by the Mondragon Congress even though both the Basque Government and Mondragon clearly and quickly affirmed "total and absolute respect" for the decisions of both cooperatives.

Mondragon's formal leadership response placed "emphasis on mutual cooperation and solidarity" empowering Mondragon cooperatives to "carry out their business projects in a completely autonomous and sovereign way by expanding and counting on the solidarity of the group in case of adverse circumstances." Mondragon also communicated its hope based on past and future activity projections "in future projects that are currently being tackled and in the confidence that the cooperative model is suitable to meet the challenges of the market and to build more cohesive and sustainable societies."

Ulma and Orona cooperative leadership pledged "maximum willingness to work hand in hand" with MONDRAGON Corporation "in all those actions that benefit the successful model that we all represent." Gipuzkoa provincial officials highlighted three points: "the contribution that the cooperative model has made to Gipuzkoa is and will remain indisputable;" "the values that inspire cooperatives are the values of the territory, and, beyond the business or legal configuration that acquire the real challenge to keep them alive every day and project into the future;" and, maintaining "competitive companies … is our collective responsibility, the legacy we must preserve and leave to the next generations" (Wayne, 2022).

Orona (industrial elevators and escalators, sustainable vertical mobility) is based in the Gipuzkoa capital of San Sebastian, while Ulma Group (scaffolding greenhouse construction, conveyor and forged components, electronic system consulting, handling and packing systems) is headquartered in Oñati, the largest municipal area within Gipuzkoa, consisting of 16 distinct neighborhoods of which Arantzazu is the most visited. There are roughly 46 miles on the road that bends from Legazpi to Oñati, and then to Mondragon before arriving at San Sebastian with its La Concha bay and beach just over the frontier line from the French resort city, Biarritz. All three Basque municipalities are located in different parts of adjoining Gipuzkoa valleys: Legazpi within the Alto Urola region, Oñati as one of the most Gipuzkoa monumental towns situated in the Alto Deba region at the foot of Aloña Mountain, and Arrasate/Mondragón also located in the High Deba with Udalaitz mountain as a commanding backdrop.

In 2008, Mondragon Corporation confronted emerging globalization challenges and opportunities by deciding to change its 15-year-old operating brand to MONDRAGON Corporation, with the goal of more firmly connecting its cooperative identity with its place-based origins, highlighting the theme of "humanity at work" and four focus areas: Finance, Industry, Distribution and Knowledge (Lezana, 2008; *El Confidencial*, 2008). Perhaps a rising Gipuzkoa cooperative ecosystem regional brand resting on the Mondragon-San Sebastian-Oñati municipality triangle will generate new business and societal transformation synergies and formulas.

In a growing global social economy context, and as Mondragon itself has experienced responding to pandemic-distorted market realities, success goes to agile, values-aligned and mission-driven performers. The idea in 2008 of equating then 52 years of cooperative ecosystem experiences with the place-based word identity, "MONDRAGON," seemed reasonable to those Mondragon cooperatives having previously decided in global markets to downplay their internal democratic workplace democratic and solidarity-infused structures in favor of projecting more conventional product and service brand messaging.

Another 15 years later, everything has changed with pandemic-disrupted global supply chains forming into more nationalist subdivisions; socially distanced work environments choosing home offices over office parks; a rapidly changing present and future of work in the face of robotics and artificial intelligence (such as ChatGPT) (2023); the "electrification of everything," which impacts transportation sector factory capacity and purpose; and the *sine qua non* of clean energy and climate security in the face of Europe's most intensive and threatening military conflict since World War II.

Focusing less on cooperativism limited to specific place, and more on rebuilding and renewing cooperativism regardless of place and in place, may appear more healing and opportunistic. Gipuzkoa's potentially emerging Mondragon-Oñati-San Sebastian place-based trifecta may serve as the next decade's exportable, enriching, regional inter-cooperating regional model.

Successful and sustaining worker ownership's first axiom is that rights inextricably link to responsibilities. In this newly proclaimed, intentional Gipuzkoa regional-cooperative frame, the rising importance of Tier II supporting-cooperative infrastructure (bank-university-insurance mutual) may necessitate tomorrow's *á la carte* cost/pricing strategy, rather than today's legacy *prix fixe* approach. The former is usually more expensive than the latter, unless economies of scale elevate outcomes — just as expensive weddings contribute to greater precarity when they cause even more costly, destructive divorces.

Mondragon's hoped-for, common-good answer is always more ecosystem, more reinvention, more renewal. This time the answer also lies in spiritual as well as economic and productivity values, to align Mondragon ecosystem solutions *as a portal* to greater inter-generational prosperity capable of inspiring rising generations. Lifting the purpose and practice of hope through dignified, productively profitable, equitably shared and democratically governed work inspires deeper insourcing for greater outpouring.

Tomorrow's realization is that Mondragon is not just an ecosystem for those cooperatives needing group intercooperation (size and strength) when facing adversity; it is also a structurally recurring reinvention of how intercooperation and ecosystem solidarity drive individual cooperative marketplace successes. This creates the pluralistic *E Pluribus Unum* economy, where the whole is so much greater than the sum of its parts. The US activist Heather McGhee (2021) defines this phenomenon as the "solidarity dividend," which is measured by the extent that each part is lifted up by its fullest expression.

Monetizing solidarity dividends requires the courage of foresight and the forbearance of faith, two of Mondragon's initial ingredients. Devolution does not imply demutualization, and the strength of shared-services Tier II cooperatives might form a more elastic and relevant trampoline infrastructure for multi-located cooperative businesses and their sectors. Within this transformation can come new expressions of collective, synthesizing, intergenerational, spiritual and civic-society aspirations together with socioeconomic equality, servant-leader intellectual and lifestyle wayfinding, material sufficiency, and community prosperity. Whether inside or outside Tier I or Tier II Mondragon, and sooner rather than later, "by their fruits you will know them" (Matthew 7:16).

Rob Witherell, the veteran United Steelworkers organizer, 1worker1vote cofounder, and primary author of *Sustainable Jobs, Sustainable Communities: The Union Co-op Model* (Witherell *et al.*, 2012), shares a labor-insider perspective that:

> As an outsider, I wonder if a better analogy than "Coopexit" might be when seven US unions split from the AFL-CIO in 2005 to create Change to Win. Some of them returned to the AFL-CIO a few years later, some still haven't (Change to Win is now [a] strategic organizing center). The reasons to stay in the AFL-CIO generally seem to track the reasons to stay offered by Inigo Ucin, Mondragon's President, as to why Ulma and Orona should not leave (Tulankide, 2022b), but no one would characterize that split as a rejection of trade unionism or collective bargaining, but rather that the leadership of these Unions had different ideas on how to allocate resources, both people and money, to attain what are ultimately similar goals. Union members are probably less focused about how their union affiliates with other unions, than they are about how their union affects their job and their lives. Just like those unions rejected a centralized union of unions, not trade unionism and collective bargaining, the Ulma and Orona votes sound like a rejection of a centralized co-op of co-ops, not the cooperative model or worker ownership.

Gipuzkoa's "Coopexit" accelerates the ongoing debate over more or less Mondragon, with this latest example advocating for more local autonomy by city and valley against the backdrop of rapidly changing globalization and supply chain structures. An opportunity now exists for Mondragon second tier coops (*e.g.*, bank, university, insurance mutual, several research entities, think tanks, LKS) to become more externalized and compellingly competitive, more vital and more "treasured" amid the changing roles of "place" in a post-pandemic global economy.

The complaint risks becoming cliché, that the world doesn't get to vote in US elections even indirectly, but is existentially pre-condemned to suffer US electoral outcomes without representation. The reverse is also true for Mondragon's globalizing workforce, who do not benefit from the right to vote in the overseas subsidiaries of individual cooperative general assemblies of 141 productive subsidiaries with sales in 150 countries. Perhaps Orona and Ulma Group can serve as solution pathfinders, clearing away regulatory and social-inclusion obstacles, starting in their own global supply chains, so that no working community is left behind, nobody is restricted to voting vicariously and in permanent process *absentia*.

Could this inclusive internationalist approach inspire the Basque Country's rising Z and Alpha generations to rejoin and renew their professional commitment to the cooperative ecosystem model, despite the global appeal of hybrid gig economy work-life balance and start-up culture emphasizing rewards over risks? So far these generations, compared to Boomers and Generation X, are less attracted to both the Mondragon and Emilia Romagna ecosystems, making this a preeminent challenge to their future viability. Equally thought-provoking, why does this fly in the face of what's happening in the US and in developing economies, where hybrid and localized cooperative structures and a fight for the right to unionize receive overwhelming local population support percentages (upwards of 70% in the US) (Diaz, 2022; McCarthy, 2022)? This is how peripheries might inform the center in the interplay between centrifugal and centripetal learning journey forces.

Will Mondragon reach more deeply into its spiritual and moral-values tool kit and inspire others as it re-inspires itself — with quantifiable spillovers into production, innovation, profits, people, purpose, planet — and set up newly inspiring virtuous cycle structures wherein the whole re-energizes all component parts? Will Mondragon's solidarity vision — of worker-owners as much more than just employee owners in a full-cycle industrial democracy peopled by inter-connecting industries, sectors, and markets — reinforce and uplift lessons that Mondragon as "humanity at work" in living practice has already earned and learned in its 70 years of challenging and changing history?

HUMANITY @ WORK & LIFE reveals only a first and partial glimpse of what the world outside of the Mondragon cooperative ecosystem aspires to, while striving eclectically to localize the solidarity art of Mondragon's cooperative ecosystem practices within geographically diverse and culturally distributed operating contexts.

Will Mondragon continue to elevate its discourse and thinking (as it already has in many national and global leadership forums) beyond just cooperative sectors and into the even larger social economy sectors through a revitalized and inclusive global practice of "humanity and work and life"? If so, will this progression give rise to more hybrid shared ownership and workplace governance models in receptive geographies and cultures, such as the union-coop template?

Will the Mondragon cooperative ecosystem optimize its earned and natural structure and cultural practice advantages, anticipating the importance of human- and social-capital assets driven by ESG metrics and SDGs? Will resulting global capital flows on behalf of Spain's and the EU's rising social economies (already representing 10% of GNP in many countries) help to finance global adoption of these social economy enterprise and ecosystem models?

Perhaps "Gipuzkoa Coopexit" is not a moment to retrench but instead an opportunity to shine ever more brightly, become more transparent, more courageous, more visionary, more values-driven, more humble, more open, showing not telling, demonstrating through performance instead of proselytizing (which has always been the Mondragon way). The mustard-seed parable is of the smallest and simplest becoming the largest of garden plants — and then a tree "so that the birds come and perch in its branches" (Matthew 13:31-21). As described in **Chapter 11**, the simple Erreka industrial screw has become the fastener-sensor of choice for next-generation oil- and wind-energy platforms by combining the most basic, operationally hardened and tested engineering principles with data-innovation-driven qualities.

Perhaps it is only by reaching beyond mountaintops through the courage of progressive innovation and faith — in oneself and one's community — that everyday fears are dispelled so that valleys are uplifted, and highly competitive rural-based products and services flow into regional, national, and global markets. The world (and not only by industrial tourism) now comes to the Mondragon cooperative ecosystem just as much as Mondragon has gone into the world since the mid-1990s.

A starfish involuntarily sheds its appendages and intentionally grows back new ones. Similarly, attracting rising generations to the cooperative ecosystems starts with derailing performative values and virtue-signaling, in exchange for brand authenticity and the promise, premise, and power to participate in demonstrable societal transformation towards the greater common good.

Writing in *Wired*, Rose Eveleth (2022) discerns that hope is neither emotion nor optimism:

> We are being pitched futures all the time. Every advertisement, every political campaign, every quarterly budget is a promise or a threat about what tomorrow could look like. And it can feel, sometimes, like those futures are happening, whether we like it or not — that we're simply along for the ride. But the future hasn't happened yet. We do, in fact, get a say, and we should seize that voice as much as we possibly can … Like greenwashing and pinkwashing, hopewashing offers a way for corporations and people with power to make it seem like they're making the world a better, more hopeful place, while in reality they're doing the opposite … Chasing this kind of druglike hope is not how we build a better future. You cannot wait to feel hopeful before you begin trying to build something better … Hope should be a place to start, not a feeling to marinate in. Not a warm bed, but the alarm that gets you out of it.

"Gipuzkoa Coopexit" sounds that alarm but hope is the right place to start. Vertical office towers and the patriarchal corporate cultures they represent are ever more rejected by Generation Y, Z, and Alpha workers (Lynch, 2023; Royle, 2023), who choose more economic instability and diversity in return for family solidarity and the pursuit of personal and professional freedoms with gig jobs and side hustles filling in gaps until better, collectively supportive, mutualist structures evolve. The art of the emerging post-pandemic social compact, and its accompanying vocation to practice daily hope as discipline, means workers no longer can afford to be just along for the ride, because the costs are prohibitive when the music stops.

Fortunately, rising generations refuse to be along for the ride, but also insist they represent what the ride can become and where this ride must go beyond 2008's Great Recession, Covid-19, the Great Resignation, Brexit, MAGA civil-society insurrection, inflation, and the Ukraine war pitting energy against climate security and resiliency with democracy and cultural sovereignty in the balance. Whether the world's solidifying multipolar order includes all of its stakeholders or leaves winners and losers in vastly different places is entirely up to those rising in spite of adversity to steer humanity towards better destinies.

There is no better time to ignite this practice than now (Daniel, 2023; Pope Francis, 2022; Roden, 2022). The so-called "Year of the S" (for social and human capital) intends to hold shareholders turning stakeholders into shareholders accountable to the progress proclaimed and then achieved through democratic workplaces distributing equity and other forms of solidarity remuneration.

ImpactAlpha (impactalpha.com), a thought-leader "source for all things impact investing and sustainable finance," reported that its 2022 "Agents of Impact" (Price & Bank, 2022) chose the winning word "abundance" from all other options, reflecting:

> … a palpable desire to escape scarcity-driven, zero-sum and inherently divisive storylines. The runners-up trended in the same direction: "ownership," in the sense of both shared prosperity and active stewardship; "resilience" to persist and flourish in the face of obstacles; and "community," a stand-in for empathy and collaboration … To invert an old saying, lifting all boats creates a rising tide. As the abundance agenda creates its own political and economic momentum, corporations and asset owners will want to make sure they're on board. Workers, customers, and communities can hold them accountable.

Seventy years of the Mondragon cooperative ecosystem experience (MCE[2]) shows that structuring *a priori* democratically governed stakeholder ownership produces and scales abundance towards inter-generational prosperity, self-sufficiency, inter-cooperation, and ecological sustainability.

The mission-aligned investing world should be coming to Mondragon for solutions. Again from ImpactAlpha (Bank, 2022):

> It's not about the scores. It's about the solutions. ESG — shorthand for environmental, social and governance considerations in enterprise operations and investment decision-making — has taken a beating from all sides this year. ESG is either a barely disguised conspiracy to undermine capitalism or a toothless box-ticking fad designed to pump up wealth-management fees. When history is written, ESG will be remembered instead as a transitional stage that established the materiality of factors previously considered external to business and finance. The historians may also say that ESG trends, rough as they were, helped distinguish the leaders who ushered in an economy built around sustainability, inclusion and equity from the laggards who tried to block it … The shift from ESG inputs to impact-oriented outputs, as shown by a company's revenue mix, is increasingly central to how investors are valuing a company's prospects in the 21st century … Along with corporate accountability, better treatment of workers is the ESG plank with the most bipartisan popular support.

Every one of these investor-valued inputs — stakeholder ownership, socio-economic justice, and focus on innovative, impact-oriented goods and services outputs demonstrated by revenue mix — proclaim Mondragon cooperative ecosystem's comparative advantage. DNA-embedded, cultural, and operational strengths deliver profits undergirded by inter-cooperating industrial connectivity and inter-cooperation between sectors and processes, showcasing resiliency, and unbreakable solidarity. The net results transform adversity into singular opportunities.

A world on fire learns from those able to put fires out about how best to regenerate, repair and restructure. The opportunity mandate facing Western democracies, after learning the hard way that everything is downstream from culture, opens multiple, maybe innumerable doors to mutualist strategies that are desperately needed to restore and renew human work and life on behalf of the common good. This is the year to rise, shine, and lead the practice.

Enlightened investors able to rise above ideological jackal and hyena partisanship are beginning to prioritize and restructure worker voice and power. They're starting with treating workers better, and focusing on more aspirational and dignified job creation by understanding, after the Great Resignation, that workers are each company's most vital stakeholder. "One way to highlight corporate accountability to workers … is upgrading ESG to 'EESG' to put employees at the forefront" (Bank, 2022).

The markets — for those with commensurate values and structures to embrace their complexity and create solutions — offer unparalleled possibilities to innovate. As an example:

> The UN-backed Principles for Responsible Investment initiative (unpri.org; Inevitable Policy Response, n.d.), is forecasting that new policy aimed at protecting nature will lead to the creation of voluntary **markets where companies could trade biodiversity credits.** It points to an existing Australian initiative (the Threatened Species Action Plan) where the involvement of the financial sector would lead to the creation of a biodiversity market. Globally, the IPR anticipates that biodiversity credits could generate annual revenues of up to $43bn in 2050 … From this year, companies in Germany will also need to focus on the risks of not **preventing human rights breaches and environmental damage throughout their supply chains,** as the Supply Chain Due Diligence Act came into force in January.

"Goodness" standards are on their way to become practical, specific, meaningful metrics based increasingly on universal and local moral, ethical and even spiritual principles.

Mondragon, while never perfect but empirically and organically in the process of becoming more perfect, can repurpose into a spiritual, common good, purpose-driven, universally experienced platform that drives ESG-SDG investments in social enterprises, ecosystems, and economies everywhere. By doing so for itself, it can inspire others to do likewise. Perhaps an ESG-SDG Mondragon Team Academy (mondragonteamacademy.com) approach, focused on human- and social-capital assets investment, would attract and motivate new generations of young people from all over the world to participate in this virtuous-cycle conversation.

In this process, Mondragon would once again reinvent itself, as it knows it must, remaining true to its founding ethos of socioeconomic transformation.

"Revolution can take a while. Resistance can be fierce. And yet, it moves" (Gessen, 2022; Saric, 2022; Schmemann, 2022; Steele, 2022; Thomas, 2022).

In a world starving for moral and spiritual leadership to transform practice into mission, every Mondragon discussion, even 70 years later, inevitably returns to the singular inspirational and visionary role of the founding village priest, José María Arizmendiarrieta. This conversation is equally essential to Mondragon's future as to its beginnings.

Ironically, there's not a single first-tier US business school (Bloomberg, 2022), to my imperfect knowledge, that teaches José María Arizmendiarrieta's brand of leadership. What global school combines spiritual and social justice with a social-enterprise business curriculum that includes how to manage and scale multi-formatted cooperatives — perhaps an ecumenical, multi-denominational Business-Divinity School might jumpstart this better way of enterprise thinking and doing? Perhaps a future Mondragon reinvention will inaugurate a school curriculum of "Entrepreneurial and Practical, Spiritual and Moral, Mission-Driven Business Transformation Practices," or something similar with a shorter, more catchy and more compelling brand?

Mondragon's knowledge sector includes Mondragon University, Mondragon's Management and Engineering consultancy cooperatives, LKS Next — Mondragon's corporate dissemination outreach center, Otalora, and other entities comprising 20 different brands and 500 patent offshoots. Inter-cooperation can only spring sustainably from shared values, aligned vocabulary, and common experiences — all of which demand interlocking practices leading to societal equalities in public and private sector practice. Participation is the central value and intercooperation, social responsibility, and reciprocity allow Mondragon to create as much wealth as possible and distribute it as equally and fairly as possible. Ordinary people together achieving extraordinary things shows how structure becomes destiny.

Two recent innovative teaching-by-doing precedents to build upon might start with the Basque Culinary Center (bculinary.com) in San Sebastian, innovated in part by Mondragon University in collaboration with local chefs — because *El Pais Vasco*, in addition to many other attributes, fields more three-star Michelin restaurants than any other region in the world. Mondragon Team Academy represents another local-to-global learning journey with breakthrough momentum, dedicated to the generational, entrepreneurial repositioning of Mondragon's legacy foundational insights into the emerging social economy.

Perhaps future pilgrims will arrive in the "Basque Threshold" between the Cantabrian and Pyrenees ranges, with Udalaitz mountain framing the city of Mondragón, to take an industrial tour of worker solidarity and interdependent, inter-cooperating, multi-located, cooperatively structured and democratically governed, omni-sectoral social enterprises.

As so many before, they will depart already feeling called upon — as veterans in their civic-spiritual, activist, entrepreneurial, artisan, aspirational, organizing souls — to inspire anyone, anywhere, who commit to these transformational practices for "humanity at work and life."

Beyond the winter of 2022-2023, the EU will lead globally in integrating climate and energy security indices and practice, because "necessity is the parent of invention," and surviving the war in Ukraine demands nothing less. Beyond the war, rebuilding Ukraine's social economy stands to become one of the most expansive Marshall Plans of our times (Collins, 2022; Frum, 2022; Shapero, 2023; Twining, 2023).

On March 8, 2022, Ukraine President Volodymyr Zelensky, in his address to the British Parliament, said: "To Shakespeare's elemental question, 'to be or not to be,' Ukrainians have decided 'to be'" (Adam *et al.*, 2022).

As a former Mondragon International President wrote to me after the December 2022 "Gipuzkoa Coopexit": "They've decided, which is their right. We have to respect each other. The future will be our witness. Now we are going to work for the best: to create a more equitable community with stronger commitment."

Like Ukraine defending global democracy and freedom, the Mondragon cooperative ecosystem experience (MCE[2]), standing for universal solidarity, socioeconomic equality, democratic governance, and shared, intergenerational prosperity "has decided to be."

End-note

[1] DC LERA President and 1worker1vote Advisory Board member, Steve Sleigh, hosts Oskar Goitia, Chairman of Mondragon International, in conversation about Mondragon – May 2021. https://lerachapter.org/dclera/video/ - "Ordinary people together achieving extraordinary things" shows how structure becomes destiny. The quote is by Goitia, the event is hosted by Sleigh.

References

Acemoglu, D., Naidu, S., Restrepo, P. & Robinson, J. A. (2019). Democracy does cause growth. *Journal of Political Economy*, *127*(1), 47–100.

Adam, K., Suliman, A. & Berger, M. (2022, March 9). Zelensky receives standing ovation, calls for more support in address to UK Parliament *via* video. *Washington Post*. https://www.washingtonpost.com/world/2022/03/08/zelensky-uk-parliament-address-war-ukraine/.

Allen, M. (2023, January 16). 1 big thing: Business gains trust. *Axios*. https://www.axios.com/newsletters/axios-am/.

Andrew Breitbart. (2023). In *Wikipedia*. https://en.wikipedia.org/w/index.php?title=Andrew_Breitbart&oldid=1143334946.

Bamburg, J. (2018, July 11). Mondragon through a critical lens. *Employee Ownership News*. https://medium.com/fifty-by-fifty/mondragon-through-a-critical-lens-b29de8c6049.

Bank, D. (2022, December 22). Using ESG and impact to sort leaders from laggards in 2023. *ImpactAlpha*. https://impactalpha.com/using-esg-and-impact-to-sort-leaders-from-laggards-in-2023/.

Basque Country (Autonomous Community). (2023). In *Wikipedia*. https://en.wikipedia.org/w/index.php?title=Basque_Country_(autonomous_community)&oldid=1141167651.

Bloomberg (2022). US B-schools rankings. *Bloomberg*. https://www.bloomberg.com/business-schools/regions/us/.

Boffo, R. & Patalano, R. (2020). *ESG investing: Practices, progress and challenges*. OECD: Paris.

Bogage, J. & Davenport, C. (2022, June 17). SpaceX fires workers who criticized Elon Musk in open letter. *Washington Post*. https://www.washingtonpost.com/business/2022/06/17/spacex-workers-fired-elon-musk/.

Bonta, E. & Patni, M. (2022, February 8). Companies disclosing the highest level of workforce diversity data – EEO-1 report – saw higher 2021 returns. *Just Capital*. https://justcapital.com/news/companies-sharing-eeo-1-data-saw-higher-returns/.

Brandenburg, M., Eccles, B. & Strine, L. (2022, October 19). Employees: The missing 'E' in ESG. *ImpactAlpha*. https://impactalpha.com/employees-the-missing-e-in-esg/.

Brooks, D. (2021, August 2). How the bobos broke America. *The Atlantic*. https://www.theatlantic.com/magazine/archive/2021/09/blame-the-bobos-creative-class/619492/.

Brooks, D. (2022, October 6). The triumph of the Ukrainian idea. *New York Times*. https://www.nytimes.com/2022/10/06/opinion/ukraine-liberal-nationalism.html.

Cadelago, C. & Olander, O. (2022, August 25). Biden calls Trump's philosophy "semi-fascism." *Politico*. https://www.politico.com/news/2022/08/25/biden-trump-philosophy-semi-fascism-00053831.

CaixaBank (2021, November 5). *Basque Country*. CaixaBank Research. https://www.caixabankresearch.com/en/publications/autonomous-community-profiles/basque-country.

ChatGPT (2023). In *Wikipedia*. https://en.wikipedia.org/w/index.php?title=ChatGPT&oldid=1143301908.

Christensen, J. (2019, April 16). The amount of plastic in the ocean is a lot worse than we thought, study says. *CNN*. https://www.cnn.com/2019/04/16/health/ocean-plastic-study-scn/index.html.

Cohen, E.A. (2022, October 22). The words about Ukraine that Americans need to hear. *The Atlantic*. https://www.theatlantic.com/ideas/archive/2022/10/volodymyr-zelensky-ukraine-speech-churchill/671836/.

Cohen, P. (2022, September 1). Portugal could hold an answer for a Europe captive to Russian gas. *New York Times*. https://www.nytimes.com/2022/09/01/business/economy/portugal-russia-natural-gas.html.

Collins, P. (2022, November 20). A message from Ukraine by Volodymyr Zelensky review – A winner in the war of words. *The Guardian*. https://www.theguardian.com/books/2022/nov/20/a-message-from-ukraine-speeches-2019-2022-by-volodymyr-zelensky-review-a-verbal-freedom-fighter.

Cornwalls (2016, January 6). *Surfing terms glossary*. Cornwall Guide. https://www.cornwalls.co.uk/surfing/dictionary.htm.

Cortese, A. (2021a, August 25). Is your fund serious about climate? Show me your scientists. *ImpactAlpha*. https://impactalpha.com/is-your-fund-serious-about-climate-show-me-your-scientists/.

Cortese, A. (2021b, September 14). Move over SPACs. Here come NACs to turn ecosystem services into tradable assets. *ImpactAlpha*. https://impactalpha.com/move-over-spacs-here-come-nacs-to-turn-ecosystem-services-into-tradeable-assets/.

Cortese, A. (2022, November 15). New narrative of climate action: Unstoppable progress and immense opportunity. *ImpactAlpha*. https://impactalpha.com/new-narrative-of-climate-action-unstoppable-progress-and-immense-opportunity/.

Cortese, A. & Price, D. (2022, August 24). Riskwashing: How the crusade against ESG is hurting businesses, taxpayers and retirees. *ImpactAlpha*. https://impactalpha.com/riskwashing-how-the-crusade-against-esg-is-hurting-businesses-taxpayers-and-retirees/.

Daniel, W. (2023, January 7). The "everything bubble" has popped & the experts on Wall Street & in Silicon Valley were spectacularly wrong about a ton of things. *Fortune*. https://fortune.com/2023/01/07/forecasts-gone-wrong-wall-street-bitcoin-stock-market-everything-bubble/.

Deneys-Tunney, A. (2012, July 15). Rousseau shows us that there is a way to break the chains – from within. *The Guardian*. https://www.theguardian.com/commentisfree/2012/jul/15/rousseau-shows-us-way-break-chains.

Diaz, J. (2022, August 31). Support for labor unions in the US is at a 57-year high. *NPR*. https://www.npr.org/2022/08/31/1120111276/labor-union-support-in-us.

Duda, J. (2016, February 18). Learning from Emilia Romagna's cooperative economy. *The Next System Project*. https://thenextsystem.org/learning-from-emilia-romagna.

Economy of Spain. (2023). In *Wikipedia*. https://en.wikipedia.org/w/index.php?title=Economy_of_Spain&oldid=1138331346.

Elliott, L. & Wearden, G. (2023, January 16). Almost two in five CEOs "fear their global firms will be unviable within 10 years." *The Guardian*. https://www.theguardian.com/business/2023/jan/16/almost-two-in-five-ceos-fear-their-global-firms-will-be-unviable-within-10-years.

Eveleth, R. (2022, December 29). The case against hopewashing. *Wired*. https://www.wired.com/story/prediction-futures-politics-hope/.

EY Global (2021, January 4). Why sustainability has become a corporate imperative. *EY*. https://www.ey.com/en_gl/strategy/why-sustainability-has-become-a-corporate-imperative.

EY Reporting (2018, May 3). Why more companies are measuring their natural and human capital. *EY*. https://www.ey.com/en_us/assurance/why-more-companies-are-measuring-their-natural-and-human-capital.

Fagor (2023). In *Wikipedia*. https://en.wikipedia.org/w/index.php?title=Fagor&oldid=1142619944.

Fowers, B.J., Novak, L.F., Calder, A.J. & Sommer, R.K. (2021). Courage, justice & practical wisdom as key virtues in the era of Covid-19. *Frontiers in Psychology*, *12*, 647912. https://doi.org/10.3389/fpsyg.2021.647912.

Friedman, T.L. (2022, February 25). We have never been here before. *New York Times*. https://www.nytimes.com/2022/02/25/opinion/putin-russia-ukraine.html.

Frum, D. (2022, December 22). Zelensky recalled us to ourselves. *The Atlantic*. https://www.theatlantic.com/ideas/archive/2022/12/volodymyr-zelensky-us-congress-address-ukraine/672546/.

Galston, W. A. & Kamarck, E. (2022, January 4). Is democracy failing and putting our economic system at risk? *Brookings*. https://www.brookings.edu/research/is-democracy-failing-and-putting-our-economic-system-at-risk/.

Gessen, M. (2022, August 31). Mikhail Gorbachev, the fundamentally Soviet man. *The New Yorker*. https://www.newyorker.com/news/postscript/mikhail-gorbachev-the-fundamentally-soviet-man.

Gibson, W. (1984). *Neuromancer*. Penguin.

Gilbert, G. (2015, August 6). Cincinnati's experiment with an economy that works for everyone. *Waging Nonviolence*. https://wagingnonviolence.org/2015/08/cincinnatis-experiment-with-an-economy-that-works-for-everyone/.

Goodman, P.S. (2020, December 29). Co-ops in Spain's Basque region soften capitalism's rough edges. *New York Times*. https://www.nytimes.com/2020/12/29/business/cooperatives-basque-spain-economy.html?smid=em-share.

Grover, P. & John, R. (2015, February 1). A virtuous cycle for top-line growth. *McKinsey*. https://www.mckinsey.com/capabilities/growth-marketing-and-sales/our-insights/a-virtuous-cycle-for-top-line-growth.

Hadfield, M. (2019, April 29). Unions & co-ops—A new way forward for workers? *Co-Operative News*. https://www.thenews.coop/138577/sector/worker-coops/unions-co-ops-new-way-forward-workers/.

Henderson, R. (2020). *Reimagining Capitalism in a World on Fire*. Public Affairs.

Henderson, R. & Norris, M. (2015). *1worker1vote: Mondragon in the US*. Harvard Business School. https://drive.google.com/file/d/1Bjri47Z_RrCpxuGnu0VI7YrZ8HdeSRe4/view?usp=embed_facebook.

IEA, IRENA, UNSD, WHO & World Bank. (2022). *Tracking SDG7: The Energy Progress Report*. World Bank. https://trackingsdg7.esmap.org/data/files/download-documents/sdg7-report2022-full_report.pdf.

Inevitable Policy Response (*n.d.*). *IPR: Forecast policy scenario + nature*. https://www.unpri.org/download?ac=17705

Junkus, J., & Berry, T. D. (2015). Socially responsible investing: A review of the critical issues. *Managerial Finance, 41*(11), 1176–1201. https://doi.org/10.1108/MF-12-2014-0307.

Kempf, A. & Osthoff, P. (2007). The effect of socially responsible investing on portfolio performance. *European Financial Management, 13*(5), 908–922. https://doi.org/10.1111/j.1468-036X.2007.00402.x.

King, M.L., Jr. (1963). *Letter from Birmingham jail*. The Martin Luther King, Jr., Research & Education Institute. https://kinginstitute.stanford.edu/encyclopedia/letter-birmingham-jail.

Kishan, S. (2022, February 3). ESG by the numbers: Sustainable investing set records in 2021. *Bloomberg*. https://www.bloomberg.com/news/articles/2022-02-03/esg-by-the-numbers-sustainable-investing-set-records-in-2021.

Knight, W. (2022, November 4). Elon Musk has fired Twitter's "ethical AI" team. *Wired*. https://www.wired.com/story/twitter-ethical-ai-team/.

Larsen, K., Pitt, H., Grant, M. & Houser, T. (2021, May 6). China's greenhouse gas emissions exceeded the developed world for the first time in 2019. *Rhodium Group*. https://rhg.com/research/chinas-emissions-surpass-developed-countries/.

Lezana, C. (2008, April 1). MCC is renamed Mondragón. *El Correo*. https://www.elcorreo.com/vizcaya/20080401/economia/pasa-llamarse-mondragon-20080401.html.

List of countries by GDP (nominal). (2023). In *Wikipedia*. https://en.wikipedia.org/w/index.php?title=List_of_countries_by_GDP_(nominal)&oldid=1140258662.

List of sovereign states in Europe by GDP (nominal). (2023). In *Wikipedia*. https://en.wikipedia.org/w/index.php?title=List_of_sovereign_states_in_Europe_by_GDP_(nominal)&oldid=1135592158.

Lowenstein, A. (2022, November 20). The savior CEO & the empty promise of "stakeholder capitalism." *The Guardian*. https://www.theguardian.com/business/2022/nov/20/stakeholder-capitalism-jp-morgan-walmart.

Lynch, S. (2023, January 7). How Gen Z social media managers became the new CMOs. *Fast Company*. https://www.fastcompany.com/90827081/gen-z-social-media-managers-tiktok-taco-bell-duolingo-dunkin.

Macmillan Dictionary (*n.d.*). Virtuous circle (noun) definition and synonyms. In *Macmillan Dictionary*. Retrieved March 6, 2023, from https://www.macmillandictionary.com/dictionary/british/virtuous-circle.

Madrigal, A.C. (2019, March 6). The servant economy. *The Atlantic*. https://www.theatlantic.com/technology/archive/2019/03/what-happened-uber-x-companies/584236/.

Malik, K. (2022, November 20). Beware self-made "genius" entrepreneurs promising the earth. Just look at Elon Musk. *The Observer*. https://www.theguardian.com/commentisfree/2022/nov/20/beware-self-made-genius-entrepreneurs-promising-earth-just-look-at-elon-musk.

Mathiesen, K., Jack, V., Coi, G. & Cooper, C. (2022, October 12). Putin's war accelerates the EU's fossil fuel detox. *Politico*. https://www.politico.eu/article/vladimir-putin-war-ukraine-accelerates-eu-fossil-fuel-detox/.

McCarthy, J. (2022, August 30). US approval of labor unions at highest point since 1965. *Gallup*. https://news.gallup.com/poll/398303/approval-labor-unions-highest-point-1965.aspx.

McGhee, H. (2021). *The sum of us: What racism costs everyone and how we can prosper together*. Random House Publishing Group.

Meredith, S. (2022, September 2). Russia's energy influence over Europe "is nearly over" as bloc races to shore up winter gas supplies. *CNBC*. https://www.cnbc.com/2022/09/02/winter-gas-russias-energy-influence-over-europe-is-nearly-over.html.

Merriam-Webster (*n.d.*). Virtuous circle definition & meaning. In *Merriam-Webster*. Retrieved March 6, 2023, from https://www.merriam-webster.com/dictionary/virtuous%20circle.

Molloy, T. (2019, October 15). Bernie Sanders says 3 people are wealthier than half of all Americans. Here's who they are. *The Wrap*. https://www.thewrap.com/bernie-sanders-says-3-people-are-wealthier-than-half-of-all-americans-heres-who-they-are/.

Mondragon (Director) (2012, April 27). *What does the world think about Mondragon?* https://www.youtube.com/watch?v=F2S78cLoJb4.

Montanaro, D. (2022, July 19). 14 key moments from the Jan. 6 committee hearings—So far. *NPR*. https://www.npr.org/2022/07/19/1112177450/14-key-moments-from-the-jan-6-committee-hearings-so-far.

Morford, S. (2023, January 15). Climate disasters cost the US more than $165 billion in 2022. *Fast Company*. https://www.fastcompany.com/90834205/climate-disasters-cost-the-us-more-than-165-billion-in-2022.

Morgan Stanley (2019). *Sustainable signals: Individual investor interest driven by impact, conviction and choice.* https://www.morganstanley.com/pub/content/dam/msdotcom/infographics/sustainable-investing/Sustainable_Signals_Individual_Investor_White_Paper_Final.pdf?mc_cid=8ecb1b5307&mc_eid=72c50a6d0d.

NationMaster (n.d.). *Spain vs United States: Economy facts and stats.* http://www.nationmaster.com/country-info/compare/Spain/United-States/Economy.

Neumann, J. (2022, June 30). How a worker-owned business model in Spain is keeping inequality in check. *Bloomberg.* https://www.bloomberg.com/news/features/2022-06-30/worker-owned-business-model-in-spain-is-keeping-inequality-in-check.

Norton, R. (n.d.). Unintended consequences. *Econlib.* https://www.econlib.org/library/Enc/UnintendedConsequences.html.

NYSE (n.d.). *Natural asset companies (NACs).* https://www.nyse.com/introducing-natural-asset-companies.

O'Connor, S. (2022, June 14). Farewell to the servant economy. *Financial Times.*

Packer, G. (2022, September 6). Ukrainians are defending the values Americans claim to hold. *The Atlantic.* https://www.theatlantic.com/magazine/archive/2022/10/ukraine-invasion-civilian-volunteers-survival/671241/.

Padilla, D.F. (2022, June 5). *Talent is the X factor in limiting warming to 1.5°, young people everywhere are trying work in climate and that type of talent is undefeated.* [Tweet]. Twitter. https://twitter.com/dfp2017/status/1533251654719447040.

Pandey, E. (2022, May 6). The Great Resignation has no end date. *Axios.* https://www.axios.com/2022/05/06/great-resignation-turnover-lasting-remote-hybrid-work.

Paxton, R.O. (2004). *The Anatomy of Fascism.* Knopf Doubleday Publishing Group.

Peck, M. (2014, May 28). Mondragons in Appalachia. *Daily Kos.* https://www.dailykos.com/stories/2014/5/28/1302558/-Mondragons-in-Appalachia.

Peck, M. (2020, March 23). Covid-19 & America's extreme solidarity deficit. *1worker1vote.org.* https://1worker1vote.org/covid-19-americas-extreme-solidarity-deficit/.

Peck, M. (2022, December 8). Leaving Twitter. *1worker1vote.org.* http://1worker1vote.org/leaving-twitter/.

Peshawaria, R. (2020, October 12). Stewardship: The core compass of enduring organizations. *Forbes.* https://www.forbes.com/sites/rajeevpeshawaria/2020/10/12/stewardship-the-core-compass-of-enduring-organizations/.

Peshawaria, R. (2022, October 17). ESG: Will G save us from E and S challenges? *Forbes.* https://www.forbes.com/sites/rajeevpeshawaria/2022/10/17/esg-will-g-save-us-from-e-and-s-challenges/.

Philip, P., Ibrahim, C. & Hodges, C. (2022). *The turning point: A global summary.* https://www.deloitte.com/global/en/issues/climate/global-turning-point.html.

Polman, P. & Winston, A. (2021, September/October). The net positive manifesto. *Harvard Business Review.* https://hbr.org/2021/09/the-net-positive-manifesto

Pope Francis (2022, December 27). *Address of His Holiness Pope Francis to managers and delegates of the Italian General Confederation of Labor (CGIL).* https://catholiclabor.org/address-of-his-holiness-pope-francis-to-managers-and-delegates-of-the-italian-general-confederation-of-labour-cgil/.

Pothering, J. (2022, May 27). Olu Oyinsan, Oui Capital: Investing in Africa's mass market. *ImpactAlpha.* https://impactalpha.com/olu-oyinsan-oui-capital-investing-in-africas-mass-market/.

Power, R. (2022, August 21). 3 ways businesses can avoid greenwashing. *Forbes.* https://www.forbes.com/sites/rhettpower/2022/08/21/3-ways-businesses-can-avoid-greenwashing/?sh=2cc8f43b46f4.

Price, A. (2021, May 23). How startups can benefit from a virtuous cycle. *HuntClub.* https://www.huntclub.com/blog/how-startups-can-benefit-from-a-virtuous-cycle.

Price, D. & Bank, D. (2022, December 23). Next year in impact investing: Abundance. *ImpactAlpha.* https://impactalpha.com/next-year-in-impact-investing-abundance/.

Protzer, E. & Summerville, P. (2022, April 20). Reclaiming populism. *Persuasion.* https://www.persuasion.community/p/reclaiming-populism.

Reed, S. (2022, August 30). Russia halts natural gas flows to Germany again. *New York Times.* https://www.nytimes.com/2022/08/31/business/russia-natural-gas-germany.html.

Rich, B. (2020, January 6). Sustainability in a small place: The Spanish Basque Country as a 21st century model. *Open Democracy.* https://www.opendemocracy.net/en/oureconomy/sustainability-small-place-spanish-basque-country-21st-century-model/.

Richardson, H.C. (2022, October 16). *Letters from an American.* https://heathercoxrichardson.substack.com/p/october-15-2022.

Ritholtz, B. (2017, May 28). Transcript: Andreessen MIB Podcast. *The Big Picture.* https://ritholtz.com/2017/05/transcript-andreessen-mib-podcast/.

Roden, R.D. (2022, December 7). In a violent economy, people of faith try cooperatives. *Sojourners.* https://sojo.net/articles/violent-economy-people-faith-try-cooperatives.

Romeo, N. (2022, August 27). How Mondragon became the world's largest co-op. *The New Yorker*. https://www.newyorker.com/business/currency/how-mondragon-became-the-worlds-largest-co-op.

Rorschach test (2023). In *Wikipedia*. https://en.wikipedia.org/w/index.php?title=Rorschach_test&oldid=1141344307.

Rose-Smith, I. (2022, October 12). How Patagonia's private plan for the public good inadvertently reveals the limits of impact investing. *ImpactAlpha*. https://impactalpha.com/how-patagonias-private-plan-for-the-public-good-inadvertently-reveals-the-limits-of-impact-investing/.

Rott, N. (2023, January 10). Extreme weather, fueled by climate change, cost the U. $165 billion in 2022. *NPR*. https://www.npr.org/2023/01/10/1147986096/extreme-weather-fueled-by-climate-change-cost-the-u-s-165-billion-in-2022.

Roy, A. (2020, April 3). Arundhati Roy: "The pandemic is a portal." *Financial Times*. https://www.ft.com/content/10d8f5e8-74eb-11ea-95fe-fcd274e920ca.

Royle, O.R. (2023, January 9). What CEOs are most worried about going into 2023, including a Gen Z culture clash with unretiring boomers. *Fortune*. https://fortune.com/2023/01/09/ceo-worries-2023-gen-z-culture-clash-unretiring-boomers-esg-short-term-fixes/.

El Confidencial (2008, April 16). The MCC group changes its corporate identity to Mondragón, which will be shared by its 246 companies. https://www.elconfidencial.com/mercados/fondos-de-inversion/2008-04-16/el-grupo-mcc-cambia-su-identidad-corporativa-por-mondragon-que-compartiran-sus-246-empresas_828984/.

Saric, I. (2022, September 1). Gorbachev was "shocked and bewildered" by Russia's war in Ukraine, interpreter says. *Axios*. https://www.axios.com/2022/09/01/gorbachev-war-russia-ukraine-interpreter.

Scheiber, N. & Mac, R. (2022, November 17). SpaceX employees say they were fired for speaking up about Elon Musk. *New York Times*. https://www.nytimes.com/2022/11/17/business/spacex-workers-elon-musk.html.

Schmemann, S. (2022, August 31). Gorbachev freed the Soviet Union but could not save it. *New York Times*. https://www.nytimes.com/2022/08/31/opinion/gorbachev-death-soviet-union.html.

Seth, E. (2021, June 4). Why is cyberpunk relevant today? *Medium*. https://ethanseth.medium.com/why-is-cyberpunk-relevant-today-cb4f40789e09.

Shabad, R. (2022, August 26). Biden blasts MAGA philosophy as "semi-fascism." *NBC News*. https://www.nbcnews.com/politics/2022-election/biden-blasts-maga-philosophy-semi-fascism-rcna44953.

Shapero, J. (2023, January 15). Zelensky draws comparisons between "Ruscism" and Nazism in Saturday address. *The Hill*. https://thehill.com/policy/international/3813697-zelensky-draws-comparisons-between-ruscism-and-nazism-in-saturday-address/.

Singletary, M. (2022, December 8). Elon Musk showed us how not to fire people. *Washington Post*. https://www.washingtonpost.com/business/2022/11/09/elon-musk-how-not-to-fire-employees/.

Sleigh, S. (Director) (2021, May). *Oskar Goitia, chairman of Mondragon International, in conversation about Mondragon*. https://lerachapter.org/dclera/video/.

Stead, D. (2022, January 23). Natural asset companies (NACs). *Impact Entrepreneur*. https://impactentrepreneur.com/natural-asset-companies-nacs/.

Steele, J. (2022, August 30). Mikhail Gorbachev obituary. *The Guardian*. https://www.theguardian.com/world/2022/aug/30/mikhail-gorbachev-obituary.

Surfing Waves (*n.d.*). Wave terms explained. https://surfing-waves.com/waves/wave_terms.htm.

Tharoor, I. (2022a, August 22). Six months after Russia invaded Ukraine, the world is on a knife edge. *Washington Post*. https://www.washingtonpost.com/world/2022/08/22/global-six-months-ukraine-war-russia/.

Tharoor, I. (2022b, August 30). The debate over American fascism gets louder. *Washington Post*. https://www.washingtonpost.com/world/2022/08/30/fascism-biden-trump-american-history/.

The Matrix (2023). In *Wikipedia*. https://en.wikipedia.org/w/index.php?title=The_Matrix&oldid=1143099974.

The Matrix Resurrections (2023). In *Wikipedia*. https://en.wikipedia.org/w/index.php?title=The_Matrix_Resurrections&oldid=1140902580.

The Matrix Wiki (*n.d.*). *Agent Smith*. https://matrix.fandom.com/wiki/Agent_Smith.

New York Times (1982, February 27). Susan Sontag provokes debate on communism. https://archive.nytimes.com/www.nytimes.com/books/00/03/12/specials/sontag-communism.html.

Thomas, M. (2022, August 31). Russia: Mikhail Gorbachev changed history, but was wrong about ties to West. *BBC News*. https://www.bbc.com/news/world-europe-62735271.

Thorn, C. (2019, August 15). How do you value your social and human capital? *EY*. https://www.ey.com/en_gl/assurance/how-do-you-value-your-social-and-human-capital.

Tremlett, G. (2013, March 7). Mondragon: Spain's giant co-operative where times are hard but few go bust. *The Guardian.* https://www.theguardian.com/world/2013/mar/07/mondragon-spains-giant-cooperative.

Tulankide (2022a, May 12). "The cooperative movement has grown in recent years as people look for more equitable and democratic ways to organize economic life." https://www.tulankide.com/en/201cthe-cooperative-movement-has-grown-in-recent-years-as-people-look-for-more-equitable-and-democratic-ways-to-organize-economic-life201d.

Tulankide (2022b, December 15). Why vote No when leaving Mondragon? https://www.tulankide.com/es/por-que-votar-no-a-la-salida-de-mondragon.

Tulankide (2022c, December 16). Mondragon begins a new stage. https://www.tulankide.com/es/mondragon-inicia-una-nueva-etapa.

Twining, D. (2023, January 4). Ukraine is already paying us back. *Politico.* https://www.politico.com/news/magazine/2023/01/04/ukraine-democracy-investment-00076180.

USANews (2022, December 16). The departure of Orona & Ulma from the Mondragón Corporation convulses Basque cooperativism. *USANews.* https://www.usanews.net/breaking/the-departure-of-orona-and-ulma-from-the-mondragn-corporation-convulses-h39570.html

Vaghul, K. (2022). *Just over half of the largest US companies share workforce diversity data as calls for transparency from investors and regulators grow.* https://justcapital.com/reports/share-of-largest-us-companies-disclosing-race-and-ethnicity-data-rises/.

von Czechowski, A.S. (2020). *CDP Africa report.* https://cdn.cdp.net/cdp-production/cms/reports/documents/000/005/023/original/CDP_Africa_Report_2020.pdf?1583855467.

Wayne (2022, December 16). Mondragon emphasizes "mutual cooperation and solidarity", in its new phase without Ulma & Orona. *Today Times Live.* https://todaytimeslive.com/world/182546.html.

Wilson, E. (2021, October 1). The United Nations free-thinkers who coined the term "ESG" & changed the world. *Euromoney.* https://www.euromoney.com/article/294dqz2h1pqywgbyh3zls/esg/the-united-nations-free-thinkers-who-coined-the-term-esg-and-changed-the-world.

Witherell, R., Cooper, C. & Peck, M. (2012). *Sustainable Jobs, Sustainable Communities: The Union Co-op Model.*

Wolfe, T. (1940). *You can't go home again.* Scribner.

World Health Organization (2022, May 5). 14.9 million excess deaths associated with the Covid-19 pandemic in 2020 & 2021. https://www.who.int/news/item/05-05-2022-14.9-million-excess-deaths-were-associated-with-the-covid-19-pandemic-in-2020-and-2021.

Zugasti, I. & Peck, M. (2021). *ESGs & SDGs meet their Port Alegre moment.* https://www.asbcouncil.org/sites/main/files/file-attachments/esgs_and_sdgs_meet_their_port_alegre_moment_-__michael_and_ibon_-_march_2021.pdf.

CHAPTER 2

What's in a Name? Conceptual Frameworks for a Cooperative World

Jason Spicer

Approach & Method

Popular interest in transitioning to a more environmentally and socially sustainable alternative to capitalism and the investor-owned firm has risen over the last decade, advanced by global social movement actors in the face of multiple crises: record economic inequality, environmental degradation, racial and caste injustice, and the coronavirus pandemic (Milkman, 2017; Della Porta, 2020). In conjunction, scholars and intellectuals have increasingly questioned how capitalism might end and what might come to replace it (Fergnani, 2019; Streeck, 2016; Davis, 2016a). Crises and interest in alternatives have long been historically connected, of course, reflecting well-worn theories of legitimation and conjunctural crises (Gramsci, 1926; Habermas, 1973; Fraser, 1997, 2015; Hall & Massey, 2010). At the heart of these alternatives are cooperatives, which are by definition not motivated by investor profit or exchange value (not M-C-M, in the notation of classical Marxism), but rather are motivated by the substantive values and use value concerns of member-owners. Alongside the formal cooperative are a host of other alternative enterprise models, such as community land trusts, solidarity enterprises, mutual benefit corporations, community interest companies. A host of frameworks are used to more broadly conceptualize such alternatives. Avoiding the state-centric connotations of the well-worn term socialism, they include alternative, diverse, and community economies (ADCE); commons/commoning; community wealth and control; collectivist/democratic organizations and alternative enterprises; economic democracy; the social and solidarity economy (SSE/ESS); post-capitalism; and degrowth, among others. In academic and popular settings, these frameworks can appear both separately and together. Are there differences among these frameworks? And if so, does it matter?

To address the last question first: we know frames and frameworks matter, especially for phenomena like alternative enterprises, which are closely related to and incubated by social movements. This is because sociologists have established how and why frames matter to the success of social movements (Snow & Benford, 1988; McAdam *et al.*, 2001, Ganz, 2009). They shape and condition how people find and connect to others to collectively act. To this end, framing is heavily cited across the social sciences (Benford & Snow, 2000), in research which has shown how frames evolve and align through processes of extension, bridging, amplification, and transformation, with universalizing frames often serving to broaden the reach of socio-political movements (Almeida, 2019; McAdam, 1982). Frames also matter in determining economic outcomes, as a generation of research on economic-related organizing and movement-based projects has shown (Soule, 2013; Fligstein & McAdam, 2019). Beyond affecting real-world collective action in the economy, frames also likely matter to academic scholarship on the economy, and on economic-related social movements beyond the academy. If academic study of the economy is a multi-field "contest of economic ideas" (Stilwell, 2002), one which shapes the hearts and minds of students who go on to become the public, then how those ideas are framed in academic classrooms is likely to bear on how well different ideas about the economy are received by and utilized by the public. With respect to economic alterity, certain frames may be more influential and have broader reach than others, affecting both patterns in academic discourse about alternatives, as well as the success of real-world attempts to build a more sustainable, ethical, and cooperative economy. Simply put: frames are not just a matter of semantics. They are what grab people's attention and move them to action. Frames thus need to capture the attention and imagination of the multiple publics with which cooperatives and their allies must engage. So, the way we talk about cooperatives and their sibling organizational forms matters. Are they part of a diverse economy? A degrowth agenda? A social economy? A collectivist-democratic one? A commons? This matters to the shared, long-term success of cooperatives and other alternative enterprises.

Despite rising popular, movement-based interest in economic alternatives today, and despite development of overlapping frames to conceptualize such alterity, there has been little systematic review of these various frames, of their comparative strengths and limits, or of their consequence. I analyze and review these various conceptual frames listed above, yielding two key findings of interest not only for academics and scholars, but for real-world practitioners as well. First, though they vary in their breadth, depth, and degree of overlap, each frame remains shaped by distinct meso-ontological orientations, national/linguistic traditions, and academic disciplinary foci, which shape their bounds and limits. What this means is that these frames aren't all just talking past each other about the same things: there are differences in what they privilege, what they value, and what they discuss. But in as much as a universalizing frame is desirable, however, as to enable cooperators and allies to organize to build a better world, the persistence of multiple frames may undermine the long-term success of alternatives like the cooperative. Multiple frames may fragment and splinter efforts, or needlessly create division.

Second, regardless which particular frames are deployed, academic research within and across these frames has not often empirically articulated the specific macro-conditions under which various alternatives proliferate, succeed, or fail, nor has it examined the appropriateness of different models for use to address different problems or contexts: when should one utilize a consumer cooperative model, for example, as opposed to a mutual benefit corporation? This is unclear. Nor, to this end, has empirical research examined whether certain *frames* might be more appropriate or desirable for use in some settings than others. Social science-based research on these questions might remedy this oversight, and in so doing, help those in the real world through actionable findings.

To begin to answer these questions, a traditional review article approach of discursive analysis of leading texts for each frame was supplemented with descriptive statistics on academic and popular uses of the frames listed above. I conducted targeted keyword searches in the Web of Science's (WOS) main social science-based Core Collection Citation Indices for known frames (**Tables 1 and 2**). Records were manually cleaned to eliminate extraneous results before descriptive statistics of publication and citation counts were generated. To examine popular use, frame hashtags were analyzed using Hashtagify,[1] which ranks and classifies Twitter hashtag usage, to generate details on relative popularity, top languages, and nations of use. Where known non-English variants of hashtags appear in the literature, these were also analyzed. **Table 3** summarizes frame differences across key dimensions, including disciplinary focus, national/linguistic tradition, and meso-ontological focus, based on content analysis of tweets, highly cited WOS articles, and other sources referenced in both. Additional frames were considered but excluded because they did not *primarily* center alternatives, or they considered alternatives *equally* alongside strategies which center working complementarily to capitalism (e.g., labor unions, community development corporations). Instead, using Fraser's (1997) distinction between affirmative *vs* transformational reforms, I selected frames focused on transforming capitalism, rather than merely making it more livable.[2]

Table 1 Web of Science Core Collection: Citations and Record Counts by Frame

Frame	Keywords Searched	Citations Total	Publication Records Count Total	Top Languages >2.5%	Top Countries (Top 4)	Fields >10% of Publications	# of Publications by Field
Alternative, Diverse, and Community Economics	"alternative economies" or "diverse economies" or "community economies" or "diverse and community economies"	5,805	388	English 93.3% Spanish 3.9%	USA 108 UK 94 Australia 76 Canada 21	Geography Environmental Studies Economics	148 65 44
Commoning	"commoning"	1,497	233	English 94.0% Italian 3.4%	USA 47 UK 40 Netherlands 25 Germany 22	Geography Environmental Studies	59 45
	"the commons"	41,119	2,397	English 93.3% Spanish 3.8%	USA 896 UK 309 Canada 178 Spain 102	Environmental Studies Economics	501 472
Economic Democracy	"economic democracy"	1,025	386	English 90.2% Spanish 3.1% German 2.6%	USA 139 UK 44 Canada 27 Germany 14	Economics Political Science Industrial Relations Sociology	98 77 65 51
Social and Solidarity Economy	"social and solidarity economy" or "economie sociale et solidaire" or "solidarity economy" or "economie solidaire" or "the social economy" or "economie sociale"	4,607	1,110	English 54.8% Spanish 27.1% Portuguese 10.5% French 4.3%	Spain 219 Brazil 130 Canada 114 USA 93	Economics Social Science Interdisc.	309 120
Alternative Enterprises/Organizations and Collectivist/Democratic Organizations	"collectivist-democratic" or "collectivist/democratic" or "collectivist organization" or "democratic organization" or "collectivist rationality" or "democratic rationality" or "alternative enterprise" or "alternative organization"	1,272	133	English 82.7% Spanish 4.5% Russian 3.8% Portuguese 3.0%	USA 43 UK 18 Canada 7 France 7 Spain 7	Business/Management Political Science Sociology	22 17 17
Post-Capitalism	"postcapitalism" or "post-capitalism"	727	149	English 80.5% Russian 8.7% Spanish 6.7%	UK 43 USA 21 Russia 15 Australia 14	Political Science Sociology Economics Geography	32 20 15 15
Degrowth	"de-growth" or "degrowth" or "decroissance" or "decroissant"	10,135	723	English 93.4% Spanish 2.8%	Spain 119 Germany 111 UK 101 US 94	Environmental Studies Environmental Science Economics Green Sustainable Science Technology Ecology Environmental Engineering	288 256 185 172 100 74
Community Wealth and Control	Community Wealth	578	43	English 100.0%	USA 30 Canada 4 UK 4 Italy 3	Economics Development Studies Public Administration Environmental Studies	9 7 5 4
	Community Control	2,523	249	English 96.4%	USA 135 UK 27 Australia 14 Canada 13	Political Science Urban Studies Sociology	49 44 32

Note: Web of Science Core Collections searched include: the Social Science Citation Index, Emerging Sources Citation Index, and the two Book Citation Indices (Sciences and Social Sciences)

Table 2 Twitter Usage by Frame

Term	Hashtag	Hashtagify Score	Top Languages 1%+	Top Countries 5%+
Alternative, Diverse, and Community Economies	#alternativeeconomy	4.2	English	Netherlands
	#alternativeeconomies	1	Norwegian	N/A
	#diverseeconomy	4.2	English	N/A
	#diverseeconomies	--	English	--
	#communityeconomies	6.7	English, Italian	N/A
	#communityeconomy	1	English	N/A
	#takebacktheeconomy	1	English	N/A
Commons/Commoning	#commons	46	English, Japanese, French, German Spanish, Italian	UK, Spain, US, Italy
	#commoning	19.2	English, Japanese, French	UK, France
Economic Democracy	#economicdemocracy	22.7	English	US, India
	#democraciaeconomica	12.7	Spanish	Argentina
	#democratieeconomique	1	French	N/A
	#democraziaeconomica	N/A	Italian	
	#wirtschaftlichedemokratie	--	Germany	--
Social and Solidarity Economy	#ess	53.3	French, English, Arabic, Spanish	France, UK, US
	#socialeconomy	37.4	English	Belgium, UK, Spain, Indonesia
	#solidarityeconomy	26	English	US
	#economiesociale	21.6	French, Indonesian, English	France, Canada
	#economiesolidaire	18	French, English	France
	#economiasolidaria	31.7	Spanish, Portuguese, Italian	Spain, Argentina, Colombia, Ecuador, Paraguay
	#economiasocial	38.6	Spanish, Portuguese, Italian, English	Spain, Argentina, Colombia, Ecuador, Paraguay
	#economiesocialeetsolidaire	15.7	French	France
	#solidarwirtschaft	--	German	--
Collectivist/Democratic Organizations and Alternative Enterprises/Organizations	#collectivist	21.9	English	US
	#alternativeenterprises	--	English	--
Community Wealth and Control	#communitywealth	18.6	English	UK
	#communitycontrol	18.6	English	US, Australia
Post-capitalism	#postcapitalism	32.6	English, Spanish, French	UK, Spain, Netherlands, Ireland, Australia
Degrowth	#degrowth	38.6	English, German, French, Spanish, Finnish	Germany, UK, US, France, Spain, Italy
	#decroissance	26.5	French, English, German	France, Canada, Germany, US
	#postwachstum	24.2	German, English	Germany, US

Table 3 Content Analysis Summary of Major Frames

Frame	Primary Academic Discipline/Area	Dominant Language and Nat'l Tradition	Focus: Factor of Production	Focus: Meso-ontological
Alternative, Diverse, and Community Economies	Geography	Anglophone	Land, Labor, Capital	Post-structural; Transactions, Enterprises, Labor, Finance, Property
Commons/Commoning	Resource/Public Economics	Anglophone	Land	Micro-Structural; Nature, Ecology, Public Goods/Resources
Economic Democracy	Political Science	Anglo-American, Anglophone	Labor/Capital	Micro-Structural; Firm Rules/Governance, Political Participation
Collectivist/Democratic and Alternative Enterprises	Sociology, Organizational Studies	Anglo-American, Anglophone	Labor/Capital	Micro and Meso Structures; Hypothetico-Deductive; Organizations, Institutions, Enterprises
Social and Solidarity Economy	Economics; Social Science Interdisciplinary	France, Quebec, Latin America, Spain, Italy; Francophone/ Romance Languages	Land, Labor, Capital	Micro, Macro Structural; Networks/sectoral ecosystems
Community Wealth and Community Control	Urban Studies and Planning; Urban/Public Affairs	Anglo-American, Anglophone	Land, Labor, Capital	Micro, Meso-Structural; Place/Spatial scale: Local Areas/Neighborhoods
Degrowth/Decroissance	N/A	France/Francophone; Anglo-American/Anglophone	Land, Labor, Capital	Material Resources
Post-capitalism	Political Science, Sociology, Economics	Anglo-American, Anglophone	Labor, Capital	Meso-structural; Networked, decentralized production; Technology

Review & Analysis of Frames

Alternative, diverse & community economies (ADCE)
Most associated with a pair of geographers writing under the pen-name Gibson-Graham (1996, 2006, 2008), ADCE argues that academic economic discourse historically privileged capitalism, delegitimizing

other economic practices in study of the economy (Leyshon, 2003). By decentering capitalocentric language and integrating non- and more-than-capitalist economic practices (Gibson-Graham & Dombroski, 2020) into study of the economy, ADCE seeks to reconstruct a more ethical economic paradigm for theory and practice. At its heart is a call to participate in and perform a community economy, one embedded in society. To that end, ADCE researchers work with, not on, community economies *via* participatory action research (PAR) to make "other worlds possible" (St. Martin *et al.*, 2015, p.1), often through its action-oriented Community Economies Institute (CEI).

ADCE invokes a distinct ontological orientation, reflecting Laclau's and Mouffe's post-structuralist politics of language. A new economy requires new language for praxis, with action researchers constructing new imaginaries (Sarmiento, 2017). This is not to deny structural forces exist; rather, such forces are contingent (Gibson-Graham, 2006; Miller, 2019). Further, ADCE's post-structuralist approach does not entirely abandon structural elements, but adopts a "loose grammar" for "weak theory" (St. Martin *et al.*, 2015). At the new language's center is a typology of diverse activities in a community economy. Economic activities are conceptualized through a two-dimensional typology divided into capitalist, alternative/more-than-capitalist, and non-market/non-capitalist categories, across meso-level focal objects of transaction, labor, and enterprise (subsequently expanded to add property and finance, *cf.* Gibson-Graham & Dombroski, 2020). ADCE does not deterministically pre-assign enterprise or transaction types to a particular typology cell, however. A "capitalist" investor-owned firm (IOF) can engage in non/more-than-capitalist practices (Gibson-Graham, 2006, p.75) whilst ostensibly "more-than-capitalist" firms, like consumer cooperatives, might engage in capitalist practices; each contains unique Deleuzo-Guattarian site-assemblages of practices. Scale as a meaningful concept is also interrogated and questioned (Gibson-Graham, 2002), with practices expected to achieve widespread proliferation through economic and political "geographies of ubiquity" (Cameron & Hicks, 2014), rather than realize prevalence through economies of scale. Further, ADCE has increasingly jettisoned the word alternative, because the word itself centers capitalism (Williams & Pierce, 2019). Nonetheless, its adherents have inventoried diverse economic practices worldwide (Gibson-Graham & Dombroski, 2020; Roelvink *et al.*, 2015), across all factors of production, whilst also directly addressing a popular audience (Gibson-Graham *et al.*, 2013).

ADCE has three major limitations, the first two of which also apply to most other frames reviewed. First, linguistically, it is highly Anglocene (Alhojärvi & Hyvärinen, 2020), a claim which both Twitter and WOS data affirms: 93% of WOS citations to the frame are in English. Given post-structuralists' concerns with language, this is problematic: if language is a Wittgensteinian cage, is the ADCE framework an English one, limiting broader usage potential? Second, there has been scant ADCE research *measuring* the uneven development of diverse economies, or empirically *explaining or theorizing* their variable formation, persistence, and prevalence (Fuller *et al.*, 2010). This matters for at least two reasons: measurement is how practices are made legible to the state (Scott, 1998). In as much as non/more-than capitalist legal forms require enabling policy for to succeed, lack of legibility is problematic. Second, measurement of the existing *size* and prevalence of these firms and practices also matters. Social scientists have shown what Pareto realized long ago (the 80-20 rule or power law, Gabaix, 2016), that large entities/observations drive aggregate outcomes more than many small ones. Material, productive economies of scale remain powerful in explaining differences in economies, especially in today's ever more technologically clustered and regionally unequal world (Gertler, 2003; Storper *et al.*, 2015; Delgado *et al.*, 2014; Moretti, 2012). If it is more difficult for community economies to achieve such scale, a point acknowledged despite ADCE's general abandonment of scalar ontologies

(Gibson-Graham, 2002; Cameron & Hicks, 2014; Diprose et al., 2017), can such practices actually become more prevalent *via* small-scale ubiquity if they are less efficient, even under efficiency definitions which internalize externalities? Under what conditions? Measuring ADCE practices' collective economic role and scale, would seem important — particularly for those not operating from a post-structuralist lens — as to empirically understand how this was achieved. Such empirical measurements of ADCE prevalence and scale are rare (see North, 2005, 2014, for an exception), though from a post-structuralist view, measurement might seem unnecessary and misguided, and perhaps counterproductive and harmful. Finally, as WOS and Twitter data suggest, ADCE has little presence in other social sciences or cognate professional-school fields, and appears limited in non-academic usage, too. Business school and sociological scholars have made attempts to apply ADCE to analyze alternatives' institutional logic/structure (Campana et al., 2017), but such usage beyond geography is rare, as WOS citations of Gibson-Graham's work affirms. Twitter data also shows virtually no hashtag use of ADCE framing language or of its "take back the economy" (Gibson-Graham et al., 2013) term, suggesting lack of real-world take-up.

The commons/commoning

Drawing on public/natural resource economics, the commons is associated with Nobel economics laureate Ostrom and ecologist Hardin. Reflecting these historical roots, the literature has been driven by environmental science and environmental studies, as WOS data affirm. Among all frames examined in this article, the commons has the strongest academic presence, as measured by citation and publication count data in WOS, ranking first in both. Its popular usage, based on Hashtagify data, is stronger than most other frames, with presence across languages and countries.

Ostrom won the Nobel prize in economics for showing groups could collectively self-solve Hardin's (1968) "tragedy of the commons", in which shared resources lacking clear property/access rights are destroyed through overuse. Though the idea of the commons is old and wide-ranging (McCarthy, 2009), Hardin shaped its modern development as a term centered on natural resources and public goods (i.e., non-rivalrous, non-excludable goods). Ostrom identified eight design principles/conditions under which commons management of pooled resources succeed (Ostrom, 1990, 2010; Wilson, 2015). Subsequent research, emanating from environmental studies, has examined localized efforts to pool common resources, and often examines enterprises and organizations which may not be formally incorporated as cooperatives. Core commons literature has often focused on the enabling micro-conditions for shared or cooperative institutional practices, or the role of institutional rules in their maintenance (Fennell, 2011). It has largely avoided macro-questions of how political-economic conditions affect commons management, though some have recently questioned whether Hardin's micro-diagnoses were accurate: Brinkley (2020) provocatively called Hardin's tragedy supposition "pig shit," arguing that the commons' loss is macro-political in nature, while Mildenberger (2019) affirmed Hardin's argument was historically inaccurate and misguided: the specific commons Hardin examined were indeed well-regulated by community institutions, with Hardin's argument fueled primarily by racism and xenophobia.

Also central to the framework is historian Linebaugh (2009), who traced implications of the oft-overlooked English *Magna Carta*-era *Charter of the Forest* for subsistence access to forests and land, a right severely abridged during the enclosures (18th/19th century Parliamentary acts which converted about one-fourth of cultivated English land from common to private property; Thompson, 1991; Williams, 1973). Linebaugh's contributions include active promotion and use of commons as a verb, commoning

(Diprose *et al.*, 2017) normatively calling for action to reconvert public goods, including land, to be held collectively and in common, and reflects the oft-explicitly normative stance of this scholarship, and its connections to practice.

The commons/commoning frame appears to enjoy broad popular usage in English, and in Romance and Germanic languages as well (Euler, 2016), as the geographic range and levels of usage in the Twitter data suggests, as noted earlier. Frame usage has been clearly extended beyond natural resources to include conceptualizing postcapitalist information, data, and digital peer-to-peer commons (Lessig, 2002; Hess & Ostrom, 2003; Beagle, 2012; Morell, 2014; Bauwens *et al.*, 2019), labor commons (Azzellini, 2018), housing commons (Aernouts & Ryckewaert, 2019), black commons (Roane, 2018), and urban commons (Huron, 2018).

But are such frame extensions appropriate? While all of these other, commons-labeled resources, if pooled, may generate positive externalities, they are not necessarily classical public goods (*i.e.*, non-rivalrous/non-excludable like air, oceans, and other natural resources), which was the domain to which Ostrom (and Hardin's) original approach was intended to apply. Further, there is little in this literature to indicate the economic sustainability or efficiency of commoning such non-public goods. This begs the question: how comprehensively can this frame be applied to conceptualize alternatives more broadly? Can all factors of production be meaningfully conceptualized using the framework of the commons? Can all factors of production be organized, in practice, according to the principles of commons management? If so, under what macro-conditions, and how? Though many normative public scholarship works have proposed efforts to prospectively create commons, such questions have not been meaningfully asked or empirically answered in the commons/commoning literature.

Community wealth/community control

Though it appears to have some conjoint usage with other frames (such as the commons/commoning (McCarthy, 2009; Thoms, 2008), economic democracy (Casper-Futterman & DeFilippis, 2017), and ADCE (Huron, 2018), suggesting efforts at frame alignment, this frame primarily reflects the multi-disciplinary traditions of urban studies, including urban policy and planning, as WOS data affirms, spanning sociology and political science. The community control frame does not appear to be originally academic in origin, however, having gained prominence in the 1960s Civil Rights movement, as African-American communities sought community control over local schools, as well more generally in local politics and economics (DeFilippis, 2004). As the 1960's radical visions of Black community empowerment gave way to institutionalized community development and Black capitalism by the 1980s (Stoecker, 1997), the community control achieved was limited. Nonetheless, structuralist scholarly work persisted (Williamson *et al.*, 2002; Gunn & Gunn, 1991; DeFilippis, 2004) and is today experiencing a popular and scholarly revival (Rahman & Simonson, 2020), building from DeFilippis's (2004). He argued community control over land, labor and capital offered a route by which local communities and neighborhoods might escape cycles of corporate investment followed by disinvestment and abandonment, detailing how different forms, including community land trusts, worker cooperatives, and credit unions, achieve community economic control. Today this interest in community control has appeared simultaneously with work on community wealth building forms (Dubb, 2016; Spicer, 2020; Spicer & Casper-Futterman, 2020), a term associated in practice with the Democracy Collaborative, which advocates for such models, primarily in US communities, and its UK equivalent, the Centre for Local Economic Strategies.

Notwithstanding DeFilippis's (2004) conceptualization of community economic control, research has largely been descriptive and case-based, documenting benefits, outcomes, and challenges, with recent work focused on land (e.g., DeFilippis et al., 2019). Implicit in this work, and reflecting its academic roots, are local notions of place-based community. As "community without propinquity" (Webber, 1963, Calhoun, 1998) is ever-increasing through virtual, networked economic forms, do peer-to-peer and non-hierarchical virtual models which transcend place (e.g., open-source software and platform cooperatives; Schneider & Scholtz, 2016) fit this frame? This is unaddressed. This tradition has also failed to fully identify macro-political-economic and social conditions under which community economic control can be achieved, despite calls to do so by urban regime theorists (cf. Rast, 2005 on the Stone-Imbroscio debates). It also has not addressed the issue of scale, which DeFilippis (1999) also raised: can these approaches achieve economic scale, or are they destined to remain trapped as highly localized, Lilliputian phenomena? If they can transcend the localist trap, when and how? This also remains unaddressed. The frame also is highly Anglocene, with Twitter and WOS data suggesting a lack of take-up beyond the Anglo-American world.

Economic democracy

As an academic frame, economic democracy is often associated with political scientist Dahl (1986), who argued political democracy cannot be sustained without corollary economic democracy. Echoing Schumpeter and Marx, he argued capitalism's search for monopoly super-profits produced concentrated ownership of enterprises, resulting in deeply unequal political and economic power, threatening political democracy. As an antidote, he advocated economic democracy, where individuals exert both democratic control and voice (Hirschman, 1970) in economic institutions. He defined these as enterprises owned and controlled by constituent members, to achieve workplace or industrial democracy. For much of the 20th century, political scientists and sociologists referred to economic democracy conjointly with industrial democracy, a related, more expansive concept in which workers democratically control industry by a range of means, including trade unionism and co-determination, and the Germanic notion of Wirtschaftsdemokratie (Muller-Jentsch, 2008). Dahl also built on democratic theorists and empirical research on political and economic participation's effects, from Macpherson (1942) to Carol Pateman (1970, 2012). Echoing Marshall (1920) regarding cities' knowledge spillovers, Pateman theorized civic spillovers from workplace democracy: it would inspire workers to participate in civic life. Subsequent scholars across the academy have further developed these arguments (Schweickart, 1992; Davis, 2013).

In practice, ownership and control/voice considerations led Dahl to argue worker-owned and controlled cooperatives were the most practical way to achieve economic democracy. But he failed to articulate the macro-political or social conditions/mechanisms implementing such visions might require, reflecting a surprisingly micro-structural orientation. This frame has often remained focused on how well certain organizational forms embody economic democracy, and measuring their participatory benefits (Carberry, 2011). Subsequent research has largely examined labor and employer-employee relationships within firms (Michael, 2015), sometimes eliding over the specifics of land/housing (which often lacks employees) and capital (which lends itself to customer, not employee, ownership; Hansmann, 1996). Scholars have, however, begun extending the frame to address these gaps (Johanisova & Wolf, 2012; McGaughey, 2020), examining community currencies, communal land and property, and self-employment, among others, as embodying economic democracy. Though political science (Malleson,

2014) and sociological research has continued to deploy the term, as WOS data affirms, other disciplines have directly engaged with this frame. Geographer Amin (1996), building on Hirst's (1994) more expansive "associative democracy," offered description of the forms and policy fronts, including reinvigorated public ownership (Cumbers, 2012), though there has been little subsequent empirical examination of outcomes. Finally, as with the commons, frame extension is evident: "energy democracy," for example, examines and conceptualizes democratic, community ownership of the energy sector (Burke & Stephens, 2018; Becker & Naumann, 2017). Meanwhile, as Twitter data suggests, though Anglophones have widely used economic democracy to advocate for its organizational forms, and despite the related Germanic notion cited above, the form has little usage in other languages. In conjunction, notable real-world organizations promoting and deploying the term – the New Economics Foundation and its allies (UK and US, *cf.* Dubb, 2016), Center for Economic Democracy (Boston), and the Bronx Cooperative Development Initiative (New York), are Anglophone and US-based.

Collectivist/democratic organizations & alternative enterprises

Organizational and economic sociologists have developed a rich tradition examining democratic enterprises and organizations, which they often refer to as collectivist/democratic organizations or alternative enterprises. Building from Weber, sociologist Joyce Rothschild (1979) identified a different rationality in certain organizations like worker cooperatives: a collectivist/democratic one, particularly in cooperatives, which make it possible for substantive values to dominate instrumental ones (*e.g.*, profit). The research emerged in organizational studies across sociology, industrial and labor relations, and business, which has thoroughly studied "hybrid" enterprises (Battilana & Dorado, 2010) and "hybrid" fields (Spicer *et al.*, 2019), like social enterprise and entrepreneurship, which attempt to combine competing commercial and social logics. This structuralist research has examined how collectivist organizations embody values through specific rules and practices (Chen *et al.*, 2013), often to participants' benefit, and how alternative organizations and alternative enterprises, terms often used interchangeably, are incubated by social movements (Schneiberg *et al.*, 2008) and technological change (Schneiberg, 2017; Davis, 2016a,b). Other research has argued alternative ownership forms like cooperatives (Spicer & Lee-Chuvala, 2021) embed governance rules which may be necessary, if not sufficient, for these organizations to avoid mission drift. Unlike ADCE-related geographers' usage of the term alternative enterprises (*cf.* Coe *et al.*, 2020), sociologists' usage is generally structural, and presumes alternative legal forms and structures, while not sufficient to secure alterity, may be necessary and may serve to increase the probability of organizational alterity.

This research has largely focused on enterprises' internal dynamics, and the mechanisms used to manage conflicting rationalities and values. It has on occasion addressed the external political-economic and social factors which enable alternative enterprises to succeed (Schneiberg *et al.*, 2008), to examine how, when, and where these models diffuse, proliferate, and scale, reflecting organizational scholars' engagement with diffusion processes (DiMaggio & Powell, 1983) and related social movements' scholars work examining scale shift (Soule, 2013). Practices occurring outside of formally structured, permanent organizational enterprises, however, are not typically addressed (Chen (2009) is a notable exception). As with economic democracy, there has been scant academic application to housing or land. The frame also has limited real-world reach, and is almost entirely Anglophone, with little to no usage found in Romance or Germanic languages. Though the #collectivist handle is fairly widely used on Twitter, content analysis revealed little connection to its organizational studies usage; rather it simply describes collectivist practices. Alternative enterprise tweets are virtually non-existent.

Social & solidarity economy

Development of the social and solidarity economy frame (*économie sociale et solidaire* or ESS) can be traced to 19th century France. In the French Revolution, the state eliminated feudal corporations and economic organizations which might come between the people and the state (Sewell, 1980). Over the course of France's "long 19th century" (Hobsbawm, 1962), new forms grew into this void, including cooperatives/mutuals and economic associations. These organizational experiments, often illegal, slowly achieved state sanction. In conjunction, the structural idea of a social economy rooted in these forms emerged, developed by early economists led by Gide (Moulaert & Ailenei, 2005). Gide, who today would likely be labelled an activist-scholar, popularized the concept of the social economy (*vis-à-vis* political economy) as rooted in cooperative enterprises and associations, which he also helped build in practice (Gide, 1905).

The notion of a coherent social *and solidarity* economy emerged after the 1968 Paris uprisings, as one of two pillars of a Socialist Party plan for a Jacobin France (Duverger, 2016). The social economy frame was extended to include the solidarity economy, a related term believed to have originated in Spain in the early 20th century. After the Socialist Party achieved national power in the early 1980s, France systematically worked with advocates to knit together various alternative economic forms into a coherent sector. New organizational forms, such as legally defined solidarity enterprises, multi-stakeholder cooperatives, and work integration cooperatives, were introduced as part of a formally, legally recognized ESS sector of France's economy. Regulation of these disparate forms, which include more than a dozen entity types, had evolved gradually over two centuries (Seeberger, 2014), each with their own laws and advocacy organizations. The ESS frame legally encompasses all these forms, which have kept their own advocacy organizations, but benefit from supplemental shared laws, financing organizations, and national/regional policy advocacy councils (Duverger, 2016; Laville, 2010). A similar structure exists in Quebec (Lévesque, 2013; Spicer & Zhong, 2022).

Often published in Romance languages, as WOS data affirms, research focuses on cataloguing ESS practices in different cases and settings.[3] ESS research of a hypothetico-deductive, explanatory nature is limited. Scholars have, however, exhaustively measured the size, scope and geographic density and coverage of France's ESS, in contrast to researchers in other Anglophone frameworks, and in contrast to Anglophone context usage of ESS. It is possible that this reflects a generally weaker and less-developed policy and legal structure for ESS forms in Anglophone countries, but this is an empirical question that has not been addressed. In English, sociologist Bruyn (1977) produced many works on ESS, as did geographer Amin (2002). Across fields, other scholarship has combined ESS with explicitly green/environmental elements of the commons/commoning as well (Smith, 2005; Healy *et al.*, 2018; Shear, 2019). Finally, ESS is in popular use across Romance language-dominated countries in Latin America and Europe, as Twitter data affirms, not surprising given the terms' origins. English usage on Twitter is also high; in multiple languages the terms are tweeted separately (social economy, solidarity economy) and together (social and solidarity economy, or social solidarity economy), suggesting the frame has potential for broad and flexible use across more contexts than Anglophone-originating frames. In the WOS citation data, nearly half of the publications referencing the terms do not originate in English, and instead are driven by

Romance Languages. Organizations such as Rencontres Mont Blanc in France, the Chantier de L'Économie Sociale in Québec, and CIRIEC's (International Centre of Research and Information on the Public, Social and Cooperative Economy) chapters in Spanish-speaking countries are particularly active in studying and advocating for greater use and development of ESS forms. Notably, however, while Anglophone usage appears on the rise in popular settings, as evidenced by development of groups such as the US Solidarity Economy Network and the adoption of the term Solidarity Economy by the New Economy Coalition in 2020-2021, the term may be saddled with well-known challenges of socialist-sounding frames in Anglophone settings, particularly the US (*cf.* Sombart, 1906).

Post-capitalism & degrowth

Two other frames have rapidly emerged as significant in both popular and academic settings, as affirmed by their quickened pace of reference in WOS citation data, and warrant brief analysis. Though the idea of post-capitalism has an established history, including in the ADCE framework (*cf.* Gibson-Graham, 2006), the term's broader current usage was stoked by economics journalist Mason's (2016) work on technological developments in enabling post-capitalism, complementing related academic work (Srnicek & Williams, 2015). This usage has overlapped somewhat with the economic democracy and alternative enterprises scholarship, with conjoint appearance of all three terms evident in the literature (*cf.* Johanisova & Wolf, 2012; Boillat *et al.*, 2012), suggesting efforts at frame alignment by scholars. Post-capitalist scholarship also builds on the legacy of research examining flexible, decentralized networked production, argued a generation ago to be looming in dominance (Piore & Sabel, 1984), as technological advancements reduced the benefits to fixed-cost investment at scale. If 3D-printing replaces factories, benefits of economic scale might disappear (Rehnberg & Ponte, 2018), undermining traditional corporations. Sociologist Davis (2016b) notes jobs from the Big Three automakers have not been numerically replaced by high-tech GAFA (Google, Amazon, Facebook, Apple) successors. But economies of scale clearly still matter: GAFA dominate as the Big Three once did, and as industrial conglomerates before them. Davis has concluded alternatives like peer-to-peer networked production (Benkler, 2007) and cooperatives could rise in the void. The role of politics, however, remains undertheorized in this work, though it is emerging (Miller, 2015; Zanoni *et al.*, 2017).

From French anti-growth activists' *decroissance* in 2001, the English variant degrowth was further popularized in academia after a 2008 Paris conference (Demaria *et al.*, 2013); the term also has older roots in political ecology and 1970s French scholarship (Gorz, 1975; Gorz & Bosquet, 1977), and in ecological economics, with the tradition led by figures in the latter field today, most notably Barcelona-based Giorgos Kallis, as WOS citation data affirms. Like the commons/commoning, degrowth focuses on the environment, but did not initially focus only on natural resources/public goods, but rather on how material limits of a finite-resource earth necessitate a shift to a degrowth economy based on decentralized, local production, because endless growth is materially impossible. While this has, theoretically, always been the case – growth cannot continue forever – implicit in degrowth is that the end is imminent, and another future is and must be at hand. Scholars and activists have attempted to apply degrowth across factors of production, though as with the other frames, there is limited effort to measure degrowth practices, and to empirically identify conditions which might enable successful transition to degrowth, though work on this is emergent (Kallis *et al.*, 2012, 2018; Ott, 2012). Twitter data suggests strong popular use cutting across multiple linguistic traditions, including English, German, and Romance languages, and WOS citations have rapidly overtaken those of almost all other frames reviewed. Nonetheless, practically, the frame suffers from a popular perception problem: as Chomsky noted, degrowth is incorrectly taken to mean a decline in living standards (Drews & Antal, 2016), instead of offering alternative to green growth, which is unlikely to result in climate improvements (Hickel & Kallis, 2020).

Discussion & Conclusions

Despite conjoint use which indicates some evidence of alignment and bridging between frames, each retains clear bounds reflecting its disciplinary and national/linguistic roots, and associated limitations. While ADCE helped reveal the presence of diverse economies, for those interested in empirical social science on alternatives, or applying research to build a scaled-up non-capitalist global economy, the framework's post-structural and Anglophone orientation are limiting. Though the commons lacks such limitations, its applicability to or appropriateness for rivalrous, excludable goods is unclear. Meanwhile, economic democracy has not been well applied to the third factor of production (land/physical structures), and its appeal for use beyond English-language contexts is also unclear. Community control/wealth framing appears to apply across types of goods and factors of production, but it is unclear whether it can transcend the localist trap, or appeal beyond Anglophone worlds. While the social and solidarity economy has broad global appeal, and Anglophone usage appears on the rise, it remains unclear whether the term sounds too socialistic for success in liberal Anglophone democracies today.

Academically, while research in the ADCE, community wealth/control, and social and solidarity economy traditions have sought to systematically describe and catalogue practices, none have measured or empirically explained how, why, where and when alternatives proliferate and scale. Nor have they considered which alternatives work best for different types of situations or contexts. Social scientists studying the economy across multiple fields, however, have excelled at asking and answering these types of questions, using both qualitative and quantitative empirics. How might they advance such understandings of alternatives? Scholars could work within these frames to measure and explain prevalence and scale of their practices and forms, and consider how their prevalence and scale is conditioned by different contextual factors. To that end, I recently published a study (Spicer, 2022) which attempts to start to do exactly this, for large-scale cooperative enterprises: I examined how a range of social, economic, and geographic factors condition the cross-national prevalence of large scale cooperative enterprises across the rich democracies. But this was just one study, covering a particular alternative model, only for some countries, and only in a single moment in time. There is much more work to be done on this front. Scholars could also seek to measure how well various alternative economic forms, including the cooperative, embody pro-social, community-oriented economic traits. Modern statistical techniques make this possible, and can even accommodate a degree of post-structural orientation. For example, the degree to which different alternative forms embody idealized community economy features, such as social equity or environmental sustainability, could be measured, to see how strongly, if at all, each form is associated with these traits. One could also measure the degree of alterity lost as practices scale, if at all. These are empirical questions which can be addressed using Bayesian techniques (e.g., mixture, mixing, and random effects models).

Some frames have the added benefit of originating in the real economy and have proliferated in multiple languages, avoiding extreme Anglocentrism, potentially yielding a broader global provenance and resonance, as Twitter data affirmed. The commons and ESS stand out as particularly notable in this regard. While commons/commoning may be limited by its goodness-of-fit beyond public/natural resource goods, as noted above, this might be overcome by bridging to the community wealth/control frame, which lacks this problem. Both come from the same Latin root, a basis for such a bridge. ESS has already undergone such bridging between the social and solidarity components of the term, and, like community/commoning frames, has provenance across the academy and beyond. These frames' names also directly address the twin forces sparking recent interest in alternatives: record inequality and climate change. In as much as a universal frame is desirable, both seem promising for further study and popular use, as well. Academics, however, need not drive frame selection at all: this can be empirically asked of those building real alternatives. What frames do they find most useful? Consistent with PAR's ontology, this is not merely an academic question: indeed, the idea for this study was suggested by practitioners of alternatives, including cooperators involved with the cooperative movement, I have encountered in research. Their experiences affirmed that "made here" local labels can have stronger valence in local movements (Miller & Nicholls, 2013), while also affirming that frames' content matters to movements' success. Community frames may suit liberal Anglophone settings less hospitable to socialistic-sounding concepts; social labels may fit sites more open to democratic socialism. But these are unanswered empirical questions, as is the notion that the lack of a unifying, global frame to complement local ones may undermine economic organizing of global solidarity at scale.

As noted, less alternative-centric frames have not been examined here, thereby missing opportunities to review relations between what Fraser conceptualized as transformational and affirmative strategies. I have not examined explicitly either feminist economic perspectives (Mies, 2014; Mies & Shiva, 1993; Waring & Steinem, 1988), or indigenous/decolonizing economic lenses (Amoamo et al., 2018; Curchin, 2015; Kuokkanen, 2011); as most examined frames were born of the twinned forces of capitalism and colonialism, they may accordingly be limited in transcending them (Sengupta, 2015). Non-capitalist frames such as Ujamaa and Ujima (Swahili for extended family and cooperative economics; Mushi, 1970), are inspiring alternative practices in the US and elsewhere (Jimenez, 2018; Shear, 2019), and may also offer more promise in overcoming such limitations.

End-notes

[1]   Scores ranges 1-100, with 100 the maximum. Black Lives Matter registers 77.5, for comparative purposes.
[2]   Frames excluded on these grounds include social enterprise/entrepreneurship, sharing economy, circular economy, third sector/non-profit/voluntary sector, alterglobalization/altermondialization, community economic development, just transition, and Polanyian substantive economies. Other frames (New Economy, Next System, Participatory Economics, and Cooperative Ecosystem) were excluded due to newness, limited development, or lack of substantive academic usage.
[3]   The leading ESS academic journal, indexed in EconLit, is *RECMA/Revue Internationale de l'économie sociale*. English special issues are occasionally available. Beyond *RECMA*, Québec-based Professor Marie Bouchard and her collaborators are among the leading English-publishing ESS scholars.

References

Aernouts, N. & Ryckewaert, M. (2019). Reproducing housing commons: Government involvement & differential commoning in a housing cooperative. *Housing Studies*, 34(1), 92–110.

Alhojärvi, T. & Hyvärinen, P. (2020). Translating diverse economies in the Anglocene. In J.K. Gibson-Graham & K. Dombroski (eds.), *The Handbook of Diverse Economies* (pp.467-475). Edward Elgar.

Almeida, P. (2019). *Social Movements: The Structure of Collective Mobilization*. University of California Press.

Amin, A. (1996). Beyond associative democracy. *New Political Economy*, 1(3), 309-333.

Amin, A. (2002). *Placing the Social Economy*. Routledge.

Amoamo, M., Ruckstuhl, K. & Ruwhiu, D. (2018). Balancing indigenous values through diverse economies: A case study of Māori ecotourism. *Tourism Planning & Development*, 15, 1–18.

Azzellini, D. (2018). Labor as a commons: The example of worker-recuperated companies. *Critical Sociology*, 44(4–5), 763–776.

Battilana, J. & Dorado, S. (2010). Building sustainable hybrid organizations: The case of commercial microfinance organizations. *Academy of Management Journal*, 53(6), 1419–1440.

Bauwens, M., Kostakis, V. & Pazaitis, A. (2019). Peer to Peer. In M. Bauewens, V. Kostakis & A. Pazaitis, *Peer to Peer: The Commons Manifesto*. University of Westminster Press.

Beagle, D. (2012). The emergent information commons: Philosophy, models & 21st century learning paradigms. *Journal of Library Administration*, 52(6–7), 518–537.

Becker, S. & Naumann, M. (2017). Energy democracy: Mapping the debate on energy alternatives. *Geography Compass*, 11(8), e12321.

Benford, R.D. & Snow, D.A. (2000). Framing processes & social movements: An overview & assessment. *Annual Review of Sociology*, 26, 611–639. JSTOR.

Benkler, Y. (2007). *The Wealth of Networks: How Social Production Transforms Markets & Freedom*. Yale University Press.

Boillat, S., Gerber, J.-F. & Funes-Monzote, F.R. (2012). What economic democracy for degrowth? Some comments on the contribution of socialist models & Cuban agroecology. *Futures*, 44(6), 600–607.

Brinkley, C. (2020). Hardin's imagined tragedy is pig shit: A call for planning to recenter the commons. *Planning Theory*, 19(1), 127–144.

Bruyn, S.T.H. (1977). *The Social Economy: People Transforming Modern Business*. Wiley.

Burke, M.J. & Stephens, J.C. (2018). Political power & renewable energy futures: A critical review. *Energy Research & Social Science*, 35, 78–93.

Calhoun, C. (1998). Community without propinquity revisited: Communications technology & the transformation of the urban public sphere. *Sociological Inquiry*, 68(3), 373–397.

Cameron, J. & Hicks, J. (2014). Performative research for a climate politics of hope: Rethinking geographic scale, "impact" scale, and markets. *Antipode*, 46(1), 53–71.

Campana, M., Chatzidakis, A. & Laamanen, M. (2017). Introduction to the special issue: A macromarketing perspective on alternative economies. *Journal of Macromarketing*, 37(2), 125–130.

Carberry, E.J. (2011). Employee ownership & shared capitalism: Assessing the experience, research & policy implications in E.J. Carberry (ed.), *Employee Ownership and Shared Capitalism: New Directions in Research*. Ithaca: Cornell University Press.

Casper-Futterman, E. & DeFilippis, J. (2017). On economic democracy in community development. In M. van Ham, *Entrepreneurial Neighborhoods: Towards an Understanding of the Economies of Neighborhoods & Communities* (p.179). Edward Elgar.

Chen, K.K. (2009). *Enabling Creative Chaos: The Organization behind the Burning Man Event*. University of Chicago Press.

Chen, K.K., Lune, H. & Queen, E.L. (2013). How values shape & are shaped by nonprofit & voluntary organizations: The current state of the field. *Nonprofit and Voluntary Sector Quarterly*, 42(5), 856–885.

Coe, N.M., Kelly, P.F. & Yeung, H.W.C. (2020). *Economic Geography: A Contemporary Introduction* (3rd edition). Wiley-Blackwell.

Cumbers, A. (2012). *Reclaiming Public Ownership: Making Space for Economic Democracy*. Zed Books.

Curchin, K. (2015). Two visions of Indigenous economic development & cultural survival: The "real economy" & the "hybrid economy." *Australian Journal of Political Science*, 50(3), 412–426.

Dahl, R.A. (1986). *A Preface to Economic Democracy*. University of California Press.

Davis, G.F. (2013). After the corporation. *Politics & Society*, 41(2), 283–308.

Davis, G.F. (2016a). Can an economy survive without corporations? Technology & robust organizational alternatives. *Academy of Management Perspectives*, 30(2), 129–140.

Davis, G.F. (2016b). *The Vanishing American Corporation: Navigating the Hazards of a New Economy*. Berrett-Koehler Publishers.

DeFilippis, J. (1999). Alternatives to the "New Urban Politics": Finding locality & autonomy in local economic development. *Political Geography*, 18(8), 973–990.

DeFilippis, J. (2004). *Unmaking Goliath: Community Control in the Face of Global Capital*. Routledge.

DeFilippis, J., Williams, O.R., Pierce, J., Martin, D.G., Kruger, R. & Esfahani, A.H. (2019). On the transformative potential of community land trusts in the United States. *Antipode*, 51(3), 795–817.

Delgado, M., Porter, M.E. & Stern, S. (2014). Clusters, convergence & economic performance. *Research Policy*, 43(10), 1785–1799.

Della Porta, D. (2020). How progressive social movements can save democracy in pandemic times. *Interface*, 12(1), 355–358.

Demaria, F., Schneider, F., Sekulova, F. & Martinez-Alier, J. (2013). What is degrowth? From an activist slogan to a social movement. *Environmental Values*, 22(2), 191–215.

DiMaggio, P.J. & Powell, W.W. (1983). The iron cage revisited: Institutional isomorphism & collective rationality in organizational fields. *American Sociological Review*, 2, 147.

Diprose, G., Dombroski, K., Healy, S. & Waitoa, J. (2017). Community economies: Responding to questions of scale, agency & Indigenous connections in Aotearoa, New Zealand. *Counterfutures: Left Thought & Practice Aotearoa*, 4, 167–184.

Drews, S. & Antal, M. (2016). Degrowth: A "missile word" that backfires? *Ecological Economics*, 126, 182–187.

Dubb, S. (2016). Community wealth building forms: What they are & how to use them at the local level. *Academy of Management Perspectives*, 30(2), 141–152.

Duverger, T. (2016). *L'Économie Sociale et Solidaire: Une Histoire de la Société Civile en France et en Europe de 1968 à Nos Jours*. Editions Le Bord de l'Eau.

Euler, J. (2016). Commons-creating society: On the radical German commons discourse. *Review of Radical Political Economics*, 48(1), 93–110.

Fennell, L.A. (2011). Ostrom's law: Property rights in the commons. *International Journal of the Commons*, 5(1), 9–27.

Fergnani, A. (2019). Scenario archetypes of the futures of capitalism: The conflict between the psychological attachment to capitalism & the prospect of its dissolution. *Futures*, 105, 1–16.

Fligstein, N. & McAdam, D. (2019). States, social movements & markets. *Socio-Economic Review*, 17(1), 1–6.

Fraser, N. (1997). *Justice Interruptus: Critical Reflections on the "Post-socialist" Condition*. Psychology Press.

Fraser, N. (2015). Legitimation crisis? On the political contradictions of financialized capitalism. *Critical Historical Studies*, 2(2), 157–189.

Fuller, D., Jonas, A.E.G. & Lee, R. (eds.) (2010). *Interrogating Alterity: Alternative Economic & Political Spaces*. Routledge.

Gabaix, X. (2016). Power laws in economics: An introduction. *Journal of Economic Perspectives*, 30(1), 185–206.

Ganz, M. (2009). *Why David Sometimes Wins: Leadership, Organization & Strategy in the California Farm Worker Movement*. Oxford University Press.

Gertler, M.S. (2003). Tacit knowledge & the economic geography of context, or The undefinable tacitness of being (there). *Journal of Economic Geography*, 3(1), 75–99.

Gibson-Graham, J.K. (1996). *End of Capitalism (As We Knew it)?* Wiley.

Gibson-Graham, J.K. (2002). Beyond global vs local: Economic politics outside the binary frame. In A. Herod & M.W. Wright (eds.), *Geographies of Power* (pp.25–60). Blackwell Publishers Ltd.

Gibson-Graham, J.K. (2006). *A Postcapitalist Politics*. University of Minnesota Press.

Gibson-Graham, J.K. (2008). Diverse economies: Performative practices for "other worlds." *Progress in Human Geography*, 32(5), 613–632.

Gibson-Graham, J.K. & Dombroski, K. (eds.) (2020). *The Handbook of Diverse Economies*. Edward Elgar Publishers.

Gibson-Graham, J.K., Cameron, J. & Healy, S. (2013). *Take Back the Economy: An Ethical Guide for Transforming Our Communities*. University of Minnesota Press.

Gide, C. (1905). *Coopération Économique et Sociale 1886-1904*. Editions L'Harmattan.

Gorz, A. (1975). *Socialism & Revolution*. Allen Lane.

Gorz, A. & Bosquet, M. (1977). *Écologie et Liberté*. Éditions Galilée.

Gramsci, A. (1926). *Selections from the Prison Notebooks* (Q. Hoare & G.N. Smith, eds.; Later printing edition). International Publishers Co.

Gunn, C. E. & Gunn, H.D. (1991). *Reclaiming Capital: Democratic Initiatives and Community Development*. Cornell University Press.

Habermas, J. (1973). *Legitimation Crisis*. Beacon Press (MA).

Hall, S. & Massey, D. (2010). Interpreting the crisis. *Soundings*, 44, 57–71.

Hansmann, H. (1996). *The Ownership of Enterprise*. Belknap Press.

Hardin, G. (1968). The tragedy of the commons. *Science*, 162(3859), 1243–1248.

Healy, S. (2009). Alternative economies. In *International Encyclopedia of Human Geography* (pp.338–344).

Healy, S., Borowiak, C., Pavlovskaya, M. & Safri, M. (2018). Commoning & the politics of solidarity: Transformational responses to poverty. *Geoforum*.

Hess, C. & Ostrom, E. (2003). Ideas, artifacts & facilities: Information as a common-pool resource. *Law & Contemporary Problems*, 66(1/2), 111–145.

Hickel, J. & Kallis, G. (2020). Is green growth possible? *New Political Economy*, 25(4), 469-486.

Hirschman, A. (1970). *Exit, Voice & Loyalty*. Harvard University Press.

Hirst, P. (1994). *Associative Democracy: New Forms of Economic & Social Governance*. University of Massachusetts Press.

Hobsbawm, E. (1962). *Age of Revolution: 1789-1848*. Hachette UK.

Huron, A. (2018). *Carving Out the Commons: Tenant Organizing & Housing Cooperatives in Washington, D.C.* University of Minnesota Press.

Jimenez, S. (2018). *The Emergence of the Boston Ujima Project.* Tufts University.

Johanisova, N. & Wolf, S. (2012). Economic democracy: A path for the future? *Futures*, 44(6), 562–570.

Kallis, G., Kerschner, C. & Martinez-Alier, J. (2012). The economics of degrowth. *Ecological Economics*, 84, 172–180.

Kallis, G., Kostakis, V., Lange, S., Muraca, B., Paulson, S. & Schmelzer, M. (2018). Research on degrowth. *Annual Review of Environment & Resources, 43,* 291–316.

Kuokkanen, R. (2011). Indigenous economies, theories of subsistence & women: Exploring the social economy model for indigenous governance. *The American Indian Quarterly*, 35, 215–240.

Laville, J.-L. (2010). *L'Économie Sociale et Solidaire: Théories, Pratiques, Débats.* Seuil.

Lessig, L. (2002). *The Future of Ideas: The Fate of the Commons in a Connected World.* Knopf Doubleday Publishing Group.

Lévesque, B. (2013). The social economy wins recognition in Québec at the end of the 20th century. In M.J. Bouchard (ed.), *Innovation & the Social Economy: The Québec Experience* (pp. 25–70). University of Toronto Press.

Leyshon, A. (2003). Scary monsters? Software formats, peer-to-peer networks & the specter of the gift. *Environment & Planning D: Society & Space.*

Linebaugh, P. (2009). *The Magna Carta Manifesto: Liberties and Commons for All.* University of California Press.

Macpherson, C.B. (1942). The meaning of economic democracy. *University of Toronto Quarterly*, 11(4), 403–420.

Malleson, T. (2014). *After Occupy: Economic Democracy for the 21st century.* Oxford University Press.

Marshall, A. (1920). *Principles of Economics.*

Mason, P. (2016). *Postcapitalism: A Guide to Our Future.* Macmillan.

McAdam, D. (1982). *Political Process & the Development of Black Insurgency, 1930-1970.* University of Chicago Press.

McAdam, D., Tarrow, S. & Tilly, C. (2001). *Dynamics of Contention.* Cambridge University Press.

McCarthy, J. (2009). Commons. In *A Companion to Environmental Geography* (pp.498–514). John Wiley & Sons, Ltd.

McGaughey, E. (2020). Economic democracy in the 21st century: The vote in labor, capital and public services. *Capital & Public Services* (August 22, 2019).

Michael, C. (2015). *Building Bridges: Economic Democracy & Cooperative Alliances.* Grassroots Economic Organizing (GEO). https://geo.coop/story/building-bridges-economic-democracy-and-cooperative-alliances.

Mies, M. (2014). *Patriarchy & Accumulation on a World Scale: Women in the International Division of Labor.* Zed Books Ltd.

Mies, M. & Shiva, V. (1993). *Ecofeminism.* Fernwood Publications.

Mildenberger, M. (2019). The tragedy of the tragedy of the commons. *Scientific American Voices*, 12.

Milkman, R. (2017). A new political generation: Millennials & the post-2008 wave of protest. *American Sociological Review*, 82(1), 1–31.

Miller, B. & Nicholls, W. (2013). Social movements in urban society: The city as a space of politicization. *Urban Geography*, 34(4), 452–473.

Miller, E. (2015). Anticapitalism or postcapitalism? Both! *Rethinking Marxism*, 27(3), 364–367.

Miller, M.A. (2019). B/ordering the environmental commons. *Progress in Human Geography.* Online First.

Morell, M. (2014). Governance of online creation communities for the building of digital commons: Viewed through the framework of institutional analysis & development. In B.M. Frischmann, M.J. Madison & K.J. Strandburg (eds.), *Governing Knowledge Commons.* Oxford University Press.

Moretti, E. (2012). *The New Geography of Jobs.* Houghton Mifflin Harcourt.

Moulaert, F. & Ailenei, O. (2005). Social economy, third sector & solidarity relations: A conceptual synthesis from history to present. *Urban Studies*, 42(11), 2037–2053.

Müller-Jentsch, W. (2008). Industrial democracy: Historical development & current challenges. *Management Revue*, 260–273.

Mushi, S.S. (1970). Modernization by traditionalization: Ujamaa principles revisited. *Taamuli: A Political Science Forum*, 1(2), 13–29.

North, P. (2005). Scaling alternative economic practices? Some lessons from alternative currencies. *Transactions of the Institute of British Geographers*, 30(2), 221–233.

North, P. (2014). Ten square miles surrounded by reality? Materializing alternative economies using local currencies. *Antipode*, 46(1), 246–265.

Ostrom, E. (1990). *Governing the Commons: The Evolution of Institutions for Collective Action.* Cambridge University Press.

Ostrom, E. (2010). Polycentric systems for coping with collective action and global environmental change. *Global Environmental Change*, 20(4), 550–557.

Ott, K. (2012). Variants of de-growth and deliberative democracy: A Habermasian proposal. *Futures*, 44(6), 571–581.

Pateman, C. (1970). *Participation & Democratic Theory.* Cambridge University Press.

Pateman, C. (2012). Participatory democracy revisited. *Perspectives on Politics*, 10(1), 7–19.

Piore, M. & Sabel, C. (1984). *The Second Industrial Divide: Possibilities For Prosperity*. Basic Books.

Rahman, K.S. & Simonson, J. (2020). The institutional design of community control. *California Law Review*, 108, 679.

Rast, J. (2005). The politics of alternative economic development: Revisiting the Stone-Imbroscio debate. *Journal of Urban Affairs*, 27:1, 53-69,

Rehnberg, M. & Ponte, S. (2018). From smiling to smirking? 3D printing, upgrading & the restructuring of global value chains. *Global Networks*, 18(1), 57–80.

Roane, J.T. (2018). Plotting the black commons. *Souls*, 20(3), 239–266.

Roelvink, G., Martin, K.S. & Gibson-Graham, J.K. (eds.) (2015). *Making Other Worlds Possible: Performing Diverse Economies*. University of Minnesota Press.

Rothschild. J. (1979). The collectivist organization: An alternative to rational-bureaucratic models. *American Sociological Review*, 509–527.

Sarmiento, E.R. (2017). Synergies in alternative food network research: Embodiment, diverse economies & more-than-human food geographies. *Agriculture & Human Values*; Dordrecht, 34(2), 485–497.

Schneiberg, M. (2017). Resisting and regulating corporations through ecologies of alternative enterprise: Insurance & electricity in the US case. In A. Spicer & G. Baars (eds.), *The Corporation*. Cambridge University Press.

Schneiberg, M., King, M. & Smith, T. (2008). Social movements & organizational form: Cooperative alternatives to corporations in the American insurance, dairy & grain industries. *American Sociological Review*, 73(4), 635–667.

Schneider, N. & Scholz, T. (2016). *Ours to Hack & Own*. OR Books, LLC.

Schweickart, D. (1992). Economic democracy: A worthy socialism that would really work. *Science & Society*, 56(1), 9–38.

Scott, J.C. (1998). *Seeing Like a State: How Certain Schemes to Improve the Human Condition Have Failed*. Yale University Press.

Seeberger, L. (2014). History of the evolution of cooperative law from its origins to the present day. *Revue Internationale de l'Économie Sociale*, 333, 63–79.

Sengupta, U. (2015). Indigenous cooperatives in Canada: The complex relationship between cooperatives, community economic development, colonization & culture. *Journal of Entrepreneurial & Organizational Diversity*, 4(1).

Sewell, W.H. (1980). *Work & Revolution in France: The Language of Labor from the Old Regime to 1848*. Cambridge University Press.

Shear, B.W. (2019). From worker self-directed enterprise analysis to solidarity economy movement. *Rethinking Marxism*, Forthcoming.

Smith, P.M. (2005). *A Concise History of New Zealand*. Cambridge University Press.

Snow, D.A. & Benford, R.D. (1988). Ideology, frame resonance & participant mobilization. *International Social Movement Research*, 1(1), 197–217.

Snow, D.A., Rochford, E.B., Worden, S.K. & Benford, R.D. (1986). Frame alignment processes, micromobilization & movement participation. *American Sociological Review*, 51(4), 464–481

Sombart, W. (1906). *Why Is There No Socialism In The United States?* https://www.goodreads.com/book/show/3508735-why-is-there-no-socialism-in-the-united-states.

Soule, S.A. (2013). Diffusion & scale shift. In *The Wiley-Blackwell Encyclopedia of Social & Political Movements*.

Spicer, J. (2020). Worker & community ownership as an economic development strategy: Innovative rebirth or tired retread of a failed Idea? *Economic Development Quarterly*, 34(4): 325-342.

Spicer, J. (2022). Co-operative enterprise at scale: Comparative capitalisms & the political economy of ownership. *Socio-Economic Review*, 20(3): 1173-1209.

Spicer, J. & Casper-Futterman, E. (2020). Conceptualizing US community economic development: Evidence from New York City. *Journal of Planning Education & Research*. Online First.

Spicer, J. & Lee-Chuvala, C. (2021). Alternative enterprises, mission drift & ownership: The case of values-based banking. *Research in the Sociology of Organizations*, 72: 257-291.

Spicer, J. & Zhong, M. (2022). Multiple entrepreneurial ecosystems? Worker cooperative development in Toronto & Montréal. *Environment & Planning A: Economy and Space*, 54(4): 611-633.

Spicer, J., Kay, T. & Ganz, M. (2019). Social entrepreneurship as field encroachment: How a neoliberal social movement constructed a new field. *Socio-Economic Review*, 17(1), 195–227.

Srnicek, N. & Williams, A. (2015). *Inventing the Future: Postcapitalism & a World Without Work*. Verso Books.

St. Martin, K., Roelvink, G., Gibson-Graham, J.K. (2015). Introduction: An economic politics for our times. In K. St. Martin, G. Roelvink & J.K. Gibson-Graham. *Making Other Worlds Possible: Performing Diverse Economies* (pp.1–25). University of Minnesota Press.

Stilwell, F. (2002). *Political Economy: The Contest of Economic Ideas*. Oxford University Press.

Stoecker, R. (1997). The Cdc model of urban redevelopment: A critique & an alternative. *Journal of Urban Affairs*, 19(1), 1–22.

Storper, M., Kemeny, T., Makarem, N. & Osman, T. (2015). *The Rise & Fall of Urban Economies*. Stanford University Press.

Streeck, W. (2016). *How Will Capitalism End?* Verso Books.

Thompson, E. P. (1991). *Customs in Common*. New Press.

Thoms, C.A. (2008). Community control of resources & the challenge of improving local livelihoods: A critical examination of community forestry in Nepal. *Geoforum*, 39(3), 1452–1465.

Waring, M. & Steinem, G. (1988). *If Women Counted: A New Feminist Economics*. Harper & Row.

Webber, M. (1963). Order in diversity: Community without propinquity. In L. Wingo (ed.), *Cities & space: The future use of urban land* (pp.23–54). Johns Hopkins University Press.

Williams, O. & Pierce, J. (2019). Trialing analytic metaphors for socio-political economic alterity. *ACME: An International Journal for Critical Geographies*, 18(6), 1283–1299.

Williams, R. (1973). *The Country & the City*. Oxford University Press.

Williamson, T., Imbroscio, D. & Alperovitz, G. (2002). *Making a Place for Community: Local Democracy in a Global Era*. Routledge.

Wilson, D. (2015). Generalizing the commons. In D. Bollier & S. Helfrich (eds.), *Patterns of Commoning*. Common Strategies Group in cooperation with Off the Common Books.

Zanoni, P., Contu, A., Healy, S. & Mir, R. (2017). Post-capitalistic politics in the making: The imaginary & praxis of alternative economies. *Organization*, 24(5), 575–588.

CHAPTER 3

The Racial Equity Collaborative: "Undesigning" American Racism through Cooperative Community & Workplace Democracy

Charles Chawalko, Sandra McCardell, Elroy Natuchu, Kandis Quam, April de Simone & Damien Goodmon

Introduction

As has already been noted, capitalism, defined as the primacy of shareholders, is not working *for anyone*. It should not be surprising that a system which assumes "what I want for myself is good for everyone" will bring harm to many. As Steve Denning observed in *Forbes* magazine, stakeholder capitalism will fail:

> While MSV (maximize shareholder value) delivered a gargantuan transfer of assets to the existing owners of shares, it didn't deliver for the rest of society. The best analysts could see that MSV was a toxic mix of soaring short-term corporate profits [and] astronomic executive pay, that led to stagnant median incomes, growing inequality, periodic massive financial crashes, declining corporate life expectancy, slowing productivity, declining rates of return on assets and overall, a widening distrust in business. (Denning, 2020)

Forward motion, improvement, impact — they must come from a different direction, as highlighted in a brief video (https://www.youtube.com/watch?v=8wLvYa1xC7M) by the Racial Equity Collaborative (REC), a partnership to build cooperation, community, and cooperative economies between three grassroots organizations located in Trenton, New Jersey, Los Angeles, and the Pueblo of Zuni.

In the video, Niki Okuk (of Los Angeles-based Downtown Crenshaw Rising) and Kandis Quam (of the Zuni Arts Cooperative) describe REC's vision. They point out that, in the United States, the *Declaration of Independence*'s promise of "life, liberty, and the pursuit of happiness" has not been achieved in any of the REC community-partner home regions; all three are disproportionately affected by interlocking crises. Okuk and Quam propose to "undesign" the racism that's component to this crisis, by using cooperative community models and a five-pronged approach:

1. Center communities.
2. Invest in ownership.
3. Use supportive webs of mentors and investors.
4. Advocate for transformation.
5. Document the work.

Indigenous, Black, and immigrant communities, working collaboratively and from their own experience in a supportive web, uplift people outside of current systems. Together — and with support, expertise and funding from others — these communities both define and co-create success for long-lasting impact.

Separate Worlds

A 2020 Pew Research Center report highlighted increasing inequality in the US: median household income for lower-income households has gone from $20,000 in 1970 to $28,700 in 2018, while upper-income household income has increased from $126,100 to $207,400 (Menasce Horowitz, Igielnik & Kochhar, 2020). Over the same period, the share of US aggregate income held by lower-income households decreased slightly, from 10% to 9%, and the share held by upper-income households increased from 29% to 48% at the expense of middle-income families, whose share decreased from 62% to 43%. This phenomenon has become known as the "hollowing out of the middle class."

The report also highlighted the fact that income inequality in the US was at that time rising faster than in other countries. The authors note that "Most Americans say there is too much economic inequality in the US, but fewer than half call it a top priority." On the other hand, most Americans do seem to prioritize what *Investopedia* calls some of the effects of income inequality, including "higher levels of crime, stress, and mental illness."

Covid-19 intensified that economic inequality:

> The coronavirus exposed and exacerbated the fragility and inequity of the global economic system. Many countries, including the US, proved unable to manufacture simple products such as face masks, let alone more complicated ones such as ventilators. Multiple supply chains broke. The resulting ordeal will surely lead to the creation of more onshore production facilities. An ugly nationalism displayed by countries that have hoarded vaccines and put profits over lives shows no sign of abating, despite its potentially devastating consequences for the world.

The pandemic's most significant outcome will be a worsening of inequality, both within the US and between developed and developing countries. Global billionaire wealth grew by $4.4 trillion between 2020 and 2021, and at the same time more than 100 million people fell **below the poverty** line. Just how bad the situation will become depends on how long the disease rages and what policymakers do to control it and its consequences.

In part because of its huge income and wealth inequalities, the US suffered the most COVID-attributed deaths of any country. SARS-CoV-2 went after those with poverty-related health conditions and with jobs that cannot be done in isolation. Surviving from paycheck to paycheck and not having even the most basic rights of health care and paid sick leave, many Americans lacked testing to know if they were infected and either went to work, spreading the virus, or sought help too late. (Stiglitz, p.52)

The gaps in income between upper-income and middle- and lower-income households are rising, and the share held by middle-income households is falling

Median household income, in 2018 dollars, and share of U.S. aggregate household income, by income tier

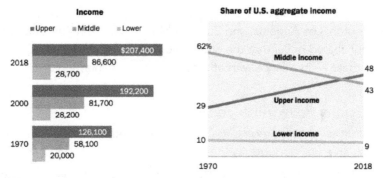

Note: Households are assigned to income tiers based on their size-adjusted income. Incomes are scaled to reflect a three-person household. Revisions to the Current Population Survey affect the comparison of income data from 2014 onwards. See Methodology for details.
Source: Pew Research Center analysis of the Current Population Survey, Annual Social and Economic Supplements (IPUMS).
"Most Americans Say There Is Too Much Economic Inequality in the U.S., but Fewer Than Half Call It a Top Priority"

PEW RESEARCH CENTER

Income inequality in the U.S. is rising ...

Ratio of income at the 90th percentile to income at the 10th percentile (90/10 ratio)

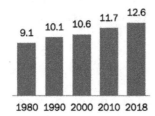

... and it is the highest among G-7 countries

Gini coefficient of gross income inequality, latest year available

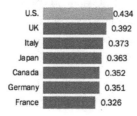

Source: U.S. Census Bureau and the Organization for Economic Cooperation and Development.
"Most Americans Say There Is Too Much Economic Inequality in the U.S., but Fewer Than Half Call It a Top Priority"

PEW RESEARCH CENTER

We are a nation of youth, rural community members, city dwellers, unemployed workers, single mothers, citizens returning from prison, government officials, refugees, immigrants, elders, business leaders, nonprofit executives, and many other groups — people of different races and income levels. We often live in separate worlds, with little contact or understanding amongst us, and yet Covid and economic injustice have connected us all by baring the ugliness of embedded racism. Those with privilege are only slowly learning to recognize that they have it, and those without are impatiently hoping to breach the structures designed to oppress them, whether that be in unsafe housing, in jobs that do not pay a living wage, or on reservations without running water or power. Inequality can only grow in an economy where the rich build easily upon their wealth while others have few opportunities to begin to create wealth upon which to build. Covid creates a two-class system of people who can work from home while keeping themselves safe and people who have to go to work, often in high-risk occupations; even the experience of Covid and its effects vary by economic status (Moore *et al.*, 2022).

We are at an inflection point where people must choose, and are choosing, a different path. Realizing that only they can chart an appropriate path forward, community leaders are designing and forging a new way with supportive partners and allies, defining what success means for themselves, and working together in collaborative or mutualist ways to drive higher impacts. This chapter highlights three such communities — in Trenton, Los Angeles, and Zuni Pueblo — and the organizations which support them as part of REC. It is our shared belief that the economies of the future will be developed by, and led by, communities such as these — in alliance with other supportive organizations.

Melding Racial Equity & Workplace Democracy

Racial equity affirms that all people, regardless of their racial/ethnic group identification, skin color, or physical traits, deserve an equal opportunity to experience well-being in a just society. Racial healing is a process that restores individuals and communities to wholeness, repairs the damage caused by racism, and transforms problematic societal structures into ones that affirm the inherent value of all people.

Deconstructing the entrenched social constructs of race requires being in community with each other. We envision neither a singular communal identity nor a mêlée of individualistic winners and losers, but rather an interconnected and healing relationship supporting and unleashing unique capacities in each person and community. To liberate those possibilities, we must discard systems that use race, status, identity, and ability to devalue people, and instead build systems that celebrate ways we are valued by one another. Each REC partner has a firm commitment and historical practice of dismantling racism and creating equitable systems. REC and our broader network will validate the primacy of community voices, the creation of trusting relationships, and the impetus towards transformative yet practical solutions — such as cooperative enterprises in supportive ecosystems, which create opportunities that provide for families while transforming communities.

The Partners & How This Project Came To Be

REC is an outgrowth of many singular initiatives focusing on community voice, power, leadership, and opportunity, and designed to create structures and opportunities chosen by the communities. Although the original construct was developed in response to a grant request, the partners are committed to moving the initiative forward using other pathways and other resources.

The three community partners at the center of the project are quite different. All have experienced racism, and are acting together to co-design a generative future:

- In Trenton, New Jersey, the People's Studio 76 organizes a strong and long-lasting grassroots group of local residents from all walks of life. This has created a regenerative ecology which centers shared-value projects, businesses, and activities to activate a more just and equitable city. This cross-pollination focuses on revitalizing the long disinvested Coalport neighborhood and Trenton's wider community.

- At Zuni Pueblo in New Mexico, a group of artists created a cooperative, the Ancestral Rich Treasures of Zuni Cooperative (ARTZ), not only to sell their art, but to help instill pride in young artists who could receive fair value for their creations without going through intermediaries, some of whom have a history of lowballing the value of the art by demeaning the artists.

- In South Los Angeles, Downtown Crenshaw Rising (DCR) is an immigrant community working for many years to develop a community center in a mall that is slated to be sold to a developer. Against all odds, DCR is fighting to keep their space, and often succeeding.

These three very different communities have been individually developing ways to create the opportunities that they envision, and as part of REC will also collaborate in a peer network of innovation, support, and co-creation. Each project was designed to establish cooperative enterprises, generate increasing economic benefits, build leadership, and seed similar activities in other communities; they're supported in turn by essential service providers:

- The American Sustainable Business Network (ASBN, formerly the American Sustainable Business Council, Social Ventures Circle, and American Sustainable Business Institute), with its 250,000 small-business members, provides financing, mentorship, and visibility for the communities and the cooperatives they form.

- We Architect (We Arch.) works at the intersection of research, planning, design, and systems thinking to advance equitable, humane, and just frameworks within projects shaping the conditions of our society.

- 1Worker1Vote, and the Mondragon affiliate LKS in Spain, help create cooperative ecosystems across communities, by providing training that's adapted to each community, based on models tested worldwide.

- The Cooperative Catalyst of NM has a mission to improve the lives of people in the Southwest by catalyzing community-led enterprise, upholding cooperative values, and fostering a healthy cooperative ecosystem.

The REC communities will operate as a peer network that shares challenges, ideas and successes; convenes its members; and learns from different lived experiences. All activities will be documented and incorporated into a shareable teaching tool for historical context and community learning.

The Importance of the Collaborative Approach

The partners in REC build from local strength to broad, deep transformation. With a cohort of community leaders and national practitioners, change comes from bringing to the same table people with the experience, passion, and ability to work in broad stakeholder initiatives to restructure business, economy, and policies:

- In Trenton, We Arch. activated and leads a local public-research and design studio, the People's Studio 76, to work with diverse stakeholders and launch projects such as the Garden State Agri-Hood Project (GSAP), which began with an intensive community process that continues to expand.
- In New Mexico, the Ancestral Rich Treasures of Zuni Cooperative (ARTZ) changed the mindset of the Zuni community by redefining artistic value.
- In Los Angeles, Downtown Crenshaw Rising (DCR) is building a strong cooperative community of immigrants and refugees in South Los Angeles.

The role of the service agencies in supporting the REC community partners is essential: ASBN's sustainable business organizations and companies have led strong and equitable local economic initiatives with members and allies who developed, advocated for, and helped pass preferred procurement policies that favor worker ownership and community capital. The Cooperative Catalyst of NM assisted in the formation of ARTZ. 1Worker1Vote and LKS have developed and supported successful cooperatives in the Bronx, Preston, UK, Cincinnati, Colombia, and elsewhere. We Arch. has planned and implemented many community-driven "undesign" projects in the US and in other countries.

The Design

The REC project was designed with three clear phases:

1. Develop the relationship between the community partners and map the current situation in each community, including the economies and structural racism.
2. Co-define collaborative or cooperative projects, with training and mentoring for the communities as they develop them.
3. The communities expand their projects and their reach, supported by the service providers.

One of the challenges with most projects is that, funded as they are by grants from foundations or government agencies — which can be no less short-term oriented than businesses — the lifespan of a project tends to be a year or two. That makes it difficult for communities, organizations, and individuals to make a long-term commitment to the project, and also inhibits any long-term goal setting and planning. A longer term is much more conducive to success and significant impact; the REC project solution has been planned using a timeline of 10 years (see **Table 3.1**).

Phase 1:

In this initial phase, We Arch. activates a public studio to research and contextualize the community over time, to answer the question, "How did we arrive at the conditions of today?" Activities include mapping neighborhood narratives — local stories and histories told over time in that place — and community assets to build innovative actions for social and economic change.

The role of 1Worker1Vote/LKS is to facilitate training in the Mondragon system of interconnected cooperatives, and the creation of community-owned and -controlled enterprises.

Table 3.1: The Racial Equity Collaborative Model

		Phase I	Phase II	Phase III
Goal		Growing, racially diverse, mutually supportive, healthy, economically vibrant communities		
Community Engagement &		**MAP:** Existing relationships; economic activity; economic opportunities & barriers; culture including structural racism elements	**MAP:** Developing & changing relationships; people transmitting new relationships; new channels	**MAP:** Developing & changing relationships; people transmitting new relationships; new channels; increasing investments in community leadership
		COLLECT: Racism profiles, "Living Archive" materials including documentary films by community members	**COLLECT:** Metrics	**COLLECT:** Metrics
		CO-CREATE: Metrics, culturally-appropriate memberships, inter-generational leadership groups	**CO-CREATE AND BUILD:** Vision & Mission, Youth & Elder leadership, adaptations of models from other areas	**CO-CREATE AND BUILD:** Vision & Mission, Youth & Elder leadership, adaptations of models from other areas
		COOPERATIVE EDUCATION: Discussions on Mondragon system of inter-connected cooperatives		
Framework for the Future		**COOPERATIVE DEVELOPMENT:** Training on Mondragon approach and experience	**COOPERATIVE DEVELOPMENT:** Identify opportunities for developing cooperatives; Co-develop accessible, sustainable mentoring for cooperatives	**COOPERATIVE DEVELOPMENT:** Continue identifying opportunities for new cooperatives; Co-develop accessible, sustainable mentoring; expand outside original communities
		PEER NETWORK: Begin developing relationships between communities, including visits; focus on sharing and developing systems & structures that support racial equity in a mutually supportive cooperative network	**PEER NETWORK:** Continue developing relationships between communities, including visits by leadership groups and online meetings with a focus on sharing and developing systems & structures that support racial equity in a mutually supportive cooperative network	**PEER NETWORK:** Continue developing relationships between communities, including visits by leadership groups and online meetings with a focus on sharing and developing systems & structures that support racial equity in a mutually supportive cooperative network
		EXPANSION: Form & deepen community understanding & knowledge of creating vibrant communities in culturally & locally appropriate ways	**EXPANSION:** Deepen, share, & codify community understanding & knowledge of creating vibrant communities in culturally & locally appropriate ways through multiple programs including toolkits; increase number of cooperatives seeding further transformation	**EXPANSION:** Deepen, share, & codify community understanding & knowledge of creating vibrant communities in culturally & locally appropriate ways through multiple programs including toolkits; expand outside original community seeding further transformation
		FELLOWSHIP PROGRAM: Co-develop fellowship program to engage local leaders	**FELLOWSHIP PROGRAM:** Expand fellowship program for local leaders	**FELLOWSHIP PROGRAM:** Expand fellowship program for local leaders
		EDUCATIONAL & OUTREACH WEBSITE: Co-design with all communities a website for educational & outreach purposes, appropriate for each community	**EDUCATIONAL & OUTREACH WEBSITE:** Build out with all communities a website for educational & outreach purposes	**EDUCATIONAL & OUTREACH WEBSITE:** Transfer responsibility and work to all communities for continued development & maintenance of a website which fits their needs
Develop Related Relevant Programs		**TOOLKITS:** Co-develop toolkits with each community leading to deepening/expanding mindset shifts & forward thinking, with growing numbers of strong inter-generational leaders & increasing shared local expertise	**TOOLKITS:** Continue co-development of toolkits with each community leading to deepening/expanding mindset shifts & forward thinking, with growing numbers of strong inter-generational leaders & increasing shared local expertise	**TOOLKITS:** Continue co-development of toolkits with each community leading to deepening/expanding mindset shifts & forward thinking, with growing numbers of strong inter-generational leaders & increasing shared local expertise
		SUSTAINABLE FINANCING MECHANISMS: Co-develop accessible, sustainable financing systems & mechanisms that are culturally appropriate for communities, develop outside investor networks	**SUSTAINABLE FINANCING MECHANISMS:** Continue development outside investor networks & expansion of accessible, sustainable financing systems & mechanisms with funding pools that are culturally appropriate for communities, including complementary internal policies & practices	**SUSTAINABLE FINANCING MECHANISMS:** Continue development outside investor networks & expansion of accessible, sustainable financing systems & mechanisms with funding pools that are culturally appropriate for communities, including complementary internal policies & practices
		MENTORSHIP SYSTEM: Develop strong connections with outside business networks & mentorship systems with national / international business & cooperative leaders	**MENTORSHIP SYSTEM:** Expand & deepen strong connections with outside business networks & mentorship systems with national / international business & cooperative leaders	**MENTORSHIP SYSTEM:** Expand & deepen strong connections with outside business networks & mentorship systems with national / international business & cooperative leaders
		COMMUNITY BEST-FIT POLICY PLANS: Co-create policy plans that grow from community needs & goals, including advocacy program to increase support for cooperative community development programs	**COMMUNITY BEST-FIT POLICY PLANS:** Implement policy plans that grow from community needs & goals, including advocacy program to increase support for cooperative community development programs	**COMMUNITY BEST-FIT POLICY PLANS:** Implement policy plans that grow from community needs & goals, including advocacy program to increase support for cooperative community development programs
		STAKEHOLDER ENGAGEMENT PROGRAM: Develop program to engage stakeholders at the local, state, and national levels for support of all communities	**STAKEHOLDER ENGAGEMENT PROGRAM:** Deepen stakeholder engagement at the local, state, & national levels for culturally & economically vibrant communities	**STAKEHOLDER ENGAGEMENT PROGRAM:** Deepen stakeholder engagement at the local, state, & national levels for culturally & economically vibrant communities
		DOCUMENTARY: Train community members to film & produce documentaries on their communities and the evolution of this project	**DOCUMENTARY:** Support community members in sharing the documentary and the importance of this project in creating vibrant communities	**DOCUMENTARY:** Support community members in sharing the documentary and the importance of this project in creating vibrant communities
Outcomes Anticipated		Increased understanding of racial barriers		
		Development of skills to deconstruct obstacles		
		Quality narratives produced and distributed		
		Relationships between communities developed, leading to shared understanding & support		
		Co-creation of relevant benchmarks		
		Innovative structures of social & economic change built through co-creation with varied communities		
		Policy campaigns developed & implemented, & beneficial local/state/national public & institutional policies gathered & supported		
		Inter/intra community social interactions & relationships deepening		
		Development, familiarization, use of tools such as connections, mentorship, tools, materials		
		Increased financing opportunities & partnerships providing attainable financing		
		Mentorship program created, utilized, shown to be effective		
		Key stakeholders engaged and supportive		

Beginning in Phase 1 and continuing throughout the project, the three community partners will design and build a peer network, sharing ideas, strategies, experiences, challenges, and successes. The collaboration between these three very different communities is a core part of the initiative, enabling deeper learning and strong relationships between people who would normally not have the opportunity to participate in a project together.

Early in Phase 1, all communities will begin to tell their stories through video and film, capturing their voices and their evolution through time.

Phase 2:

Communities will focus on building their vision and mission, adapting successful models from other areas, and identifying opportunities for co-op development. We will co-develop accessible, sustainable financing and mentoring for nascent cooperatives. Through coalition-building efforts, ASBN will develop and advocate for local, state, and national policy to support sustainable, expansive cooperative-community development.

Phase 3:

Continued community-strengthening support includes activities focused on data collection, new opportunities, increasing policy work, securing attainable financing, continuing investments in community leadership, building local economies, expanding geographically, and seeding further transformations.

It is important to note that, throughout the project, the communities are in the lead and set the direction and activities; project partners anticipate that each community will follow a quite different path, sharing their progress through the peer network, which is composed of the community partners and initially facilitated by the service providers. Service provider partners are of course expected to provide the benefit of their experience and advice, and to train and mentor the communities — but they are not the final decision-makers. This is a co-creative, community-centered approach that the partners have used in multiple projects in the past; the reason for working with these three distinct communities is to demonstrate this approach's wide applicability, and to develop additional learnings for all partners through the peer network.

There are several elements in this project that we feel to be particularly important:

- First, the intention is to map and dismantle racist structures and policies *while at the same time* developing leaders and creating cooperative economic activity to strengthen the local community.

- The peer networks provide an opportunity for the three different communities to learn from one another as equals who are quite different, lessening the challenges that come from power dynamics created when communities are working with "experts." That peer network demonstrates what equitable and mutually respectful relationships look like.

- Humans are story-making beings, and those who tell the stories have the ability to control the narrative. These communities will write their own stories. Each of the communities will be given the training, equipment, and other resources to document in video and film their stories as this process unfolds, for their own benefit and for that of the others who will follow them.

- The linkage to ASBN members and others who provide loans, grants, and support *outside* of traditional philanthropic or government funding creates a pathway for flexible funding that's responsive to the situation in each community, and not subject to the short-term priorities of traditional foundations and agencies.

- Two of the primary design elements draw upon the past to create a different future: the community-engagement element is conceived to be intergenerational, with leaders from all age groups, and a documentary film created by each community (with training from documentary filmmakers) will provide them with a voice, as well as a record of the entire process. The documentary gives each an opportunity to redefine and share their narratives. As we dismantle racist and inequitable structures, we build communities that control their social, economic, and political fates.

- Existing policy work amplified and expanded using a race and equity lens will enable REC visibility and impact on a national level — growing the impact far beyond the communities where it begins.

- The project will be managed by a Project Board that will adapt to changing circumstances, methodology effectiveness, additional community needs, and other issues and challenges. It will comprise members from each of the six partner organizations. In order to achieve the appropriate balance, an extra two Board members will be chosen from the communities so that the communities are in the majority.

- Funds, when secured, will be allocated so that two-thirds of the total goes to the community members; the remaining one-third will be allocated to the supporting service providers.

As we dismantle racist and inequitable structures, we build communities that control their social, economic, and political fate. REC provides an extraordinary opportunity to turn the learnings, expertise and leadership of Indigenous, Black, immigrant, and refugee communities and service providers into a transformative ecosystem. Racial equity and stakeholder economy talk is popular, but it must be turned into action, and it is this that REC plans to do. REC partners will not wait for historically unjust institutions to transform themselves; we will create new ones, and work through policy to enable a shift in practices that have undermined communities, families, and local, small, and medium businesses, co-designing a future that should belong to us all equally.

Community Stories

Ancestral Rich Treasures of Zuni — created from tradition & a sense of community
The Pueblo of Zuni, the largest out of the 19 New Mexican Pueblos, has always been rich in tradition, culture, and art. The area itself is nestled in a beautiful valley and surrounded by gorgeous mesas. In addition to the enchanting landscape, Zuni Pueblo artwork is renowned throughout the world, with the majority of Zuni people considering their primary occupation to be an artist. Unfortunately, with the nearest town (Gallup) being 36 miles away and the closest city 150 miles away, the physical isolation and lack of employment means that there are few ways for Zuni people to earn income and build economic wealth. These factors provide ample opportunity for outsiders to take advantage of the situation.

In the 1970s, a group of traders came into the village with hopes of selling their goods. Of course, with little money, Zunis traded their art for these goods. This began the Zuni art market and the rise of jobbers. Jobbers are the wholesale buyers; they often come to the Pueblo to buy artwork directly from the artist at half or less of the retail price, ultimately selling to the jobber's customers at a higher price than retail. The new, cooperative market for Zuni art brought the limelight to Zuni artistry, with good and bad effects. On a positive note, the demand for Zuni art grew to an all-time high; that period was the golden era for Zuni artists, where everyone had a chance to make a decent living for the first time without going outside of the village for a job. Every household in Zuni was working day and night to supply the demand.

However, the production rate and price of Zuni art were insufficient to meet demand, in the eyes of the jobbers and other intermediaries. In response, these people recruited non-Zuni, non-Indigenous people to recreate Zuni art, to the point where there are villages in China and the Philippines named "Zuni" that are solely dedicated to reproducing "Zuni" art with artificial materials at a quarter of the cost in half the time. The cheaper options available for customers led buyers to demand more for less, making the profit for artists significantly less. In addition, the high demand created hostility among Zuni artists. Before capitalism came to the Pueblo, artists were more than willing to teach each other their techniques. In the aftermath, artists are very protective of their practices and techniques to the point where passing on information and techniques became exceedingly rare.

In response to the unjust and unequal art market, with the help of Cooperative Catalyst of NM, a small group founded the Ancestral Rich Treasures of Zuni Cooperative in 2019 (zunipuebloart.com). ARTZ is the solution created by Zuni people *for* Zuni people to develop a healthy art market that adheres to their culture and her people. Since the cooperative's inception in 2019, ARTZ has hosted several training and conferences to educate fellow Zuni artists in the community, and has given ARTZ members a fair price for their artwork. With no marketing, the ARTZ Cooperative's first year was wildly successful. Then, when Covid hit the largest Pueblo in New Mexico, it hit hard, and the art market predictably plummeted. The cooperative immediately had to switch gears to survive, for the good of both the community and the co-op members. ARTZ created multiple ways to bring in revenue for the gallery and its members. The cooperative established monthly auctions and an online store, and created facemask designs with members' artwork. The ARTZ Cooperative has always strived to serve and protect its artists and community, even amongst the worst circumstances. In a larger sense, the Pueblo of Zuni has survived and thrived for thousands of years through the strong ties of working together as one for the greater good. ARTZ, as a Zuni owned and operated organization, is and will be no different.[2]

Two recent newspaper articles highlight both the importance of what the Zuni artists who form the ARTZ Cooperative have accomplished, and the resilience shown by Native artisans. 77% of Zuni households have at least one artist at home, an indication of why ARTZ has been so transformational (Leigh Brown, 2020). In an article in the *Albuquerque Journal*, co-op member Elroy Natuchu says that artists did not have many options for selling work, and that "What we're trying to show is that there's another way" (Hamway, 2020).

Trenton, New Jersey — The power of community-informed systems

Background:

Architecture ascribes human value to space and place. A sense of worth, connection, and identity is defined through connection with our spatial, psychological, and social surroundings. Upon closer examination, architecture and the culture that creates it reinforces undemocratic values which are revealed in the way community spaces are designed and built.

"Life, liberty, and the pursuit of happiness" are more than just words describing democratic values. They are foundational principles of what is planned, designed, and activated into the environments and systems we build around us.

From the moment we step outside our door to the moment we return home, our everyday life is a journey through many layers of culture, environment, economy, politics, and society, where our actions and words create ripples in an ocean of systems. These designed systems — which make up the world we live and work in — are products of decades and centuries of thought, decision, and practice.

The choices and decisions about designing and building our environments affect us greatly. They cause ever-widening disparities between people and their communities, and can make us financially unstable, physically unhealthy, or even psychologically traumatized. These effects can be felt on a grand scale, making some communities fall behind others on socioeconomic and health metrics.

This inequity is a threat to our democracy, and only through progressive action, embracing our ethnic, racial, and religious diversity, and critical thinking can we create change.

We Arch. stands in alignment with those who see themselves as stewards of universal values like integrity, dignity, empathy, honesty, respect, responsibility, and fairness, all critical to advancing democracy and humanity. We advance equitable, humane, and just opportunities to shape the conditions of our society, using participatory research, planning, and design; project incubation and management; collaborative methods; and impact evaluation and evolution.

Case study:

Trenton, New Jersey, stands at an intersection of the nation's most pressing social, economic, and environmental challenges. By relearning its history, including the violent appropriation of land from the Lenape Nation, toxic industrialization, redlining, urban renewal, deindustrialization, service cuts, environmental degradation, and now the specter of gentrification and speculative investment, we can develop *agency through architecture* to heal these impacts on the local community. The design process will not replicate the methodologies of the past, where topical solutions were applied to systemic issues and generated a new set of unintended consequences. What must be broken is the routinization of purported solutions that recycle the same outcomes for each generation.

This work supports the strong and creative people of Trenton in search of allies to realize *their* vision of an equitable, thriving community, collaborating with partners who genuinely believe in healing undemocratic legacies, while advancing new strategies to meet the social and spatial challenges of the 21st century.

In 2015, the John S. Watson Institute for Urban Policy & Research at Kean University and We Arch. launched an innovative, collaborative, public-design studio in Trenton, to advance initiatives and projects cultivating an ecology of equity. A two-year process brought forth a conversation involving community stakeholders that revealed underlying anxieties about the future, questions about opportunities for the youth of the community, and concerns that the neighborhood was neglected and unsafe.

With an active farm — initiated by a collaboration between the Watson Institute, D&R Greenway Land Trust, the Trenton Area Soup Kitchen, and the City of Trenton — operating within a space originally slated to be a junkyard, this collective effort grew the local ecosystem, providing a space for farmers, volunteers, and neighbors to invest their time, sweat, and energy to build a new community asset. Created out of this context, GSAP is a 501(c)3 organization promoting community-based land tenure with a focus on food security and access via planned community design. As it grows and new stakeholders and organizations become a part of it, its role in setting deeper and stronger roots of equitable social change and shared value in Trenton becomes even more pronounced. This GSAP space is not just a farm — it's a *shared-value ecosystem* that's already spinning off new projects and endeavors, such as a partnership with the Iroquois Valley Farm, a farmland-finance public benefit corporation and B Corp. It's a partnership that has yielded critical technical and financial support; it also exemplifies how real estate investment trusts (REITs) can be used to attain socially beneficial outcomes.

Moving from collaborative work to a renewed set of shared values exemplifies the critical and social importance of co-authoring our ecosystem. An informed and contextual research, planning and design practice produces three critical and desired impacts:

- A deeper understanding of the complex societal challenges rooted in equity, healing, and justice, to foster the creation of new entities and platforms.
- Interventions producing improved social determinants of health.
- Opportunities to build a cohesive network to support sustainable and scalable strategies into practices shifting systemic inequity.

These impacts go hand-in-hand with democratizing our built environment. Each project demonstrates how system change occurs concurrently with new opportunities for leadership, teaching, and volunteering.

Another opportunity that has come out of the public studio endeavor is a proposed teaching hospital developed in partnership with Kean University in Trenton. Colleges of medicine, and the communities they serve, have benefited by using teaching hospitals as integral elements of their programs. The hospitals provide services to their communities, and emphasize connections with the public for their doctors-in-training. They are also an economic resource.

Our proposal would utilize this model to connect Trenton's underserved communities with professional skills and academic resources, and bring together Kean faculty, students, and recent graduates; local community members; and professionals from the private sector and nonprofit organizations to work on the region's economic, social, political, design, and environmental issues. It would be an institution of the community where it is located, a resource to the state, and a valuable component of higher education.

One of the tools the teaching hospital model will help establish is land tenure for the community, in the form of a hybrid of REIT, which can address the almost 3,000 vacancies created by the predatory subprime-mortgage crisis of 2008 that deeply impacted communities such as Trenton. This type of REIT land trust enables a collective stewardship of land while tailoring the financial tools necessary to jump-start impact investment that builds community. A teaching hospital and land-tenure model will advance racial equity and serve four major tasks:

- Democratize land tenure to meet the needs of the community.
- Restore the social fabric of the community devastated by historical policies.
- Encourage economic growth and innovation in local economies.
- Scale environmental stewardship of land and soil through regenerative and organic practice.

Imagine 10, 20, or 30 years into the future: the work at hand is assuredly a trial of time, sweat, unlearning, relearning, investment, and monitoring outcomes. The outcomes produce enough tangible and intangible change that newer generations do not experience the conditions of past generations. We Arch. sees this engagement in Trenton as one link in a greater chain to affirm and uphold democratic and humanizing values. It embodies the greater struggle to be involved, educate ourselves, and collaborate to tackle the challenges facing precarious communities in our nation's cities and counties.

Such engagement does not just "happen," however. It requires deliberate and targeted investments and efforts by the nonprofit, philanthropic, public, and private sectors. It also calls for cultivating and equipping individual leaders to forge and strengthen connections among constituencies, neighborhoods, organizations, and/or sectors. And finally, it requires all of us to create an atmosphere of trust, respect, shared goals, and mutual responsibility.

> ... it is important to keep in mind that systems change, as a way of making real and equitable progress on critical social and environmental problems, requires exceptional attention to the detailed and often mundane work of noticing and acting on much that is implicit and invisible to many but is very much in the water. Making big bets to tackle a social problem without first immersing yourself in understanding what is holding the problem in place is a recipe for failure. (*The Water of Systems Change*, FSG Consulting, 2018)[3]

Our work over the past six years in Trenton represents that greater democratic-visioning process "of the people, by the people, for the people." It's a process with a table large enough for diverse stakeholders ready to co-create strategies that impact the very buildings, sidewalks, and services where we build equitable and inclusive communities.

Los Angeles, California — A neighborhood claims its space[4]

The nonprofit Downtown Crenshaw Rising was launched in 2020 to counter efforts by CIM Group, development partners of then-US President Donald Trump, to purchase the Baldwin Hills Crenshaw Plaza — *a.k.a.* The Crenshaw Mall — located at the intersection of Crenshaw and Rev. Dr. Martin Luther King Jr. boulevards in South Central Los Angeles. The iconic economic center of Black Los Angeles, Crenshaw Mall had been undergoing rampant gentrification, and the proposed sale to CIM in 2020 sent shockwaves across the community and America. Los Angeles' Black community did not want Crenshaw's economic anchor put into the hands of a company with such a troubling history, in a community already undergoing severe displacement pressures.

Just hours after the article announcing CIM's intent to purchase was published in the *LA Times*, #Crenshaw was trending on Twitter, and community-based and -focused leaders, with over 200 collective years of experience in finance, acquisition, and development, began collaboratively identifying strategies to stop the sale and quickly acquire Crenshaw Mall for the community.

The effort was seeded by the all-volunteer Crenshaw Subway Coalition (CSC), which had become one of the region's most noteworthy Black-led anti-gentrification groups advancing the solidarity economy. Focused on coalition building across Black LA, the organization's roots date back to 2006 with a focus on transportation and environmental justice. By 2020, CSC had become an advocate of community-wealth building. Cooperative development, community land trusts, and community investment funds were seen as vehicles necessary to address systemic economic and racial injustice, and now significant displacement pressures. The Crenshaw Mall gave the group and community partners the opportunity to put the principles in practice, and the local community and nation responded.

In short order and with laser-like focus, the historic Downtown Crenshaw Rising development team identified financing partners and began to work with stakeholders on a community-driven development plan for a community-controlled, 40-acre urban village. National award-winning architecture firms worked with local real estate advisers and the community to put forth an alternative vision for the site. And national experts in the solidarity economy, cooperatives, community land trusts, and community-based development began to identify unique structures that would give a local Black-led nonprofit the ability to raise nearly $200 million in capital for the massive real estate project, while remaining under community control.

The group successfully stopped the sale to CIM in June of 2020. LivWrk, a Brooklyn-based development group and another Trump affiliated developer was selected over DCR in the second round of bidding, and the group stopped that sale in December 2020. During the third round of bidding, a historic coalition of high-net-wealth individuals and foundations responded to an ambitious demand. In February 2021, with less than two weeks to submit a bid with proof of a $10 million deposit, a national call to wealth advisors and major solidarity economy donors was made. The result was the largest fund raised for a community-based organization for a real estate effort in American history. DCR raised over $34 million in philanthropy, with $25.6 million in social-impact investor commitments, and a mission-aligned debt partner to round out the $122 million bid. Downtown Crenshaw Rising had submitted the highest offer with the best terms, but Deutsche Bank subsidiary, DWS, which was chosen by the owner/investors of the mall (public pension funds) to manage the sales process, selected a once-bankrupt developer David Schwartzman of Harridge Development Group backed by a company owned and controlled by billionaire Len Blavatnik, a Soviet-born oil oligarch on Putin's List. They completed the purchase in August 2021.

Since the sale of the Crenshaw Mall, Downtown Crenshaw Rising has focused on transitioning to a long-game strategy of preventing the Schwartzman-Blavatnik gentrification plan from being developed and forcing the sale of the mall to the community group. Resources raised for the Crenshaw Mall purchase have been reprogrammed towards a variety of community initiatives, including a "scattered site," community-owned real estate plan of residential and commercial properties to preserve affordability. The properties are purchased with funds by DCR and placed into the Liberty Community Land Trust (LCLT). All three organizations — DCR, CSC, and LCLT — operate as part of the broader Liberty Ecosystem (libertyecosystem.org/).

REC: A Holistic, Systemic Program Leading to Systems Change

The REC project creates a new path, one focused on addressing racial inequality and creating cooperative economic opportunities in a systemic way. It is not enough to say "Let's cure racial inequality" without undoing the inequitable structures and systems created. The codification of racism in American capitalism has built structures to maintain white supremacy. Racist policies, laws, and mindsets are cemented in place, resulting in a lack of economic opportunity, healthy food, housing, financing, and a widening wealth gap — all symptoms of the deeper problem. Dominant frameworks and systems cannot address the complex intersectionality of these systemic challenges. The disastrous impact of the pandemic, racial unrest, growing disparities, rising costs, and unmet basic needs emphasize this urgent need. The REC communities are deeply affected by these issues and know we cannot build equity on hostile frameworks; we must together deconstruct the systems that allowed these conditions to flourish, transforming communities into places where self-determination, community control, and models of cooperation can thrive. White supremacy and conventional capitalism have fed each other for mutual benefit for centuries, but the cooperative model provides a powerful and proven counter-approach.

What's necessary is a healing methodology that acknowledges generational/genetic trauma, fosters accountability, and intentionally advances equity, ecological regeneration, and democracy. That requires a deliberate, interconnected process of transformation that trusts communities to know what is in their best interest and creates the new narrative and direction for the path forward. Partners must steward a deliberative, co-creative process, relying on cultural heritage and traditions, forming infrastructure to support a larger "we" secured with public policy to protect a revitalized, regenerative community.

- The first step in this co-creative approach is to strengthen and build the relationships amongst all community partners by focusing on specific action-oriented tasks and activities, and building stepping stones of success — a space to work together, systems of communication, project ideas, etc.

- That work then morphs into examining the current situation in each community, including the barriers to forward motion or success caused by racist structure or policies. As those structures and policies are known and understood by the local leaders, the community should be included in determining how to demolish them.

- The next step, in a supportive and systemic way, is to rebuild systems that have been proven to work. During the course of the REC project in each community, cooperative structures that give primacy to the community partners (supported by the service providers) will create a system to develop leaders, learn methods of working and relating in a non-hierarchical way, and enable economic benefit that provides direct benefit to the communities and the cooperative members.

The biggest risk is not to act.

Using this co-creative and intersectional approach with the community partners at the center, REC can be successful. But what does that mean? Who defines what that success should look like, and when it will have been reached? Philanthropic funders and governments often specify in minute detail what should be accomplished by the end of a project period, and these metrics rarely take into consideration what the grassroots organization or community would want and need.

At the very beginning of the project, the entire team will work together to define what success looks like *for each community*; from those goals will flow discussions and decisions on the metrics that show the community what has been a success and what has not. This approach works because both the communities and the service providers are likely to be more enthusiastic about meeting criteria and metrics that everyone feels are important to the communities.

The Importance of a Cooperative, Collaborative Structure

The shareholder economy and institutionalized racism bring threats to individual and collective health, economy, democracy, society, the environment and climate, by themselves and in combination. REC challenges the supposed necessity of choosing between racial equity and the good of business, economy, democracy, country; countless issue and public policy campaigns have shown they are inextricably linked and mutually supportive.

Cooperatives can ameliorate concrete barriers for communities, such as a lack of internet connectivity and other resources. More deeply, the process of unpacking trauma-laden topics in a difficult time requires safe spaces to explore and deconstruct racism. By co-developing and implementing cooperative projects in impacted communities and mobilizing support from businesses, investors, and other institutions, the REC partners are building a power base to ensure the necessary shifts. That experience will be drawn upon during the course of the project. That deep approach contributes to community rebuilding on a more comprehensive scale than most existing methods and practices. The shift toward an economy that works for all will be an intersectional, community-led process, with a peer network for learning and support, linked to regional and national networks of BIPOC business leaders, equity-focused sustainable businesses, investors, and legislators, enabling long-term equitable relationships, and complementary public policy.

In this way and through the Yoruba spirit of *ubuntu* ("I am because we are") and the Indigenous perspective of "all my relations," REC's three community partners will form a supportive intergenerational peer network within and between their own communities that both transcends and honors geography and culture. The transformation creates a growing web of sustainable, community-owned enterprises reverberating through social, economic, and environmental systems. Throughout the project, REC members will host visits from other communities, thereby expanding their circle of peers. Each community will also produce a documentary film of stories and their developmental process as a resource to benchmark milestones, share during the project, and seed inspiration in other communities.

Cooperative Impact Radiates Out from the Communities

REC's path to impact connects the reality of inequality in communities to constructs in government and other institutions. The cooperative movement has grown as a way to create community well-being outside these inequitable structures. Local leadership, enabled to deconstruct embedded racism and draw strength from tradition and culture, coupled with the creation of cooperative enterprises, leads to reclaiming local economies. Linked to wider networks, they bring an aggregated and powerful voice for systems-wide transformation.

The goal of our approach is to demonstrate and document why and how cooperatives are transforming communities, by shifting away from crippling disparities and toward a more equitable, shared, secure, healthy ecosystem.

- In the near term, REC's community partners will identify and deconstruct systems of racism and extractive capitalism, reimagining local ownership and control while documenting the process.

- In the medium-term, they will create cooperative businesses to meet their own needs, developing strategic relationships with groups providing resources, support, investment, and market access for sustainable growth.

- Lastly, long-term outcomes will be successful cooperatives that will help grow additional enterprises, joining with others in a robust and sophisticated network to advance local, state, and national policy change supporting successful anti-racist community development that, when expanded, shift towards a web of cooperative enterprises and communities that restructure the economy.

The ASBN in particular is supporting the community partners with access to funding and business mentors. As a triple-bottom-line trade association advocating for and developing an economy that works for all,

ASBN sees REC as a way to build multiple social enterprises that are connected and impactful, demonstrating that working together confers a clear business advantage.

For example, in supporting passage of the *Pro Act* to support union organizing, ASBN affirmed that:

> When employers and employees work together, there is a clear business advantage … Business benefits when workers who have a voice and vote are better trained, exhibit higher morale and retain at higher and longer rates and are more resilient, putting the country on a path to a more inclusive and sustainable economy … A safe, healthy, fulfilled, inclusive, informed workforce which values family-supporting wages and benefits is business's indispensable competitive asset. (American Sustainable Business Network, *The Protect the Right to Organize Act* (PRO Act), https://www.asbnetwork.org/protect-right-organize-act)

The Racial Equity Collaborative charts a path from communities through cooperative businesses and economic development, driving systemic change and social enterprise that has the power to change our world.

Endnotes

[1]   This chapter is based on a response to a grant application prepared by multiple partners, all of whom contributed to the original document. The partners (and authors) include the American Sustainable Business Network, asbnetwork.org (David Levine, MaryAnne Howland); LKS/Mondragon International, www.lks.es/en/ (Ibon Zugasti); 1Worker1Vote, 1worker1vote.org; the MAPA Group, mapa.group (Michael Peck); We Arch., we-arch.com, (April De Simone); Downtown Crenshaw Rising, downtowncrenshaw.com (Niglmoro (Niki) Okuk); Cooperative Catalyst of NM, coopcatalystnm.org (Bijiibah Begaye, Caitlin Kundrat, Sandra McCardell, Robin Seydel); and Ancestral Rich Treasures of Art Cooperative, zunipuebloart.com (Kandis Quam, Elroy Natuchu). The authors also thank Brian R. Corbin from Catholic Charities USA for insights and networking.

[2]   Story written by Kandis Quam and Elroy Natuchu, members and officers of the Ancestral Rich Treasures of Zuni Cooperative.

[3]   Case study prepared by April de Simone and Charles Chawalko.

[4]   Case study written by Damien Goodmon.

Projects & Partner References

Denning, S. (2020, January 5). Why stakeholder capitalism will fail. *Forbes*. Retrieved May 10, 2022, from https://www.forbes.com/sites/stevedenning/2020/01/05/why-stakeholder-capitalism-will-fail/?sh=70ed9f00785a

Hamway, S. (March 23, 2020). Cooperatives Work to Keep Money in the Community. *Albuquerque Journal*. https://www.abqjournal.com/1435286/cooperatives-work-to-keep-money-in-the-community.html.

Leigh Brown, P. (June 5, 2020). On Tribal Lands, a Time to Make Art for Solace and Survival. *New York Times*. https://www.nytimes.com/2020/06/05/arts/design/native-americans-art-coronavirus.html.

Menasce Horowitz, J., Igielnik, R. & Kochhar, R. (2020, January 9). Trends in US income and wealth inequality. Retrieved from Pew Research Center: https://www.pewresearch.org/social-trends/2020/01/09/trends-in-income-and-wealth-inequality/.

Moore, S., Burns, C., Carter, N., Clamp, C., Amendah, E. & Martin, W. (May 2022). *Understanding Vaccine Hesitancy Amongst Frontline Workers — the Influence of Trade Union and Community Representatives*. Retrieved from the British Academy: https://www.thebritishacademy.ac.uk/documents/3752/Understanding-Vaccine-Hesitancy-Amongst-Frontline-Workers.pdf.

Stiglitz, J.E. (2022, March 1). Covid has made global inequality much worse. *Scientific American*, pp.52-53. Retrieved from https://www.scientificamerican.com/article/covid-has-made-global-inequality-much-worse/.

GSAP: Garden State Agrihood Project http://www.designingthewe.com/capital-farm.

ARTZ: On Tribal Lands, a Time to Make Art for Solace and Survival — Ramsay de Give / *New York Times*, June 5, 2020; Cooperatives work to keep money in the community, Stephen Hamway / *Albuquerque Journal*, March 23, 2020

DCR-LE: Vernon Oakes, *Everything Coop* — Radio Show / Podcast: Niki Okuk and Damien Goodmon, members of Downtown Crenshaw Rising, discuss plans to reinvent Crenshaw Mall as an urban village. https://everything.coop/episodes/.

ASBI: *The High Road Workplace: Route to Sustainable Economy* report — https://www.ASBIouncil.org/sites/main/files/file-attachments/ASBI_building_the_high_road_report_2017.pdf ; Creating an economic system that works for All – https://www.ASBIouncil.org/post/creating-economic-system-works-all; Social Economy Europe and American Sustainable Business Council announce global collaboration to mark 5th anniversary of Paris Accord, *prnewswire*, December 12, 2020 – https://www.prnewswire.com/news-releases/social-economy-europe-and-american-sustainable-business-council-announce-global-collaboration-to-mark-5th-anniversary-of-paris-accord-301191534; State and Local recommendations — https://ASBI.salsalabs.org/businesscasereportsign-inrecommendationsforstatelocalg/index.

1W1V / LKS: *Reimagining Capitalism in a World on Fire*, Rebecca Henderson (Hachette, April 2020) Multiple citations. https://www.publicaffairsbooks.com/titles/rebecca-henderson/reimagining-capitalism-in-a-world-on-fire/9781541730151/ (Download and Intro) and https://www.getabstract.com/en/summary/reimagining-capitalism-in-a-world-on-fire/39594 (abstract); Humanity at Work – MONDRAGON, a social innovation ecosystem case study. The Young Foundation, Putting People at the Heart of Social Change. Youngfoundation.org Humanity-at-Work-online-copy.pdf; Harvard Business School Case Study on 1Worker1Vote/Mondragon https://drive.google.com/file/d/1Bjri47Z_RrCpxuGnu0Vl7YrZ8HdeSRe4/view.

dtW: NPR Amy Scott, *Marketplace*, Inequality By Design – https://www.marketplace.org/2020/04/16/inequality-by-design-how-redlining-continues-to-shape-our-economy/; Harvard https://www.hks.harvard.edu/centers/wiener/news-events/undesign-redline.

PART 2

Social Innovation in the Mondragon Cooperatives

This section provides an overview of the Mondragon cooperatives, the development of the networked group and the current involvement in the world.

CHAPTER 4

The Power of Social Innovation in the Mondragon Experience: Setting the Stage

Christina Clamp

If you ask me what is so compelling about the Mondragon Cooperative Corporation (MCC), I would say their success as innovators is the "secret sauce." When I first travelled to Mondragón, the region of Basque Country where this co-op movement first emerged, I was struck by how "off the beaten path" the town was in 1982, but how connected the Mondragon cooperatives were to the larger world. Today, with its modern turnpike that runs through the Alto Deva Valley, one would be surprised that it used to take hours over winding mountain roads to get there.

What has motivated so many people to visit Mondragón over the decades? Clearly it has been a touchstone of inspiration for many of its visitors. "The Mondragon Experience" (as it was fondly referred to when I first visited) spoke to the concerns that others had with the rise of neoliberalism, the decline of trade unions, and the rise of social inequality. I was told that there was even a Chinese delegation to Mondragon that year. They were interested in whether Mondragon was a model that could work within Chinese state socialism. Community activists in Western democracies saw in Mondragon a model for democratizing ownership of the workplace and creating a commitment to a geographic location — important at a time when many factories were moving offshore to lower cost labor markets.

When the ICA Group, an American developer of worker cooperatives (icagroup.org/) visited Mondragón in 1982, they learned about how members' ownership stakes were held in internal capital accounts; these were monies that would leave with them when they retired but also provided a cushion for lean years. In the use of internal capital accounts for worker members, David Ellerman, a staff economist with the ICA Group, saw a solution to the overvaluing that occurred in ownership transfers in firms such as the US plywood cooperatives and waste management cooperatives in California that resulted in worker-owned firms selling to outside investors over time. Ellerman referred to this as the "Mondragon solution" to the problem (2007). Internal capital accounts are a key innovation that has translated well into the practice of worker co-op development in the US ever since. In large and small ways, those of us committed to creating worker cooperatives could see how there were lessons to be learned and solutions to recurring problems that Mondragon had overcome. Mondragon continues to be a social innovator that we can learn from and a source of inspiration in addressing the challenges facing our own communities.

In 2017, the Young Foundation released a report, *Humanity at Work: Mondragon – A Social Innovation Ecosystem Case Study* (Heales, Hodgson & Rich, 2017) in which they define the elements of successful social innovation: "Social innovation refers to the process, relationships and products engendered in creating unique solutions to entrenched or emerging social need or problems" (p.1). They identify three dimensions to social innovation:

- A social innovation is an articulation of expressed or latent "social demands" and "social values."
- Whether something is a social innovation is dependent upon the context in which it has developed.
- A social innovation is frequently driven by specific social practices that emerge from those social values (*e.g.*, collaboration and cooperation, or democratic participation) (p.19)

The articulation of demands or needs reflect market failures and typically are driven by inequalities, vulnerabilities, or uneven power dynamics. Social innovations are grounded in solutions to those institutional or systemic failures and are context-dependent (Heales, Hodgson, & Rich, 2017). Inherent in social innovations is the incorporation of new behaviors and interactions. What's noteworthy is the way that this impacts the ability of others to adopt these same innovations in a new setting. It is why efforts to replicate Mondragon have found that they cannot create the exact same model (Heales *et al.*, 2017).

In this chapter, the role of social innovation in the case of Mondragon is revisited with a particular focus on the role of Caja Laboral Popular (CLP) in the development of the Mondragon cooperatives. In the early development of the cooperative group, CLP played a key role as a development bank. Today CLP does business as Laboral Kutxa and has become a more conventional bank in its operation. Therefore, my purpose here is to focus on the early years of CLP's operations and contributions to the creation of what is now Mondragon. In brief, the CLP was instrumental in the creation of the Mondragon cooperatives, its health care insurance, revitalization of Basque education, language and culture, and the financing and development of many of the worker cooperatives.

Social Innovation as a Lens for Examining Mondragon

In examining Mondragon through the lens of social innovation, the work of Heales *et al.* (2017) is the most extensive recent research. They conducted interviews with members of the cooperatives to document how and why Mondragon has been a wellspring of ideas for so many seeking to create social transformation in the creation of new jobs on a cooperative model. Their analysis identified several key themes in successful innovation:

1. Social impact through shared values.
2. A networked organizational model grounded in those shared values.
3. An ongoing commitment to social means and ends that guide their working practice.
4. Democratic and egalitarian governance.

5. An ecosystem of intra and inter-cooperation.

6. Success grounded in disruptive business ideas, profit sharing and member mobilization.

7. Internal development of complementary institutions serving the wider mission; and commitment to the sovereignty of labor.

Mondragon has faced challenges, such as the failure of Fagor Electrodomésticos in 2013. Yet even in that crisis, the group was able to rely on its core values to work together to minimize the impact of the losses on the workers and to reflect on lessons learned.

What is noteworthy about the Mondragon case is that it is the largest network of worker-owned cooperatives in the world. The scope and scale of its social innovation is considered iconic and has inspired people for decades to study its experience and to draw inspiration from and elements of its model for development elsewhere in the world. Shared values are critical to the Mondragon cooperative ecosystem. All who work in the Mondragon cooperatives recognize the importance of maintaining shared ownership as a cooperative. The alignment of their values creates one out of many.

While an outsider will see Mondragon Corporation as monolithic, the group is a network of firms able to support one another and to achieve their goals through sharing of risks and benefits. This approach has enabled the cooperatives to weather recessions and to remain viable and competitive in their business sectors. This cohesive set of values fosters their democratic system and ensures that firms both large and small are accountable to their members through the principle of "one member, one vote."

The significance of this was brought home to me in 1998 when I was in the Basque Country for a sabbatical. My older daughter, who was then 12 years old, accompanied me to a machine-tool fair in Bilbao. As we walked through the exhibit hall, she suddenly said to me how exciting it was to her that the largest of the machine tool firms at the fair was the cooperative. I knew that there were multiple MCC affiliates under one banner, which she in turn saw as one single cooperative.

Mondragon's relevance is more than just the shared values. Intercooperation is a core principle that has led to strategies that have insured a commitment to cooperation rather than competition amongst the affiliated cooperatives. Collaboration is key. One sees this in the everyday interactions where a sales representative of one firm sees an opportunity for another in the group and acts as the bridge to open that relationship for the second firm. It is also evident at a strategic level through the coordination of the group at the level of governance for MCC. Heales et al. (2017) identified an approach to MCC's socially driven cooperative system based on "good and disruptive business ideas" that inform its economic performance and how wealth is distributed. Gallego-Bono & Chavez-Avila (2020, p.3110) refer to this as a form of "collective entrepreneurship" that ensures coherence in the group. Mondragon operates at a remarkably high level of coherence in its stated principles and alignment of core values. Gallego-Bono & Chavez-Avila refer to this as a macro-order that operates within clearly defined rules at a meso level (2020, p.3111).

Innovation in the case of Mondragon is always geared to the preservation of the sovereignty of labor while pursuing opportunities for new development. Labor sovereignty is Mondragon's *credo* and its people are the group's greatest asset. Heales et al. (2017) found that Mondragon has grown and been sustained internally through the establishment of complementary institutions that support its development. Specifically, Laboral Kutxa, which began as Caja Laboral Popular, was key to that early growth and success (Gallego-Bono & Chaves-Avila, 2020, p.3114; Heales et al., 2017, p.37).

Heales *et al.* (2017) see three key drivers to the innovation inherent in Mondragon's model: the first is incrementalism to address "market failures;" second is the will to disrupt – to develop models that are entirely new and "which come to change our framework of understanding" (p.35); last is social innovations that are structural and reconfigure markets and organizations or institutions in the process of the innovation (p.35). In this next section, we briefly revisit the early history of the CLP and examine it utilizing these three drivers.

A Brief History of the CLP's Early Years

In 1959, Don José María Arizmendiarrieta saw the need for a bank (Altuna Gabilondo, 2008, p.116). His concern was that, while the first cooperatives were doing well, there was a need to create a financial intermediary that could capture additional resources to promote cooperative and community development (Altuna Gabilondo, 2008, p.116) beyond those early successes. There was good reason to assume that no help could be expected from the Spanish government and its financial allies, since the Basques had not supported Franco in the Spanish Civil War. The creation of the CLP itself was a response to market failure and disruptive in its form as a development bank. The focus on community reinvestment served to generate a number of additional social innovations and changes to the local markets.

The CLP was created as a second-tier cooperative and served as the hub of the cooperative group from 1959 to 1991 (Altuna Gabilondo, 2008, p.165). As a second tier cooperative, CLP's membership was comprised of the workers in CLP; workers of cooperatives affiliated with CLP and the affiliated cooperatives (Caja Laboral Popular, 1979, p.1; Caja Laboral Popular, 1959, *Capitulo II, Art. 6*). Governance included 12 representatives — four worker representatives and eight from the affiliated cooperatives (Caja Laboral Popular, 1979, p.31; Caja Laboral Popular, 1959, *Capitulo VI, Art. 44*). This innovation adapted the democratic governance of the industrial cooperatives but recognized the importance of accountability to both workers and the affiliated industrial cooperatives. It also ensured a role for the consumer cooperative, Consumo San José (today known as Eroski), as a founding member.

As well as a banking division, CLP had an entrepreneurial or business division devoted to providing technical assistance to start-ups and ongoing support of associated cooperatives. The bank also had a general services division that managed personnel, food services, buildings and equipment, and services and programs for the individual worker members of CLP. A technical department provided technical assistance in the form of urban planning and construction projects, including a land bank and a social project that became Lagun Aro, the social insurance co-op (Altuna Gabilondo, 2008, p.117).

In the early years, the cooperative group was based on their association with the CLP. Each cooperative agreed to a contract of association that outlined both obligations and rights. The advantage was that CLP served as their financial advisor and financier. Terms of association for each co-op outlined the form of governance, democratic structure, and capital structure (Clamp, 1986, pp.69-70). There was a one- to two-year trial period for cooperatives new to the association. This was especially important in times of economic downturns.

Another condition of association was that all cooperative members were to become enrolled in the social services of Lagun Aro, established in 1967 (Altuna Gabilondo, 2008, p.118). The Spanish government had passed legislation that made members of a worker cooperative ineligible for the national health program. This led to the creation of Lagun Aro by the CLP (Heales *et al.*, 2017, p.37). Lagun Aro adopted the second-tier cooperative structure with dual membership as in the CLP.

By 1970, under CLP's leadership, 45 cooperatives and four regional cooperative groups were created. Each cooperative group established a way to share both profits and losses and the ability to relocate workers to other firms to avoid layoffs. The groups were also able to achieve some economies of scale by reducing redundancies in the firms' operations. Where cooperatives were in a regional group, the CLP served a more conventional banking function (Clamp, 1986, p.67).

By 1982, leadership recognized the need to restructure the group. The transition was driven both internally and externally. A recession in the 1970s and early 1980s saw unemployment rise to over 16% in 1981 (Clamp, 1986, p.147). The CLP and the cooperative groups relocated workers from firms with excess workers to those that could absorb additional workers.

The bank had an exportation department in its entrepreneurial division and resources were devoted to developing a uniform trademark (Clamp, 1986, p.156). The transition was both to position the cooperatives for entry into a European common market and to engage in global markets. This led to the reorganization into business sectoral groups instead of geographic groups.

Additionally, there was external pressure from the Central Bank of Spain, as well as internal pressure, to lower the risk of the CLP portfolio through investments beyond the associated co-ops. The bank was lending to associated cooperatives at 8% while the market rate was 15% in 1983 (Clamp, 1986, p.176). This set of push/pull factors led to a re-examination of the role of CLP and a transition that was finalized in 1991. The sectoral groups took on a greater role with their member cooperatives and the bank stepped out of the development of new firms. The entrepreneurial division was spun off as a separate consulting firm, LKS. Mondragon Cooperative Corporation was formed.

In the course of that period of 37 years, the CLP was able to nurture significant growth in the Mondragon cooperatives. Employment increased from 4,211 in 1965 to over 22,860 in 1990 (Ormaechea, 1993, p.93). As of 1990, there were 99 associated cooperatives; 45% were created by CLP (1993, p.101). CLP captured not only resources from the associated cooperatives but also from community members' Individual savings accounts. The bank and co-ops contributed social funds for the development of a hospital, schools, and resources to preserve the Basque language and culture. In turn, all worker members benefited from the creation of the social security system in the form of Lagun Aro.

The transition in the role of the bank led to the separation of the entrepreneurial division into a separate cooperative, LKS. Today, LKS continues to provide technical assistance for incubating new companies. Its activities have included international as well as domestic projects in other nations, including the Preston Model in the UK (see **Chapter 14**).

The bank devoted resources to promoting and preserving Basque culture and language that had suffered greatly under the Franco dictatorship through Hezibide Educational Group and the promotion of the *ikastolas* — Basque language cooperative schools which today have 4,500 teachers, 500 non-teaching staff, 60,000 students and an impact on over 40,000 families (Ikastolen Eklartea, 2018). The investment in education has resulted in the establishment of Mondragon University and its LEINN program that is part of Team Academy.

CLP's activities were consistently focused on social innovations to respond to market failures, the recovery of the economy after the war, the anti-Basque efforts to de-develop the region by the Franco government, and to preserve Basque language and culture. The Spanish government excluded them from the national health system and in response, they developed their own health insurance. The public education system did not offer instruction in the Basque language — so they created their own schools.

Even the very establishment of CLP was to ensure that there would be financing available for new cooperatives in the Basque Country. These social innovations illustrate how the CLP exercised incrementalism to address market failure and disruptive strategies to overcome government policies through new organizational structures. Lastly, in the development of the worker cooperatives, the CLP exercised a structural approach to develop locally owned and controlled economic institutions committed to the development of Basque communities.

Today, Mondragon continues to be innovative, as we will see in the cases of LEINN and the Erreka co-op. Heales *et al.* (2017) address the question as to whether Mondragon is still innovative. They point to the factors that influence the ability to be innovative: the length of time that an innovation has been in place; whether it has achieved market share or scale; whether it has become institutionalized; and whether it is able to continue to adapt or change. In examining these elements, they conclude that Mondragon has achieved market share and scale. Critics (Bretos, Errasti & Marcuello, 2018; Errasti, Heras, Bakaikoa & Elgoibar, 2003; Flecha & Ngai, 2014) assert that there are ways that Mondragon's response to globalization has caused some drift from the cooperative model. They conclude that this is more problematic than indicative of becoming more traditional. This was evident in the adaptive and innovative response to the failure of Fagor Electrodomésticos in 2013 where the group redeployed most of the workers (Heales *et al.*, 2017, p.40). Mondragon has become a "social innovation ecosystem" that demonstrates an ability to generate both internal and external innovations. These innovations are key to the sustainability of the existing firms, as we will see in the case of the Erreka Group, and the novel approaches to creating opportunities for a future generation of co-operators as intrapreneurs and entrepreneurs.

References

Altuna Gabilondo, e.L. (2008). *La experiencia cooperativa de Mondragon.* Eskoriatza: Lanki.

Bretos, I., Errasti, A. & Marcuello, C. (2018). Ownership, governance, and the diffusion of HRM practices in multinational worker cooperatives: Case-study evidence from the Mondragon group. *Human Resource Management Journal, 28*(1), 76-91.

Caja Laboral Popular (1959). *Estatutos Sociales* (Social Statutes). Mondragón, Spain: Caja Laboral Popular.

Caja Laboral Popular (1979). *Estatutos Sociales de Caja Laboral Popular* (Social Statutes of Caja Laboral Popular). Mondragón, Spain: Caja Laboral Popular.

Clamp, C. (1986, March 20). Managing Cooperation at Mondragon. *Unpublished doctoral dissertation.* Chestnut Hill, MA: Boston College.

Ellerman, D. (2007). On the Role of Capital in "capitalist" and in labor-managed firms. *Review of Radical Political Economics, 39*(1), 5-26. doi:10.1177/0486613406296895

Errasti, A.M., Heras, H.I., Bakaikoa, B. & Elgoibar, P. (2003). The internationalization of cooperatives: The case of the Mondragon Cooperative Corporation. *Annals of Public & Cooperative Economics, 74*(4), 553–584.

Flecha, R. & Ngai, P. (2014). The challenge for Mondragon: Searching for the cooperative values in times of internationalization. *Organization, 21*(5), 666-682.

Gallego-Bono, J.R. & Chaves-Avila, R. (2020). How to boost clusters and regional change through cooperative social innovation. *Economic Research-Ekonomska Istrazivanja, 33*(1), 3108-3124. doi:10.1080/1331677X.2019.1696694.

Heales, C., Hodgson, M. & Rich, H. (2017, April 5). *Humanity at Work.* Retrieved from The Young Foundation: https://www.youngfoundation.org/our-work/publications/humanity-at-work-mondragon-a-social-innovation-ecosystem-case-study/.

Ikastolen eklartea (2018). *Ikastolak, Transforming Education.* Retrieved October 5, 2021, from Basque Country Schools: https://ikastola-eus.translate.goog/ikastola/zer_da?_x_tr_sl=eu&_x_tr_tl=en&_x_tr_hl=en&_x_tr_pto=nui,sc.

Ormaechea, J.M. (1993). *The Mondragon Cooperative Experience.* Mondragón, Spain: Mondragon Cooperative Corporation.

CHAPTER 5

An Interview with Julio Gallastegui

Christina Clamp

Julio Gallastegui Is the former general manager of Laboral Kutxa. I first met Julio in 1982 while I conducted the field research for my dissertation on the Mondragon cooperatives. Given his involvement over the years, I asked him to share his reflections on the transition from a development bank to its current banking priorities.

Julio: It is very appropriate to frame our discussion in a context of social innovation to discuss the history of Caja Laboral and the group as a whole, as you have described in your introduction. You know very deeply Caja Laboral and the Mondragon Group; I can only make some reflections from my point of view. You rightly point out that Caja Laboral played a key role as a development bank at the beginning of what we know today as the Mondragon Corporation.

Today it has become a more conventional bank in its operation. This responds to the necessary adaptation of all financial institutions, regardless of their legal structure, to an activity as regulated as banking. Renew or die! Today, a development bank and a commercial bank cannot coexist in a single entity. Nor can they have shared governance, even if differentiated entities are established. Not to understand it that way would lead, in my view, to a dead end.

It is, therefore, about designing instruments, mechanisms, and ways of doing that replace the historical role that Caja Laboral has played in the development of the group. We could classify as social innovation the adaptation carried out, and that will undoubtedly have to continue to be carried out, without losing the signs of identity and connection with the group.

A long time ago it became clear that a credit institution could not be the head of an industrial and distribution group. The creation of the Mondragon Corporation, which includes some of the activities carried out by the business (entrepreneurial) division of Caja Laboral,[1] is a relevant milestone in the evolution of the group, as it was certainly atypical and innovative, because it does not correspond to being the owner of cooperatives. Caja Laboral's economic support to the industrial cooperatives was decisive for their consolidation. It evolved over time and had a structural character. It was certainly something new, not only for a bank, but also a credit union. The initial economic impulse and support to what is now a consulting cooperative [has transferred to] LKS [which] has assumed the role of the entrepreneurial division of Caja Laboral, and once segregated has experienced vigorous development.

Lagun Aro, the social [health] insurance provider, has experienced profound changes, as workers were able to participate in the national pension system. It is quite different from what was in force in the first period of the group when Mondragon cooperators were excluded from the national system. Lagun Aro's health insurance adapted to the changes in the financing of the national public health system. It is also a clear example of innovation in its adaptation.

Caja Laboral, as a credit union that developed into a commercial bank, could not be maintained as a development bank. But it has not abandoned that function. It promoted the creation of Mondragón Inversiones[2] and Fundación Mondragón,[2] with decisive economic support. These economic supports evolved over time and were made possible through the distribution of net profits. Structurally, there is a clear separation of the governance of the commercial bank which Caja Laboral became and the newer corporate instruments. All this is a continuous adaptation that allows us to maintain our principles, contribute to the development of the group and make our "experience" sustainable over time.

When we say that Caja Laboral develops a more conventional type of banking than the one it previously developed, it may seem that this has a pejorative character. That is not my opinion.

Caja Laboral has focused its present activity on commercial banking, which is the one that has had the greatest development. And commercial banking responds to operating rules and regulation that one must inevitably take care of. Its performance in the market corresponds to that of any company, whether cooperative or not.

However, it maintains very different elements if we stick to its internal organization, its cooperative nature, the existence of working partners, its governance, or the distribution of its results. Those are distinctive elements that have characterized Caja Laboral throughout its history, with the necessary adaptations, and that do not challenge, in my opinion, any of the fundamental elements or cooperative principles that have guided the group as a whole.

Caja Laboral's specialization in commercial banking does not at all imply an abandonment of the functions that it has historically developed. These functions, suitably adapted, have been assumed within the group, illuminating the institutions that can perform them in a way more in line with regulatory evolution and with the changes in the environment that have been taking place. In my opinion, this global adaptation is a real innovation, not only of Caja Laboral but of the group as a whole, and that can make the Mondragon experience a more sustainable reality.

Sometimes we tend to yearn for the past and do not perceive the importance of the momentous changes that are being developed to make the Mondragon experience a sustainable success over time. Gaztenpresa is an innovative activity. Undoubtedly, this is not a central activity in Caja Laboral. However, this does not detract one iota from the importance of this action, even recognizing the modesty of its contribution. The impulse in the creation of the Gaztenpresa Foundation, the establishment of agreements with public institutions, or the collaborations established with the commercial network of Caja Laboral, are added elements to the direct economic collaboration that is carried out.

The activities promoted by Caja Laboral in its history have certainly been varied. If we refer to its Social Division, we must mention pensions, health care, or temporary disability, as the most significant. In its Entrepreneurial Division, we see auditing, information and management control, engineering, consulting in its various facets, intervention in cooperatives in difficulties, international trade or study services. It also promoted the constitution of educational cooperatives, housing cooperatives, and the acquisition of land (land banking) for new cooperatives, as well as the creation of training and technological research centers. As is logical, all these actions respond to a historical context that has evolved over time. The Mondragon Group and Caja Laboral are business realities fully integrated into the market and responsive to the evolution of the socio-economic context.

As we can see, the development of the regional public administration has greatly influenced the changes produced in these activities. The regulatory evolution of health and social security have conditioned, and will continue to condition, the management of the benefits of Lagun Aro, as heir to the Social Division of Caja Laboral. Today, the reforms in pensions or health care are a clear outcome of this evolution. The assumption by the autonomous governmental institution for the competences in the educational field, and the corresponding financing of the public system, has impacted the *ikastolas* (educational cooperatives) and will be a clear determinant of their evolution. The financing of public, private, and charter education is a controversial aspect and subject to changes conditioned by the external socio-political context. The maintenance of a land exchange for the promotion of cooperatives ceased to be valid in the context of public support in this arena. The promotion of housing cooperatives ceased to be a central element linked to the group. It remains in the market as an alternative promoter, but without greater link with the group.

The opening to the market of engineering, auditing and consulting activities constitutes a successful development from the embryo that was constituted in the Business Division of Caja Laboral.

The function of intervention in cooperatives in difficulty was transferred to the divisions of the corporation, and the information, management, and international trade were assumed by the corporation.

All this transformation had an intense economic support from Caja Laboral in a first phase, in order to make it viable and sustainable. Support has become structural through the distribution of results to the Fondo de Educación y Promoción (FEP) and Fondo Central de Intercooperación (FCI). Financial support to the Training and Technological Research (FEP) centers is maintained through contributions to the FEP.

On the other hand, and in this same context, we must not fail to mention that there is an intense collaboration with the public administration, within the framework of its economic policy, which enables agreements and the transfer of important public resources to cooperative business initiatives.

Surely, we have commented previously on some of the practices of the Mondragon group that, in my opinion, are in an important respect responsible for the success of their business experience. Classifying them as values is not something for me to judge.

As a prominent element, consider the cooperative as its most important partner. The cooperative, its sustainability as a company, must prevail over the particular interests of the members. As always, you have to look for balance, because a cooperative pursues the interest of its members. But the greatest interest is in its development and sustainability. Economic management and results-sharing mechanisms should be oriented in that direction.

The search for efficiency in the organization of the business, the adequacy of wages for economic evolution, the adequate distribution of results towards reserves and capital, the capitalization of cooperative returns, remuneration limited to capital, etc. They are all elements that guide our direction.

Not always, and not in all the cooperatives of Mondragon, have these elements been effectively managed. We could describe different examples. But I would dare to say that, in general, management has been successful. Although, of course, past successes do not guarantee future successes. Hence the importance of the structural mechanisms established to guarantee it. Otherwise, it will never be a good time to reduce wages, reduce or eliminate the remuneration of capital, adjust personnel ... and yet, they are decisions that have proven to be right. Painful, but necessary.

Chris: In line with these reflections, I would like to ask you about the system of relocation or recycling of personnel in the Mondragon group.

Julio: Indeed, it is a system that is still in operation within the framework of Lagun Aro's employment assistance for redundant workers. It is a mutual commitment between cooperatives, whereby those that require a staff adjustment commit to relocate their members as a priority to reduce unemployment, and receiving cooperatives prioritize this relocation over any other alternative.

It is a complex and certainly differential action with respect to the operation of the other companies within the framework of the unemployment benefits of the social security system. It has an economic advantage for cooperatives because it greatly reduces the cost of unemployment benefits. On the other hand, it is a relevant effort for the relocated partners (displacements, change of job ...) and also for host cooperatives that are limited in their access to the labor market. These relocations are temporary, although they may be permanent when the crisis is structural.

In addition to the cooperatives affiliated with the Mondragon Corporation, Lagun Aro has other cooperatives that also belong but are not MCC affiliates. Managing this benefit is more difficult in a different organizational context. In my opinion, it is a valuable and complex mechanism, very differentiated from the conventional business context.

End-notes

[1] The entrepreneurial administrative unit in Caja Laboral is referred to as the "business division" by the Mondragon cooperators. In the American literature about Mondragon, it has been referred to as the "entrepreneurial division."

[2] Fondo Central Intercooperativo (FCI) administers 10% of net profits allocated by the Mondragon cooperatives and 20% from Caja Laboral to the Permanent Commission of MCC for deployment through Mondragon Inversiones in projects to strengthen the economic prospects of cooperatives such as international investments or new activities as determined by the preferences of MCC's General Assembly annually.

[3] Fondo de Educación y Promoción (FEP) is the fund for education and development, formerly the Fondo de Educación y Obras Sociales (FEOS). It has been the destination for the legally obligated 10% of net profits destined per cooperative law for social development.

CHAPTER 6

The "Own The Metrics" Campaign: ESGs & SDGs Meet Their Porto Alegre Moment

Ibon Zugasti & Michael Peck

Introduction

Better metrics are essential to defining, measuring and building on the achievements of social economy practitioners, and thereby advancing stakeholder primacy in a circular and caring economy. Metrics already show that worker-owned social enterprises and cooperatives are more stable, equitable, democratic, ecologically sustainable, productive, and competitive, with fewer job losses, especially during downturns.

Yet the powers of the shareholder-primacy economy can co-opt rising human- and social-capital asset metrics measuring the greatest common societal good we advocate for, and putting on a show of "doing good" through virtue signaling and green and "purpose washing" at the direct expense of "humanity at work and life."

ESG/SDG standards represent a critical but as yet still emerging tool at scale to create a more just society and economy that works for all. We believe those who are developing these tools and proving their results should lead the way in qualifying and benchmarking performance metrics that drive more equitably shared investment. Social economy practitioners at every level of global society need to righteously and factually assert ownership over these metrics, and push back vigorously against the omnipresent shareholder-primacy, corporatist-plantation economy mindset that would dictate the opposite. This campaign requires the permanent, decision-making presence of stakeholder practitioners on the various regional, national and international forums and bodies that deliberate about and track sustainable development goals, and which define economic, social and governance protocols for financial, human, social, and environmental investment worldwide.

This is the goal of the "Own the Metrics" campaign, which we launched in Q1 2020 to flatten extractive and predatory curves and transform how regional, national and global forums measure inequity, social progress, and the economics of environmental sustainability, health and healing. In this chapter we issue a call to arms that lays out the issues and crises that threaten the health and future of people and planet; we describe the successful business models and measures that can lead us to a better future; and share the process by which the Own The Metrics campaign has moved forward, and will continue to do so.

Call to Arms

The World Economic Forum in Davos (www.weforum.org/) began in 1971 on Switzerland's highest mountain peaks, overlooking the rest of the world in real and presumed physical and intellectual majesty. Confusing heights with might is not a new Western concept: New York City and London skyscrapers also command global financial fealty and enshrine vertical-hierarchy culture. In Paris, the Sacré Coeur Basilica at Montmartre and the libertine Quartier Pigalle stand as another *"caritas to cupiditas"* example of church-to-barrio, "sinner look up to be saved" communion, symbolizing revelations from on high trickling down to the children of lesser gods below.

Yet the Covid pandemic has inspired resistance in the workplace to these elevated powers. Just as the call to arms of the pandemic was to use masking, vaccinations, and social distancing to flatten Covid's terrible mortality curves — the spikes or dramatic increases in infections and fatalities caused by the disease — so a fuller mosaic of social economy practitioners, which includes individuals from all classes and backgrounds, can flatten the terrible inequity curves produced by Davos-style shareholder primacy.

In 2001, 30 years after the first Davos Summit, a counterpoint to its ever-rising global inequality was born in Porto Alegre on the Brazilian coast, when the World Social Forum gave visible voice to the disenfranchised and downtrodden (en.wikipedia.org/wiki/World_Social_Forum).

It is urgent that the promise of the original Porto Alegre conference continues to grow, especially in light of the embryonic but growing importance given to human and social capital as assets to invest in instead of commodities to outsource and offshore. Today, our world reels from one existential threat to the next — a lethal pandemic, climate crisis, and predatory capitalism cocktail surging and mutating from 2020 through 2022. An additional pandemic layer of political-military authoritarianism arrived with Putin's latest invasion of Ukraine in February 2022, further crippling existing and fragile energy-climate imbalances.

Half a century after Davos (from 1971–2021), the world's global elite persist in neither understanding nor caring that "nothing about us, without us, is for us." Reactionary "social libertarians" addicted to passive income power cling to shareholder-primacy privilege to impose individual will over common good. Governments dedicated to hegemonic empire through totalitarian and even genocidal practices inflict unconscionable human and ecological devastation with Orwellian implications.

The goose-step march and Roman salute are back in vogue. The world on fire graduates to serial, spree and mass civic arson: daily climate and socioeconomic crimes against humanity commoditize and arbitrage the poverty index on a planet where 1.89 billion people — 36% of humanity — live under the most inhumane definitions.

Cumulative effects threaten human survival on a planet submerging under rising seas and melting glacial ice, roasting from increasing temperatures, and dehydrating due to spreading regional drought. Carbon and methane emissions choke Earth's atmosphere until George Floyd's "I can't breathe" becomes the ubiquitous climate and social justice norm pinned down under a boot long in the design and making,

Those who would vertically rewire the wounded but defiantly resistant 21st century into an 18th century plantation continue winning many regional, national and even continental battles. Yet still they fail in the aggregate to convince global hearts and minds to abandon hope and resolve. Seductive authoritarianism and terrifying military fury cannot reverse resilient, resolute tides of sociocultural healing and progress.

Policy, Structure & Practice: Our Growing Mutualist Hopes

Fortunately, there are three positive transformations in policy, structure and practice that provide an organic, mutualist way out of this top-down vicious cycle.

First through policy, as described in the Millennium Project's *State of the Future* report:

> World leaders have agreed to achieve the UN Sustainable Development Goal (SDG) of eliminating extreme poverty by 2030. Meanwhile, the concentration of wealth is increasing (the wealth of just eight billionaires equals that of 3.6 billion people, the poorer half of humanity), income gaps are widening, employment-less economic growth continues, returns on investment in capital and technology is usually better than returns on labor measured as an expendable asset in the technologist belief that future innovation can replace, displace, and improve much of human and social capital asset value. (Millennium Project, 2017)

Second, a new structure is emerging with the recent rise of global social economy movements that reach beyond the divided legacies of the World Economic Forum and World Social Forum. With a focus on enterprise and ecosystems, this socioeconomic phenomenon occurs by deploying more enlightened stakeholder ownership and democratic governance structures to quicken the transition from extractive *shareholder-primacy* to regenerative *stakeholder-centric* thinking and doing. Consider the growth of the sustainability sector in the Global North alone:

- The United Kingdom has an estimated 471 social enterprises.
- Social Economy Europe (socialeconomy.eu.org/) has 2.8 million members.
- The American Sustainable Business Council (asbnetwork.org/) with its newly merged Social Venture Circle partner, has grown to more than 250,000 quadruple-bottom-line (people, planet, purpose, profit) member businesses and business organizations.

Third, through practice, global social impact capital allocation combined with emerging fair and transparent public standards — and performance metrics are on the rise. ESG (environment, social, governance) fiduciary transactions together with wider, verifiable adoption of UN SDGs (sustainable development goals) collectively serve as performance-based blueprints and profit-seeking mandates. These can restructure the global, post-pandemic precariat into an equally rising social-economy citizenry through more compelling and relevant externalities, key performance indicators, and investor metrics.

"Free at last, free at last, thank God Almighty we are free at last": the prophetic words of two Nobel Peace Prize recipients and civil rights icons, Dr. Martin Luther King and Nelson Mandela, both imprisoned as leaders of color in their respective countries, mark the changing socio-economics of post-pandemic liberation, and set the standards for the rest of us to "level-up" in the most democratically just sense.

For the first time in collective human history, what we call "social impact investing" establishes four ESG capital sources (human, social, environmental, and financial) as fundamental to investing practice, starting with climate resiliency and safety. Putin's invasion of Ukraine puts this transformational potential to the test, demanding a Hobbesian choice between energy and climate security, when the answer is not either, but both. Already, disillusioned practitioners and cynics are calling out the distractions of partisan politics, self-serving virtue signaling, and investor confusion over credible metrics.

So far, evidence shows that ESG and SDG impact investors are learning that human, social, and natural capital can make or break financial capital margins. This process of flattening the inequity curves of shareholder primacy starts with solidarity and mutualist culture, which drive shared profitable returns. The goal is to uplift those who do the work, together with their families and communities, equalizing labor and capital returns on investments, and ending the feudal/plantation practice of privatizing profits while socializing losses.

It's necessary to elevate the "S" both in the social part of ESG metrics and the "sustainable" mandate for SDG goals to flatten shareholder primacy inequity curves so that stakeholders can become shareholders in their own local, living economies. For ESG capital providers, the "S" dominates: resiliency and stakeholder ownership are inseparable; one provides the roots and rationale for the other.

Hope translates John Elkington's triple bottom line — "profit, people, and planet" as "a genetic code for tomorrow's capitalism, spurring the regeneration of our economies, societies and biosphere"[4] — into mutualist ESG/SDG standards and performance metrics. These transform aspirational capital allocation and define a new quadruple bottom-line of people, planet, purpose, and profit.

We believe it is possible to frame an international "bubble-up to gusher-up"™ model that reverses economic exclusion: more profitable, regenerating, renewing, circular economy deal-flow aligns local stakeholder and community-based values with purpose-driven businesses collaborating beyond borders to prod and inspire truly "free" markets towards virtuous instead of vicious cycles.

With this purpose in mind, we envision a global social-economy forum to build mutualist voice and agency, and in the process earn a full seat at all national, regional, multinational, and international decision-making forums on performance indicators, metrics, and standards. An aggregated, global social economy community — which *already includes* cooperatives, mutualist organizations, social enterprises, and organized labor — discards the leftover externalities of shareholder primacy. These externalities are predicated on exclusion, economic and social injustice, accidents of birth and postal-code addresses; they leave workers behind on a burning planet.

As presented during the 2021 World Cooperative Congress (icaworldcoopcongress.coop) in Seoul, this call to action centers ESG/SDG metrics so that, as 1worker1vote declares: "everything cooperatively, mutually about us and with us, can be for all of us" (the reverse of the "nothing about us, without us, is for us" slogan). We define this as an example of Heather McGhee's "solidarity dividend," and its power is both synergistically global and local, so that the whole becomes more upwardly transformative and impactful than the sum of all parts (McGhee, 2021).

Goals, Models & Actions

Our first goal is to convene a reimagined conversation on the "Social Economy ESG/SDG Metrics Toolbox;" this will help build an inclusive and measurable approach to business and the social economy. We want to go beyond the Davos/Porto Alegre divide to create a profit-seeking universal platform that is caring economy compatible in design, practice, measurement, and enforcement. The newly announced United Nations Research Institute for Social Development (UNRISD, 2018-2022) Sustainable Development Performance Indicators (SDPIs) help significantly to serve this purpose.

Our second goal is to design a roadmap for a global, social economy "just transition" from shareholder primacy to stakeholder capitalism, using capital, social and human resources metrics, and key performance indicators (KPIs) to inspire and channel uplifting financial investment.

Our purpose in deploying both goals is to outline social economy protocols echoing both the reimagining capitalism framework developed by Harvard Business School, which envisions "caring/sharing ecosystems where profitability affords, sustains, and proves values and purpose" (Henderson, 2020), and the Oxford/SAID Economics of Mutuality (EOM) definition of company purpose to "solve problems faced as individuals, communities, customers, societies, and the natural world in ways that are commercially viable, profitable, and sustainable" (Ellis, Colin-Jones & Zugasti, 2021).

Bringing "shop floor" participants to the fore enables righteous, profit-seeking claims to achieve equal policy consideration and impact on ESG/SDG formation, and guides their performance metrics for virtuous cycle/social economy business ecosystems that transcend borders, markets, and silos.

Academic methodologies justifying this approach are on the rise: our collaboration with Harvard Business School professors Rebecca Henderson and George Serafeim from 2013 to 2019 focused on their acclaimed *Reimagining Capitalism* classes for second-year students; many of these students volunteered for 1worker1vote movement projects in Cincinnati (coopcincy.org). Ibon Zugasti co-published *Mondragon: Maintaining Resilience through Cooperative Strategies* with principals from the SAID Business School (Ellis *et al.*, 2021) who, together with the British Academy (2019), pioneered a global movement on "putting business purpose into practice" (purposeintopractice.org/).

A recent, well-received (Fraser, 2022) report from the Business Purpose Commission for Scotland outlines how this might work on a regional basis, starting with the British Academy standard that "the purpose of a business is to find profitable solutions to the problems of people and planet, not to profit from creating problems for either." In this approach, a purposeful business:

> … adopts and commits to a purpose by law; adopts a social license to operate (if regulated); seeks shareholders committed to the purpose; has inclusive governance and values that support delivery of purpose; measures delivery of the purpose; states profits, net of failures, to fulfil purpose; raises risk capital aligned with purpose from shareholders (to increase investment in purposeful businesses by establishing a world leading ESG investment hub); establishes partners to make investments for purpose. (Business Purpose Commission for Scotland, 2022)

What if we modified one part of this far-reaching prescription for greater common-good economics by focusing on a more mutualist approach that centers worker equity and workplace democracy? Pursuing 2023 as the first ESG "Year of the S" prioritizing social and human capital assets compels us to consider purposeful social economy businesses and ecosystems with these qualities meriting equal regulatory and tax consideration. This way, aspiring worker owners and their host communities can freely choose the enterprise structure locally and culturally best suited for them.

This approach shares risks and rewards, including worker and employee equity to build community wealth; and hybrid, localized models for fulfilling fairly and transparently earned and distributed "citizen share" (Quirk, 2022) prosperity for stakeholders as shareholders. Such structural innovation is already occurring in Scotland, in Preston in adjacent northern England, in Spain and Italy's Basque and Emilia

Romagna regions; and in other proliferating, social economy ecosystems across Europe, the United States, Canada, Japan, Republic of Korea, Latin America, the Caribbean (such as Puerto Rico), and, increasingly, Africa.

A generic example outlined below shows a purposeful, worker-owned, mutualist, social economy business models from the British Academy and purposeful business Scotland models integrated with almost 70 years of Mondragon cooperative experience:

- **Law:** Adopts and commits to a purpose by law:
  - o Mondragon example: UNIVERSALITY — The co-op supports all efforts to promote workplace democracy, the cooperative model, individual freedom and self-fulfillment through ownership, and higher, broader, and deeper levels of civic equity.
  - o 1worker1vote goal: An 18th UN SDG goal of "universally inclusive, individual and community, stakeholder equity and democratic governance." This acknowledges that the foundational policy for a fair and aspirational economy rests on inclusive local-stakeholder (worker and employee) ownership undergirded by workplace democracy practices.
- **Regulation:** Adopts a social license to operate (if regulated).
- **Ownership:** Seeks shareholders committed to the purpose:
  - o Mondragon example: DEMOCRATIC ORGANISATION — The principle of "one worker, one vote" shall prevail throughout the co-op, including the annual General Assembly and the election of the Board of Directors. Every worker-owner owns an equal share and has an equal vote through "one class" ownership.
- **Governance:** Has inclusive governance and values that support delivery of purpose:
  - o Mondragon example: PARTICIPATION IN MANAGEMENT — The goal is for "ownership" to become more than just the value of a share. Workers undertake the responsibilities of ownership in their co-op by participating in management positions and as members of the co-op's board of directors, by striving for inter-cooperation and competitive excellence, and by ensuring that the co-op remains accountable to its worker-owners.
- **Measurement:** Measures delivery of the purpose:
  - o Mondragon example: SOCIAL TRANSFORMATION — A key part of the co-op's mission is to support and invest in the economic, social, and cultural development of its community. Creating jobs, funding development projects, pursuing education, and providing opportunities cooperatively brings about a freer, fairer and more caring society. Mondragon co-ops reinvest a high proportion of their profits, including regular investments, in community funds for job creation – for example, 10% of the net profit of the cooperative is donated to non-profit organizations; Mondragon's Lagun Aro mutual cooperative (owned by other cooperatives) provides social security, unemployment, and health insurance benefits; and Mondragon cooperative members serve as committed community activists.
- **Performance:** States profits (and failures) to fulfil purpose.
- **Finance:** Raises risk capital aligned with purpose from shareholders.

- Mondragon example: INSTRUMENTAL AND SUBORDINATE NATURE OF CAPITAL — Only profitable enterprises provide the workplace freedom for Mondragon cooperatives to align principles with practice. Generally, a corporation sells shares of ownership and management to raise capital, and then hires labor: Mondragon Cooperatives do not sell shares to raise capital. Instead, workers own their cooperative enterprises, choose their management and rent sustaining capital. Within the Mondragon ecosystem, capital is labor's instrument, not its master.

- **Investment:** Establishes partners to make investments for purpose:
  - Increase investment in purposeful businesses by establishing a world-leading ESG investment hub (Webb, 2021).

Deploying localizing versions of this model can help social-economy practitioners to deflect and expose ESG/SDG "purpose-washing" and "virtue signaling" on the part of large multinationals wanting to jump on the latest "doing well by doing good" bandwagon. The stakeholder ownership and governance template we advance achieves this by defining and measuring the good that must be done properly at the onset and then by equitably sharing the "wellness" produced.

Setting fair trade ESG disclosure standards will have a huge impact on how transparency is practiced to benefit future generations. This process will include a bottom-to-top reevaluation of social and environmental externalities in business, and of governance practices that impact frontline, underserved communities, enable systemic racism and poverty, and cripple Earth's capacity to heal.

Research reveals that combining an equity stake with participatory-ownership culture (essentially the definition of a worker cooperative) creates upwardly transformative, shared-purpose businesses and societies. The basic democratic principle valued in nation states and stakeholder economy social enterprises is one human/one vote. An equity share is the right to vote and provides the basis for paradigm-changing culture, combining inclusive and caring community, individualistic civic solidarity mutualism, stability, and self-reliance, leading to flatter inequity curves facilitating more equally fulfilled lives and dignified retirements.

A competitive stakeholder economy marketplace innovating products and services contributes to the collective good, prioritizes strategies and tactics, accelerates entrepreneurial drive, and rewards ability to execute. Profit motive is uplifted beyond the individual to the community, beyond naked self-interest to enlightened societal interest. Shareholders as local stakeholders reject traditional assumptions promoting harmful climate redlining and other societal injustices that produce regressive, extractive practices and outcomes.

These new competitive equations thrive on higher-purpose values and compatible operating structures, and they create sequential downstream virtuous cycles that are aspirational and inspire others.

Already some of the most progressive thinkers and doers throughout global cooperative and organized labor communities see hybrid models (union-coops in the US and UK), workplace solidarity equations (worker councils in Germany), and other practices as offering pathways for workers to become equity and/or values-driven stakeholders. Additional examples (there are many) include the growing use of B Corporation standards (bcorporation.net/certification/meet-the-requirements); the 10 Mondragon and seven International Cooperative principles; as well as the use of open book bargaining, open book participatory budgeting, and open book management by several US union locals.

These modernizing and democratizing tools (potentially a "cooperative-labor ESG" formulation) can represent a more relevant, agile, competitive, and encompassing hybrid shared-ownership future. These approaches become even more impactful and sustaining when buttressed by single-class worker equity and workplace democracy, guaranteeing a voice and a vote through a seat at the enterprise-ownership table (aligning with almost 70 years of the Mondragon cooperative experience).

Increasingly now that investors are paying attention, metrics confirm that companies operating from long-term, purpose-driven, stakeholder primacy models are outperforming those that do not:

- An Oxford/SAID webinar in 2021 pointed out that corporate laggards — those publicly traded, shareholder primacy companies that chase short-term interest rates to capture more than their fair share of $70 trillion sloshing around in the wastelands of the global economy — average less than 17 years' listings.

- Bank of America reported in Q1 2021 that "$4 out of every $10 globally invested go to ESG missions and companies" (Webb, 2021), showing how this new framework can begin to serve as a primary catalyst towards global healing and transformation goals if transparently, relentlessly, and consistently measured.

Expanding on the "economics of mutuality" (eom.org/), Freelancer's Union founder Sara Horowitz asserts: "Mutualism: it's not capitalism and it's not socialism. It's the future" (Horowitz, 2021). This future awaits social economy practitioners working to rebuild a more perfect civil-civic society based on shared community risks and rewards. Consolidating earnings and liabilities leads to mutually beneficial profit distribution, and can integrate stakeholder social, human, and natural capital into societal transformation that is additive, not divisive.

During the 2021 Davos forum, a pandemic-driven "Great Reset" saw 61 companies representing $4.3 trillion in market cap and 7 million employees announce that they had adopted an evolving ESG metrics framework consisting of 21 core metrics and 34 broader ones. Inspired by this, Deloitte, EY, KPMG, and PwC volunteered to ensure that all corporate participants calculate these metrics in the same way. This uniformity is critical: publicly-exposed corporate "purpose-washing" and "green-washing" reveal how shareholder primacy democracy so often becomes something else in practice, with one dollar equaling one vote (echoing America's "pay to play" political system) perfected during publicly-traded shareholder annual meetings (Sorkin, 2019, Kenan Institute, 2021).

At the time, Axios noted that the Davos goal is to allow investors to compare their progress against each other on key environmental, social and governance standards, and to make life a lot easier for regulators and investors to judge companies not just on carbon emissions but on many other areas — from water consumption to the amount they pay in taxes. However, there's no guarantee that any of these savings and benefits will trickle down to stakeholders and their communities. This is because rating compliance does not include net outcome distribution, starting with the most precarious communities and places (Salmon, 2021).

In July 20202, Ra Criscitiello, the SEIU-UHW's deputy research director, observed that Covid-19 has exposed the inherent contradiction of the "servant economy":

Essential workers are often people of color and, because largely misclassified as independent contractors, are denied the protections and benefits of formal employment that are currently so needed. Now more than ever is a time to focus on creating a different kind of economy that centers worker voice, pooled advocacy, employment benefits, and focuses on better work lives for low-wage workers who have historically been undervalued in many undeserved and unproductive ways. (Bird *et al.*, 2020)

It soon became clear in 2021 that goals 8 ("Decent Work and Economic Growth") and 10 ("Reduced Inequality") of the 17 UN SDGs are still necessary but woefully insufficient. Even more clear, the KPIs, values, and purpose metrics imposed by biased standards-setting organizations, publications, and conferences excluded the 99% of humanity that once again would bear the *status quo* burden in traces designed by others more fortunate.

Shouldn't a post-multi-pandemic economic reordering dedicated to flattening unhealthy inequity curves formulate an 18th UN SDG goal? One acknowledging that the foundational policy for a fair and aspirational economy rests on inclusive, broadened, and deepened local-stakeholder (worker and employee) ownership, undergirded by workplace democracy practices?

A purpose-driven "call to arms" must drive an organic campaign to establish mutualist summits where KPIs, metrics and standards are co-established with practitioners. As the Indian novelist Arundhati Roy noted, the quintuple pandemic's five plagues — climate change, Covid, capitalism, un-civic and uncivil democracy, and cultural "originalism" that drives authoritarianism — can serve as catalysts for inclusive, generational, post-pandemic change led by dirt-spoon socioeconomic classes and their social economy allies "ready to imagine another world. And ready to fight for it" (Roy, 2020).

Armed with Purpose: The Campaign Begins
A conversation with Jonathan Sumption and Yascha Mounk in *Persuasion* warns:

Democracies depend on two things. They depend on an institutional framework, and they depend on a cultural background. It isn't usually the institutional framework that fails. That's still there. What fails is the cultural background, which is the desire of people to make it work, the desire of people to respect plurality of opinion, and to accept that sometimes they can't get their way, however important the issue and however right they think they are. In most countries which have lost their democratic status, the institutions are still there, there are still elections of a sort, there are still parliaments — but they are largely meaningless because the culture that sustained them disappeared. (Mounk, 2022)

We took this warning to heart, validated globally on a daily basis, to help start a movement that could restructure and refinance "humanity at work and life" enterprise culture, starting with human- and social-capital allocation that is defined by its practitioners. We decided the best next step would be to kick off a campaign to convene and empower global social economy leaders who are building next-generation human/social capital metrics on climate-security capital investments that correspond to ESG/SDG risk-washing urgency.

Earlier in 2020, we had partnered with Victor Meseguer, director of Solidarity Economy Europe (SEE), and David Levine, president and cofounder of the American Sustainable Business Network (ASBN), to build a working mission and values-aligned framework. The following December 12, on the fifth anniversary of the Paris Accord, SEE and ASBN announced this precedent-setting transatlantic partnership (consisting of over 3.5 million social enterprise and triple-bottom-line business members) to advance business sustainability on all fronts (asbnetwork.org/media-release/social-economy-europe-and-american-sustainable-business-council-mark-fifth-anniversary).

Our goal is to build movement power through convenings around human and social assets, capital, and metrics. We frame this in the context of the global social enterprise-ecosystem-economy, which can encompass for-profits and non-profits, and may take the form of cooperatives, mutualist societies, social businesses, voluntary and charity organizations, foundations, and unions.

Our vision is to unite global social impact investors with mosaic social economy practitioners who are innovating, including, deploying, measuring, and scaling human and social assets as high-road capital. Sara Horowitz describes this process as "a way to build our next safety net in America through local cooperative organizations and practice. Today it exists in four principal areas: unions, cooperatives, mutual aid groups, and faith-based institutions," with global adherents and protocols already leading the way (Horowitz, 2021).

Together with globally distinguished and committed colleagues, we presented, and Ibon chaired, a competitively-awarded panel at the International Cooperative Alliance (ICA) World Cooperative Congress in Seoul, South Korea, in November–December 2021. Attendees, including UN and ICA organizing officials, subsequently called for a global social-economy forum to build mutualist voice and agency, and earn a decision-making seat at all national, regional, multinational, and international forums for ESG/SDG decision-making around performance indicators, metrics, and standards.

Starting in Q1 2022, our consensus-based working group of global forum conveners has grown to include uniquely qualified, innovating pioneers in defining ESG/SDG metrics (UNSSE, 2020) in an SSE (social solidarity economy) context, and specifically by deploying UNRISD SPDIs (UNRISD, 2018-2022). Our campaign-convening team has considerable background and expertise analyzing corporate SPDI omissions, blind spots in the reporting process that can stop human and social capital asset allocations from reaching critical mass, and developing performance metrics from measuring income gaps, tax evasion, gender-income gaps, and workplace governance.

Our campaign purpose is to establish a full-system accounting framework that embeds all of the GAIA (generally accepted integrated accounting) principles (sustainableorganizations.org/GAIA-Principles.pdf) advanced by the Center for Sustainable Organizations; and that also includes UNRISD SDPIs such as "thresholds, allocations, (context-based) materiality, duties and obligations, and commensurability." An aspirational, two-year timeline for the "Global Social Economy SSE Sustainability, Human and Social Capital Convening Campaign," re-branded as the "Own The Metrics" campaign, breaks down as follows:

2022:

1. Convened the conveners to build consensus on an alternative ESG approach to KPIs, metrics and standards which sheds light on neglected dimensions such as human and social dimensions, and prepares for the 2023 Global Social Economy SSE Sustainability, Human & Social Capital Convening Campaign convention.

2. The campaign developed mutualist and inclusive momentum on designing an alternative approach to an SSE sustainability-reporting roadmap, focusing on defining metrics to guide investor-driven profit-seeking, profit-bearing and profitable capital allocation for the common good.

    o   The campaign mission is to build a collective, cooperative, and mutualist voice and agency for development and promotion of sustainability measures, indicators, metrics, and standards from the social-solidarity economy perspective.

    o   The campaign goal is to earn a mandatory, decision-making social economy seat at all national, regional, multinational and international global forums making decisions about sustainability indicators.

3. In the name of full democratic inclusion and prosperity for all, this campaign calls for a global, social economy convening forum to build mutualist voice and agency.

    o   Setting fair trade disclosure standards will have a huge impact on how transparency is practiced to benefit future generations. This process will include a bottom-to-top reevaluation of social and environmental impacts, and how governance practices most acutely impact frontline, underserved communities; disable systemic racism and poverty; and enable Earth's capacity to regenerate.

    o   This campaign convenes the UNRISD SDPI manual as the beginning of a "social economy toolbox" to build an inclusive and comprehensive social enterprise/cooperative business approach that can go beyond the zero-sum Davos/Porto Alegre divide to become more equitable, inclusive, proficient, and caring-economy-compatible in design, practice, measurement, and enforcement. The SDPI manual and process objective is to push the envelope and lead the stakeholders to alternative approaches (context based, trend analysis and transformative indicators), collaborating and not competing with other similar attempts.

2023:

4. Launching the 2023 Own The Metrics Convention for Global Social Economy SSE Sustainability, Human and Social Capital event, most likely in Brussels or Spain Q4 2023; venue, date, time and program to be decided Q2 2023.

In full alignment with our campaign, Social Economy Europe revealed the Spanish government's four-part commitment — announced June 1, 2022, and backed by a budget of more than €800 million, mostly coming from Next Generation EU funds. Goals include:

•   Support workers' buyouts under social economy forms (as workers' cooperatives) to save jobs and companies (in a situation of crisis, or without a successor);

•   Improve competitiveness among social economy SMEs in order to face the green and digital transition with more guarantees to boost digitalization and specialized training in business skills that improve the competitiveness of social economy SMEs;

•   Promote the development of advanced inter-cooperation mechanisms in social economy SMEs to improve their competitiveness and guarantee their sustainability, as well as creating a "hub" to ensure the transfer of research and advances knowledge to social economy enterprises; and

- Strengthen the caring economy and boost short consumption circuits (socialeconomy.eu.org/2022/06/01/a-decisive-moment-for-the-social-economy/).

America's mostly competing and occasionally collaborating worker-buyout conversion leaders could take note and do likewise "to save jobs and companies in a situation of crisis." Federal and state enabling policies could help, starting with two transformative legislative initiatives in the next year:

- Collective Guarantee (proposed US Small Business Administration language to "fund $100 million for a pilot program for eligible cooperatives and employee-owned businesses to receive SBA loan products without the requirement of a personal or entity guarantee");
- California's Power Act (asbnetwork.org/pod/support-california-power-act).

The possibility of a collective guarantee combined with the 10 Mondragon principles (including the seven International Cooperative principles) enshrined in hybrid shared-ownership structures, such as a union-coops with a collective bargaining agreement, demonstrates business model creativity, agility, and inclusivity. It offers a compelling socioeconomic-justice framework that can respond competitively to all four ESG capital sources: societal, human, climate, and financial.

In tandem, a universal social and solidarity economy (SSE) definition, aligned with the EU Social Economy Action Plan (ec.europa.eu/social/main.jsp?catId=1537&langId=en), and clarity from US Securities and Exchange Commission regulations and Congressional legislation, undergirds what Social Economy Europe describes as the "primacy of people and social-environmental purpose over capital, the reinvestment of most profits and surpluses, and democratic and/or participative governance in the form of leading social-economy structures (cooperatives, mutuals, associations/charities, foundations, social enterprises, and emerging models with similar purpose, mission, and values)."

Such transformative thinking is not limited to business school re-imaginers, boardroom visionaries, serial entrepreneurs, movement organizers, academic seers, political leaders, or executive pioneers. In the words of Harvard Business School's Rebecca Henderson, "We are all pebble rollers intending to start an avalanche" towards purpose-driven, values based, high-impact directions.

Activating the avalanche on November 1, 2022, UNRISD, an "Own the Metrics" campaign leader, released its breakthrough *User Manual for Sustainable Development Performance Indicators*, followed by a press conference in Geneva on November 4. The SDPIs, and now its manual, which UNRISD has been "developing collaboratively since 2018," have been heralded as "a major inflection point" (Jonathan Morris, Business for Social Responsibility) and "sustainability history in the making" (Kees Klomp, THRIVE Institute).

On the following day, Wednesday, November 2, choreographed joint press statements (*Better Signals With Less Noise*) by SEE and ASBN highlighted UNRISD's SDPIs as alternative ESG manual as well as the SEE-ASBN-UNRISD Own The Metrics campaign. Together, SEE and ASBN represent well over 3.5 million social-economy and quadruple-bottom-line businesses and business organizations.

On Tuesday, December 13, 2022, the campaign was invited to present Better Signals With Less Noise: UNRISD's Sustainable Development Performance Indicators (SDPIs) Manual and the accompanying SEE-ASBN-UNRISD Own The Metrics 2023 Campaign to the UN multistakeholder meeting: *Social and Solidarity Economy & the SDGs, How can the International Recognition of Social and Solidarity Economy (SSE) Help Achieve the SDGs through Social and Inclusive Innovation?*, United Nations Headquarters, NY.

Own The Metrics's campaign voice contributes to defining and fulfilling the performance standards for "humanity at work and life," so that those doing, innovating, and proving the work earn a proportionally equal seat at the rules-making tables. The UNRISD SDPI manual cooperatively "rocks and rolls" sustainability metrics and conforming capital flows forward into practice (more than 200 companies have adopted these standards since the launch of the SDPI manual in November 2022 and this number should only grow exponentially through the associated Own The Metrics campaign). Concurrently, virtuous cycles are outperforming and out-humanizing shareholder-primacy capitalism's inveterate trickle-down, demeaning, and unsustainable *status quo*.

Together, this is how we begin to leave virtue-signaling and greenwashing in the corporate-retread dust, to reclaim communal and community ownership and sovereignty of stakeholder metrics. The next three mission steps are clear:

- First, mutually convene and act in solidarity on behalf of the most vulnerable with their consent and full stakeholder participation;
- Second, start with natural (climate), human, and social-capital asset design, performance, and measurements;
- Third, do not cede ground no matter how fierce the challenge but "leave it all on the campaign field" by "deciding to be."

References

Bird, A., Conaty, P., Mangan, A., Mckeown, M. Ross, P. & Taylor, S. (2020, July). *Manifesto for Decent Work*. union-coops.uk/a-manifesto-for-decent-work/.

British Academy (2019). *Principles for Purposeful Business*. https://www.thebritishacademy.ac.uk/publications/future-of-the-corporation-principles-for-purposeful-business/.

Business Purpose Commission for Scotland, The (2022, June 28). *Now is the Time for Purpose: Putting Purpose at the Heart of Scottish Business*. https://www.scdi.org.uk/policy/commission-calls-for-purpose-led-recovery-and-growth/.

Ellis, J.E., Colin-Jones, A. & Zugasti, I. (2021). Mondragon: Maintaining resilience through cooperative strategies. In C. Mayer & B. Roche (eds.), *Putting Purpose into Practice: The Economics of Mutuality*. Oxford University Press.

Fraser, D. (2022, June 28). Doing Business on Purpose. *BBC News*. https://www.bbc.com/news/uk-scotland-61975166.

Henderson, R. (2020). *Reimagining Capitalism in a World on Fire*. Hachette.

Horowitz, S. (2021). *Mutualism: Building The Next Economy From The Ground Up*. Random House.

Kenan Institute (2021, November 16). *Is Shareholder Primacy the Democracy of Capitalism?* https://kenaninstitute.unc.edu/kenan-insight/is-shareholder-primacy-the-democracy-of-capitalism/.

McGhee, H. (2021). *The Sum of Us: What Racism Costs Everyone And How We Can Prosper Together*. One World.

Millennium Project (2017, October). *State of the Future 19.0*. http://www.millennium-project.org/state-of-the-future-version-19-0/.

Mounk, Y. (2022, February 12). Jonathan Sumption on the limits of state power. *The Good Fight with Yascha Mounk*. https://www.persuasion.community/p/sumption?r=7y9tn.

Quirk, J. (2022, March 29). The citizen's share. *The Distributist Review*. https://distributistreview.com/archive/the-citizens-share.

Roy, A. (2020, April 3). The pandemic is a portal. *FT.com*. https://www.ft.com/content/10d8f5e8-74eb-11ea-95fe-fcd274e920ca.

Salmon, F. (2021, January 26). Larry Fink to CEOs: Climate risk is investment risk. *Axios*. https://www.axios.com/larry-fink-blackrock-climate-change-48849f32-baa8-4acb-954d-0edb0eda826d.html.

Sorkin, A.R. (2019, August 20). How shareholder democracy failed the people. *New York Times*. https://www.nytimes.com/2019/08/20/business/dealbook/business-roundtable-corporate-responsibility.html.

UNRISD (2018-2022). *Sustainable Development Performance Indicators*. https://www.unrisd.org/en/research/projects/sustainable-development-performance-indicators.

UNSSE (2020, August 5). *Social and Solidarity Economy (SSE) and the Sustainable Development Goals (SDGs)*. https://unsse.org/2020/08/05/social-and-solidarity-economy-sse-and-the-sustainable-development-goals-sdgs/.

Webb, D. (2021, February 26). *Friday Funds: '$4 out of Every $10 of Global Equity Inflows are now in ESG*. https://www.responsible-investor.com/Friday-Funds-4usd-out-of-every-10usd-of-global-equity-inflows-are-now-in-ESG/.

CHAPTER 7

The Footprints of the Catholic Church's Social Doctrine in Mondragon's Experience: Its Future Projection

Jésus María Herrasti

Cooperatives must not be closed worlds, but instead centers of social radiation. We do not live in a world we have conquered but in a battlefield for social justice and for a more human and just order. (*Reflections 433*, Arizmendiarrieta, *n.d.*)

Introduction

The objective of this chapter is to make a brief presentation of Mondragón's experience, to point out the relevant role of D. José M. Arizmendiarrieta as the person inspiring all of its development, and to make reference to the principles of the Catholic Church's social doctrine that had great importance in the motivation of D. José M. and his closest collaborators.

Mondragón's experience has been a practical fashioning of an economic and business reality for over 50 years. It is also an aspiration to provide a theoretical frame that can then be applied to new situations and future challenges and to motivate other possible leaders to assume the commitment and leadership needed to work together for fairer and more equitable society, that can extend to enterprises and society, especially those realities with whom communities can be configured.

Mondragón's Experience: History, Foundation & Context

We do not aspire to economic development as an end but as a means. (*Reflections 029*, Arizmendiarrieta, *n.d.*)

Mondragón's reality today is not the result of a premeditated and detailed plan, but of a continual process of decisions that were adopted and adequate to each moment's demands, concretized in acts that responded to the aspirations of its members. This included overcoming competitor challenges, attending to new social and organizational needs with the purpose of achieving growth and development that provided social coverage to a major part of society, and resulted in the construction of a framework of regulations, norms, and habits that make up what can be considered an organizational and business model that extends to its social environment.

The Mondragón reality was named for many years "The Mondragón Experience." In my view, the expression "experience" reflects better what happened in its process of development. Experience means learning. In reality, it implies that you open the door to new knowledge and extend the aspirations to new objectives. One is always in search of the collective betterment, facing new challenges, and trusting people and their commitment. Don José María Arizmendiarrieta inspired the development of this Experience that was projecting the systematic improvement of the person and society based in the principles of the Catholic Church's social doctrine.

It all started in 1941 with the arrival of Don José María Arizmendiarrieta to Mondragón, where he was recently assigned as a diocesan priest. He found a reality traumatized by the devastating consequences of the 1936-1939 Civil War. The economy was destroyed. Society was divided by the gravity of the conflict and as a consequence, there was a great need for regeneration of the social structures, recovery of coexistence and to make possible a future that could offer development options for everyone.

Don José María identified areas that he considered important and critical such as education, work, and health, which are the base to strengthen social justice and equal opportunities. He created the *Escuela Profesional* (Professional School), the seed of Mondragón University, to make youth education accessible to all, many of whom became future cooperative worker members. He created a new business model for the working world, characterized by the participation of workers and by its democratic functioning. His first step into the health system was oriented towards mothers with the installation of a maternity ward, which he later expanded to a concern for health in general, by opening a hospital.

In his first efforts, his conviction was not enough to modify the then businesses' posture. He thought that participation from workers was needed in the common project of the enterprise, in the property and in the results to build a more harmonic society. Given the impossibility of the transformation of the existing enterprises, he decided to create a new type of enterprise able to adhere to the cooperative formula, due to the fact that the law that regulated cooperatives offered the only framework with that possibility. That is how the first cooperative was created in 1956.

A few years later, the need to strengthen the financing capacity arose and D. José María suggested the creation of a credit cooperative (Caja Laboral Popular, known today as Laboral Kutxa) to be able to dedicate popular savings to the promotion of cooperatives. Caja Laboral Popular was established in 1959. The first slogan of "*Libreta o maleta*" (checkbook or suitcase), meaning savings or emigration, was very well known and expressive. This banking alternative was rewarded with important resources that helped significantly in the creation of new cooperatives.

By the end of the 1960s the commercial cooperative groups were created to coordinate and create cohesion between the cooperatives and create a common fund to address downturns in the economic cycles, as well as to create new cooperatives and more job opportunities. In this way, through intercooperative agreements, they shared their results and met their financial needs, strengthening their development, and reducing the risks to their businesses.

The cooperatives also committed to social contributions of 10% of profits to promote education and culture. This fostered the creation of Mondragón University, and numerous primary and secondary schools (*ikastolas*) for promoting the Basque language, *Euskera*. This resulted in a vast network of educational cooperatives in the Basque Country.

We have been able to see different instances that were key and focused on a future vision – attending to the common interest, risking innovative solutions, and based in trust and commitment of everyone. Many of these decisions have been embodied in the different norms, procedures, and organizational decisions that constitute the heritage of the "Experience" and have been the subject of much research.

The *Annual Report* numbers for 2020-2021 reflect the dimension attained by the Mondragón Group (Mondragon Corporation, 2022). Today, it is amongst the most important enterprises in the world within the cooperative sector, with annual total income of €11,482 million and 81,507 jobs (*Fortune*, 2022). Noteworthy is the presence of the industrial group that bills €5,271 million a year and employs 40,729 workers, of which 74% are cooperative partners. Also, their activities extend through different countries in Europe, America, and Asia, producing high technological value goods, including equipment and components, which compete against worldwide industry leaders. There are 14,455 industrial jobs in plants outside their territory (Mondragon Corporation, 2022). Sales from the distribution sector are also remarkable, reaching €5,595 million, close to the volume of the Industrial Area, with 38,523 jobs. Its sales are directed to the Spanish Market (Mondragon Corporation, 2022).

Naturally, the social impact that comes from the 81,507 jobs is remarkably high. The corresponding profit sharing generated from the distributions and possible capitalized benefits offer a considerable level of wellbeing to each person. Also, their effect on society is greater for the concentration of cooperatives in certain provincial counties. According to the study *Datos de Pobreza de Euskadi* (EUSTAT, 2022), led by the Basque Government, the presence of poverty oscillated between 10.6% of Gasteiz county to 1.8% in Alto Deba county in which some of the most important cooperative enterprises are located and where the share of cooperative workers is greater than the total of other workers. Another contribution to this reality is the worker compensation policy in the cooperatives governed by a ratio of one to six between the lowest and highest paid members.

All of these facts occurred in changing and challenging environments. We have to remember that they were initiated during the post-war period in an impoverished and divided society, in which religion served to maintain solidarity within the community. In the 1950s, the process involved moving from an autocratic economy to a more open free market. The political regime was not ruled by democratic principles until the approval of the *Constitution* in 1977 (D. José María had died the previous year). Later, the entry to the European Union produced a notable increase of competition and inroads into the national economy with accelerated incorporation of technology and expansion of markets due to globalization.

The cooperative model already included many novelties within the organization of an enterprise, in the extension of the organizational spirit to the group of workers: the directors, technicians and the rest of the workers. Growing complexity of the environment of these businesses made management of them ever more demanding. Notwithstanding some flaws, we can say that the outcome has been satisfactory judging by the results obtained; for being able to renew principles, ways, and conducts, for having achieved relevance and a social knowledge of democratic management; whose result can be observed in the present reality.

The Presence of the Footprints of the Catholic Church's Social Doctrine

Through the study of the history of the Experience, we have had the opportunity to cite some important moments, the risks and opportunities and the broad participation of the partner workers that assumed their responsibilities with generosity. They excelled in their general interest and in orienting their efforts towards the growth and extension of the Experience to reach more workers and society.

D. José M. Arizmendiarrieta approached young people who later became the founders of the Experience through church institutions such as *Hermandad Obrera de Acción Católica* (HOAC), a Catholic Action Workers Movement. They shared with him a commitment to work for a society with more options for personal development and social solidarity in the community.

As a reflection of the source of inspiration of the first cooperatives, we offer the text of the *Social Statutes* of the cooperative Fagor Electrodomésticos in 1975 which states the following in its third article of *Normas Fundamentales*:

> The cooperative formula is adopted for its ideal characteristics for the aggregation of and the rule of the production factors, to be done in harmony with the dignity and aspirations of human work within a frame that is human and Christian. (Fagor Electrodomésticos, 1975)

In later versions, due to demands of a legal nature, these explanatory articles were set aside. On the other hand, the cooperative group members have become more secular and diverse ideologically. Nevertheless, it maintains in its core, the relevance of its cooperative formula, the importance of work, its dignity and solidarity.

The Mondragon Experience has developed in detail and practical terms the contents of the framework of human and Christian solidarity. If we look at Chapter VI of the Catholic Church document, the *Compendium of the Social Doctrine of the Church* (*Compendio del la Doctrina Social de la Iglesia*) titled, "The Human Work," we see that the Mondragón "Experience" is reflected in many of its sections (Pontifical Council for Justice & Peace, 2005). Here are some examples:

- Work represents a fundamental dimension of human existence.
- The dignity of work.
- The intrinsic social dimension of work.
- Work is superior to any other production factor.
- Participation of workers in the property.
- Public and private property to guarantee the economy to the service of humans.

- The instruction and educational systems should not neglect human and technical development.
- Dignity of workers and respect towards their rights.
- All members of the enterprise must be aware that the community in which they work represents a good for all.
- To give expression to humanity at work at a global level.

We can also find other shared themes in Chapter VII: "Economic Life" (Pontifical Council for Justice & Peace, 2005):

- The moral dimension of the economy allows us to understand that economic efficiency and the promotion of a solidary development are goals that are linked to each other.
- The right to economic initiative.
- The creative dimension is an essential element of human action, also in the entrepreneurial arena.
- The components of a business must be conscious that the community in which they operate represents a benefit for everyone.
- Recognizes the proper function of the proceeds.

All of these aspects are evident in everyday functions of the enterprises. They are not consciously embedded in Christian norms, and habits but have been incorporated historically in the cooperatives through the influence of D. José M. Arizmendiarrieta. In the history of the Mondragon Experience, it is possible to point out the important developments for the betterment of society and in the accumulation of a social capital that shapes its core values.

Times Accelerate; Start and Renew

If one desires that economy activity attain its human objective, multiple reforms and, better yet, a change of mentality, are indispensable. It is definitely the human person who is the author, center and end of all economic and social life (*Reflections 007*, Arizmendiarrieta, *n.d.*)

We need to pause for a brief moment in our activities to contemplate the reality and the trends that mark our future. We need to see the inconsistencies, to be conscious of the pleasing and conformist postures, to elevate the vision and aspirations, without rejecting them due to their difficulty or their superficial analysis. Do it with an interested eye, imagining and designing paths for its continuity. Almost everything is possible; especially if its goal is worthy. We are in search of general well-being and we act constantly, dedicating the necessary time and resources.

We live better than in any other era, but at the same time, poverty and inequality persist. We enjoy more resources than previous generations, but we are not sure that we will be able to keep them in the future. Growth is on hold while businesses struggle to survive.

We are investing in education and we have the best prepared population in history but we cannot secure these opportunities for everyone. Employment forecasts are become worse. All of that is accompanied by accelerated changes and with the sense of being dragged, sometimes run over, more than being able to maintain our own rhythm.

We must ask ourselves if, with the simple application of the current rules, and the repetition of past experiences, without facing renewed aspirations, whether we can respond to our changing world. Can we respond to new demands arising from technological development, communications, exchange between countries and people, and globalization, with all its overwhelming capacity for transformation of the world?

To think and reflect on the challenges that concern our society, the commitments that could arise, is not an act that we can simply do in our spare time. It is something necessary. It is the base upon which our future aspirations and actions rely. Nothing can be changed or improved without starting from firm and current convictions.

For that, we need an activator mentality that motivates us, a transformative attitude which leads us to improve, reduce problems and to improve the social situation and that of the people who are a part of it. A mentality that will give us strength to overcome inertia based on difficulty or ignorance of the solutions to adopt, or in false priorities that tend to justify our lack of activity. How many times have we recited that phrase: "Actions equal love" (*obras son amores*)...It is the actions that will shape and will finalize the theoretical proposals, offering us the opportunity to acquire and add new ways and experiences.

The Need to Transform the Principles into Practical Functions

We need to face realities rather than hypotheses. We also need to reflect more on facts and concrete action than a pure ideological formulations. (*Reflections 390*, Arizmendiarrieta, *n.d.*)

The diverse studies and documents that illustrate the Mondragón Experience tend to have historical content, a certain degree of analysis of the circumstances that motivated the many experiences, and evaluation of results. We can safely assume that its main orientation is to highlight the positive legacy and with that, to provide evidence to support the interest and convenience of similar initiatives with the commitment of the people who get to know the impact of the transformations that result in new experiences.

Nevertheless, for the successful completion of all processes of change, besides obtaining a shared conviction of principles and values that motivate it, it is necessary to develop complementary procedures and organizational rules. We need to assure that in everyday work, small and big decisions rely on a value relevant frame. In the same way it is necessary to deploy application of formulas to care for the great aspirations such as internal democracy, equal opportunities, the fair distribution of the social results, solidarity, etc. We need to establish guides to the exercise of personal and social responsibility and the definition of a governance model.

Many of these aspects have been collected from legal and normative frameworks for general applications. In addition, each co-operative has their unique particularities, their internal bylaws and other social norms. All of these constitute the heritage or social capital of organizational knowledge, and of regulation of singular aspects of cooperative enterprises and that develop social specificities in relation to other companies.

When we try to take advantage of a specific social experience for its transferability and potential of application in a different reality, we find that the efforts of transmission are centered in a labor of sensitizing, transforming or diffusing our principles and values. Even the essential ones may not be applied sufficiently.

Below, a brief consideration of some of these aspects is illustrated:

- Favorable fiscal regulation of cooperatives according to degree of workers participation as shareholders in the company.
- Legal demand of the application of Reserve Funds so the cooperative can respond to financial requirements.
- Dedicate funds to the formation and social promotion of the environment.
- Statutory definition of the governing aspects: the role of the Administrative Council and Direction. In my opinion, this needs a more elaborated construction for large enterprises and entrepreneurial groups.
- Status of cooperative groups along with their diverse ways of integration: strategic, functional or service (commercial, purchase, Inspection + Delivery (I+D), etc.).
- Mixed cooperative status where the partners are workers and an enterprise cooperative or non-cooperative.
- International cooperative, without current experience.
- The right to promote and its regulations: status and bylaws.
- Evaluation of the work according to responsibility and contribution to annual results
- Rules for the regulation of the retributive level, refer to the actualization of the level of annual retribution depending on the economic situation, business forecast, balances and financial needs, etc.
- Definition of the maximum level of retributive level; these last three elements are fundamental to the definition of the retributive policies and the personalized distribution of the results. They are defined in every company's bylaws.
- Rules for General Assembly, Social Council and other ways of participation.

Some of these are located in areas of decisions to be adopted by the cooperatives themselves and others correspond to other institutions that decide on fiscal and regulatory aspects that shape the legal framework of cooperatives. What is intended to be highlighted is that, in addition to their conceptual definition, they incorporate their quantitative ideas for a greater clarification of the objectives to be achieved and the improvement of their capacity for commitment. For example, these quantitative measures include fixing the levels of tax contribution, the share of profits allocated to reserve funds, the amount of resources allocated to training, the setting of valuation indices for the various jobs, the relationship between maximum and minimum remuneration, the exercise of the right to vote and indicating the amount necessary for decision-making according to its importance, etc. Some other important rules or procedures may be missing, but at least, some representative and particular ones of the Mondragón Experience have been pointed out.

We know that the definition, development and, in some cases, revisions or actualizations of experiences such as Mondragón are done from the moment of their creation and continue with the incorporation of new inputs. Additionally, changes will follow the evolution of initiatives taken in the presence of new challenges in the economic environment and the market, or due to the surge of modern technology and lastly, the acquisition of social goals deemed desirable and developed.

The coordination of these tools, organizational forms, and experiences are key to formulating practical ways for the ideological commitment to be transformed into a work plan that is achievable and that proves its goodness in the results obtained. All of them could be called "functional practices."

In the same way, it is useful when we note the areas to cover in new research and areas in which the improvement of the development of the social experiences will be demanded in the future, as an instrument to compare similar schemes among different cooperatives situated in their respective social environments and be able to tell them apart based on their respective advantages. This way, we can move forward progressively from a general knowledge that normally serves to promote a first interest to continue with its gradual implementation in the other fields such as the constitution of society, its status, norms and follow up references.

> The radicalism of the cooperative proposal, in face of development, appealing to the economic, personal, communal and integral concourse of its believers, faces the alternative of success or complete failure. Cooperativism requires people with strong spirit, or at least people who are willing to risk it all. Therefore, it is not a formula that fits everyone, but the biggest mistake that we could make would be to be place our demands at the level of the weakest, since in such case it would be impossible to reach higher levels. (*Reflections 538*, Arizmendiarrieta, *n.d.*)

Mondragon's Relevance for a New Generation

One of the greatest achievements of the Mondragón Experience has been its ability to attract a diverse group of people to work together for their shared benefit. Mondragon is often viewed as a unique experience grounded in Basque culture and Catholic social justice values. In reality, it has been a diverse group that has created a safe and inclusive space for people from across the religious and political spectrum. In a world that is increasingly divided on partisan and religious lines, the norms of the Mondragon cooperators suggest that this too can be overcome when we adhere to principles and practices that allow for democratic and transparent practices in how we work together.

In this chapter we have reviewed the history of the Mondragón Experience, its foundations and its projection. Many of its characteristics were formulated and manifested in the decades of the 1960s to the 1980s. In those years the needs felt by Basque society were more immediate; they were poorer and with fewer resources, their primary aspiration was the development of basic conditions of life. We have also seen that the will to serve the community and the progressive creation of a more just society gave rise to a social impulse that made possible a considerable improvement in the socio-economic situation.

The world of work has changed dramatically since the founding of the Mondragon cooperatives. It is no longer a world that is bound by a time clock and the assembly line. Today's workers face new challenges as they seek to create a better work experience. Technology has created more options as well as more risks for workers. Today we urgently need to address global challenges in different areas: the economy, caring for nature and overcoming social inequalities.

When we look at the discourse of the solidarity and social economy, we see that on measures of sustainable development goals and socially responsible investing or ESG (Environmental, Social and Governance) factors, Mondragon has been ahead of the curve but not always "perfect." It is always in the process of seeking to become more perfect. It has demonstrated that as a business group working at scale and internationally, it is possible to be both purpose driven and guided by spiritual principles for the common good.

We know that an adequate management of desires and aspirations requires the setting of quantitative objectives but they are not sufficient to offer people all the intensity of motivation from the ethical and moral principles that answer the great questions of life. What is the foundation of our existence and what is essential for human development? What do we need to foster our creative capacity and that strengthens the personal commitment of each one of us to the larger good? In the Mondragon Experience, Father José María Arizmendiarrieta was the person who offered us this rich vision.

References

Arizmendiarrieta, J.M. (n.d.). *Pensamientos de Don José María Arizmendiarrieta* [*Reflections of Don José María Arizmendiarrieta*] (Cherie Herrera; Cristina Herrera; David Herrera; Teresita Lorenzo; Virgil Lorenzo, Trans.). Mondragon, Spain: Otalora.

EUSTAT. (2022, May 9). *Tablas estadísticas Pobreza y Desigualdades Sociales*. Retrieved from Eustat - Euskal Estatistika Erakundea - Instituto Vasco de Estadística: https://www.eustat.eus/estadisticas/tema_136/opt_0/tipo_1/ti_pobreza-y-desigualdades-sociales/temas.html.

Fagor Electrodomésticos (1975). *Normas Fundamentales*. Mondragón, Guipuzkoa, Spain: Fagor Electrodomésticos.

Fortune (2022, May 9). *2021 Change the World Mondragon*. Retrieved from Fortune Mondragon Company Profile: https://fortune.com/company/mondragon/change-the-world/.

Global Impact Investing Network (2022, September 28). *What You Need to Know About Impact Investing*. Retrieved from GIIN: https://thegiin.org/impact-investing/need-to-know/.

Mondragon Corporation (2022, May 9). *Basic Data*. Retrieved from Mondragon *Annual Report 2020-2021*: https://www.mondragon-corporation.com/urtekotxostena/datos-basicos.php?l=en.

Pontifical Council for Justice & Peace. (2005). *Compendium of the Social Doctrine of the Church*. Washington, DC: United States Conference of Catholic Bishops (USCCB PUB).

Wylie, M. (2020, January 15). *How Much it Costs to Start a Business in Every Industry*. Retrieved from LendingTree.com: https://www.lendingtree.com/business/startup-costs-by-industry/.

CHAPTER 8

Mentoring Practices from Spain's Basque Region – 1: The Gaztenpresa Case Study

An Interview with Oscar Muguerza Telleria, Vice-President, Gaztenpresa Foundation (June 28, 2022)

Chris Clamp & Michael Peck

Oscar Muguerza is a member of Laboral Kutxa (laboralkutxa.com), a co-operative bank based in Northern Spain, which is part of the Mondragon Group (mondragon-corporation.com/en/), one of the 10 largest Spanish industrial groups. He has been working there for 20 years, in various positions, most of them in branches, rising to Head of Business Banking in 2009. He is responsible for product development, marketing, pricing, commercial policy and international development for business clients, including entrepreneurship and microfinance. Oscar is also responsible for intermediary programs of the European Investment Fund, such as Employment and Social Innovation (EaSI) and InnovFin.

Concurrently, Oscar is vice-president and coordinator for the Gaztenpresa Foundation (gaztenpresa.org/) and serves on its board. Gaztenpresa was envisioned in 1994 to foster the creation and consolidation of jobs by creating and supporting small scale proprietary businesses in the Basque Country (Spain). The aim of this Foundation is to support the development of employment, mainly amongst young people. Its portfolio of services includes "end-to-end" consulting, training and support in the initial moment of launching the initiative, and throughout its consolidation. Gaztenpresa provides financing in situations where clients are considered high risk, according to banking standards.

Michael: Oscar, first of all, thank you so much for participating in this interview and for always being our interlocutor helping us pioneer understanding of Gaztenpresa's successful methodologies to overseas audiences. Our first question relates to your individual voice and vision regarding Gaztenpresa's mentoring of entrepreneurs based on your experiences over many years. We would like to understand what has motivated you to be a Gaztenpresa mentor?

Oscar: Well, let me start by saying that Gaztenpresa is more than 25 years old. Mentoring began in 2014. It is a relatively young project. Considering what we do, it is one of the youngest projects. Curiously, it is also one of the projects that when you are looking for collaboration, it is one of the aspects that most attracts the attention of potential outside stakeholders. It allows us to collaborate with municipalities, the Basque government, with different stakeholders. They say it's very synergistic. We can add this to practically any project.

Why did we start at Gaztenpresa with mentoring? We started because it was necessary. We saw in that phase they taught us that once the business is open, we cannot leave that project alone, to go our own way, saying "We have lent you money, we have financed you and such." We saw that projects are weak and need ongoing support for a while.

So we turned to the methodology of Youth Business International (youthbusiness.org/) and Youth Business Spain. We are the creators of Youth Business Spain (youthbusiness.org/member/youth-business-spain-spain). What's more, I'm on the board of Youth Business Spain. So, it has provided us the methodology and at the same time a process.

The first thing is the training for the mentor. We have seen that it is a particularly important phase because in the end when you say to a person "Do you want to be a mentor of Gaztenpresa?", many people say "Yes." Then they say "What do I have to do? I have to design a business plan; how do I do that? No, you have to do this, this and that." It is the phase in which we tell them what it means to be a mentor, what it means to accompany an entrepreneur – which means not to intervene too much.

We've had mentors who have not been effective. I'm going to describe a case of someone who was also my collaborator, at one point one of the most powerful people I have had as a collaborator, but an inflexible person, very rigid like an Excel sheet. Then he went to the first interview and when he saw the financials, he said "You have to close." I said, "Closing? Iñaki (his name was Iñaki), you can't tell him that. You have to help him." He replied, "No, I help him by closing." It can't be. So sometimes those sorts of things have happened to us.

The relationship between the mentor and the mentee is just as important. There are two parts -- there is a feeling, and there is understanding, synergy, that all this flows. This is important. In the matching phase, the Youth Business methodology helped us a lot. We are investing in that training every year, even now with a pandemic we are also investing in training. Every new mentor has to go through a training process, which takes six hours, more or less, to complete. At the same time, we also do an important follow-up. There are people within Gaztenpresa who are in contact especially in relationships at the beginning; the standard relationship is one year.

We are talking to the two (mentor/mentee) as a pair, individually also a little, to see how it goes. We think that's very relevant. Then we usually leave enough freedom to the two parties to determine the nature of the assistance. That's something I've learned a lot about in my personal experience. We try to match experience of a sector, for example when a farmer needs a mentor.

As an example, I am going to tell you about three cases in which I have participated. The first case was a Brazilian musician, who participated in the World Talent. Jairo, his name was Jairo, and he was a snake oil salesman. I don't know if that translates into English. A very commercial person, friend of everyone, hugs, super friendly. That for a musician is very good. He knew how to sell super well. For a musician that is super important.

So he knew how to sell very well. What was missing? He lacked financial management and management knowledge. The example I always give is that the first few times he did weddings, he played at weddings. I asked him "How do you decide how to quote the price of weddings?" Answer: "I look at the bride and groom like that and I say it is worth so much." Well, that's a system like any other, but let's review that system.

So we looked at the Excel sheet. We said, let's see how many musicians have you taken? Four. How much do you pay each? €100. Let's consider how many kilometers away, car, petrol, food, other expenses. You have just lost €100. No way. Either reduce expenses or raise income, there is not much mystery there. Then he started trading higher. There were weddings that he didn't get but he really did well. Then there was another issue. This was how to identify his business segment with companies to which you will be able to charge more. In fact, I play in one of our assemblies and well that part also helped him develop another line of business. In this case, the help was financial management, and management.

In the second case, it was luxury bicycles, worth €8,000 or €10,000, custom made. On the first day, the entrepreneur came to me with 20 Excel spreadsheets. He had plans, his cash position, everything. In this case he didn't know how to sell. His problem was that he knew how to produce, he produced in a carpentry shop, he did it very well, he had everything very well controlled financially, but he lacked marketing. All the efforts we made were concentrated on how to sell, selection of the public, such as approaches to the market, all the marketing portion. You have to look for the complementary part that may be missing.

The third project during the pandemic was a Microsoft installation software company. Well, actually what they were looking for were ways to see that what they were doing was OK. Then we did a review, due diligence, audit. They were very friendly, we went over all aspects of the company, financial, commercial, hiring people and we were commenting, here's how you do this. It was like an audit process. Well, he told me you've helped me a lot. I told him I haven't contributed much. He told me the tranquility that you are giving me is very great. You don't know what that is. In fact, Luis, which is the name of this person, we have engaged him as a mentor.

I believe that the key to success is in seeking complementarity, in filling the gaps. You have to have well defined profiles of the mentors -- what they can contribute. But as good as our mentors are, most are management profiles, financial profiles, marketing profiles. It costs us more, for example, when we have a very nice project that is agricultural with solar energy and though we have been looking, we did not have in our mentor profile someone who knew the agricultural world well. We have already found someone and we have looked for a mentor almost tailored to this project. We really thought that what was needed was someone who knew technically about that particular business. For us, that's the key, complementarity, synergy and then monitor the process both at the beginning and later so that the project flows.

Michael: This so interesting because when Caja Laboral started in 1959 and spun off all the other Mondragon cooperatives, like LKS, that is exactly what Caja Laboral was doing, it was mentoring. So, we are sort of "back to the future." Except now you are reaching the community outside Mondragon. I really think this approach aligns the past and present. I remember when we had those discussions with the municipal government of Bilbao about the immigrant communities and how the success of cities and neighborhoods depends on how well they integrate and bring people together instead of pushing people apart. In the USA, we have so much recent experience separating people where what we need are more reasons to come together. What is your assessment of how well Gaztenpresa fulfils that role?

Oscar: I would say we don't do anything special. For us a person who was born in Bilbao, or a person who was born in Africa, Germany or Pakistan, are the same. There is no difference, not in color, not in gender, not in age, nothing, zero. That means we don't do anything special either. If we still develop that relationship with these stakeholders that we talk about, we approach stakeholders to collaborate with stakeholders who are dedicated to working with immigrant people. Then internally we do nothing special. For me the difference is that there is a higher level of need in the person. That's very good, because it makes people strive harder. It makes people have to fight more. That's very good.

Then on the other hand the challenge is that they are people who are more rooted in friends, family members who at some point can help you. That in practice for me implies two things. That they get into micro projects which are small which is self-employment with far less impact. That phenomenon is not a problem, but sometimes it's a bit limiting. Then sometimes it also creates financing problems since the costs of administering the loan may not be adequately covered by the percentage charged on the project and there are no guarantees. That is what happens with Laboral Kutxa as a financial institution and is the part we have to work. There we are using a lot the European Investment Fund, a line of €125 million for microcredits. The European Investment Fund endorses an important part of the project. That allows us to help people who have recently arrived.

In addition, we are participating in a pilot project of the European Investment Fund that combines financing with business development services. They are very interested in how we are doing also in Gaztenpresa. I believe that 15% of Gaztenpresa's credits correspond to non-native people.

We have very nice cases; in fact I think it was last Christmas we had a meeting with the participants of the European Investment Fund telling them what we were doing and it generated a lot of interest in their part. In the end I think that in the case of immigrants what you have to pursue is to have more layers, more elements, more tools that help to fill the gaps in those things that happen to them. Support is critical, not just financial support.

Normally, very few immigrants come to mentoring. Jairo is an example, but I think the work is in the initial part, in the pairing of the mentor with the person. These are very simple businesses: it is a bar, a shop, a stall in a flea market, it is a hairdresser, it is a taxi driver. These are the types of projects to which mentoring is applied. Well, to a taxi driver what you are going to tell him or her, to drive kilometers? That's kind of the first thing you have to say. But for the aspect of pairing, coaching is important. Perhaps also to help with guarantees of other types that these people do not have access to.

Michael: The United States is seeing what we call "The Great Resignation," people leaving their jobs and not wanting to return to office buildings. They prefer to work from a home or neighborhood base. What we are talking about is people need better, more affordable and sustainable housing, but we can also help by creating a more fulfilling and productive work experience from the home. What some call here the hybrid work office formula. There is a major public and private sector debate on how best to do this. It seems to me that Laboral Kutxa has always been at the forefront of sustainable housing, affordable housing, cooperative housing and that now with the amount of social distancing everyone has experienced, have people been thinking about this?

Oscar: Not really. Here there has been some talk about that movement, but it does look more like a movement in the United States. I don't think there has been much of that here. Yes, there is a lot of movement of teleworking, of working from home. We ourselves in Laboral Kutxa have implemented a telecommuting program 40% of the time since May 2022. I telecommute two days a week. Today I am in the office, but on Friday I will be working from home.

Here, more, there has been the phenomenon, what we have seen, that people have become more timid. People who could think about starting their own business because they were not comfortable in their work has decreased. In Spanish we say, "Better the devil you know than the devil you don't." But our experience has been the opposite. Almost more has been produced and we have seen in Gaztenpresa projects, in 2020 and 2021, they have been years in which we have done something less than half of the normal, that is it has been reduced a lot. Just as 2022 started very well, in January, February and March we have made almost pre-pandemic levels. But April and May are very weak again and we are all attributing it to the issue of Ukraine. That again people say, well, crisis is coming, energy has gone up a lot, everything is going up a lot, inflation is almost at 10%, so people are apprehensive.

In what you said about the conditions of housing and such, is that we are working a lot in Laboral Kutxa but more from an issue of environment and sustainability. Here we have in Europe what they call the "Next Generation" funds, which is a very important program of the European Union in which there are many millions of subsidies and aid for installing many solar panels, both in companies and in homes, housing rehabilitation for the energy issue, there is a real boom. But we are facing that a little more from Laboral Kuxta, seeing a little more information, processing of projects and financing. We are very focused on both the company and individuals.

Michael: This is so interesting. It would be nice to revisit in two or three years and see what has changed here and what has changed there. Because it is not the first time that we have gone in completely different directions for similar reasons. So far, we have talked a little bit about why Gaztenpresa is unique, now how do you see it beyond the geography of the Basque Country or maybe Navarra, or Cataluña or Spain, even beyond those borders?

Oscar: I believe that Gaztenpresa because it is a union between a bank, in this case a cooperative bank or financial institution and a provider of non-financial services or business development services, is the key. For example, we are members of the European Micro Finance Network. We have the General Assembly in June. There you see either banks, financial institutions or small financial institutions that give microcredits or you see foundations, associations, many things that give business development services.

So, of course, if you only give the microcredits because you lack the other part, if you only give business development services or even some micro-credits because you lack all the power of a financial institution… I think that mix is what makes Gaztenpresa powerful. I remember the last meeting was in October, we were there and those from Spain who were there went to dinner and there were people from foundations and such and they said as you have here Laboral Kutxa, this allows you another uplift, another power.

Although of course Gaztenpresa has a budget of almost €1 million per year that is not a giant budget, it has funding bases similar to those that a foundation can have, but then within what is the activity, that combination for me is the powerful thing. It is a combination based on mutual trust that we have been working on for many years and not only is it a long term trust, but when we have done this social impact, we have really done it between three people from Laboral Kutxa and two people from Gaztenpresa that we have designed with external help throughout this whole process.

We have invested a lot of time; we have a risk map with Laboral Kutxa. For example, an important risk is that business plan I talked about before and Gaztenpresa says it is viable; the project is reliable and Laboral Kutxa that has a risk department says "No, no, I think not." We have set indicators of what percentage of companies that are viable for Gaztenpresa do not end up receiving financing. We've always followed that up informally, because hey, what's wrong? But now we decide we're going to create an indicator and we're going to measure it. Now we are at 11% which is not much, but it seems like a lot to us. To me it seems a lot.

So we're going to start working on that to reduce, so that 11% this year is 7%, 8%, 3% or 2%. I mean, we're going to do things to make that work. Also when there are incidents, in the end when you work with 2,000 people, 400 projects and many people, incidents arise and we solve them, we seek to solve, and you have to dedicate yourself a lot to that. Being very close, I have two hats, because I am Vice President of Gaztenpresa and I am the one who leads the coordination of Gaztenpresa in Laboral Kutxa and at the same time, I am the Director of Business Development in Laboral Kutxa.

Sometimes I wear the hat of Gaztenpresa and sometimes I wear that of Laboral Kutxa and Gaztenpresa. I have to say some things to Gaztenpresa and sometimes I have to say things to Laboral Kutxa. That mix, I think it is also important, that people have double vision because that makes you empathize a little more and when you have to put things on the table that are not pleasant you also have to do it with empathy. And if I were someone who provides business development services that has nothing to do with local needs, someone from 100 km away, that would be complicated.

Michael: To have this creative duopoly of the Laboral Kutxa position and the Gaztenpresa position, do you think it is forming a new kind of banker? Here we talk about restorative finance, extractive finance, community finance as lending practice silos. Could there be more positive outcomes from integrating different kinds of lending practices into each project, intersectionality, where the whole is greater than the sum of the parts?

Oscar: Of course, because in the end what the silos generate is a lot of efficiency within the silo but little additional crosscutting vision. I think this multitasking we have is key, but here there are also silos and more in projects of these, but we have to try to do transversal things that intersect. I will give you another example. For us at Gaztenpresa, the Basque Country is a small place. Gaztenpresa was born in Vizcaya, in Bilbao, and then later to the rest of the Basque Country. So in Vizcaya, Gaztenpresa has much more soul than it has in other places. That hurts me, it hurts a lot. So now we are going to take advantage of this social impact of Gaztenpresa to raise it also in the soul of Gipuzkoa province.

I talk to office colleagues who say Gaztenpresa is a tool, it helps me. But I want them to tell me that they have clients who without Gaztenpresa would not have opened that business. Tell me that thanks to Gaztenpresa those businesses are open. Tell me that people have encouraged you, that they have brought you some chocolate bonbons because of Gaztenpresa. So I think that's where we have to get to. Of course, something we have to work on. There are so many people wanting and needing this help. We are designing an internal action plan to give soul to territories that have less. All day, as Arizmendiarrieta said, "There is always one more step to take." We are always thinking about what more steps because in the end if you stay still you take a step down.

Michael: Very much appreciate that answer. When you look at Laboral Kutxa and you see Gaztenpresa in Basque provinces and you see Mondragon Team Academy abroad, they are both doing the same thing with completely different audiences: jointly fulfilling the initial vision of José María Arizmendiarrieta, the whole socio-economic impulse of reaching out to people where they are and helping them help themselves, and on the other hand encouraging entrepreneurs to learn everything they needed to succeed in stand-alone businesses integrating through local and regional ecosystems that was so important for the formation of Mondragon back in the day. Even more important today and tomorrow when collaboration will be driven not just by technology but by common good values and purpose-driven societal imperatives to save the planet and protect the most vulnerable.

Oscar: By chance I just had a team meeting with the people of Team Academy, with the Polytechnic school, the engineers, the people who lead entrepreneurship, just this afternoon. Because we are working precisely on this. Because in the end we say Team Academy does entrepreneurship in its own way and sometimes Gaztenpresa too. Sometimes it seems that one is Mondragon and the other Siemens.

The truth is that we have sat down many times and it is not easy to reconcile because there are many ways to do this work and one approach is very financial, one more management, the University is more formative. But what I told them is that in the end and I am very clear about this, we intervene in different phases of the process. That is, a junior coop of Team Academy is in a very preliminary phase to what Gaztenpresa can do. Why? Because in Gaztenpresa we usually treat the project when it is practically ready to go to market, when it is almost ready to go to invoice, to go to the sell phase.

In Team Academy, they deal with very preliminary phases. What we have to achieve is synergies. That Gaztenpresa's project can go and rely on the people of Team Academy and that this continuity in the financing we are going to put in Gaztenpresa projects of Team Academy from the beginning and even with the school of engineers. I mean, we're going to do things in three bands. In that sense and projects that come out of Team Academy that are in the phase of investment, financing, we are already managing. Well the same thing one has to commit, you have to see. Instead of saying they do different things differently, we must look for a spirit of collaboration with Mondragón.

Sometimes it doesn't happen because in the end we are many people with different priorities, with different realities, with very different short-term agendas. I believe that in the end between Laboral Kutxa and Mondragón we already have opened six lines of work: entrepreneurship, innovation, training, people, we have teams dedicated to entrepreneurship and teams dedicated to seeking synergies. I think that is the part that touches us, the part where Mondragón comes in and the part where we are going and finally take advantage of the kind of group we are. Sometimes it was happening that projects of Team Academy ended up in Banco Sabadell or University of Deusto. This can change and we are building better ways to collaborate going forward.

Chris: What makes a good coach? What kind of preparation is done with the mentors?

Oscar: How do we create a super mentor? First one has to have the will. For us that it is voluntary is very important. In our model, we would not have mentors that we have to pay. Another good thing is that it is a payment in a symbolic way. Above all, that you have the will to help. The will that this is a teacher of two. Because I personally believe that I have gained more from the people I have tried to help. Others in my team may think differently, but for me it has been super enriching. Above all, that willingness to help. Because in the end you have to dedicate time to it, you have to dedicate mental space to it.

You have to think, you have to worry, that thing that you have asked me, those things that worry you, that you have told me that it does not let you sleep, to see how I can help you. Then you have to have skills. You have to know what skills you have. Because I would say it almost doesn't matter what kind of skills I have because it's the matching that fill the gaps as I said. The initial formation that is expected of people is important. You have to know why there are times it is thought that Google is mentoring, that more person-to-person mentoring is not worth it. We have to look for someone who is an expert in training. Training determines what it is to be a mentor. Also for the mentee. It's not worth it that you're calling the mentor every day. "Hey, I have a problem here with a customer who has told me to lower the price, what do I tell him? What do I say?" Well you will see what you say. But you, be yourself.

That is, there are things that can happen to you on a day-to-day basis. I think people are important because both have mentor and mentee have to volunteer. It is important to work well on the training process, then matching and then get it all to flow. Be a little aware of problem solving. We are looking above all for people with aptitude, people who feel like this is essential. Then we will see what profile they have. Because then we will have someone to match and fill the gaps with those profiles. One will know how to sell, another will not, one will know about numbers, another will know about management, another will know about people management. Well that's kind of the concept.

Chris: So, for the vision, the future of Gaztenpresa in five years, what would you like to see?

Oscar: Well I'm quite ambitious, I think you are at the point where Gaztenpresa Digital has to give us growth, the leap. I tell Inma Ramos, who is the CEO of Gaztenpresa, that if we now treat 2,000 people, we have to support 5,000. If we support 400 projects, we have to support 1,000. Because I think that is what should allow us an important qualitative leap. Because we have many years working on organic growth, to improve the process, this is leading you to more growth, to help more people, but I think we are in a position now to make a qualitative leap, because we have means. We have a budget. Last year we earned €180,000. We don't have to earn €180,000, we have to invest that €180,000 in helping more. We have good partners. We have Mondragón partners, we have Basque government partners. The next step is to open Laboral Kutxa to other sites. Then we have to open geographically where Laboral Kutxa is. Laboral Kutxa is in Navarra, Madrid, Barcelona. That I think will not cost us much and will be for next year. In the end to be able to be better, to improve every day, to know the impact we have and to know that Gaztenpresa Digital has to be the qualitative leap.

CHAPTER 9

Mentoring Best Practices from Spain's Basque Region – 2: The Ahalbidetu Case Study

The Experience of Learning by Doing

José Arturo Villanueva Barriocanal, José Miguel Martínez Urquijo & José Antonio López Egaña

Summary

It was 2012 and unemployment among recent graduates was very high. It occurred to us that one way to help might be to give graduates a competitive advantage through a "Learning by Doing" program.

This became the first initiative of Ahalbidetu — an association of professionals from diverse fields with a mission to provide young university graduates with a differentiated (specialized) qualification to help them get their first job in competitive job markets, and to help them adapt to workplace demands faster and more effectively.

The idea was original and risky, and required skilled professionals to mentor the graduates. It also involved the novel concept that most of the professional mentors were retired, and volunteers. Many of them had previously worked with José Miguel Martínez Urquijo, whose inseparable collaborator, José Arturo Villanueva Barriocanal, died shortly before the publication of the Ahalbidetu book in 2021. (The book is now available through Amazon in print or ebook editions.) Ahalbidetu enabled these professionals to give back to society some of what they had received from it.

Graduates acquire general knowledge at university, within their specialty, and not specific knowledge required by the companies that hire them. Yet even specific technical knowledge alone is not enough for an employee to achieve results within a company. Some graduates do not achieve effective results because they lack the cross competencies of a highly sought-after executive skill set — such as oral and written communication, planning an assignment, time and information management, participating in a meeting, making decisions, etc. — that turn specific knowledge into effective results.

Cross competencies are directly related to behaviors, and provide skills to competently perform specific jobs or activities: In other words, they provide the requirements for success. This led to two new questions:

- What cross competencies should be taught?
- How could they be taught in a reasonable period?

Regarding the first question, and like most people, the retired professionals volunteering for our program had learned various skills through practical experience — by trial and error, learning by doing, and making mistakes repeatedly, without being fully aware that this was happening. They learned to organize tasks by breaking them down into parts and scheduling them. They also learned to manage information as a way to avoid getting lost in the tangle of data found in the books and reports available at the library (back when there were no computers or Internet). They learned, by making endless mistakes, how to behave in meetings. They learned to work as a team through group assignments, all without any guides, mentors, or shortcuts.

To select the most effective cross competencies, we grouped them into three categories: "leadership," "social," and "learning to learn" competencies, to which we added "problem solving" and "critical thinking."

In response to the second question, our volunteers reflected on what they could do to reduce the amount of time it took the graduates to learn.

Based on some of our own experiences and others taken from American methodologies, we set up the Learning by Doing program to teach cross competencies using these six strategies:

1. Graduates develop a business plan on a specific product they choose.
2. Graduates are organized by departments, as if in a real company, with a multidisciplinary group of around 20 in each group.
3. Graduates work in-person with four to six mentors, who ask questions that encourage the graduates to find the answers.
4. Graduates explore group dynamics by constantly working as a team, learning from and with each other, planning collaboratively, assigning managers, coordinating tasks, presenting their progress to each other and to mentors, and listening to questions.
5. Each mentor acts as a tutor by personally monitoring the learning of four or five graduates, agreeing on objectives, and accumulating and evaluating evidence of progress.
6. Summary documents and lectures provide the minimum essential conceptual support.

The program consists of around 200 teaching hours, takes place in 24 weeks (two four-hour days a week), and requires about another 300 hours of individual work.

How It Works

Learning by Doing is a 24-week program that helps college graduates integrate into the business world and optimize their long-term value to society by improving their preparation for finding a job or becoming self-employed. It combines learning in teams and multidisciplinary groups, as well as mentoring, and also uses reports and business plans on emerging issues. It also connects graduates with potential employers, or with potential funders interested in the problem-solving business plans the graduates create as part of the program. In addition, graduates who finish a six-month internship with participating companies may be awarded a six-month paid contract, which 70% of the time is extended to a permanent contract.

The primary participants are the graduates, whose credentials are their values and eagerness to learn, and who are organized into peer groups of 20 to 24 individuals each.

The second agents are the mentors, who accompany and inspire graduates in their learning process. The program has 16 experienced mentors and volunteers.

Graduates play the roles of professionals in the practice companies they create; they learn by doing business activities and, above all, they learn to take action to achieve results. They learn with others and from others, contrasting, presenting, and listening, having conversations, making the proposals of others their own, compromising, and finally arriving at a common plan of action, which they execute and continually evaluate.

In practice, participants experience situations that occur in real jobs, but with the advantage of having mentors to support their learning process. In this manner ,the program is a gateway for graduates between university and employment.

The difference

The Learning by Doing program has a number of distinct advantages:

- It is not a training program; it combines mentoring with group dynamics, complementary training teams, and internship contracts.
- Its aim is to improve the "employability" of participants, by providing them with skills necessary to work effectively in any type of corporation or organization, and that are learned not in undergraduate and graduate studies, but rather in practice.
- The focus, design, content, and mentorship provide graduates, in 24 weeks, with a complete perspective on the various activities of a company and an experience far superior to what is normally achieved after several years on the job.
- Companies agree beforehand to provide internship contracts for graduates.
- The cost of the program is much less than its value, since the mentors' input is free.

The keys

Effective employees solve problems by applying knowledge they've learned traditionally, and using the skills and perspective they've gained through practice. Ordinary people perform extraordinary actions in emergency situations, revealing capabilities that they didn't know they possessed. The Learning by Doing program is intended to be a detonator of these capabilities.

The keys are the graduate and the group, the mentor, and the methodology of the program.

The main character is the **graduate** looking for a job, who must meet the following requirements:

- Be willing to investment in himself/herself, dedicating the time and effort necessary to carry out their individual work.
- Be proactive in understanding the role of the team, group, and mentors, and be open to feedback.

- Find and select relevant information, process it, and present it clearly to the team and the group.
- Be willing to adopt the personal and professional changes that will come from the program.

The **group** is where graduates contribute individual and team work, helping them learn to:

- Present, contrast, listen, and engage in dialogue.
- Bring positions closer together, compromise, and make the proposals of others their own.
- Assume individual and joint responsibilities to establish deadlines, prioritize objectives, meet commitments, obtain results, and evaluate them to continue learning from successes and failures.
- Use group dynamics to maintain interest, engage, motivate, and challenge each other.

Mentors facilitate the process by:

- Listening carefully to the presentations and interventions of the graduates to understand their worries, problems, and concerns.
- Participating in group dynamics.
- Helping graduates learn through dialogue and questions that help the graduate and the group to develop, offer different perspectives, present alternatives, establish objectives, and take responsibility for their fulfilment. Mentors do not instruct; their function is not to teach but to help to learn.

The methodology of the program is designed around the graduates playing technical, commercial, economic, strategic roles, etc., and joining teams to design and execute a project.

The basic ingredients

Virtual company. The program recreates the atmosphere of a real company. It is actually a virtual company, the purpose of which is to develop two projects or business plans by the team of graduates with complementary skills and education. The virtual company is organized into departments which the participants rotate between over the course of the program. Special task forces help coordinate and pool the work of the various departments.

Multidisciplinary teams. Graduates with complementary training and skills — such as technical, scientific, social, or humanistic — are organized in groups to enrich the program and learn with and from each other. In this manner, new ideas, insights and methods of analysis are opened for all. These multidisciplinary teams are configured according to the different departments of a company, which helps to:

- Enrich viewpoints.
- Provide unexpected questions on topics far removed from each discipline.
- Complement technical, economic, commercial, and legal expertise with humanistic and social perspectives.

Mentoring. Mentors facilitate personal and professional development through listening, questioning, feedback, reformulation, synthesis, and stimulation. At least four mentors attend each group during all teamwork sessions, and mentors in charge of follow-up observe the behavior of graduates during group sessions. Each graduate is also assigned a mentor, who interviews them individually every three to four weeks. Throughout the program, graduates have five to seven interviews with their assigned mentor, who monitors and evaluates their work, and issues a final report on each graduate's progress. All meetings are recorded with their corresponding reports and data.

Business plans. Each group prepares two business plans, then establishes the corresponding teams. In some cases, the plan is a project commissioned by one of the collaborating companies, which provides experience in real situations.

Presentations in joint sessions. Specialized mentors or speakers give lectures on skills, methodologies, disciplines, activities, and experiences.

Presentations. Each week a spokesperson from each team presents a progress report to the rest of the group, thus improving communication skills.

Group dynamics. These are constantly applied throughout the program, and promote assertive communication, teamwork, and leadership, among other cross competencies. By sharing what has been done, future goals are set, managers are assigned, approaches are refined and progress plans are established.

Data management. Sharing information in real time is one of the basic conditions of the program. Digital platforms allow sharing and access to all materials during office and non-office hours; this increases the effectiveness of in-person meetings. Through individual work and teamwork in departments, task forces, and groups, graduates learn how tasks *should* be done, thus acquiring skills necessary for any business activity.

Since acquiring these skills is achieved by "doing" a business project, graduates perform the main functions of any company individually and in teams. Participants get a total sense of a company's operations, something that would otherwise take years to acquire in a real work setting.

Time dedicated to the program

During the 24 weeks of the program, each graduate invests 192 in-person hours and about 12 hours per week of personal or group work. This brings the total time commitment to 480 hours. Each mentor also dedicates 192 hours of direct work with the graduates, not including the hours of online attention, analysis of weekly reports, personal interviews, and final reports.

The Competencies

The Learning by Doing program provides cross competencies, common to all types of activities, that empower graduates to perform productive tasks in different work settings, using different resources that ensure quality results. These are essential for all stages of professional development, from their first time in the job market, to promotion within the company, to career changes.

A competency is defined as an "integrated set of knowledge, skills, and attitudes that allow the person to act effectively to achieve an objective." We break down the competencies we teach in four chapters: Leadership, Social Skills, Learning to Learn, and Synthesis:

- **Leadership**
  - Initiative: Willingness to take actions, create opportunities, and improve results without an external requirement.
  - Goal setting and planning: Ability to translate general intentions into clearly defined goals, programming (time and term), intermediate products, and procedures to achieve the objectives.

- o Decision-making: Ability to choose the best option among several, following defined criteria, to act and achieve the objective.
- o Market orientation: Ability to identify internal and external clients, satisfy their needs, build a network of contacts, and learn about market trends.

- **Social skills**
  - o Teamwork: Ability to collaborate in an interrelated way, sharing responsibilities to achieve a common goal.
  - o Business communication: Ability to transmit ideas and projects, both orally and in writing; to listen with interest and interact with initiative and team spirit; all promoting the harmony of the company or the business project.
  - o Meeting effectiveness: Ability to be a committed player in a team activity, in which a group tries to carry out a job.

- **Learning to learn**
  - o Results orientation: Ability to focus available resources on achieving essential results.
  - o Time management: Ability to organize time based on priorities, which requires differentiating and prioritizing tasks.
  - o Information management: Ability to improve individual and organizational effectiveness by developing a culture of continuous learning; ability to locate, use, and take advantage of the information *via* sources such as libraries, databases, or the Internet.

- **Synthesis**
  - o Critical thinking: Group dynamics and teamwork to learn to prove facts, form arguments, and draw conclusions.
  - o Problem solving: Initiative, results orientation, decision making, and teamwork to identify situations, obstacles, and opportunities, and develop effective solutions.

The Stages & Structure of the Program

The Learning by Doing program involves five stages:

1. Introduction to the program, for graduates to understand the methodology and process, in preparation for learning the competencies.
2. Definition of business models that will serve as the basis for the development of each project.
3. Obtaining information and basic concepts that allow one to have the necessary criteria and data to design and feed the business plans of each project in the proper conditions of quantity and quality.
4. Preparation of business plans that correspond with the different needs of an overarching plan.
5. Preparation and presentation of the final documentation for each project.

The goal is to train 40 graduates in two groups of about 20 individuals. Each group is organized into multidisciplinary teams that carry out activities characteristic of a company by developing two projects.

At each stage, different work teams are formed in each group, with the graduates all rotating through each distinct team.

The following table provides an overview of the structure and timeline of Learning by Doing for each group, with more detail thereafter.

Figure 7.1: The Structure of the Program – Overview

STAGES	PROCESS OF EACH PROJECT	WORK TEAMS	DURATION
Introduction	Presentations on methodology and competences. Analysis of proposed sectors. General description of the selected projects. Group dynamics. The search and selection of information for each team begins.	Four work teams are created to start the analysis of each project.	Two weeks.
Definition of business models	Two business models are defined for each project, a total of four. Two business models are selected, one per project, on which the business plans will be developed.	Each team defines and defends its business model.	Three weeks.
Obtaining information and basic concepts	Ideas and concepts to consider in the company are presented and clarified. Reference companies in different sectors are presented. Information on the market and resources is obtained, necessary to carry out business plans.	Work teams are formed for business plans. Two teams per project, mixing components of the active teams in each model in the previous stage.	Four weeks.
Development of business plans	Presentations are given on topics, concepts, and criteria to be considered in each department of the company. Two business plans are drawn up (one for each business model) considering the specified contents and thematic schemes.	The company is organized into business lines and departments, and the teams responsible for each of them are formed. Coordination mechanisms are established.	Ten weeks.
Preparation of the final documentation	The final documentation for each project (business plan and annexes) is prepared and presented to executives of the prescribing companies.	The teams from the previous stage are maintained, the interaction mechanisms are established and the teams in charge of presenting the projects are assigned. Each project is presented by three designated graduates who have participated in its development.	Five weeks.

The Program Schedule

The program takes place over 24 weeks between October and March (excluding two weeks for the Christmas holidays), and is divided into five stages.

Except for the first stage, in-person sessions happen weekly on Mondays and Wednesdays from 4pm to 8pm. Each week, participants also get 12 hours of personal work. Thursdays from 4pm to 8pm are also available for in-person team meetings.

Each stage of the program breaks down as follows:

1. Introduction

For the first two weeks, over the course of four four-hour, in-person sessions, participants prepare for their roles in the virtual company and the competencies they'll be developing. Each four-hour session explores the following topics:

- Explain the methodology of the program.
- Illustrate the rules that should guide the role of the professional in the company.
- Present in detail each of the competencies to be learned, and criteria for evaluating achievement throughout the program.
- Researching information on the proposed base projects.

In this stage, work teams begin to explore the two projects to be analyzed in the next stage. At the end of each session, the groups discuss and collaborate on the topics discussed in the session. Also, work teams have four hours per week for voluntary, in-person coordination meetings.

At the end of this stage, a presentation on business models sets up the next stage.

2. Definition of the business model for each project

The objective of this second, three-week stage is to define and select the models for the business plans participants will develop. Four teams are organized, two for each project and balanced for gender and educational background; members should not have worked with each other in the previous stage. Two four-hour in-person sessions are held each week and each graduate dedicates another 12 hours of individual or group work.

In the Monday sessions, each team shares and reviews their work of the past week, before presenting it at the full meeting. The second part of these sessions involves the first 180-degree assessment of competencies by graduates and an evaluation of their literacy and numeracy.

On Wednesdays each team submits its report to the larger group for feedback. In the second part of the session (6pm to 8pm), the teams plan their work through the following Monday. The mentors meet individually with the graduates assigned to them, so that every three weeks they complete a cycle of meetings with all participants.

On a voluntary basis, teams can hold in-person coordination meetings on Thursdays to share and contrast information, strategies, and ideas, and clarify and resolve issues or problems, ensuring their goals are achieved ahead of the following Monday's group session.

The last in-person session of this stage is devoted entirely to the selection of business models that will serve as the basis for developing the business plans. Each team presents its final report and submits it at the plenary meeting. Each team has 15 minutes to submit their report and 30 minutes for group questions, observations, and comments. Following this process, the group selects two models to serve as the basis for the actual business plans.

To close this stage, participants review the next stage's process and corresponding work teams.

3. Obtaining information & basic concepts

Creating a good business plan requires each team to understand the key concepts and criteria that comprise that plan. This stage opens with presentations on:

- The Company.
- Objectives.
- Principles and functions.
- Human resources.
- Competitiveness at work
- Critical thinking and problem solving.
- Doing well by doing good.

Participants also study and visit companies from different sectors, analyze their business activities, and conduct research to increase the reliability of their plans as much as possible. The duration of this stage is four weeks, with eight in-person sessions of four hours each, and with an additional (individual or group) commitment of another 12 hours per graduate each week. The proceedings are similar to the previous stage, except that the second part of the Monday session is devoted to presentations, talks, and group dynamics, to help get everyone aligned around defining the basic concepts and principles of the company.

At the end of the last session of this stage, the methodology for the fourth stage and the new team assignments are presented.

4. Elaboration of business plans

During the 10 weeks devoted to this stage, each group is organized into teams or departments corresponding to the structure of a company and business plans.

Market analysis, necessary resources, required investments, and economic forecasts will be analyzed and determined in the business plan itself. These depend on the strategic guidelines and objectives adopted by the team. To begin with, each business project must clearly specify its basic principles (vision, mission, and core values), and propose the strategic guidelines and objectives it must assume for the development of its internal and external activities.

From this, the content of the business plans responds to the following thematic scheme:

- Description and characterization of products and services.
- Market analysis; customer segmentation; preliminary SWOT (strengths, weaknesses, opportunities, threats) analysis.
- Legal and tax implications.
- Objectives and strategic actions.
- Production process; organization and resources required.
- Marketing plan; promotion, sale, and distribution.

- Human resources plan.
- Investment plan.
- Financial plan; annual and at five years.
- Creation of value.
- Risk analysis.

This stage also includes presentations on:
- Business case for the project.
- Marketing.
- Planning and risk management.
- Accounting status.
- Financing a start-up.

To ensure that business plans follow appropriate channels, two mentors are assigned to each of the plans to observe and support the process. Mentors coordinate with each other to reach consensus on how to avoid contradicting each other.

5. Preparation & presentation of final documentation
The last five weeks of the program are dedicated to preparing the final documentation and to present it to the board of directors of the corporate clients.
  This documentation is structured in three blocks:
- Summarized PowerPoint presentation.
- Business plan:
  o Executive summary.
  o Introduction.
  o Business model.
  o Basic principles and strategic guidelines.
  o Products and services offered; production process.
  o Market recognition; SWOT analysis.
  o Marketing plan; objectives and strategic actions.
  o Organization and resources required.
  o Investment plan.
  o Financial plan.
  o Value creation and risk analysis.
  o Conclusions.
- Appendices:
  o Marketing plan.
  o Specification of material and technological resources.

- o Human resources plan.
- o Detailed financial plan; annual and at five years.

Documentation is prepared by teams responsible for each of the topics, and coordinators review and correct any style issues. Mentors remain in supportive and guiding roles throughout this stage.

Support & Follow-up by Mentors

In principle, the Learning by Doing program is designed to be taught to two groups of 20 graduates, who are monitored by 12 mentors — professional managers with extensive experience from various disciplines and activities, both retired and active. Their participation is entirely voluntary, with the aim of giving back to society part of what society has given them during their professional lives.

The role of mentors

The role of mentors is based on listening, questioning, reformulating, and synthesizing. Mentors provide alternatives in a work environment that uses group dynamics as motivating tools. Their functions can be summarized as follows:

- Listen carefully to the presentations and interventions of the graduates to understand their problems and concerns.
- Help the graduate, the team, and the group to develop, perceive issues from different perspectives, consider alternatives, establish objectives, and take responsibility for fulfilment. The mentor does not instruct; his/her function is not to teach but to help learn.
- Cooperate in the practice of group dynamics as an instrument of "learning by doing" in the teamwork competition.
- Interview the graduate individually on a regular basis to follow their progress in learning competencies.

All mentors assume these roles. However, to optimize their contribution, some focus on project development and others on monitoring the development of competencies by each graduate.

Of the 12 permanently dedicated mentors, four are more directly responsible for ensuring that projects are properly channeled and developed, continuously monitoring them, ensuring that teams understand the concepts and criteria, and keeping the schedule up to date.

In addition to observing the progress of the projects and the response of the teams, the other eight closely monitor the progress of the graduates they are assigned to, support them personally, and meet with them every three weeks. They constantly assess the development of each graduate's competencies and help them direct their efforts well.

The weekly cycle

With the criteria outlined, mentors channel their performance through weekly cycles that typically respond to the following scheme:

- **Monday sessions:** In the first part of the session (from 4pm to 6pm), the mentors responsible for monitoring projects attend each team meeting and presentation of weekly objectives. They confirm alignment with guidelines and the criteria, make observations, ask questions, and/or provide suggestions for Wednesday reports and presentations to the plenary group. In the second part of the session (from 6pm to 8pm) mentors go in-depth on the competencies and business environment and mechanics. Some Mondays, graduates are evaluated to assess their understanding, self-awareness, and personal profiles, as well as 180-degree awareness of competencies.

- **Wednesday sessions:** The first part of the session (4pm to 6pm) is dedicated to the presentation of each team's reviewed Monday reports. All mentors are in attendance, and provide observations, guidance, and direct check-ins with their graduates' progress in developing the various competencies. In the second part of the session (from 6pm to 8pm), each team meets to guide and plan the work to be done until the following Monday, while the mentors meet with their assigned graduates. Each week they meet individually with two of them, so that all graduates have a personal interview with their mentor every three weeks.

- **Outside of in-person hours:** Mentors also help graduates outside of in-person hours. First, they review the information that was submitted to the group work tool and make pertinent comments. Then they respond through said tool to questions directly posed by graduates.

CHAPTER 10

The Mondragon Team Academy & TAZEBAEZ

Ana Aguirre

Introduction

When I was first asked to contribute to this book with a piece from the perspective of Mondragon Team Academy and TAZEBAEZ, the cooperative I am co-founder and worker owner at, I was taken aback. It is true that over the last year or so I have been playing around with the idea of writing, and maybe even embarking on the adventure of trying to follow the PhD path, but sitting in front of a blank paper and writing the story of the entrepreneurship community within Mondragon University Business faculty seemed like a huge step.

I postponed writing this chapter to the edges of the impossible, giving the editors some headaches and even almost falling out of the project as a whole, probably because I felt like there is a lot to say, but I was not sure it was my story to share. So, I have decided that I will make it mine. I will share this part with you from my voice. Not from an academic perspective, but from an action-based, experience-like, adventure tale that has brought me and us (TAZEBAEZ) to where we are today. This may clash with the rest of the chapters, but it is the one way I know how to do this. I hope it brings you, the reader, some joy and insight as well as some memorable anecdotes. We all know it is the useless funny stories that remain easier in our brains. So, let's start.

First, let me tell you a little bit about me. The person behind this piece is Ana Aguirre, me, 31 years old, originally from San Sebastian in the Basque Country, co-founder, and worker-owner at TAZEBAEZ S. Co-op. I also just started serving as the Global Youth President and Youth Representative to the board of the International Cooperative Alliance (ICA), a term that runs from 2022 to 2025.

My role in this book is to share with you about Mondragon Team Academy. In reality, this has a lot of my personal story, as TAZEBAEZ was first founded as the tool for learning within the first generation of the Leadership Entrepreneurship and Innovation degree (LEINN) that launched the community. TAZEBAEZ today is a worker-owned cooperative home to almost 30 people and present in five countries. But let's start from the beginning.

A quick reminder that this is no academic text and that most of what you are going to read are personal takes, ideas shaped during conversations, perceptions, and a lot of my personal opinion. As you see, I am set to be a great candidate for research.

A Jump in Time

In order to do this right and understand the creation of Mondragon Team Academy, one almost needs to jump to the beginning of Mondragon. When José María Arizmendiarrieta first pictured the group, he was certain that the first step towards a socio-economic revolution that would reshape the Alto Deva Valley, as it was known, started with education. "...In order to democratize power, one must socialize knowledge beforehand..." is one of my favorite quotes from him (brace yourself, I have many and you will read them here) (Arizmendiarrieta, *n.d.*, p.48).

Arizmendiarrieta spent 10 years educating the community and the youth before the founding of the first cooperative, ULGOR. He understood that education was key to fostering participation, solidarity, and responsibility. These features are undoubtedly present in a worker-owned cooperative environment, where shared ownership and participation in management are structurally embedded. And his commitment to education and dignifying labor did not stop there. There are a couple of concepts that I would like to highlight here about J.M. Arizmendiarrieta's understanding of education that we take for granted today, and yet they settled the foundations of what Mondragon Unibertsitatea would become.

First, he committed to an education and methodology that remained close to the labor market and to the companies in the area. An education that answered to the needs of the market and that would prepare the students to fit into it as well as to transform it – practical education.

Second, he wanted no one to be left behind. Education should not be an obstacle in people's life but an enhancement of their journey. For many people, their education finished when they needed to contribute economically to their family. Many young people in the valley needed to leave school early or after basic education, which is after age 16 in Spain. Arizmendiarrieta created ALECOP, a cooperative where students could work part-time and study part-time so they could make money through a flexible job contributing to their family and yet receive professional training beyond the basics – what we call today "dual education."

Third, in order to contribute to more technical profiles and further education for people that would become the workers and managers of the future, he understood that basic education was not enough. He encouraged some of the youth to go on and study further. There was no university or higher education institution in the valley, and the problem of not being able to leave due to family commitments remained. Arizmendiarrieta arranged with a Spanish university where he would teach the students in Mondragon and then send them there to take the tests locally – remote education.

This shows that he truly was a visionary – a generator of innovative ecosystems, and a strategist. He was someone who had a clear understanding that training people was the best way to ensure business success and therefore community growth. Adding to the mix was a commitment to social impact, solidarity in compensation, sharing of wealth and selflessness. To end with another quote, he was a problem/challenge solver, a man of action under the belief that "the world hasn't been given to us to contemplate it but to transform it and this transformation is not accomplished only with our manual work but first with ideas and action plans" (Arizmendiarrieta, *n.d.*, p. 19).

Internationalization & Search

For years Mondragon and the companies continued growing, and by the early 2000s most of the cooperatives had started to internationalize. As more of the companies went to establish their businesses in different countries, cultures and business environments, a clear need started to take shape. It was not the same to manage and lead a company in the valley as it was in valleys far away. The people that were sent to establish the new businesses needed to have a specific set of skills that were not necessarily the same as those of the great managers "back home." It was time to set the machinery of innovation of the university to roll again, and to search and find interesting schools, degrees and methodologies that were "producing" a different kind of graduate.

Fast forward to 2008. The economic crisis started hitting the US first, and Europe soon after. There was a huge uncertainty at both the local market and international levels and the university was deep in the search for that "different" without a rigid idea of what that meant exactly. In a congress in San Sebastian, with a couple of companies of Mondragon in attendance, some Finnish students were presenting about their program of study and their methods, which struck the directors. "That's the kind of people I want to be graduated from our university. That's what we are looking for" seems like someone said. And thus, Tiimiakatemia Finland became the main subject of interest for the university team.

Three young professors at the university were selected as the "founding team," and a graduate from the Finnish program was hired to become the fourth member of the team. José María Luzarraga, Aitor Lizartza and Sain Milena Lopez were joined by Sari Veripä to form the team that would take this adventure forward.

The Beginning of the Mondragon Team Academy (MTA)

Once the focus was set it was time to start understanding and creating a way to introduce the Tiimiakatemia Finnish education model into the reality of Spain. Finnish education was already well-respected in the world, so this was an advantage. Yet, what the Finnish Ministry of Education considered valid was not necessarily aligned with or even close to what the Ministry of Education of Spain was ready to consider official. This was also at the start of the European unification of degrees with the agreement of Bologna.

Mondragon Unibertsitatea was very clear on something: the new degree needed to be considered official. They would take as long as was needed to make it happen, otherwise it was not going to be a significant innovation in entrepreneurial education. The degree would comply with the new education framework of the European Union. A degree that, even if adopted within the frame of the ministries was set to be disruptive, would unify the Mondragon Cooperative way with the Finnish program. It was a game changer.

The core team was sent to start the Team Mastery, the Finnish program to train the team coaches. These were the people that were to accompany the students in their four-year entrepreneurial adventure. In order to experiment while training, an elective subject was set into place within the business faculty, the host of the program. This subject contained some of the methodology that would be used in the future, testing how Basque students reacted and which features were more or less successful, generating an "end of the year" event where last year students from schools in the Basque Country participated, and could try the new methodology first-hand.

At the same time, the university team defied time to have an official European degree presented to the Spanish Ministry and approved before the beginning of the school year in September 2009. The marketing and outreach team of the university that was touring schools all over the territory, incorporated LEINN – Leadership, Entrepreneurship, and INNovation – in the menu of options presented to potential students. I was one of those in my school, sitting in the back row, barely paying attention, speaking to my friends until some key words reached my ear.

Spoiler. The university team succeeded in passing the degree through the Education Ministry. The marketing team succeeded in having 27 people sign up to the adventure. September 2009 was the time of the kick-off.

MTA Methodology & Work

The first and most important thing to understand about LEINN and the MTA methodology is that it is not for everyone. As a Finnish student said to us once: "It can be both the easiest and the hardest course to take. It all depends on how much you want to invest yourself in it." This aligns with the "the more you give, the more you get" spirit that we were introduced to later while in Mother Teresa's mission in India.

LEINN is based on trust and self-management, but also working in teams and shared responsibility. Most people that graduated from LEINN will say it is a learning experience, yes, but mainly a transformative journey.

It is a team learning experience. All of it is based on dialogue, practice, work, and reflection in entrepreneurial teams. Students are learning entrepreneurship by doing team entrepreneurship. The first perception is that of freedom and a little bit of feeling lost. The base that attracts a lot of people is that there are no classes, no teachers, no exams and quite a bit of traveling. There is no academic structure as one might expect it. Yet, there are projects, teams, team coaches and Key Performance Indicators that measure development; and the travel turns into the so-called learning journeys.

The main tool for the learning process is the team and the team company. That means that the teams, generated at the very beginning of the first semester of the first year by the team coaches, are "home" for the next four years. Students become "teampreneurs" and they become responsible not only for themselves but for each other. Teampreneurs cannot change from one team to another and they do not choose their team; they are assigned based on the perceptions of the coaches.

The team company is created in the first year, normally in the form of an association under Spanish law that is a legal form that allows you to start a business without initial capital. The team entrepreneurs name and register the team company themselves, in this way having their first encounter with public administration and bureaucracy. They need to learn about the structures, the roles and the responsibilities needed for it and the working and participatory structure and flow they want for their newly founded company.

The methodology is based on three different main pillars: the individual, the company/business, and the environment/community. Within each of the three pillars are plenty of categories and within each category specific indicators. All of them add up to close to 100 indicators a year. All of this is compiled in the study plan or syllabus, that for all LEINNers is called the "Falkon Model." The last review of the Falkon

Model was done in 2022. Changes, updates, and reviews are annexed to the public records of the Ministry of Education that has it stored for any institution or person to search.

Some of the main features are dialogue, practice, and self and team assessment. Teams have mandatory dialogue sessions, or training sessions of four hours twice a week where they meet along with the coach and discuss progress, projects, learnings and follow up with each other. The training sessions are used to share, ask, and support each other as well as push each other for the better. The more activity in projects, customers, and learnings there are, the better and deeper the dialogue and the better the learning experience.

The more "traditional" learning occurs in bootcamp or workshop-like seminars where the concepts are practical and can be implemented in the companies throughout the different processes. Subjects like accounting, law or technology are tailored directly to the company and project needs, including structures, functions, and legal support for the teams. Another significant source of theoretical content is the approximately 20 books a year that each entrepreneur needs to read. MTA has a book list that contains books from a variety of fields of interest and rated 1 to 3 according to complexity (content or language). Team entrepreneurs and team companies generate aligned reading plans for people to not only reach the mandatory 40 points a year but to do so with books and content that is relevant for the team company and its projects or structural needs.

And business is business. In visits to Mondragon Corporation and while in university, the vision of Arizmendiarrieta was shared as being as much business-oriented as philosophy-oriented, underlying the idea that there are no cooperative members and cooperators without cooperatives and that cooperatives would not exist unless they were profitable and well-managed businesses. And this is a concept that LEINNers learn "the hard way." Business indicators are ever present in any team company's dialogues. The amount escalates year to year as projects become more robust, meaningful, and ambitious. Every year, a team company needs to reach common and individual indicators of business size and profit that leads to the possibility of investment in the company and other projects and opens the door to better travel budgets.

And why travel? Because within the Falkon Model there is a process focused on the acquisition of international awareness and learning. All teams take a yearly learning journey to different global economic-cultural ecosystems to learn about the differences in business development. The selection of the ecosystem depends on the global situation, the pros and cons of places and the development of the teams. These trips are covered by the team companies, so the experiences vary depending on the expanding capacity of each of the teams. Budgets are made yearly with concrete goals from each of the "financial leaders" in order to set a target for the learning journey.

Here are the trips past, present and future:

- Year 1: A European ecosystem. Four to six weeks. Currently Berlin. Originally Finland.

- Year 2: An American ecosystem. 25 days. Currently Costa Rica. Originally San Francisco and later Seattle (USA). Potentially going back (maybe NYC).

- Year 3: An Asian ecosystem. Six to eight weeks. Currently Seoul. Originally Shanghai and Mumbai (China and India). India has been included again in 2022 after the pandemic.

- Year 4: Final degree project. The teams and teampreneurs choose their destination based on their project.

Cultural intelligence and the cooperative form were two of the main additions from Mondragon to the original Finnish model.

The First Cooperative, TAZEBAEZ & LEINN International

In 2013, we, the first generation of LEINNers, graduated. We were two different team companies. Out of the 27 people that started, 22 finished. Out of the two team companies created through the program only one transitioned into a cooperative, ours, TAZEBAEZ.

After four years together, nine of us decided to go on and generate a cooperative and work together for the future. The cooperative form seemed only right as we had multiple experiences through the years that made us believe more and more in the model. We wanted to create the cooperative for ourselves but also to create employment, as those were not great days for youth employment numbers in Spain (youth unemployment peaked at almost 50% those years).

We wanted to set an example for the ones to follow that it was possible to believe and make it happen. We believe that young people can create social transformation change through a socio-economic reality like cooperatives. Of course, being part of the Mondragon University and our understanding of the Mondragon ecosystem reinforced that feeling. We knew we wanted a worker-owned cooperative. We knew we wanted a company that, while excellent in management and for profit, remained social, fair, participatory, and shared.

TAZEBAEZ today is home to more than 30 people in five different countries. It is an innovation group that focuses its activity in the creation of learning and training ecosystems for companies and education institutions (TravellingU); visual communication (MakeItVisual); and participates in various companies in emerging sectors through a specific structure (Innkubo). As a company, we are also very committed to the international cooperative movement. In 2015, we were part of the co-founding of the Young European Cooperators Network where I served as a board member. In 2017, when the president of the European network became Global Youth President of the ICA, I took over as VP for Europe in the Executive Committee of the ICA. In 2022, I was elected as Global Youth President, where I am currently serving.

One of the lines of TAZEBAEZ, Travelling University, has been consistent all through the years. When we graduated back in 2013, our experience had been quite unique. We had been trained to push the system to its limits, to show that anything is possible and to work together with the university team, as partners, to improve the system for the better. It crystalized today in the MTA value: "leave it better than you found it." Some of us, in our last year, took part in the Team Mastery program and our final degree project had us engaged in the creation of new laboratories of MTA-LEINN in different locations (Madrid and Amsterdam at first, but later Barcelona, Valencia and São Paulo).

Under that pretext, we toyed with the idea of generating a new version of LEINN that was really loyal to the "global citizen" feature of the LEINNers. In 2016, after much talk and debate, a solid agreement was reached with the university, the creation of LEINN International. A new LEINN that aspired not to generate new ecosystems of LEINN in labs, but to generate truly international-minded people through having multinational and multicultural teams as well as a completely itinerant program. There were no longer learning journeys, LEINN International was going to be "always on the road" with much longer stays (at least six months) that allowed the teams to truly incorporate some of the cultural features to their understanding of the business work and the way they operated. The teams have at least five different nationalities among the 15 members, which leads to a huge capacity for cultural empathy. The different backgrounds of the team entrepreneurs allow reflection and better understanding and appreciation of each other's reality, which leads to much more socially responsible projects. LEINN International has graduated two generations since its inception, as of June 2022.

Current Reality & Challenges

Over the last decade and a half, there has been a lot of development in the way things are done in the community. Mondragon Team Academy has expanded, its offerings with more than "just" undergraduate programs. A program in team coaching on intrapreneurship and open innovation (MINN) and another one in Team Coaching (Team Mastery and later TMINN) quickly followed LEINN in 2011 and 2013, respectively.

The networks of labs around the world also grew. The Basque family that had started in Irun grew to add Oñate and then Bilbao. Spain joined first with Madrid, and then Barcelona and Valencia. Worldwide, the strongest partner was China and Shanghai was the first international Lab, followed by Korea. The last one to join the family was Berlin. Itinerant labs were also established in India, the US, and now Costa Rica, to host learning journeys and potentially become a steady lab.

The community has reached more than 1,500 team entrepreneurs, with people from all walks of life. The entrepreneurship rate has risen to almost 45% and the employment of graduates exceeds 90%. A big success! Not only is MTA creating entrepreneurs but also people that are well suited for the current market.

The pandemic times have been interesting for the MTA community which has a very offline kind of model as well as all the traveling, so the community saw its very core of learning shaken. But most of the labs managed to continue working and not stop traveling during any of the pandemic years. TAZEBAEZ, as the learning journey partner, moved well over 400 people around the world yearly despite the pandemic. The TravellingU team moved fast and was able to identify feasible new destinations and generate in-depth programs for the teams to keep experiencing alternative ecosystems.

The university also moved fast and was able to generate digital support for all teampreneurs, adapting to their dynamics and supporting all the teams and the coaches.

Many challenges will keep coming. As a sentence attributed to both Confucius or Eleanor Roosevelt says, "It is better to light a candle than to blame darkness" – and that is the spirit that the community breathes.

Here are some questions that we are asking ourselves:

- Can we do more to foster a more cooperative outcome? Not all companies are cooperatives after graduation, but many remain very social spirited.

- What is education going to look like in the future? Will our program continue to make sense?

- How can we generate more flexible, more accessible, more outreach programs that grow in scale to serve those who aren't able to access education?

- How do we make sure that alumni remain connected and increasingly more engaged in the community and stay as active builders of new realities?

- Where next? Are learning journey destinations the ones to visit? When and how can we incorporate destinations?

- How do we answer and connect with the needs of the new generations? What part of their needs do we need to cover and how much do we need to shape?

- How are we championing inclusion, cultural empathy, social change, and community impact?

We do not know, but we are surely trying to look for answers and remain open as new questions arise. Because following Arizmendiarrieta's spirit of evolution and growth, he believed that although humans aren't perfect, we are perfectible. And work is part of that development process, as he shares in some of his reflections. (Arizmendiarrieta, *n.d.*, p. 18).

References

Arizmendiarrieta, J.M. (*n.d.*). *Pensamientos de Don José María Arizmendiarrieta* [*Reflections of Don José María Arizmendiarrieta*] (Cherie Herrera; Cristina Herrera; David Herrera; Teresita lorenzo; Virgil Lorenzo, Trans.). Mondragón, Spain: Otalora.

CHAPTER 11

The Erreka Co-op Reimagined:
The Industrial Screw Case Study

How Mondragon's values and structure lead to continuous
innovation in mature industries over decades in the most
competitive environments

Imanol Olaskoaga

Introduction

In this chapter we examine how Mondragon's values and structure lead to continuous progress in mature industries. Erreka is a traditional screw-manufacturing company that has been forced to reinvent itself as the business culture around it changed, even as its business environment remained the same for decades. Now the environment is *also* changing — locally, regionally, and globally. How can the company remain relevant?

At Erreka, we transitioned into the wind power industry from 2000–2010, a period of exponential growth of the industry in Spain's Basque Country. During those years everything that could be produced was absorbed. Manufacturing gigantic screws for propellers and turbines for the wind-energy sector in a mainly local market was not risky, because the local market was able to absorb more than was being produced. Clients would reserve capacity to guarantee production, and the company could contract only with local clients and remain highly profitable.

Spain was in a recession by 2010, and the renewable-energy market froze. Traditional clients stopped stocking-up locally because their projects had shifted to other regions around the world. In other European countries the wind-energy crisis was less dramatic, but they were purchasing from other OEMs (original equipment manufacturers) to assemble those wind farms, and not from Erreka. In order to keep working, Erreka had to lose money; without our usual clients, it was difficult to remain competitive in the market unless we lowered our prices.

In this complex context we started looking for solutions from within the company, based on our knowledge of the technology and the high value of our products. Even if clients had started to undervalue the fact that we sell an expertly milled industrial screw, a windmill that costs a few million euro will still end up failing with a poorer-quality screw.

Looking back at the history of the Matz-Erreka Cooperative is where we find the essence of our adopted solutions.

An Enterprise for the People

Matz Erreka S. Co-op, was founded in 1961 by four partners in Bergara, in the Basque Country. The Basque Country was starting to recover its economic and social well-being; entrepreneurial initiatives surged, many of them within a cooperative formula in Mondragon. It's an entrepreneurial model in which human and social values are strong. Erreka started in the screw business — what's now called "fastening solutions." It was a manufacturing business from the start, focusing on hot-steel stamping, mainly for industrial applications.

In 1968 there was a brief pause. The team made a deep strategic analysis of the direction that they wanted for the cooperative. The focus was, and still is, the well-being of people and their environment, with a goal to create more jobs. In order to achieve this, they needed to open the market; it was clear that staying within the fastening market was not sufficient. After studying different diversification options, they finally settled on plastic injections — an industry so far from their initial business that anyone unfamiliar with the spirit of this particular cooperative would be surprised they considered it an option.

The first products that were manufactured in this new environment were heels and soles for shoes, directed mainly to clients in the Mediterranean Basin. These were still commodity products, but very different from the previous in design, production, marketing, and relationships with clients.

This diversification of products and markets has proved to be one of the great strengths of the company, allowing it to organically resist a challenging environment. Matz Erreka's worker-owners have concluded that the more diverse their products and markets, the more protected they are from economic declines: when one of its businesses is in a valley, another can be on a peak. It's a very different vision from the hyper-specialization that makes other businesses so vulnerable to shifts in the market (something that has been recently demonstrated during the Covid-19 pandemic; many enterprises with one product targeting one sector are suffering, as we can see in the automotive, aeronautics, and even tourism industries, or in companies focused on component casting).

Approximately a year later, in 1969, Erreka's association with the Mondragon Cooperative Group was formalized. It became part of the enterprise group that was creating Mondragon, and has gained worldwide recognition as part of the cooperative group.

In 1982, Erreka began developing its automation business after purchasing a patent for the manufacture of motors for lifting window blinds. The business evolved to include automated garage doors, and then, in 1994, the design, manufacture, and installation of automatic pedestrian doors.

Besides these businesses, Erreka has a spinoff delivering solutions for people in wheelchairs, and is investing in job creation in high-technology medical equipment.

Workers at Erreka still think that there is no better way of generating value for people than to create projects in different sectors, and diversifying within a worker-owned company.

From Traditional to Smart Products

In 2011, Erreka's original business operations in the manufacture of forged screws was in a difficult environment. It had been centered in the production of basic steel products for Spanish clients that built wind farms in Spain. Those clients shifted their operations to other countries and employed low-cost local suppliers. Erreka was unable to compete: sales were down by a third, threatening jobs in the core manufacturing business that the company had been in for the last 50 years.

The team saw the need for a turnaround and took a deep dive to analyze the essence of the business. They tapped into the collective's historic knowledge to build something new and different that would spur another 50 years of value creation.

We started with a moment of self-reflection, to build up self-esteem and get the team aligned around our values and identity. We produce a product that our clients tend to undervalue — screws — but that are essential. They are basic, traditional, made from steel, and mass produced. They can stand enormous weights and work very close to their structural limits, and bring more expensive components together, enabling their optimal functionality.

Erreka's industrial screws are exposed to variable loads that generate fatigue in the components — stresses that in many instances are not very well known, nor anticipated at the time of design. This includes the way screws are tightened to hold more expensive components together. According to one analysis, 75% of the failures in wind turbines, including tower collapses, are caused by inconsistent screwing.

It became clear that wind energy is a conventional business that was vulnerable to inconsistent assembly using our products. Yet our many years of expertise have turned this weakness into a strength.

Erreka's R&D team has been researching the best way to tighten screws. The wind industry makes indirect measures of the "tightening twist," and is incapable of measuring the tension to which the screw is subjected, nor of measuring the tension during assembly. Without reliable measurements there's a great deal of variation in the tightening of each screw that, instead of strengthening the entire assembly, can cause fatigue and weaken structural integrity.

To add value to the existing product, Erreka's R&D team developed a method of verifying the tightening process by making ultrasound measurements of the screw load. Yet it turned out that two other companies had already patented this process. The next step was to negotiate with the patent holders, which eventually produced an agreement with one to implement the ultrasound-measurement technology in the Erreka plant in Basque Country.

The change that this creates is profound. Erreka updated its very traditional manufacturing process to include high-end electronic processes using ultrasound sensors that can take measurements in picoseconds, enabling the company to bring to market a "smart product."

The leap goes even further: Erreka is now not only managing products; we are now managing data. Downstream, we're manufacturing the screw, supporting the assembly and maintenance of the whole component, and following up over time to prevent problems before they happen. Upstream, we're involved in the design of the entire process.

When we started commercializing our screws with sensors, a completely new world opened up. We acquired *data* that we could also commercialize beyond our traditional OEMs in the wind-energy sector.

Now the energy sector's biggest utilities — the ones that would buy power from the wind farms we served — were interested in tracking the moment-by-moment state of the critical connections our screws enabled.

We started commercializing this solution with our clients' clients, and our existing OEM clients began considering Erreka as not merely a parts supplier, but a data-services provider.

We gained access to the manufacturers of high-value components for the wind-power industry, such as the bolts for the blades on wind turbines, and many other services that would benefit from data control.

In this manner, we can rescue client-business sectors that only focused on screw attachments, and that had been in decline. They can now offer Erreka's smart components, with all the linked data. This includes oil and gas concerns, motor manufacturers, or construction that uses pre-tightened screws.

A leap from traditional products to smart products has also enhanced workers' self-esteem: they now know how to reposition the company in tough times.

From Smart Products to Smart Services

It took us some time to realize that the real differentiation is not the sales of sensor-equipped products. Clients do not buy a sensorized screw because it is a "smart product," but because of the overall benefits that the product offers. So we started thinking about how we sell services. We had not previously considered services, but our new strategies were bringing us closer to this idea.

As we introduced our sensors into the market, the technical level of our sales team has changed. We are no longer accessed through our purchasing department. We had to start involving the technicians in charge of designing the new wind-power systems.

These technicians started designing more powerful turbines with screwed connections that would be submitted to greater stresses, and in which fatigue of materials and structures becomes complex. During the first years of the 2010s, wind generators were producing one megawatt; by the end of the decade they were up to 12 megawatts. The technological leap in that time was huge.

These design challenges require profound engineering advances in the screwed connections — challenges that emerge in every phase of energy production. How do we develop designs that can take greater loads, and are subjected to greater fatigue, if they cannot handle the challenges in tightening the screws? How do we guarantee a good tightening process during assembly, with bigger screws that are harder for operators in the field to manipulate and tighten under very harsh conditions, such as the assembly of an offshore wind farm in cold northern waters? How do we guarantee the integrity of the screwed connection during huge winter storms over the next 25 to 30 years?

The case of the offshore wind farms is particularly interesting. The wind generators are huge; their designs are taken to their engineering limits; they have to operate in very aggressive environments, full of temperature changes, humidity, salts, winter storms; and also they are very far apart from each other, covering large areas. It becomes very expensive to have to adjust something, and sometimes impossible due to weather conditions. In these situations, monitoring the screws is very helpful. It identifies the lifespan of the screws, and enables quick, prioritized interventions if specific turbines need to be fixed or adjusted after a big storm. It's much more efficient than having to check each turbine, and helps avoid more serious damage.

We focused on selling services linked to the integrity of custom-engineered industrial fasteners. Our sensors differentiate us, but we can use other types of commercial sensors that measure other factors, and develop new strategies that respond to other challenges that emerge among our current clients, as well as clients outside of the wind-energy sector.

We created a system for studying our clients' different challenges, and developing solutions to each case. This has allowed Erreka to create a catalogue of high-end industrial services, including real-load measurements, optimized tightening, predictive and corrective maintenance strategies, fatigue characterization, design-to-cost, joint design and tightening for severe thermal conditions, leak prevention for high-pressure systems, high risk fluid-failure analysis, and designing maintenance operations without having to use cranes.

Orienting Erreka towards services means that workers have to change their orientation as well, which would be impossible without their full commitment in a process that creates jobs and values those workers. As a service provider, new needs are always arising, which attract valuable new team members, and some workers even change their job responsibilities. Historically, co-op workers operated forging machines, and some still do; Erreka's new service offerings also require people capable of throwing themselves from a wind tower, or finding patterns in data. These are big leaps that could not have been possible without the combined knowledge of the team. That's the value at the core of Erreka's business.

Can a Screw Generate New Businesses?

Erreka has demonstrated, through its fastening solutions business, that the future of traditional and local companies can emerge from a united team of workers that think about the essence of what they have been doing, and then explore ways of adding new value propositions.

The company has gone from offering a traditional product to a smart product, and from there to offering integrated services, all without abandoning the original product. In fact, that original product is used as leverage, so that the whole team remains united, rowing together, allowing the new roles and businesses that can guarantee the future of our social environment as we grow from a local business to a global business that offers valuable work.

Our lessons learned:

- Look for the essence of our business: even if our product is a commodity, knowing that our team's knowledge can get us closer to more valuable solutions.

- Work through the quick commercialization of our ideas, and work around any external barriers, such as with the owners of existing patents outside the company.

- The market looks for solutions to problems, not more sensors.

- If we work with data, our future clients may be different from our current clients. Working with our clients' clients is risky, but puts us at a different sales level.

- To sell services, we have to rapidly adapt our internal capacity and team structures, in order to respond to new needs, and incorporate valuable new roles.

- Most important is our team's self-esteem and ability to row all together; everyone has a place in the new business model, even the workers who remain in the traditional side of the business.

CHAPTER 12

Ten Reasons for Mondragon

Agustín Markaide Soraluce

These are my 10 reasons for a cooperative to decide to be, or remain, part of Mondragon:

1) Because I am part of Mondragon

It represents me and I am a constituent part of the project. I have inherited it, they gave it to me, it is my patrimony. It is my responsibility. I appreciate it and I must improve it and give it to future generations.

When I joined my cooperative as a member, I also secured my participation in the cultural heritage represented, in *Euskadi* (Basque Country) and in the world, by the "Mondragon Cooperative Experience." It was given to me by those who created and improved it and I received it almost unconsciously, perhaps because it was free, giving it less value and recognition than it deserved.

This heritage is a gift, but it is also a responsibility. I can turn to it, but I must also take care of it and increase it. It alone does not sustain itself; it is sustained by actions consistent with its values of people that are part of it.

Losing that value for the future would be irresponsible. If we see that the values we have proudly claimed are at risk, we should act to preserve them.

I owe it to those who preceded us and, above all, to those who follow us, to whom I cannot deny it for selfish reasons or for carelessness or negligence.

2) Because by putting our voices together, we can be heard louder and farther

Ideas of cooperation to solve problems small and large are not fashionable or expanding. Liberal ideas for the economy, those that extol individualism and personal enrichment, are the ones that win all over the world, and the confrontation of interests — between workers and employers, for example — is the expected way of approaching relationships.

Therefore, cooperatives are strangers and generate distrust in financial markets and other agencies. Not even in Euskadi are we social partners in many matters that affect us.

Only by joining forces and voices can we give our ideas a chance, and we cannot just make them last — we must also expand their relevance. Ours are useful ideas, put to work in practice; they are imperfect learnings but based on facts, not on mere words.

3) Because people are the most important thing

People are important in any project, but in our cooperatives there is nothing else that is as important as the people we are today and those who will be in the future. Every well-run company will make sure that its people feel like they are at home. But the cooperative *IS* our home and only *WE* can build it and determine its future.

Training cooperative people and cooperative leaders is essential to function in cooperation — and is not an easy task. Our environment does not educate us to work in favor of the whole, to think of others, or of "us." The management demands on the members of the cooperative are extreme; the governance of advanced companies is much more demanding than in the past, and cooperatives cannot act like traditional, competitive companies.

In many moments of life, we have seen how each cooperative cannot alone continuously create the human capacity necessary to remain among the best. An isolated cooperative project will have to periodically overcome problems of this kind in order to survive.

In addition, we have a primary responsibility to the people who work with us who are not members of the cooperative. We have to advance management models that will allow us to apply the same values and practices in all the societies we work with around the world. It's a difficult challenge without collective enthusiasm and learning.

4) Because we help each other

Especially in challenging times, there is no other group, outside of Mondragon, that will give part of its profits to a company that it does not have an ownership relationship with, and relieve that company of social expenses, and support it financially, without asking for anything in return.

We have seen, quite often, how cooperatives that went through major difficulties support each other, not only financially, but also with *people* — with staffing and personnel who strengthened their capacities. And, later, they have become important projects that we are all proud of, and with which we identify.

(Unfortunately, we have not been able to solve difficulties in all such cases.)

And also, of course, we help each other throughout our business and cooperative life when things are going well. Intercooperation is an essential principle.

Some define it as "one for all and all for one."

5) Because society needs it

Society needs the company to share its hopes for change, for property that is not appropriated by a few. It needs cohesion. It needs a more equitable distribution of wealth. It needs co-responsible people, not victims.

Yet the society that surrounds us displays strong individualistic tendencies; it victimizes, and doesn't encourage the shared responsibility of searching for solutions to problems, especially for those who do not constitute a profitable market.

This happens while technology offers us greater capabilities and when human challenges are enormous and growing.

What kind of solutions will we as a society create for these challenges?

Many people who see these problems worldwide agree that it is necessary for companies to take a more relevant, more human, more responsible, more cohesive social role. Cooperatives do that, all over the world. The Mondragon cooperatives were created for that purpose, and we represent that hope.

6) Because we have a "home"

We cooperative members and our cooperatives have a "home." Finance capital has no home, it has only "interests."

Our house is not only our cooperative, but also our family, our people, our culture. And all this lives, together, in the same "home." Therefore, we defend what we are, our identity, *gure aitaren etxea* ("our parents' home").[1]

And this happens in every place where we are. The cooperative has members around the world. Thus, when we go through difficulties, we often resist giving up, when giving up could be the simplest and most advisable thing to do. But we will not so readily put our "home" at risk.

This could be considered as a weak point compared to others. When faced with risk, the traditional business perspective packs its bags right away.

But our history is full of cases in which tenacity and professionalism have managed to find a way to overcome difficulties, and weaknesses, and turn them around, before abandoning or relocating becomes the only option. Often, Mondragon has been part of the answer — although, unfortunately, this does not happen in all such cases.

7) Because it is useful for any size of cooperative

If I am a small cooperative, in Mondragon I find community. I can use the common instruments, created and financed by and for cooperatives. Cooperative delegations working abroad and at home help me to open new markets and get customers. Other business mechanisms and services help to finance me or improve my management, and not make the mistakes that others made before me. I can act, in many cases, as if I were bigger.

Whether I am small or large, I get referrals and educational resources for the most diverse situations socially and in business, and I contribute my learnings to others. Cooperatives share their experiences in all important fields.

And throughout this cooperative community, I explain who I am, and what I want, just by saying where I come from, because I am preceded by the reputation built by everyone before me. They know and appreciate me before they see me.

This is how I build, with others, the best collective form of mutual support that I have ever imagined.

8) Because Mondragon is a permanent university of social co-responsibility

We are all permanent learners at this university. New cooperative members join with all the rights of membership, each one coming from their own environment, and entering the larger Mondragon environment together. The diversity of situations and approaches provides a wealth of learning that makes us more resistant to new problems. Biology shows us how diverse populations are able to overcome difficulties better and faster than homogeneous ones.

We learn by facing problems. We learn more in difficult situations. Comfortable situations are bad for learning how to work in support of others or for the future. In fact, in these cases, generosity often becomes an impossible subject and self-centeredness prevails: We want everything, *now*. Like spoiled children.

In this university of cooperative life, we get used to curbing our immediate impulses, and instead think and act in favor of a common future — with others, and for future generations. And over time, and after overcoming different challenges, we graduate with successive "degrees" in social co-responsibility. (Although, as always, there are some who do not.)

In short, we learn to apply family lessons to the company — and in the end to society as well, as if to a larger family.

What we learn is not limited to working and cooperative life; we also use it in our social lives. And, where cooperative density is most important, the social impact is most noticeable and society changes.

Which, after all, is one of our essential purposes.

9) My aspirations are added to those of Mondragon

We all look for ways to give meaning to our lives and our actions. We like to be an active part of the stories that happen around us, and we set ourselves personal and professional challenges to gain satisfaction from.

Mondragon is not the football club of my passions. It is not the NGO into which I pour my free time and my donations. It doesn't help me overcome personal sporting challenges. Nor does it need to be.

Through my daily work, together with thousands of other cooperative members like me, I build a meaningful, more egalitarian, and supportive reality. This helps advance many of the things that are important to me and society. It's a reality that, sometimes, I take for granted, as if it were a landscape, in which nothing had to be done to maintain and improve it. That is not the case.

Participation in Mondragon is additive, it is not disjunctive. To participate in any affiliated cooperative is to participate in Mondragon. Participation happens at different levels; they are added, not excluded or competed. If one wins, the other does not lose — *both win*.

Cooperative members and cooperatives join forces to strengthen Mondragon; on the other hand, the result of competing to damage the other company would be that we would all lose. Nobody would win.

The participation of each one in this Mondragon Experience is an opportunity to expand the meaning of the work to which we dedicate a large part of our time and our efforts. It is an opportunity for non-alienating work.

The sense of the social, participatory and solidarity inherent in the Mondragon Experience surpasses simple daily work: it turns into the construction of a "cathedral." And this utopian effort has the capacity to shape reality: it questions, elevates, and modifies it.

10) Because vitality and cooperative "soul" are in Mondragon

There are many cooperatives in the world that are not in Mondragon. In fact, in Euskadi there are more than 1,400 cooperatives, but only 100 are in Mondragon.

However, Mondragon is the global standard. It is the one that attracts Nobel laureates and international analysts (Stiglitz, Krugman, Chomsky); the one that annually provokes dozens of studies in universities, and reports in the most prestigious news media; the one that generates an intense pilgrimage to know and learn from the Mondragon Experience.

It is not the model of perfection, nor has it solved all its problems. Far from it. Mondragon is the standard because it represents the permanent struggle for utopia *and also* for the evident results achieved in that struggle ("Mondragon will change the world," reports *Fortune* magazine in its ranking of companies with social commitment).

All this, against the dominant currents in the world of finance and business.

And it will continue to be the benchmark because time is showing that the values we declare (which lead to "changing the company to change society") really matter to the people who constitute Mondragon.

This is the "soul" of Mondragon.

Hopefully, time will show that these values also matter to cooperatives that are not in Mondragon and to all kinds of companies that have a genuine commitment to change, and to improve society.

End-note

[1] The original expression is taken from *Euskera*, the language of the Basque Country, and is the title of the best-known poem by the Basque poet Gabriel Aresti, in which he refers to the defense of the Basque Country and its culture. The literal translation is "our father's house."

PART 3

Mondragon's Global Influence

Mondragon has earned an outsized mission and values-based influence far beyond its regional home in Spain. Today, the group annually hosts between three and four million industrial tourism visitors (returning to pre-Covid levels) from all parts of the world through Otalora, Mondragon's Center for Management & Cooperative Development, housed in a rural mid-14th century manor. This section examines how Mondragon continues to inspire and catalyze local stakeholder ownership, creating and preserving good worker cooperative and union jobs in Preston, UK, Germany and in South Korea.

CHAPTER 13

The Role of Faith in Civic Renewal: Pope Francis, Catholic Social Justice & Mondragon

Paying It Forward – Moral Populism & America's Solidarity Dividend

Brian Corbin & Michael Peck

It is easier for a camel to go through the eye of a needle than for a rich man to enter the kingdom of God. (Mark 10:25)

Writing in her 2021 book *Mutualism: Building the Next Economy from the Ground Up*, Sara Horowitz observes:

> Religious institutions have always been some of the most powerful incubators of mutualist activity. After all, religion gives us the world's first labor story: Exodus. Pharaoh was the first bad boss. Moses was the first labor leader, and the Exodus was the first strike. (Horowitz, 2021, p.7)_

By this reckoning, Jesus was the first social democrat, distributing fish and bread to the masses, demonstrating that faith in the miracle of sufficiency equal to the needs of all feeds the hungry and heals the sick.

This chapter is about scholarly activism expressed at a basic level and not the reverse. Its mission-driven purpose connects moral populism with new labor organizing, and links legacy definitions of

Catholic social justice thinking and doing, outreach, and movement building (Catholic Social Teaching, 2023) to the tense present in present tense. It seeks to define and outline a higher regenerating, transformative societal ethos through cause and effect, tenet, and practice, to heal a multi-pandemic economy reeling from Covid-19, climate, and predatory capitalism.

This chapter warns of losing defining freedoms to resurgent authoritarianism. It recoils from the encroaching digital Metaverse, which would aggregate, monetize, and commoditize what remains of the civic commons by data mining and co-opting every formerly unalienable right and freedom — including religious convictions. It hopes to uplift proven inspirational pathways showing how to heal an information-manipulated country where voting citizens willingly step through a cultural Carrollian looking glass in search of more authentic tribal identity.

Both co-authors claim equal inspiration from the living Mondragon cooperative ecosystem. One of us (Brian) is a devout Catholic from Midwest Ohio, fulfilling a frontline servant-leader role in one of America's most impactful charities. The other (Michael) is from mixed Jewish and Catholic religious heritage, raised in the US Northeast as a multi-denominational Protestant (Episcopal, Congregationalist, Christian Science), who served as Mondragon International's USA and Canada delegate from 1999-2019.

What we believe in unison by reading the "signs of the times" past, present, and future, starts with Catholic social doctrine's moral methodology based on "See, Judge, Act." Pope Francis refers to this viewpoint explicitly and in measuring purpose against practice, and the Mondragon cooperative ecosystem example provides the world's leading industrial reference.

During the past 70 years, Mondragon has organically risen to fulfil its originating mission, serving as the backbone of a Basque regional economy successfully, competing locally within Spain, and today on a global scale.

Mondragon and the Basque Region continue to mark GINI index social equality, cultural solidarity, and climate resiliency metrics (2021), leading to upward socioeconomic transformation — all underpinned in Mondragon's case by 10 foundational worker-cooperative principles, accompanied by first-rate education and training, technology innovation and adoption, and consistent reinvestment in its "one worker, one vote" workplace democracy ecosystem.

The debate continues both within and external to Mondragon, whether this living model is exportable beyond its borders or simply indigenous to its historical and socio-cultural legacy.

We believe this question is moot, a false choice. Instead, we hold that the global pandemics of Covid, climate and predatory capitalism compel localized, hybrid adoptions of the Mondragon ecosystem to build mutualist voice and agency that can begin healing our world and our planet.

What We See

Religious faith in America's present and immediate future is haunted by a widening dichotomy between Jesus the Christ and militant nationalist Christianity.

The former distributes fish and bread to the masses, showing how the grace of moral and spiritual solidarity leads to the miracle of sufficiency equal to needs, feeding the hungry, healing the sick, dying under torture while forgiving tormentors and the sins of this world. The latter convenes and condones the Insurrection of January 6, 2021, carrying Nazi and Confederate flags into the US Capitol edifice for the first time in its erected history to ignite deeper rifts between grace and grievance.

The Old Testament common to three of the world's leading religions (Judaism, Christianity & Islam) declares that "faith is the substance of things hoped for, the evidence of things not seen" (Hebrews 11:1 KJV). Human history is replete with examples of how belief activates faith into practice, transforming results.

A principal New Testament differential describes Jesus as the first divine being who showed that God cared enough about the human creation to be present in the moment, incarnated in human flesh, not as a distant or abstract deity. Jesus as the second Person of the Trinity willingly sits and suffers at humanity's table, one of us in but not of this world, preaching and practicing solidarity with the most vulnerable and marginalized, recruiting them as disciples, healing their redlined neighborhood diseases, inspiring souls to join in the table and the cross.

Somehow, this core teaching has been lost. Heather Cox Richardson (2022) observes, "American evangelicals are converting to the Russian Orthodox Church out of support for its nativism, white nationalism, rejection of LGBTQ rights and abortion, and support for authoritarian Russian president Vladimir Putin." Like him, they object to the diversity inherent in democracy. Axios reports on how politics is poisoning Christian evangelism to the point where "the Church is not a victim of America's civic strife. Instead, it is one of the principal catalysts." Polls show that when organized religion hotly pursues political power, spirituality retreats from the civic commons, believers in tow (Alberta, 2022).

Similarly, America's social compact fails forward if it lacks inclusive healing that transforms rank individualism into a promised unifying "solidarity dividend" (McGhee, 2021). The absolute shareholder primacy of the Old Testament's "dominion over the fish of the sea, and over the fowl of the air, and over the cattle, and over all the earth and over every creeping thing that creepeth upon the earth" (Genesis 1:26) commoditizes human beings and brings the American Republic's democratic expression to a creeping halt.

Under Chief Justice John Roberts, the US Supreme Court "has become the most pro-religion it's been since at least the 1950s, and it appears to include the six most pro-religion justices since at least World War II" (Philbrick, 2022). However true, the net effect has not translated into greater majority public support for the Court as an institution, nor for its decisions, and neither has such outward religiosity, which blurs distinctions between church and state, helped to sit more attendees in Sunday church pews.

Already more than 21% of all Americans do not identify with any religion, similar to the acceleration rate in the rise of political independents (40% to 50%) over faithful adherence to and identification with any political party (B. Walsh, 2021; Reilly, Salit & Ali, 2022). Only 47% of Americans currently belong to a church, cathedral, synagogue, temple, mosque, or other holy institutions "not of this world," falling from 70% at the turn of the century (B. Walsh, 2021). Emma Goldberg in the *New York Times* (2021) highlights Harvard University's new chief chaplain, an atheist, symbolizing this growing trend of religious refugees seeking cooperation instead of conflict between people of different faiths, thirsting for authentic spirituality without vertically organized religious hierarchies getting in the way.

There are signs that both religious institutions and multilateral organizations are recalibrating relationships, and that both institutions and the public can change for the better. For example, the United Nations supports an interfaith coalition with shared roots in the Old Testament putting pressure on banks to end "all financing towards any new oil and gas projects exploration and extraction projects," including coal in Europe and the OECD, by 2030 and by 2040 worldwide (Sauca *et al.*, 2022).

Rounding out the introductory Sara Horowitz quote on biblical bad bosses, labor leaders and strikes are additional Old and New Testament stories, as well as from the Koran, of prophets feeding starving and desperate multitudes and proclaiming a year of jubilee.

If offered, America would welcome this nonpartisan, multi-denominational approach to spiritual and civic healing. We sense the country, and the planet, might be healed if only the pounding of the drums would stop; if the demagogues caterwauling scorn, hatred, fear and violence from their media and political golden thrones could be silenced not by fiat, but by massive moral rejection. What we see is that the emerging marketplace for inclusive common good can actively, individually, and collectively tune out cacophony in favor of relearning and pursuing how solidarity can produce the harmony needed to redesign, rebuild, uplift, and heal America's battered civic soul. It can be profitable, purposeful, participative, inclusive and harmonious.

We believe humanity can step back from the brink created by the crises of Covid, climate, and predatory capitalism, and take new, decisive steps towards healing, freedom, peace, and civic salvation. We are witness to how faith produces miracles of certainty so that:

> … alongside profit-oriented private enterprise and the various types of public enterprise, there must be room for commercial entities based on mutualist principles and pursuing social ends to take root and express themselves. It is from their reciprocal encounter in the marketplace that one may expect hybrid forms of commercial behavior to emerge, and hence an attentiveness to ways of civilizing the economy. (Pope Benedict XVI, 2009, para.38).

This is about purpose-driving the macroeconomics of the many to pursue a stakeholder-as-shareholder economy benchmarked by mutualist ESG (environment, social, governance) standards and UN-inspired sustainable development goals (SDGs) and metrics. This is about casting aside shareholder-primacy externalities and replacing them with assumptions that are more fair, shared and virtuous cycle-structured; about how to be "spiritual without being necessarily religious;" about reimagining and communicating restorative, regenerative, respectful language that seeds better practice by "meeting people where they are with love and respect," as Rebecca Henderson shared with the co-authors. It is a language grounded in ethics and grace, molding spiritually secular-civic movements dedicated to sharing and expanding the common good.

What We Judge

The heart of "judging" requires the revelation of what a just and peaceful society looks like, and how it is organized. The Old Testament prophets reminded Israel about their heritage from Genesis onwards to celebrate being a "People in covenant with their Lord," wherein no one feels abandoned, rights are redressed through jubilee years and Zion celebrates its splendor.

The Christian community goes further and claims that the Covenant has been fulfilled with the Incarnation, where everyone is welcomed to the Table, and no one suffers from unmet needs, since the community shares generously and the political-economic paradigm has shifted from exile to abundance.

In Catholic social thought, the four values of truth, justice, freedom, and love — along with four principles of human dignity, common good, solidarity, and subsidiarity — provide the operative analytical lens. In this context, we "judge" current reality regarding its distance from or closeness to the original sign of covenant or blessing found rooted in the sixth day of creation as each person was made in God's very image and likeness (Pontifical Council for Justice & Peace, 2006).

What we "see" appears to indicate that we may be far from that moment of original blessing and insight of abundance found in the proverbial holy Garden of Eden located metaphysically in our heart, mind, and soul.

Though 46 years apart, the falls of Kabul, Afghanistan, in August 2021, and Saigon, Vietnam, in April 1975, challenge America's basic social compacts (Risen, 2021). The lessons are never learned, and too many inconvenient truths cloud, obscure, and obliterate the definitions of winning and losing. America applauds returning war veterans still in uniform, only to abandon them to post-service joblessness, PTSD, housing evictions, and "deaths of despair" suicide rates 50% higher than their peers who never served (Stop Soldier Suicide, *n.d.*). Half an American century after Saigon, America is still unable to answer John Kerry's historic questions to the Senate Foreign Relations Committee on April 22, 1971: "How do you ask a man [or a woman] to be the last man [or woman] to die in Vietnam?," and, "How do you ask a man [or woman] to be the last man [or woman] to die for a mistake?" (C-SPAN, 1971). Likewise, David Paul Kuhn's painful and unanswerable questions demand a moral clarity that we must reclaim: "Amid historic wealth and cultural gaps, is this once-iconic meritocracy increasingly dependent on a small worker class to do our suffering? Have we now become a society of 'expendables'?" (Kuhn, 2020).

The expendables of the opioid crisis are now the expendables of the pandemic — well over 600,000 Americans murdered by opioids so far, while the Covid death toll already exceeds 1.13 million more domestic victims with no end yet in sight (Glenza, 2022; White *et al.*, 2022). This reliance upon "expendability" is driven by predatory economic systems and violates the cry of justice echoed through the centuries by the Prophets — and re-called into prominence recently by Pope Francis.

Moral inclusion is the opposite of expendable or deplorable "lepers." All are made in God's image and likeness.

Yet the global precariat's struggles with exclusion, systemic racism, and socioeconomic inequalities are among the first battles to win if the pandemic is to serve as a portal into a more just, virtuous-cycle planet. "Covid-19 has exposed these gaps in our public solidarity, not caused them" (Carroll, 2021). The world collectively witnesses all physical, moral, political, cultural, ideological, and religious infections "tracing the routes of inequality."

Ra Criscitiello, Deputy Research Director, SEIU-UHW, in the July 2020 Union-Coops UK & UK Cooperative College *Manifesto for Decent Work 22*, observed Covid-19 has exposed the "servant economy's" inherent contradiction. Essential workers are often "people of color and, because largely misclassified as independent contractors, are denied the protections and benefits of formal employment that are currently so needed. Now more than ever is a time to focus on creating a different kind of economy that centers worker voice, pooled advocacy, employment benefits, and focuses on better work lives for low-wage workers who have historically been undervalued in many undeserved and unproductive ways."

Consider the contrasts between the vicious and virtuous cycles.

Predatory gig-economy companies (*e.g.*, Uber, DoorDash, Lyft) are investing hundreds of millions of dollars in ballot campaigns across the country to drive down wages and increase profits through misclassification schemes that "define-down" gig workers as independent contractors rather than employees. Some are successful, such as 2020's Proposition 22 in California (2020 California Proposition 22, 2023); others don't gain traction, such as the Massachusetts gig-worker initiative that was found by the state supreme court to violate state law, and was therefore ineligible to go before voters — a major win for labor rights activists who argue that companies have been failing to provide proper worker protections and benefits, like workers' compensation or even a basic minimum wage (Bellan, 2022b). Yet Uber CEO Dara Khosrowshahi has stated multiple times that the company would support and promote similar proposals across the US (Bellan, 2021). Uber and other companies are actively working to do just that in states such as Illinois, New Jersey, New York and Washington (Bellan, 2022a).

Contrast this predatory approach with a virtuous-cycle alternative: The Drivers Cooperative (drivers.coop), based in New York City, uplifts and empowers over 2,500 driver-member-owners of a ride-hailing enterprise through their Co-op Ride app. This includes a free, online course (drivers.coop/academy) where prospective driver-owners can meet like-minded drivers and allies from around the world. The company has already raised over $1 million through regulation crowdfunding, while maintaining 100% driver-ownership (Conger, 2021).

Look what happens when the profits flow sideways, to stakeholders as shareholders.

The "Great Resignation," "Great Attrition," and by default, "Great Reflection" and "Great Reset," serve as prologue to entirely new concepts of human and social assets, resources and capital centered around working-class lives and sustainable destinies, their families and communities who depend on equal access to decent remuneration from dignified work.

Celebrating a resurrected spirit of "humanity at work" is compatible with believing, declaring, and advocating on behalf of worker rights to basic equalities such as workers becoming stakeholder-owners with a voice, a vote, a seat at the decision-making table, and a union to represent them if they so vote.

Otherwise, driving and living without agency means feudally serving those with agency from serf-farming someone else's land to gig-driving as part of someone else's app. Nothing changes except the extraction platform.

The co-authors confess to professing an enthusiastic, underlying loyalty to the ever-evolving Mondragon cooperative ecosystem's seven decades of "ordinary people doing extraordinary things" through secular shared purpose, values, and performance (Mondragon Corporation, n.d.).

Likewise, Pope Francis's deliberate acts of love open minds and hearts to more transparent, inclusive, and mutualist structures and outcomes.

How We Act, Part 1

There is no Catholic teaching called "common good capitalism." It's simply the common good. Furthermore, the history of such teaching has been very concerned about the "logic of the state" versus the "logic of the market" and wanting an alternative way to think about political economy.

Pope Benedict XVI (2009) calls it "logic of gift" wherein new forms of organizations with stakeholder-centric structures work for the common good with co-ownership as a critical thought and process.

Pope Francis frames this as the disregarded lives of the margins now coming to center stage and increasingly adopted into mainstream thinking. In a trifecta pandemic world (of Covid, climate change, and predatory capitalism) the peripheries equally inform the centers across borders and oceans, time zones and space. Market forces can uplift all stakeholders as shareholders once the markets themselves are no longer shareholder primacy owned, commoditized, and arbitraged.

Moral populism dismantles this hierarchy in favor of combining workplace democracy, technology innovation, constant cross-training, and retraining, allowing shared purpose-driven businesses and their ecosystems in hybrid permutations to reflect and optimize local culture and well-being. In the moral populism of Mondragon, ecosystem dynamics permit the market-influenced transfer of capital and labor between cooperatives of all categories, starting with sector-influenced spin-offs, producing start-ups as well as competitive products and services.

Rapidly evolving ESG standards and UN-inspired SDGs (sdgs.un.org) — while suffering through predictable waves of "greenwashing" and counterfeiting — inspire a global social-impact investing community that identifies, commits, and measures human, social, climate, and financial capital flows which, for the first time, are created equal in recognized impact, if not yet practice. (Claims of one-third or half of the world's money committing to net zero metrics come up short against actual practice. Amy Cortese of Impact Alpha informs that "being committed to net zero is not the same as being Net Zero.")

Pope Francis insists that it is time again for people of faith and goodwill to re-ask the question posed in the biblical story of the Tower of Babel (Genesis 11:1–9): "Which was more valuable, the brick or the worker? Which was considered an expendable surplus in the pursuit of endless growth?" (Pope Francis & Ivereigh, 2020). Francis worries about the prevalent ideologies that have trapped global humanity pre-pandemic in cause, effect, and prophecy of reappearance by writing:

> It is striking how neoliberal currents of thought have sought to exclude from the political arena any substantive debate about the common good and the universal destination of goods. What they promote instead is essentially the efficient management of a market and minimal government control. But the problem is that when the economy's primary purpose centers on profit, it is easy to forget that the earth's resources are for all, not the few. The obsession with profit weakens the institutions that can protect people from reckless economic interests and the excessive concentration of power. The increasing social conflicts are in large part fed by inequality and injustice, but their underlying cause lies in the fraying of the bonds of belonging. An atomized society can never be at peace with itself because it fails to see the social effects of inequality. Fraternity is today our new frontier. (p.108).

How can "fraternity" confront and overcome the 2021-2022 trifecta-pandemic economy? How can it help transition "humanity at work" from shareholder primacy to stakeholder centric interconnecting and ecosystem enabling virtuous cycles? Francis also notes:

> We have worldviews — such as the various kinds of populism — that deform the meaning of the word "people" by hitching it to ideologies that focus on perceived enemies, internal and external. If one worldview exalts and promotes the atomized individual, leaving little room for fraternity and solidarity, the other reduces the people to a faceless mass it claims to represent. (p.107-108)

The 1worker1vote movement (1worker1vote.org) declares that worker-ownership and the democratic governance that comes with it create fraternity, unity, caring, and healing rather than the "atomized individual" and the "faceless mass."

In August 2018, Michael Peck co-authored a *Harvard Business Review* article with Ibon Zugasti and Peter Walsh that predicted:

Within the next decade, we expect worker- and employee-owned companies to grow in popularity thanks to three mutually reinforcing trends: First, renewed interest in ensuring the economic viability of local communities suggests that Baby Boomer owners about to retire are increasingly likely to want to sell to workers. Second, evidence is mounting that worker- and employee-owned enterprises outperform their competitors, especially during economic downturns… Third, as a result of strong performances by worker- and employee-owned companies, it is becoming easier for workers to overcome arguably the biggest hurdle to worker buyouts: financing. (P. Walsh et al., 2018)

Pope Francis highlights this specific understanding about an appropriate role for populism in the World Meeting of Popular Movements in Bolivia in 2015, here noted in a speech to various groups of organized low-income and working-class persons that:

> … popular movements play an essential role, not only by making demands and lodging protests, but even more basically by being creative. You are social poets: creators of work, builders of housing, producers of food, above all for people left behind by the world market. (Pope Francis, 2015a, 2015b)

Francis continues with a specific definition for his vision of an authentic populism rooted in the reality of poverty, and the need for leadership from below and from those most impacted by decisions:

> I have seen first-hand a variety of experiences where workers united in cooperatives and other forms of community organization were able to create work where there were only crumbs of an idolatrous economy. I have seen some of you here. Recuperated businesses, local fairs and cooperatives of paper collectors are examples of that popular economy which is born of exclusion and which, slowly, patiently and resolutely adopts solidary forms which dignify it. How different this is than the situation which results when those left behind by the formal market are exploited like slaves!
>
> Governments which make it their responsibility to put the economy at the service of peoples must promote the strengthening, improvement, coordination and expansion of these forms of popular economy and communitarian production. This entails bettering the processes of work, providing adequate infrastructures and guaranteeing workers their full rights in this alternative sector. When the state and social organizations join in working for the three "Ls," the principles of solidarity and subsidiarity come into play; and these allow the common good to be achieved in a full and participatory democracy. (Pope Francis, 2015a)

The three Ls referred to by Pope Francis are "land," "lodging" and "labor." He continues his reflection on these three Ls, on the use and abuse of populism, and his insights about a "solidarity dividend" form of ethical and political economy. In his book, *Let Us Dream: The Path to a Better Future* (Pope Francis & Ivereigh, 2020), specifically calling upon leaders to recognize the importance of voice and engagement of those most impacted, Francis writes:

An authentic politics designs those changes alongside, with, and by means of all those affected, respecting their culture and their dignity. The only time it is right to look down at someone is when we are offering our hand to help them get up. As I once put it in a talk to some religious men and women: "The problem is not feeding the poor, or clothing the naked, or visiting the sick, but rather recognizing that the poor, the naked, the sick, prisoners, and the homeless have the dignity to sit at our table, to feel 'at home' among us, to feel part of a family. This is the sign that the Kingdom of Heaven is in our midst." In the post-Covid world, neither technocratic managerialism nor populism will suffice. Only a politics rooted in the people, open to the people's own organization, will be able to change our future. (p.113)

Pope Francis leaves no doubt as to why he believes peoples have risen up around the world to demand change:

The Neo-Darwinist ideology of the survival of the fittest, underpinned by an unfettered market obsessed with profit and individual sovereignty, has penetrated our culture and hardened our hearts. The successful growth of the technocratic paradigm so often demands the sacrifice of innocent lives: the child abandoned in the streets; the underage sweatshop worker who rarely sees the light of day; the worker dismissed because his company has been asset-stripped to generate dividends for shareholders; the refugees denied the chance to work; the elderly abandoned to their fate in underfunded care homes. (p.116)

Francis then segues to the heart of his social analysis of the populism phenomenon, the globalization of indifference:

Populisms are often described as a protest against globalization, although they are more properly a protest against the globalization of indifference. At bottom they reflect pain at the loss of roots and community, and a generalized feeling of anguish. Yet, in generating fear and sowing panic, populisms are the exploitation of that popular anguish, not its remedy. The often-cruel rhetoric of populist leaders denigrating the "other" in order to defend a national or group identity reveals its spirit. It is a means by which ambitious politicians attain power. In the name of the people, populism denies the proper participation of those who belong to the people, allowing a particular group to appoint itself the true interpreter of popular feeling. A people ceases to be a people and becomes an inert mass manipulated by a party. (pp.117-118)

Francis' searing words and resilient principles erect a bulwark of moral reason against today's performative populism facilitated by invasive social media platforms devouring and perverting every previously known and accepted truth in sight.

In that spirit, Facebook formally rebranded as Meta on October 28, 2021, anticipating a global, pandemic-inspired need to exchange a punishing physical world for a virtual one. This coincided with an Axios piece on "self-described Evangelicals" deciding to break away "from evangelical Christian churches" using "social media to engage tens of thousands of the former faithful" — representing a rich business opportunity for the recently announced Metaverse.

To that end, the New York Times reported, Meta is:

> ... intensifying formal partnerships with faith groups across the United States and shaping the future of religious experience ... Facebook has nearly three billion active monthly users, making it larger than Christianity worldwide, which has about 2.3 billion adherents, or Islam, which has 1.8 billion ... Many of Facebook's partnerships involve asking religious organizations to test or brainstorm new products "including exclusive content, like messages from the bishop; and another tool for worshipers watching services online to send donations in real time. (Dias, 2021; Hackett & McClendon, 2017)

The Bible, both the Old and New Testaments, chronicles never-ending examples of false prophets confusing outreach with impact. Concerted efforts to sell God to humankind while pursuing revenue streams is to chase Mammon, representing a false communion.

In stark contrast to Metaverse algorithmic religion, moral populism ontologically, empirically, and transcendentally invokes spiritual love and its inspiring triumph over the physical world. Revolutionary moral populists such as Mahatma Gandhi declared (Fischer, 1962), "to see the universal and all-pervading Spirit of Truth face to face, one must be able to love the meanest of all creation as oneself."

Nelson Mandela in *Long Walk to Freedom* (1995) stated:

> No one is born hating another person because of the color of his skin, or his background, or his religion. They must learn to hate, and if they can learn to hate, they can be taught to love, for love comes more naturally to the human heart than its opposite.

In his March 31, 1968, *Remaining Awake through a Great Revolution* speech at the National Cathedral in Washington, D.C., Martin Luther King Jr., predicted, "We shall overcome because the arc of the moral universe is long but it bends toward justice. Change takes a long time, but it does happen... Each of us who works for social change is part of the mosaic of all who work for justice; together we can accomplish multitudes" (King, 1968).

Pope Francis in his "Believe in Love" message, said:

> To love the poor means to combat all forms of poverty, spiritual and material. And it will also do us good. Drawing near to the poor in our midst will touch our lives. It will remind us of what really counts: to love God and our neighbor. Only this lasts forever, everything else passes away. What we invest in love remains, the rest vanishes. (von Stamwitz, 2018)

Sara Horowitz's mutualism thesis reflects this understanding. This is not about right or left, capitalism or socialism, but rather the living, reconciling, inclusive middle of a country desperately needing to return to basics and a more-perfecting union fairly based on shared community risks and rewards (Horowitz, 2021).

Heather McGhee in *The Sum of Us* (2021) refers to the "solidarity dividend" that America earns — and then can spend as healing capital. Tankersley & Deparle (2021) argue, similar to McGhee's vision, that there seems to be a new awakening to the role of government for social justice and equity that can unify workers and other middle-class families, noting that when groups are not pitted against each other, and both can obtain the public "investment" they need for a stable life, circumstances caused by divisive populism can be bridged.

This new "solidarity dividend" awakening arrives just in time to combat current civil society dystopia where all sides lose faith in origins, process, and outcomes. As the existentialists recognized almost a century ago, there is more solidarity in the shared destiny of absolute death than in discordant, relative life.

"Free marketplace" and civic-solidarity principles can combine with broadened and deepened workplace ownership to produce an operative, resilient, secular, and spiritual faith on which to construct new and improved virtuous cycles supporting more transparent free markets, stronger and resilient free governments, climate-friendly materials and processes, and more inclusive, local stakeholder-centric and equal-democratic societies.

Democracy, solidarity, equality, and other forms of caring human connections make a difference. They amount to friendship in human community. The New York Times reports that "a study of 21 billion Facebook friendships — about 84% of US adults aged 25 to 44 — uncovered a key to reducing poverty: friendships between the rich and poor (Miller et al., 2022).

How We Act, Part 2: Past, Present & Future Praxis

Father José María Arizmendiarrieta, the social justice village priest and co-founder (1956) of the Mondragon cooperative community, faced even more severe, reactionary populism and harsh political realities in the form of Spanish fascism and anti-Basque sentiment under Franco.

His rootedness in a moral vision of the common good, human dignity, solidarity, and subsidiarity that were developing as recognized Church teaching over 80 years ago engaged him to organize others in becoming artisans of their own destiny.

The body of Catholic social teachings that informed Mondragon's mid-20th century leaders progressively reinspire church and community leaders alike today to lead a transformational exodus from economic suffering and depravity into a more mutualist and inclusive community.

The moral populism inherent in this exodus is reflected by Mampilly (2021), who says:

> The presence of simultaneous uprisings in countries with a range of income levels, government types and geopolitical significance indicates a deeper disillusionment: the loss of faith in the social contract that shapes relations between governments and their people. Put simply, the governments of today seem incapable of offering both representative and effective governance. And ordinary citizens have had enough.

Aligning with Sara Horowitz's call for a "new mutualism," moral populism offers regenerating transformation through tenet and practice for bipartisan consideration. Horowitz (2021) observes that contemporary mutualism already exists in four principal areas: unions, cooperatives, mutual aid groups, and faith-based institutions.

Pope Francis, calling for a new form of mutual relations and solidarity, echoes this when he reflects:

> Now, more than ever, what is revealed is the fallacy of making individualism the organizing principle of society. What will be our new principle? We need a movement of people who know we need each other, who have a sense of responsibility to others and to the world. We need to proclaim that being kind, having faith, and working for the common good are great life goals that need courage and vigor; while glib superficiality and the mockery of ethics have done us no good. (Pope Francis & Ivereigh, 2020, p.6)

Francis continues:

> What ties us to each other is what we commonly call solidarity. Solidarity is more than acts of generosity, important as these are; it is the call to embrace the reality that we are bound by bonds of reciprocity. On this solid foundation, we can build a better, different, human future. It is an understanding sadly absent from contemporary political narratives, whether liberal or populist. (p.107)

This solidarity framework can help committed local stakeholders co-create safer, healthier, more rewarding, and personally fulfilling environments and ecosystems, both aspirational and lived, mutually accepted through a vote, a voice, and place-based equity share. It means uniting DIY-style self-reliance with synergistic, network-based sustainability as the focal point of every social compact equation ("for the people, by the people, of the people").

This is not new thinking, but it is dangerously missing in action on all levels — public, private, philanthropic, academic, and nonprofit. The condition and opportunities of women speak to this. From a social-justice perspective, the author Isabel Allende (2007) observes that "the poorest and most backward societies are those that put women down ... although women do two-thirds of the world's labor, they own less than 1% of the world's assets." In a similar vein, Baylor University historian Beth Allison Barr challenges the patriarchal Christian doctrine that God "wants women to support men but never lead them" (Barr, 2021; Griswold, 2021).

This patriarchal doctrine is not borne out in reality. According to an Impact Alpha newsletter (Isenberg & Neichin, 2021):

> Faith-based institutions were among the original impact investors._Congregations of religious women, for example, were instrumental in early efforts to hold public companies accountable and provide low-interest loans to nascent community development finance institutions, or CDFIs ... extending a hand to those in need is critical to an ethical society, even when it requires sacrifice.

Many of these early investments by women-sponsored religious orders utilized free-market capital to ensure inclusion of women, especially those disenfranchised and low-income, in economic circles and ownership structures. When women, as well as other marginalized persons, required a voice, capital investment in their projects and processes cemented their place at the table, a mutual winning formula to enhance and repeat.

Moral populism prepares the pathway for a world of rising, inclusive, and equalizing opportunities, where liberated cultural definitions of gender power and promise open on to limitless horizons of spiritual grace.

An inclusive moral populism also makes logical demographic sense. America's near-future "majority minority" workforce will be more race- and gender-diverse, older, and with higher education levels, starting with women. This workforce, and especially its essential-worker precariat — which lacks just compensation, benefits, and the right and ability to organize for self-betterment — suffered disproportionately during the pandemic (like their fallen and serving military comrades). Fortunately for America's vulnerable-but-vital civilian working class, ground-breaking legislation points the way forward.

California's proposed Power Act, formerly the Cooperative Economy Act (cooperativeeconomyact.org; American Sustainable Business Network, n.d.; McCarty Carino, 2023) empowers "gig and freelance" workers as owners. An economy that works for all must envision a new form of labor market intermediary, representing a new employment paradigm where both traditional employees and gig workers not only receive employment protections, but also own and govern their workplaces.

The Cooperative Economy Act defines a new class of worker, a "Cooperative Labor Contractor" status that protects workers, adds worker ownership, provides employment protections and benefits (such as minimum wage, paid sick leave, and unemployment), and accelerates misclassified workers' economic recovery from the Covid pandemic, and from structural inequalities, including systemic racism. As an antidote to misclassification by corporate gig-economy predators, it empowers a strategically positioned staffing intermediary in each affected industry sector that does pay living wages and benefits, is unionized, and facilitates worker ownership and workplace democracy practices.

Legacy remedies already exist. Following World War I and the global flu pandemic of 1918, the Catholic Bishops of the United States released a major document connecting efforts to defend political democracy with the lack of economic democracy (United States Catholic Bishops & National Catholic War Council, 1984). In their *Program of Social Reconstruction*, the bishops argued for social security, pensions, health care, worker safety, labor rights, and issued a clarion call for worker-owned cooperatives and other means for laborers to own the means of production. They wrote:

> The full possibilities of increased production will not be realized so long as the majority of workers remain mere wage earners. The majority must somehow become owners, at least in part, of the instruments of production.

Father José María Arizmendiarrieta's discovery of the body of Catholic social teachings fashioned his understanding of how to recreate forms of worker relationships that moved beyond — ethically and practically — the binds of industrial capitalism and fascist ideology. The Mondragon leaders heard about the radical call found in Pope Leo XIII's *Rerum Novarum* in 1891, that labor and capital "each needs the other: Capital cannot do without labor nor labor without capital (Pope Leo XIII, 1891). Leo XIII famously defended the rights of workers to a living and just wage, the right to strike, the right to form unions and bargain collectively.

Certainly, Father José María read about developments in Catholic social thought, especially after the publication of Pope Pius XI's *Quadragesimo Anno* (the 40th anniversary of Rerum Novarum) in May of 1931 (Pope Pius XI, 1931). In this document, the Church articulates its understanding of the need to find an alternative political-economic theory that differs from the collectivism of communism and the radical individualism of *laissez faire* capitalism.

Another important contribution in this document relates to the social-theoretical construct of mediating institutions and the proper role of subsidiarity. This principle maintains that decisions ought to be made by those persons and institutions closest to the situation. When a local group cannot solve the problem alone, it then has a right to call upon higher-level institutions who have an obligation to provide needed help — but without mandatory absorption into the greater whole. Subsidiarity in many ways echoes the refrain "nothing about us, without us, is for us," in a manner that recognizes both local rights and global responsibilities.

Before the death of Father José María in 1976, he would have heard the call of Pope Paul VI in his *Populorum Progressio* (1967) in which he called upon world leaders to recognize that people require an integral human development that incorporates material, physical, and spiritual goods, and that each person and group must be allowed to be "artisans of their destiny." We can make these assumptions, given the Mondragon Cooperative Corporation's adoption of the seven recognized cooperative principles (Cooperative Identity, Values & Principles, *n.d.*), while adding three more to create 10 founding and enduring principles in 1987.

These are also the principles behind the United Steelworkers-Mondragon International union-cooperative collaboration agreement signed in October 2009. Principles 3 and 4 of Mondragon's 10 principles (as paraphrased by the 1worker1vote movement) are specifically germane:

- **Sovereignty of labor:** The co-op is centered around labor, around the people doing the work. Created wealth is distributed in terms of the labor provided and there is a firm commitment to new family and community sustaining jobs. Worker-owners receive competitive and just salaries and dividends based on the profitability of the cooperative.

- **Instrumental and subordinate nature of capital:** Only profitable enterprises provide the workplace freedom for Mondragon cooperatives to align principles with practice. Generally, a corporation sells shares of ownership and management to raise capital, and then hires labor. The Mondragon Cooperatives do not sell shares to raise capital. Instead, the workers own their cooperative enterprises, choose their management, and rent sustaining capital. Within the Mondragon ecosystem, capital is labor's instrument, not its master.

Pope John Paul II celebrated the 90th anniversary of the publication of *Rerum Novarum* with his own reflection, rooted in his personal experience with Poland's Solidarity movement. In *Laborem Exercens* (Pope John Paul II, 1981), he goes beyond the mere collaborative and equal footing between labor and capital noted by Leo XIII and asserts the "priority of labor":

> The principle of respect for work demands that this right should undergo a constructive revision, both in theory and in practice. If it is true that capital, as the whole of the means of production, is at the same time the product of the work of generations, it is equally true that capital is being unceasingly created through the work done with the help of all these means of production, and these means can be seen as a great *workbench* at which the present generation of workers is working day after day. Obviously, we are

dealing here with different kinds of work, not only so-called manual labor but also the many forms of intellectual work, including white-collar work and management.

In the light of the above, the many proposals put forward by experts in Catholic social teaching and by the highest Magisterium of the Church take on special significance: proposals for *joint ownership of the means of work* [emphasis added], sharing by the workers in the management and/or profits of businesses, so-called shareholding by labor, etc. Whether these various proposals can or cannot be applied concretely, it is clear that recognition of the proper position of labor and the worker in the production process demands various adaptations in the sphere of the right to ownership of the means of production. (para.14)

Subsequently in the United States, the US Catholic Bishops integrated these papal teachings, in light of their 1919 Program, and published their 1986 *Economic Justice for All: Pastoral Letter on Catholic Social Teaching & the US Economy* (United States Catholic Bishops, 1986). In that document, the bishops continue the traditional teaching of worker rights to strike, form unions, and bargain collectively, as well as the need for living and just wages. Equally important, the bishops maintain that there needs to be a new "American experiment" wherein political democracy fuses with economic and workplace democratic practices.

They argue, forcibly, that new organizational arrangements with meaningful worker participation are required. Their message merits full citation:

New forms of partnership between workers and managers are one means for developing greater participation and accountability within firms. Recent experience has shown that both labor and management suffer when the adversarial relationship between them becomes extreme. As Pope Leo XIII stated, "Each needs the other completely: Capital cannot do without labor nor labor without capital." The organization of firms should reflect and enhance this mutual partnership. In particular, the development of work patterns for men and women that are more supportive of family life will benefit both employees and the enterprises they work for. (para.298)

Workers in firms and on farms are especially in need of stronger institutional protection, for their jobs and livelihood are particularly vulnerable to the decisions of others in today's highly competitive labor market. Several arrangements are gaining increasing support in the United States: profit-sharing by the workers in a firm; enabling employees to become company stockholders; granting employees greater participation in determining the conditions of work; cooperative ownership of the firm by all who work within it; and programs for enabling a much larger number of Americans, regardless of their employment status, to become shareholders in successful corporations. Initiatives of this sort can enhance productivity, increase the profitability of firms, provide greater job security and work satisfaction for employees, and reduce adversarial relations. In our 1919 Program of Social Reconstruction, we observed "the full possibilities of increased production will not be realized so long as the majority of workers remain mere wage earners. The majority must somehow become owners, at least in part, of the instruments of production." We believe this judgement remains generally valid today. (para.300)

None of these approaches provides a panacea, and all have certain drawbacks. Nevertheless, we believe that continued research and experimentation with these approaches will be of benefit. Catholic social teaching has endorsed on many occasions innovative methods for increasing worker participation within firms. The appropriateness of these methods will depend on the circumstances of the company or industry in question and on their effectiveness in actually increasing a genuinely cooperative approach to shaping decisions. The most highly publicized examples of such efforts have been in large firms facing serious financial crises. If increased participation and collaboration can help a firm avoid collapse, why should it not give added strength to healthy businesses? Cooperative ownership is particularly worthy of consideration in new entrepreneurial enterprises. (para.301)

Several US Catholic dioceses and Catholic Charities agencies, along with various unions and social movements, took this pastoral letter to heart and developed mechanisms for new worker-ownership and cooperative structures. Many religious orders ratcheted up their social investment portfolios and sought instruments to invest in worker cooperatives and other community-development organizations (Corbin, 1989). The US Catholic Bishops' anti-poverty funding program — the Catholic Campaign for Human Development (CCHD; usccb.org/committees/catholic-campaign-human-development) — reorganized some of their work to invest in long-term cooperative and community development efforts. Church leaders promoted these long-held teachings about worker cooperatives and worker-community ownership structures by creating collaborative efforts to provide technical assistance and policy advocacy.

One such group is the Ohio Employee Ownership Center (OEOC; oeockent.org) located at Kent State University. Bishop James W. Malone, the Bishop of Youngstown, Ohio, who served as the President of the US Conference of Catholic Bishops at the time of the Pastoral Letters on Peace & Economic Justice, also served as the first OEOC chairman. Bishop Malone actively shaped this Pastoral Letter on the US Economy due to his own experience during the closing of the steel mills in Youngstown in the late 1970s and early 1980s, and his attempt, with the Ecumenical Coalition and the Save our Valley Campaign, to buy and convert several abandoned steel mills as worker-community union based owned cooperatives (Fuechtmann, 1989).

That experiment failed, but the lessons learned shaped the work of the OEOC along with many others seeding subsequent successes. One of the authors of this chapter (Brian Corbin) remains an active member of the OEOC board. An OEOC principal (Chris Cooper, currently its executive director) was one of the two principal authors of the Mondragon-United Steelworkers union-coop model (Witherell et al., 2012), together with steelworker organizer Rob Witherell.

Concurrently, the OEOC continues its decade-plus collaboration with Coop Cincy (coopcincy.org) to serve as the living lab and national prototyping center for the 1worker1vote movement, additionally supporting a highly successful Coop Cincy spin-off in its own right, Coop Dayton (coopdayton.org). Both Coop Cincy and Coop Dayton consistently earn nationwide recognition for their worker ownership ecosystem achievements and practices (Coop Cincy, 2021; Dubb, 2021).

In 2020, organizations from across Ohio formed the Ohio Worker Ownership Network (OWN; oeockent.org/the-ohio-worker-ownership-network) with the aim of supporting worker-owned businesses. OWN increases awareness about the benefits of worker-ownership among business owners, economic development agencies, public officials, and the public. OWN also connects stakeholders while offering training and assisting with transitions. OWN is composed of Co-op Cincy, the OEOC, Co-op Dayton, The Fund for Employee Ownership (evgoh.com/tfeo), The Center for the Creation of Cooperation (athensenergyinstitute.org), Cleveland Owns (clevelandowns.coop), the CFAES Center for Cooperatives at Ohio State University (cooperatives.cfaes.ohio-state.edu), the Junction Economic Transformation Center (junctioncoalition419.org), Co-op Columbus (coopcolumbus.org), and Co-op Nelsonville (ohiocoopliving.com/taxonomy/term/398).

The impacts of Catholic social teaching in Ohio, at the center of the historic and also deindustrializing heartland over the past 50 years, are instructive.

Following the financial crisis that wrecked markets and homes during the 2007–2008 Great Recession, Pope Benedict XVI used the occasion of his 2009 *Caritas in Veritate* to reflect on the political-economic situation and its post-crisis reconstruction (Pope Benedict XVI, 2009). He continued the quest to secure a new way of thinking about society that avoided the errors of collectivism and atomized individualism. He argued that this continuum had morphed into two "logics" that held sway over political-economic reality — the logic of the state and the logic of the market. Rather, he offers a new logic that many do not recognize or understand — the logic of gratuity as generosity, wherein new models of mutualism can emerge:

> Today we can say that economic life must be understood as a multi-layered phenomenon: in every one of these layers, to varying degrees and in ways specifically suited to each, the aspect of fraternal reciprocity must be present. In the global era, economic activity cannot prescind from gratuitousness, which fosters and disseminates solidarity and responsibility for justice and the common good among the different economic players. It is clearly a specific and profound form of economic democracy. Solidarity is first and foremost a sense of responsibility on the part of everyone with regard to everyone, and it cannot therefore be merely delegated to the State. While in the past it was possible to argue that justice had to come first and gratuitousness could follow afterwards, as a complement, today it is clear that without gratuitousness, there can be no justice in the first place. What is needed, therefore, is a market that permits the free operation, in conditions of equal opportunity, of enterprises in pursuit of different institutional ends. Alongside profit-oriented private enterprise and the various types of public enterprise, there must be room for commercial entities based on mutualist principles and pursuing social ends to take root and express themselves. It is from their reciprocal encounter in the marketplace that one may expect hybrid forms of commercial behavior to emerge, and hence an attentiveness to ways of civilizing the economy. Charity in truth, in this case, requires that shape and structure be given to those types of economic initiative which, without rejecting profit, aim at a higher goal than the mere logic of the exchange of equivalents, of profit as an end in itself. (para.38)

Conclusions

The task of moral populism, Brooks concludes in *How the Bobos Broke America* (Brooks, 2021), is first to recognize the uncrossable inequality chasm of "financial inequalities and more painful inequalities of respect," and then to "dismantle the system" that built the societally imploding monster whose DNA is now becoming metaverse algorithmic.

Moral mutualism and populism counter these inequalities with the core sororal and fraternal values of the civic commons, even as multi-denominational, ecumenical religious spirituality cares for the everyday sense of self and ministers to a nation's soul. Nothing could be more relevant to solving the multiple, concurrent pandemics plaguing economy, society, democracy, and public health.

As Mondragon-model adherents, both chapter co-authors believe that hybrid shared ownership and democratic governance models, starting with single-equity-class social enterprises and corresponding ecosystems, stand out as proven, worthy paradigms deserving of scale. Not only are workplace ownership and democracy indivisible to America's recuperating moral, spiritual, and commercial civic society, and marketplace health; they represent a productive and innovative culture that can prevail against authoritarian, statist competitors.

Workplace ownership and democracy transform vicious into virtuous cycles, and allows a reconstituted American social compact to emerge, rise, and scale. A foundational step in this civic recuperation and revival is to promote mutuality, shared risks, and rewards. Local, inclusive stakeholder ownership within commercial markets serves as handmaiden to a more socio-politically harmonious and values-aligned national culture that practices what it preaches.

To unite the country and reconstitute its authentic moral soul, America can redefine and enlarge social and cultural common ground, and rebuild the moral mission and ethical values that connect "we the people."

One example is *Rich Christians in an Age of Hunger*, by Ronald J. Sider (2015), which argues that vast global wealth inequality is a moral failure resulting from systems of oppression and sin.

Pope Francis, who worked with slum dwellers in Argentina, reminds us of that experience when he refers to the marginalized and vulnerable as persons who have a deep sense of agency and mutuality (Pope Francis & Ivereigh, 2020), writing:

> I mean those who lack regular work living on the margins of the market economy. They are landless peasants and smallholders, subsistence fishermen and sweatshop workers, garbage pickers and street vendors, sidewalk artisans, slum dwellers, and squatters. In developed countries, they are the ones who live from odd jobs, often on the move, poorly housed, with poor access to drinking water and healthy food: both they and their families suffer all kinds of vulnerability.
>
> Yet if we manage to come close and put aside our stereotypes we discover that many of them are far from being merely passive victims. Organized in a global archipelago of associations and movements, they represent the hope of solidarity in an age of exclusion and indifference. On the margins I have discovered so many social movements with roots in parishes or schools that bring people together to make them become protagonists of their own histories, to set in motion dynamics that smacked of dignity. Taking life as it comes, they do not sit around resigned or complaining but come together to convert injustice into new possibilities. I call them "social poets". In mobilizing for change, in their search for dignity, I see a source of moral energy, a reserve of civic passion, capable of revitalizing our democracy and reorienting the economy. (pp.119–120)

Francis continues, echoing the critical nature of organizing persons for mutuality through their own agency, when he notes that:

It is not the Church's task to organize every action of the people but rather to encourage, walk with, and support those who carry out these roles. Which is quite the opposite of how elites of all kinds think as in "All for the people, but nothing with the people," whom they suppose to be faceless and ignorant. It is not true. A people know what it wants and needs, and has an instinct. (p.122)

Francis further calls upon those who have formally organized through labor unions to open their horizons. He observes: "Sadly, nowadays few unions look out for those on the margins. Many are remote from the edges of society." He demonstrates the power of those on the edges as being "social poets" in pointing out:

... the dignity of the cartoneros: how hard they worked to maintain their families and feed their children, how they worked collaboratively, as a community. In organizing they entered their own kind of conversion, a recycling of their own lives. And along the way they changed the way Argentines viewed their garbage, helping them to understand the value of reusing and recycling. (p.125)

Francis delves into the social theory behind work, labor, and the role of business, calling for a new way of seeing, thinking, being and acting. He writes:

Many words in the business world suggest the fraternal purpose of economic activity we must now re-establish: "company", for example, comes from sharing bread together, while "corporation" means integration into the body. Business isn't just a private enterprise; it should serve the "common" good. Common comes from the Latin cum-munus: "cum" means together, while "munus" has the meaning of a service given as a gift or out of a sense of duty. Our work has both an individual and a common dimension. It is a source of personal growth as well as being key to restoring the dignity of our peoples. Too often we have it the wrong way around: despite the fact that they create value, workers are treated as the most expendable element of an enterprise, while some shareholders — with their narrow interest in maximizing profits — call the shots. Our definition of the value of work is also far too narrow. We need to move beyond this idea that the work of the caregiver for her relative, or a full-time mother or volunteer in a social project, is not work because it pays no wages. Recognizing the value to society of the work of nonearners is a vital part of our rethinking in the post-Covid world. (p.131)

Summarizing his reflection on the nature of populism, politics and a new solidarity, Francis concludes:

All this means having common-good goals for human development rather than the false assumption of the infamous trickle-down theory that a growing economy will make us all richer. By focusing on land, lodging, and labor we can regain a healthy relationship with the world and grow by serving others. In this way, we transcend the narrow individualist framework of the liberal paradigm without falling into the trap of populism. Democracy is then reinvigorated by the concerns and wisdom of the people who are involved in it. Politics can once again be an expression of love through service. By making the restoration of our people's dignity the central objective of the post-Covid world, we make everyone's dignity the key to our actions. To guarantee a world where dignity is valued and respected through concrete actions is not just a dream but a path to a better future. (p.132)

Today, the Catholic Labor Network has been training priests to perform critical card-check duty, where many workers sign up to join a union and the company in question bargains openly with the union chosen. "In the past few months, their work has enabled nearly 1,000 low-wage food service workers in six locations to secure union membership" (Catholic Labor Network, 2021).

The inclusive nature of this work is critical. Sara Horowitz (2021) calls out the false dichotomy characterized by those who believe unions are for people other than themselves:

> This misperception, that unionization is only for low-wage workers, couldn't be further from the truth. Unions were historically intended to protect all workers. Low-wage and middle-wage workers need to stand together. Without this solidarity, vulnerable workers will not have the leverage they need to achieve meaningful change for themselves. Why do so many middle-class workers believe the labor movement isn't for them?

Former US Labor Secretary Robert Reich "imagines a world where workers have power" (Reich, 2021), but any trajectory from this vision to a more modern and compelling reality isn't linear, uncontested, or going to happen through some magical entropic process. Too many first-tier labor union structures resist worker ownership with the same resolute energy and intensity reserved for union-organizing campaigns targeting corporate employers. The answer lies in how best to inspire and define change so that labor perceives the concrete value of belonging to and supporting the March 2012 USW-OEOC-Mondragon International North America union-coop/worker-ownership hybrid model (Witherell *et al.*, 2012), with its trifecta benefits of single-class equity, democratic governance, and a progressive collective bargaining agreement (CBA). The goal is to transform the foreseeable future into present tense empowerment tools delivering socio-economic justice, productivity, resiliency, sustainability and agency to the benefit of collaborating local worker, cooperative and union communities.

Sara Horowitz (2021) understands this truth better than anyone, having predicted the rise of the gig economy worker decades before it occurred and pioneered cooperative and solidarity-enhancing structures through the Freelancers Union (freelancersunion.org):

> The division of workers into "employees" and "independent contractors" is just one example of a larger trend that dates to the Taft-Hartley Act of 1947: an attempt by anti-labor capitalism to weaken the labor movement from within by dividing the workforce. Over the past half century, politicians, policy makers, labor leaders, foundations and workers alike have internalized these divisions. Today, rather than asking if someone is a worker who deserves our society's protection, we ask instead what kind of worker they are first: Blue or white collar? Low- or high-wage? Skilled or unskilled? Knowledge or service worker? Employee or independent contractor? But in 2021, if you're a worker of any type, you're exposed.

James Baldwin lays down a social justice condition: "We can disagree and still love each other, unless your disagreement is rooted in my oppression and denial of my humanity and right to exist."

Ecumenical theology calls for better angels among us in living and proving unconditional love even in the face of extreme hatred, prejudice, and disposability. Inklings of tomorrow's overpowering resolve can be learned from precariat communities where those who practice such love in the face of pure evil or cultural rejection nevertheless prevail, and will not be deterred.

The theological virtues of faith, hope, and love bear witness to the deeply-held, multi-denominational religious conviction that each person is indeed created in the image and likeness of an Almighty God. Still, today, too many false gods and human demagogues would cage immigrant babies as "children of lesser gods," and ask their followers to surrender conscience and abnegate spiritual responsibility.

Multi-global pandemics reveal a world where gardens are despoiled, where land is inappropriately seized from its original owners, where only the privileged have access to fresh sustaining produce and water, and the time to cultivate such at will.

In contrast, the story of the original Garden of Eden's blessing continues to provide grist for moral imagination and prophetic witness of what the common good can look like and become, rooted in the action of mutualist gratuity and economy of climate-resilient abundance.

There is much to be angry and dismayed about in America's endless and constant need for moral and spiritual grace. In First Corinthians 13:13, Paul counsels civic partners entering into a more and always demanding but perfecting civic union that, "three things will last forever: faith, hope, and love — but the greatest of these is love."

Mondragon's founder understood that selfless, metaphysical, or spiritual love is what propels "the heart, the work, the life" (inscription on Father José María Arizmendiarrieta's tombstone) to reach for and fulfil the process of the culture's perpetual work of becoming its better self. One worker, one vote, single share, single-class equity ownership coupled to workplace democratic practices, with a progressive collective bargaining agreement, or a Mondragon social committee, serving as structural check and balance.

Pope Francis supports an economy founded on and sustained by "moral obligation" that is accomplished through a "just distribution of the fruits of the earth and human labor" — suggesting that Americans can find their true moral compass by reinvesting more fairly in themselves:

> The goal must be to enable networks of belonging and solidarity to flourish by restoring the bonds of community and fraternity, engaging institutions rooted in the community together with people's movements. When organizations act together beyond boundaries of belief and ethnicity to achieve concrete goals for their communities, then we can say that our peoples have claimed back their soul.

For America's 21st century populism to ring true, morally, and spiritually, its peoples must claim back their collective soul. As Francis believes, a faith-infused, inclusive, and renewed Bill of Rights and updated Constitution leads to uniting, honoring, and renewing the country's civic-union identity not as barely envisioned in the 18th century but as fulfilled in the 21st.

During public appearances in Greece, the world's birthplace of democracy and refugee flashpoint, the Pope decried an "era of walls and barbed wire" supported by ideological politicians and jurists whose "obsessive quest for popularity, in a thirst for visibility, in a flurry of unrealistic promises," trumpet "siren songs of authoritarianism."

We must learn and relearn, individually and collectively, how to act in unison, how to believe together again. Moral populism mandates we cannot "retreat from democracy" but "must turn away from authoritarianism, individualism, and indifference," rededicating ourselves "to the common good and strengthen democracy." We must return to "good politics," where "fraternity is today our new frontier" and where salvation is found, expressed in solidarity, and shared.

The path forward is inwardly clear and outwardly blessed. We must acknowledge and ask forgiveness for our original sins and then sin no more. We must agree to listen, respect, forgive, love, and practice open-ended, unceasing civic communion to heal beloved communities in every corner of the beloved nation. We must strive mightily to become one mosaic people engendering "solidarity dividend" miracles of vision, promise, commitment, and enactment becoming daily occurrences of grace.

This chapter and book joins with Pope Francis and with all framers and signatories of the recently ratified *Economy of Francesco Covenant* below (Watkins, 2022), that echoes the 10 Mondragon principles. Our collective spiritual and hands-on mission: to build an ecumenical and universal practice judged by performance metrics as the everyday miracles of progress in our lifetimes and in the names of those taking up the mantle so that memory becomes a beacon.

> We, young economists, entrepreneurs, and changemakers, called here to Assisi from every part of the world, aware of the responsibility that rests on our generation, commit ourselves today, individually and all collectively to spending our lives so that the economy of today and tomorrow becomes an economy of the Gospel, and therefore:
>
> an economy of peace and not of war,
>
> an economy that opposes the proliferation of arms, especially the most destructive,
>
> an economy that cares for creation and does not misuse it,
>
> an economy at the service of the human person, the family and life, respectful of every woman, man, and child, the elderly, and especially those most frail and vulnerable,
>
> an economy where care replaces rejection and indifference,
>
> an economy that leaves no one behind, in order to build a society in which the stones rejected by the dominant mentality become cornerstones, an economy that recognizes and protects secure and dignified work for everyone,
>
> an economy where finance is a friend and ally of the real economy and of labor and not against them,
>
> an economy that values and safeguards the cultures and traditions of peoples, all living things and the natural resources of the Earth,
>
> an economy that fights poverty in all its forms, reduces inequality and knows how to say with Jesus and Francis, "Blessed are the poor,"
>
> an economy guided by an ethics of the human person and open to transcendence,
>
> an economy that creates wealth for all, that engenders joy and not just riches, because happiness that is not shared is incomplete.

We believe in this economy. It is not a utopia, because we are already building it. And some of us, on particularly bright mornings, have already glimpsed the beginning of the promised land.

References

2020 California Proposition 22 (2023). In *Wikipedia*.
https://en.wikipedia.org/w/index.php?title=2020_California_Proposition_22&oldid=1138281914.

Alberta, T. (2022, May 10). How politics poisoned the evangelical church. *The Atlantic*.
https://www.theatlantic.com/magazine/archive/2022/06/evangelical-church-pastors-political-radicalization/629631/.

Allende, I. (2007, March). *Isabel Allende—Words*. https://www.isabelallende.com/en/words/tales_of_passion.

American Sustainable Business Network (n.d.). *Support the California Power Act*. https://www.asbnetwork.org/pod/support-california-power-act.

Authentic Basque Country (2021, March 8). *Moving to Basque Country: Everything You Need to Know*.
https://www.authenticbasquecountry.com/l/by-the-numbers/#:~:text=Basque%20Country%27s%20Gini%20is%20lower,0.307%20while%20Spain%27s%20is%200.347.

Barr, B.A. (2021). *The Making of Biblical Womanhood: How the Subjugation of Women Became Gospel Truth*. Baker Books.

Bellan, R. (2021, August 4). Uber CEO calls Massachusetts gig economy ballot measure the "right answer." *TechCrunch*.
https://techcrunch.com/2021/08/04/uber-ceo-calls-massachusetts-gig-economy-ballot-measure-the-right-answer/.

Bellan, R. (2022a, May 12). Uber shareholders get closer to passing lobbying disclosure proposal. *TechCrunch*.
https://techcrunch.com/2022/05/12/uber-shareholders-get-closer-to-passing-lobbying-disclosure-proposal/.

Bellan, R. (2022b, June 14). Massachusetts court rejects ballot to define gig workers as contractors. *TechCrunch*.
https://techcrunch.com/2022/06/14/massachusetts-court-rejects-ballot-to-define-gig-workers-as-contractors/.

Bird, A., Conaty, P., McKeown, M., Ross, C., Taylor, S. & Mangan, A. (2020, July 6). *Manifesto for Decent Work*. union-coops: UK.
https://www.union-coops.uk/a-manifesto-for-decent-work.

Brooks, D. (2021, August 2). How the bobos broke America. *The Atlantic*.
https://www.theatlantic.com/magazine/archive/2021/09/blame-the-bobos-creative-class/619492/.

C-SPAN (Director) (1971, April 22). *Vietnam War Hearing 1971* [Video]. https://www.c-span.org/video/?181065-1/vietnam-war-hearing-1971.

Carroll, A.E. (2021, September 5). We've never protected the vulnerable. *The Atlantic*.
https://www.theatlantic.com/ideas/archive/2021/09/weve-never-protected-the-vulnerable/619981/.

Catholic Labor Network (2021, November 23). Labor priests certify "card checks" for workers seeking union.
https://catholiclabor.org/labor-priests-certify-card-checks-for-workers-seeking-union/.

Catholic Social Teaching (2023). In *Wikipedia*.
https://en.wikipedia.org/w/index.php?title=Catholic_social_teaching&oldid=1140038099.

Conger, K. (2021, May 28). A worker-owned cooperative tries to compete with Uber and Lyft. *New York Times*.
https://www.nytimes.com/2021/05/28/technology/nyc-uber-lyft-the-drivers-cooperative.html.

Coop Cincy (2021). *Recordings & More from the 2021 Union Co-op Symposium*. https://mailchi.mp/coopcincy/recordings-more-from-the-2021-union-co-op-symposium?e=90b0c97995.

Corbin, B.R. (1989). Unfinished business: Community economic development & the US Catholic Bishops' Economic Pastoral. Social Thought, 15(2), 35–47. https://doi.org/10.1080/15426432.1989.10383661.

Dias, E. (2021, July 25). Facebook's next target: The religious experience. *New York Times*.
https://www.nytimes.com/2021/07/25/us/facebook-church.html?smid=em-share.

Dubb, S. (2021, June 16). In West Dayton, Ohio, a food co-op heralds a "black renaissance." *Nonprofit Quarterly*.
https://nonprofitquarterly.org/in-west-dayton-ohio-a-food-co-op-heralds-a-black-renaissance/.

Fischer, L. (1962) *The Essential Gandhi*. Vintage.

Fuechtmann, T.G. (1989). *Steeples & Stacks: Religion & Steel Crisis in Youngstown, Ohio*. Cambridge University Press.
https://www.google.ca/books/edition/Steeples_and_Stacks/ZrcCpqrv28MC?hl=en.

Glenza, J. (2022, May 15). US Covid deaths hit 1m, a death toll higher than any other country. *The Guardian*.
https://www.theguardian.com/world/2022/may/15/1-million-us-covid-deaths-effects.

Goldberg, E. (2021, August 26). The new chief chaplain at Harvard? An atheist. *New York Times*.
https://www.nytimes.com/2021/08/26/us/harvard-chaplain-greg-epstein.html.

Griswold, E. (2021, July 25). The unmaking of biblical womanhood. *New Yorker*. https://www.newyorker.com/news/on-religion/the-unmaking-of-biblical-womanhood.

Hackett, C. & McClendon, D. (2017, April 5). Christians remain world's largest religious group, but they are declining in Europe. *Pew Research Center*. https://www.pewresearch.org/fact-tank/2017/04/05/christians-remain-worlds-largest-religious-group-but-they-are-declining-in-europe/.

Horowitz, S. (2021). *Mutualism: Building the Next Economy from the Ground Up*. Random House Publishing Group.

International Cooperative Alliance (n.d.). *Cooperative Identity, Values & Principles*. https://www.ica.coop/en/cooperatives/cooperative-identity.

Isenberg, D. & Neichin, G. (2021, August 11). In search of existential answers and impact-first investors, Ceniarth finds religion. *Impact Alpha*. https://impactalpha.com/in-search-of-existential-answers-and-impact-first-investors-ceniarth-finds-religion/.

King, M.L., Jr. (Director). (1968, March 31). *Remaining Awake through a Great Revolution* [Video]. https://www.youtube.com/watch?v=okv2QSupAHk.

Kuhn, D.P. (2020). *The Hardhat Riot: Nixon, New York City & the Dawn of the White Working-class Revolution*. Oxford University Press.

Mampilly, Z. (2021, October 3). Protests are taking over the world. What's driving them? *New York Times*. https://www.nytimes.com/2021/10/03/opinion/covid-protests-world-whats-driving-them.html?smid=em-share.

Mandela, N. (1995). *Long Walk to Freedom: The Autobiography of Nelson Mandela*. Abacus.

McCarty Carino, M. (2023, January 6). New California law promotes co-ops and worker-owned businesses. https://www.marketplace.org/2023/01/06/new-california-law-promotes-worker-owned-businesses/.

McGhee, H. (2021). *The Sum of Us: What Racism Costs Everyone & How We can Prosper Together*. Random House Publishing Group.

Miller, C.C., Katz, J., Paris, F. & Bhatia, A. (2022, August 1). Vast new study shows a key to reducing poverty: More friendships between rich and poor. *New York Times*. https://www.nytimes.com/interactive/2022/08/01/upshot/rich-poor-friendships.html.

Mondragon Corporation (n.d.). *Mondragon Corporation*. https://www.mondragon-corporation.com/en/we-do/.

Philbrick, I.P. (2022, June 22). A pro-religion court. *New York Times*. https://www.nytimes.com/2022/06/22/briefing/supreme-court-religion.html.

Pontifical Council for Justice & Peace (2006, May 25). *Compendium of the Church*. https://www.vatican.va/roman_curia/pontifical_councils/justpeace/documents/rc_pc_justpeace_doc_20060526_compendio-dott-soc_en.html.

Pope Benedict XVI (2009, June 29). *Caritas in Veritate*. https://www.vatican.va/content/benedict-xvi/en/encyclicals/documents/hf_ben-xvi_enc_20090629_caritas-in-veritate.html.

Pope Francis (2015a, July 9). *Apostolic Journey—Bolivia: Participation at the Second World Meeting of Popular Movements at the Expo Feria Exhibition Centre*. https://www.vatican.va/content/francesco/en/speeches/2015/july/documents/papa-francesco_20150709_bolivia-movimenti-popolari.html.

Pope Francis (2015b, July 10). Read Pope Francis' speech on the poor and indigenous peoples. *Time*. https://time.com/3952885/pope-francis-bolivia-poverty-speech-transcript/.

Pope Francis & Ivereigh, A. (2020). *Let Us Dream*. Simon & Schuster. https://www.google.ca/books/edition/Let_Us_Dream/pQrJzQEACAAJ?hl=en.

Pope John Paul II (1981, September 14). *Laborem Exercens*. https://www.vatican.va/content/john-paul-ii/en/encyclicals/documents/hf_jp-ii_enc_14091981_laborem-exercens.html.

Pope Leo XIII (1891, May 15). *Rerum Novarum*. https://www.vatican.va/content/leo-xiii/en/encyclicals/documents/hf_l-xiii_enc_15051891_rerum-novarum.html.

Pope Paul VI (1967, March 26). *Populorum Progressio*. https://www.vatican.va/content/paul-vi/en/encyclicals/documents/hf_p-vi_enc_26031967_populorum.html.

Pope Pius XI (1931, May 15). *Quadragesimo Anno*. https://www.vatican.va/content/pius-xi/en/encyclicals/documents/hf_p-xi_enc_19310515_quadragesimo-anno.html.

Reich, R. (Director) (2021, July 21). *How Workers can Reclaim Power from Bezos & Billionaires* [Video]. https://www.youtube.com/watch?v=JSralhrpK44.

Reilly, T., Salit, J. & Ali, O. (2022). *The Rise of the Independent Voter*. Routledge.

Richardson, H.C. (2022, May 10). https://heathercoxrichardson.substack.com/p/may-10-2022.

Risen, C. (2021, August 17). Afghanistan, Vietnam & the limits of American power. *New York Times*. https://www.nytimes.com/2021/08/17/us/politics/vietnam-war-afghanistan.html?smid=em-share.

Sauca, I., Usher, E., Abu Moghli, I., Alrumithi, S. & Potasnik, J. (2022, May 9). *Climate-responsible Finance: A Moral Imperative towards Children*. UN Environment. http://www.unep.org/news-and-stories/statements/climate-responsible-finance-moral-imperative-towards-children.

Sider, R.J. (2015). *Rich Christians in an Age of Hunger: Moving from Affluence to Generosity*. Thomas Nelson.

Stop Soldier Suicide (n.d.). *Veteran Suicide Stats*. https://stopsoldiersuicide.org/vet-stats.

Tankersley, J. & DeParle, J. (2021, March 13). Two decades after the "end of welfare," Democrats are changing direction. *New York Times*. https://www.nytimes.com/2021/03/13/business/economy/child-poverty-stimulus.html.

United States Catholic Bishops (1986). *Economic Justice for All: Pastoral Letter on Catholic Social Teaching & the US Economy*. https://www.usccb.org/upload/economic_justice_for_all.pdf.

United States Catholic Bishops & National Catholic War Council (1984, February 1). Documentation: The bishops' program of 1919. *Crisis Magazine*. https://www.crisismagazine.com/vault/documentation-the-bishops-program-of-1919.

von Stamwitz, A. (2018, September 10). *Believe in Love: A Message from Pope Francis*. Franciscan Media. https://www.franciscanmedia.org/franciscan-spirit-blog/believe-in-love-a-message-from-pope-francis/.

Walsh, B. (2021, April 7). America is losing its religion. *Axios*. https://www.axios.com/2021/04/07/americans-less-religious-gallup-poll.

Walsh, P., Peck, M. & Zugasti, I. (2018, August 8). Why the US needs more worker-owned companies. *Harvard Business Review*. https://hbr.org/2018/08/why-the-u-s-needs-more-worker-owned-companies.

Watkins, D. (2022, September 24). Economy of Francesco Covenant: Building an economy of the Gospel. *Vatican News*. https://www.vaticannews.va/en/pope/news/2022-09/economy-francesco-final-covenant-pope-francis-gospel.html.

White, J., Harmon, A., Ivory, D., Leatherby, L., Sun, A. & Almukhtar, S. (2022, May 13). How America lost one million people. *New York Times*. https://www.nytimes.com/interactive/2022/05/13/us/covid-deaths-us-one-million.html.

Witherell, R., Cooper, C. & Peck, M. (2012). Sustainable Jobs, Sustainable Communities: The Union Co-op Model. https://towardfreedom.org/wp-content/uploads/2016/04/The-Union-Co-op-Model-March-26-2012.pdf.

CHAPTER 14

From Mondragón to Preston: How the Basque Experience has Influenced the Preston Model

Julian Manley

From the Collapse of Inward Investment to New Thinking

In November 2011, the major inward investment regeneration program for Preston (UK), called the Tithebarn project, collapsed, and with it the typical "dreams" of the stakeholders to that project based around consumerism and the supposed wealth associated with new shopping malls, big national department stores, mechanical escalators swishing happy families up to the swanky stores and boutiques and down to the carpark to jump into their cars and return to their well-stocked houses with yet more items of both need and luxury. This wonderland of city center regeneration was to include the demolition of the iconic Bus Station (now regarded as a gem of 1960s brutalist architecture) and the normal trappings of "progress": pedestrian streets, restaurants and cafes, and green and public spaces. The collapse of the project came about after a major department store pulled out of the project, thus revealing the centrality and dependence of such inward investment initiatives on retail and consumerist pulls. With hindsight, this inward investment scheme, typical of its time, seems less attractive than intended, and instead is more suggestive of what Baudrillard described as a moment where "through articulated networks of objects" people are conditioned in action and time "to the systematic organization of ambiance, which is characteristic of the drugstores, the shopping malls, or the modern airports in our futuristic cities" (Baudrillard, 1988, p.33). Moving from mere "ambiance" to emotional manipulation with Orwellian undertones, Byung-Chul Han interprets such palaces of consumerism as "Emotional Design" that "moulds emotions and shapes emotional patterns for the sake of maximizing consumption" (Han, 2017, p.46).

However, in November 2011, it looked as if Preston had been left with nothing. Since the 2008 economic crash, central government had been pumping huge sums of money into the failing financial system and was making the "average citizen" pay for this through a program of so-called austerity measures. Productivity and investment were low and there appeared to be little left to hope for in terms of social and economic benefits for a place like Preston. This was the context that brought about the generation of ideas that began to form in 2012 and eventually became inter-connected and enmeshed into what was dubbed the "Preston Model."

Although economically challenged, Preston had a local Council that was Labour Party-controlled and left-leaning. So, by the time of the collapse of the Tithebarn project, Preston City Council had already become the first real living wage employer in the north of England, a policy that the Council has been encouraging ever since. In other words, there already existed a possibility and potential for change. Once it became clear that inward investment was no longer an option, it became necessary to think in more radical and more alternative ways. It was a sink or swim situation for Preston. There was no "masterplan" approach from the beginning. Instead, developments were stimulated through "hunches" and good intentions, supported by "good ideas." Many of these ideas were directly or indirectly garnered from the Mondragon experience.

In November 2013, two years after Tithebarn, the University of Central Lancashire invited Mikel Lezamiz from the Mondragon Cooperative Corporation to a three-day "Distinguished Visitor" visit, with meetings and talks to various stakeholders in Preston both from within and outside the university. In the course of a public presentation, Lezamiz sowed the seeds of the cooperative features of the Preston Model. What was revelatory to Lezamiz's Preston audience, which included City Councilors, was the idea that workers could own and govern their own workplaces democratically in large scale business projects and that these cooperatives could be networked for mutual benefit, as opposed to in competition with each other, and the network of cooperatives could be sustained, supported, and developed by an important community ecosystem of services, which in the case of Mondragon consisted of four pillars: finance (a local cooperative bank), health (a local health insurance entity), education (at all levels but especially at university level), and research and development (the realization of creative and innovative projects and products for the cooperative businesses of Mondragon). The whole system was governed by the Mondragon Cooperative Corporation, acting as a "cooperative of cooperatives." From this moment onwards, Preston City Council began a fruitful collaboration with the local university, twice commissioning researchers to firstly provide a scoping review of the potential for cooperative development in Preston (Manley & Froggett, 2016), and secondly to develop a network (as recommended in the first scoping report) of cooperatives for Preston, loosely based on the Mondragón system of cooperative networks. This became the Preston Cooperative Development Network (PCDN), of which the author and Cllr Matthew Brown were two of the small group of founder members.

The Preston Cooperative Development Network

The PCDN was the first major recommendation of Manley & Froggett's 2016 report to Preston City Council. The recommendations, accepted in full by the Council, are remarkable for being clear predictors of the future development of the Preston Model, in all cases but the last recommendation, (due to the demise of Cooperatives North-West), and for their clear resonance with the Mondragon experience:

1. The formal setting up of a network of cooperative groups in Preston that would initially be facilitated and led by the Council. This would lend it status and legitimacy and link it to city-wide goals and initiatives. Although information and advice are vital, there is also scope for a pro-active developmental role.

2. The network can be developed in line with other local economic and social strategies, especially those policies highlighted by the CLES report in relation to Anchor Institutions and local wealth building and retention. Despite financial cuts, the Council exercises influence in key areas of the local economy and so retains potential as enabler.

3. In conjunction with the network, the four pillars of cooperative development – Education, Finance, R&D, and Welfare/Health – can be promoted.

4. A creative approach should be adopted in relation to Council property/offices that are currently out of use, such as renting of disused Council property to fledgling cooperative organizations.

5. National and regional links to hubs of cooperative activity should be encouraged. Connections to international cooperative organizations such as Mondragon and the Evergreen Cooperatives should be strengthened, including reciprocal study visits.

6. Existing knowledge and expertise in existing cooperative activity in Preston should be mapped, recognized, and shared with other groups and organizations.

7. A flagship/example of a worker owned cooperative in Preston could be used to demonstrate the ideas and practices that produce a successful cooperative business.

8. The offer by Cooperatives North-West to make available its knowledge and expertise in helping to start up co-ops should be taken up. A partnership could be established with Uclan to develop cooperative education and research. (Manley & Froggett, 2016, pp.27-28)

As demonstrated in these recommendations, the PCDN emerged from recommendation number 1, and the four pillars of the Mondragon experience, brought to Preston by Lezamiz, are clearly stated in number 3. From recommendation number 5, we have a mention of Mondragon, and a relationship that has been sustained throughout, as well as later connections with manifestations of Mondragon in the United States and on-going links to the Cleveland Model that is the root of the Evergreen Cooperatives.

Although progress in developing the PCDN (https://prestoncoopdevelopment.org) has been slow, the theory and concept are well established and continue to be projected forward as part of the overall Preston Model design, especially as part of the second phase of planned work of Preston City Council's Community Wealth Building strategy (Preston City Council, 2021).

Anchor institutions & procurement

In parallel to this development of (or at least the desire to develop) worker-owned cooperatives in Mondragon fashion, there was a parallel development of incentivizing local businesses, especially big, so-called "anchor institutions," to spend more money locally and to somehow encourage the retention of local economic wealth. The Cleveland initiative in the United States is often credited with the idea of generating and retaining local wealth through encouraging major local spending. In this regard, the influence from Mondragon remains significant and is acknowledged by Ted Howard, one of the principal thinkers behind the ideas emanating from Cleveland ("It has influenced the work we're doing in Cleveland.

It's illuminating to see highly democratic worker ownership done at scale." (Harvey, 2019)). In Preston, the change in anchor institutions' procurement habits and the consequent generation and retention of local wealth has been hugely impressive, with "the share of local procurement expenditure…rising from 5% to 16.2% within Preston, between 2012/13 and 2016/17, and from 39% to 79.2% in Lancashire [the region within which Preston is located]" (Whyman, 2021, p.141). In terms of financial return "at a time when austerity measures had reduced the total procurement spend for the five initial Preston Model anchor institutions, from £750 million to £620 million per annum, the realized economic boost from procurement to the Preston economy increased by £74 million and for Lancashire the equivalent gain was £200 million" (Whyman, 2021, pp. 141-142).

Behind the motivation to change procurement habit in anchor institutions is a sense of solidarity in community as a general principle. This is important because it demonstrates how the Mondragon experience is about community development. In Preston, the changing procurement habits of anchors is not simply focused on increasing local wealth through large scale procurement. Even in the case of anchors, there is always the question of why should they spend more money locally? It is possible to see this spirit of care and pride in the local in comments made by Oscar Muguerza, Director of Business Development in Mondragon's hugely successful bank, Laboral Kutxa. As a successful banking entity, there is no reason for the bank to be particularly interested in local, small-scale projects, and yet Muguerza demonstrates exactly this spirit from his position in Laboral Kutxa:

> Each and every one of us, we have to think about where we buy and what we buy… Whatever we spend close by will rebound for the benefit of all… And this is not only true of the everyday consumer, but also for banking, supermarkets … It's for all. We have to value what we have, (in) the local (Muguerza, 2020).

Similarly, an anchor institution in Preston will add social value criteria to the tendering of competitive contracts in order to acknowledge the social importance as well as the financial requirements of its spend. And this injection of social value from an anchor's perspective is in itself, even without a direct implication in actual procurement, a social act which filters through the system

Governance

Just as important as the economic regeneration of Preston through changing procurement habits, is the social, affective, and relational movement that accompanies it. In this sense, the Mondragon influence is also key, even if in Mondragon itself, this is rarely emphasized (at least until recently, when there has been a shift in priorities in Mondragon to embrace so-called "cooperative culture," as a result of the collapse of a flagship cooperative and the soul-searching that ensued (Ortega Sunsundegi & Uriarte Zabala, 2015)). As I have indicated previously (Manley & Aiken, 2020), despite the pragmatic emphasis on traditional business needs based on financial targets, the money generated in Mondragon is never an increase in economic wealth in isolation from social and cultural capital. On the contrary, there is an essence and motivation for the generation and retention of wealth in Mondragon, without which the cooperative system in Mondragon would have collapsed a long time ago (Manley & Aiken, 2020, pp.182-184). This is why it is important that whatever wealth is generated and retained in Preston as a result of changing procurement habits in anchor institutions and in the creation of jobs and new businesses, it is governed within the framework of democratic participation and ethical goals that aim to increase social and economic justice in communities. Therefore, just as in Mondragón, the businesses that are encouraged in Preston are worker-owned cooperatives, where workers have agency and power over shared decision-making and where commitment to quality jobs, local pride and attention to place are priorities. Perhaps in a place like Mondragón the importance of this localism may be showing signs of decay, due to Mondragon's ever-increasing global presence, which makes it more and more difficult to take decisions from a Mondragon perspective. For example, Imanol Basterretxea, who has studied the demise of Fagor Electrodomésticos (FeD), previously a flagship Mondragon cooperative, suggests that the global outreach of FeD caused a problem in decision-making on the part of the Governing Council, many of whom were born, bred, and had never left Mondragón. Basterretxa describes how one of the managers in FeD told him that "When I went to the Governing Council to convince them to buy Brandt – a very large French company with more than 4,000 employees – one of the members of the Governing Council told me, 'How can I make a decision to buy a French company if I never go abroad, if I've never gone out of my town? I do not have knowledge, I do not have experience'" (Basterretxea, 2021). Basterretxea goes on to recommend that the best governance practice should include the breaking up of larger cooperatives into smaller divisions, to facilitate decision-making and support the digesting of information that may appear unfamiliar to the governing bodies of the cooperatives. Be that as it may, cooperative development in Preston is nowhere near this contemporary global Mondragon experience, and in Preston, for the foreseeable future, commitment to the local and to participatory democratic decision-making, as in Mondragon's beginnings (and still true of smaller cooperatives in Mondragon), is key and central to the Preston Model.

Community

Work by Ridley (2021), in a study of community cohesion in Preston, draws attention to the way cooperative principles naturally resonate with factors that draw communities together and specifically compares this to the Mondragón and Basque spirit of "Auzolan" (pp.67-68), which roughly translates as "community work." Ridley shows the closeness of the Mondragon experience to the spirit of community cooperation in Preston, which is backed up by Manley & Froggett's 2016 report on the potential for cooperative development in Preston's communities. Although community work in Preston does not consciously draw from principles of Auzolan in the Basque tradition, I would argue that the overall conceptual framing of the Preston Model in the context of the Mondragon experience brings together a rhizomatic "flavor" to the Preston Model that I have previously compared to Raymond William's "structures of feeling" (Manley, 2021, pp.28-29). Indeed, many of the interviews drawn from studies of the effects of the Preston Model (Manley, 2021; Manley & Aiken, 2020; Prinos, 2021; Ridley, 2021) clearly allude to the community-cooperative connection in ways that echo reflections gathered from Mondragón (Manley & Aiken, 2020, pp.182-184). In turn, the sense of a cooperative community in Preston, as in Mondragón (in terms of quality rather than extent), are reminiscent of the views of the "father" of the Mondragon cooperatives, José María Arizmendiarrieta: "The cooperative enterprise is a living organism; it is a society of people in a community supported by solidarity, and the awareness of this solidarity is the driving force we should place our confidence in" (Arizmendiarrieta, 2013, p.100).

Mondragon in Preston

Since Mikel Lezamiz's visit to Preston in 2013, the ties and relationships with Mondragon have been maintained, with visits between Mondragón and Preston on a semi-formal basis, and also by contracted work and special events hosted at the University of Central Lancashire. In 2020-2021, the Mondragon consultancy group, LKS Mondragon, guided a Project Committee of a range of Preston stakeholders towards the development of a cooperative entrepreneurial system for Preston, and produced two reports for the Committee, one based on the Mondragón and Basque experience of combining Mondragon University teaching with the creation of business hubs, support and mentoring for start-up businesses, and another specifically directed at Preston, including recommendations and a four-year strategic action plan (see prestonmodel.net to download both reports). In the first of these the reader can find detailed analyses of the various start-up initiatives with their origins in Mondragón and their development in Bilbao and the Basque Country. These initiatives trace the development, successes, and challenges of the Saiolan innovation and business center; the Bilbao Berrikuntza Factory (BBF); Gaztenpresa, the social and business support system associated to Laboral Kutxa Bank; and Elkar-Lan, a development service specifically focused on cooperatives. All of these initiatives, in one way or another, have strong ties with Mondragón and are powering business growth in the Basque Country. For Preston, which is at the beginning of this journey, there is an opportunity to adopt and adapt the structures and designs of these initiatives, and it is easy to see how, for example, the work of Gaztenpresa as part of Laboral Kutxa can become part of the forthcoming North-West Mutual Community and Cooperative Bank in Preston, or how the pioneering educational designs of the BBF, including the LEINN degree (a degree in entrepreneurial leadership and innovation, designed in Mondragon University, in part based on a Finnish model), can become part of the education services of the newly-founded Preston Cooperative Education Centre. The second of the LKS reports identifies four "Challenges" for Preston. These are (1) inter-cooperation, (2) shared leadership, (3) social value approach, and (4) cooperative culture and awareness. Clearly these resonate absolutely with contemporary Mondragon preoccupations, with inter-cooperation being the very essence of the networked Mondragon ecosystem, shared leadership fundamental to cooperation, social value being embedded in the Mondragon motto, "Humanity at Work", and cooperative culture having become an important priority in Mondragon since the demise of FeD and the feeling that younger cooperators in Mondragon may not as fervently share the taken-for-granted cooperative principles of their elders. At the time of writing this chapter, a team of experts from Mondragon, including consultancy, education, banking, and global vision are arriving to Preston and meeting stakeholders in different areas, as well as the City Council and the University. As part of their visit, they will go to Rochdale, close to Preston, to visit the birthplace of cooperativism. It is interesting to see the concept of cooperation at work turning full circle in this way, with the origins being met by the outcomes, so to speak. It is also worth noting in this context, that there are some cooperators in the UK who do not share the same enthusiasm for Mondragon as many of the stakeholders in Preston, and that there are different versions of what cooperatives would look like both in the UK as a whole and also in some quarters in Preston. Nevertheless, the influence of Mondragon on the design of the Preston Model has remained consistent since the beginnings of the Model, and even became part of policy development for the Labour Party in the UK when it created its Community Wealth Building Unit (Manley, 2018).

The Union-Coop: A Bridge to Link Mondragon to Preston?

On March 16, 2012, the United Steelworkers (USW), the Ohio Employee Ownership Centre and Mondragón International announced a union-coop model that was fruit of much work by many at different levels, but especially guided by the inspiration of Michael Peck of 1Worker1Vote, representing Mondragon and continuing to work at developing the model both in the United States and the UK (Witherell, Cooper & Peck, 2012). In one of the key visits to Preston by Mondragon in 2018, Michael Peck spoke to the Preston audience about the union-coop model, and since then, the model has become an important part of the Preston Model jigsaw, leading to the creation of Union-Coops UK, and a manifesto preparing the ground for the development of this type of co-op in Preston and the UK (Bird *et al.*, 2019). The idea and purpose behind the union-co-op design, as described in the Manifesto, was followed up in 2021 by an academic commentary on the meaning and need for the active participation of the Trade Unions in cooperative development in the UK, beginning with its development in Preston (Bird *et al.*, 2021).

Details of the union-co-op design can be found in these above-mentioned publications, but the principal feature that creates the link between Preston (and anywhere else with a strong trade union presence) and Mondragon is in the substitution of the Mondragon "Social Council" for the union-co-op's Union Committee. Taking the Mondragón system of governance for worker-owned co-ops, the union-co-op design is governed ultimately by the workers in who elect a Governing Council, a Management Council, and a Union Committee. In this way, the potential antagonism between the cooperative design and the trade unions, with their history of worker support and solidarity, is diluted and the role of the trade union is honored and celebrated. In the case of Preston, the first union-co-op, both in Preston and in the UK, was the Preston Cooperative Education Centre, founded in 2021.

The Preston Cooperative Education Centre

The cooperative movement is an economic effort that is translated into an educational action, or it is an educational effort that uses economic action as a vehicle of transformation. (Arizmendiarrieta, 2013, p.100)

As described in Wright & Manley (2021), and as indicated above in the LKS Mondragon reports (Boixados & Zugasti, 2021a,b) on developments in the Mondragon and Basque entrepreneurial ecosystem, where education is central and key to this ecosystem, the role of education has been and continues to be of paramount importance to the development and sustainability of Mondragon. It is sobering and fascinating to remember that Arizmendiarrieta founded a technical school in 1943 and it was not until 1959 that the first cooperative was created in Mondragón. For Arizmendiarrieta, education had to come before the establishment of any new system of work, especially a system such as a cooperative that was so radically different from what people were accustomed to. This then was one of Mikel Lezamiz's main messages to his Preston audience in 2013, and it has taken until 2021 for the Preston Cooperative Education Centre (PCEC) to be founded.

Although in its infancy, the PCEC's mission is clear and resonates with the role and mission of the various educational establishments in Mondragón: to provide an inclusive and diverse educational experience for anybody who wants to learn about cooperation in the workplace and with the opportunity to either start up a worker-owned cooperative business or to use the skills learned as transferable skills in regular employment. As in Mondragon, therefore, the ultimate aim of education is to create and sustain new businesses, preferably cooperative businesses (Meek & Woodworth, 1990). All students will be expected to begin work with an introduction to cooperation in the workplace, and discussions are in place with the Cooperative College in Manchester to possibly use and contribute to some of the materials used in its START program (Cooperative College, *n.d.*). The Cooperative College has strong ties to Mondragon University, and it is hoped that the connections in Preston to Mondragon, and with the Cooperative College, will provide a further strengthening of the Preston relationship with Mondragon. Additionally, and in response to Wright & Manley (2021), who pointed out that the pedagogy and delivery of education in Mondragon continues to be traditional in approach, the PCEC intends to develop a transformative pedagogy that is as interested in the experience of education as in the content of the curriculum. To this end, the PCEC will adopt social pedagogical techniques, methods, and tools (Charfe & Manley, 2021). As mentioned above, the PCEC is a union-co-op and will be run as such, including trade union education, and governed with full membership participation, including the students. In this way, cooperative education will be about a lived experience and not only a theoretical discourse. This is conducive to the social pedagogical approach that embraces learning from experience. In fulfilment of one of the Challenges mentioned above as set by LKS Mondragon to the Project Committee, the PCEC hopes to work inter-cooperatively with anchor partners, potentially Preston's College, Gateway Housing Association, the Cooperative College, and the University of Central Lancashire. The range of educational partners available for education in Preston – and the ambition to form part of a future cooperative university (Woodin & Shaw, 2019) – mirrors the education on offer in Mondragón, which offers degree courses on the one hand in Mondragon University, and other types of practical cooperative education in its Otalora education center.

The North-West Mutual Community & the Cooperative Bank

One of the pillars of the Mondragon system is the role played by the cooperative bank, now known as Laboral Kutxa. As we have seen above, the Mondragon bank provides all the normal services of a bank, but in addition it provides mentoring and social support for the start-up of new businesses as part of its social mission. As many other features of the Mondragon system, the bank was started by Arizmendiarrieta in order to support cooperative development in Mondragón, and Preston is following this example in the development of the Preston Model. The bank that will serve Preston Model – the North-West Mutual Community and Cooperative Bank – was given approval and registered by the UK Financial Conduct Authority (FCA) in May 2020. The intention is to open branches across the region, including Preston. The bank will be run as a cooperative, by and for its members, and will exist to provide banking services and support to individuals as well as to businesses. As part of its care to social value (one of the LKS Mondragon "Challenges"), the bank will have a mission to address inequality and contribute to community wealth building. It will favor lending to small businesses, including cooperatives, and will revive some of the traditional, personalized banking that is currently disappearing from the High Streets.

Like Mondragon, from Theory to Practice

Looking at the Preston Model today, what we see is a huge amount of good ideas, optimism and positivity, and major progress in many areas, especially in the area of the changing of procurement habits in the anchor institutions. Many of the features of the Mondragon ecosystem are now available to Preston: the Preston Cooperative Education Centre, which may also one day perform the functions of a cooperative university, potentially performs the role of the educational establishments in Mondragon; the North-West Bank creates a cooperative bank that will have functions similar to those of Laboral Kutxa; the Preston Cooperative Development Network is an organization that theoretically is designed to mirror the role of a co-op of co-ops, such as the Mondragon Cooperative Corporation. The area of health, which in Mondragon's Lagun Aro was created to cover the health needs of cooperators at a time in Spain when the health service was not easily accessible to all, is not currently part of the Preston Model (except inasmuch as the National Health Service is an anchor institution and contributes in that way); and the area of research and development, represented in Mondragon by its various research centers, is only part of Preston *via* the university, as opposed to being specifically designed to be part of the Preston Model. It is fair to say that the major building blocks are in place and they wait to be developed. In saying this, it is important to note that the Preston Model is not an export from Mondragon, but rather an adaptation of the features and spirit of Mondragon. The Preston Model is, so to speak, "made in Preston."

The reason this is important is because one of the main challenges facing Mondragon in terms of globalization and expansion, is precisely how to export the model or "experience," often the preferred term in Mondragon. The challenges for exporting Mondragon abroad have been identified by Flecha & Ngai (2014) as economic, cultural, legal, and investment-related (p.671). The first of these, the economic issue, is clearly a problem in Preston: who is going to give preference to a cooperative as a business model compared to a standard company, especially if the people who will benefit from the investment are not shareholders, but the workers themselves? This means that the investment somehow needs to come from the workers themselves (and therefore can only be a minimal investment, suitable for a small business, quite unlike the large industrial cooperatives of Mondragon). It is amazing to think that, in Mondragón, this is exactly what happened in the beginning: the workers themselves invested in their own businesses. Perhaps in Preston investment into cooperative businesses will take off with the opening of the North-West Mutual Bank?

Culture is an essential question for Preston and elsewhere. Clearly global capitalism and the cult of the individual reign strongly in people's minds and hearts, so the radical difference that working cooperatively entails is a major challenge for cooperative development in Preston and elsewhere in the UK. This is one of the major reasons why the present Cooperative Development Network has been slow in developing cooperatives. Many people are not clear about what a cooperative is and why anyone would want to start one. The issue has been identified by the LKS Mondragon team as one of the four Challenges facing Preston. According to Flecha & Ngai, taking their argument from Altuna (2008), "The cooperative culture in the Basque Country has existed for more than a century. The 1884 constitution of the Sociedad Cooperativa de Obreros de Barakaldo… was the beginning of modern Basque cooperativism" (p.672). It is worth pointing out that while this is impressive compared to most parts of the world, Preston is located next to Rochdale, which is the seat of the Rochdale Pioneers, who set up their cooperative in 1844. So, cooperative culture, in terms of historical legacy, is not lacking in the Preston area. Perhaps this accounts for the positive attitudes research has encountered in Preston with regards cooperation, community, and social value (Manley & Aiken, 2020; Prinos, 2021), and perhaps this is hopeful for future development.

The legal question is not the greatest impediment to developing worker-owned cooperatives in Preston. The laws in the UK are not as embracing and positive towards co-ops as in the Basque Country, but they are not in themselves impediments. That this can be done in the UK is demonstrated by the success story of Suma, a highly successful ethical food products supplier, with over 200 worker-owners (Suma, *n.d.*), also located in the north-west of England; and the final obstacle identified by Flecha & Ngai is that of control over investments, clearly not an issue in Preston, since there is no investment from Mondragon (except the "social" investment of showing interest and contributing with thoughts and ideas). This final issue does, however, send a warning signal related to excessive localism and protectionism, which is a criticism that has been levelled at the Preston Model (Whyman, 2021, pp.135-141). The "danger" of excessive localism is also discussed by Russell (2019), who turns to municipalist initiatives as a way of catering to the local without falling into the "trap" of localism (Russell, 2019). Indeed, there may be an unresolved question about the Preston Model connected to the presence of the City Council and its role and influence, and it is not yet clear to what extent the Preston Model could be understood as "new municipalism" as opposed to the bottom-up development of a place like Mondragón, where the local authorities had little input into the development of Mondragon (although Mondragon initiatives in Bilbao are strongly tied to the local Council). There may be an unresolved paradox inherent in the localism of Mondragón and Preston, a localism which is both a strength and a weakness. Nevertheless, and especially in the case of Preston, which is far from global expansion, the strengths appear to outweigh the weaknesses, as demonstrated by the resilience of the cooperative to economic stress in Mondragón compared to traditional businesses (Matthews, 2012).

Unlike Mondragon, but...

As is well documented, the Mondragon experience began as a form of Catholic social action driven by the priest, Don José María Arizmendiarrieta (Molina & Miguez, 2008). The Preston of today is nothing like the Mondragón of the 1940s and 1950s. However, there are some provocative historical similarities that are suggestive of closer synergies than might otherwise have been considered. For example, according to Hepworth (2020), 19th century Preston was exceptionally Catholic in its social fabric: "By 1851, Preston was 'the most Catholic town in England,' with Catholics comprising approximately one-third of the population" (p.79). Combining this fact with the development of the first recognized cooperative in the world in neighboring Rochdale possibly suggests that the roots of working in a cooperative way are somehow weaved into a place like Preston, in much the same way as it is sometimes claimed that the Basque way of life was a precursor to the cooperative movement in Mondragón (see Thompson, 2014, who both brings up this idea and questions it). Whatever the truth of this speculation, it would certainly be an interesting area for further research. Certainly, what resonates in the hearts of cooperators in Preston, Mondragón and elsewhere are the principles and values of cooperation, whatever the place and time of their design.

Conclusion

It is difficult to conclude on a work in progress, where possibly at the time of publication things will have changed and moved on, as developments occur or unravel. What this chapter shows, however, is that from its beginnings, the Preston Model has been very much influenced by the Mondragón experience, both directly and indirectly. The direct participation of visitors from Mondragón, and their warm welcome of visitors from Preston, is a sign of welcome solidarity in a world of today that is facing multiple simultaneous crises. For this alone, we should be grateful for the Preston experiment. Perhaps it is best to understand the Preston Model as a framework and preparation for an infrastructure or ecosystem for the future, one that is inspired by Mondragón but is adapted to the realities of a northern English city. Like Arizmendiarrieta, the stakeholders of the Preston Model value education as a priority; like the Basque priest, the pragmatic need for finance through a cooperative bank is also hugely valued. And systems of work and worker ownership that are networked and supportive, rather than competitive and exploitative are givens in both Mondragón and Preston. Let us hope that the following lines written in memory of the Rochdale Pioneers can also contribute to and continue to resonate in joining Prestonians together and to Mondragón:

> True hearts still answer to the call of truth,
> And forward press, in spite of toil and ruth,
> To carry out the principles ye taught.
> Ere long those truths their world-wide way shall win,
> Cast out the demon Self, and end the strife.
> E'en now we see that glorious day begin,
> The toilers enter into larger life:
> A foretaste of the Golden Age to be,
> When men shall all be truly good and free.

(Extract quoted in McIvor, 2019, p.65)

References

Altuna, L. (2008). *La experiencia cooperativa de Mondragón. Una síntesis general*. Eskoriatza: Lanki-Huhezi, Mondragon Unibertsitatea.

Arizmendiarrieta, J-M. (2013). *Reflections*. Mondragón: Otalora.

Basterretxea, I. (2021, June 18). *A failure of cooperative governance* [Webinar]. International Cooperative Governance Symposium, International Centre for Cooperative Management (ICCM) in the Sobey School of Business at Saint Mary's University, Halifax, Canada. https://geo.coop/articles/failure-cooperative-governance.

Baudrillard, J. (1988). Consumer Society. *Selected Writings*. Polity.

Bird, A., Conaty, P., Mangan, A., McKeown, M., Ross, C. & Taylor, S. (2021). Together we will stand: Trade unions, cooperatives, and the Preston Model. In J. Manley & P.B. Whyman (eds.), *The Preston Model and Community Wealth Building. Creating a Socio-Economic Democracy for the Future* (pp. 93-111). Routledge.

Bird, A., Conaty, P., Ross, C., Taylor, S. & Mangan, A. (2019). *A Manifesto for Decent Work*. Retrieved October 30, 2021, https://union-coops.uk/a-manifesto-for-decent-work/.

Boixados, M. & Zugasti, I. (2021a). Analysis of Basque entrepreneurial initiatives: BBF, Gaztenpresa, Saiolan and ElkarLan to inspire the development of a Preston Cooperative entrepreneurial ecosystem. Retrieved April 28, 2022 at https://prestonmodel.net/reports/.

Boixados, M. & Zugasti, I. (2021b). Designing a cooperative entrepreneurship initiative for Preston: Challenges and strategic action lines. Retrieved April 28, 2022 at https://prestonmodel.net/reports/.

Charfe, L. & Manley, J. (2021). Human Learning Systems (HLS) and the Preston Cooperative Education Centre – Educating about Life with Life: Some Common Links. www.humanlearning.systems/blog/human-learning-systems-hls-and-the-preston-cooperative-education-centre-educating-about-life-with-life-some-common-links/.

Cooperative College (n.d.). *START: Cooperative Thinking, Cooperative Learning*. Retrieved October 31, 2021, from https://www.co-op.ac.uk/Event/start-cooperative-thinking-cooperative-learning.

Flecha, R. & Ngai, P. (2014). The challenge for Mondragón: Searching for the cooperative values in times of internationalization. *Organization*, 21/5, 666-682.

Han, B.-C. (2017). *Psycho-Politics*. London: Verso.

Harvey, R. (2019). Ted Howard, architect of the Cleveland Model, on the journey to a new economy. *Coop News*. https://www.thenews.coop/141559/topic/democracy/ted-howard-architect-cleveland-model-journey-new-economy/.

Hepworth, J. (2020). Between isolation and integration: Religion, politics, and the Catholic Irish in Preston, c.1829-1868. *Immigrants and Minorities*, Vol 38, 1-2, pp. 77-104

Manley, J. (2018). The Mondragon experience to the Preston Model. *Stir to Action*, Autumn issue, number 23.

Manley, J. (2021). The Preston Model: From top-down to rhizomatic-up: How the Preston Model challenges the system. In J. Manley & P.B. Whyman (eds.), *The Preston Model and Community Wealth Building. Creating a Socio-Economic Democracy for the Future* (pp. 32-48). Routledge.

Manley, J. & Aiken, M. (2020). A socio-economic system for affect: Dreaming of cooperative relationships and affect in Bermuda, Preston and Mondragón. *Organizational & Social Dynamics* 20 (2), 173-191.

Manley, J. & Froggett, L. (2016). *Cooperative Activity in Preston*, a report for Preston City Council. Retrieved October 30, 2021, https://core.ac.uk/download/pdf/42138668.pdf.

Matthews, R. (2012, October 19). The Mondragon Model: How a Basque cooperative defied Spain's economic crisis. *The Conversation*.

McIvor, L. (2019). 'O Pioneers': Presentation and meaning in the work of the Cooperative Heritage Trust. In T. Woodin & L. Shaw (eds.), *Learning for a Cooperative World* (pp. 32-71). UCL.

Meek, C.B. & Woodworth, W.P. (1990). Technical training and enterprise: Mondragón's educational system and its implications for other cooperatives. *Economic and Industrial Democracy*, 11 (4), 505-528.

Molina, F. & Miguez, A. (2008). The origins of Mondragon: Catholic cooperativism and social movement in a Basque valley (1941-59). *Social History*, 33/3, 284-298.

Muguerza, O. (2020, June 16). Tenemos que ayudar, es el momento de que la banca demuestre. *El Diario Vasco*. Retrieved October 30, 2021, www.diariovasco.com/suplementos/gipuzkoa-te-necesita/ayudar-momento-banca-20200616093556-nt.html.

Ortega Sunsundegi, I. & Uriarte Zabala, L. (2015). Retos y dilemas del cooperativismo en Mondragón tras la crisis de Fagor Electrodomésticos. *Cuadernos de Lanki* (10). Eskoriatza: Lanki.

Preston City Council. (2021). *Community Wealth Building 2.0. Leading resilience and Recovery in Preston*. www.preston.gov.uk/media/5367/Community-Wealth-Building-2-0-Leading-Resilience-and-Recovery-in-Preston-Strategy/pdf/CommWealth-ShowcaseDoc_web.pdf?m=637498454035670000.

Prinos, I. (2021). The Preston Model and cooperative development: A glimpse of transformation through an alternative model of social and economic organization. In J. Manley & P.B. Whyman (eds.), *The Preston Model & Community Wealth Building. Creating a Socio-Economic Democracy for the Future* (pp. 32-48). Routledge.

Ridley, J. (2021). Community and cooperatives: a Preston perspective. In J. Manley & P.B. Whyman (eds.), *The Preston Model and Community Wealth Building. Creating a Socio-Economic Democracy for the Future* (pp. 64-79). Routledge.

Russell, B. (2019). Beyond the local: New Municipalism and the rise of the Fearless Cities. *Antipode* (pp. 1-22). University of Sheffield repository.

Suma. (n.d.). *Our Co-op*. https://www.suma.coop/about/our-co-op/.

Thompson, S. (2014). Is the Mondragon cooperative experience a cultural exception? The application of the Mondragon Model in Valencia and beyond. *Journal of Cooperative Studies*, 47/3, Winter, 19-33.

Whyman, P.B. (2021). The economics of the Preston Model. In J. Manley & P.B. Whyman (eds.), *The Preston Model and Community Wealth Building. Creating a Socio-Economic Democracy for the Future* (pp. 128-150). Routledge.

Witherell, R., Cooper, C. & Peck, M. (2012). *Sustainable Jobs, Sustainable Communities: The Union-Co-op Model*. Retrieved October, 30, 2021, from http://1worker1vote.org/wp-content/uploads/2014/02/The-Union-Co-op-Model-March-26-2012.pdf.

Woodin, T. & Shaw, L. (eds.). (2019). *Learning for a Cooperative World*. London: UCL.

Wright, S. & Manley, J. (2021). Cooperative Education: From Mondragón and Bilbao to Preston. In J. Manley & P.B. Whyman (eds.), *The Preston Model and Community Wealth Building. Creating a Socio-Economic Democracy for the Future* (pp. 48-64). Routledge.

CHAPTER 15

As German Unions Struggle to Save Jobs, Worker Buyouts Are on the Rise

David O'Connell

Facing an unprecedented wave of mass workplace closures, Germany's leading engineering union, IG Metall, now finds itself fighting a defensive battle to protect jobs (Balhorn, 2020). At the 655-year-old Schwabische Huttenwerke steel and iron smelter in the small southern town of Koenigsbronn, the union took the radical step of supporting an employee buyout — a takeover plan developed by shop-floor workers to save their jobs by buying the firm themselves. Reopened last April as Huttenwerk Koenigsbronn GmbH, the plan has saved 74 union jobs, and is now one-third worker owned. A contractual right of first refusal further paves the way for eventual full employee ownership (Scheytt, 2020).

In some ways, this isn't entirely new. IG Metall is following in the footsteps of a number of its sister unions around the world, notably the *Sindicato dos Metalúrgicos do ABC* in Brazil (SMABC) and the United Steelworkers (USW) in America. These unions have each used employee buyouts, conversions, and cooperatives (Gowan, 2019) as early as the 1980s to successfully resist the effects of industrial decline. The German model of industrial relations and union practice itself have historically differed from each of these other contexts, placing much greater stress on sectoral collective bargaining, but as this model comes under significant pressure, unions like IG Metall are now being forced to look for other means of protecting jobs.

The German Context

Europe's largest trade union and a trendsetter in improving workers' conditions nationally, IG Metall is a force to be reckoned with. In 2018, it secured for its members the right to a 28-hour week, a 4.3% pay raise, and an extra eight days of vacation (or of extra pay) for workers with children. Unlike bargaining models in the Anglophone world, the German model has unions negotiate primarily with employers' associations rather than individual firms. This form of "sectoral bargaining" ensures collective agreements apply to vast swathes of the industry covering numerous firms. This model is based in large part on good faith and voluntary codetermination between the social partners rather than on law. IG Metall has thus tended to neglect strategies that may undermine or draw resources away from this highly successful model of collective bargaining, which has hitherto delivered increasing returns for its members.

Dependence on this model also comes at a cost. While IG Metall's own constitution commits the union to the "democratization of the economy," in practice any serious application of this policy has had to be left on the shelf. Far from seeking to establish a "cooperative commonwealth" or "solidarity economy" in which the union actively develops employee ownership, this clause has traditionally (though not universally) been interpreted as committing the union to codetermination and support for shop-floor–based "works councils" as institutions of workplace democracy. Ownership questions are subsequently not raised, and the union takes the mantle of a "loyal opposition" within the prevailing codetermination structure.

Unlike workers in most other countries, Germans have the right to elect a *Betriebsrat*, or "works council" — a body consisting of shop floor employees who represent staff interests within the company. The impressive "Works Constitution Act" (*Betriebsverfassungsgesetz*, BetrVG), which governs the practice of these works' councils, gives them significant legal powers, including insights into the firm's financial status, the right to review all hirings and firings, and to oversee the application of collective bargaining agreements at the company level. In best-case scenarios, these are composed of trusted union members and become a tool of union power within the company. A not insignificant portion of union activity is thus committed to ensuring that these works councils are able to effectively carry out their tasks on behalf of the employees, and that union candidates are elected to them every four years.

Despite the effectiveness of sectoral bargaining and the unions' efforts to maintain it, this model is now under attack from a number of directions. As union membership declines, an increasing number of firms are either boycotting negotiations or leaving the employers' associations altogether, abandoning the bargaining rounds and reducing overall coverage. Other firms are adopting an "observer status" which exempts them from actually implementing the agreements, while longstanding German manufacturers such as Volkswagen and Audi have begun relocating production to countries like the United States and Hungary, where they can avoid the codetermination system and the agreements resulting from it.

Resisting this process of offshoring was the basis for IG Metall's 2015 "transnational partnership initiative" with the United Autoworkers (UAW), which resulted most notably in the botched organizing efforts at the VW plant in Chattanooga, Tennessee — seeing workers vote twice against union representation. An obvious takeaway from this is that while German employers expound the virtues of social dialogue at home, they engage in shameless union busting abroad and seek to undermine organized labor at every opportunity. This process of workplace relocations, which was previously slow paced, has been accelerated by COVID-19, with companies like Mahle announcing over 2,000 permanent job losses nationally in a single year (*Metallzeitung*, 2020).

There is also the threat posed by newcomers such as Google or Tesla, the latter of which opened a new "gigafactory" in Brandenburg in 2021. This has sparked concerns that the firm may become a "second Amazon" in the automotive sector: busting unions, avoiding a works council, and opting out of both the employers' association and traditional models of German codetermination. Billionaire publicist Elon Musk's firm could thus set a dangerous precedent in the sector, which other firms would be keen to follow.

The shifting terrain of industrial relations is not limited to the economic sphere, either. Having hemorrhaged significant votes to the Greens in the 2020 state elections, the future strength of the Social Democrats (SPD) is also in doubt. As the Greens make further inroads among the unions' membership base, what this precisely means in terms of strategy is not yet clear, though it is hard to imagine the Greens supporting increased protections for automotive firms, even in line with IG Metall's own pro-Green transition policies. The fractures on the center left are also internal, with the SPD party leadership condemning calls by its youth leader, Kevin Kühnert, to collectivize large manufacturing plants like the Wolfsburg VW factory (*TheLocal.de*, 2019).

IG Metall has not been passive during these developments, as its transnational partnership, resistance to closures, and efforts to address the establishment of companies like Tesla have shown. In November, it elected a new bargaining commission and continues to push for higher wages, secure workplaces, and rights for workers during the pandemic. The union remains powerful, influential, and pragmatic, and is thus in many ways at the forefront of efforts to respond to these challenges. But these are significant threats — and the role of employee buyouts is an uncertain component in the response. While the IG Metall "Learning Factory for Labor Policy" has worked with the Hamburg-based NGO "h3-o" to explore the potential use of worker buyouts as a form of succession planning (where retiring owners sell the company on to their own employees rather than to a competitor), the strategy remains on the fringes of union policy.

The Worker Buyout

This backdrop highlights why the decision by workers at the Schwabische Huttenwerke GmbH to secure their employment through employee ownership is quite so significant. The ancient firm had undergone three insolvencies in only the five years leading up to the 2020 buyout. As the plant had an effective, unionized works council, workers were acutely aware of three things prior to closure: that the plant had benefited from recent investment and was fitted with modern machinery; that it was producing high-quality iron and steel products; and that it had a full order book. Thus, all the prerequisites for economic viability were there, despite the alleged financial mismanagement of the firm.

Ordinarily, the union's practice in this case would be to discuss with management the restructuring of the company, along with changes to the collective bargaining agreement. This may include some redundancies, a commitment to unpaid overtime or wage reductions, and other annulments of potentially "costly" sections of the collective agreement until the firm ends back up in the black. The principle behind this approach is to keep unionized firms in business and show a recognition that, while bargaining agreements apply broadly to the entire industry, not all firms are in the same economic position to be able to fully implement them. When such cases become more common, the union has also emphasized the political dimension of its work, pushing for macroeconomic and policy solutions to prevent shutdowns or widespread redundancy. But even this is often not enough to save a firm — in which case the union's main job is to ensure that the contractual and legal agreements regarding redundancy are honored.

In the case of Schwabische Huttenwerke GmbH, these avenues were fully exhausted by 2018. What made this case stand out, however, was the chance encounter between members of the works council and a local barman who happened to be a retired insolvency administrator. Together, they formed a draft restructuring plan which became the basis of the buyout. Having been supported by IG Metall, the union suggested collaborating further with the German-British restructuring consultancy One Square to develop a successful ownership agreement, which culminated in securing workers a one-third share in ownership. This comes with a right of first refusal over the other two-thirds, facilitating the gradual conversion of the plant to full worker ownership as private investors sell their shares.

Huttenwerk Koenigsbronn remains part of the Suedwestmetall employers' association. It maintains a collective bargaining agreement, which temporarily deviates from the standard industry agreement in order to accommodate a 15% pay cut and the forgoing of Christmas bonuses — concessions which were used to finance the buyout. While these concessions could be cited by critics as a potential threat to industry standards and an argument against the widespread use of buyouts, closure would have been undoubtedly worse. They have secured 74 jobs, and with optimistic economic forecasts, the firm has been confident enough to rehire some of those who had originally not been part of the buyout itself.

Initially, then, this risky maneuver seems to have worked on almost all counts. Unlike other insolvency concessions, the cuts faced by employees have been in exchange for tangible ownership. Whether this results in long-term success, and whether this can form the basis of a wider response to insolvencies, remains, however, an open question. As the regional IG Metall representative Ralf Willeck notes, this strategy requires a workforce willing to adopt the risk of ownership. But this is not totally uncharted territory for organized labor in the metal sector, as examples abroad show.

A Legacy of Failure?

Union-led employee buyouts have often occurred in very unfavorable circumstances. They're usually reactive, take place in economically distressed companies, are conducted at the last minute with little planning, and almost entirely depend on the individual enthusiasm of local leaders – all of which maximize the chances of failure and become, to an extent, self-fulfilling prophecies which fuel much of the reservation toward buyouts among union strategists (Delgado et al., 2014). These factors are concerningly apparent in this case, too. But successes are by no means rare, and their utilization, which stretches back to the very beginnings of the labor movement, have at times taken center stage in the fight for jobs.

The United Steelworkers (USW) have used buyouts since the 1980s, using Employee Stock Ownership Plan (ESOP) legislation — a form of employee benefit which gives workers share ownership in the company — to resist major shutdowns in American industry and bring firms under employee ownership. Their extensive experiences led USW to formalize this approach, passing Resolution No. 17 in 1986, which committed the union to actively support ESOP conversions under certain conditions — for example, requiring locals to pass through a two-step review designed to ensure the firm in question was economically viable. They began to negotiate conversion clauses into collective bargaining agreements in advance of insolvencies. This process of "investment bargaining" has subsequently played a key part in saving dozens of firms throughout the Rust Belt, including but not limited to Copper Range Co. (1983), Northwestern Steel & Wire (1988), Republic Engineered Steels Inc. (1989), Market Forge Industries Everett (1993), and Sharpsville Quality Products Inc. (1994) (Hoffman & Brown, 2016).

The primary motivation of the USW, as with the IG Metall today, had never been to create worker ownership for ideological reasons, but to save union jobs and prevent closures. This ended the "reduce pay and working conditions or we'll move shop" dichotomy faced in insolvency negotiations and meant that reductions in pay and conditions could be exchanged for ownership. In some cases, worker ownership worked as a temporary stopgap solution until the market improved and another firm could repurchase the plant. In this sense, even firms which failed to remain employee owned actually succeeded in saving union jobs and in increasing union negotiating power in critical moments (Witherell, 2013).

Where possible, USW also sought to build a more substantial "ownership culture" within these firms, which would give workers not only share ownership but also a level of shop floor democratic control. Learning from these shortfalls, in 2009, the USW partnered with the world's largest worker cooperative, Mondragon, to develop a "union–co-op model" as a template for establishing a unionized cooperative sector, both in startups and bought-out firms (Gindin, 2016). The "1worker1vote" movement, backed by Mondragon and the Steelworkers, has resulted in a number of employee ownership centers nationally, and is a model now championed by other trade unions such as the United Food and Commercial Workers Union (UFCW).

In Brazil, the SMABC — from which future president Lula da Silva would emerge as a political force — has long supported the recuperation of workplaces facing insolvency. While, as with the USW, this was primarily motivated by the need to save jobs and prevent closures, successes led SMABC to go further and establish the Union of Cooperatives and Solidarity Enterprises (UNISOL), networking cooperatives into a solidarity economy that now covers over 700,000 workers nationwide. The development of legal and financial instruments to support the expansion of the union-cooperative economy became a central plank of the Workers' Party's development program under Lula. While these policies are currently suffering from attacks by Jair Bolsonaro's ruling Social Liberal Party, the work of the SMABC, UNISOL, and the Workers' Party still stands as one of the most successful examples of workplace recuperation in the Americas.

Forging Ownership

Employee ownership, and buyouts in particular, have never been a one-size-fits-all solution to the challenges facing trade unions in the 21st century. To paraphrase Rob Witherell of the United Steelworkers, the purpose of a kind of a worker-ownership focused "Unionism 3.0" should not be to replace the current industrial relations models but to supplement them. Employee ownership can and has been used as the basis of significant union revitalization around the world. To build from the success at Huttenwerk Koenigsbronn and apply this approach more widely, IG Metall would not only fulfil its constitutional commitment to the democratization of the economy more fully but ultimately sustain rather than undermine the codetermination system currently being disassembled by the cynical machinations of the employers themselves.

Rather than leave it to last minute chance, IG Metall has the power, resources, political leverage, and infrastructure to deploy this strategy coherently at the national level and produce examples of successful employee buyouts that parallel and transcend the achievements of unions around the world, outflanking automotive employers in the process.

References

Balhorn, L. (2020). In Germany, trade unions are waking up to the climate crisis: An interview with Hans-Jürgen Urban. *Jacobin.* https://www.jacobinmag.com/2020/11/germany-trade-unions-climate-crisis-ig-metall.
Delgado, N., Dorion, C. & Laliberté, P. (2014). *Job Preservation through Worker Cooperatives.* Geneva: ILO, p.1.
Gindin, S. (2016). Chasing utopia. *Jacobin.* https://www.jacobinmag.com/2016/03/workers-control-coops-wright-wolff-alperovitz.
Gowan, S. (2019). Workers should be in charge. *Jacobin.* https://jacobinmag.com/2019/04/worker-ownership-private-equity-cooperatives.

Hoffman, R. & Brown, M. (2016). Employee ownership and union labor: The case of United Steel Workers of America. *Labor History*, 58(3), pp.350-371.

Metallzeitung (2020). Jetzt gemeinsam Abrbeitsplätze und Einkommen sichern. (D4713), p.13.

Scheytt, S. (2020). Hurra, sie leben noch. *Mitbestimmung,* (4), pp.35 -36.

TheLocal.de. (2019). *Social Democrats in uproar as youth leader calls for BMW to be nationalized.* https://www.thelocal.de/20190502/social-democrats-in-uproar-as-youth-leader-calls-for-bmw-to-be-collectivized/.

Witherell, R. (2013). An emerging solidarity: Worker cooperatives, unions and the new union cooperative model in the United States. *International Journal of Labour Research*, 5(2), 251-268.

CHAPTER **16**

Mondragon's Influence in Korea

Sang-Youn Lee & Garam Lee

Even before the birth of the Mondragon Cooperative, the cooperative movement in Korea was already beginning – from the Japanese colonial period around 1920 to the period of industrialization and democratization after liberation (Compilation Committee of 100 Year History of the Korean Cooperative Movement, 2019). Over the past two decades, however, the social economy has grown significantly as capitalism develops and various problems arise with it in the Republic of Korea. There is not yet a universally accepted definition of the social economy, and its exact scope remains a subject of controversy in the country. In addition to existing social economy enterprises (eight different types of cooperatives under their own specific acts), new types of social economy enterprises, such as general co-operatives, social enterprises, community enterprises, self-reliance enterprises and social ventures, have emerged in order to meet the new social demands, including job creation and social inclusion for the disadvantaged, social services expansion and new solutions for unsolved social problems emerging in society, and the number of these enterprises has increased significantly (Yoon & Lee, 2020).

In this chapter, we focus on the background where the introduction and application of the Mondragon cooperative model was possible and the cases where the Mondragon cooperative influenced the operation of cooperatives and social economy education in Korea.

Practical research on the Mondragon cooperatives in Korea has been happening since the late 1980s. Professor Lee Hyojae introduced William F. Whyte's 1991 book *Making Mondragon* to Sungoh Kim, who translated and introduced the book in Korea under the title of *Let's Learn from Mondragon.* Influenced by the book, production communities that applied the Mondragon principles and models began to appear for the self-reliance of the urban poor, starting in 1993, when there was then no legal framework for worker cooperatives. The Mondragon cooperative model was introduced and applied as a model to seek a new direction for alleviating poverty and labor alienation, creating common jobs in the 1990s, and regained social attention with the enforcement of the Framework Act on Cooperatives in 2012.

Context in Korea Where the Values of the Mondragon Cooperatives were Accepted

The institutionalization of the social economy in Korea can be discussed mainly around two time points:

- 1999, when Korean society experienced so-called the International Monetary Fund (IMF) foreign exchange crisis[1] and its aftermath; and

- The period of 2006-2012, when the Social Enterprise Promotion Act in 2007 and the Framework Act on Cooperatives in 2012 were enacted and effectuated.

The process of introducing and applying the values of the Mondragon cooperatives in Korea also coincides with this time in many aspects. However, Korean society's interest in Mondragon cooperatives has existed even before such institutionalization-related movements.

Interest in Mondragon before the institutionalization of cooperatives & social economy
Even before the concept of cooperatives was introduced in earnest in Korea, interest in the labor movement/student movement/Catholic priest groups in the Mondragon cooperative complex (MCC) had grown through books, materials, and field trips to Mondragón. Sungoh Kim (then president of the Workers' Cooperative Management Research Association) translated and introduced the book *Making Mondragon* in Korean in 1992. The book introduces MCC as a new alternative to Korean society. In this book, Mondragon's founder, Father José María Arizmendiarrieta, introduces cooperativism as:

> Through the unity of the humanization of power and economic democratization, we try to stop the formation of the privileged class and create a new phase of conscience and culture. Possession is valuable only when it can increase responsibility and efficiency in communal life. (Kim, 1992)

This introduction was appealing to those who wanted to seek new social alternatives after the weakening of social movements, including the labor movements and the anti-poverty movements after Great Labor Struggle in 1987. It gained additional support with the collapse of socialism in the Soviet Union and Eastern Europe in the 1990s. As an example, in a column in *Sisa Journal*, on introducing the publication of this book, Professor Mun-goo Kang, a political science professor from Kyungnam University at that time, wrote that the significance of introducing Mondragon is that the book is a foundation for realizing new alternatives in an era when "a new ruling block with the banner of neo-conservatism" is leading change and reform (Kang, 1993).

Sungoh Kim later co-authored *The Enterprise of Working People* [in Korean] with Gyutae Kim. The book raised the question of whether Mondragon is possible in Korea and contains the intention to "present a new corporate structure and culture as sufficient conditions for workers to have creative enthusiasm and feel rewarding." The book introduces companies, including workers' cooperatives (Gwangdong Taxi in Masan; Hyupseong Production Community that makes non-polluting powdered soap (Moolsarang) and laundry soap; Worker Dure, a production community of Pastor Byeong-seop Heo and construction workers' and a producer cooperative, Thread & Needle in Sanggye-dong, Seoul), worker-owned corporations (Shinah Shipbuilding and Kwanglim Group), Seoul Jupa (coil, tuner, and transformer production company) operated by the labor union, and the Korean Wheat Restoration Movement Headquarters, operated in the form of a national movement.

In 2002, the Korean Rural Revitalization Movement Headquarters affiliated with the Catholic Archdiocese of Seoul went to Mondragón as a research trip. In a news article at the time, the purpose of the training was introduced as "to learn the spirituality and dedicated leadership of Father José María, who founded the Mondragon cooperative, and to explore the complex cooperative community and Eroski consumer cooperative, which are the core of cooperative operation, into the livelihood of the rural saving movement" (*Catholic Times*, 1996).

After the institutionalization

Many cooperatives have been created since the Framework Act on Cooperatives was passed in 2012. With few exceptions, the cooperatives created this way did not expand beyond the small- and middle-scale, and often could not maintain their identity as cooperatives. This led to an increased interest in spirituality and philosophical backgrounds which drive "cooperatives as movements." In addition, people thought of Mondragon as an advanced case for cooperative management for answering the question: "Can cooperatives survive/succeed in the market?" This atmosphere of learning from Mondragon's experience as the "world's best cooperative" in realizing the success of cooperatives and cooperation among cooperatives overcoming the economic crisis continued after 2010. For example, the Korea Social Enterprise Promotion Agency organized a study visit to Mondragón in 2015. In particular, Mondragon's worker-centered management, despite the fact that the size of the Mondragon Cooperative Complex (MCC) in the Spanish economy exceeds that of many large conglomerates, or the way it achieved employment succession even in the case of bankruptcy, drew a lot of attention from cooperatives in Korea.

Influence of Mondragon on the Korean Cooperative Movement

Happy Bridge Workers' Cooperative

As of August 2022, 680 worker cooperatives have been created in Korea since the enactment of the Framework Act on Cooperatives in 2012. This is about 3% of the total 23,138 cooperatives (Korea Social Enterprise Promotion Agency, 2022). These figures show that with adequate institutional support, worker cooperatives can be successfully developed. The philosophy of the Mondragon cooperatives had a profound influence not only on the establishment and operation of worker cooperatives in Korea, but also on the operation of consumer co-ops and some joint stock companies, as will be described later.

Imagine for a moment that the head office of McDonald's, Starbucks or Tim Hortons turns into a worker cooperative, which would be incredible. Yet that is what happened to the Korean fast food chain Happy Bridge (Radio Canada, 2018). Happy Bridge started distributing food materials and operating food factories in Daejeon and the metropolitan area in 1997, and was converted from a corporation to a cooperative in 2013.

More specifically, on February 21, 2013, Happy Bridge changed from a corporation to a cooperative with 67 members. It is of great significance to Korean society in that it is the first case of such transformation (Jang, 2017). The six founders of Happy Bridge in the early days were together in the Catholic Youth Movement, and at the time of conversion, they also gave up the founder's stake, which held about 40% of the stake (*Catholic Times*, 2013). Their founding vision was "a company that gives priority to people over profits, a company that makes my dreams come true, a company that works in solidarity with social poverty," which was based on the Catholic spirit. The early founder groups of Happy Bridge are currently serving as executive directors of social and solidarity funds, president of the National Cooperatives Association, and representatives of Happy Bridge members, and are applying the spirit of Mondragon cooperatives in the Korean cooperative movement.

The transition to the cooperative did not happen overnight. From around 2007, Happy Bridge's executives believed that a joint stock corporation was the legal form necessary to do business in Korea, but that the concept of an investor-owned company had limitations in the way it operates. Thus they constantly explored alternative models. From 2011, organizational leaders began to complete external training courses for cooperatives through their human networks or worked to find alternative organizational forms through relationships with external experts.

Executives who were leading the change saw real-life examples of an organizational form called "workers' cooperatives" during overseas training in Italy (2011), France (2012), and the United Kingdom (2012). Most of the cases they learned at the time were social cooperatives and non-profits, so they thought they were not suitable for their business. During this trip, however, Happy Bridge executives got to know the Mondragon Cooperatives. Through the translations of the book and the introduction of experts about Mondragon, they concluded that the Mondragon Cooperatives could be similar to the direction of Happy Bridge in many ways, including a religious base, a worker-centered organizational model, and a group of manufacturing and various other businesses (Cho & Jang, 2021).

While the enactment of the Basic Cooperative Act was being discussed in Korea, Happy Bridge visited the Mondragon Cooperatives in 2011 and learned about their success. In this process, they received advice from those who pioneered Mondragon research, such as Sungoh Kim, who was the head of the Employee Buyout Support Center and joined the International Monetary Fund management (IMF) system after the Asian financial crisis in 1997 (SisalN, 2013).

After the enactment of the Framework Act on Cooperatives in 2012, various types of cooperatives could be established with more than five members in South Korea, and the central and local governments became more active in learning about overseas cooperatives through education and training. In addition to organizing an overseas training group to visit Mondragón, one of the representative ways to learn about the cooperative is to directly invite the experts of the Mondragon cooperatives to listen to and learn of advanced cases of overseas cooperatives through presentations and seminars.

In 2014, Happy Bridge invited professors from Mondragon University to provide cooperative education for all members. The expected role of the professors was to create educational materials for them based on the case of Mondragon co-operatives and to educate members about co-operative management and philosophy. According to the members who participated in the education at the time, based on the concept, philosophy, and principles of Mondragon, it was an opportunity to learn about the organizational form and operation of the cooperatives that had not been experienced in the organization before (Cho & Jang, 2021).

As of the end of 2020, 86 out of 178 Happy Bridge employees are members, and are operating businesses such as restaurant franchises, food production and logistics.

As of 2022, the representative brand of Happy Bridge Cooperative, Noodle Tree, has about 510 franchise stores, which is a figure that ranks in the top 1% of the franchise businesses in Korea. Happy Bridge is conducting franchise business with the cooperative philosophy, although 510 affiliated restaurants are not included as members, because not all franchisees agree and the structure of the company is too complex.

Happy Bridge also drew attention for win-win management whenever the self-employment economy fell. The food supply price has not been raised in the past eight years, and the headquarters has decided to offer a 20% discount on the price of fresh noodles to share the pain with the store owners. It not only provides tax and labor consulting, but also transmits the appropriate manpower relative to sales to teach how to manage employees. According to a Happy Bridge official, "Strengthening competitiveness through cooperation and solidarity between employees and franchisees is the biggest competitiveness and characteristic of Happy Bridge. We are creating an ecosystem," he said (Hankyung Economy, 2013).

Meanwhile, the Happy Bridge Social Cooperative, which was founded by one of the founders of Happy Bridge, has been entrusted with the LEINN education program of Mondragon University and is operating the Seoul LEINN program. Among various businesses, Happy Coop Tour Cooperative provides services such as air tickets, hotels, and car rentals necessary for overseas travel such as visiting and training at the Mondragon Cooperative.

What Happy Bridge learned from Mondragon's case is the following. Happy Bridge, which has been conducting business activities in association with various groups such as regions and businesses, has repeatedly experienced internal conflicts and agreements after being integrated into one organization called a cooperative. However, they learned from the Mondragon case that this phenomenon is natural.

Second, the necessity and process of creating a new business within Happy Bridge arose in the Mondragon case study process. Happy Bridge was a company that operated production, distribution, and franchise operation with a focus on restaurant franchises. However, in the process of learning about the Mondragon cooperatives, new businesses such as overseas training and import of educational contents were created that Happy Bridge had not previously experienced, and these businesses developed into businesses linked to Happy Bridge.

Third, the governance strategy of Happy Bridge has been realized through lessons learned and adopted from the governance structure of the Mondragon Group. For example, one was the member council. Prior to the Mondragon study and training, the role of the member council was recognized as an auxiliary role in gathering members' opinions and explaining the strategy and direction of the board and management to members. After training and learning, it was designed to increase the authority of the member council. It changed the governance system into a role of monitoring the management and the board of directors. As in the case of Happy Bridge, Mondragon's cooperative philosophy provides significant implications for cooperative management in Korea. Happy Bridge is still inspiring the social and solidarity economy sector to influence Samsung and Hyundai, both big conglomerates in South Korea.

Taxi cooperatives

The taxi industry is one of the representative businesses that can be operated as a cooperative, guaranteeing wages so that it can become a stable job for workers, and allowing workers to participate in management as the owner. Mondragon's philosophy led to the establishment of a taxi cooperative in South Korea. In the case of Sungoh Kim, who first translated and introduced a book related to Mondragon, he conducted about 100 consultations on the establishment and operation of taxi cooperatives. In addition, one of the founding members of Happy Bridge and the president of the National Cooperative Association in South Korea support the establishment and operation of the taxi cooperatives at the association level.

Unlike corporate taxi companies, which are made up of shareholders, taxi cooperatives have a structure in which drivers jointly invest, control the company, and share profits with each other. Taxi drivers are investing in kind for the taxi they will drive and investing ₩20 to 30 million (won) in cash. According to the information on the establishment of cooperatives operated by the Korea Social Enterprise Promotion Agency, among 23,133 cooperatives in Korea, 55 taxi cooperatives have registered (Korea Social Enterprise Promotion Agency, 2022.

The increase in taxi cooperatives in Korea is related to the poor treatment of taxi drivers. The average monthly income (as of 2016) of investor-owned corporate taxi companies is only ₩1.2 million per month even if they work for a full month. For this reason, investor-owned corporations imposed a daily corporate wage system on taxi drivers: money which taxi drivers have to turn over to the company out of their daily earning (now abolished), which was the cause of low wages. On the other hand, a daily corporate wage system operated by taxi companies before the amendment of the law was a method of deducting from drivers' total salary if they did not pay ₩120,000 to ₩150,000 to the company every day, causing accidents and excessive labor due to unreasonable competition among drivers to fill the quota (Lee, 2018).

As of June 2019, there were a total of 1,675 corporate taxi companies operating nationwide, and more than 50% of the total were small businesses with fewer than 50 vehicles. In particular, in the metropolitan area, the proportion of businesses with 50 or more is high, whereas in other regions, there are many small businesses with 50 or less, which is one of the causes of poor management.

Daegu is one of Korea's representative cities with a population of about 2.5 million. As of the end of 2021, there are 88 corporate taxi companies in Daegu, nine of which are taxi cooperatives. In April 2016, the Daegu Taxi Cooperative was established, signaling the beginning of cooperative taxis in Daegu. At that time, the number of cooperative taxis, which had only been around 100, increased more than 10-fold in five years since its introduction.

An interesting fact is that among 88 companies with 5,856 taxis, 4,400 are actually operated, which means that the overall utilization rate is low in Daegu. However, the number of cars owned by the nine taxi cooperatives is 1,075, accounting for 24% of all corporate taxis, so their utilization rate is very high (Hankyung Economy, 2021). Currently, there are three taxi cooperatives that are preparing to operate in Daegu. Taxi cooperatives in Korea are likely to increase in the future. The basic taxi fare in Korea is only 38% of the OECD average, which leads to a poor employment environment for taxi industry workers, so cooperatives are highly likely to solve this problem. In addition, there is an aging problem of taxi drivers. Currently, more than 70% of corporate taxi drivers are over 60 years old (Ministry of Land, Infrastructure & Transport, 2016).

As in the case of the Daegu cooperative taxi, the cooperative provides loans so workers with relatively few assets can enter to do business. Workers' cooperatives have a structure in which those in need of jobs can purchase specific assets necessary for business together. On the other hand, in the case of the taxi industry, it is generally recognized as a short-term job, so the identity as a workplace is very low. However, the cooperative type of operation can make taxi corporations a desirable identity as a workplace. In particular, it can be applied more effectively in labor-dependent industrial types such as taxis, care service and delivery.

In addition, considering that new taxi business types are emerging through platforms, worker cooperatives can be applied more flexibly to changes through the democratic agreement of their members, and thus can effectively respond to new business environments. On the other hand, taxi cooperatives can act as a counterweight to the taxi industry. This is because, if the taxi cooperatives transparently disclose their monthly expenses, it can be seen that the expenditures of the private investor-owned taxi companies are at a similar level. The data disclosed by the taxi cooperative will help transport workers throughout the taxi industry to live more humanely in various dimensions.

According to a study by Lee (2018), taxi drivers were able to secure their own time by working for a taxi cooperative, and to live a life dreaming of the future through the development of knowledge capital and vision formation. At the family level, the increase in income allowed them to build a stable foundation for the family economy and to enjoy time with their families, which was difficult to even think about before. At the organizational level, the study participants found that workers became owners and performed self-directed labor, and that all members worked in a horizontal relationship and cultivated common property with voluntary loyalty. At the social level, it was confirmed that by raising the social awareness of cooperative taxis, they took pride in their jobs, had more free time in their minds, were able to consider others, and were able to maintain social relationships that had been neglected in the past.

Consumer cooperatives & investor-owned companies

Mondragon cooperatives, which were introduced to Korea from the late 1980s, influenced not only worker cooperatives, but also consumer cooperatives such as Hansalim and iCoop, and investor-owned corporations listed on the stock market. In Korea, the Consumer Cooperation Act came into effect in 1999. All organizations that had previously functioned as consumer cooperatives operated as voluntary organizations that were not entitled to legal protection. Since the 1980s, Korean consumer co-operatives have been able to acquire information on the trends of overseas co-operatives, including Mondragon, through exchanges with Japanese consumer co-ops.

Established in 1986, Hansalim also learned about the organizational structure and governance of Mondragon since the early 1990s, and visited Mondragón in 1993 (Compilation Committee of 100 Year History of the Korean Cooperative Movement, 2019). In 1994, Hansalim was reorganized into an organizational form that could better capture the ideology and activities of Hansalim, referring to the governance of the Mondragon cooperative and the case of Japan. Specifically, it was reorganized into "Hansalim Corporation," a multi-stakeholder structure in which producers, consumers, and employees can participate together (Compilation Committee of 100 Year History of the Korean Cooperative Movement, 2019). As of 2021, Hansalim has 224 stores nationwide, 700,000 members, and 2,200 rural members of the community, with sales of about 480 billion won (Hansalim, 2022).

Mondragon also influenced iCOOP Consumer Cooperatives. Starting with the integration of six small regional cooperatives that directly traded eco-friendly agricultural products in 1997, iCOOP expanded its scale to more than 100 regional iCOOP cooperatives in 2021. Sales grew from about ₩1.52 billion in 1998 to about ₩660 billion in 2020. The number of members increased significantly from 633 in 1998 to 302,561 in 2020 (iCOOP, 2022). Like Hansalim, iCOOP also has many exchanges with Japanese consumer co-operatives, and through this, they often obtained information about Mondragon.

For reference, executives of the Japanese consumer co-op frequently visited Mondragón, and the compiled reports were often shared with iCOOP. In particular, in Japan, there is an outstanding Mondragon researcher named Hideo Ishizuka (nicknamed "Walking Mondragon"), and this researcher's point of view greatly influenced the Japanese consumer co-op, which in turn had an impact on the Korean consumer co-op (Ishizuka, n.d.).

iCOOP's management and member representatives visited Mondragón in 2013. In particular, what the management of iCOOP wanted to check at the time was the treatment of the early founder generation, capital raising and governance, and the management capabilities of the workers. The lessons learned from Mondragon helped to solve the problems that arose as iCOOP grew in size are as follows (H. Kim, personal communication, July 13, 2022).

In the case of Mondragon, the founders who failed in the cooperative were held accountable by the cooperative and transferred to another cooperative to contribute again. As a result, there was no management dispute. On the other hand, it is said that the capital raising and governance of Eroski Co-op was not suitable for iCOOP due to its complexity and high risk, so it was not adopted. In addition, they wanted to know how Mondragon overcome the inequality of management capabilities and the tendency to under-invest of worker members, but they did not get a sharp insight in this area.

In the iCOOP intranet "shared data room," a total of 14 Mondragon-related reports from 2009 to the present are stored. In particular, in the second half, Mondragon's management and capital raising were investigated in detail. The reason is that iCOOP does not stay as a consumer cooperative, but rather has built its own industrial ecosystem or supply chain. This is because iCOOP instinctively realized that it is very difficult to construct an industrial ecosystem with the dichotomous constraint (cooperative or shareholder corporation company) of a company. In such cases, iCOOP had difficulty in finding a case of creating an independent path by overcoming such limitations—and enjoying economies of scale—other than Mondragon. As such, Korean consumer co-ops also tried to benchmark Mondragon in terms of business diversification and vertical integration.

Mondragon also provided a lot of inspiration to entrepreneurs who seek to operate a joint stock company in a healthy way. KSS Line Ltd. was established in December 1969 and has been transporting petrochemical cargo, and was listed on the Korea Stock Exchange in 2007. The company's founder, Jongkyu Park, had visited Mondragón and was inspired by Sungoh Kim, who first translated the Mondragon book, and recommended him as an outside director in 2016. Sungoh Kim served as an outside director twice for six years, and served as the chair of the board of directors for the second half of his tenure. At the end of his term of office, in accordance with company regulations, he recommended Kangtae Park, co-founder of Happy Bridge, as an outside director in March 2022. As such, KSS Line Ltd. has reflected the value of cooperatives by recruiting cooperative experts to the board of directors in operating a joint stock company (KSS Line Management Disclosure, Retrieved on July 30, 2022, 2022).

In this company, employees hold about 17% of the shares through employee stock ownership and welfare fund. The company implements a profit sharing system with its employees from net income. Unlike other large corporations in Korea, the descendants of the largest shareholder are excluded from management and the president is elected by the president recommendation committee. Employee recommendation committee members participate in the President Recommendation Committee to express their opinions on the selection of the president (S. Kim, personal communication, July 14, 2022).

Jongkyu Park, the founder of KSS, already contributed 10% of the company's issued stock to the employee stock ownership association in 1999, and also contributed 300,000 units of stock to the in-house labor welfare fund in 2016. As a founder, he went against Korean tradition and did not transfer shares to his children. Since the implementation of the profit-sharing system in 2014, KSS has more than tripled in sales, ranking fifth among the world's LPG gas transportation and shipping companies as of August 2022. In addition, one of the reasons for the sales growth is that in 2016, co-operative expert

Sungoh Kim was appointed as a director and the company was run under the co-operative philosophy. In a joint stock company, the profit-sharing system can be said to be a dividend system that allows employees to participate in responsible management with a sense of ownership like a worker's cooperative, and it also includes the intention to deal with a company's difficulties with wage reduction rather than layoffs.

> The Founder Jongkyu Park explained the "employee dividend" system as follows: Human life is limited. Working in an organization is an investment in your life. It is to dedicate one's precious life to the organization. Those with money invest with money, and those without money invest with labor. Therefore, I believe that employees deserve the same treatment as shareholders. We want to see labor as an investment rather than just an expense. (News1, 2020)

Overseas, it has been a big trend for several years to expand the number of outside directors and strengthen the diversity of corporate boards of directors. However, in Korea, the purpose of improving the decision-making structure by engaging various stakeholders of the company as outside directors to monitor the major shareholder or the CEO appointed by him and to improve the decision-making structure has not been effectively implemented. Considering this, it can be said that it is a great innovation in governance structure that KSS's shareholders appointed Sungoh Kim, a preacher of Mondragon cooperative as chair of the board of directors, and Kangtae Park, president of the National Co-operative Association as an outside director.

Currently, most of the boards of directors of corporations are operating in a lax manner. In the case of larger than a certain size, reforming the board system itself so that directors representing major shareholders, employees, customers, partner companies, civil society, women, and co-operative experts participate in the composition of the corporate board is also an indirect way to spread the value of cooperatives.

KSS was able to introduce the profit-sharing system because it has been transparently managed with the will of the founder. This case is a good example showing that even an investor-owned joint-stock company can improve the lives of workers along with the improvement of the company if the company is run by reflecting the values of the cooperative. As such, Mondragon's philosophy in Korea spreads "a company of working people," not a "a company for investors," going back and forth between corporations and cooperatives. As seen in the case of KSS, it is important to spread and educate the values of cooperatives. In the next session, we will introduce how Mondragon is affecting the education of future generations.

Influence of Mondragon's Coaching Method on the Social Economy Ecosystem

Training to strengthen the capacity of local residents

Since the enactment of the Framework Act on Cooperatives in 2012, it has become possible to establish various types of cooperatives with five or more members in Korea. As the number of cooperatives increases and the direction of support for social economy revitalization moved from focusing on the number of individual social economy enterprise organizations (cooperatives, social enterprises, etc.) to the ecosystem approach, interest in how MCC fosters new actors as a component for maintaining the ecosystem has increased.

Many overseas training groups visited the Mondragon cooperative, and experts related to MCC were directly invited to give presentations and seminars in Korea. It was around this time that Mondragon University's Team Academy method (MTA) was introduced in Korea.

Won-soon Park, the mayor of Seoul at the time who played a leading role in the development of Korea's social economy, "benchmarked the case of the Mondragon cooperative group" and launched a policy to build "Resident Skill Schools" which taught residents essential life skills so that they can establish and operate companies that can directly take charge of local businesses, including residential environment management. Former Mayor Won-soon Park announced this initiative at the 3rd Global Social Economy Forum (GSEF)[2] General Assembly in 2018 and, after pilot projects were carried out in four districts in 2019, resident skill schools were officially opened in 21 districts in Seoul in 2020. A Residents Skill School is designed to provide education centered on demand for social services required in the region, such as housing management (repair, cleaning and disinfection, etc.) and care management (food, emotional, etc.) and after completion of the training, the graduates engage in local activities and encouraged to create a local management company model.

Impact of MTA method on nurturing the next generation

Mondragon's influence in terms of the social economy ecosystem, on the other hand, has been expanded to team learning and cooperative learning that raise the interest of young people in cooperatives and the social economy. The interest in education method and nurturing the next generation led to interest in the ideas and methods of the founder of Mondragon, Father José María Arizmendiarrieta. Mondragon's education method is also characterized by pursuing practical learning in a way linked to actual start-up and running business rather than theory-oriented education.

In 2016, HBM Cooperative Management Research Institute published a book titled *The Thoughts of Father José María* together with the Karl Polanyi Institute for Socio-Economics. The book played a role in raising interest in Father Arizmendiarrieta and Mondragon. Publication of this book is also significant in igniting discussions about the cooperative's identity and educational methods in large and small learning and seminar gatherings based on this book.

As mentioned earlier, iCOOP has played a key role in the creation of the social economy ecosystem in Korea in many ways. In 2016, iCOOP operated a cooperative education and start-up consulting course called "Youth Ariz Mendi School" for young people who are interested in starting up social businesses (Sapenet, 2016). The Seoul Metropolitan Government has supported the participation of teams to promote youth entrepreneurship. They participate in 60 hours of workshops and lectures for three months. Close support is provided ranging from consulting to sales in support of the growth of new young entrepreneurs in the social economy sector. The youth entrepreneurship teams could grow in iCOOP KOREA. It was a way of providing co-op to co-op support.

In 2014, Happy Bridge signed an MOU with Mondragon University and started preparing to bring the MTA course, especially the LEINN degree course, to Korea, which launched in 2020. Before that, Sungkyunkwan University started operating a start-up innovation education program called "Changemaker Lab (CML)" in the form of a pilot program with MTA Korea in 2017. The CML is operated for five months within the university with the educational philosophy of Teampreneurship and Learning by Doing (MTA Korea, *n.d.*).

MTA Seoul Lab officially opened at Seoul Innovation Park in April 2018, and Mondragon MTA's LEINN degree program started in 2020. In addition to the official degree program, the concept of learning by doing and teampreneurship as a methodology is introduced and practiced through short-term workshops, etc. For example, in 2020, a joint workshop with the Life Skill School of Seocheon-gun, Chungcheongnam-do, where 47 urban youth who want to settle and create a business model in the area, was held. The workshop introduced the MTA method as a learning and implementation methodology to young people who are seeking new opportunities in the local area (Eroun.net, 2020).

The MTA method seeks to create a process in which students train their creative abilities and dreams through innovative methods within university education (MTA Korea, *n.d.*). In particular, it emphasizes corporate management through cooperation, such as team entrepreneurship. Self-directed methodologies such as setting a relationship as a Team Coach-Teampreneur rather than a Student-Professor relationship, and learning by doing through real business, practicing various business methodologies including design thinking and lean start-up while participating in a team collaboration process rather than a simulation characterizes the MTA methods. A Teampreneur is a compound term of team + entrepreneur and refers to an entrepreneur who conducts business based on a team. Teampreneurs carry out actual business projects, travelling to China, Europe, the United States, Spain, and India for four years, and learn cooperative entrepreneurship skills and global citizenship in the process.

The educational method of MTA was also introduced in diverse media, including a documentary on KBS, a Korean public broadcaster, under the title of "University that does not exist in the world," along with Minerva School and other alternative ways (KBS News, 2017). This interest suggests that the MTA method has a message not only for nurturing talents in the social economy but also for solving social issues related to education in Korea, such as over-enthusiasm for higher education and inefficiency created by education centered on entrance exams.

In order for the social economy to develop and continue to grow, it is necessary to develop people who are active in relevant areas and bring in competent people to the sector. With the short history of the social economy and the lack of opportunities to experience it in daily life, the level of public awareness of the social economy is still low in South Korea. We hope that MTA method can help develop human resources to be active in the social economy through education and training. In addition, to aim to enable primary and secondary school students to understand the social economy and practice cooperation, we do hope the Korean government will decide to add social economy-related content with MTA method to the public educational curriculum.

End-notes

[1] The Asian Financial Crisis of the late 1990s wreaked havoc on the Korean economy, leading to massive layoffs and soaring unemployment and poverty rates. It led to the enactment of the National Basic Living Security Act in 2000, with the aim of ensuring minimum living for everyone irrespective of their ability to work. The Act also supported the creation of jobs by governmental actors, accumulation of assets, and job-seeking and entrepreneurial efforts of the working poor under a series of self-reliance policy programs.

[2] For more information about GSEF, visit at https://www.gsef-net.org/en.

References

Catholic Times (1996, May 12). *Report on Training in Mondragon, Spain, related to the Movement to Revive our Rural Areas*. No. 202,15. https://m.catholictimes.org/mobile/article_view.php?aid=239417.

Catholic Times (2013, January 20). Happy Bridge converted from a Co., Ltd. to a cooperative. No. 2829, page 13. https://www.catholictimes.org/article/article_view.php?aid=253592.

Cho, S.-M. & Jang, S. (2021). A Korean worker cooperative's learning process of global cooperatives: A case study of Happy Bridge Cooperative. *Korean Journal of Cooperative Studies*, 39(1), 131-154. http://doi.org/10.35412/kjcs.2021.39.1.005.

Compilation Committee of 100 Year History of the Korean Cooperative Movement (2019). *100 Years of the Korean Cooperative Movement II: Resistance & Alternatives*. Autumn Morning.

Eroun.net (2020, January 14). A young man who settled in a life technology school learns Mondragon's team entrepreneurship. https://www.eroun.net/news/articleView.html?idxno=9579.

Hankyung Economy (2013, January 20). Happy Bridge introduces "Spanish-style cooperative" ... Participated in 40 affiliate stores for two years. https://www.hankyung.com/economy/article/2019032838081.

Hankyung Economy (2021, January 12). Daegu taxi overcomes crisis with cooperatives. https://www.hankyung.com/society/article/2021011248891

Hansalim (2022). http://http://www.hansalim.or.kr. (Retrieved on July 30, 2022.)

Ishizuka, H. (*n.d.*). http://e-kyodo.sakura.ne.jp/ishizuka/index.htm. Retrieved on July 30, 2022.

Jang, S. (2017). Becoming a co-operative with self-organizing process: The case of Happy Bridge Co-operative. *Korea Business Review*, 21(1), 261-282. https://www.kci.go.kr/kciportal/ci/sereArticleSearch/ciSereArtiView.kci?sereArticleSearchBean.artiId=ART002202529

Kang Mun-goo (1993, September 23). Is "Mondragon" possible in Korea?. *Sisa Journal*. https://www.sisajournal.com/news/articleView.html?idxno=106500.

KBS News (2017, December 1). The school doesn't have a campus or lectures? University that does not exist in the world. https://news.kbs.co.kr/news/view.do?ncd=3577840

Kim, S. (1992). Let's Learn from Mondragon. (In Korean) Nara Sarang Publishing (republished by History Critics, 2012).

Korea Social Enterprise Promotion Agency (2022). *Cooperative Status*. https://www.coop.go.kr/home/state/guildEstablish.do?menu_no=2032. Retrieved July 30, 2022.

Lee, H. (2018). Changes in the lives of member of employee cooperative: focused on Korea Taxi Cooperative's member. *Journal of Governance Studies*, 13(1), 137-161.

Ministry of Land, Infrastructure & Transport (2016, December 15). Response to the aging of taxi drivers, open forum for discussion. http://molit.go.kr/USR/NEWS/m_71/dtl.jsp?lcmspage=66&id=95078594. Retrieved July 30, 2022.

MTA Korea (*n.d.*). http://mta-korea.co.kr/cml.html. Retrieved on July 30, 2022.

News1 (2020, January 13). Talking about "new capitalism." [Kim Soo-Jong Column] http://jeju.news1.kr/news/articleView.html?idxno=43133.

Radio Canada (2018, February 16). A Korean fast food chain transformed into a cooperative. https://ici.radio-canada.ca/nouvelle/1083943/restauration-rapide-coree-sud-cooperative-happy-bridge-nouilles.

Sapenet (2016, May 6). [Education] Opened iCOOP Cooperative Support Center "Youth Ariz Mendi School." http://sapenet.net/archives/7961764.

SisaIN (2013, May 1). What if a bakery owner and a bus driver make a cooperative? https://www.sisain.co.kr/news/articleView.html?idxno=16217

Whyte, W.F. (1991) *Making Mondragon: The Growth & Dynamics of the Worker Cooperative Complex*. ILR Press.

Yoon, K.-S., & Lee, S.-Y. (2020). Policy systems and measures for the social economy in Seoul. UNRISD Working Paper, https://www.socioeco.org/bdf_fiche-document-7512_en.html.

PART 4

Worker Ownership in America

The focus in this section is telling the stories of efforts around the USA generating new worker cooperative development, influenced by global models for which Mondragon is baseline.

CHAPTER 17

Mondragon: A Model for a
New Paradigm of Development

Dan Swinney

Introduction

In 1980, I saw a British Broadcasting Company documentary on Mondragon—*The Mondragon Experiment*. I've now come to understand that my experience was shared by many in the same way portrayed by the movie *Close Encounters of the Third Kind*, where thousands of people were mysteriously drawn to a mountain landing strip for a spaceship carrying aliens wanting to make first contact.

At that time, I was a machinist, cutting metal on big machines. Up to that point, I had seen cooperatives as a model relevant to small companies, sandal and candle stores, or marginal food cooperatives. The documentary showed worker owners working on big machines. They had a sophisticated governing model, and they were engaging thousands of workers. I was stunned. Seeing the documentary about Mondragon put me on an irresistible path of inquiry, study, and application since then—very much like those portrayed in *Close Encounters*. Here was a model of development that was democratic, efficient, and had scale.

My work at Manufacturing Renaissance (MR) has given me the opportunity to understand why there's been such a dramatic decline in manufacturing and its ecosystem and the frightening impact this has had in every aspect of our society. This experience has led me to the conclusion that our country/world needs to embrace and fight for a new paradigm (Kuhn, 1962) of development—a paradigm where the creation of wealth and the focus of our productive capacity is development that is economically, socially, and environmentally inclusive, sustainable, and restorative rather than the private accumulation of wealth.

Mondragon and the Basque Country in general provide us with a model of development that can be applied in countries like the US. The Basque Country certainly has a different history and different culture than the US, but its general experience provides important lessons that we can apply in a different cultural context.

De-industrialization & its Impact

I was a machinist and union organizer in the 1970s and 1980s and organized USW Local 8787 at Taylor Forge on Chicago's West Side. Taylor Forge was purchased by Gulf+Western—a company at the cutting edge of strategies to maximize short-term profits while destroying the company. Taylor Forge closed, as did 3,000 out of 7,000 Chicago companies in the 1980s, resulting in a loss of 150,000 manufacturing jobs in the region. This level of de-industrialization had devastating consequences that are present today—particularly in Black and Brown communities. We saw increasing income inequality, growing poverty and unemployment, mass incarceration, and a contaminated environment.

In light of the scale of deindustrialization, many began to think that manufacturing was at least dying – if not already dead. I founded Manufacturing Renaissance to answer that question. We looked at scores of companies on behalf of local government, unions, and community organizations to see if the companies had problems that could be solved or were they beyond repair. Some companies we looked at should have closed for any number of reasons. We advised our clients not to waste political or financial capital on a losing proposition.

But every publicly-traded company—including at Taylor Forge where I had worked—closed, downsized, or went off-shore under the short-term profit-making demands of Wall Street. As David Roderick, the CEO of US Steel, famously commented "I'm in this business to make money, not steel," as he closed South Works, one of the most profitable steel companies in the world.

Thousands of small companies were closing because of aging owners with no successor—a problem that could be addressed by effective government in transferring ownership to their employees or to Black and Latino entrepreneurs. In Illinois, 99% of manufacturing companies are owned by whites.

We came to the conclusion that 80% of the companies were viable and could have been retained. The crisis created by de-industrialization could have been averted. It wasn't a by-product of "blind market" forces. The crisis was created by investors and owners that unilaterally abandoned their stewardship responsibilities for the manufacturing sector. Instead they sought the highest possible financial return in the shortest amount of time, enabled by passive government, and made possible by new technologies. We were witnessing the cannibalization of our productive sector.

As we saw the destruction of our manufacturing sector, we were reminded that manufacturing is the essential foundation for a modern society:

- It is the only sector that can support a broad-based middle class. Each job in manufacturing generates five or six jobs in the larger economy; whereas each service sector job generates one or two other jobs; and each retail job creates a quarter of a job.

- It is the only sector that can solve the environmental crisis—through new technologies, processes, and products.

Today, US manufacturing represents 11% of GDP. This is the same percentage as the West Bank in Palestine, and is down from 27% in the 1960s. In other countries like Germany, and the Basque Country in Spain, manufacturing represents 25% of GDP. In China, it's 30%.

Under the traditional social contract, society had ceded to the private sector control over the means of production and the decisions regarding wealth creation—a social contract that had generally worked for decades. The broader public, including labor and other social movements, focused their attention on the redistribution of wealth, benefits, and working conditions—informed by leaders like Saul Alinsky.

This traditional development paradigm was driven by the objective of the private accumulation of wealth. Enabled by new technologies, this objective drove income inequality, contamination of the earth, discrimination and marginalization, and polarization of all kinds. This impact disproportionately affected communities of color, but also white working-class communities throughout the country in rural and urban areas.

The Need for a Paradigm Shift & the Significance of Mondragon

These conditions will give rise to a paradigm shift. The question is what political direction will guide the shift – a refined, destructive neo-liberal program of development, a right-wing fascist program, or a program for development that is socially, economically, and environmentally inclusive, sustainable and restorative.

There are models that can inspire and inform this new paradigm such as the Mondragon Cooperative Corporation in the Basque Country in Spain.

Father Arizmendiarrieta was a local priest who fought with the Republicans in the Spanish Civil war. Following the war, he was sent to serve the small, rural, and poor city of Mondragón in Northern Spain. He was a visionary. He recognized that any viable future for Mondragón would be the development of its manufacturing sector but in a way that was different from Franco's fascism, American capitalism or Soviet state socialism. In the 1940s, he organized a polytechnical high school where young people learned the technical skills required for manufacturing, but also learned social values to guide production such as that the purpose of a company is to serve the community, that work should be valued and serve to develop the individual, and that manufacturing shouldn't poison the earth.

In the 1950s, five graduates of the school bought a manufacturing company and converted it to a cooperative—a company where each worker had a vote in managing the company and the highest paid worker didn't make more than three times the lowest paid. The first company was successful, as was the second, and others that followed. Today Mondragon has 250 companies, 74,000 employees, and operates on five continents.

The objective conditions to apply such a model in the US exist—provided there's the leadership with a clear vision of the new paradigm, and the discipline needed to win over the broader society with programs that end poverty, as well as create jobs and stable communities.

- There is a dramatic increase in the decline in every aspect of our society and particularly in communities of color.
- We have millions of jobs in manufacturing going unfilled—an opportunity to transform our public education system to create a new generation of young people with the technical skills and values required by the new paradigm.
- We have millions of small manufacturing companies with aging white owners like me who must retire—Mother Nature doesn't kid around. This creates the opportunity for employees as well as Black and Latino entrepreneurs to buy, sustain, and grow these companies as the foundation for the new paradigm.

The conditions for a paradigm shift exist. The question is whether we are going to advance and fight for a bold development vision or remain oppositional and focused only on the redistribution of wealth. Are we going to choose the narrower path of Alinsky or will we choose the broader and transformative path of Arizmendiarrieta and lead in the creation of wealth?

The Arizmendiarrieta Path

I'm going for the Arizmendiarrieta path. What does this look like?

- It requires a network of leaders with a profound grasp of the features of a declining paradigm of development, and the features of an alternative model.
- It means organizing for deep institutional reform to put in place the resources needed to implement a new vision of development.
- It means creating programmatic prototypes that can demonstrate the power of a new paradigm.

These programs provide the first steps in bringing about a new paradigm of development. For example:

1. MR published *Toward a New Paradigm of Development* that describes the features of a shift as well as the programmatic prototypes that could be replicated in communities around the country (https://mfgren.org/articles-and-reports/).

2. There are organizations like the Bronx Cooperative Development Initiative that has partnered with Mondragon and is applying the model in a variety of programs in a challenged community in New York City.

3. A network of organizations who believe in these objectives worked with Congresswoman Jan Schakowsky who introduced a bill—HR 5124 (www.mrcampaign.net) in Congress that would allocate $20 billion to support programs in education and training, employee ownership, as well as economic and community development.

4. In Chicago, MR is working with Chicago Public Schools and the Chicago Teachers Union to promote education linked to careers in all aspects of manufacturing, including ownership, inspired by the polytechnic school started by Father Arizmendiarrieta in the 1940s that set the foundation for the development of cooperatives starting in the 1950s.

5. In Chicago, we also have the Young Manufacturers Association that is encouraging and supporting young people on Chicago's West and South Sides as they enter the world of manufacturing and the Ministers for Manufacturing with 70 members who are bringing this message to their parishioners—programs that contribute to the culture that's essential in bringing about a paradigm shift.

6. The Steel Valley Authority (SVA) has sustained a Strategic Early Warning Network for years that reaches out to companies that need assistance, including ownership transition in companies with an aging owner with no successor. SVA has saved hundreds of companies and 30,000 jobs.

7. The Industrial Commons in North Carolina is organizing networks of cooperatives and companies in projects like the Carolina Textile District.

8. There's the development of cooperatives in Cleveland, Ohio, the Bay Area, New York, Cincinnati, Dayton, and North Carolina and elsewhere around the country, organizations like the US Federation of Worker Cooperatives, and large networks like ReImagine Appalachia that is

advancing a new vision of development for a large region that includes the development of worker-owned companies.

Conclusion

There are lots of examples across the country of work inspired by the Mondragon cooperative experience. Mondragon provides an evidence-based model with basic principles that can be applied in any context, including urban and rural America. The challenge is to understand the full model, including the foundation in manufacturing as a concrete alternative to the current paradigm of development. We need to – and can – show how this model can compete with in the marketplace, within government, and within the culture of our society and provide a future that is hopeful and dynamic.

References

Kuhn, T.S. (1962). *The Structure of Scientific Revolutions*. University of Chicago Press: Chicago.

CHAPTER 18

Platform Co-ops & Emerging Possibilities: An Interview with Doug O'Brien

Christina Clamp & Michael Peck

Doug O'Brien is President & CEO, National Cooperative Business Association CLUSA International (NCBA CLUSA).

Christina Clamp: You are uniquely positioned to think about where the movement is trending, and think about this more broadly, and not just in terms of Mondragon's influence. What are the emerging areas for new co-op development and of the co-op movement changing in the United States? Do you see any breakthroughs with the current administration and Congress?

Doug O'Brien: I will focus on three: platform, small-business conversions, and the care economy.

Platform cooperatives occur using new information technology that captures, analyzes, and distributes information. The people or businesses who use these platforms, many times known as gig workers, are the potential members of cooperatives. There is huge potential for these cooperatives given that the use of big data, inevitably, will have a much larger impact on our economy and our society and cooperatives. We need to make sure that the cooperative business model is understood, and that people can use it on platforms. I think that dynamic is going to push some of our notions on how to do cooperative development. There are some great things happening. For example, the New School's Trebor Scholz and others are exploring and really pushing what is possible in terms of cooperative development. But I feel like we haven't hit that tipping point and have yet to find momentum.

Another area of focus is the care economy.

Christina Clamp: Before you go into the care sector, if you could say something about how you see platform co-ops having a particular advantage when structured as a cooperative.

Doug O'Brien: First would be the traditional advantages of a co-op: the people who use the business — whether they're workers or consumers or producers — own, control, and benefit from the business. Without this type of cooperative organization, platforms make it easy for those in a relatively weak bargaining position to be exploited. For example, highly skilled gig workers find it nearly impossible to bargain for decent benefits or any type of job security. If the workers joined together in a co-op, they would be able to set more rules that benefit the workers — those who are creating the real value. Perhaps more importantly to many workers, it means that they actually could begin to come together to make sure that they have better job security, how much they work, and on a particular day or particular week. It means that they'd have some stability.

So, for gig workers, co-ops are better. They will be better paid, receive better benefits, and enjoy better work conditions. These kinds of co-ops are in essence worker co-ops, or perhaps producer or small business co-ops.

Platforms also afford consumers to use the cooperative business model. Currently, individual consumers have essentially no say whatsoever in how they engage with the platform and what is done with their information. People have no control over how their information is used and whether the value that is being created from that information is flowing back to the consumer. Capturing value is what cooperatives are designed to do. Co-ops also ensure that the business is engaging in community in a way that matches the values of the individuals. That's what they're made for, and the platform economy is in dire need of more cooperatives.

Christina Clamp: Excellent. If you'd like to move on to talking about the care sector?

Doug O'Brien: In Italy, communities look to cooperatives to meet the needs of families who need dependent care — elder care, childcare, or care for the differently abled. In Italy, cooperatives make up nearly 50% of the care sector. And many of those co-ops are multi-stakeholder that include as members both the workers and the families. The funding streams are varied — public funding from federal or national government, philanthropic funding, or funding from the families themselves. The literature indicates that these kinds of cooperatives are actually more affordable and yield better outcomes than non-co-ops.

Here in the US, one of the glaring failures of both the market and of government intervention is being able to really meet basic needs of these families. Cooperatives can serve this purpose. They could be worker co-ops, consumer co-ops (where the families are the members), or multi-stakeholder co-ops.

Much would need to be done to make this vision a reality. First, we would need to build up the ecosystem of co-op development for this special kind of cooperative. Then we would need to ensure that there are funding streams in place, primarily from the public sector, to ensure viability.

An example in the US is around home care — typically for the elderly. The <u>Cooperative Development Foundation</u>, an affiliate of <u>NCBA CLUSA</u>, has been working in coalition with a number of other groups for seven years developing an ecosystem of cooperative development so that more and more people can use cooperatives for home care.

According to the data in terms of worker members, it is almost all women. And these home care cooperatives tend to be significantly overrepresented with women who are Black and brown, who are able to create a business and then have a leadership ladder. Co-ops provide these women the ability to have a say in what is a very hard job, and in many ways some of the most important work in a community. The co-ops result in better pay and, even more significantly, better working conditions.

And the co-ops provide better outcomes for the families and those being cared for, because the workers stay a lot longer in a sector that otherwise has very high turnover rates. With lower turnover comes better care.

Better outcomes for the workers, the families, and the communities. So, we have an example to point to in the US in terms of the efficacy of a cooperative in the care sector.

Christina Clamp: I think you've captured the needs around social cooperatives. I put together a study trip with help from Legacoop in Italy a few years back to visit some of their social cooperatives and the care sector. The caregiving sector is clearly an area where there has been failure in the US of the public sector. The Italians have shown that it can be done, and done affordably — more affordably than having it totally handled by the public sector.

Doug O'Brien: Regarding small business conversion: *Nonprofit Quarterly* reported earlier this year that of the 2.34 million businesses owned by people ages 58 to 76, which employ 24.7 million people nationwide, a whopping 83% do not have written succession plans (Dubb, 2020) or view such plans as a topic too complex to approach (Butler *et al.*, 2021). While the term perhaps is a bit overused, these numbers show the "silver tsunami" is real. We are on the front end of it right now; it is a huge opportunity for people who could work at or patronize these cooperatives to be able to own and control their own business. This is a cooperative development opportunity. As with the platform co-ops and care sector co-ops, it will require a different approach to co-op development. In the case of conversions, not only are the prospective new members stakeholders — but the current owner of the business in many ways is the most integral person in the co-op development journey. For the conversion to be successful, the co-op developers will need to balance the needs and priorities of both the seller (the current small business owner) and the prospective members. And unlike much of current co-op development that focuses on start-ups, conversions are a bit of a hybrid in terms of the business' maturity. In one way, the business is established. In another, there are new owners and a completely different ownership and management structure, thus making it feel more like a start-up. All of this requires new skill sets from the co-op development community.

The opportunity for these millions of businesses to be converted into cooperatives is absolutely a priority. For example, in many rural communities in the US, anchor main street businesses might be a perfectly viable going concern, but there is no one person interested in buying the business. If this grocery store, hardware store, or restaurant folds, it could be a fatal blow to the community. It may be the only buyer for that grocery store in a small town of 700 people, who will be either the people who are working there or the people who are its patrons. This is a strategy that the public sector should be interested in because it maintains these anchor businesses while providing ownership opportunities for workers. And it's not only in rural communities, but also in more urban neighborhoods that private investors ignore.

Christina Clamp: I think you're right. It's not just a rural issue. It clearly is an issue in rural communities in terms of preserving services and a community. But I remember, oh, probably a couple of years ago, there was a Korean grocery store in my neighborhood. And the woman who owned it was ready to retire. So, she shut the store down, and people were really bemoaning the loss of the store. It's a shame, because it probably had sufficient business that with the right transition it could have continued to serve the community.

Michael Peck: Here's another approach to this, based on the union Workers United and their groundbreaking Starbucks campaign, with whom 1worker1vote joined forces starting with the Gimme Coffee debacle in Ithaca, NY, two years ago.

A well-known consultancy working with co-ops and ESOPs represented the owner; the coffee shop had a preexisting union, and the consultancy went on video and said, "Well, you don't need a union for workplace democracy. We can replace that with a worker co-op." They actually helped the owner achieve that goal. Together they decertified the union, and it became a real scandal. The US Federation of Worker Cooperatives and their union Co-op Council really got into it. And then everybody apologized, but the damage was already done. Like with the New York City Owner to Owners initiative — it's a jackal's ball, in the sense that the so-called good faith co-op developers are transition experts, and the owner pays the transition experts. So, no one really represents the workers, and no one is letting the workers know if they're getting the right deal for them.

There's so many ways to structure hybrid deals, so many options now that workers intending to be owners should be made aware of all the alternatives out of fairness and best practices. And there's no guarantee of that in these kinds of approaches.

So, 1worker1vote has come up with a concept called the Workers Guarantee Lab, which would offset this, being a third party to a conversion transaction, to make sure the workers are equally represented by experts without a client agenda.

Another principle that you know we've insisted on in our movement is tax parity, because we feel that the way business conversions are set-up now, the playing field is not level and departing capital wants to have an ESOP for the tax advantages. Even in the co-op world, conversions reach out to the ESOP community because that's where the money is, and this US Treasury line-item distortion (because it's not equally shared) allows imbalances to take place when the issue is an arbitrary federal government line-item benefitting only one kind of structure. If you want to do something big, you'll do an ESOP. If you're small, you'll do a co-op — and it doesn't have to be like that at all. All of us know exceptions to that statement, such as, historically, Cooperative Home Care Workers (CHCA), and recently The Drivers Coop, Lobster 207, and New England Loggers Cooperatives. And my point is that if federal tax treatment was equal, if everybody had the same tax benefit as the ESOP community, then the workers that are going to take over running, building, and owning the opportunity and responsibility of growing the enterprise, and the community that's hosting them, get the opportunity to choose the culture that's best for them, instead of having it imposed by the outgoing owner. Tax parity would allow freedom of choice facilitating enterprises structured by inclusive stakeholder choice with values and a culture more aligned in community. ESOP advocates respond that it's too complicated. It's too complex for those smaller worker co-ops. And my point is that shared-services co-ops where you can bridge the services and drive the cost down could solve that issue. So, I just wanted to get your thoughts on that.

Doug O'Brien: Co-ops certainly need tax parity with ESOPs. Without it, workers — and perhaps more importantly financial and legal advisors — will continue to steer away from worker co-ops.

On shared-service — or federated — co-ops, I'm fully on board with that idea. To those who say "Well, it's big and complicated," I point to the 900 rural electric co-ops that have created federated co-ops to solve wickedly complex supply and service challenges, and the over 4,500 credit unions that work together to ensure even small credit unions have the opportunity to stay on the cutting edge of financial member services.

Michael Peck: Yes, that's exactly the point.

Doug O'Brien: For example, rural electric cooperatives need back-office support for IT. Cloud services. Well, that sounds kind of big and complicated when you're talking about 20 million homes and businesses. They have a co-op for that: the National Information Solutions Cooperative (NISC). Meanwhile, credit unions are working together to solve highly complex IT security and service delivery challenges.

The home care sector that we discussed earlier is now working on a shared services co-op to drive down the costs and increase the back-office sophistication of these very small businesses. One interesting service that a co-op can provide is brand. Think of Ace Hardware, one of the more prominent purchasing cooperatives that is made up of small hardware stores. These small-business owners certainly enjoy the buying power of the co-op, and they also capture value by branding and advertising in the same way. If small businesses are looking for this kind of solution, co-ops can deliver.

Christina Clamp: In a study that I did looking at shared-services cooperatives, we examined its application across sectors. We looked at what was happening with credit unions and cooperative financial services and the business sector. I had previously done work on Carpet One. It's very clear that there's lots of wonderful, successful applications of a shared services model. And I think that if you look at the structure of Mondragon Cooperative Corporation (MCC), it is a shared services model.

Doug O'Brien: Right.

Christina Clamp: MCC does the same thing that shared services co-operatives would do, and that's part of their secret sauce if you will. It's what makes it possible for them to be out in the world successfully.

Doug O'Brien: Yes, right. Your point makes me think of another example. Almost a contra-example of MCC. You know the name Murray Lincoln. His memoir *Vice President in Charge of Revolution* tells the story well. He ended up leading CLUSA for over 20 years. He was also the force behind the creation of what became Nationwide Insurance. I just reread the book in the last six months or so, and it's still a little bit fresh in my mind. I refer the book to key leaders at NCBA CLUSA because he was truly one of the great co-op entrepreneurs, "co-op-preneur," if you want.

He came from hardscrabble New England in the early 20th century and cut his teeth on co-op organizing as one of the first county co-op extension officers. Before long, he ends up at the nascent Ohio Farm Bureau, and he just starts spinning out all kinds of co-ops to solve every conceivable problem for farmers. The original was the kind of classic farmer cooperatives — farmers coming together to market their commodities — but quickly he uses co-ops to obtain farmer inputs and electricity, and to insure their cars, which was the new thing; that's how Nationwide came about. And it wasn't just in Ohio either. It was happening in other states where there was a generation of co-op leaders too; for example, State Farm Insurance started this way as well.

To compare it to today, that generation included a set of stakeholders who aggressively sought to innovate and determine how co-ops could help solve that next problem. At the end of the day, it was always about helping their members be economically viable. Over time things went a different direction — the way people thought about co-ops in Ohio, as opposed to the Basque region.

So that would be an interesting research topic — to compare those two eras of intense co-op development given they evolved in different ways. In the Ohio Farm Bureau, an organization I think highly of, as I did a lot of work with them in a former life, they no longer think of cooperatives as the first option to solve a problem. Why did Ohio evolve in a different direction? And has it made a difference to the people who live in those regions? What's it mean to the communities in the Basque region *versus* the rural communities in Ohio? That would be an interesting paper. For reference, I recently had an opportunity to spend time with a professor from the University of Bologna in Italy, Flavio Delbono. Professor Delbono showed, through rigorous economic analysis, that regions more robust in co-ops enjoy greater prosperity — defined as greater wealth (GDP) and more equal distribution.

Christina Clamp: Well, if you refer back to the questions that we proposed for you, you'll see that the Spanish government allocated €800 million for strengthening the social economy in their country, and one has to ask: Why is it that the Spanish government has seen the wisdom of investing in the social economy? And why is it that we are still struggling in the US to essentially hold on to the limited resources that we've got now in the federal budget?

Doug O'Brien: Right.

Michael Peck: And in Spain, the government's "go to" conversion solution is worker co-ops. Clearly stated.

Doug O'Brien: Well, the experience that the government has with worker co-ops in Spain *versus* here in the US is significantly different. While we have a growing worker co-op sector here in the US — by most measures the fastest growing cooperative sector — it has yet to gain broad recognition. It still does not compare to Spain. It's not necessary, but it helps to have that example. Sadly, policy-makers in the US do not tend to put too much credence in examples from places outside the US. I suppose that is yet another expression of the supposed US exceptionalism. That only means we need to work extra hard to show people how the experiences from other places in fact do have applicability in the US.

We, as a cooperative advocacy community, need to be more effective in doing exactly what you're doing with this book. We need to tell the MCC story, and other stories from around the world, on how co-ops can really be effective tools for economic and social improvement. At the same time, we need to be wide eyed that the US does have its unique context. Change in the US will be iterative — until a tipping point. It takes place in the context of a strong preference for free market solutions. Yet we are in a moment when more people are asking questions on whether relatively unfettered capitalism yields the best societal outcomes. Whatever policy changes we seek will likely need to be bipartisan — especially if we want those changes to stick.

Christina Clamp: I've been thinking about the issue of the form of ownership in a cooperative, and how I've often had people say to me, "Well, workers understand stock, but they don't understand a membership share and how that is going to be advantageous for them".

Well, in the years I've been on the ICA Group's board, they have done both worker co-ops and democratic ESOPs as a solution. I had done some case research on worker co-ops back in 2005 and visited King Arthur Flour, and was really struck by how Steve Voight, the CEO, and Frank Sand, the former owner, worked on the conversion. They really did take very seriously the importance of making membership democratic, and so they actually convened ownership meetings quarterly.

They also created ways even for high school students to become share owners in the business. When I visited, I had a woman on the shop floor come up to me and she said, "We're so excited about the fact that we are now the owners of our own company." You know, maybe the solution is because of the cultural structure here being so individualistic that there has to be some way to convincingly show people that shared ownership can be every bit as effective as stock ownership.

Doug O'Brien: I think those are great examples. I think that language of ownership in the US probably has a connotation that we can take greater advantage. This is pretty fertile ground these days in terms of people's desire for greater stability and a greater say in their business. We do, however, need to be careful about not pigeonholing the word "ownership" into simply an investment vehicle, which can happen in the US context. There's so much more to what worker cooperatives are. I think that we have yet to pierce the larger public conscience on what co-ops are, have done, and are capable of doing. So, there is a lot of good work to do for the co-op community — or on a cynical day, a lot of frustration that we haven't figured out how to really increase the visibility of co-ops yet given their significance and potential.

Michael Peck: None of us invented any of the issues associated with the US cooperative community, but we inherit them. Starting with public recognition of voice and agency, how the seven universal cooperative principles serve the greater common good and undergird the fullest expression of inclusive civic democracy. Why does everyone still operate in silos, instead of coming together in expressions of broader, deeper, multi-stakeholder critical mass power? There is a huge opportunity before us. Polls show consistently that rising generations want to be part of unions and they want to form and join cooperatives, and they feel comfortable innovating hybrid structures of both.

Dr. Phil Thompson, former deputy New York City Mayor in the De Blasio Administration, told me that at MIT the #1 structure preferred by student-teacher spinoffs from internal research was cooperatives by far; so many academics from other schools have told me the exact same thing, and we have a great opportunity now that some in the private sector have decided to "equity wash" by jumping on the worker- and employee-ownership bandwagon — which is a good development in that it induces "ownership" competition into all competing (should be collaborating) models to help them become their best selves. If the worker- and employee-ownership formula fundamentally doesn't change the structure of stakeholder wealth and power control, then the conversion equation is just not good enough.

Doug O'Brien: Right.

Michael Peck: We're in this world where Generation Z and Alpha, much more than Millennials or Boomers, are looking for authenticity and aspirational reality, given what they've gone through so far with pandemics, the Great Resignation, the after effects of the 2008 Great Recession, all the societal bait-and-switches, getting shot and killed while trapped in their classrooms across the country, everything of value breaking down. What they want are structures that are more real, more agile, more inclusive, more promising and deliver on the hope of commitments made. And so, we have this opportunity to actually collaborate across generational divides to redesign the social compact starting with stakeholder equity and democratic governance.

But instead we're offloading bait and switch. Performative populism in sound bites without legacy substance. We're using the words, but we're not clothing, feeding and sheltering these words with policy options and values-aligned, purpose-driven innovation. And that's what the private equity people are understanding — that the status quo US "ownership" community can be disintermediated because it's not living up to its fully shared potential. It's like a semi-hostile takeover of an inert object.

The people that private equity "ownership" innovators are worrying first and foremost is the ESOP structuring class, who've been doing that same deed forever and making big fees in the process. Where the transaction is everything, and where fees are paid upfront (ESOPs are after all a Wall Street invention) and the incoming worker-owners get to figure the rest out. Multiclass stock formulas don't really care if the employees have any control whatsoever. They don't really care if workers participate. The focus is on complying with underlying regulations (IRC section 401(a); qualified defined contribution plan regulations; Employee Retirement Income Security Act of 1974). People drive up in Porsches to do these transactions, and people who are on the worker side of the transaction are carpooling to shoulder all the subsequent burdens with much greater risk — there's this huge economic class difference. And I think we can do so much better. This is so solvable. And that's one of the reasons why many of us have reached for the social economy as a more mutualist community. As Chris said, it's a bigger footprint, and includes labor, cooperatives, enterprises, mission-based enterprises, faith-based groups. Social Economy has become a huge movement outside of the US that's pretty well organized. In the European Union, it's really powerful. For some countries, it's 10% of their GNP, not in all, but some in the EU.

And it's got major support from the European Commission and from the European Parliament. So far in the US, it hasn't materialized in the same way, but maybe our "Own the Metrics" campaign outlined in **Chapter 6**, *focusing just on social and human capital, can help make this happen. We want the global social economy community to impact the ESG/SDG performance metrics process so that we can actually participate to drive the funding — instead of being driven by the funding and the funders, like always before. Arbitraged and commoditized. Doing this trench work today allows this kind of transformation to take place tomorrow where we actually can deliver massive tipping-point change in the foreseeable, immediate future with a lot of international support.*

Doug O'Brien: I agree. At NCBA, we want to work with this big tent — and we have been. We have been involved with the OECD's solidarity and social economy (SSE) work, and I have been involved with Sarah Horowitz on the mutualism network. Co-ops have such a huge role to play. My inclination is that co-ops need to be in that tent as a best example of what we mean by SSE.

Michael Peck: Great. Thanks, Doug, for stating this.

Doug O'Brien: That forces people like me to be clear on the distinctions of what it means to be a co-op — these entities that have a shared set of values and principles that include democratic ownership and control. That demands the question: How do we as a cooperative movement stay true to the values and the principles, while seeking to innovate and be relevant in today's context? For example, some people are pushing to have non-members exert some level of control of the co-op in the name of attracting outside capital. I understand that people will sometimes need outside capital to get the business going — but co-ops already have strategies to address this need, especially the use of preferred shares that carry no voting rights for the outside investor. While it is great that more people are looking at inserting more democracy into businesses, not every one of these businesses can be called a co-op unless they truly are owned, controlled by, and benefit the user of the business.

I do want to bring up another important item when considering our cooperative roots. I'll say I've evolved in the last few years, particularly in light of the focus on inclusion and equity, which was long overdue. The Rochdale Pioneers are an important touchstone, as are the cooperative economies of Native Americans and Black communities — the first of which has been here well before any European set eyes on North America and the second that arrived on our shores with the people in bondage and enslaved.

We need to really understand and embrace that as part of the cooperative story. And I think here in the US we should be able to do that more quickly in a more authentic way than maybe in some other places. We need to face these dynamics as a cooperative community. Not only face them but embrace them.

Michael Peck: That's so well said, Doug. But there's also so many pitfalls that you have to navigate. In this country, for the African American population, it was either the church, some unions, and local cooperatives serving as three transformational vehicles allowing for growing workplace and societal agency and resiliency to build prosperity and community.

The problem is, if you go to the cooperative boards that are positioned, in some cases, in closed communities, we still witness systemic racism. We still lack inclusion and socioeconomic justice. Cooperatives are not always democratically represented and governed. We're fighting the same legacy problems over and over again, seeing ourselves in the cracked mirrors and broken windows scarring the indivisible, E Pluribus Unum nation and short-changing its solidarity dividend potential.

There are important vested interests that just don't want to allow everyone knocking on the door to get in, and you have to make these compromises all the time and compromises can clip wings that need to fly. We have to find compelling, multi-partisan Venn diagram intersections; for example, there's this incredible briefing that the polling expert, Stanley Greenberg, put together that shows that if we can just avoid the vocabulary and the cultural triggers, there's this huge bipartisan mandate in our country for climate — but you wouldn't know it, reading the press or listening to politicians speak. We have to reframe the middle so that we can be incredibly impactful without culturally irritating each other. And I think that the cooperative movement can play a decisive role in this transformation, because we have these basic principles already in place, we already operate on principles emphasizing intellectual and morally aligned cohesion and inter-cooperation. This is something where a reframing focused on how and where the benefits are defined is where we find the win; that tire is kickable, and it can help pull us across the line. Like the US Small Business Administration's federal loan collective guarantees, or US Treasury tax parity among all hybrid ownership structures.

Doug O'Brien: Yeah.

Christina Clamp: I served on the NCBA board for nine years, and I was really struck by that on the CLUSA side of NCBA. The scope of connections operate more broadly around the social economy and solidarity economy. We're very clearly a part of the work that NCBA's been doing overseas. I had a chance to go to Ghana and to see the work that was being done around civic engagement and building civil society there. And to the extent that you build the civil society, you create a framework that allows for greater engagement with cooperatives in a way that we would see as appropriate, desirable. And I do think that the organization has been doing this internationally.

Doug O'Brien: For almost 70 years. I knew you had served on the board — I didn't realize it was a nine-year tenure or that you had a chance to go to Ghana.

One of my goals with the board of directors — and I haven't figured out how to implement this — is to get essentially all of them to visit one of our international projects. As you know, Chris, once you see the power of the cooperative business model in a developing region, your eyes are opened to the potential in the US. For example, I just spent time in Guatemala, where the most effective means of economic empowerment for the indigenous population is cooperatives. This group of people makes up 40% of Guatemala's 17 million people, and have suffered a terrible legacy of discrimination. Co-ops are their lifeline. And co-ops not only provide a way for people to participate in the economy, but they also teach the fundamentals of democratic governance — lessons that are then applied in civic life.

Christina Clamp: It's powerful. Yeah, I went on two trips. One was Ghana and the other was to Indonesia to visit northern Sumatra after the tsunami, and so we actually went into an area that was post-conflict. Rebuilding after the Civil War. The conflict had gone on since World War II. It really stayed with me as a very powerful experience of the way in which it was combining, bringing together a coffee co-op and a credit union and … So yeah, I think those opportunities are really important for leadership in the NCBA to understand our place in the larger world.

Doug O'Brien: Co-ops can play such a pivotal role in helping communities transition from crises. Again, referring to Guatemala. We are working with communities there who are exploring something they call an "immigrant co-op" that seeks to help families address the refugee crisis at its root — in the rural Guatemalan communities where families lack economic opportunity. They are considering how to use cooperatives to capture remittances — the dollars that Guatemalans in the US send back to Guatemala — so that those dollars can be invested in the Guatemalan communities. By using the cooperative model, those dollars can be invested in businesses and jobs that will bolster those communities so that fewer people have to make the difficult choice to leave their homes.

Michael Peck: And I think also, Doug, given the back and forth via email of what's happened collectively so far in Ukraine, I think there's a huge opportunity to collaborate between the social economy work that we're doing through the American Sustainable Business Network with Social Economy Europe, and the cooperative work that you're doing through NCBA and cooperatives in Ukraine – there's so much rebuilding to do. We can really put things together for greater social impact. In this case, there's clearly assets on all sides and just an endless need.

Doug O'Brien: Just a quick update on what's happening in Ukraine. Their consumer co-op sector is vibrant. You know, it's a little bit more like the UK with a major consumer co-op system known as Co-op Ukraine. It has 12,000 food retail establishments, hundreds of restaurants and three universities. We hosted a delegation from Co-op Ukraine in October to learn from their work and to ensure that the US government understands how co-ops can play a major role in the reconstruction of the country.

We as a global community face some enormous challenges: climate change, the changing nature of work, an information economy that is not really serving people — rather people seem to be serving the data platforms. There could be reason to be cynical at this moment. But at the same time, there are reasons for real hope.

There are pioneers in information technology seeking to empower people. By some important measures, women and historically under-underrepresented communities are gaining more power, gaining more economy.

And there's some real progress on policy to fight climate change, so that's good. That's the context where co-ops can show up as proven solutions that have gone to scale, whether in farmer co-ops, where rural families have used co-ops for over 100 years to have a stake in our food system; in rural electric co-ops where nearly 50 million people own and control their energy utility; or credit unions that see over 100 million people own and control their financial institution.

When most successful, co-ops innovate and evolve. This is what we need to do as a cooperative community to make sure that people have this tool in a way that's most impactful in these years and generations to come. The magic will happen as we embrace our core values and principles, as we engage in these new economic opportunities, and evolve to be more relevant to those most in need of economic and societal solutions.

This has been hugely enjoyable for me.

Christina Clamp: Thank you, Doug.

Michael Peck: Yes, thank you so much, Doug.

This interview took place on August 4, 2022 and has been lightly edited for clarity.

CHAPTER 19

"Co-op Cincy": A Living Lab for the 1worker1vote Movement

Kristen Barker & Ellen Vera

So many of us throw up our hands and feel that the problems of poverty and wealth inequality are intractable and will always be with us. At Co-op Cincy, we believe that, together, we can not only move the needle on wealth inequality and poverty, but we *must*. We are living through a climate crisis, runaway inequality, the impacts of systemic racism, as well as a crisis of institutions. We need to shift. We cannot do it alone, but we can do it together. We can help shift the economy with structures and businesses that center people and the planet at their core. Communities of co-ops can begin to transform our world. It is already happening in Ohio.

Mondragon – A Guiding Light

Mondragon serves as a guiding light and a proven example of what is possible: how an interconnected community of co-ops can profoundly move the dial on poverty, unemployment, and inequality. The Mondragon cooperatives, in the heart of the Basque region of Spain, transformed the area from one that was poverty-stricken and full of unemployment to a thriving community that even 60+ years later continues to weather economic crises. From humble beginnings, five graduates of a polytechnic school founded by a Catholic priest who imbued the school with cooperative principles, launched the first of a network of co-ops, a kerosene stove co-op in 1956. Today Mondragon is the largest industrial network of cooperatives in the world and the 10th-largest business group in Spain. With more than 100 worker-owned cooperatives on five continents, the federation has more than 80,000 employees!

Is It Possible in the United States?

In Cincinnati, a non-profit based on Catholic social teaching, called the Intercommunity Justice and Peace Center (IJPC) sponsored trips to Mondragon in the 1980s and 1990s. The goal of those trips was to investigate what it looked like when an economy put people before profits. The consensus? That the Mondragon integrated network of worker-owned co-ops was an extraordinary model. The question that arose: how could we introduce that model to a new context? It seemed like a significant challenge, maybe even impossible.

A key to the Mondragon system thriving over the years is deep solidarity. Its resilience over time has been supported by its deeply integrated network where individual co-ops share profits with the larger whole, and where co-ops that are thriving are willing to take on and retrain worker-owners from co-ops that are struggling.

In the Basque region, there is a cultural emphasis on solidarity and the whole community thriving. In the US, on the other hand, people tend to value the individual and the family thriving. For example, the ideal here is the American Dream—upward social mobility, homeownership, a white picket fence, etc.—and achieving this dream is seen as the result of individual achievement. Material success and accumulation of wealth are more common goals here than job creation, employment stability, or community enhancement (Democracy at Work Institute, 2017). In order for the Mondragon system of interconnected co-ops to thrive here in the US, this would need to be addressed.

A Seed Planted

One of the people that went on those IJPC trips to Mondragon in the 1990s was Jerry Monahan, also known as "Moose," who was the head of the Building Trades in Cincinnati at the time. When he returned, he gave an impassioned speech at the Central Labor Council meeting during which he said that if the labor movement ever had a chance to bring the Mondragon model to life in the United States, it needed to jump on it. He was amazed at the level of worker solidarity, worker voice, and worker control in the worker-owned cooperatives. He saw it as fully aligned with the goals of the labor movement.

One of the Labor Council delegates in attendance that night was Phil Amadon, a railroad mechanic and peace activist whose roots go back to Vermont, Arkansas, Colorado, and Ohio where he finally landed. Accustomed to the Building Trades' more traditional ways of thinking, Phil was struck by Jerry's invitation to engage in a whole new paradigm. Phil never stopped thinking about how transformative a Mondragon-style system could be, and how many working-class people could benefit from it.

A Game-changer

Fast forward more than a decade to October 2009. Phil sees a New York Times article highlighting a historic agreement between the United Steelworkers and Mondragon. He recognizes the significance. He intuitively understands that connecting the solidarity inherent in the best practices of the labor movement to the Mondragon business model gives the model a fighting chance in the US.

Phil, at the age of 57 in 2009, immediately convened a small group of like-minded souls to explore this possibility. The group included Kristen Barker, at that time, a 32-year old Cincinnatian working at IJPC as a Peace and Nonviolence Coordinator and Ellen Vera (at the time Ellen Dienger), another Cincinnatian, who was a 26-year old organizer at United Food and Commercial Workers. Ellen, in turn, invited her boyfriend, Flequer Vera, an immigrant from Lima, Peru, aged 31, who worked as an immigrant rights organizer. (Flequer and Ellen later married.) The four began to meet and study at 9pm at Kristen's house after her daughter went to bed. As a single parent of a child with special needs, this arrangement made it possible for Kristen to participate.

Each approached the study group with overlapping but distinct desires. Kristen's goal was to find effective ways to build the beloved community, a place where all people are valued, where resources are shared more equitably, the earth revered, and conflicts handled constructively. She had spent years organizing against war and other injustices. The need to resist and uproot injustice is necessary, and yet she feels drawn toward experimenting with how to positively build toward the future she wants to see. Ellen was getting disillusioned with labor laws being so anti-labor and where she kept working with workers who were putting everything on the line. So many of them were losing their jobs in the process, or just getting minor increases despite their efforts. She saw the union co-op as a way to move away from the lowest common denominator and to start with the highest, best possibilities for workers. Flequer has a small business family background. He loves finance and believes business should be used as a tool for promoting the common good in support of social justice. His finance classes did not share that viewpoint. He saw Mondragon as validating and as direct proof that business can both be profitable and move society forward.

Worth Pouring Heart & Soul Into

After about a year of studying the books and videos on Mondragon (procured from the IJPC library), the small group determined it was worth pouring their hearts and souls into this effort. It was time to reach out to others.

In contemplating the tens of thousands of workers in the Mondragon system (the Basque population is 2.1 million) and the few thousand workers in worker-owned cooperatives in the US (population 330 million), our small group came to believe that Mondragon's incredible success had a lot to do with the ecosystem, the deeply integrated co-op of co-ops network approach as compared to the more isolated one-off ways worker-owned co-ops had principally been developed in the US. Specifically, Co-op Cincy's "Founding Four" began to conceptualize the keys to Mondragon's success in the following ways.

Keys to Mondragon's Success & Resilience

Interconnected, integrated resilient network, a community of co-ops
Mondragon is a federation of cooperative, worker-owned businesses as opposed to a collection of solitary companies being buffeted by the global economy. By joining together, the businesses are stronger and more resilient. By sharing at least 10% of the profits back to the whole and then the co-ops democratically deciding where it goes (towards a rainy day fund, new co-op development, education, research and development, etc.), the co-ops have a safety net during business downturns. Similarly, worker owners enjoy much more stability because of the solidarity between co-ops allowing co-ops doing well to retrain and hire worker members from other co-ops that are in a downcycle.

Focus on education, 10 Cooperative Principles and intergenerational wealth creation
Education is the foundation of the Mondragon system. Without a significant focus on education, people do not have a chance to develop their full potential and to effectively participate as workers and owners

and full community members. Mondragon's focus on its 10 cooperative principles is also key to its long-term success. While most of the principles dovetail with the seven International Cooperative Alliance principles, Mondragon adds three more to further emphasize the dignity and importance of the worker, the role of capital as a necessary tool but subordinate to workers, and the solidarity between workers.

Mondragon's 10 basic principles are:

- **Open admission:** Cooperatives will not discriminate in hiring.
- **Democratic organization:** One worker, one vote.
- **Sovereignty of labor:** Workers run the cooperative.
- **Participation in management:** Development of adequate systems for participation, transparency, consultation, and negotiation.
- **Instrumental and subordinate nature of capital:** Providing and creating jobs is prioritized over increasing the marginal return on investments.
- **Wage solidarity:** Highest paid workers earn no greater than three to seven times more than the lowest paid.
- **Inter-cooperation:** Working cooperatively with other cooperatives is valued and essential.
- **Universality:** Solidarity with all those who work for economic democracy.
- **Social transformation:** Support and invest in social change.
- **Education:** To promote establishment of these principles.

Two of the most important principles are sovereignty of labor and the subordinate nature of capital.

The principal reason that the Mondragon cooperatives were founded was to create good, family-sustaining jobs, not to maximize profit for individual owners. The goal is to create broad-based intergenerational wealth. Mondragon's focus on creating jobs and intergenerational wealth rather than solely increasing wealth for current work-owners has served as a big purpose and mission that has inspired many people to participate in something bigger than themselves.

While a focus on creating jobs and intergenerational wealth is paramount, individual worker owners share in the profits as well in proportion to the work they have contributed. This practice creates powerful impacts, including a better quality of life for the workers, who then spend and invest in the local economy. This in turn sustains more jobs and builds community wealth.

Reinforcing structures that encourage its co-ops to scale with its values

The Mondragon model promotes conflict resolution and facilitates smooth business operations in a way that is distinct from many in the international cooperative movement. In addition to the typical corporate bodies such as a Board of Directors, and management team, it includes a third body or space that is atypical. When a cooperative reaches 50 people, it activates a Social Council, a defined space for dealing with conflicts and facilitating day-to-day information flow and dialogue between workers and management.

The Social Council can suggest policies in areas such as compensation, human resources, and working conditions. It can also inform management on issues related to the business, from work hours to suspensions. It is a reinforcing structure that helps Mondragon cooperatives scale with their values intact. As a cooperative grows and people are less in touch on a daily basis, information flow can be stymied. In the 1970s one of Mondragon's cooperatives had a strike when there was a large enough disconnect between the management and people on the production line. As a result, Mondragon doubled down on this Social Council in order to support optimal functioning and scale with the values intact. This creates defined processes and spaces for information to flow freely and ensure all voices continue to be heard.

Bringing the Idea to the US

A key breakthrough in successfully adapting the Mondragon model to a US context happened in 2009 when Mondragon International made a historic agreement with the United Steelworkers, North America's largest industrial union—to launch unionized, worker-owned businesses in the US. By combining the deepest solidarity practices from the United Steelworkers with the Mondragon cooperative model, the union cooperative model was catalyzed.

A worker-owned business that is unionized has the advantage of solidarity with the labor movement and support from the broader union system. The labor movement represents more than 17 million workers in the US, and union members have the ability to amplify the cooperative movement's voice. In addition, a union cooperative can draw on shared experience and knowledge, as well as tap into union benefits, such as health insurance plans. Collective bargaining can lead to clear expectations and clear human-resource policies in the union cooperative, helping morale and creating a more harmonious, collaborative work environment through day-to-day dispute resolution. Like the Social Council in Mondragon's co-ops, the union can help ensure that all voices are heard and that there is a defined space for dealing with conflicts and facilitating day-to-day information flow and dialogue between workers and management. It can create a reinforcing structure that can help co-ops scale with their values intact.

The cooperative model also offers a way forward for the labor movement in the US. In a modern capitalist economy, a cooperative is the only means by which workers can own their own means of production, an important safeguard in a society with high unemployment and a constant threat of layoffs. By embracing the cooperative model, unions and workers can take greater control of their economic futures.

A Union Co-op template emerged from the agreement between Mondragon International and the United Steelworkers. In that template, the Union Committee replaced the Social Council of Mondragon's cooperatives.

Bringing the Union Co-op Model to Life in Cincinnati

The "Founding Four" reached out to labor, community, and faith allies for an event in February 2011. Soon, about 30 to 35 people were meeting regularly to bring this vision to life. By the end of 2011, the group was "off to the races." They had connected with Michael Peck, the North American delegate for Mondragon, through the Ohio Employee Ownership Center's excellent conference. They had begun working to bring three co-ops to life and had incorporated the Cincinnati Union Cooperative Initiative (today known as Co-op Cincy).

What did the group have?

- Hope. Belief. Conviction. Grit. Tenacity. A Big Dream.
- A willingness to engage and build the road as we were walking.
- A belief we could learn what we needed to know with help.
- Purpose.

What didn't stop us?

- **Money and access to financial resources:** Everyone was working other jobs and contributed little bits here and there from their own pockets to be able to fly Michael Peck to Cincinnati each month and cover other expenses as we advanced three co-op business possibilities. Excitingly, we were able to get some small, meaningful grants through various partnerships (even though we were not yet a 501c3 non-profit) to help get feasibility studies underway. By 2013, the board was used to looking at profit and loss statements of just a few dollars. Once, we showed a $6 loss and a board member contributed on the spot to bring us back up to $0!

- **Lack of time:** All of us were working full-time jobs and bringing Co-op Cincy to life on the side. There were so many meetings each month to advance the three co-op businesses! The "Founding Four" met at Kristen's house at 9pm until midnight or 1am most nights of the week to move these efforts forward.

- **Lack of business acumen:** Our goals were so big! They must have sounded outlandish to people in the financial world. While our lack of business acumen hurt us in a number of ways (including how we launched Our Harvest so early (April 2012) and with so much debt in a low margin industry), it definitely helped us think big, think creatively and connect various partners in exciting ways that are leading to longer term potential. It helped us jump in rather than get stuck in analysis paralysis.

- **Other people's doubts:** At one meeting when we described a plan to reach out to a Mondragon manufacturing cooperative, Danobat Group Rail (DGR), and invite them to expand to Cincinnati, a member of the Mondragon delegation, Fernando Fernandez de Landa, told Kristen that would never happen, it would be like landing on the moon. "So, possible, then," she said. Remarkably, while we did not land DGR, we got closer than many imagined. Representatives of DGR visited Cincinnati twice. We introduced them to key stakeholders including elected officials, the Mayor, workforce development professionals, economic development professionals, the European Chamber of Commerce, and connections to potential clients. Cincinnati's Mayor also visited DGR in the Basque region.

10 Years of Co-op Cincy – Highlights & Some Key Lessons Learned

Co-op Cincy was the first cooperative developer to emerge in the US from the Mondragon and United Steelworker agreement. We formed around a powerful desire to help create an economy that works for all, especially those who have been historically excluded. We celebrated our 10-year anniversary in November, 2021. Currently, we have 12 co-ops in our network, with a number of new ones in process. We are an experiment. We have had both successes and setbacks, and we are learning as fast as we can, trying to determine how to make the biggest impact.

Some Key Moments:

2011

- Co-op Cincy incorporated the Cincinnati Union Co-op Initiative with 14 board members representing faith, community, and labor groups and held an event (that became an annual event) in November attended by Fernando Fernandez de Landa and Michael Peck of Mondragon

International. This followed a meeting at the United Steelworkers (USW) headquarters in Pittsburgh on developing the Union Co-op model.

2012

- Our Harvest, the first Mondragon style union co-op under the USW-Mondragon International agreement, began operation in April, just one month after the Union Co-op Template drafted by the USW, Mondragon International, and the Ohio Employee Ownership Center was released. Our Harvest is a farm and food hub co-op with a mission to create access to healthy local food in a way that honors land and labor. The United Farm and Commercial Workers (UFCW) provided critical financial and strategic support in making this effort happen.

- Also in March, two DGR representatives, accompanied by Mondragon International representatives, visited Cincinnati for two days of meetings with city officials (including the Cincinnati Mayor, City Manager, Economic Development Team, and Chamber of Commerce), Cincinnati State, OEOC, and USW to explore expanding to the Cincinnati area. The Steelworkers provided a key loan to support a feasibility study for the DGR expansion.

- Renting Partnerships, a land trust with resident control, which provides affordable housing for tenants, was established.

2013

- In March, the Mayor of Cincinnati visited DGR in the Basque region.

- Co-op Cincy got its first paid staff! In July 2013, Kristen switched from working for the IJPC to working for Mondragon International North America (MINA), the organization run by Michael Peck who was the North American Delegate for Mondragon (1999 – 2019) which, at the time, was majority owned by Mondragon International Cooperative (55%) and MAPA Group (45%).

- Sustainergy Co-op incorporated and launched in November, with a focus on commercial energy retrofitting services.

- Co-op Cincy hosted the first Union Co-op Symposium with presentations from three Mondragon representatives. The Los Angeles Union Co-op Initiative (LUCI) was formed afterward. 1worker1vote was also launched at this event as a way to connect union co-op networks throughout the country.

2014

- By January, organizing for Apple Street Market co-op, a worker and community-owned full-service grocery co-op in a food desert, was in full swing. In May it was incorporated.

- In July, disappointingly DGR decided not to expand to Cincinnati.

- Our Harvest Co-op experienced multiple crises after taking on too much debt. Co-op Cincy offered more support and leadership, increased worker training, and began helping to find ways to deal with debt.

2015

- Sustainergy pivoted from commercial to residential energy efficiency work.

- Over 150 people attended Second Biennial Union Co-op Symposium.
- Apple Street Market secured more than 1,100 community owners at the end of 2015 and hired a General Manager. UFCW grocery specialists consulted on the business plan, store design, and more.

2016

- Co-op Cincy supported the launch of the Greater Dayton Union Co-op Initiative and its efforts to replicate Apple Street Market.
- Co-op Cincy launched a Focus on Transitioning Manufacturing Companies to Worker Ownership in Southwest Ohio. The IUE-CWA helped kickstart and fund this effort.

2017

- Isabel Uribe, author of *De La Idea Al Negocio* (*From an Idea to a Business*), who worked at Saiolan, one of Mondragon's incubators, spent time supporting Co-op Cincy in developing Co-op U.
- Hosted 3rd Biennial Union Co-op Symposium drawing 200 participants from across the US and as far away as the UK, Australia, and Argentina.
- Joined Seed Commons, the financial cooperative, as a local peer loan fund to be able to offer our co-ops non-extractive capital.
- After months of advocacy and organizing, Cincinnati City Council unanimously approved funding for NEST, Northside's community development corporation, to purchase the building to house Apple Street Market.

2018

- Published the *Worker-Owner Workbook*, a resource for working with union co-op workers to build co-op and labor knowledge, solidarity culture, and business and financial literacy.
- Childcare organizing became a focus. Co-op Cincy explored ways to increase wages in Childcare through a Care Share model, a shared services support co-op for family childcare and small centers, and worked on the *Childcare Wage Implementation Report* (168 pages), as part of the organizing effort in tandem with the Cincinnati Federation of Teachers and the AFSCME union around a universal pre-school effort in Cincinnati.
- We hosted the first two Co-op Us (12 week co-op start-up bootcamps) and learned a lot.

2019

- 4th Annual Union Co-op Symposium brought together more than 200 people from across the country and the world to launch union co-ops.
- Completed two rounds of Co-op U – Queen City Commons was formed and Olive Tree Catering explored becoming worker-owned.
- Apple Street lost its financing package in January.
- Our Harvest debt was restructured through Seed Commons, allowing it to survive and hopefully thrive!

2020

- Launched the $3 million Business Legacy Fund with Seed Commons. Twelve companies applied; six were selected as finalists for the 6-month cohort
- Completed Co-op U for Bhutanese refugees, who launched Bhutanese Bari, an agricultural and grocery delivery co-op.
- A Touch of TLC Home Health Care LLC launched.
- Launched the Statewide Worker-Owner Network with Co-op Dayton and Ohio Employee Ownership Center.
- Apple Street searched for a location.

2021

- Released our revised and updated *Worker-Owner Workbook* and translated it into Spanish.
- Launched National Childcare Co-op U with Wellspring Cooperative, Cooperation Jackson, and Cooperacion Santa Ana. CareShare Santa Ana co-op and Wellspring worked on a possible Childcare Transition. Shine Nurture Center in Cincinnati moved forward in its transition to worker-ownership.
- Launched Power in Numbers, Black-led Co-op U, and Queen Mothers Market, a buyers club working to be a full service grocery store. Hopes Fulfilled Farm to Table food truck incorporated as did Body for Bodji, a swim apparel co-op.
- Completed Co-op U for Swahili-speaking refugees, who are working on launching a DJ co-op and an East African restaurant co-op.
- Ohio Worker Ownership Network expanded to include 10 co-op developers in the state.
- Massage for the People Co-op launched.
- Unable to secure a new location, Apple Street was dissolved. CareShare Cincinnati dissolved as well.

Successes

- Our Harvest continues to survive and be a significant resource for food access and training the next generation of farmers through being a practicum site for Cincinnati State Sustainable Agricultural Management program.
- Sustainergy is growing substantially and poised for expansion across the state and beyond.
- We have improved co-op support processes with the release of the *Worker-Owner Workbook* in English and Spanish.
- Union Co-op Symposiums foster union co-op development, innovation, partnerships and deeper connection to the Mondragon USW union co-op model
- We have become part of Seed Commons Financial Cooperative as a local peer loan fund and have lent more than $350K to members in our cooperative network.
- Co-op U, the 12 to 14-week co-op bootcamp launched in 2018, became increasingly effective at launching cooperatives. During 2019 Queen City Commons, a composting co-op was launched.

During 2020, in partnership with Our Harvest we launched a permutation of Co-op U for refugees, which led to the formation of Bhutanese Bari. In 2021 we launched Power In Numbers which focuses on Black led co-ops, which led to the launch of three co-ops.

- Business Legacy Fund launched and multiple businesses are transitioning to worker-ownership at this time.

- We are proud of our role in starting OWN – Ohio Worker-Ownership Network and 1worker1vote.

- Grateful for our deep connections with the labor movement. Co-op Cincy benefits from deep ties and strategic support with the Central Labor Council, the United Steelworkers USW, the Greater Cincinnati Building Trades (all of whom have had their leadership on our board), the United Food and Commercial Workers who helped kickstart Our Harvest and who represent the workers there, the representation of the USW at multiple co-ops in our network, the strategic and financial support of other players including the Cincinnati Federation of Teachers and the IUE-CWA, LIUNA, the IBEW.

Setbacks

- Our Harvest almost died. We share the lessons from Our Harvest over and over again!

- Apple Street dissolved. This felt fairly crushing after so many hundreds of volunteers poured so much time, talent, and heart into this effort for years. Losing our financing, then a cascade of events that resulted in losing our location, and not being able to find a new location was heartbreaking. Positive aspects include that the business model we developed served as a blueprint for Gem City Market in Dayton which opened in May of 2021. Also our experience led to the formation of a buyers' club in Cincinnati and dissemination of our lessons learned to other grocery co-ops in formation

- The dissolution of CareShare was super sad but what we learned informed the startup CareShare Santa Ana and our work on childcare co-ops like Shine Nurture Center in Cincinnati that is successfully transitioning to a worker-co-op.

- Our impact remains so insignificant compared to our desires! Ugh!

Over the last decade, we have learned a number of lessons related to launching, nurturing and sustaining worker-owned cooperatives. They include the following:

Key Lessons

1. Bringing a cooperative to life is tough, just like starting any business:
   - It requires grit and fortitude and people willing to stick through the peaks and the valleys. It usually works better when we have a team who has grit and passion and own their idea *versus* trying to incubate a co-op and recruit others to lead it.
   - The team is crucial. Armin Isasti and Isabel Uribe of Mondragon's cooperative incubators, Saiolan, taught us the following equation: (Business Idea + Business Model + Resources) x Team = Business Opportunity. The team is the multiplier. We could not agree more!

- o Technical assistance makes a substantial difference in helping start-ups be successful. Supporting people in identifying and clarifying their assumptions and the risks they pose to the co-op business is crucial.
- o Allies and mentors are incredibly helpful!

2. Education:
- o Even though co-ops have pressing business concerns, It is essential to take the time to build cooperative culture. Consistent and intentional building of cooperative culture, solidarity, conflict resolution, communication skills, and financial and business literacy skills is critical to success.
- o In order to deepen cooperative education, one of the foundations of Mondragon's success, we have created resources such as the *Worker-Owner Workbook*, and the Mondragon Principle cards with artist Caroline Woolard. We have created the Co-op U course, the Business Legacy Transition program, and have partnered with Xavier University to create a Cooperative Management Certificate.

3. Access to financial capital:
- o Finding the right capital is critical. Debt can be deadly and almost killed Our Harvest Co-op.
- o In order to create pathways to capital for our co-ops (such as Laboral Kutxa, Mondragon's bank), participating in the Seed Commons Financial Cooperative where our co-ops can tap into our own proprietary funds as well as the national funds has been a game changer.

4. On plans and setbacks:
- o It is helpful to create a plan and be prepared, but it is also important to get going, building the road as you go and not getting bogged down in structure or letting the "perfect be the enemy of the good."
- o Setbacks lead to lessons that can be shared, benefitting upcoming projects around the country.

5. We need each other!
- o A union cooperative coming to life anywhere helps all our efforts!
- o Collaboration is paramount. We cannot build an economy that works for all on our own.
- o It is indispensable to have a long-term vision. Rather than build a single cooperative, nurture an interconnected family of cooperatives to achieve transformational change.

We have a lot of room to grow! Today Mondragon employs over 80,000 people in the Basque region, which has a population of about 2.1 million. Cincinnati, Ohio, has a metro population of 2.5 million, similar to the Basque region. So, our goal is to have as many worker-owners in 50 more years.

What will Effectively Increase the Impact of the Union Cooperative Model?

At Co-op Cincy, we are experimenting with the following four strategies.

1. Co-op U.
2. Business Legacy Fund.

3. Support of existing co-ops.

4. Statewide/national networks and policy.

Co-op U

Co-op U is a 12 to 14-week co-op development course offered to teams interested in launching a worker-owned business. Co-op U is designed to be a hands-on, interactive class that helps participants identify assumptions and refine their business idea and consistently strengthen their cooperative business so it can become the highest value version of their idea, the most feasible version with the greatest impact. In addition to our general Co-op U, we have launched some specialized versions of Co-op U. In 2020, through a Health and Human Services grant we launched a Co-op U in tandem with Our Harvest Co-op that focuses on refugees with agricultural backgrounds and delivering the content in a way that transcends language. In 2021 we launched Power in Numbers, a Co-op U designed especially for Black-led co-ops.

Through the Co-op U courses, we help teams increase awareness and understanding of the worker-owned model in the Cincinnati area and beyond, and help the teams build cooperative culture and participatory management practices into their business. We enjoy connecting teams to mentors and are grateful that through our participation in the Seed Commons financial cooperative, we are able to help fund new worker-owned businesses through our Co-op Cincy Loan Fund. Our loan dollars allow us to fund earlier stage and riskier loans.

We use two key tools to guide participants on their way to launching their own cooperative: the Co-op Canvas and Co-op Map.

Co-op Canvas: The Co-op Canvas is a dynamic tool utilized to generate a business model. We created the Co-op Canvas tool by combining aspects of three different frameworks, each of which is designed to help participants express their business ideas in a specific and productive manner. The frameworks are called the Business Model Canvas (developed by Alex Osterwalder), the LEAN Canvas (developed by Ash Maurya) and the CoStarters Canvas (created by the CoStarters organization). While these three frameworks overlap, they have unique elements. Based on our experience, we selected the elements most useful for guiding co-op teams.

After participants have a first draft of their Co-op Canvas plan, they explore different elements of their plan each week. They experiment, test their assumptions, and identify ways to reduce risk. The Co-op Canvas document is dynamic and evolves with the understanding of the participants.

Co-op Map: The Co-op Map is a tool that helps participants shape their own co-op experience. One of the wonderful things about forming a co-op is that participants choose what works best for them, as well as what is most important to them and their team.

Using the Co-op Map tool, participants determine their co-op's mission and values, the roles of their team, work on the bylaws to structure how money and information flow through their co-op, how membership is determined, how decisions are made. They begin to identify opportunities and practices for participatory management as well as ongoing co-op education and culture building. A *Co-op U Manual* and *Co-op U Facilitator Guide* are currently being written. We are also adding a "train the trainer" course for communities who would like to be trained on how to run their own Co-op Us in their cities. We plan to regularly update these texts as a result of our experiences and developments elsewhere.

For our Co-op U, we plan the following:

- Make the *Co-op U Manual* and *Facilitator Guide* available in multiple languages and update them regularly.

- Take multiple groups through Co-op Us, help them co-facilitate their own Co-op Us, then support them as they lead their own Co-op Us.

- Provide four or five Co-op Us a year locally and nationally, with two or three co-ops participating in each Co-op U, for a total of eight to 15 new co-ops completing the training annually. To facilitate the process, some of these Co-op Us would be virtual.

- Dedicate grant funding for each Co-op U cohort to be able to reward participation and have a grant that the teams can compete to receive.

- Fund earlier-stage and riskier loans through local dollars, including money raised from local faith communities.

- Train a group of mentors to support each co-op team.

- Offer technical assistance for Co-op U trainers.

- We would like to see Co-op 101 courses offered at local high schools and business schools throughout Cincinnati, with a curriculum that could be taken to schools around the country.

- We want courses and train the trainer courses for co-op development (Co-op U), co-op culture building (WOW), and Cooperative Business Management Certificate through our partnership with the Xavier Leadership Center) for hundreds of organizations and individuals around the country.

- Further developing our legal and education toolkits and providing ongoing technical assistance to groups that are working to start union worker co-ops and networks in their communities.

Business Legacy Fund

Around two-thirds of all businesses are owned by baby boomers, many of whom are in the process of retiring or are nearing retirement. As a result of this wave of retirements, 80% of these businesses are at risk of shutting down.

Through our Business Legacy Fund, we are working to transition businesses whose owners are retiring. We have partnered with the Seed Commons, a national network of non-extractive loan funds, to create a multimillion-dollar continuity fund for small and mid-sized businesses. With technical assistance from Co-op Cincy, the fund will help business owners design a viable succession plan to transition their businesses into worker ownership.

We are also raising money locally to help finance transitions. We are hoping to transition at least four to six businesses a year locally in the near future. With these transitions, we will enable people who have historically been excluded from business ownership to become cooperative business owners and build long-term wealth.

As part of the Business Legacy Fund, we have taken a proactive strategic approach in which we collaborate with business brokers, investment bankers and business services professionals. This approach also allows us to target larger companies in specific sectors that have a strong potential to create family sustaining jobs over the long term and build on the industries and successful companies we already have within our network. Some of the sectors we have identified for our region include manufacturing, industrial services, the care economy, and the green energy sector.

Co-op Cincy will continue to have an open call for local businesses to apply to our transition cohort program in the fall of each year. During our first cohort in 2021 we had 12 companies apply, six of which were accepted with a total of 110 workers who took tangible steps to explore transitioning their company to worker ownership over a six month period.

Finally, we have cultivated a robust Board of Advisors and bench of professional managers with industry expertise to help Co-op Cincy evaluate potential deals and help these businesses succeed as they transition worker ownership. Sometimes this support will include sustained coaching on a certain aspect of business to help the co-op up its game and other times this may go as far as stepping in as an interim manager when needed.

For our Business Legacy Fund, we plan the following:

- Steward the transition of at least four to six companies to worker ownership to start each year and growing capacity and staff over time to transitioning four to six companies per transition staff per year.

- Support business transitions and acquisitions through our statewide network, with at least four co-op developers outside Cincinnati supporting two to four transitions per year, for a total of eight to 16 new co-ops annually. For these efforts we expect the average company size to be five to 20 workers, meaning that 40 to 320 workers would be impacted annually.

- To ensure the sustainability of the Business Legacy Fund program, Co-op Cincy is developing a fee for service and loan fee structure that will make the program self-sustaining as we increase the number of deals and businesses we can support each year.

- Through case studies, earned media, annual reports and key partners (business services economic development professionals), Co-op Cincy plans to dramatically increase the awareness of worker ownership as a mainstream option for small business owner succession, substantially increasing the number of co-ops and worker-owned companies in our region.

Support for existing cooperatives

We provide support for culture building, financial literacy, business analysis, and business planning for existing worker-owned cooperatives. We also help worker-owned cooperatives solve challenges, access financing, and grow. In addition, we offer Cooperative Management Training Certification to all managers.

We currently support 12 co-ops directly. We meet regularly, often weekly, with our cooperative teams to support them, and we also meet with cooperative management regularly. In addition, as needed, our loan fund offers financial support to our network of cooperatives. We utilize the *Worker-Owner Workbook* we first published in early 2018 and then updated and translated to Spanish in 2021 to support this work. It helps co-op workers understand co-ops, labor, the union-co-op model, through practical hands-on solidarity-building exercises, communication and conflict resolution resources, financial and business literacy exercises, and more.

To sustain worker-owned businesses, we help build and strengthen a culture of solidarity within cooperatives. In our discussions with cooperatives, we analyze reflections on solidarity from famous leaders such as Cesar Chavez and Audre Lorde. We emphasize that solidarity means recognizing that whatever happens to one directly affects all indirectly. We use activities to help worker-owners understand their own needs, leadership styles, and hopes. We also help them develop skills in understanding the needs, desires, and styles of others. Finally, we introduce communication, conflict management techniques, and offer exercises that explore power and privilege. Conflict is an unavoidable part of life and can be a gift, a signal that something needs to change for things to work better for all. Conflict management techniques ensure innovative ideas and different approaches get heard. We use nonviolent communication methods to productively navigate internal and external conflict.

To support the success of worker-owned cooperatives, we also build skills related to financial literacy, business analysis, and business planning. We teach workers:

- What business success looks like.
- How to track, measure, and improve performance.
- How to collaborate as a team.

Open book management is one of the key components of our training. The basis of this approach is to give employees key financial information about their company so they can make informed decisions (Stack & Burlingham, 2014). Such information not only helps employees do their jobs effectively, it also helps them understand how the company is faring as a whole. This management style is new and is described in detail in Jack Stack's and Bo Burlingham's book *The Great Game of Business*, which uses the familiar concept of a game. Turning open book management into a game is a fun, dynamic way for employees to better understand their business. The game includes exercises and discussion of key business concepts like a balance sheet, profit and loss statement, and cash flow statement.

We expect to strengthen existing co-op support through the following:

- By continuing to improve and update the *Worker-Owner Workbook*.
- Provide group training and mentorship beyond Co-op Cincy staff that supports co-op workers sharing their skills with one another.
- Facilitate connections and deeper co-op of co-op connection between our network of cooperatives.
- Keep improving business planning and organizational supports.
- Work to help each co-op keep growing itself and its workers so the co-op functions like a living organism where everyone is sensing and responding to opportunities and crises, and where people's potentials are fully unleashed.
- Offer Cooperative Management Certificate Training for all business managers through our partnership with Xavier Leadership Center.
- Further refine our efforts to accelerate the growth of cooperatives.
- Start businesses within existing co-ops and then help them incorporate on their own.
- Accelerate existing co-ops such as franchising Sustainergy across Ohio and around the country with the goal of creating over 1,000 new jobs in energy efficiency and solar in the next 10 years. We also have plans to accelerate co-ops in residential cleaning, apparel, and personal health services.
- Develop and standardize performance metrics for social, financial, and human capital for our co-op network that could be used as a template for impact by other co-op networks to become a standard for excellence.

Statewide/national networks & policy

Co-op Cincy deeply believes our liberation, our destiny, is bound up with all others, and believes we will all do better when we all do better and union co-ops proliferate across the US and world. So, we felt like a national network group was needed to help learn together and share experiments and templates that work. The union co-op agreement template creators agreed and 1worker1vote was officially launched at the first Union Co-op Symposium held in Cincinnati in 2013. 1worker1vote is building a national network of hybrid, shared ownership, regional and municipal ecosystems starting with unionized worker-owned cooperative businesses to overcome structural inequalities of opportunity, mobility, and income. Building pathways out of poverty leading to pathways toward prosperity. With the CUNY Law Foundation serving as a fiscal sponsor, 1worker1vote.org collaborates with a growing network of like-minded local and national organizations to help businesses transition to union cooperatives and launch new union cooperatives. 1worker1vote.org provides technical assistance, education, mentoring, templates, and access to supporting finance.

Since the first symposium sponsored by Co-op Cincy, 1worker1vote and Co-op Cincy have cosponsored the Union Co-op Symposium, a national gathering of people interested in practical tools on how to start and run union cooperatives, every two years. The goal is to help support the growth, development, and experimentation of the union co-op movement. New union co-op networks form after each one.

We continue to collaborate with organizations across the country to increase awareness of the worker-owned cooperative model, develop and nurture worker-owned cooperatives, reduce barriers to worker-owned cooperatives and implement policies that support such cooperatives. We have earned significant media coverage in Greater Cincinnati highlighting our work and the advantages of the worker-owned cooperative model. Through the assistance of the Greater Cincinnati Foundation, we have attempted to get worker ownership policies passed in Cincinnati. In addition, we have created new cooperative development materials and webinars to reduce barriers to launching and sustaining cooperatives.

With the support of a grant from Google, we recently formed the Ohio Worker Ownership Network with 10 organizations from across Ohio, including Kent State University's Ohio Employee Ownership Center, Ohio State University's CFAES Center for Cooperatives, Co-op Dayton, Co-op Nelsonville, and Co-op Columbus. Our goal is to help launch 15 to 25 worker-owned cooperatives a year across the state as the network matures.

We hope to achieve the following:

- Continue to build OWN (the Ohio Worker-Ownership Network), a network of co-op developers and support organizations across Ohio, with nodes in Toledo, Columbus, Cleveland, Kent, Dayton, Nelsonville, Athens, Cincinnati, and elsewhere. We anticipate that each co-op developer will support one or two Co-op Us annually and train three to five co-ops each year. With at least five co-op developers, we could support 15 to 25 new co-ops in Ohio annually, building an increasingly resilient network.

- Ensure our statewide and national networks of co-op developers have access to funding through Seed Commons, a national network of locally-rooted, non-extractive loan funds.

- Replicate our statewide network across the country, starting with geographically close states and then expanding from there.

- Do joint advocacy to promote pro-co-op policy at a statewide and local level to include co-op development technical assistance as a part of the standard business mentorship repertoire through government funded networks such as SBDC. Potentially, pushing through legislation like the *Cooperative Economy Act*.

- Collaborate with national networks of co-op developers to fundraise, support trainers, offer Co-op Us, and share knowledge and resources such as the *Worker-Owner Workbook*. We expect to work with Common Future (a national network striving to shift capital, uplift local leaders, and strengthen the development of equitable economies) and 1worker1vote (a national network supporting unionized worker-owned cooperative businesses).

References

Democracy at Work Institute (*n.d.*). The Benefits of Worker Cooperatives. Accessed November 28, 2017.
    https://institute.coop/benefits-worker-cooperatives.
Stack, J. & Burlingham, B. (2014). *The Great Game of Business: The Only Sensible Way to Run a Company*. London: Profile Books.

CHAPTER 20

Citizen Share Brooklyn: Addressing Structural Racial & Economic Inequality *via* Economic Democracy

Roger Green

A thoughtful observation of American history instructs that the Covid pandemic created the most consequential social and economic emergencies faced by the African American community and the larger American citizenry since the 19th century.

Furthermore, that same observation will demonstrate that the worst effects of the pandemic were exacerbated by the unhealed wounds of American history: the socioeconomic disparities and injustices that weaken individual and community health in African American and other marginalized communities. In our Brooklyn community, a key example of this is the breakdown during the pandemic of medical-supply chains that procured medical furniture — examination tables, hospital beds, etc. — from an abusive prison-labor scheme that enriched plutocrats but failed to serve communities in need.

Citizen Share Brooklyn is our response, and is self-organizing and co-creating cooperative and community-based alternatives to this ongoing disaster.

Looking Back: Roots of the Problem

It was in the 19th century that the seeds of today's struggles and solutions were planted — specifically the Civil War, the epochal conflict that eventually moved a renewed US federal government to enact a monumental law to abolish that "peculiar institution," chattel slavery.

A growing body of knowledge concerned with this time period reveals how the 13th Amendment, a Constitutional amendment passed at the end of the Civil War and a covenant that abolished chattel slavery, did not immediately resolve the long-burning economic and social contradictions found within the US republic. In spite of this law, US sovereignty continued to sustain some forms of *de facto* oppression, even after beleaguered and stateless Africans were defined as a newly freed people.

The federal government's initial failure to define an authentic and more expansive American democratic project was inclined to engulf the newly freed and stateless African population (my ancestors) in a precarious social and political domain, wherein the values of citizenship, due process, and participatory democracy were absent. This intentional negligence of the democratic aspirations of formerly enslaved people did produce human suffering, including afflictions that eroded public health imperatives, while accelerating premature deaths and contributing to long-term illnesses.

Contemporary medical anthropologists and social historians have confirmed that the 4 million stateless Africans who transitioned from bondage were set adrift into a fragile and hostile "post-Confederacy" — a realm ruled by men who continued to give voice and power to the interest of former slave owners. It did not take long for the newly freed Africans to conclude that they had entered an adverse environment where they could barely subsist. This precarious post-bondage domain continued to be shaped by public policies originating from the advocates of racial supremacy and oligarchy. Poor sanitary conditions, poverty, disease, and starvation were byproducts of an oppressive political and economic tradition that obstructed people of African heritage from achieving health and wealth, and integrating into an authentic democratic order.

Consequently, this failure to empower stateless Africans with equal citizenship, and to integrate this substantial population into a larger society, upended the vision quest for "a more perfect union." It also placed the stateless Africans, and other vulnerable US citizens, within the vortex of the greatest public health crisis of the 19th century. The toxic stressors of penury, environmental degradation, and a traumatic transition from slavery to stateless inequality all produced an epidemic of premature deaths, long term illnesses, cholera, smallpox, dysentery, and starvation, contributing to a quarter of all African American deaths from 1862 to 1870.

Here's a question: Does this seem familiar? I posit that contemporary African Americans and the larger US citizenry should explore and contemplate all the serious questions and solutions that may emanate from this history. We must place this political, social, and economic inquiry in context with the challenges and opportunities that the Covid pandemic presents to our present-day democratic republic.

We may ask:

- Why did the Covid pandemic cause disproportionate deaths and long-term illnesses among African Americans and other marginalized US constituencies (Indigenous, Latinx, East Asian immigrants, poor whites, etc.) given the nation's inherent wealth?

- Can the tax dollars invested within our health-care system's infrastructure, which in part originates from poor, working poor, and working-class citizens, be orchestrated *via* a distributive justice policy, to build community health and shared wealth for those in need?

- What does it mean for an avowed democratic-republic wherein concentrated and disproportionate wealth originating from industrial and technological advances, including the health care sector, fails to address the structural, racial, and economic inequality that's causing poor health outcomes?

What to do in response to the COVID crisis? What to do for an increasingly fragile democratic republic?

Confronting the Crisis: New Visions

In 2015, prior to the Covid pandemic, I committed to joining a community-labor coalition. It was a civic effort that united the social and political capital of the 1199 SEIU United Healthcare Workers East, and the New York State Nurses Association, with progressive actors associated with health justice, community empowerment, participatory scholarship, and economic justice causes.

This coalition is determined to co-create a "community of inquiry and action" that will explore the aforementioned questions concerning definitions of democracy and shared wealth, while advocating for public policies and programs that are intended to define a new vision for community health. Our coalition is particularly concerned with those Central and East Brooklyn communities wherein 61,000 union members and their neighbors are challenged by structural racial and economic inequality — a phenomenon that we believe contributes to poor health outcomes.

A central focus of our community-labor coalition is a desired transformation of the health-care sector's supply chain and its group purchasing network, a system that enacts contracts estimated at $30 billion per year. This supply chain and its group purchasing network is responsible for purchasing food, furniture, laundry, pharmaceuticals, and a host of other essential products, as well as services that are needed for the daily operation of our public health care sector.

This supply chain and group-purchasing network is allegedly organized to benefit patients and health care workers in Brooklyn and citywide. However, the Covid crisis made incandescently clear that this system prioritizes the profits of corporations that exploit unprotected labor located in the Global South and the "right to work for less" regions of the United States.

During the height of the COVID surge, health care workers were morally obligated to serve patients from the marginalized neighborhoods of Central and East Brooklyn. However, a distant, inequitable, inefficient, and probably unethical supply chain failed to provide masks, gowns, incubators, pharmaceuticals, and other essential products to the beleaguered frontline workers and their patients. While health care workers did their duty to save their neighbors' lives, a dysfunctional supply chain most likely contributed to the premature deaths and long-term illnesses that disproportionately harmed frontline workers and their patients from areas where traditional economic and social stressors contribute to poor health. The sight of medical practitioners and frontline health care workers donning plastic garbage bags as substitutes for undelivered medical gowns from the Global South demonstrated how a distant and dysfunctional health-care supply chain benefits wealthy one-percenters at the expense of "we the people."

These contradictions of this failed emergency response that, in part, originated from disaster and extractive capitalism, inspired our community-labor coalition to embrace a progressive imagination, and organize to build health and wealth in Central and East Brooklyn

With this came more questions about the health-care supply chain and group purchasing system, including:

- What if contracts were redirected to a localized supply chain, and a reformed group purchasing network that enhanced shared wealth for citizens in economically distressed communities?

- Can these reforms include principles that expand democratic values (e.g., economic democracy) within our political economy?

- Can a reformed system incubate and accelerate localized worker-owned enterprises that ensure a living wage, and shared wealth for citizens in economically distressed communities?

- Will these reforms ensure that workers have a share of profits and/or equity, and incorporate equity benchmarks that build generational wealth for families? These are the essential means that a person must have in order to mediate or reverse the toxic triggers of poverty, chronic unemployment, wage stagnation, and depressed wealth.

Our progressive imagination ultimately seeks to transform the health-care supply chains and purchasing systems so as to mediate the structural, racial, and economic inequality that cause poor health outcomes in marginalized communities. We envision a better way to rebuild (*i.e.*, Build Back Better) our neighborhoods, and our larger democratic republic, by enacting public and private policies to co-create an economic laboratory that is founded on the moral imperatives: *Democratize labor! Democratize capital! Democratize wealth!*

Our community-labor coalition is determined to co-create a civic and economic infrastructure that would actively address how we might expand democratic values and practice in a reformed health-care supply chain, and its group purchasing network. Our proposed economic-development strategy and complementary business model intends to ensure a local and equitable administration of opportunities needed to sustain innovative enterprises owned by people of color. We believe this effort must include unionized, worker-owned enterprises that are designed to enhance shared wealth to address the polarizing effect of wage stagnation. As envisioned, these innovative enterprises will participate in a community-hiring program to recruit, train, and employ people residing in neighborhoods challenged by structural racial and economic inequality.

Building & Organizing New Structures

In 2017 our community-labor coalition collaborated with MIT CoLab and 1worker1vote at the City University of New York School of Law to incorporate a cohort of Central Brooklyn, East Brooklyn, and South Bronx elected officials into a "community of inquiry" process. This process concerned the feasibility of creating an economic-democracy policy and practice strategy for New York City.

Our coalition organized a 10-day study group and tour of the Mondragon Cooperative Corporation in Spain, the world's largest worker-owned cooperative system, with 75,000 worker-owners in a solidarity economy. At the conclusion of this rigorous deliberative process, the Central Brooklyn elected officials resolved that it would be feasible for them to enact public policies that supported the co-creation of a furniture manufacturing company, in collaboration with the Mondragon-affiliated Inea Furniture and Design Cooperative. This new enterprise would produce hospital beds, bedside tables, operating tables, office furniture, etc., for local health-care providers, using an economic model that promotes equity, economic security, and social solidarity within an authentic market economy.

This proposed enterprise could also serve as an ethical alternative to CorCraft, a state monopoly designed to exploit convict labor within the New York State Department of Corrections by paying incarcerated people a maximum of $0.60 per hour to manufacture furniture that New York state plutocrats sell to private companies and government agencies (*e.g.*, hospitals, colleges, public schools, etc.). A recent procurement analysis authored by one of our community-labor coalition's ventures (Brooklyn Community Collaborative) found that the State University of New York Downstate Medical School purchases all of its furniture from CorCraft.

Our community-labor coalition discerns a direct historical link between a contemporary prison-industrial complex, as reflected in the CorCraft convict labor model, and the egregious examples of penal servitude (e.g., chain gangs) that were enacted by former slaveholders and oligarchs in 1865 after stateless Africans transitioned from chattel slavery into a fragile and marginal definition of freedom.

We acknowledge that contemporary forms of convict labor are the living legacy and institutional heir to an oppressive system of <u>Black Codes</u> that were designed to exploit and profit from human bondage after the enactment of the 13th Amendment, and prior to the ratification of the 14th Amendment. With this in mind, we are determined to break the chains connecting an earlier form of human oppression with a contemporary typology of economic repression, a phenomenon that we believe contributes to a tradition of mass incarceration, poor health, and depressed wealth within marginalized communities of color.

We have concluded that our proposed strategic partnership with Mondragon's Inea Furniture Design and Manufacturing Cooperative will serve as a national model to reverse the worst forms of racial and extractive capitalism. It will also plant the seeds for an economic democracy ecosystem (Health Enterprise HUBs) that will include the unionized worker cooperative developed in a strategic partnership with the Mondragon Cooperative Corporation. To achieve this worthy goal and more, our community-labor coalition has determined to co-create a comprehensive civic and economic infrastructure, by launching the following economic-democracy ventures:

Citizen Share Brooklyn EDC

Citizen Share Brooklyn is a 501c3 economic development corporation dedicated to reversing the structural racial and economic inequality that contributes to poor health outcomes impacting residents of Central and East Brooklyn.

This economic development corporation prioritizes collaborating with the Brooklyn health care sector to build three Health Enterprise HUBs. As proposed, these economic democracy domains will serve as progressive engines for a transformed New York City health-care supply chain and group-purchasing network. The Health Enterprise HUBs will incubate and accelerate <u>unionized worker cooperatives</u> that are positioned to produce and distribute essential products and services for Brooklyn's hospitals, medical schools, nursing homes, homecare services, and ambulatory care centers.

Citizen Share Brooklyn proposes that engaged worker-owners associated with these economic-democracy enterprises will originate from marginalized neighborhoods. Furthermore, we anticipate that these worker-owners will secure a "citizen's share" as aggregated from a living wage and shared wealth.

Our Citizen Share Brooklyn priorities will co-create a transformed supply chain that includes a Local Strategic Stockpile (LSS) containing PPEs and other essential products needed for the health care sector. In addition, we foresee a manufacturing base designed to support the fabrication of essential health care products, including medical furniture. As envisioned, the health hubs will implement localized "surge preparedness" efforts in anticipation of a future health crisis or natural disaster.

Brooklyn Community Collaborative

BCC is a nonprofit, nongovernmental, 501(c)3 (tax-exempt) organization that coordinates a place- and sector-based mission to address the structural racial and economic inequality found in some Brooklyn neighborhoods that we propose to define as "health and wealth domains."

BCC concludes that individual and community health outcomes are shaped by the social determinants of health (SDOH), factors that include the distribution of money, power, and resources at the local, state, and national level. Given this knowledge, BCC proposes that the inherent value of the borough's health-care sector must be reformed by a program for distributive justice to build health and wealth in distressed neighborhoods.

BCC works to achieve this moral imperative by collaborating with Brooklyn's health care institutions (hospitals, medical centers, nursing homes, home-care services, ambulatory care, etc.), to co-create policies and programs informed by an inclusive community needs-assessment. As practiced the BCC effort incorporates a "participatory action research" method that gives voice to neighborhood residents who aspire to promote public policy interventions that enhance health and wealth. Since 2016 BCC has sponsored five participatory action research efforts. In 2017 this PAR process moved the New York governor and state legislature to enact VITAL Brooklyn (ny.gov/programs/vital-brooklyn-initiative), a $1.5 billion comprehensive place- and sector-based health care initiative.

Accordingly, BCC is committed to developing a local human development index (LHDI) to define and assess public, private, and philanthropic investments that can improve health outcomes within distressed neighborhoods. As proposed, initiatives organized around public health, workforce development, and progressive procurement covenants will be assessed for their impact in mediating or reversing structural racial and economic inequality, and in achieving equitable health and wealth outcomes over time.

In 2019 BCC launched the Strong Communities Fund, a philanthropic program informed by the principles inherent in community self-determination and self-governance. In response to the Covid pandemic, a cohort of community leaders and organizers collaborated to appropriate $3 million to sustain fragile, community-based NGOs that were challenged and under-resourced because of the Covid crisis.

Citizen Share Global LLC

Citizen Share Global is a for-profit enterprise that will facilitate strategic partnerships with local, national, and international corporations (such as Mondragon LKS) who seek to reach markets *via* a network of economic democracy entities associated with the Citizen Share Brooklyn ecosystem. This limited liability corporation (LLC) will prioritize harvesting investment capital (*i.e.*, special purpose vehicle) and aligning this effort to enhance research and development for the benefit of the emerging economic-development corporations that are affiliated with the Citizen Share Global ecosystem. Citizen Share Global will operate as a "triple bottom line" corporation that works for three goals: community health, the environment, and shared wealth. As envisioned this business model will mediate structural racial and economic inequality.

Society for Effective Economic Democracy

SEED is a new 501(c)4 social enterprise dedicated to uniting community empowerment actors and union members within a progressive civic infrastructure that values critical citizenship and participatory democracy.

SEED activists propose to organize and mobilize the social capital inherent within a community-labor coalition on behalf of policies, legislation, judicial precedents, and programs intended to advance economic democracy within communities traditionally challenged by structural, racial, and economic inequality. A central component of the SEED civic engagement strategy is an effort to include and empower a new generation of activists originating from unions, community empowerment organizations, prison moratorium efforts, student associations, interfaith traditions, and economic justice movements, among others.

SEED organizers propose to launch an initial grassroots campaign in support of a distributive justice policy that is intended to redirect state-taxpayer dollars from the CorCraft convict-labor scheme. SEED envisions that the active and critical citizenship originating from this campaign will move public officials to invest in an alternative enterprise — a unionized worker cooperative with an economic-democracy mission. SEED anticipates that successful implantation of this campaign will create an organizing model and progressive civic infrastructure that attracts broad public support for additional economic-democracy initiatives impacting health care and other sectors in the economy.

Economic Democracy: Evolution & Progress

As our community-labor coalition continues its journey to build community health *via* an economic-democracy mission that promotes shared wealth, we are committed to looking back so that we may move forward. We are compelled to acknowledge that the Covid pandemic emerged out of a historic trajectory in which structural, racial, and economic inequality was never effectively mediated, and instead helped germinate and exacerbate the co-morbidities that cause premature deaths, massive illnesses, and extensive economic disruptions among African Americans, and other marginalized communities.

We posit that the unattended maladies originating from structural racial and economic inequalities of the 19th century did seed a host of socio-economic afflictions found in the 21st century. However, we believe our effort to co-create a healthy and competitive alternative to the CorCraft convict-labor scheme will demonstrate how contemporary socio-economic contradictions must be mediated by expanded democratic practice within the economic sphere — and the health-care sector, specifically.

Furthermore, the moral and socioeconomic philosophy of economic democracy should guide this important mission. It proposes to shift decision-making power from the exclusive control of corporate managers, and corporate shareholders, to a larger group of public stakeholders, including workers (*i.e.*, union members), community empowerment actors, consumers, suppliers, and the broader public as represented by an active and critical citizenry. The core values motivating economic democracy are equity, shared decision-making, self-governance and democratic accountability. Advocates for economic democracy (myself included) believe that these values, when operating within the political economy, will prioritize the instrumental, yet subordinate, nature of capital to human labor, and to a community's common good.

When the moral philosophy of economic democracy is applied to the New York City health-care system it should encourage a public confirmation that poor, working poor, and working class taxpayers residing in distressed neighborhoods are, in fact, citizen stakeholders who consistently invest their tax dollars to support our public hospitals and nonprofit, voluntary health-care institutions (medical schools, nursing homes, homecare services, ambulatory care centers). These public and nonprofit institutions secure 89% to 100% of their operating capital from citizen taxpayers. Therefore, citizen taxpayers residing in distressed areas should be empowered through democratic accountability, and not restrained by an anti-democratic standard that gives life to a modern version of "taxation without representation" that mostly benefits plutocrats and bureaucrats.

To the point, advocates for economic democracy propose that a new regulatory system of equity, shared decision-making, self-governance, and democratic accountability should be enacted to ensure that when any public, private, or nonprofit enterprise secures essential investments (grants, subsidies, operating capital, tax breaks, etc.) from citizens, the profit imperative within these organizations should include a "citizen share."

To this end, Citizen Share Brooklyn prioritizes a distributive-justice initiative that redirects taxpayer dollars away from the CorCraft convict-labor scheme, to instead assist in the co-creation of a local furniture manufacturer that will serve the needs of New York City hospitals, university medical centers, nursing homes, homecare providers and ambulatory care centers, while providing a living wage, and shared profits, for residents of communities impacted by structural racial and economic inequality.

Thus, the Covid crisis is a teachable moment. Our community-labor coalition continues to imagine that progress can be achieved when unobstructed memory merges with prescient and progressive vision. As we see it, the United States was founded as an aspirational experiment. This extraordinary pilot created a procedural republic that in its inception constrained participatory democracy within a system of political governance. This system was initially designed to benefit, in part, a select cohort of white male property owners, who defined other humans as their exploited chattel and as denigrated commodities. This limited vision constrained democratic values and practice within the economic sphere of such a new nation.

However, the United States evolved — somewhat. Two steps forward and one step back. Political sovereignty is inexplicably linked to a continuous evolutionary force. Democracy is more than a structured political institution where a command bureaucracy manages a stagnant government on behalf of a passive citizenry. Our community-labor coalition proposes that *democracy is a moral philosophy* with inherent ethical ideals that advance equity, shared decision-making, self-governance, and democratic accountability. This, we argue, should empower a regenerative process for a nation that avows to become "a more perfect union," even in our economic system.

The African American legacy in the US serves as a penultimate example of this dynamic phenomena. Within the heart and soul of this human experience you will find an ongoing history of awakenings, reckonings, and protracted struggles concerning the meaning of freedom and its essential relationship to democratic values and practice. This history includes a public trial concerning the status of enslaved humans that inspired an epic political and armed civil battle that gave birth to a second republic, through which an expanded definition of democracy was eventually enacted. This ethical campaign inspired an active and critical citizenry to embrace the fact that their procedural republic should transition to become an evolving democratic republic. This new democratic republic would eventually repeal the notion that US citizenship authorizes an atavistic political and legal standard that enthrones blood and soil, or racial superiority — and instead works for liberty for all, equal protection for all, and a right to vote for more.

Today, we conclude that the lessons learned from the African American's struggle to define authentic freedom, and to expand the definition of democratic practice, must be applied to address the contradictions challenging all US citizens, as we enter the 21st century.

We propose that the contemporary aggregation of concentrated, and disproportionate, wealth for a few has again distorted and devolved the US democratic republic's egalitarian values. The social contract needed to provide domestic peace and prosperity for the whole is fragile, as exemplified by a violent attempt to overturn a peaceful transfer of presidential power on January 6, 2022; by a growing number of mass killings directed at communities of color; and by a culture of violence that increasingly threatens a diverse group of disinvested post-industrial communities.

Our community-labor coalition believes that this existential threat is inextricably linked to growing human alienation and anomie originating, in part, from economic polarization. We observe a common "misery index" that connects the white youth who murder the innocent based on a racist "replacement conspiracy" theory, and the youth residing in disadvantaged communities of color who kill the innocent because despair has replaced prosperity.

To this and future generations we must bequeath a commitment to expand the values inherent in our democracy into our economic system. Democratize labor! Democratize capital! Democratize wealth!

We must learn from and be inspired by the past as we organize and mobilize to ensure that all citizens in our human family, regardless of race, sex, ethnicity, religion, gender, or national origin, can protect and sustain their inherent dignity by building health and shared wealth within an evolving democratic republic.

In Central and East Brooklyn, we are building a civic and economic infrastructure that will serve as a laboratory to democratize our economy, starting with our health-care sector. We launched this journey at a time when the Covid pandemic caused over 1 million deaths, and an economic crisis that gave rise to additional unemployment and wealth inequality within traditionally marginalized communities.

We acknowledge that our drive occurs when citizens in the 21st century are bearing witness to intensified social and political polarization. This phenomenon causes tears in the social fabric of our nation. These divisions within our citizenry have contributed to the realization that a nation judged "pandemic impregnable" is in fact most vulnerable. Our community-labor coalition believes that a lack of national memory concerning the meaning and scope of democratic values and practice has obscured the fact that a citizen can have no "life, liberty, and the pursuit of happiness" without a virtuous and rigorous commitment to common good and commonwealth.

With these all important values in heart and in hand, we seek to unite "We the People" of Central and East Brooklyn around a 21st century movement to address structural racial and economic inequality by building health and wealth with an economic-democracy imperative.

CHAPTER 21

Building Mondragon in Detroit: An Interesting Context for an Interesting Translation

Terry Lewis

Introduction

This chapter proceeds from a particular vantage point. It is important, before beginning the analysis that is the heart of what is attempted, to set out just what that vantage point consists in.

First, the project is embedded in a particular physical, political, cultural, and demographic location at a particular point in time.

Second, while the project shares values and aspirations with what I think of as the "worker ownership movement." It is not just about ideas. It is also about the pragmatics of bringing into being a development organization and a constellation of enterprises and connecting structures through fits and starts, triumphs and disappointments, to a point that is (hopefully) a good beginning.

Consequently, I will proceed by laying out the context and then lay out the ideas, pragmatics, and quandaries of our attempt to build Mondragon in Detroit.

Context

There are two elements to the context: the City of Detroit and the Center for Community Based Enterprise, the 501(c)(3) community development enterprise of which I am the CFO and whose goals and actions this chapter will chronicle.

Detroit

If you want to understand the deep history of the City of Detroit, I commend to you *The Origins of the Urban Crisis: Race and Inequality in Postwar Detroit*, by Thomas J. Sugrue (Princeton University Press, 1916, 2005). Sugrue's master work lays down an almost comprehensive exposition of the major forces and events that moved Detroit into its decline at the end of the 20th century. Sugrue, however, neglected the role of housing mortgage and property tax defaults and the failure of both HUD and the City to take possession of the defaulting properties in order to resell them. This began the spiral of vacant and deteriorating properties in a city that had once led the nation in homeownership. Otherwise, his analysis is (in my opinion) spot on.

In describing the city as context for this chapter, I will leave the deep history to Sugrue and sketch a description of the city as it has existed and evolved over the past few years.

On July 18, 2013, the City of Detroit, Michigan, filed for Chapter 9 bankruptcy. By debt, estimated at $18bn to $20bn, it was the largest municipal bankruptcy filing in US history. An interesting historical depiction of the bankruptcy can be found in *Detroit Resurrected: To Bankruptcy and Back*, Nathan Bomey (W.W. Norton & Co., 2016).

Detroit came out of the bankruptcy in a far better position than might have been expected, though still troubled in many aspects. The city itself had stabilized its finances and positioned itself for renewal, but the people of the city were and remain at risk.

The city's population has continued the fall that began in 1950. Then, it was the fifth largest city in the nation, with a population of 1,849,568. On July 1, 2019, its population was estimated to be 670,031, little more than one-third of what it had been at its height. Its homeownership rate had fallen from over 80% to 47.2%. Its BIPOC (largely black) population was 89.5%. Its median income from 2015 to 2019 was $30,894. Its poverty rate in 2019 was 35% (US Census Bureau, *n.d.*). And all of that was before the pandemic.

Any understanding of Detroit's current condition must also consider the epidemic of empty lots and decaying structures that mark its 139 square miles. Once, that space was filled to bursting with single-family homes, vibrant schools and other public spaces, factories, stores, and warehouses. Depending upon what you classify as "vacant," between 26 and 40 of those 139 square miles (that is, between 19% and 29%) is empty land without any structures (Gallagher, 2019). Add in the many vacant and deteriorating homes, factories, retail spaces, and public structures (especially schools), and you have a clear picture of urban physical decay.

All is not lost. This time, the city has created the Detroit Land Bank to take title to properties foreclosed by failure to pay property taxes and to resell them to others who, it is hoped, will restore them to use. One can argue, righteously, about the gross over-assessment of properties – especially single-family homes in the poorest neighborhoods – that has led to many of those foreclosures and the large number of families who have lost their homes as a result. Anyone working on the ground to revitalize neglected neighborhoods will be sure to point out how difficult it is for ordinary Detroiters to register with the Land Bank to purchase properties and the prevalence of outside investors employing a "buy and hold" strategy to flip properties without improving them. It could be worse.

In some areas of the city, real revitalization is taking place. Within the downtown core, extending up Woodward (the iconic semi-diagonal street that divides east from west in Detroit), revitalization is explosive. Both commercial space and retail income soared before the pandemic. Housing prices in proximate areas continue to soar. Quicken Loans' CEO Dan Gilbert is a key driver of the commercial revitalization, though his record of foreclosures during the financial crisis is deplored by many.

For community developers like myself, the strategy of the Duggan mayoralty and of Dan Gilbert, which imagines that revitalization requires the in-migration of outside people and entrepreneurship, both misses the point and leaves most neighborhoods without much support. Recently, there has been administration support for a traditional urban planning approach that imagines a "community" process that does not foresee or encompass much indigenous entrepreneurship.

There are, however, a variety of economic development entities working within the city that support entrepreneurship, though that support remains focused largely on an individual entrepreneur model.

That is the Detroit context.

The Center for Community Based Enterprise (C2BE)

C2BE was founded in 2007 by Deb Groban Olson, a Detroit attorney with a deep understanding of worker-ownership, ESOPs, and the Detroit auto industry. Deb understood that, as the auto industry left Detroit, as it sought vertical integration of parts of its supply chain, and as it jettisoned elements of its manufacturing structures to reduce costs, jobs would be lost that could be retained through worker-buyouts.

C2BE was unable to scale rapidly enough to capture those opportunities, but Deb's vision began to gather momentum as United Way of Southeastern Michigan (UWSEM) and the W.K. Kellogg Foundation (WKKF) were moved to invest in C2BE. Those first investments were small and focused on education – creating awareness of worker-ownership as a powerful tool in the entrepreneurial/economic development toolbox.

C2BE gathered steam, both through increased investment by grantors and an accretion of dedicated staffers. At first, staffers were unpaid board members. Gradually, funds became available to pay Deb, and then others, all of whom were part-time independent contractors.

People became engaged in C2BE's work as Detroit deteriorated, drawn in by the idea of worker-ownership and its ability to create wealth, empowerment, and good-paying jobs in Detroit's disadvantaged communities. I was one of them, joining the C2BE board in 2015 and then exiting the board and becoming part of its staff a few years later.

C2BE worked as quickly as possible to expand its remit from education and community awareness to providing actual technical assistance: creating and supporting a widening variety of worker-owned enterprises.

Today, C2BE is working to expand both its grants and its fee-based funding. We are focused on both start-ups and the conversion of existing businesses and we have expanded our vision a bit beyond worker-ownership to encompass a few producer supply and marketing cooperatives and some innovative community collaboratives.

The Ideas

Mondragon, as an icon of worker-ownership, was part of the C2BE *zeitgeist* from the beginning.

As C2BE built its capacity, its notion of creating Mondragon in Detroit began to solidify into the notion of "a cooperating network" of enterprises. Also central to our zeitgeist from the beginning was the notion of the "community based enterprise".

Mission statement

C2BE's mission is to build a sustainable, more equitable and inclusive living-wage local economy, by developing a cooperating network of worker-owned businesses and increasing the number of worker owners.

The Community based enterprise

Central to C2BE's ideations and its efforts is the notion of a community based enterprise (CBE):

- A sustainable business or business idea;
- Involving the collaboration of multiple individuals through worker-ownership or some other form of collective ownership;
- Rooted in the community;
- Paying living wages; and
- Willing to participate in a network of similar enterprises.

The critical elements are the notions of:

- *Sustainability*: the ability of the organization to fund its operations on an ongoing basis;
- *Enterprise*: that is, engagement in some form of business operation;
- *Collaboration*: an enterprise founded on the equality and the contributions of many, rather than the notion of the single hero entrepreneur;
- *Community* and of *rootedness*: for an enterprise to fall within C2BE's self-defined wheelhouse, it must have some community connection that is non-trivial and unlikely to change;
- A *living wage*: as fundamental to the idea of good and empowering work; and
- The *network*: that is, Mondragon in Detroit.

The Practicum

Building sustainability

When C2BE began, the roots of its founder in law and legal structuring dominated its notion of, first, building awareness of worker-ownership and, later, building actual CBEs. As C2BE gathered resources and built capacity, grants (rather than fee income) became its primary source of funding. Its focus shifted from the conversion of existing businesses to the development of start-up enterprises, and then back toward conversions, though both paths to the creation of CBEs were always part of its strategy.

These shifts demanded an evolution in C2BE's technical assistance provision from legal and governance structuring to full business development. The creation of CBEs (especially from the ground up) requires rigor in both organizational structuring and business development. C2BE began exploring partnerships with other economic development organizations, in order to avoid both the resource drain of reinventing the technical assistance wheel and the need to supply all of the elements (particularly financing) necessary to develop or expand CBEs. At the same time, we added internal capacity to oversee business development and guide what partnering we could develop.

Lessons learned

We also learned a lot of lessons and are continuing to do so. We have made great strides in defining and operationalizing a crisp development process: timelines; process stages and decision points; how to engage with existing employees and what is expected of them and offered to them at each stage; and subscription services to support project partners after the CBE is established.

We have spent considerable focus on scaling. This focus is in part about the sustainability of our own organization and in part a response to what we see as the coming "Silver Tsunami" – the wave of enterprise and employment loss that could easily result from the retirement of business owners from the Baby Boom generation. Baby Boomers own fully half of the privately held businesses in Michigan. Between 66% and 88% of small businesses don't have a succession plan. Nowadays, fewer than 30% of businesses are transferred to family members. And fewer than 20% of businesses put up for sale actually sell. Many of those will sell to competitors who will utilize their suppliers, cannibalize their customer base, and use neither the original location nor the existing employees to carry out the buyer's businesses.

C2BE needs to scale up to meet this crisis. And C2BE is using this crisis to scale up by marketing its services to governmental entities. Our recent contract with the Lansing Area Economic Partnership (LEAP) will allow us to expand our scale and is, hopefully, the precursor to several more.

Because we understood early on that our enterprise development involved something other than top-down creation, we learned to engage in active partnering with the collection of individuals who would be its beneficiaries. We call and treat them as Project Partners.

In looking at the grant funding needs of some of our start-ups and community-owned collectives, we realized that C2BE's 501(c)(3) status could be used to receive that funding on their behalf. One of the first lessons we learned in that regard was not to act as a "fiscal sponsor" (taking responsibility for carrying out the funded project), but only as a "fiscal agent" (receiving funds on behalf of and disbursing those funds to the beneficiary Project Partner). Those Project Partners are signatories to the grant agreements and hold the ultimate responsibility for carrying out their funded projects.

Defining enterprise

This task is largely a matter of organizational choice. It comes from the necessity to narrow one's desired field of operations to an accomplishable set of desired outcomes. We call the parameters in which C2BE has chosen to work its "wheelhouse." The way in which C2BE has defined its wheelhouse has shifted over time, especially in its choice of target enterprises.

Should the wheelhouse be limited only to self-sustaining businesses and business ideas? What about the emerging art community, its relevance to place-making and overall development in Detroit, and the very low costs of making and displaying art in this inexpensive city?

What about the notion of community enterprises? Could we envision an enterprise owned by a community, developed to build community structures, institutions, and processes, and financed, at least in part, by community resources as a sustainable idea?

In the end, at least to date, C2BE has not excluded either the artist collaborative or the community enterprise from its wheelhouse. But each must demonstrate some measure of sustainability. As described above, we have also allowed ourselves to cast a widened net by offering services as a fiscal agent to non-tax exempt enterprises partially or wholly funded by grants.

The need for a driver

One of the qualifications that C2BE set in place early in defining its wheelhouse was the necessity of a driver – at least one individual within the enterprise group that is committed to seeing the process of creation through from start to finish.

In conversions of existing businesses to worker-ownership, the driver is initially the selling business owner. But there needs to be sufficient commitment within the employee base to partner with C2BE and drive the conversion through to completion.

In the case of a start-up, a driver is even more essential. Start-ups are hard. There are a lot of good business ideas out there. Ask any business incubator. But the dropout rate is enormous! Yes, building a worker-owned or other collaborative/cooperative business is greatly advantaged by the multiple sources of energy, experience, and financial contribution the enterprise can draw on. Still, the start-up enterprise requires a huge quotient of commitment to drive it.

In both cases – conversion or start-up – that commitment will be necessary to carry on the enterprise once its creation in partnership with C2BE is accomplished, even though it will by that time be spread out among multiple individuals rather than a single driver.

Centering on collaboration

This has never been a question. The idea of collaborative ownership – whether through worker cooperatives, other forms of worker-ownership, other forms of cooperative or community ownership, or some other legal structure – has been at the heart of the C2BE idea. It is a central part of the broad notion of a Community Based Enterprise and of the version of Mondragon in Detroit that C2BE is seeking to build.

Community

The notion of community and community rootedness is far more nuanced and more elective. In thinking about these ideas in relationship to C2BE, there are two aspects that spring immediately to mind. Which community or communities? And what defining elements of a community are necessary to root an enterprise within it?

C2BE has grounded its choice of communities on social justice. Within the City of Detroit, the fight for social justice is ongoing. It is racialized, is based in and focused on neglected neighborhoods, and is deeply and daily confronted with the alternative possibilities of grass-roots empowerment *versus* displacement.

In describing the City as context, the racial composition of the population and the economic hardship experienced by much of that population become clear. Choosing to serve BIPOC and economically disadvantaged communities within the City gives C2BE huge scope within which to focus its work. In reaching out beyond Detroit, C2BE has chosen to maintain that focus, looking for conversion targets located within or near similar communities, with majority BIPOC or economically disadvantaged employees or both.

In thinking about the idea of community rootedness, I am drawn to the work of Josefina Figueira-McDonough in *Community Analysis and Praxis: Toward a Grounded Civil Society* (2001). Figueira-McDonough (2001) employs the idea of "high communalism," which she defines as "…a locality whose residents and local organizations are linked by dense networks of exchange and who identify strongly with the community" (page xv). Before I read her book, I thought of what Figueira-McDonough is describing as an effective community. I will use my own term rather than hers, but we are speaking of pretty much the same thing.

In requiring that CBEs be rooted in the community, C2BE is essentially requiring that the enterprise be part of an effective community or do its part in building one. In looking at our social justice focus, we are attempting to tip the balance toward the support and engagement an effective community can bring to our partner CBEs.

One last element that I want to address here is conflict within Detroit and among elements seeking various forms of community development between grass-roots empowerment and displacement. Inherent in the idea of an effective community is one in which grass-roots groups coalesce to attract resources and promote social justice for community members. Those members are not transient.

The notions of community membership and of advocacy on their behalf are antithetical to notions of displacement, even in a city like Detroit with much vacant land. Even if no occupied structures are torn down or sold to and rehabilitated by incomers, the process of gentrification increases property values, thereby increasing occupancy costs, thereby forcing out economically disadvantaged community members. C2BE's own Bryce Detroit says all this far more effectively than I can through the "Hood Closed to Gentrifiers" campaign he initiated in his own community and that is spreading across the city and the nation (Click On Detroit Local 4 WDIV, 2020).

The idea of good & empowering work:

We call it "Just Work". Payment of a living wage just scratches the surface of the Just Work idea. It is a social justice concept. Worker-ownership gives form to it, necessarily including both worker voice in the structuring and valuing of work and a worker financial stake in the success of the enterprise. It is a concept that contrasts significantly with many notions of "job creation." It can even be distinguished from the "good union jobs" that created Detroit's post-WWII middle class. I owe a great debt to my C2BE colleague, Michael J. Friedman, for raising my understanding of this issue. Before becoming a lawyer, retiring, and becoming a part of C2BE, Michael had been deeply involved with unions for many years. He is a founding member of Teamsters for a Democratic Union (TDU).

A little Detroit union history is in order here.

Detroit is the home of the United Auto Workers (UAW), of which Walter Reuther was the President from 1946 until his death in 1970. In 1950, Reuther negotiated a collective bargaining agreement with General Motors that was dubbed by *Fortune* magazine as "The Treaty of Detroit" and was forever after known as such.

Previous UAW agreements were negotiated annually. They had increased wages and even added a cost of living formula (COLA) to labor contracts. In 1949, Reuther began a campaign to add company-funded pensions and medical care to his contracts with the auto companies.

After successfully negotiating a company-funded pension plan with Ford, the union carried out a strike against Chrysler, which capitulated by offering its workers an equivalent company-funded pension after 104 days of work stoppage.

In moving on to General Motors, the UAW sought not only the same pension rights but also company-funded medical care. Seeking to avoid the losses that Chrysler had experienced due to the strike, General Motors agreed to both. In return, General Motors sought and received a five-year term for its contract, avoiding the cost of negotiating a new contract each year. In addition, the company regained control over its shop floor, its long-term scheduling of production, model changes, and tool and plant investment (Barnard, 1983).

At the outset of the union movement, workers wanted more than bread and butter. They wanted and often fought for control over their day to day working conditions: shop safety; output quotas/line speed; emergency medical treatment; and the ability of individual workers to stop the line when shop conditions warranted it.

These were not the things that unions focused their collective bargaining on after the Treaty of Detroit.

In a more generalized societal fight, state and federal laws imposed Worker's Compensation, Wage and Hour Laws, Unemployment Compensation, and Occupational Safety and Health Codes from outside the employer/employee relationship.

The nature and shaping of work otherwise became a prerogative of the employer.

Then there is the concept of "Workforce Development." Again, I owe a great debt to one of my C2BE colleagues – this time our current Executive Director, Karen Tyler-Ruiz – for developing my understanding of this issue. Karen has been involved in Workforce Development in many roles and across many organizations for chunks of her career. My conversations with her have allowed me to understand many of the contrasts in operations and objectives between what she used to reckon with and what C2BE does.

Workforce Development is not Job Training. Job Training teaches people specific skills to enable them to perform particular jobs. It is like apprenticeship programs, but without the wages and on-the-job training. The Workforce Development concept arose to socialize people around becoming part of the workforce.

Let me take a moment to discuss socialization, the learning process all individuals go through that allows them to fit in to and understand the expectations of the cultures and communities in which they live. Socialization takes those cultures and communities as a given. But there is a ragged edge any time a culture or a community bumps up against the insights and demands of social justice.

Like the admonition to women to "lean in" to misogyny/patriarchy, to minority group members to be "exemplary," or like the tension between grassroots empowerment and gentrification/displacement, Workforce Development begins with the notion that, to enter the workforce, one must conform to its every element – including its underlying injustices.

Paired with the transformation of Aid to Families with Dependent Children (AFDC) to the time-limited Temporary Assistance for Needy Families (TANF) and the complete exclusion of able-bodied men from any income support, Workforce Development supported the need for people (especially mothers) to take any job and to be "hirable" at the most basic level.

Over time, Workforce Development began to broaden its desired outcomes to include "good jobs" – meaning well-paying (or, at least, better-paying) jobs and even jobs with benefits. Advocates within or adjacent to Workforce Development programs began to build in financial coaching and financial tracking, the former to aid clients in shepherding their earnings well enough to save some part of them, and the latter to compile data to prove to policymakers that a poorly paying job left clients and their families worse off than with the income support they had been receiving.

As unions became less and less powerful and their operations more and more constrained by right to work laws and the denial of mandatory dues, their bread-and-butter focus dovetailed with that of Workforce Development programs.

Then there is the phenomenon of "outsourcing," which divides the worker completely from the owner/manager of the enterprise by hiring a third-party company to supply labor. The enterprise is enabled by out-sourcing to completely structure all of the elements of work without either input from or consent by the workers who (as employees of the third-party company) are unable to bargain with them. Outsourcing also often reduces overall compensation to workers, as their new third-party employers siphon off cash while trying not to unduly raise costs to the enterprise itself.

In a similar fashion, the gig economy has stripped workers of power to structure their work. Gigs are take it or leave it. The platform owner sets the price and pays only for the actual performance of the service while the worker carries all of the costs of service-provision along with the drag of down time while on call.

Contrast all of this with the notion of Just Work that C2BE is building.

Of course, C2BE is not alone in what it seeks. As this book so richly demonstrates, we march in parallel with the entire worker-ownership sector. And we are encouraged by a growing institutional awareness and support of worker-ownership (witness the Aspen Institute, among other "think tanks"). We are also delighted by current efforts among, for example, teachers and nurses, to bargain about conditions of work as they effect desired outcomes.

Nevertheless, there remains a significant sector of workers who fall within the parameters of a new acronym, ALICE: Asset Limited, Income Constrained, Employed.

Quandaries

Who do you collaborate with?

I am not talking here about the choice of enterprises to incubate or transition. I am talking about the choice of economic development partners. Some choices are easy – there can be a joyous intersection of values and goals among C2BE's potential partners. Even in those cases, finding specific joint projects and allocating authorities and responsibilities require time, effort, and energy and may not lead to either commitment or outcome.

Other cases are more difficult, especially when the context in which C2BE is working requires collaboration with institutions or actors whose values and goals share little with ours. Working within the City of Detroit often involves competition with rapacious property investors and owners. Institutions created by the City to deal with vacant and abandoned properties and increase economic activity may involve shared goals but include little in the way of shared strategies. Extractive models abound and working in such contexts means walking a tightrope between economic outcome and social justice.

What does it mean to build a network In Detroit?

Mondragon is a powerful model well worth emulating, but there are a few significant differences between the Mondragon context and the context within which C2BE works in Detroit.

To my mind, a key difference is in the predominant force operating on (and devastating) the existing communities of the post-WWII Basque region as opposed to present-day Detroit. Both contexts lack(ed) opportunities for improving quality of life for existing (especially young) community members. In Mondragón, a cultural setting in which generation after generation had remained in place, the draw of distant opportunities was leading the younger generation of Basques to leave the region. In the United States, it is rare for multiple generations to remain together within a single community. Here, economically viable individuals and families move often to advance within their professions. Staying in place is an undesired outcome. Often, people stay in place because they are trapped, and some who are trapped and others who are committed to the work are willing to focus their energy on making their communities better places to live.

But in Detroit, neighborhood gentrification is bringing in a flood of wealthier, whiter, outsiders (some from the Metro Detroit area, many from more expensive locales across the US). This influx of outsiders is causing wholesale displacement of existing residents. While Detroit's gentrification can in some sense be considered "neighborhood improvement," it is not creating opportunities for or improving the quality of life of existing residents. Nor is it strengthening existing communities.

C2BE is committed to strengthening existing communities. C2BE works to create community-based enterprises (CBEs) that provide living-wage jobs for community residents and, above and beyond that, a profound financial stake for the worker-owners of those CBEs, plus significant voice in their strategic direction. Displacement undercuts all of that.

So what does it mean to build a network in this quite different context? How can networks create strength and resiliency among enterprises located within communities whose residents will tend to be in flux?

In building a network, there needs to be a nexus, a central idea or institution that is persistent, understood, and valued, and that can tie the network together over time.

In Mondragón, the powerful nexus was the church. And the network that was created was among cooperatives that were structurally very similar. That is not what is happening in Detroit. While the Black church has power as a network and a social institution in Detroit, we see the opportunities it represents as the potential for one or more partnerships within a scattering of neighborhoods. An important instance is our partnership with Church of the Messiah, located in Detroit's Island View neighborhood.

When we first envisioned our network, we imagined that the CBEs within it would have clusters or nodes centered on similar industries: sewing/fabrics; art; childcare; home care; retail; food; and so on. We quickly understood that we would not be able to develop such nodes quickly.

Later, we began to understand the power of effective communities both in fostering rootedness and serving as nexuses. There are several effective communities that can work with us in this way, and we work hard to build relationships with and within them. But many of our existing or prospective Project Partners are not or will not be centered in an effective community.

Along the way, we began to consider the power of providing shared services (accounting; purchasing; marketing; bargaining; and perhaps others) to hold a network together. This will be complex, but it shows promise if we can obtain the resources to build it out.

While all of our Project Partners agree to become part of our network, and many are delighted by the prospect of "paying it forward," we've learned that it takes more. A network has to be dense enough to function day to day. As our CBEs push to sustain themselves and to grow, they often lack resources to also sustain and grow a network. We are beginning to suspect that we will want to use all of the potential nexuses I have described to create a network that can sustain itself and add value to the enterprises of which it is comprised.

Conclusion

So there you have it, a portrait of the origins and development of a worker-ownership development organization seeking to create its own vision of Mondragon in Detroit. I have given you the story so far: the context, the ideas, the organization, the practicum and the quandaries. I will leave you *in medias res*. The rest of the story has yet to be written.

References

Barnard, J. (1983). *Walter Reuther and the Rise of the Auto Workers*. Little, Brown.

Click On Detroit, Local 4, WDIV. (2020, November 18). "Hood Closed to Gentrifiers" street sign gains popularity in Detroit neighborhood [Video]. *YouTube*. https://www.youtube.com/watch?v=8A-eiQn42ag

Figueira-McDonough, J. (2001). *Community Analysis and Praxis: Toward a Grounded Civil Society*. Brunner-Routledge.

Gallagher, J. (2019, October 26). Social media is arguing about how much vacant land is in Detroit—And the number matters. *Detroit Free Press*. https://www.freep.com/story/money/business/john-gallagher/2019/10/26/detroit-vacant-land/4056467002/.

US Census Bureau (*n.d.*). *US Census Bureau QuickFacts: Detroit city, Michigan; Michigan*. Retrieved January 16, 2023, from https://www.census.gov/quickfacts/fact/table/detroitcitymichigan,MI/PST045222.

CHAPTER 22

Reflection: What Then Shall We Do?

The Past, Present & Future of Worker Ownership

Chris Cooper

Rising "workplace-workforce" ownership is one of those very rare issues that enjoys broad, across-the-aisle support from a wide majority of Americans, including warring political parties and their polarizing politicians.

What explains the disconnect between public support and private practice, and what shall we do to bridge the difference?

Over the last 30 years or so, employee ownership has proven itself as a concept. Employee-owned companies on average are more productive, more profitable, more resilient — and better for businesses, their communities, and our economy. Employee owners tend to make more money, have better benefits, generate more personal wealth, have more opportunities for continuing education and advancement, and are usually happier on the job.

Employee and worker ownership is broadly supported by Americans — surveys show that we prefer doing business, and spending our money, at employee-owned businesses. It is broadly supported by the political class — employee ownership is one of the few (maybe the only) policies with broad bipartisan support. The sector as a share of workers has consistently grown over the last 20 years, through good times and bad. The broadening number of models that are built on the concept of greater ownership of productive assets is heartening, and a sign the sector is maturing — perhaps even settling into the collective consciousness and becoming commonplace.

At a systemic level, there are also some very positive things happening. For the first time in my 20+ years of working in the field there seems to be real momentum, on multiple fronts, to bring worker and employee ownership out of the corner and into the center of the room. Political momentum for laws, policy, and programs friendly to employee ownership is growing. The number of public and private organizations providing development resources has never been bigger: 20 states now have employee-ownership centers, and more will be coming online soon. In Ohio, 10 development organizations (including the Ohio Employee Ownership Center) have created a network of mutual support and collaboration dedicated to growing employee ownership in every region and every community in the state

And yet, the level of employee ownership is still relatively low as a percentage of both the number of firms and only marginally better in the number of employee owners. Why is this? Some of the answers to this question are matters of policy and politics, and some are internal to the practice community. In matters of policy, there are a number of very practical ideas that can help grow the worker and employee-owned sector; on the surface these shouldn't be too difficult to accomplish:

- We need tax parity — incentives that promote worker and employee ownership should be available for all models, not just a few.

- We need to update the rules to allow majority-minority worker-owned businesses to take advantage of government contracting preference programs for publicly funded projects.

- We need to create capital support programs that take into account the unique structures of worker-owned businesses, and don't place extra burdens on them.

- We need to continue our work in "mainstreaming" the idea of worker and employee ownership, both in the business community but also in the community of business advisors and support services. Employee ownership need not be the option of last resort for business owners who are planning for their succession.

Of course, this is not a complete list, and there have been a number of other great ideas and examples put forth in the volume you are now reading.

We also face challenges of our own creation that require broad-minded solutions. As a community, there is still too much time spent in disagreements about which form, or which aspects, of employee ownership represents the ideal. All forms of worker and employee ownership have many strengths, and each has their weaknesses too. Some models do a better job at addressing the wealth gap; others provide workers with more control over their work life and how their job is structured — both are valuable.

Spending precious time and resources on debating whether this or that model represents "real" employee ownership means we've likely relegated ourselves to the margins for the foreseeable future. There is no reason to fortify the silos that already keep us running in place. Too often, a specific employee-ownership model is defined in relation to another employee ownership model, rather than to other conventional or investor-owned businesses.

It's long past time to release worker and employee ownership from the political, policy, and ideological purgatory in which it's often been stuck. We all have our preferences, and our principles, and they will determine where we spend our time and focus our efforts — as they should. But as worker and employee ownership expands and gains traction as an idea, our ability to control or define what it is (and what it isn't) will shrink. Some will expropriate the term, and the idea, to create examples that we may find less than ideal. Still others may create hybrid models that will have great value. We will have to decide if these are collective weaknesses worth lamenting or strengths worth celebrating. Employee and worker ownership should not just be bipartisan, it should be non-partisan, and living within the broadest and biggest of big tents.

Even so, will doing all these things *substantially* increase the number of worker and employee-owned businesses, and the number of worker and employee owners? How do we cease being a niche of a niche? Is there something more (or larger in scope) being asked of us?

Two weeks prior to sitting down to write this piece, I was in a room with about 40 non-managerial employee-owners from ESOP companies — everyday working people — engaged in a training program on the basics of business finance. True to its name, it was indeed about how the basics determine outcomes. As we were beginning a discussion of assets, debt, and liabilities, I threw out a question to the group: what are some examples of assets in your company? A quick answer came back from several attendees — the employees!

It is not the first time this has occurred, and I did have a return answer at the ready based on Generally Accepted Accounting Principles. Most of us know that the standard accounting methods don't consider workers as an asset, but only as an expense or liability. But it's an unsatisfactory answer — for them, and for me. This is not a new observation, nor an original complaint, and it would be a mistake to take this example too far or have it mean too much. But surely it says something that the "language of business" is incapable of describing, let alone measuring, the full financial value of a person's labor to an organization. Strikingly, there is a sort of internal logic to this approach when considered from a strictly accounting perspective. Unfortunately, the idea has completely embedded itself into the moral calculus of how we do, and talk about, business.

One of the forms of employee ownership that we work with a lot is an ESOP, or employee stock ownership plan. I won't get into too many technical details about ESOPs (you may already know many of them), except to say that one of more momentous annual events for ESOP participants is when the independent valuation of the company is complete, and employees learn what the value of the company, and what their individual ESOP account is worth. So we talk about value in ESOP companies quite a bit.

Of course, the word "value" has multiple meanings, and we talk about values quite a bit too. In the context of employee ownership, this usually means that employees should be able to participate in the financial performance of their company, and the work they do; and they should have a voice and a say in how their company is run, and how their job is structured.

Thankfully, most, if not all, the employee-owned companies we work with share these values to one degree or another. In fact, many of them probably held to some version of these values prior to becoming employee-owned, and this was one of the factors in their eventual conversion to full employee ownership. Most of them do consider their employee owners their most important asset — and live those values during good times and bad — even if their accounting system doesn't allow them to measure it that way.

In the end, this must be our clarion call as we go forward. We must shine a spotlight on the *values* of worker and employee ownership. These are *fundamental and profoundly human values* — hard work, dignity of labor, a stake in the outcome, and fundamental fairness. These qualities seed profitability (and its positive ramifications) but also are a true value-added approach to how business is done. As the Mondragon example (upon which this book is based) shows, profitable enterprises based on our shared values provide workers — and all of us — the freedom to align principles with practice.

CHAPTER 23

Structuring Worker Ownership in America: Coming Clean & Going Long

Michael Peck

Since the 1970s, America has counterbalanced high *per capita* GDP with rising unequal income distribution, producing a "winners-take-all" economy of stagnant wages, declining mobility, increased economic-class divisions, and racial tensions at levels not experienced since the Great Depression. America is increasingly politically polarized, economically unequal and socially on edge — recalling the turbulence of the 1960s, and anticipating the outlines of ongoing civil disruption, with the January 6, 2021 insurrection on Capitol Hill setting a new low in American history.

Our solution to this catastrophe is competitive worker-ownership structures, which are evolving, innovating, and need advocacy for better federal policy.

The modern co-op movement originated with the Rochdale Principles in the 1840s in Manchester, England — as did industrial unionization. Cooperatives and unions evolved separately — but today's extreme solidarity deficit imperatives compel renewing and scaling the union-coop bond.

An example is the current gap between new jobs and new worker and employee ownership: The *New York Times* notes that manufacturing jobs are returning to America with a vengeance (Tankersley, Rappeport & Swanson, 2022). Heather Cox Richardson observes that instead of outsourcing and automation doubling down during recessions, a rebirth of over 67,00 factory jobs (as of September 2022) combining "federal stimulus spending, along with a new skepticism of stretched supply lines, has created a rebound in American manufacturing … Yet those numbers would be higher if the labor market weren't so tight, a condition leading employers to offer higher wages and better benefits" (Richardson, 2022).

It's worth reflecting on the irony that worker and employee-ownership is not exploding or even keeping pace during today's pandemic-sparked Great Resignation. A singular organizing opportunity arises to converge burgeoning public enthusiasm and support for unions (despite no commensurate rise to date in traditional union membership), and make worker-ownership real in practice providing undergirding conversion and investment metrics. Insisting on uplifting societal values — starting with an equity share, democratic governance, and humane work conditions — make worker-ownership real in practice.

Meanwhile, private equity (Harris, 2022; Zerbe, 2022) has figured out that it's good business to enter the employee-ownership and social-capital marketplace, which creates competition for those who thought they had this space to themselves.

Yet market-driven private equity ups the domestic and global ownership-economy *ante*, however imperfect in its incipient stages, and brings more resources and power to the negotiating table. My bet is the return on taxpayer dollars will be marked by innovating ownership-structure mergers, acquisitions, and conversions. Once fully and equitably unleashed, more diverse investor advocates can drive the uplifting changes that human-social capital asset markets will develop to stabilize, and sustain both workplace and civic democracy. Competition between worker ownership structures will prove meaningful in light of incoming regulatory and financial instrument innovations in the natural-capital enterprise arena, bridging the intersection between climate and energy security.

Let us welcome competition, however imperfect, to wake up the entrenched, self-serving *status quo*. As a direct result of private equity's newfound interest in worker and employee ownership, US tax structure now commands a unique opportunity to throw open its doors, level its playing field for once and for all, and let all market-viable ownership structures compete to show who succeeds best, why, and how — but on equal footing.

Innovative pioneers pushing in these directions include Trillium's July 2022 *Investor Case for Supporting Worker-Organizing Rights* and its direct impact on the nationwide Workers United Starbucks union-organizing campaign starting in Buffalo, NY; the 2016 *Responsible Investor Handbook* co-written by long-time movement ally Tom Croft; and creative spin-offs such as New York City's The Drivers Coop, under the financial leadership of Steve Sleigh (1worker1vote advisory board, Amalgamated Bank board, and Heartland Capital Strategies board member).

Collective guarantee is one of the more interesting federal legislative innovations that didn't get passed last year, but perhaps will in 2023 if bipartisanship can prevail. Once enacted, the envisioned Cooperative Lending Pilot Program could level the playing field for cooperatives and other mutualist and social-economy organizations (US Federation of Worker Co-ops, 2021), uniting ownership for the many instead of ownership by the few in sectors such as home-based care, childcare, retail grocery, and manufacturing to create good-paying jobs and locally owned businesses. Collective guarantee (for the first time ever in federal lending) can integrate with progressive collective-bargaining models to form new structures repurposing and defining social-economy enterprises and ecosystems to pursue common-good missions and projects.

Tax parity is another innovation, as Chris Cooper mentions in **Chapter 22**, for all rising ownership models, to ensure that aspirational worker-owners and their hosting communities can freely choose the enterprise structure best-suited for their local culture. Much of what passes for proposed US "ownership economy" legislation discusses equal-funding deployment outcomes for cooperatives and ESOPs — but this promise turns out to be a bait and switch. Empirical facts show that the inherent, exclusive and built-in ESOP US Treasury line-item tax benefit ensures that the majority of owners wishing to convert will continue to choose ESOPs over worker cooperatives. Each year seems to bring more legislative advocacy focused on squeezing greater federal financial benefits for converting owners at the expense of doing the hard work of building workplace democracy and stakeholder equity.

Tax parity can seed a level playing field for deserving, competing enterprise structures committed to inclusivity, transparency, and equality for all aspiring worker and employee owners. It can help level the playing field for those workers wishing to unionize (*i.e.*, the union-coop hybrid model that 1worker1vote advances). Its repercussions will lead the way towards a fairer and more integrated workplace and civic culture as well as a more locally empowered and democratically enabled workforce.

Menke & Buxton (2010) note:

> The first ESOP (employee stock ownership plan) came into being in 1956. During the 50+ years since then, ESOPs have become a popular alternative to a sale or merger as a tool of business succession, and there are now more employee owners — approximately 10 million of them — than union members in the private sector.

If true, clearly this trend is not going in the best possible direction and is leaving unions and workers behind. As Chris Cooper affirms, achieving tax parity with ESOPs will ensure market-based, emerging hybrid structures get an equal chance to earn investing adherents and practitioners seeking to identify, sustain, and increase enlightened, purpose-driven, inclusive human and social capital assets within enterprises and their hosting ecosystems.

A third innovation, workers guarantee labs (WGLs), ensures that incoming worker-owners are equally represented and apprised of best possible and most relevant ownership structure options before committing their lives and livelihoods to any conversion contract. At present, departing owners of capital, their co-investors, and consultants (paid by outgoing owners at transaction closing) choose the future worker/employee-owned NewCo structure, which almost always reconfirms existing, privileged tax benefits protecting vested financial and related socio-political interests.

Working with Ra Criscitiello (Deputy Director of Research at SEIU-UHW – United Healthcare Workers West, a labor union of over 100,000 healthcare worker members across California, part of SEIU's 1.9 million members, and a 1worker1vote advisory board member), the 1worker1vote movement believes the organizing future belongs to "hybrid worker-ownership structures rooted in the solidarity economy and worker autonomy — best exemplified in unionized worker co-ops, charitable purpose trusts that embed worker-centered values, and other cooperative and social enterprises practicing workplace democracy and equal-equity share distribution for all stakeholders."

Hybrid worker ownership structures in a hybrid-culture nation will become the norm, not the exception, as this practice-community expands. Investors should be encouraged to cash out based on company performance over time. Anti-demutualization and outsourcing/offshoring provisions can ensure that local jobs and enterprises remain local (more important now in a pandemic-recovering economy than at any time since the 1929 Great Depression).

Robert Reich (2023) notes that US President Biden has "revived democratic capitalism — and changed the economic paradigm." Shareholder primacy driving "free market" (oxymoron of the first order) capitalism ceded ESOPs to American financial culture as a Wall Street formula that prioritizes tax breaks over true employee and worker ownership and democratic governance development. More often than not, when successful, these create material wealth for employees and workers but do not deepen enough and broaden into a more inclusive generational ownership culture that can uplift and outshine America's chronic civic, social compact disorder.

Post-Great Recession and Resignation, we can hope and organize so that democratic capitalism and the growing global social economy example enables US tax parity for equally valid market structures such as worker cooperatives, union-cooperatives and other hybrid worker ownership models. American culture "wins when it can show the world that it's an open and democratic country" (Gerstell, 2023).

It turns out that "woke capitalism" is simply more enlightened and inclusive capitalism empowering stakeholders — and it's good for business (Leach, 2023). Let us awake from our complacent slumber, unplug from the privilege matrix and affirm the right to equal local individual and collective enterprise structuring choice opportunities. Ensuing and scaling "solidarity dividends" will showcase aspiring worker owners and their communities, re-inspiring the world by social economy example starting with worker owners benefitting from an equity share and workplace democratic governance, a voice, a vote, and a frontline seat at the head human and social capital assets metrics table.

References

Croft, T. & Malhotra, A. (2016). *The Responsible Investor Handbook: Mobilizing Workers' Capital for a Sustainable World* Routledge.

Fifty by Fifty (2022, October 12). *Guidelines for Equitable Employee Ownership Transitions.* https://www.fiftybyfifty.org/2021/10/guidelines-for-equitable-employee-ownership-transitions/.

Gerstell, G.S. (2023, February 1). The problem with taking TikTok away from Americans. *New York Times.* https://www.nytimes.com/2023/02/01/opinion/tiktok-ban-china.html.

Harris, L. (2022, May 6). Private equity firms want to give workers ownership stake. The *American Prospect.* https://prospect.org/power/private-equity-firms-want-to-give-workers-ownership-stakes/.

https://ssir.org/articles/entry/the_case_for_investing_in_employee_ownership.

Leach, R. (2023, February 3). "Woke capitalism" is simply capitalism — and it's good for business. *The Hill.* https://thehill.com/opinion/congress-blog/3843428-woke-capitalism-is-simply-capitalism-and-its-good-for-business/.

Menke, J.D. & Buxton, D.C. (2010, January). *The Origin and History of the ESOP and Its Future Role as a Business Succession Tool.* The Menke Group. https://www.menke.com/esop-archives/the-origin-and-history-of-the-esop-and-its-future-role-as-a-business-succession-tool/.

Reich, R. (2023, February 6). Biden has revived democratic capitalism – and changed the economic paradigm. *The Guardian.* https://www.theguardian.com/commentisfree/2023/feb/06/joe-biden-democratic-capitalism-changed-economic-paradigm-reagan-free-market?CMP=share_btn_link.

Richardson, H.C. (2022, September 26). https://heathercoxrichardson.substack.com/p/september-26-2022.

Tankersley, J., Rappeport, A. & Swanson, A. (2022, Sept. 26). Factory jobs are booming like it's the 1970s. *New York Times.* https://www.nytimes.com/2022/09/26/business/factory-jobs-workers-rebound.html.

Trillium (2022, July). *The Investor Case for Supporting Worker Organizing Rights.* https://www.trilliuminvest.com/whitepapers/the-investor-case-for-supporting-worker-organizing-rights.

US Federation of Worker Co-ops (2021, September 10). *The House Small Business Committee passes $500 million Co-op Lending Pilot Program.* https://www.usworker.coop/blog/the-house-small-business-committee-passes-500-million-co-op-lending-pilot-program/.

Zerbe, D. (2022, May 5). Employee ownership: Wall Street agrees that ownership works. *Forbes.* https://www.forbes.com/sites/deanzerbe/2022/05/05/employee-ownership--wall-street-agrees-that-ownership-works/?sh=642269c1d242.

PART 5

Resource Challenges for New Worker Cooperative Development

In the United States, the infrastructure for developing new worker cooperatives has lagged behind large scale European Union social economy (reaching 10% of GNP in some countries) and solidarity taxonomy progress. Here, we have asked leaders in the US cooperative movement to reflect on what it will take to grow similar movement scale throughout the US.

CHAPTER 24

Our Humble Harvest: Gathering the Right Lessons from Mondragon to build a North American Cooperative Ecosystem

Esteban Kelly

I spent many years immersed in cooperative conferences and reading report-backs and dispatches from delegations to the Basque Country, most of which extolled the accomplishments of Father Arizmendiarrieta, and some of which indexed what was possible for worker cooperatives "at scale." This volume itself is evidence that there is so much that is remarkable about Mondragon for a North American audience, but the pieces I read usually left me haunted by the question: Are we learning the right lessons from Mondragon?

When considering the experience of the Mondragon Corporation and the cooperative ecosystem in that part of the Basque Country, work from researchers and practitioners, while admittedly important, usually focused on questions of how to *replicate* the model of scaled regional cooperativism. Only more recently have more critical voices emerged to shift that inquiry, encouraged interestingly enough by fresh delegations to Mondragon. In 2016, I had the privilege to join one such trip. Among my biggest takeaways was the consistency among Mondragon's representatives of the uniqueness of Mondragon's origins, and that replication would be a futile endeavor. Honor and adore it, but stop puzzling through how to set this up elsewhere.

Not to be dispirited, I want to rescue the entrepreneurial instinct from Americans, because I don't think the goal ever really was replication *per se*. That might have been lost in translation or otherwise a misinterpretation of the kind of questions cooperators from the US tend to pose while onsite at Mondragon's headquarters. The reason some Americans like myself are curious to visit Mondragon is less to be voyeuristic about the marvels of Mondragon's systems (although there's plenty of that among a typical international delegation to the Basque Country, to be sure). Rather, some of us are interested in harvesting the right lessons from both what Mondragon set up and how to inform the strategies for our own economic freedom within the constraints of our own countries. The first thing you learn upon a visit to Mondragon is about the constraints under which an innovative Catholic priest was able to nurture what would become the most accomplished cooperative ecosystem supporting worker-owners in the world. Too much attention goes to the outcome of that work, and not enough to the constraints and context in which Father Arizmendiarrieta had to labor.

Most of the communities I work with are walled in by stark constraints. But not enough has been made of the dire circumstances that birthed Mondragon's cooperatives. Instead of aspiring to *replicate* the Mondragon model, we should start by situating the origins of that cooperative ecosystem, and then considering our own conditions and what elements or strategies we require to catalyze a sophisticated solidarity economy among our own communities. That necessitates a contemplation of the particular needs of a country, the context of those needs, and how a cooperative system, or elements inspired by the Mondragon "model" might successfully meet them. This reorients our task to making more strategic use of Mondragon, not as "fetish" but as a case study for what is possible when we root into considering our own needs, context, and the cooperative models that will fit best.

I situate this chapter from my vantage point in the US cooperative ecosystem to place some of the vast and layered communities I'm embedded in and apply my experience of Mondragon in order to derive a more strategic orientation for how we can be similarly successful. Although I hold connections to many local, regional, and industry or socially connected communities, I am keeping my assessment to a fairly high, mostly national level for the sake of deriving conclusions that generally apply to the legal, financial, political, and labor conditions shared across the United States. I've been a founder or key leader during "turn around" periods of a dozen cooperative businesses and institutions. At the time of this writing I have the privileged responsibility of being the Executive Director for the US Federation of Worker Co-ops, a board member of the Democracy At Work Institute and CICOPA, and the Board Vice Chair of NCBA-CLUSA. Even here, I want to be clear about the limitations of my perspective. While my experience is substantial, I continue to learn heaps from our movement elders, and from cooperators who have practiced or researched worker-ownership for a decade or more before I was even born. I've only been immersed in cooperative workplaces since the late 1990s. In my early experiences of the ecosystem there really wasn't easy access to data, maps, information, or anything amounting to an assessment of worker cooperative infrastructure in the US. Because the early days of worker co-op institution-building were so lean in those days, my attempts to baseline the status of our ecosystem are fairly limited. Indeed, that's part of why I realized – even at a young age, just freshly graduated from college – the significance of the founding of a national organization for the worker co-op "sector," and had the presence of mind to attend that conference earlier this century when I had only been a worker-owner for five years.

Why do We Need Cooperation in the US?

Origin stories for worker co-ops in the US vary widely, but motivations for founding co-ops often come down to just a handful of considerations. First-time entrepreneurs find the shared risk of a co-op to be advantageous. It's difficult to wager that draining family savings for a new business will pay off. Sole proprietorships often bankrupt the founder if, as with a majority of traditional startups, the business does not survive the brutal formative years. Pooling risk and investment among a group of co-founders is less risky to any individual, and is also more accessible to source start-up capital beyond one person or family. Some founders open their own co-op because they've been locked out of the job market and need to employ themselves in order to gain income from their skillset. Similarly, contract and contingent workers see merit in collaborating as one cooperative, rather than navigating the vulnerabilities of individual freelance or gig work. Banding together also stabilizes revenue streams, mellowing out the feast-or-famine dynamic that plagues freelance workers. Cooperatives in that context also provide easier marketing and a platform for clients to find contractors. Meanwhile, contractors are able to insist on better prices, and therefore wages and ultimately benefits, by incorporating as a co-op rather than freelancing.

The benefits of collectivizing labor also inspire founders in particularly labor-intensive industries, such as childcare, food and farm work, home healthcare, and certain types of human (rather than machine) driven light manufacturing – which explains part of the concentrations we see of worker co-ops in such fields. Of course many founders also pursue a cooperative structure based on ideology and the values of wage solidarity, sustainable or ethical business, or democracy itself.

The last motivation worth noting is for local businesses to remain viable and even to grow. Many existing small businesses face a crisis when a founder or owner seeks to exit, whether through retirement or a change of interest. Founders might also seek to leave their business if they feel threatened by gentrification, competition or other challenges that would demand more capacity than they have to offer. A transfer of ownership or "conversion" of the business into a cooperative by selling to the existing employees multiplies the number of local owners, and recruits a new team of leaders who might have more gusto to stabilize the business through its succession.

Ultimately people start worker co-ops to address social problems, whether those are for the workers themselves, the conditions of the industries they operate in, or the communities and value chains in which they are embedded. Regardless of their motivation, co-ops are usually founded in one of four ways:

- A wholly new start-up.
- Chartered by an existing organization like a nonprofit or incubator, in hopes of hiring in workers along the way.
- Converted to worker ownership from within an existing business through some type of worker buyout.
- Established by an existing cooperative as a new or spun off business, either as a franchise of their brand, a supplier or client within a related value chain, or a project for some of its members to pursue something new, interesting, or suited to their skills and passions.

From the situations above, one can imagine any number of stories in which a group of founders sets out to start a new worker co-op. There have been countless examples for nearly 200 years in the United States alone. Today there are barely 1,000 worker cooperatives in the US (which has roughly tripled in the past decade), and despite a rich history, they had not previously managed to become mainstream. And it's no wonder. As recently as 20 years ago, any founders in the aforementioned circumstances would be hard pressed to find the kind of business support services that exist for traditional businesses, or even for other types of cooperatives (for example, insurance, farmer or consumer owned). Here's where Mondragon comes into the picture. I believe the most important contributions from Mondragon to the US are first, helping to identify the need for a cooperative ecosystem, and subsequently, parsing some of the elements required for a minimally viable, and ultimately a maximally thriving, ecosystem in order for any new worker co-op project to come to fruition and prosper. If you try to start a co-op, where is the capital coming from to finance it? Who will help you incorporate your business and develop by-laws and cooperative structures? Who can advise you on your business plan, including market and feasibility studies? What about training the founding owners in taxes, decision-making, financial management, or team management? Who will advocate for a more favorable business environment for co-ops to thrive, when existing US law often penalizes consumer and worker-owned co-ops, whether inadvertently or outright?

We've essentially had to reverse-engineer a co-op ecosystem in the US based on lessons and advice that leaders brought back from places like Mondragon. By co-op ecosystem, I mean an economic network of loosely or directly interconnected leaders, projects, institutions, legal and policy frameworks, practitioners, patrons, trainers, organizers, technical assistance providers, lenders, funders, activists, business leagues, and advocacy coalitions who together steward and participate in the maintenance, growth, and development of cooperative businesses. In comparing the US to the Basque Country, co-op activists realized that very few of the elements in Mondragon's ecosystem – what they describe as a "table" – were present in the US in any recognizable form. Many of them kept their discourse on this to academic publications or newsletters like *Grassroots Economic Organizing* (GEO), while others sought to build what they could, which usually translated as "acting locally."

These efforts developed slowly and without much coordination throughout the 1990s and early 2000s, ultimately culminating in a keystone in the US ecosystem – the establishment of a national federation to map worker co-ops and gather data, harness their economic solidarity through dues to fund movement-building infrastructure, and to both connect and represent co-ops and democratic workplaces among various stakeholders. I've heard people present the founding of the US Federation of Worker Cooperatives (USFWC) in two different ways. If you're newer to worker co-ops, we say we've been around *since* 2004. But there's a smaller set of us who have been familiar with worker co-ops since the last century. Among that latter group, we often say that *it took us until 2004* to *finally found* a worker co-op federation in the US. To newcomers and outsiders, it seems strange that we would have had hundreds of worker co-ops before ever getting around to federating at a national level.

We could speculate endlessly about the timing and ingredients for why things finally coalesced in the spring of 2004, but in my view, three factors tower over the rest. One is that by the early 2000s, the existing, fully operational worker co-ops in the US had outpaced whatever support the local, informal DIY networks could offer. Several efforts had emerged throughout US history and by the late 1990s, just a couple of these remained, none as an incorporated or staffed organization. Worker co-ops needed more than what a few volunteer gatherings or DIY skill shares and conferences could satiate.

A second factor is that more and more co-op enthusiasts were antsy to bring lessons home from Mondragon to the US. These architects were inspired in part by the thundering success of the Mondragon Corporation and the worker co-op ecosystem in that part of the Basque Country. What Father Arizmendiarrieta accomplished there was – and remains – one of the most powerful monuments to worker power, self-determination, communal wealth-building, and demonstrations of the impact of the cooperative model. From afar, Mondragon played a catalytic role in the North American co-op field, primarily among revolutionary academics and labor visionaries. Researchers and activists made pilgrimage to the Basque Country in the late 1970s, starting shortly after the fall of the Franco dictatorship, and those delegations only grew in subsequent decades. Much of that is explored in depth in this book, which offers a glimpse of the many types of thinkers who not only went to experience Mondragon with their own senses, but more importantly to bring back elements of what they learned to seed initiatives in the US.

The third factor bridged the two. Some of us were part of an even smaller group of cooperators, active members of worker-run cooperatives who similarly held a vision for scaling workplace democracy through cooperative development in the US. As worker-owners with a larger vision for building a movement, we brought forth the types of pragmatic workplace needs of our co-workers in the existing co-op businesses, but also had the same twinkle in our eyes of the academics and co-op enthusiasts who were sure that – however special Mondragon was – there were elements we could infuse into a US context.

Those last two factors merit a closer look. If the foundation of a worker co-op federation is a signal of the rise of this ecosystem, the underlying cause is owed to the framework of a cooperative business ecosystem itself, and that should primarily be credited to that second and third factor – the iteration of lessons from Mondragon. Because of that, things did eventually coalesce into a modest, nation-wide worker co-op ecosystem – one stewarded by dozens of organizations, and hundreds of leaders – such that co-op development has been gaining momentum to this day.

Stable Ground for the Table

The "table" that Mondragon now stands on is meant to be a base upon which a thriving cooperative ecosystem rests. But leaders in Mondragon themselves are quick to emphasize how social history and political economy shaped their experience, and indeed anybody else's context for cooperative development. I think that deserves more attention than is often paid by visitors to the Basque Country seeking to return home with strategies from Mondragon. That is to say, the creation of any foundation for cooperative development is predicated on the social conditions and the political economy of a given place, including how those conditions constrain or enable cooperative solutions.

Though it goes back centuries, the Basque people cite the centrality of the Franco dictatorship in strengthening their ethnic solidarity. When their culture and language were, respectively, repressed and outright banned for decades, it cultivated deeper pride in the face of Castilian-Spanish hegemony. Further, from a materialist perspective, Franco's protectionist economic policies meant that Father Arizmendiarrieta's fledgling industries were insulated from foreign markets. Industrial cooperatives had ample time to develop in a domestic market where they were virtually the only game in town. At that time, Spain was attempting what many postcolonial economies of the Global South were also trying to do: "Import Substitution Industrialization" (Jackson & Jabbie, 2021). Like economists throughout Latin America, Sub-Saharan Africa, and Asia (particularly South, East, and Southeast Asia), the Franco's regime's domestic economic policies were aimed at incubating homegrown manufacturing in order to reduce dependency on imported goods. We therefore cannot separate out the triumph of Mondragon's Cooperatives from decades of government procurement and subsidies for domestic consumption. This fueled the cooperatives' nascent enterprises, further buoyed by the town of Mondragon's proximity to the industrial city of Bilbao.

In addition to trade protectionism, Franco's regime was isolationist in most other dimensions. Not even charitable nonprofit efforts were tolerated. The permissiveness of a robust Catholic Church and certain fields of academia and research were notable exceptions, as were cooperative businesses. Mondragon's founder managed to yoke all three together, connecting them to a repressed public who had few options for public life or outlets for their social talents beyond the church, the university, and his cooperatives.

It's probably difficult for people in the US to imagine if there were almost no nonprofits in their community, and that most social services and altruistic work flowed either through a Catholic diocese or cooperative businesses.[1] It doesn't discount the genius of Arizmendiarrieta to recognize that cooperatives were given every imaginable support and were almost assured some measure of success. They also attracted the Basque community's most creative and intelligent thinkers, given how few alternative career options were available to them, not to mention the opportunity to invest in the prosperity of their marginalized ethnic community. With a score of years as a runway, it's little wonder that by the time the Franco dictatorship ended with his death in the 1970s, Mondragon's cooperatives already had a sturdy table for their workers and co-ops to flourish. Here I hope outsiders are taking away the right lessons, which demands we set aside fetishization and amazement.

Contrast the rise of Mondragon under Franco's post-war protectionism with the Anglo-American political economy of the 1970s. The United Kingdom and United States were being rocked by the so-called Chicago School's neoconservatives like Milton Friedman, all assiduous about dismantling a social safety net. These neoliberal economists ushered in the era of privatization, wage stagnation, and anti-union attacks that we are still reeling from today. Commensurately, the sprawling reach of Thatcherism and Reaganism undermined domestic industrial output. Financialization and "free trade" made it easier for companies to shutter northern sites of production to areas with cheaper labor, ones without union protections in locations overseas that lacked environmental regulations and worker protections. Cooperatives in the UK and US were ultimately swept up in the tide of deindustrialization, even if there were efforts to seize this opportunity for worker buyouts of the distressed manufacturing industries. Thus, throughout the 1970s and 1980s, worker cooperatives shrunk, closed, or realigned around a service-based economy that would become dominant by the 1990s. Culturally the wave of worker cooperatives born in this era echoed the counterculture consumer co-ops of the 1960s and 1970s, espousing values of localism, self-sufficiency, and participatory democracy. They emphasized the importance of self-determination, a critique of hierarchy, and took pride in being an "alternative" to the scourge of neoliberal corporatism that devalues workers, communities, and the environment for the sake of exponential profit.

While we have seen some bright spots during the neoliberal era (ranging from Equal Exchange's global solidarity model to the Argentinian factory takeovers that birthed The Working World in their 2001 financial crisis), we are about to witness the surge of a new, much larger co-op wave. Following the 2008 financial crisis, the rumblings for a new system stirred by Occupy Wall Street and the Movement for Black Lives, and the popular upswing of Democratic Socialism, including that bolstered by politicians like Senator Bernie Sanders and Congresswoman Alexandria Ocasio-Cortez, more people have begun to see the social potential for worker co-ops in a more democratic and equitable economy. With previous avenues to generational wealth like housing and education closed off by generational debt, democratically-owned firms are more attractive than ever as a way to build economic security. Social media and new modes of communication allow more people than ever before to learn about the whats, whys, and hows of cooperatives. Questions of democratic public ownership of energy, housing, banks, and other key sectors are on the political agenda. With the decade of the Green New Deal upon us, the conditions are ripe for an explosion in co-op growth, but the question remains: are we sufficiently organized to capture these opportunities?

Setting the Table for Cooperative Development

Visitors to Mondragon learn that there are a few core areas of cooperative support that are foundational for how Mondragon developed and continues to grow. They use an image of a table, which has four legs that prop up a healthy cooperative ecosystem upon which everything else relies. The legs of the table are:

1. Education.
2. Research & development (R&D).
3. Finance
4. Social Services.

Though Americans have been borrowing from this table model for decades, we haven't consistently attributed these borrowed elements of US co-op infrastructure to their roots in the Mondragon model. Our Basque friends may not have been the first or only group to assemble a framework like this, but they sure got it right. I would like to share my sense of what the US answer is to each of those elements, because I think it helps us understand more about the foundation and efforts to further develop the US worker co-op ecosystem, including the remaining gaps that the USFWC and our constituent member organizations are attempting to fill in to build a robust, democratic economy.

Education and R&D

The importance of education is both weighty and self-evident. I think that's one of the reasons why one of the first things cooperatives do in the US is come together to share knowledge through workshops, skill shares, training, and strategy sessions, ranging from one-off gatherings to multi-day conferences. Focusing just on recent decades, small groups of worker co-op developers have been gathering since the mid-1980s to offer peer advice and support as a community of practice. Co-op conferences, like the Western Worker Co-op Conference and the Eastern Conference for Workplace Democracy, both predate the founding of the USFWC and demonstrate the growing audience of co-op members, developers, financers, TA providers, and other supporters. Indeed, as those events grew and organizers began work on a Midwestern worker co-op conference, leaders from the other coasts took that as a sign that we were ready to elevate that into our first national conference. Embedded in that larger educational forum, our first National Worker Co-op Conference, was simultaneously a founding convention and a general assembly of the field. In that way, education is what sparked the creation of a national association of worker co-ops, which became the USFWC.

From its earliest days, the founding board of the USFWC recognized that education would continue to be a crucial pillar for advancing the worker co-op field. In the US, this went hand in hand with research and development. Years before we incorporated the Democracy at Work Institute (DAWI), the founding USFWC board made a plan to create a charitable nonprofit arm of the USFWC. This group would partner with the USFWC to catalyze growth of the field by developing programs and institutions in line with all four legs of the table. In addition to the toolkits and training programs that DAWI and the USFWC developed, we collaborate to gather data for our field through an annual worker co-op census, which scaffolds maps, a directory, and a state of the sector report. We also collate the information we gather into longitudinal data, which enables us to track trends in development, resilience, and diversification of worker co-ops. R&D is more than just data of course. Whether it's quantitative or qualitative data, the USFWC, DAWI, and other partners in the field like ICA Group, Cooperation Works!, the University of

Wisconsin Center for Cooperatives, Co-op Cincy, the National Cooperative Business Association (NCBA-CLUSA) and many, many others have stepped up responsibility to share anecdotes and experiences, as well as hard numbers to test and report on what works and what doesn't in the US adaptations of Mondragon's wisdom.

The needs for worker co-op education in the US are bottomless. Beyond any of the start-up information and guidance that one would assume newer projects require, established co-ops and worker owners have an ongoing need for leadership development, operations, governance, and management training, industry specific skill-building, and curriculum for orienting new members to the running of their own co-op alongside the broader cooperative field and its constituent allies and resources. The latter might sound aspirational, but many a co-op has gone under as a cautionary tale for the vulnerabilities of a business unaware of the support and resources that make an ecosystem resilient. Too many have shuttered their operations due to neglect over taxation and compliance, unaddressed internal conflict and founders syndrome, inability to adapt in a crisis or changing market environment, and otherwise through isolation and a lack of connection to solidarity loans and a community of practice and learning.

R&D is another matter. While it might not seem as dire, the chasm between the existing positioning in the market and a more innovative and competitive one is considerable. Beyond the management, tax, leadership succession, and other internal areas where stagnation can take down a co-op internally, there are only a few industries supported by an explicit application of cooperative research, and how it might inform products, pricing, supply chains, emerging markets, customers, technology, efficiency, and margins. These are basic themes inside of business schools, but are rarely addressed outside of the initial feasibility, launch, lending, and occasional expansion for cooperative businesses here, especially when compared to the multiple R&D institutes within Mondragon's ecosystem, such as Saiolan, Mondragon's business incubator institution.

Finance

One of the gaps we worried about early on was the finance leg. Access to capital was such a limiting factor in the US that an entire branch of co-op development pivoted solely to launching low-capital intensive businesses, which is how we've wound up with such a large portion of new co-ops concentrated in the service sector. It doesn't require much upfront capital to clean homes, offer bookkeeping or other business support services, develop websites, or offer language interpretation or meal catering for events. Service-based industries such as these have had the fastest growth in the past couple of decades, followed not too distantly by relatively low-capital intensive industries like landscaping, carpentry, wellness, and home health care. Co-ops with higher capital needs in the food, manufacturing, laundry, retail (books, breweries, groceries, etc.), and transportation industries would require a shift in the ecosystem in order to get off the ground.

As the oldest firm dedicated to developing employee-owned businesses and co-ops, the ICA Group was keenly aware of this. They founded the Local Enterprise Assistance Fund (LEAF) to lend to worker co-ops, and it is still functioning to great effect even today. But it was insufficient to the needs of a growing field. Five years after our founding, the USFWC worked with the community development financial institution (CDFI) Shared Capital Co-op (formerly Northcountry Cooperative Development Fund) to seed a Worker Ownership Fund. I was a board member of the USFWC in 2010 when we were figuring this partnership out. The USFWC didn't have the capital to seed the fund itself. Instead, we launched a campaign to galvanize our members to invest some of their operational reserves or surplus capital to seed and then replenish a pool of funds that could exclusively fund the expansion, development, or founding of worker co-ops and other 100% employee-owned or operated democratic workplaces. Within a couple years, this money had already been lent out to viable co-op projects. Thankfully, other CDFIs, led by the cooperative ones like National Co-op Bank, the Cooperative Fund of New England, and Shared Capital, entered the growing field and trained their staff up to make more loans to worker co-ops specifically. These groups are all part of a financial ecosystem that is working together to figure out how to exponentially increase the amount of capital in the field as well as the vehicles for processing such deals, from underwriting and portfolio balancing to specific institutions, pooled funds, and other financial instruments that either do not yet exist or needs to be amped up through government support or new allies in the philanthropic or private sector. The sophistication of these conversations is something we were not positioned to broker prior to the 2020s. That's part of what it means to nurture an ecosystem, and is one sign of our progress.

In the preceding era, a decade prior, The Working World (TWW) came back to the US. TWW was inspired by Mondragon's financing might, exemplified by institutions like their Caja Laboral Popular (which became Laboral Kutxa).[2] TWW was birthed in the early 2000s economic crisis while industrial worker buyouts flourished throughout Argentina. After a few years, TWW expanded to Nicaragua, building on its success in Argentina. Between 2008-2010, TWW opened up US offices in New York. This began with an effort to finance New Era Windows, a worker buyout of a window factory (Republic Windows and Doors) in Chicago, a story that garnered national attention during the Obama-Biden presidential campaign of 2008.

It's important that we recognize how intentional this strategy was. Brendan Martin, the founding Executive Director of TWW, speaks to this explicitly. It's not that TWW coincidentally plays a similar role to that of Caja Laboral Popular; Martin talks about his journey of learning how Caja Laboral functioned in the Basque context, and his deliberate attempt to mimic this with La Base (the capital fund in Argentina), and eventually Seed Commons. Seed Commons is the expanded iteration of TWW, containing local peer loan funds throughout the US, powered by a shared backend and a non-extractive loan model that brings the power of finance under community control. In partnering with these groups in a decentralized lending network, they link into local co-op ecosystems and go deeper than a national CDFI like TWW might be capable of, given the wrap-around technical assistance and open book management approach in TWW's non-extractive finance model. In this way, Seed Commons plays a complementary role to the rest of the co-op lending ecosystem, and to the USFWC and DAWI, in effect holding up the financing leg of the table through a translocal co-op financing structure that mirrors the USFWC's membership and programs.

The mere existence of a financing pillar of the table is not the same as having strength within that leg. (The same holds true for the even weaker "social services" pillar, which I will shift to in a moment.) By the time the USFWC was 15 years old, DAWI was about five years old and TWW had been in the US for a decade. When I visited Mondragon myself, I had a chance to learn about the lesser-discussed history of how Father Arizmendiarrieta and Mondragon's early leaders lobbied the Spanish government in order to create better conditions in their table of development. For me, that reinforced the paramount importance of the USFWC's advocacy program and similar ones that co-op leaders nationally and regionally are spearheading to create better conditions for a thriving solidarity economy.

Joining a coalition of other co-op advocacy groups like the National Cooperative Bank and NCBA-CLUSA, the USFWC's highest financing priority has been unlocking access to the federal government's Small Business Association (SBA) 7(a) loan program, the primary public financing option for small businesses. Doing so would enable consumer, purchasing, and worker co-ops to tap into the already existing infrastructure of a robust federal financing program, including the administrative guidance and support of government workers in thousands of Small Business Development Centers (SBDCs) distributed throughout the country. Currently, a provision in the SBA 7(a) loan program requires that all borrowers – in this case, every member of a worker or consumer co-op – sign as co-guarantors and list all of their personal, private, family assets as collateral on a business loan that they are co-signing. For a tiny worker co-op of three or four members, that might still be feasible, but this provision is prohibitive to the vast majority of co-ops who have more than five members. Thus billions of dollars in federal financing are practically unavailable to cooperative businesses. By contrast, the Basque government has offices in Vitoria which serve start-ups and are a one stop shop for anything a group needs, such as information for any licensing that is required, incorporation, and consulting services for co-ops in any industry.

But pushing for financing goes beyond public policy work. Figuring out more opportunities to unleash patient capital for feasible co-op projects also brings us into conversations with philanthropy, venture capital, and social impact investment. So we advocate in other spaces to create structures for groups or individuals with wealth who are trying to divest from war, prisons, and fossil fuels, to move their money into the regenerative economy. In the summer of 2021, DAWI announced the creation of a Legacy Business Investment Initiative, launched with $30 million of seed capital. This fund is a capital tool which our ecosystem can tap into to finance the worker buyouts where a small business owner is interested in selling their business to the workforce. Many workers of color, especially Black workers, miss out on the wealth-building benefits of a potential co-op conversion because Black workers here often lack the accumulated wealth to purchase even their individual share of an owner buyout (since wealth has been systematically stolen from us through various schemes over hundreds of years). This is the type of infrastructure that DAWI and the USFWC are mission-bound to create in the US, despite the context varying so drastically from the Basque Country.

Social services

Whether it's fringe benefits and pensions, personal and home finance support through their credit union, or a full employment program, one thing that is eminently clear when you learn about the workers in Mondragon's cooperatives is that both the workers and the cooperatives are well taken care of. That's true by the standards of any comparable position outside of their cooperative complex, but the strength of their benefits and services puts the rest of the cooperative world, as well as the corporate world, to shame. That contrast is only starker when you put Mondragon side-by-side with US cooperatives. Of the four legs of the thriving ecosystem "table," the pillar of social services for worker-owners is perhaps the weakest aspect of co-op development in the US. I think that's also because it's the aspect that's had the least amount of attention from leaders, funders, and other allies in the US.

What Mondragon calls "social services" encompasses quite a lot and is scaffolded by close to half of the institutions in their ecosystem's table. Otalora is the cooperative and management training center. In addition to its banking and financing function for the cooperative businesses, Laboral Kutxa is a credit union providing banking services for the workers themselves. Ikerlan (a R&D center), Mondragon Innovation and Knowledge Research Center, and Mondragon University each straddle a mandate of traditional corporate market and product-based R&D and workforce-oriented research to develop services, benefits, and HR programs for cooperative members.

This alone would be enviable, but even without that background support, Lagun Aro on its own is a form of solidarity-based Human Resources on steroids. Lagun Aro helms a sophisticated suite of social services (HR) that cradles the worker-owners throughout the Mondragon Complex. They have 230 insurance specialists who offer car, home, life, and accident insurance to worker owners. In addition to insurance, Lagun Aro dedicates 175 employees to marketing, IT, admin, personal finance, health benefits, and other HR support. They also employ 530 mediators to address business disputes and workplace conflicts through professional mediation. Lagun Aro's "full employment" program functions as a kind of job guarantee. Rather than sticking workers on government "unemployment," their program takes on the responsibility of partial pay and job placement directly. That means if a co-op has to cut your position or your department for whatever reasons, Lagun Aro has a case worker who is there to make sure you receive some salary and benefits without disruption. Meanwhile, Lagun Aro finds new positions for workers whether they were laid off or seeking a transfer for other reasons. This also eases the process of absorbing a given worker from one cooperative to a different one since the agency gets to work finding a place for you at another one of the affiliated cooperatives. They are incentivized to do so because the sooner they set you up at a new job, the sooner they can remove you from the unemployment payrolls. From what I understand, those services are unrelated to government programs, with the exception of whatever socialized healthcare and pension social programs the Basque or Spanish government ensures.

Together with the other R&D institutions affiliated with Mondragon (and there are a handful), Lagun Aro's role in developing and strengthening cooperatives and the workers within them is powerful and boosts a virtuous cycle. If cooperative businesses and products are developed, marketed, and profitable, the business grows, the workforce expands, and the surplus from sales is reinvested in the salaries, benefits, and conditions of the workers themselves. They've also created a stabilizing web of interdependence by transferring trained workers among the Mondragon Cooperatives, thereby attracting talent to the ecosystem, given the superlative quality and conditions of work. Considering this combination of job placement, the ongoing development of the workers themselves, and the responsibility to improve the social environment around them, it's clear that workers and co-op businesses are of equal priority to Mondragon. I wish that were true in the US, but the incentives are out of balance.

However we address these gaps, the lesson from Mondragon is coordination, not disparate DIY projects. Noticing an embarrassingly delinquent gap in worker benefits, pensions, jobs guarantee, or other such programs in the US workforce generally, and, by extension, pervasively throughout the co-op sector is not necessarily a call for developer organizations or start-ups to attempt to fill in that gap themselves. Our field is already fractured and balkanized. However effective a small organization might be for local users, they remain incapable of meeting the needs of cooperatives governed by the health care, labor, pension, and corporate laws of another state or territory (with at least 50+ different sets of State, Commonwealth, and territorial policies).

For myriad reasons, including the metrics and deliverables from their funders in the government and philanthropy, cooperative developers and CDFIs in the US are primarily motivated to incorporate new business or create new jobs, but have very little incentive to additionally support the social services or worker benefits that worker-owners ultimately require. That's not to imply that developers don't care. Quite the contrary, the worker co-op development field pumps more resources into training and technical assistance than sheer grant deliverables would merit. It's clear that they are among the biggest cheerleaders for the workers and the best interest of their families—once the deal is done and the co-op has either been founded or converted (or in other words, sold to the workers from the owner under an established, traditionally structured business). But cheerleading doesn't amount to much more than moral support where worker-owners need material benefits. The creation or conversion of a worker co-op is itself a massively heavy lift for a thin, heroic bench of co-op development organizations. They lack the capacity and financial (not to mention scholarly) resources to build out the kinds of social programs fostered in Mondragon. I hope that our field comes to understand how that puts national cooperative development and support organizations in a unique position to do precisely that.

Technical assistance, mediation, and training make more sense locally, which might explain why this is one of the few social services that have some presence everywhere you find worker co-ops. To me, the most promising breakthroughs are with the union co-ops strategy, and what groups like Co-op Cincy (formerly the Cincinnati Union Co-ops Initiative) have developed. Co-op Cincy both argues for and directly develops co-ops whose workers join union locals. It does this both for labor solidarity, and so its worker-owners can tap into the power of such highly specific social services as workplace disputes, OSHA and job training, and access to pensions and free community college.

Union co-op organizing contrasts to much of the nonprofit development field. In the instances where they do exist, the latter seem best suited to those prior pillars; either anchoring education, research, and development, or finances but doing so for the sake of the cooperative as a business overall, rather than pursuing services for the workers as laborers themselves. Our members formed a USFWC because we needed a member-owned institution that could balance those interests, lifting up workers alongside their cooperative businesses, and they realized the limitations of a purely local co-op association's ability to accomplish this.

My biases are no doubt clear, but I see a clear role for achieving this at the scale we need by channeling resources to our only grassroots national, membership organization for worker co-ops in this country. Not that the USFWC should take on R&D, admin, brokerage, training, and direct HR for the whole worker co-op field, but coordination at the very least would be appropriate, including to assist with referrals and connections to allied unions on the ground. Certainly with a diverse membership spanning dozens of industries across the economy, the USFWC and DAWI are better off striking partnerships with industry or location-based groups to figure out and improve upon worker benefits and services than threadbare local co-op networks on their own.

Food on the Table

With all that said, the question then becomes how can we use lessons from Mondragon to strategically equip the next generation of worker-owners and labor leaders in the US? Additionally, what kind of ecosystem would need to be in place to foment that growth, and enable thriving synergies? My questions for how to nurture a democratic economy are not posed in the abstract. On the contrary, my provocation is that we need to engage them with specific consideration to the times, that is to say, the political economy that we live in; and perhaps more importantly, the one that will define the coming decades. Until quite recently, the 21st century has generally left workers and communities stripped of resources and agency, disproportionately so in the Global South. Even with a renewed labor militancy in North America and an overdue attitude that communities are fed up, people in the US are left more vulnerable to economic and natural shocks now than in the first few decades of neoliberal economic policy. Our first task, then, is to leverage cooperative structures to meet people's increased needs. That means cooperatives need to be more than pure entrepreneurial fantasy. I won't argue against those who say it is great if existing infrastructure allows for those with means to fulfill their dreams of founding a small business, and doing so cooperatively. Setting that aside, there are some clear community needs that we can address as we proactively design the next foundations of a robust worker co-op ecosystem that matters for workers in this economy.

The real inspiration from Mondragon should be a motivation to re-root in the times and places we find ourselves. Their examples should be less of a "model" and more of an example for what is possible when we assess our needs and develop a supporting cooperative ecosystem surrounding them. The truth is that most people have neither heard of nor would they, upon learning, care much about Mondragon. As readers of this volume grow to admire the founder of that cooperative complex, let us remember that its founder was primarily driven by a deep and spiritual devotion to focus on things that matter to everybody. I see that as the real secret to unlock in making cooperative solutions, not only effective, but relevant to people today. What Father Arizmendiarrieta created was an ecosystem that met the educational and material needs of the Basque community. Today, we are presented with opportunities to similarly foreground cooperative solutions directly within industries that have left our communities insecure, but motivated to reclaim: food, housing, early childhood education, health care. In the interstices left by this social abandon – food apartheid and food insecurity, failing and underfunded childcare, a spiraling crisis of houselessness and unaffordable housing, and near neglect of the elderly and people with disabilities – there are innumerable examples of mutual aid and community care efforts to relieve the most dire circumstances. People are already predisposed to move into action and care for those in need. Cooperatives don't need to feel alien. Some of them should probably work in tandem with, or be embedded within, some of these organic projects. The other takeaway from Mondragon is that one-off projects are not enough. Building a robust ecosystem requires us to design models across various sectors that, in aggregate, get us to be more "like Mondragon," in the sense that they will be effective because they matter and they meet a specific need.

We aren't starting from nothing. In the food system there are already dozens of worker co-ops up and running, some – such as Equal Exchange – for many decades navigating complex supply chain imports and quality control of coffee and cocoa beans, while setting a national standard for fair and direct trade commodities. Others, such as Brooklyn Packers, address food security in communities of color by sourcing, packing, and distributing food for small food delivery companies and organizations that champion fresh and healthy food. Many people are familiar with the worker-run grocery cooperatives sprinkled throughout the US, but worker co-op farms are a more recent phenomenon, especially gaining traction among Black and Indigenous Land Back movements and among Asian-American /Pacific Islander and Latinx farmworker organizers. Worker co-ops have long been a feature of cafes, restaurants, bakeries, and increasingly breweries and farm to table eateries but now, more and more "artisans" are taking raw agricultural products and layering in the value add to make health and medicinal products (especially with the decriminalization and legalization of cannabis in many states) alongside grocery and ready-made foods.

There are similar strengths in childcare and healthcare – especially home health care – fields. The groundwork has been laid for cooperative businesses who have been innovating for many years. Why aren't those innovations being replicated? The missing pieces continue to be limitations in the ecosystem. Early childhood educators lament state government limitations for the Head Start per-child reimbursement rate, which forces childcare businesses to either cater to wealthy market-rate unsubsidized clients, or struggle with higher turnover professionals who burnout from underfunded, yet community-serving facilities for poor and working class families. Such problems are addressed through advocacy and organizing. That's a primary function of the USFWC in tandem with local partners and political coalitions relevant to certain issues and industries, or otherwise to the cooperative or employee-ownership structure as a whole. At the enterprise level, Union Co-ops Initiatives (such as Co-op Cincy, or the LA Union Co-ops Initiative) work closely with unions to incubate co-ops in specific industries. At a secondary level, the USFWC convenes peer networks of co-ops who operate in the same field. Beyond the connections and solidarity, this creates a platform for leaders to identify needs within that industry, and opportunities to collaborate for shared purchasing, internal worker training, advice on sourcing, pricing, and markets, and on occasion they feed information through the USFWC to co-op developers or funders that results in secondary co-ops, or new enterprises along a related value chain. While I'm far from impartial, these efforts do start to feel "Mondragon-esque" to me. What's more, beyond filling in for specific immediate communities needs, there's a burgeoning horizon of platform co-ops, multi-stakeholder co-ops, and new endeavors in the tech and digital space that also feedback, albeit not as immediately, into serving community and worker needs. There is much innovation afoot, even if that isn't the point I'm mainly illustrating here.

The last piece that should not be missed is the centrality of solidarity within the Mondragon model, but maybe more so in its culture. You don't get to a robust ecosystem without solidarity and cooperation in building it out. North American culture struggles with membership and affiliation. People don't part with dollars for dues any more easily than they do with dollars for tolls, taxes, or utilities. That's starting to change as grassroots organizers reconnect with the long traditions of union membership and voluntary dues to organizations like the Democratic Socialists of America (DSA). The erosion of solidarity in the US was an intentional response to the strength of 20th century student movements, organized labor, and multi-racial (including immigrant) opposition to a repressive racist state, profiteering and patriarchal capitalists, and the war machine. It's critical that we rekindle this interdependence and link it to the solidarity economy in order to build both political and economic power for the kind of impact we see in the Basque Country.

On that final note, I'll recapitulate a point I've written elsewhere about just how crucial solidarity figures into the Basque culture in which Mondragon is situated, and what the stakes are for our own efforts in the US. When we exalt the depth of solidarity they demonstrate and then weave into an economic ecosystem around Mondragon, it is important to distinguish between the relatively ethnically homogenous Basque Country and the multiracial and geographic disparities of North America (and indeed among other multi-ethnic contexts looking to learn from Mondragon). Whereas North Americans learn from a disposition toward development, initiative, entrepreneurship, and movement building, Mondragon's history and culture (going back to a nearly 7,000 year old language) forged a sense of interdependence, trust, solidarity, and a drive for self-sufficiency. The crucible, as explored earlier, was a fraught political landscape ruled by Franco, which sought to suppress unique ethic identity and transform multicultural regions into a unified nation-state (Spain). The particular situation of an economically insulated ethnic minority facing political repression is intrinsic to the models that Mondragon developed. As we adapt the useful lessons from their context to ours, our challenge is to learn how to similarly assess and act within our own contexts, and to build the structures and interconnected systems that amplify such programs. At the end of the day, is that not the primary expression of economic solidarity?

End-notes

[1]   While the organizational environment was narrow, there was also a cultural environment that was dominated by values of cooperation and community manifest in the *cuadrillas* – peer social groups, and gastronomic social clubs and the *txikiteo* custom that provided a strong sense of community and shared social and economic engagement, as described in Caitlin Gianniny's chapter of this book.

[2]   Laboral Kutxa is now a conventional (albeit ethical) bank but previously it was a development bank in the early years of the development of the co-ops, a topic explored in **Chapter 5** of this book.

References

Jackson, E.A. & Jabbie, M.N. (2021). Import substitution industrialization (ISI): An approach to global economic sustainability. In W. Leal Filho, A.M. Azul, L. Brandli, A. Lange Salvia & T. Wall (eds). *Industry, Innovation and Infrastructure.* New York: Springer.

CHAPTER 25

Labor Unions & Worker Co-ops: Democratizing the Economy

Mary Hoyer & Rebecca Lurie

Labor is prior to and independent of capital. Capital is only the fruit of labor, and could never have existed if labor had not first existed. Labor is the superior of capital, and deserves the much higher consideration. (President Abraham Lincoln, in his first State of the Union address, 1861)

Worker co-ops and labor unions are natural allies in the fight for economic and social equity. Workers spend a significant portion of their daily lives struggling to make a living, whether employed by a corporation or in contracted gig work. Participation in decision-making and share in profit is limited, if it occurs at all. Excess profit is funneled into the pockets of business owners and investors, while workers are left with barely enough to live and raise a family healthily and sustainably.

Pay for the vast majority of Americans has stagnated while the wealthiest among us have grown richer, leading to a dramatic rise in income inequality. All the while, deeply-rooted racial wealth gaps have persisted. According to 2019 data from the Federal Reserve Bank, Black and Hispanic median household wealth remain staggeringly low, at $24,100 and $36,100 respectively compared to $188,200 for white households. The Covid-19 pandemic has exacerbated these inequities, exposing the long-standing failures in social and economic policies that fail to provide workers meaningful income and voice from ownership in addition to wages (Lurie & King Fitzsimons, 2021).

In this chapter, we will explore labor's current dilemma, its historic and recent involvement with cooperative businesses, and the extraordinary recent increase in institutional efforts, including the role of Mondragon, to help these two important sectors of the economy work together to enhance their efficacy.

While labor unions have historically been and are currently the main fortification against inequality in the United States, for the past 40 years they have been under severe duress with capital in the ascendency. Corporations have moved overseas and to states hostile to labor. During the 20th century, workers and small businesses endured 12 recessions/depressions, with two already in the 21st century. Many businesses have consolidated through merger, which concentrates power and makes labor organizing more difficult, especially in the legislative arena. Large corporations with funds in reserve have been able to take advantage of these crises to aggregate more and more power in their hands economically and politically.

Recent catastrophes related to environmental damage caused by unbridled capital development have exacerbated the chaos. "Unemployment, indebtedness, and precariousness...have become the fundamental human experience of capitalism over the past several decades" (Winant, 2021; Elliott, 2021). The US is lurching from one crisis to another, which is no way to run an economy.

Prior to the ascension of neoliberalism in the US with Reagan's election to the presidency in the early 1980s, organized labor, with wind at their backs from the New Deal and some progressive legislation, functioned for the most part using a business unionism model with a focus on wages and benefits, and on limited improvements in working conditions when they could be won (Post, 2015; Curl, 2009). More radical forms of worker participation (for example, worker ownership of enterprise and democratic management) were minimized. Many unions focused on terms of employment and stopped organizing workers and the broader community for policy changes that would benefit the entire economy rather than just workplaces.

The Wagner Act in 1935 resulted in rules of the road for organized labor that excluded largely black and brown domestic, service, and agricultural workers (National Labor Relations Board, n.d.). These exclusions embedded racism and divisions in US labor law that continue to have multiple implications to this day. The unemployed were left out of labor's equation altogether.

Coming out of World War II and moving into the Cold War, with damage to the European and Japanese economies, the US economy flourished. Anti-communism dominated foreign policy and influenced domestic policy, and labor as well as capital viewed worker control as a form of communism. The ruling class consolidated their control over the economy, and labor leaders took advantage of the economic opportunities that were available. This resulted in reluctance on the part of organized labor to engage in any radical organizing for ownership and control of industry.

But in recent years, there has been an increase in work stoppages and strikes in the US. After decades of reduced strike activity, the number of workers involved in stoppages and strikes increased by almost 20 times from 2017 to 2018. 2018 and 2019 saw the largest two-year increase in 35 years. Despite a decrease in the number of unionized workers, strikes before the Covid pandemic were up 257% (Keshner, 2020; Shierholz & Poydock, 2020).

Nevertheless, workers continue to be afraid of losing their jobs and healthcare coverage, risking financial ruin for their families if they organize publicly. "A lot of people truly just feel lucky to have a job" (Nolan, 2020). Simply put, employers have too much power over workers' lives. Policy decisions at the local, state, and national levels supported by business owners have reinforced that power (Weisman, 2021).

One solution to the problem of uncertain jobs and careers is for workers to create, own, and manage their own businesses. Quietly, over the last 30 years, the innovative worker co-op movement has been gaining strength. Between 2013 and 2019, before the Covid pandemic hit, data show a 36% increase in the number of verified worker co-ops (Prushinskaya, 2020), although most worker co-ops are small businesses with few workers. Many of these businesses and their support organizations (which provide training, funding, and networking opportunities) have aggregated organizationally into the US Federation of Worker Co-ops (USFWC), a membership self-help association. Over time, the USFWC created the Union Co-ops Council (UCC), a national group of volunteers, and the Democracy at Work Institute (DAWI), a non-profit affiliate that focuses on strategic planning and training for the wider movement. In addition, the Mondragon network of cooperatives in Spain has been working in the United States with such organizations as 1worker1vote, Co-op Cincy, and the City University of New York School of Law Community Economic Development Clinic. Organizations such as these that encourage mutual efforts between unions and worker co-ops discussed later in this chapter, have broadened the influence of this emerging union co-op sector.

Lower and middle income workers, including most people of color, women, and immigrants, provide an expanding social base for these changes. Legislation related to worker co-op development over the last several years demonstrates that this is not a utopian fantasy (Committee on Small Business, 2021; US Federation of Worker Co-ops, 2021; International Labor Office, 2013).

The worker co-op movement is looking to enhance its influence in the economy and labor is looking for new strategies to fight back against capital (Witherell, 2021; Hoyer, 2015; Geoghegan, 2014; Ness, 2014; Cowie, 2010; Flanders, 2012; Hoyer et al., 2011). Recent developments indicate that organized labor and the worker co-op movement can strengthen each other in exciting new ways. They represent a remarkable response to labor's repression after more than 40 years of capital's ascendancy, and build on a strong national and international foundation with important implications for the future of a more egalitarian and cooperative economy.

In the interest of clarity, we've included a glossary of abbreviations and terms at the end of this chapter.

Potential Problems between Unions & Worker Co-ops

It is often thought that unions and co-ops are mismatched. Some have queried whether worker co-ops need to be unionized since workers own and manage their businesses. Others may posit that workers in labor unions aren't entrepreneurial, but instead are oriented to "resisting the boss," setting the terms for employment and fighting to maintain them. In addition, unions and workers may be familiar with large agricultural co-ops in the United States that fight unionized workers, or with food co-ops that resist worker unionization.

In order to address this last issue, it's important to differentiate who the members and owners are of any co-op, and who has control. What many people don't realize is that there are basically four types of co-ops: producer (such as big agricultural co-ops in which the owners of farms are the members/owners); consumer (such as food co-ops in which the people who purchase goods at the co-op are the members/owners); worker (in which the people who work in the co-op are the members/owners); and hybrid/solidarity/multi-stakeholder co-ops (in which each of these groups comprise a class of members/owners).[1] In the first two types of co-ops, workers are not empowered with ownership and management control. In hybrid co-ops, workers share ownership with other stakeholder groups (consumers and producers). Only in worker co-ops do workers have full power and control. Additionally, there are some producer and consumer co-ops in which workers are unionized but are not owners.

Unions may be leery of worker co-ops due to their experience with Employee Stock Ownership Plans (ESOPs) in the 20th century, some of which were undemocratically organized and eventually failed due to unequal allocation of profits to workers and to external buyouts (Curl, 2009; Leikin, 2005). ESOPs are predominantly vehicles for the retirement of owners who are selling, and pension plans for workers who buy in. They are managed by rules of profitability for those outcomes, and member decision-making is bound by those limits.

Some aspects of co-op development may give unions and workers pause when considering co-op business development. During enterprise planning and operational start-up, workers typically put in considerable amounts of sweat equity. Wages and benefits may be limited during early stages, and the financial buy-in required of workers may seem daunting. Workers and unions may be concerned when retirement assets are heavily invested in a single enterprise rather than across a diversity of investments. Role clarity, too, can be a problem when workers are at the same time owners, managers, and employees. Friction and role confusion between technical assistance consultants, enterprise owners, union staff, and workers can pose difficulties. Worker co-op technical assistance consultants can be very unfamiliar with unions, adding another complication to the mix. These issues and their solutions, however, are increasingly familiar in the union co-op arena now, and can be addressed through careful planning and choice of technical assistance provision.

How Unions & Worker Co-ops can Strengthen One Another

Despite these concerns, there is a good deal of room for optimism. Labor and co-op values overlap considerably (Witherell et al., 2012, pp.4-5). Both honor democratic election of leadership based on one person, one vote and make efforts to promote leadership among members. Both encourage education and training for job skills and self-management. Both believe in solidarity and collective effort. Both work with like-minded organizations in the community to ensure benefit for poor and low- to -moderate income workers and the unemployed. Both operate based on democratically-decided principles and negotiated agreements. In a unionized workplace, daily work operations are codified in collective bargaining agreements. In worker co-ops, codified agreements are reflected in the enterprise by-laws, policy, manuals, and, when unionized, in collective bargaining agreements.

Unions have much to offer worker co-ops (Lurie & King Fitzsimons, 2021, pp.6-7, 12-13, 26-27, 35-36). Affiliation with a labor union and the labor movement in general gives worker cooperators access to broad and deep economic analysis and understanding of their market sector and political trends. Unions can provide access to organizing expertise and capital for enterprise initiation, including research, planning, and legal issues. They can provide space for meetings, and funding through staffing, grants, and loans. They can help aggregate capital for enterprise initiation and expansion. Unions can facilitate access to pension and health benefits and provide access to model collective bargaining agreements, operating procedures, rules, compensation structures, and model grievance procedures, thus contributing greatly to the smooth running of new worker co-op businesses, which often "reinvent the wheel" as operations commence, pick up speed, and become increasingly complex. Union representation can assure that worker protections and interests are secured and stewarded, and can train workers in how to handle misunderstandings and grievances. Unions can involve workers in conceptualization and promotion of legislation and interaction with elected officials. They can connect worker co-ops to national and international efforts to improve the lives of working people, and offer opportunities for action in solidarity with worker and community issues in the broader economic arena.

And worker co-ops have much to offer unions (Lurie & King Fitzsimmons, 2021, p.15). Unionized worker co-operators add to labor union membership, although on what may seem like a small scale when compared with large corporations. But this can be a strategy to organize many small firms and independent contractors under a union umbrella. In an era of increased gig work and independent, contracted employment, unions organizing cooperatives can expand their market and advocate for good jobs that resist elimination. Union members involved in worker co-ops enjoy enduring empowerment that involves both ownership and control of management, aspects of worker control that labor in the US has too often sacrificed in the interests of "business unionism" (Post, 2015). Business unionism, believed to be of American origin, is opposed to class or revolutionary struggle and has the principle that unions should be run like businesses. Worker co-ops help to build member and community wealth in the form of enterprise ownership.

Businesses incorporated as worker co-ops are less susceptible to attack and decimation from capital, a scenario all too common as corporations abandon unionized areas of the country. They allow the labor force to respond to economic downturns with more flexibility than traditional businesses. If workload drops off, worker owners can agree to shift workloads and schedules. This contrasts with workers in traditional businesses that are forced to accept lay-offs and contract cuts to keep the company (and its owners) in business. As a result, labor in worker co-ops is more loyal and experienced (long-term) than in traditional businesses. Crucially, worker co-ops increase workplace stability during economic downturns, thus ensuring unions continued membership. Businesses owned by employees don't "run away" to find cheaper labor or shut down when profit fluctuates.

Worker co-ops can teach unions about democratic governance, worker participation, and leadership development, which in turn can strengthen union contract and legislative campaigns. Worker co-ops and the movement for a new economy provide a broad eco-system of organizations working for community interests (small business developers, funders, churches, lawyers, journalists, academicians, etc.) that can strengthen labor's standard agenda.

Last but not least, the worker co-op strategy offers unions a creative organizing strategy beyond the endless fight back against corporate owners—the chance to build something that we own rather than eke out minimal concessions on wages and benefits. This can enhance worker morale despite the fact that entrepreneurial work can be difficult.

Historical Collaborations between Unions & Co-ops

An elaboration of the long history of unions and co-ops can help inform collaborations moving forward. Contrary to the perception that organized labor and co-ops are at odds with one another, the labor movement in the US has a long and committed history of involvement in co-op development.

Beginning in the late 18th century and blossoming after the American Civil War in the late 19th century when industrialization in the US gained momentum, there has been a rich movement in which virtually every important American labor reform organization advocated cooperation over competitive capitalism, and several thousand cooperatives opened for business (Curl, 2009, Part 1; Leiken, 2005).

As early as 1791 in the US, carpenters in Philadelphia, Pennsylvania, struck against a factory owner, forming a co-op. In 1794, shoemakers in Baltimore, Maryland, formed a co-op that paid higher wages (Curl, 2009, p.33). In the mid 1800s, unions began to grow and workers began to withdraw their labor from industry in the form of strikes (Curl, 2009, pp.31 *ff*). Some workers became proactive about setting up their own businesses before waiting for workplace crises. In the 1830s, workers and unions began to federate. The resulting National Trades' Union posited a new cooperative economy, including many stores and warehouses. In 1866, after the Civil War, the National Labor Union formed. This first American union federation included co-op workplaces and stores, and worked for co-op laws in all states.

In 1869 the Knights of Labor (KOL) formed. Industrial cooperation was one of their main principles (Curl, 2009, pp.87 *ff*). The KOL created a support organization called the General Co-op Board to provide model legal documents and articles on how to form and operate co-ops. In the 1880s the KOL co-op movement was at its height, but capital didn't remain quiescent (Curl, 2009, pp.90-93; Leiken, 2005). It fought back, often with state help and often resorting to violence. Police and capitalist vigilante activity spread throughout the country, and anti-communist red-baiting tarnished labor's image.

As time went on, workers found it increasingly difficult to take over their workplaces, since existing machinery was becoming obsolete and new machinery was becoming more advanced and expensive (Curl, 2009, pp.104 *ff*). KOL membership declined when members felt the organization was unable to support and protect them in the face of capital's pushback. Business unionism, with a focus on wages and benefits rather than control of the workplace and influence on the broader economy, gained power. This retreat from broad control allowed unions to circumvent capital's fight against progressive labor. America began to develop along different lines from Europe where workers still saw the big picture and pushed for democratic control of industry (Curl, 2009, pp.105-108). Meanwhile, low-income immigrant and minority groups used cooperatives to gain economic strength throughout the 19th and into the 20th centuries. In 1907, W.E.B. Du Bois documented a number of African-American co-ops, identifying how the cooperative model could be a structured response to build community wealth in the face of economic exclusion (Gordon Nembhard, 2014; Curl, 2009, pp.109-10, 359-60).

In 1929 the Great Depression hit the United States and the world. The AFL supported consumer co-ops as a way to help workers get more purchasing power, calling "trade unionism and cooperation…twin sisters" (Curl, 2009, pp.139-142). The US government set up a Division of Self-Help Co-ops to provide technical assistance and funding in the form of grants and loans to co-op initiatives (Curl, 2009, pp.172-173).

Several developments in Europe mid-20th century eventually had enormous impact on worker co-ops in the US and around the world. In 1947, the International Organization of Industrial, Artisanal, and Service Producers' Co-ops (CICOPA), was created. CICOPA is comprised of representative worker co-op organizations from countries throughout the world and is itself part of the International Cooperative Alliance, which represents co-ops of all types. Crucially, in 1956 the Mondragon cooperative project in the Basque region of northern Spain was formed (Whyte & Whyte, 1991). Although very well known in the worker co-op arena in the US and around the world, Mondragon has not been as well known among labor activists in the US until the development of the United Steelworkers/Mondragon Collaboration in 2009 and the Union Co-op Model in 2012 (see below).

In the second half of the 20th century, labor (particularly the United Steelworkers) began looking at worker ownership using Employee Stock Ownership Plans (ESOPs) that often involved exchanging contract concessions for worker ownership shares in order to retain jobs (Logue & McIntyre, n.d.). The Ohio Employee Ownership Center (OEOC) at Kent State University (Logue & Yates, 2008) has provided expert guidance to more than 700 firms on Employee Stock Ownership Plans (ESOPs) and more recently to worker-owned cooperatives. OEOC also developed rapid response guidelines for firms that are facing difficulties or up for sale. To date, this has helped to create about $350 million in wealth for their employee owners. Nevertheless, much to the chagrin of affiliated unions, a number of ESOPs went under. Voting power in ESOPs is determined by how many stock shares workers own, resulting in unequal influence among workers. In addition, an original owner who creates an ESOP for tax purposes may or may not exit the company. If they choose to stay as an employee, they can retain a controlling interest and even continue as manager. Since the CEO is an employee, the company would still be considered 100% employee owned (Ryssdal, 2010). Older workers in some of the earlier ESOPs voted to sell their shares (which had greatly increased in value over the years) and even the business itself when they retired. Workers and unions came to see ESOPs as simply another way to extract concessions.

These realities, among others mentioned earlier, contributed to labor union hesitancy around worker ownership, and encouraged workers to think more deeply about what was needed in the workplace for sustainability and equity.

Mondragon & the Union Co-ops Model in the US

At the close of the 20th century in 1999, Mondragon Cooperative Corporation entered the United States as Mondragon International USA (later Mondragon International North America or MINA). MINA was 55% owned by Mondragon International (itself a wholly owned subsidiary of Mondragon Cooperative Corporation) and 45% owned by Michael Peck, a principal at MAPA Group in Washington, DC and at 1worker1vote, a nonprofit founded in 2015 to develop shared ownership enterprises based on the union co-op model (Peck, 2021). When Peck retired from MINA in 2019 (an age requirement of Mondragon), 1worker1vote continued the work that was being done by MINA including collaborations with several Mondragon entities and with Co-op Cincy, the "prototype living lab" for 1worker1vote.

Co-op Cincy (CC) was founded in 2011 as Cincinnati Union Co-op Initiative (Zoller, 2021). It has been uniquely important in developing union co-ops in Ohio, and has served as a model for projects around the US. CC has developed several unionized worker co-ops, including Our Harvest Food Hub, Sustainergy home energy retrofitting, and Apple Street Market, a multi-stakeholder co-op. In 2013 Co-op Cincy sponsored the first ever gathering of labor, worker co-op, and community activists at the Union Co-op Symposium in Cincinnati.

Co-op Principles

It is important for labor unions to understand that Mondragon in Spain and union co-ops in the US are governed by 10 principles that preference the humanity of workers and the primacy of labor over capital. This makes these enterprises quite different from traditional businesses, which are governed by the principle of the "bottom line," or the profit motive.

The 10 principles are:

1. **Open admission** (non-discrimination in hiring);
2. **Democratic organization** (every worker-owner owns an equal share and has an equal vote);
3. **Sovereignty of labor** (the co-op is centered around the people doing the work; profit is distributed in terms of labor provided);
4. **Instrumental and subordinate nature of capital** (workers own their enterprise, choose their management, and "rent" capital to help sustain the business; capital is labor's instrument, not its master);
5. **Participation in management** (workers are engaged in management, or select and oversee managers; participation includes transparency, consultation, negotiation, and accountability);

6. **Wage solidarity** (disparities between the highest and lowest paid workers are minimized to a just ratio);
7. **Inter-cooperation** (co-ops work with other co-ops, sharing information and resources);
8. **Social transformation** (co-ops support and invest in social change in the broader community);
9. **Universality** (co-ops support economic justice and individual self-fulfillment through deeper levels of civic equity);
10. **Education** (training is continuous and essential both inside and beyond the workplace; understanding complex ideas allows workers to adapt and improve their businesses and communities so they can endure and prosper for coming generations).

These principles represent significant steps in co-op development, establishing clear rules that differentiate them from traditional businesses. These principles help define how a new, more equitable economy can operate. As a testimony to their value, they have been adopted and promulgated by various national and international organizations. They can also make worker co-ops acceptable as a model for labor unions.

The United Steelworkers/Mondragon Collaboration
In 2009, the United Steelworkers (USW) signed a landmark agreement with Mondragon Corporation (Witherell et al., 2012; Truthout, 2013). MINA was instrumental in this pivotal effort. Also involved were the Ohio Employee Ownership Center and the City University of New York School of Law's Community Economic Development Clinic (CUNY CEDC). In 2012, the USW/Mondragon Collaboration was elaborated into the Union Co-ops Model.

The Union Co-op (UC) Model
Smaller worker co-ops often function much like collectives, with designated worker owners playing specific operational roles, sometimes in rotation (Witherell et al., 2012; Witherell, 2013; Hanson Schlacter 2017; Cooper, 2015). As worker cooperatives gain members, worker owners commonly elect a board of directors from among themselves, which then appoints or hires managers to oversee day-to-day operations. The board of directors' model tends to look out for the day-to-day interests of worker-owners as owners but less so as workers. Cognizant of this, Mondragon cooperatives established social councils that offer shop floor worker-owners more day-to-day input on issues such as wages, benefits, and working conditions. However, this input is generally limited to an advisory role (Whyte & Whyte, 1991, pp.38 ff).

In the Union Co-op (UC) Model in the US, the social council is replaced with a Union Committee that ideally includes all non-supervisory worker owners in the co-op. As in traditionally incorporated businesses, management in a union co-op is required to engage in collective bargaining with the Union Committee, thus strengthening and affirming worker-owner power. Within the UC Model, these separate but equal groups—the board of directors, management, and the Union Committee – no worker-owner serves in more than one capacity at a time. However, worker-owners may serve consecutively in various roles. This provides a form of worker education, since those who serve in a variety of roles better understand the competing demands of the business and industry.

The union co-op committee negotiates a collective bargaining agreement (CBA) with designated or hired management (Cincinnati Union Co-op Initiative, n.d., p.110; Witherell et al., 2012, pp.11-14). The CBA provides guidelines over wages, benefits, and working conditions, and ensures that all worker-owners are treated fairly through due process. It also ensures that worker-owners as workers are engaged in the business on an ongoing basis. This negotiated agreement helps avoid the common friction that arises in newly formed co-ops that haven't taken the time to clarify these issues before commencing operations.

Mondragon, the Union Co-op Curriculum & Financing in the US

In addition to developing structural and legal applications for union co-ops, MINA, 1:1, and the Community and Economic Development Clinic at the City University of New York School of Law (CEDC) worked jointly on a worker ownership curriculum that helps unions and workers work together. Both CEDC and Co-op Cincy offer adapted versions of this curriculum.

Since worker co-ops, like all enterprises, need loans, Mondragon has also been involved in finance in the US. In 2013 Mondragon's co-op bank, Laboral Kutxa, and the US-based National Cooperative Bank headquartered in Washington, DC, agreed to partner, combining market-driven performance goals with best practices in social and solidarity-oriented lending (PRNewswire, 2013). Both entities now support each other's customers regarding charges, payments, financial services, online banking systems, and other commercial banking practices. While this agreement isn't limited to union co-ops, this is one of a number of funding sources UCs can use to their advantage.

Other Recent Union Co-op Collaborations in the US

In addition to Mondragon's work in the US, the worker co-op and union co-op movements in the US have gained considerable momentum in the past few decades. This is due in no small part to the emergence of a rich network of leading support organizations and labor unions described below that have made an enormous difference to workers and community activists involved in these efforts. Other national and international developments have contributed as well.

Worker co-op and union co-op support organizations

Moving into the current century, the Ohio Employee Ownership Center at Kent State University has increased support for worker co-ops in addition to ESOPs (Logue, 2005), and, as mentioned before, was a partner in 2009 and 2012 in developing the Mondragon/United Steel Workers Collaboration and Union Co-ops Model.

In 2004, the US Federation of Worker Co-ops (USFWC) incorporated as a non-profit membership organization for existing and aspiring worker co-ops and affiliated organizations and individuals.[2] In 2007, the Union Co-ops Council of USFWC was formed to provide networking support and resources for unions, co-op members, and activists around the country. In 2013 the non-profit training and strategic planning affiliate of USFWC, Democracy at Work Institute (DAWI), began operating. USFWC and DAWI serve both non-unionized and unionized worker co-ops, providing an array of worker co-op resources to both. Each of these organizations has been instrumental in supporting worker co-ops in general and unionized worker co-ops in particular.

In 2012, the United Nations declared the International Year of Cooperatives with three main goals, including increasing awareness about cooperatives, promoting growth of the cooperative model, and establishing appropriate policies to support cooperatives (International Year of the Cooperative:

https://www.un.org/en/events/coopsyear/). This created a spotlight on the cooperative model in the International Labor Organization.

In 2015, workers and staff from unions, community groups, and local businesses formed the Los Angeles Union Co-op Initiative (LUCI) after exploring information from Mondragon and other sources. It incubates worker co-ops in the southern California region. LUCI's affiliates include the US Federation of Worker Cooperatives, Union Co-op Council of USFWC, Sustainable Economies Law Center, United Steelworkers Union Local 675, the California Center for Cooperative Development, and Rutgers School of Management and Labor Relations.

In 2016, the Community and Worker Ownership Project (CWOP) of the City University of New York School for Labor and Urban Studies began operating. CWOP uses educational formats to support and expand efforts in New York City and nationally, to examine worker-owned cooperatives, economic democracy, and community planning. A broad array of stakeholders (unions, worker centers, community-based organizations, businesses, elected officials, and worker cooperatives) are involved in discussions and implementation strategies. CWOP sponsors non-credit workshops and has established a graduate level Certificate in Workplace Democracy & Community Ownership through the Urban Studies Department at CUNY. CWOP provides public programming, research on the economic and social justice impact of cooperative ownership and democratic engagement, and support to unions interested in co-ops and co-ops interested in unions.

In 2018, the Main Street Employee Ownership Act passed in the United States. This legislation directs the Small Business Administration of the federal government to provide loans to Employee Stock Ownership Plans (ESOPs) and worker co-ops, and directs Small Business Development Centers to provide services to enterprises converting to ESOPS and worker co-ops. It was the first worker ownership legislation to pass Congress in 40 years.

Also in 2018, the Institute for the Study of Employee Ownership and Profit Sharing at Rutgers School of Management and Labor Relations was launched. The Institute studies a wide variety of employee share ownership and profit sharing models. It provides technical assistance and education to businesses and individuals exploring employee stock ownership. The Institute convenes scholarly conferences on these issues (in recent years on labor involved in employee ownership), and develops and disseminates educational materials on employee ownership. It is affiliated with the non-profit National Center for Employee Ownership, and research fellows of the Institute serve as editors and associate editors of the academic *Journal of Participation & Employee Ownership*.

Labor unions involved with worker co-ops

With these support organizations available to assist, several labor unions have become involved in developing worker co-ops. The current period of labor involvement in worker co-ops is still very young, but actual enterprises are functioning or in the planning stages. Some of the most well-known are described here.

The United Steelworkers, in addition to being the lead union in the Mondragon/United Steelworkers Collaboration and Union Co-op Model, has been involved in several worker co-op ventures. In Pittsburgh, Pennsylvania, USW explored developing a new, environmentally friendly, high volume, competitive industrial laundry, utilizing local "anchor institutions" – large businesses such as hospitals and universities as purchasers of goods and services (CUNY CED, 2013). In Worcester, Massachusetts, Worx Printing

Cooperative provides an alternative to sweatshop-made and -printed textile products (United Steelworkers, 2015). Their printing process uses environmentally friendly inks, which has virtually no waste. USW is also involved in projects in Cincinnati *via* Co-op Cincy and in Reading, Pennsylvania, via 1worker:1vote. USW via Local 675 was involved in a carwash conversion to worker ownership in Carson, California. The biggest hurdle for USW is creating sufficiently sizable enterprises with large, stable clients to justify required capital investments. With the recent involvement of Laboral Kutxa and National Cooperative Bank in supporting Mondragon-connected co-op projects, funding may be less the issue than operational feasibility and allocation of precious staff time.

United Food and Commercial Workers (UFCW) is also involved in a number of union co-op projects (Lurie & King Fitzsimons, 2021). UFCW Local 75 is one of the principals in Our Harvest Coop in the Cincinnati area, a worker-owned farm and food hub that launched in mid-2012. UFCW is also involved in the planning and implementation of Apple Street Market, a hybrid consumer- and worker-owned food co-op with projected branches in several underserved Cincinnati neighborhoods. In Springfield, Massachusetts, UFCW Local 1459 is involved in Wellspring Coop Corporation's greenhouses project, which provides organic greens and herbs to local health care and higher education anchor institutions, among others.

In Cincinnati, Ohio, the International Brotherhood of Electrical Workers (IBEW) Local 212 and the Pipefitters Union Local 392 are involved in Sustainergy, a worker-owned residential green energy business developed by Co-op Cincy (Hanson Schlacter, 2017, p.134). Several IBEW members in Los Angeles established their own worker co-op – Pacific Electric Worker-Owned – in 2014. After working for many years as traditional, unionized electricians, they wanted to avoid the specter of layoffs and the frictions typically found in traditional businesses.

Service Employees Union International (1199SEIU) represents worker owners at Cooperative Home Care Associates (CHCA) in the Bronx, New York (Lurie & King Fitzsimons, 2021, pp.9-16). CHCA started with 12 workers in 1985 as a project initiated by Community Services Society, a large non-profit dedicated to anti-poverty work. In 2003, when their expanding workforce numbered over 500, CHCA approached SEIU with two over-arching needs: help with New York State public policies that impact home health delivery and help developing a collective bargaining process that included grievance procedures and due process, mediation and arbitration, and clear operating procedures. This also gave the members of CHCA access to 1199SEIU's benefits and training programs. Association with the union has contributed to leadership development and co-op management capacity, as well as to a sense of community among workers, which had weakened as the company grew. Participants in these processes are compensated with regular wages for time spent on decision-making and planning. In various California cities, SEIU-United Healthcare Workers West is assisting home health agencies set unionized worker co-ops (Pinto *et al.*, 2021; Lurie & King Fitzsimons, 2021, pp.32-36). SEIU-UHW serves as an example of how a union can assign staff to worker co-op activity, allowing innovations to take root.

SEIU has also been involved in a very powerful tangential development in Washington State, which serves as a model for preserving union power in the public sector when authorities move to privatize their workforces. In this case, home care workers were employed by the state and represented by SEIU Local 775 when the workforce was privatized. In response, a consortium consisting of SEIU representatives, workers, the ICA Group (a technical assistance provider), Cooperative Health Care Associates (CHCA; the country's largest worker co-op), and the Paraprofessional Health Care Institute (affiliated with CHCA) put together a co-owned, labor-friendly joint venture using a public authority model called Trust for Workers that functions as a holding entity. In 2019, after three years of research and development, the joint venture won the right to administer the state's $1 billion, 40,000-worker home care program in Washington State. Under this arrangement, workers – nearly 90% of whom are women that are disproportionately people of color – are covered under a collective bargaining agreement with SEIU 775, and have enhanced wages, health insurance, retirement, paid time off, and access to an excellent training program. While not formally structured as a worker co-op, this is a worker-friendly effort built on CHCA's worker co-op model (Lurie & King Fitzsimons, 2021, p.10; Pinto et al., 2021, pp.10-11).

United Electrical, Radio and Machine Workers of America (UE) is an independent, national union that is led by rank and file members. At its 2019 convention, the union passed a resolution to:

1. Convert traditional businesses to worker co-ops, and create worker co-ops;

2. Create unionized worker and consumer co-ops;

3. Establish a co-op sector of UE;

4. Promote products and services of co-ops;

5. Develop educational materials for co-op development;

6. Develop UE's relationship with Frente Autentico del Trabajo (an independent, democratic union in Mexico also working on co-op development); and

7. Build a sustainable economy (https://www.ueunion.org/ue-policy/build-union-co-ops).

One of UE's most dramatic accomplishments involves the factory take-over (twice) of Republic Doors and Windows in Chicago, and the successful transition of this business to a worker co-op renamed New Era Windows (Lurie & King Fitzsimons, 2021, pp.20-23; Goodman, 2013). After a struggle that began in 2008, the workers – with help from UE and the power of a factory occupation by workers – bought the company and reopened it as a worker co-op in 2013. Another UE success story involves Collective Copies, a UE-affiliated design and print shop as well as a local publishing company in Amherst, Massachusetts (https://www.collectivecopies.com/about-us/history/). In 1983, workers dissatisfied with working conditions and compensation at Kinko's, a national copy shop chain, unionized and went on strike. They proceeded to buy the business and form a worker co-op. Today the original staff has tripled in size, and the organization has become a leader in local, regional, and national worker co-op movements.

Communication Workers of America (CWA) and the Pacific Media Guild represent Design Action Collective (DAC) in Oakland, California, which offers print and electronic design services for strategic communication (https://designaction.org). They are a diverse, multilingual, 11-person shop that provides graphic design and visual communications to clients. In Denver, Colorado, CWA Local 7777 has been a principal in the worker-owned Union Taxi Co-op, formed in 2009 after much protesting and lobbying as well as formidable resistance from existing cab companies (Palmer, 2015; Ji, 2014). In 2015, more than 1,000 drivers joined CWA Local 7777 to set up Green Taxi, a second worker-owned company supporting Uber and other drivers in Denver's tightly controlled taxi industry. Subsequently, both taxi companies ran into difficult competition from gig economy rideshare programs and, even with union help, were unable to address state regulations related to decent wages and benefits of the industry. When the Covid pandemic struck, both withdrew from the union and are much reduced in size (Bolton, 2020).

Working Systems, a company that writes software to support labor unions across the United States, converted to a union co-op in 2019. The buyout committee included one of the two CWA shop stewards, and the company is now represented by CWA.

In recent years, the American Federation of Labor – Congress of Industrial Organizations (AFL-CIO) has shown interest in alternatives to traditional workplace organizing, as demonstrated by staff participation in the Union Co-op Council of USFWC and 1worker:1vote. The AFL-CIO also supports Worker Centers (local non-profits around the country that organize and support the unemployed and unorganized), which have engaged in the worker co-op model as a strategy for empowerment and equity.

This is just a partial list of support organizations and labor unions that are involved in worker co-op development in the 21st century, organizing to make inroads into a more democratic and equitable economy.

Tools for Union Co-op Collaboration

In addition to the many organizations mentioned above, a number of crucial and successful organizations and technical assistance providers have developed training manuals that support union co-op collaboration, which represents another significant strengthening of the Union Co-op movement in recent years.

The US Federation of Worker Co-ops and its non-profit arm Democracy at Work Institute have a wealth of online materials and resources that can be used in general worker co-op development. Membership in USFWC, which is based on a sliding fee scale, makes these materials readily available. Information on planning, enterprise incorporation and organizational by-laws, democratic decision-making, conflict resolution, feasibility studies, financial projections, funding, and marketing strategies all can be found here and apply equally to union and non-union worker co-ops.

Co-op Ventures Worker Co-op, along with several other Canadian institutions and the Ohio Employee Ownership Center, offers a set of four manuals entitled *A Co-operative Solution to the Job Crisis: Worker Co-op Buy-Out Guide* (Co-op Ventures Worker Co-op, 2009). Volume 1 addresses co-op basics of union-led buy-outs of existing enterprises; volume 2 includes a checklist; volume 3 lists steps; and volume 4 discusses markers of success.

Co-op Cincy provides a number of documents useful for unions working on co-ops. *The Worker Owner Workbook* (https://coopcincy.org/resources) discusses the co-op and labor movements, the Mondragon network of cooperatives in Spain, business financials, conflict management, and team building skills. *Union Co-ops: Exploring the Potential* addresses how to form a planning team and how to undertake a business feasibility study. *The Union Co-op Model: Sustainable Jobs, Sustainable Communities* is the 2012 elaboration of the 2009 Mondragon/United Steelworkers Collaboration, including an explanation of collective bargaining agreements in worker co-ops.

In order to assist worker co-op developers who are working in a union environment as well as union members themselves, in 2021 the Union Co-ops Council of USFWC developed a statement of *Principles and Guidelines for Co-op Developers in Union Environments* (Union Co-ops Council of USFWC, 2021). This document informs worker co-op development consultants who often are uninformed about and inexperienced with unions and helps them avoid unnecessary friction, and work productively with union staff and rank-and-file members.

In 2021, the Community and Worker Ownership Project (CWOP) of the City University of New York School for Labor & Urban Studies published *A Union Toolkit for Cooperative Solutions*, which describes seven case studies of unions involved in co-ops around the US and identifies ways unions can support development in union co-ops.

In addition to these tools, a number of technical assistance consultants and funders (grantors, lenders, and investors) are involved in supporting mutual union worker co-op work.

Toward Worker Control

Organized labor in the United States continues to play a unique and crucial role in progressive politics and in the economy, despite the beating it has taken from the political and corporate sectors since the 1970s. For low- and moderate-income workers and the unemployed, few if any other movements are as widespread, solvent, well organized, and well connected as labor unions and their affiliates. Worker understanding of how work can and should be organized to be most productive and rewarding has for a while not been considered a strategic arena for the labor movement. But the groundwork that labor has laid over centuries to improve work processes can help worker co-ops avoid reinventing the wheel for managing work relationships and influencing industry practices. Stimulated by the economic recession and the attack on labor unions, labor is singularly positioned to devise and promote new strategies for overcoming capital's grip on the economy.

But labor has been weakened and understands the need to employ new methods of organizing. Worker co-ops represent one such strategy to help regain control of ownership and management. There is increasingly clear evidence that uncontrolled capitalism is badly damaging the planet, causing wide disparities in wealth, health, and democratic government, and has become ineffective in creating good jobs in the changing economy. Labor must think deeply about alternative economic strategies to solve these persistent problems. Complicity with capital has not been a fruitful strategy. A much better ally is the worker co-op sector.

Workers around the world, beginning with industrialization in the late 1700s and continuing to this day, have struggled to take control of their workplaces in all kinds of historical situations, under different political systems, and through a range of political and economic crises. They have done this without benefit of historical knowledge of the efforts of others or of socialist consciousness. This appears to be an "inherent tendency" of rank-and-file workers, one of the great "underreported stories" of the past two centuries (Azzellini, 2015, pp.1-4). Worker ownership and management of enterprise resonates with important human values of self-reliance, opportunity, upward mobility, local responsibility, community solidarity, ownership, competitive business practices, and private enterprise, productivity, efficiency, and accountability.

Lower and middle income workers (that is, most people of color, women, and immigrants) constitute an expanding social base for these changes. Thirty percent of the US workforce are now independently contracted workers (Kalita, 2021). Many don't want to be gig workers for the rest of their working lives, and instead regard themselves as independent actors and entrepreneurs (Lim et al., 2019). They think they deserve better and imagine themselves as owners and managers. The cooperative business model can be a vehicle for them to achieve the agency they desire via self-employment and the camaraderie and power of being in a business together. As John Curl observes, "Once considered marginal, worker co-ops are now looked at by many in the international community as central to the hopes of economic progress in numerous communities round the world" (Curl, 2009, pp.90, 254). When linked to unionization, efficacy and solidarity are magnified.

Given this emerging reality, the Union Co-op Model can facilitate the transition to a more equitable and democratic economy in the US.

End-notes

[1] In the US, producer co-ops are comprised of business owners (such as farm owners, not farm employees) who aggregate in order to purchase supplies or market their products, etc. Members of worker co-ops are the workers themselves who are also the business owners. At times, these distinctions can be murky: producers work and workers produce. As an example, in Britain, worker co-ops were traditionally known as producer cooperatives.

[2] The Western Worker Co-op Conference and the Eastern Conference for Workplace Democracy preceded USFWC and continues to function. In 1994, the Network of Bay Area Worker Co-ops was founded in the San Francisco area.

Glossary and Abbreviations

Consumer co-op   A collectively owned enterprise in which the consumers of products on offer are the members and owners.
ESOP   Employee Stock Ownership Plan; a form of worker ownership that is less democratic than worker co-ops.
Hybrid co-op   A collectively owned enterprise with several classes of members such consumers, producers, workers; also known as multi-stakeholder co-ops.
Producer co-op A collectively owned enterprise in which the owners of member businesses are the members and owners.
Worker co-op   A collectively owned enterprise in which the workers are the members and owners; in Britain, worker co-ops are sometimes called producer co-ops.

1:1 1worker1vote; non-profit in Washington, DC.
AFL-CIO   American Federation of Labor-Congress of Industrial Organizations; national labor organization in the US.
CBA   collective bargaining agreement; operating procedures negotiated between workers and management.
CEDC   Community and Economic Development Clinic at the University of New York School of Law.
CHCA   Cooperative Home Care Associates; worker co-op in the Bronx, NY.
CICOPA   International Organization of Industrial, Artisanal, and Service Producers' Co-ops.
CUCI   Cincinnati Union Co-op Initiation; now Co-op Cincy.
CWA   Communication Workers of America.
CWOP Community and Worker Ownership Project of the City University of New York School for Labor and Urban Studies.
DAC   Design Action Collective in the San Francisco Bay Area of California.
DAWI   Democracy at Work Institute; non-profit research affiliate of US Federation of Worker Co-ops; in Oakland, California.
IBEW   International Brotherhood of Electrical Workers.
KOL   Knights of Labor.
LUCI   Los Angeles Union Co-op Initiative.
MINA   Mondragon International North America.
OEOC Ohio Employee Ownership Center at Kent State University in Ohio.
SEIU   Service Employees International Union.
UE United Electrical Union.
UFCW   United Food and Commercial Workers Union.
USFWC US Federation of Worker Co-ops.
USW   United Steelworkers Union.

References

1worker 1vote (2021). http://1worker1vote.org/
Azzellini, D. (ed.) (2015). *An Alternative Labour History: Worker Control and Workplace Democracy*. London: Zed Books.
Bolton, L. (2020). *Stories from the Organizing Front: Denver, Colorado's Union Taxi & Green Taxi Union Co-ops*. 1worker:1vote. http://1worker1vote.org/stories-from-the-organizing-front-denver-colorados-union-taxi-green-taxi-union-coops/.
Cincinnati Union Co-op Initiative (*n.d.*). *Worker-Owner Workbook: A Guide to Embracing the Worker-Owner Culture*. Cincinnati, Ohio: Co-op Cincy.

Collective Copies (2021). *Collective Copies History*. https://www.ueunion.org/ue-policy/build-union-co-ops.

Committee on Small Business (2021, September 9). *Committee Advances $25 Billion in Funding for Small Businesses* [Press release]. https://smallbusiness.house.gov/news/documentsingle.aspx?DocumentID=3930.

Cooper, C. (2015). *What Is a Union Worker Co-op?* 1worker:1vote. http://1worker1vote.org/what-is-a-union-worker-cooperative/.

Co-op Ventures Worker Co-op (2009). *A Cooperative Solution to the Job Crisis: Worker Co-op Buy-out Guide Volumes 1-4.* Calgary, Alberta: Canadian Worker Co-op Federation.

Cowie, J. (2010). *Stayin' Alive: The 1970s & the Last Days of the Working Class.* New York, NY: The New Press.

CUNY CED (2013). *'Clean and Green' Industrial Laundry Comes to Pittsburgh as a Worker Co-op.* Beaver County Blue. https://beavercountyblue.org/2013/05/19/clean-and-green-industrial-laundry-comes-to-pittsburgh-as-as-worker-cooperative/.

Curl, J. (2009). *For All the People: Uncovering the Hidden History of Cooperation, Cooperative Movements & Communalism in America.* Oakland, CA: PM Press.

Design Action Collective (2021). *About Design Action Collective.* https://www.ueunion.org/ue-policy/build-union-co-ops.

Elliott, L. (2021, August 25). The pandemic-induced global slump is just part of a 20-year financial crisis. *The Guardian.*

Flanders, L. (2012). Worker ownership for the 21st century? *The Nation.* http://www.thenation.com/article/worker-ownership-21st-century/.

Geoghegan, T. (2014). *Only One Thing Can Save Us: Why America Needs a New Kind of Labor Movement.* New York, NY: The New Press.

Goodman, A. (2013). *Chicago Workers Open New Cooperatively Owned Factory Five Years After Republic Windows Occupation.* Democracy Now. http://www.democracynow.org/2013/5/9/chicago_workers_open_new_cooperativeowned.

Gordon Nembhard, J. (2014). *Collective Courage: A History of African American Cooperative Economic Thought & Practice.* University Park, PA: Pennsylvania State University Press.

Hanson Schlacter, L. (2017). Stronger together? The USW-Mondragon Union Co-op Model. *Sage Labor Studies Journal.* https://journals.sagepub.com/doi/abs/10.1177/0160449X17696989?journalCode=lsja.

Hoyer, M. (2015). *The Power of Collaboration: Labor Unions & Worker Co-ops in the US.* Unpublished manuscript. ICA/ILO Conference, Antalya, Turkey.

Hoyer, M., Ryder, L., Adams, F., Curl, J. & Groban Olson, D. (2011). The role of unions in worker co-op development. *Grassroots Economic Organizing.* http://geo.coop/node/630.

International Labor Office (2013). Trade unions & worker cooperatives: Where are we at?, *International Journal of Labor Research,* Vol. 5, Issue 2.

Ji, M. (2014). Denver's immigrant taxi drivers build unionized workers co-op. *Labor Notes,* Oct 30, 2015. http://www.labornotes.org/blogs/2014/10/denvers-immigrant-taxi-drivers-build-unionized-workers-co-op.

Kalita, S.M. (2021). The rise of the independent worker: Why everyone wants to work in the gig economy now. *Fortune.* https://fortune.com/2021/04/21/gig-workers-covid-independent-contractors-remote-work-c-suite-executives/.

Keshner, A. (2020). *Strikes Are 275% Up in Two Years, Even Though Labor Union Membership Is Down—Why More Workers Are Taking a Stand.* MarketWatch. https://www.marketwatch.com/story/strikes-are-up-but-union-membership-is-down-and-that-could-be-a-good-sign-for-the-economy-2020-02-13.

Leiken, S. (2005). *The Practical Utopians: American Workers & the Cooperative Movement in the Gilded Age.* Detroit, MI: Wayne State University Press.

Lim, K, Miller, A., Risch, M. & Wilking, E. (2019). *Independent Contractors in the U.S: New Trends from 15 Years of Administrative Tax Data.* US Internal Revenue Service.

Logue, J. (2005). *Productivity in Cooperatives & Worker-Owned Enterprises: Ownership & Participation Make a Difference.* Kent, OH: Ohio Employee Ownership Center at Kent State University. http://dept.kent.edu/oeoc/OEOCLibrary/Preprints/LogueYatesProductivityInCooperativesAndWorkerOwnedEnterprises2005.pdf.

Logue, J. & McIntyre, B. (n.d.) *Selling Your Business to Your Employees: Employee Stock Ownership Plans (ESOPs) & Employee-Owned Cooperatives.* Kent, Ohio: Ohio Employee Ownership Center at Kent State University.

Logue, J. & Yates, J. (2008). *The Evolution & Impact of Democratic Practice in Ohio Employee-Owned Companies Over 20 Years.* Kent, Ohio: Ohio Employee Ownership Center at Kent State University. Prepared for the Biennial Conference of the International Association for the Economics of Participation.

Lurie, R. & King Fitzsimons, B. (2021). *A Union Toolkit for Cooperative Solutions.* New York, NY: City University of New York School for Labor & Urban Studies.

National Labor Relations Board. (n.d.). *1935 Passage of the Wagner Act.* https://www.nlrb.gov/about-nlrb/who-we-are/our-history/1935-passage-of-the-wagner-act.

Ness, I. (ed.) (2014). *New Forms of Worker Organization: The Syndicalist & Autonomist Restoration of Class-Struggle Unionism*. Oakland, CA: PM Press.

Nolan, H. (2020, October 7). A bunch of union organizers explain what's wrong with unions. *In These Times*.

Palmer, T. (2015). *TAXIS: Worker Cooperative Industry Research Series*. Oakland, CA: Democracy at Work Institute.

Peck, M.A. (2021). The pandemic changes everything: Hybrid stakeholder shared ownership models in the USA, starting with the union co-op movement. In J.Y Manley & P.B. Whyman (eds.), *The Preston Model and Community Wealth Building: Creating a Socio-Economic Democracy for the Future*. Routledge.

Pinto, S., Kerr, C. & Criscitiello, R. (2021). *Shifting Power, Meeting the Moment: Worker Ownership as a Strategic Tool for the Labor Movement*. New Brunswick, New Jersey: Rutgers School of Management & Labor Relations Institute for the Study of Employee Ownership & Profit Sharing.

Post, C. (2015, June 6). *The New Militant Minority*. Jacobin. *https://jacobin.com/2015/06/american-unions-labor-aronowitz*

PRNewswire (2013). *Laboral Kutxa & National Cooperative Bank to Partner*. https://www.prnewswire.com/news-releases/laboral-kutxa-the-mondragon-bank-and-national-cooperative-bank-ncb-to-partner-in-growing-domestic-worker-owned-cooperatives-222376341.html.

Prushinskaya, O. (2020). *Worker Co-ops Show Significant Growth in Latest Survey Data*. FiftybyFifty. https://www.fiftybyfifty.org/2020/02/worker-co-ops-show-significant-growth-in-latest-survey-data/.

Ryssdal, K. (Host) (2010, February 18). Man gives company to his employees. In *Marketplace*. Minnesota Public Radio. https://www.marketplace.org/2010/02/18/man-gives-company-his-employees/.

Shierholz, H. & Poydock, M. (2020). *Continued Surge in Strike Activity Signals Worker Dissatisfaction with Wage Growth*. Economic Policy Institute. https://www.epi.org/publication/continued-surge-in-strike-activity/.

Truthout (2013). *Can Unions & Cooperatives Join Forces? An Interview With United Steelworkers President Leo Gerard*. Truthout. http://www.truth-out.org/news/item/16418-can-unions-and-cooperatives-join-forces-an-interview-with-united-steelworkers-president-leo-gerard.

Union Co-ops Council of the US Federation of Worker Co-ops (2021). *Principles & Guidelines for Co-op Developers in Union Environments*. https://docs.google.com/document/d/1YDFQN5jLM1huro0FCrKAK5wYzqm9cZ2Z6GwG2Qua54M/edit#heading=h.4nlr66oriryy.

United Electrical (2019). *Build Union Co-ops*. https://www.ueunion.org/ue-policy/build-union-co-ops.

United Nations. (2012). *International Year of Cooperatives*. https://www.un.org/en/events/coopsyear/.

US Federation of Worker Co-ops (2021). *Public Policy & Advocacy*. https://www.usworker.coop/programs/advocacy/.

United Steelworkers (2015). *Worx Printing Cooperative Changing the Face of Customized T-Shirts*. https://www.usw.org/news/media-center/articles/2015/worx-printing-cooperative-changing-the-face-of-customized-t-shirts.

Weisman, J. (2021, September 13). In Social Policy bill, businesses find muck to like. They oppose it. *The New York Times*.

Whyte, W.F. & Whyte, K.K. (1991). *Making Mondragon*. Ithaca, New York: Cornell University Press.

Winant, G. (2021). *The Next Shift*. Cambridge, MA: Harvard University Press.

Witherell, R. (2013). An emerging solidarity: Worker cooperatives, unions & the new union cooperative model in the US. *International Journal of Labor Research*, Vol. 5, Issue 2.

Witherell, R. (2021). *Union 3.0: Worker Ownership & the Future of the Labor Movement*. https://owningabetterfuture.com/2020/08/02/union-3-0-worker-ownership-and-the-future-of-the-labor-movement/.

Witherell, R., Cooper, C. & Peck, M. (2012). *Sustainable Jobs, Sustainable Communities: The Union Co-op Model*. Ohio Employee Ownership Center. http://www.oeockent.org/download/cooperatives/sustainable-jobs-sustainable-communities.pdf.pdf.

Zoller, H. (2021). *Re-Imagining Localism and Food Justice: Co-op Cincy & the Union Cooperative Movement*. Frontiersin.org. https://www.frontiersin.org/articles/10.3389/fcomm.2021.686400/full.

CHAPTER 26

Worx Printing Cooperative:
A Union Worker Co-Op Case Example

Kevin O'Brien

Here's How Worx Works

Worx is a union, worker-cooperative printing and fulfilment shop based out of Worcester, Massachusetts. We offer high-quality — and beautiful! — merchandise using the most advanced direct-to-textile digital printing technology available on the market. All without exploitation.

Imagine that.

Every person at Worx is a member of the United Steelworkers Union — we share a mission underpinned by the Knights of Labor legacy and the renowned Mondragon-Steelworkers collaboration.

Our vision is prismatic, simple, and radical — an ethical, on-demand supply chain — which, as it turns out, isn't so radical at all when we look at America's history. Not only do we believe merchandise can champion the message — art can exact social change! — but merchandise can also be the message. Worx makes merchandise that is riotous, righteous, ethical and outstanding.

And we recognize that one of the greatest lies the Devil ever told is the idea that quality and quantity, or ethics and efficiency, are mutually exclusive.

Union co-ops (the platinum standard of ethical labor) believe: "Instead of one, many." The arc of justice — and a successful, sustainable business — is bent and created by the volume of people and cooperatives participating in the energy of the movement.

As for Worx? We have three key elements that support our vision and future:

- **On-demand offerings:** Worx's print-shop echoes the needs and visions of the progressive left. Our ability to offer merchandise without risk to non-professional merchandisers — incredible orgs and activists like AOC, Elizabeth Warren, Joe Biden, the Green Party, Malala, DNC, you get the idea — means their vision isn't compromised when trying to spread the good word. It's strengthened. We only print if a product is ordered and paid for, meaning every cent goes back into the movement, not into some dusty basement or predatory overseas manufacturer.

- **A collaborative ecosystem:** Worx's partnership with the United Steelworkers Union, coupled with their network of cooperative technical assistance agencies, is the backbone of our success and the labor revolution. This is not an exhaustive list of all our partners, but a vital one:
  - The Boston Center for Community Ownership (training, education, conversion strategies).
  - The Cooperative Fund of the Northeast (lends money to burgeoning co-ops).
  - Worcester Roots (community-focused environmental, social and economic-justice co-op).
  - USFWC Union Co-op Council (national grassroots membership organization for worker cooperatives).
  - Co-op Cincy (supporting family-sustaining jobs and providing ownership opportunities to people from historically marginalized groups).
  - Ohio Employee Ownership Center (OEOC)-Kent State (provides guidance to business owners considering the two major forms of employee-ownership: employee stock ownership plans (ESOPs) and worker-owned cooperatives.
  - 1worker1vote (a national non-profit designing and fostering hybrid worker-owner empowerment models).

  Every one of these organizations toggles between teacher, leader, funder, and champion offering support and guidance to one another. And in turn, they're also Worx clients — we provide them ethical, beautiful products — and this means the chain is never broken. Every interaction strengthens our shared vision of employee dignity and a healthy bottom line.

- **Worx + F.i.i.:** F.i.i. is the leading supplier of American-made and union-made merchandise — they help companies with ecommerce shops, direct mailings and events, and Worx supplies the on-demand merchandise. When we first started out, we figured we'd work with small entities with a shared mindset, but F.i.i. wanted to bring Worx's story to a nationwide audience and help us coalesce a movement. This mutualism is part and parcel of Worx's lifeblood and where we're headed next.

But in all honesty? It wasn't easy to get here. Like every good story, there was a bit of drama and a lot of lessons learned.

The Guts of Worx

In 2002, Kevin O'Brien worked with Worx's predecessor SweatX — a brand-new garment business in Los Angeles — alongside ice-cream activist Ben Cohen (of the famed Ben & Jerry's brand) who, through the Hot Fudge Social Venture Fund, invested $2 million. This marked the first attempt at a modern union co-op in direct response to the ravages of globalization.

Kevin spent the bulk of two years fighting to keep SweatX alive amid an ugly, exhausting bloodbath of mismanagement — bank accounts being raided, water being shut off, stealing from Peter to pay Paul. And in April 2004, just as the flame was fluttering out and the decision had been made to close the doors, the US Federation of Worker Cooperatives emerged, ushering in a new beginning. And while SweatX was decidedly plagued by exploitative pressures and bad business decisions, the real reason it failed was that there was never official ownership by the cooperative — and that's because the collaborative infrastructure didn't exist.

SweatX was ahead of its time, but it started too big and aimed to be a national brand overnight. It was a fledgling organization, and it was being asked to run a marathon before it could even walk.

In fact, we believe that SweatX helped lead to the development of the USFWC, and the building out of its amazing network — from attorneys, accountants, and technical-assistance providers with business education strategies to connections with the other co-ops — everything that didn't exist when SweatX tried to do it on its own.

A decade later, Kevin took the hard-learned lessons from the closure of SweatX, leveraged the groundswell of the union-cooperative ecosystem, and co-founded Worx.

Where Worx & Work is Headed

What we're doing at Worx is the same business model, but 20 years later. These days we're working without startup capital and Ben's infusion of $2 million. We're self-funded and that's because of the 800-pound gorilla in the room the movement doesn't often talk about — the infrastructure we're all leaning on.

The truth is, as soon as you turn on the light, many businesses are moths to the ethical flame. Everyone wants to be associated with a high bar of manufacturing. It's very difficult to have a clean supply chain and progressive organizations understand that they're co-branding with the merchandise provider they choose. And when you're an AOC or a Malala, when everything you're about is fighting exploitation, union cooperatives — such as Worx — are the only way to walk the walk.

And it's going to get so much bigger than t-shirts.

If Worx can maintain and increase its service offerings, we have a legitimate chance to help redefine the national dialogue on worker ownership simply by being a successful provider of services. Together with F.i.i., we can extend our collective supply chains and build an even richer ecosystem with artists, agency partners, and buyers themselves to create a multi-stakeholder platform: We imagine a future where those groups can be organized into artist, agency/influencer and buyer cooperatives in their own right while creating a virtuous cycle merchandise offering.

So many great organizations are underfunded and can't have their own store, but by splitting the share of money — by creating art, by buying something, by spreading the good word about the cause, all actions will directly impact the very thing the merchandise is aiming to solve or comment on to begin with. (And all the merchandise is made in our union worker-owned co-op, of course!)

People view the world through the lens of "me" and "I," and we need to get to "we" and "us"! There's a future where everyone is doing what they love, and they're making money doing it. It's an ethical merchandise empire and we're building it hat by hat, worker by worker.

CHAPTER 27

Placing Where We Place Value: Cooperatives, Cultural Norms & Challenges Co-ops Face in the US

Caitlin Gianniny

People over Profit

When you go to a bar in the Basque Country — an autonomous community in Spain with a thriving cooperative economy — groups of friends often put the same amount of money upfront into "the pot," known as *bote*.[1] One person is in charge of the pot of money and placing orders for the group that night. So, unless it's your turn, you don't have to worry about pulling out money or keeping track of who got what.

The group has a bar that they meet at, but after one drink and *pintxo*,[2] pronounced "pinch-oh" (small appetizers similar to tapas; Escobar, 2015), you move on to the next bar, and so on – one drink and pintxo per bar – until ready to call it a night. If there is money left over, the change is kept in the pot for next week, since friends typically meet up weekly and repeat the same route of bars.

As an American, I marveled at how efficient this was in comparison to all of the times I had sat at a table while we passed around the receipt laboriously divvying up each person's tab. Or the times I had been out and suddenly had folks announce "Let's just split the bill" even though I had carefully ordered only what I could afford. Pooling money upfront means you always know what you are going to pay so there are no surprises, but there is also no nit-picking about exact amounts — it is OK if one drink costs a little more than another.

There is also shared responsibility. The role of who orders and pays rotates every week, so folks get to relax and enjoy visiting most of the time. By moving from bar to bar, you are spreading business around to multiple local establishments and are more likely to run into other people as you go, so there is a component of greater economic and social connectedness, beyond the group as well (Hess, 2018).

Folks familiar with the worker cooperative model can probably tell why I love this example for thinking about the cultural underpinnings of co-ops — there is essentially a buy-in, a sharing of resources, responsibilities that rotate so that labor is shared amongst the group, and close ties to the local culture and economy — sound familiar? At a very stripped-down level, these are the basic principles of how a cooperative operates, embedded into the social fabric of how people spend time with their community.

This tradition of meeting up with a group of friends and moving around to the local bars for drinks is called *Poteo* or *Txikiteo*[3] or *Pinxto-Pote* when bars offer happy-hour specials (San Sebastian Tourism, *n.d.*). The groups that meet up weekly are called *kuadrillas* (Spanish, cuadrilla), a social formation that is the cornerstone for social life in the Basque Country. Kuadrillas are groups of friends usually from the same town or neighborhood, around the same age, and often the same gender identity (Hess, 2018).[4] While on the surface it could seem like kuadrillas are similar to any tight-knit group of friends or just another word for "clique" (and they can be insular, much like a clique) they were actually created in reaction to societal changes spurred by capitalism.

Their roots trace back specifically to the transition from rural farming communities or *baserris* (farmstead) to urban environments, as the Basque Country started to become industrialized with the development of capitalism in the mid-19th century (Zallo & Ayuso, 2009, p.12). They were created to strengthen communal bonds and reciprocal relationships that were lost as people moved to larger towns or cities for jobs. According to an analysis by Goicoechea (1984), kuadrillas are an informal group that play an interstitial role somewhere in between family and friend groups from work or school, that help to connect people to their local community and culture.

Despite making other groups of friends, people will only have one kuadrilla, and typically are part of that group for their lifetime. Members of the kuadrilla primarily interact around social activities like poteo and are usually only close friends with a few members of the group. But despite the group connection not being very intimate, they will take significant action to support each other by doing things like lending cars or money, visiting each in the hospital or jail. Kuadrillas also became an important means for political organizing and cultural preservation when the Basque language and culture were banned under the Franco regime (Hess, 2018).

My personal experiences match the dynamics Goicoechea described.[5] There is an amazing willingness from people within a kuadrilla to support other members of the group. When I got a job teaching English in the Basque Country, members of my mom's kuadrilla insisted that I stay with them. They took me in and treated me like family for the length of my stay. We have returned the favor and hosted their daughters in the US while they studied English. It's just …what you do.

Sharing of financial cost and labor also happens for larger group outings, like going to *sargodotegis* (cider houses). The kuadrilla that adopted me while I was living in Mondragón (*via* a niece of one of my mom's kuadrilla members) pulled straws for who would coordinate logistics for the cider house that year. That person then calculated the cost for a bus, the meal, and drinks afterwards, and then told us how much each person's share was and we transferred our portion of the cost to their bank account. They took care of all of the bookings and told us when and where to be for the bus. The rest of us just showed up for the cider and delicious meal of *tortilla de bacalao* (quiche with cod), cod in garlic sauce, steak, cheese, *membrillo* (quince paste) and walnuts. I was again in awe of the efficiency and that no one person was stuck shouldering the cost when making bookings.

I tend to think of kuadrillas as behaving more like we expect family to in an American context (only a little more organized). This is not to say that there aren't groups of friends who interact in this way in the US. I have managed to find some, but my experience more broadly has been that friends tend to be a more loose-knit collection of people from different times and places in my life, without as much cohesion or sense of responsibility. I know that my experience is also specific to growing up a white, cis, middle-class woman, in an urban environment, and moving between different urban centers in the Northeast during my adult life. There are undoubtedly differences based on class, race, and geography, as well as factors like being a first- or second-generation immigrant or part of a marginalized group that has formed tight-knit communities or networks of support that have an enormous impact on these kinds of experiences in the United States.[6]

Looking back at how kuadrillas laid a cultural framework for formal institutions, out of the informal grouping of kuadrillas came traditions like *poteo* and more formal groups like *txokos* (gastronomic societies), private dinner clubs where members have access to a shared kitchen and can host large group dinners (see Prichep, 2012, for a brief history). I would argue that worker cooperatives are another formal group structure that overlays on these cultural traditions very clearly in a way that laid strong cultural foundations for the success of the Mondragon Cooperatives in the Basque Country.[7]

Put more succinctly, these are examples of structures that prioritize people and human connection and cooperatives are a formal structure for organizations that operate on those principles. They point towards a practical path for how you can create functioning businesses and economies that are people-centered — those that strengthen connections to other people and to the local context; where the goal is success/financial stability of all group members — rather than profit-centered, where the only measure of success is financial gains, especially for the people at the top of the existing socio-economic hierarchy.

That foundational belief comes through in the writing of Father Arizmendiarrieta, a Catholic priest and founder of Mondragon Corporation, who was strongly influenced by the Catholic Church's social doctrine. He wrote about the philosophy behind his approach to social transformation (as cited by Clamp, 2003, p.7):

> The key to our future is not the revolution or conservatism, it is the noble calling to the demands of the time, by virtue of the ample educational action and the process of association that integrates men as brothers in whichever field of application.
>
> The people and communities just like the flowers and other species live and triumph not alone but in groups.

This philosophy stands in stark contrast to the dominant cultural philosophy of individualism in the US that goes hand-in-hand with capitalism, characterized by private ownership and distribution of goods determined by competition in a free market (Merriam-Webster). This is a foundational belief system that encourages social isolation rather than connection, while couching it the language of "self-actualization" (Illing, 2018).[8]

According to James and Grace Lee Boggs in their book, *Revolution Evolution in the 20th Century*, the US was founded on the fundamental contradiction of technological and economic overdevelopment and human and political underdevelopment. Which is to say, that there is a core belief that technology and economics will resolve crises, *versus* focusing on the human and social and as a way to resolve crises in our country. They argue that Americans have been "profoundly damaged by a culture that for over 200 years has systematically pursued economic development at the expense of communities and of millions of people at home and abroad" and our challenge is to grapple with that contradiction in order to evolve (Boggs & Boggs, 2008, p.*ix*).

We have all witnessed throughout the Covid-19 pandemic how detached our current financial and economic systems are from the well-being of people in our country. As millions of people lost jobs, and faced housing and food insecurity due to the pandemic, the stock market soared. We have wrongly conflated "the economy" (or more specifically, capital markets) succeeding with the security and well-being of people. What if we were able to redefine economic success to mean that those needs were met?

There is undoubtedly a reciprocal influence between institutional structure and culture, and debates about which one shapes the other, but I think focusing on one *versus* the other is less important than recognizing that when a culture and institutional structures align they can be mutually reinforcing, and when they are at odds they create friction.

In contrast to the example above, worker cooperatives intertwine personal needs with that of our workplaces and build the understanding that one cannot thrive without the other; the co-op cannot succeed if we as individuals are not doing well and *vice versa*. By having the people who are impacted as the decision-makers, co-ops structurally incentivize more humane and thoughtful decision-making.

But cooperative values are at odds with the dominant culture and institutional logic of our economic system of capitalism in the US. So by building organizations that reinforce cooperative values, we can work towards creating the culture we want, but in order to create cooperatives in the US we have to contend with a lot of structural and material barriers (more on this below).

Jason Spicer's analysis, *Exceptionally un-American? Why co-operative enterprises struggle in the United States, but scale elsewhere* (2018, p.268), puts a finer point on this, stating that co-ops rely on social solidarity or use-value (providing employment or services) as a motivation instead of profit-maximization for growth, and this is at odds with the logic of the government of the United States.[9]

Spicer's extensive review of the barriers facing US co-ops points to the legacy of race-based slavery and federalism as presenting unique challenges to the growth of the cooperative movement in the US, finding that:

> Co-ops are often formed in response to marginalization or a crisis. Historically, co-ops in the US were developed by socially or ethnically homogenous groups with a shared experience of marginalization, such as "Finns, Jews, Mormons, African Americans." (p.268)

The US faces some unique challenges when mobilizing groups *via* social solidarity because of greater social diversity and the structure of industry, which may act to divide the labor force.

Both historically and currently, the legacy of race-based slavery in the United States posed challenges to cooperative development. Since cooperatives rely on social solidarity for growing or achieving scale, on-going race-based divisions pose a challenge for building and maintaining those bonds, when institutional racism still creates real material divides today.

Most importantly, cooperatives need a supportive political environment in order to grow and achieve scale, which has not happened in the US. The institutional logic of co-ops (solidarity or use-value based) is at odds with the profit-maximization logic that the US government operates in accordance with. Since governments actively shape the economy and markets, the US context is relatively more hostile to cooperatives.

Cooperatives in the US also face another challenge in that they are a kind of "hybrid" field — they operate both as businesses in the economy/market and a social movement within civil society, whereas joint-stock corporations as competitors have no need to navigate this balance, since they operate almost entirely in the economy/market. Furthermore, in a federalist system – where states share governing powers with the federal government – changes need to happen from the local to national level, with varying needs based on the region, so Spicer notes that this creates a coordination cost that is not faced by cooperative advocates in other countries.

> Cooperatives thus face a unique coordination problem in the US: to create a truly "national" cooperative ecosystem, they must leverage their civil society-based solidarity to "scale up" like a social movement, from "local" problems to national scale, and achieve affirmative access to national economic policy tools. But as enterprises, they also must also coordinate a 50-state strategy to achieve harmonized cooperative state law, and reduce the costs of operating across state lines. (p.288)

I am not a policy expert on cooperatives, so I cannot speak to exactly what large-scale policy changes should look like, but I can speak to the challenges and opportunities that we saw in founding the cooperative I co-founded, Samara Collective, and in my experience personally as an employee-owner.

What's "Easy" is Another Way of Saying "That's What We Incentivize"
The policy structures that we create can either support or inhibit growth.

Samara's startup story
In 2018, I co-founded Samara Collective,[10] a worker-owned cooperative, with three other women to provide strategic communications support to mission-aligned organizations. We named our co-op Samara after the papery winged seed of maple trees, which are carried far and wide by the wind. We primarily work with advocacy organizations such as community-led organizations, non-profits, coalitions, labor unions, other cooperatives, and some small businesses. I am continually convinced, the more I learn, that worker co-ops are an extremely smart business model that could serve many more people in the US who do not have the workplace protections or culture that they deserve.

Before getting started, we spent a lot of time mapping out what we wanted to do (and not do) professionally, and the values and practices we wanted in a workplace. In keeping with Jason Spicer's observation that co-ops are often formed in response to crisis, one of the key defining factors for us was that we had worked in too many organizations that were doing advocacy or social justice work in some way, but where the external values and campaigns did not match how employees were being treated — whether that be sexual harassment, race-based prejudice, wage theft or abuse of power in any number of ways from those who held leadership positions. So, making sure that our internal practices and external work on those issues matched became a cornerstone for what we envisioned creating. We also wanted to create a space that centered traditionally marginalized groups, especially BIPOC, women, and queer folks.

As two women who identified as white and two women who identified as Black, and a majority queer group starting Samara, we agreed that the culture of white, male-dominant organizations is something that we have all experienced and did not want to replicate. We have intentionally tried to create a workplace that moves away from many of the ways that white supremacy shows up such as withholding information, unwillingness to confront problems, and false urgency. We try to embody those values through transparent management, recognizing that conflicts will always happen and having healthy ways to address them, speaking up when we need support, and by stopping ourselves and recognizing when we need to slow down. We all have to work to train ourselves out of ingrained habits, and it is a constant process, but I know as founders we all glow every time we hear a newer staff member comment on how special Samara is as a place to work, pointing towards the culture we have cultivated.

Over the past few very difficult years, it has proven to be the safety net and solid foundation for us that we hoped it would be in creating a sustainable means of doing the work that we love. We have grown from the initial four founders to a staff of 10 employees — eight full-time, seven of whom are co-op members. But it has not been easy. There is a lot we have had to learn about just running a business (any kind of business), but there have also been some challenges that are unique to running the organization as a worker-owned cooperative.

We also walked into the process with a lot of resources and access to support. One of the other co-founders had previously worked at a worker-cooperative and knew folks in the community. And I had grown up learning a lot about cooperatives just by being around my mom's work, volunteering at one of the Eastern Workplace Democracy conferences when I was in college, and then living and working in the Basque Country with lots of folks who worked in the co-ops there. But despite all of those advantages, it still took a lot of time, running around, and headaches to get the business set up.

Start-up challenges

One of the first big hurdles we encountered was simply incorporating the business in the state where we lived. Massachusetts is actually a relatively more co-op friendly state, because there is a statute that allows businesses to formally incorporate as a worker-owned cooperative known legally as an Employee Cooperative Corporation (ECC) (General Laws of Massachusetts, *n.d.*).

Stepping back, there are a few bigger picture things to mention about incorporation and taxes for worker cooperatives that set the stage:

- Businesses are registered with the IRS at the **federal level for taxes. Incorporation happens at the state level** through the Secretary of State's office. This is true for all businesses. It's important to say this up front, because part of what is confusing is that the two systems (federal *versus* state law) sometimes don't align clearly for co-ops.

- **State Level – Incorporation:** Regulations for worker cooperative business formation vary widely by state, so in some states you can incorporate as an ECC, but in states where there is no cooperative statute (or sometimes due to other legal considerations), cooperatives legally incorporate as LLCs, C-Corps, or S-Corps, but they must include cooperative governance in their by-laws to be classified as such for tax purposes.

- **Federal Level – Taxes:** The US has no federal worker cooperative policy nor legislative framework. So, when you go to register with the IRS for a business tax ID (EIN), unless you're forming an agricultural cooperative, there's no option to select on the form for "co-op." Since we were planning to incorporate in MA as an ECC, we chose C-Corp which is a general for-profit corporation.

However you choose to incorporate, as long as your by-laws meet the requirements for cooperative governance, when filing your taxes you ask the IRS to tax you as a worker cooperative under Subchapter-T — which governs *Cooperatives and their Patrons* This ensures that worker/owners aren't taxed twice for the same income.[11]

Yes, you read that correctly — there is no co-op option when you are applying for your business tax ID from the IRS, but there is a section of the tax code on taxing cooperatives (personal income taxes as an employee-owner are similarly confusing. More on that later).

- **Business Set-up Steps:** There is also some sequencing to setting up a business to keep in mind (that we didn't know about in advance). The quick and dirty is that you need:

  o A business tax ID known as an Employer Identification Number (EIN) from the IRS before you can incorporate.[12]

  o To talk to a lawyer to draft your articles of incorporation (sometimes known as certification of formation or a charter).

  o To incorporate with the Secretary of State's Office before you can open a bank account.

  o A bank account before you can set up payroll.

There are a lot of ducks to get in a row before you are able to begin working and pay yourselves and it is important to know that there is likely a multi-month runway where all of this is happening before you can get the business up and running.

Okay, so back to where we were, incorporating in Massachusetts. We were excited that we lived in one of the few states that has a cooperative statute, and figured that would make things way easier. We tried to look online for information and found the portal for business registration on the Secretary of State's website and were like "Great, we can do this online" and then noticed that it said you have to come in person in order to register a cooperative (so, barrier #1).

One of the other women I was working with went in person to the office, not once but twice trying to determine the documentation and forms we needed. The staff she talked to did not truly understand how to best advise her, and sent her to a different office where she was told to go back to the first office. They admitted to never having done the paperwork for a co-op. In fact, only one person in the office was really familiar with cooperative incorporation. She managed to get some forms and instructions emailed to her with some instructions. After two physical visits, she handed the duties off to me to try a third time (barrier #2).

She sent me an email with the info she had and what we needed. I read the instructions and tried to follow the steps they laid out. I noticed that it looked like the form in the email was different from what was on the Secretary of State's website, but figured the forms on the website were probably correct ones. When I got to the office and spoke to the person who knew co-ops, I found out that the form on the website was in fact the wrong form. Apparently there was an update to the statute that governs incorporation for all business types, except co-ops that are still governed by the old statute language and therefore use the old form — which isn't on the website (barrier #3).

So, I sat in the hallway with my laptop while I filled out the correct form and emailed it to them. They then had to race to review it, get it signed and stamped before the office closed for the day.

Is your head spinning yet? Because ours certainly were. We figured that having a cooperative statute would make things smoother, but it was clear that most of the staff were very unfamiliar with the process, that legislators didn't prioritize co-ops when implementing changes, and the Secretary of State's office had the information so buried and inaccessible on their website that it took three visits to their office to complete the right paperwork instead of being able to fill out forms through the online portal like all other businesses would.

After going through all of that, if I could do anything differently, it would have been to do some initial reading on our options and then talk to a CPA and a lawyer to help us decide what type of legal entity made the most sense for us before doing anything else. When we finally worked closely with a lawyer on our by-laws, he knew all of the weird quirks around incorporation (that the right form wasn't on the website, etc.) and would have made that whole process much smoother.

If the system doesn't work unless you happen to talk to the people who know its ins and outs, then by design it will disenfranchise minority and poor communities who are not already well connected. And despite facing far fewer barriers to entry than many folks who are looking to start co-ops, we were still wildly confused at times. The point is, you should not have to talk to someone with institutional knowledge to know that the wrong form is on the state government's website. All of those small barriers de-incentivize new potential cooperatives. It is the definition of a structural barrier.

There are similar issues when it comes to filing taxes as an individual employee-owner. When a co-op is profitable, co-op members take part in profit-sharing. These profits are called "patronage." The IRS has a 1099 form for cooperatives to report the profits they have paid out to members, the 1099-PATR. Cooperatives need to file 1099-PATRs with the IRS and send them out at the beginning of the year, like any other 1099s. Yet when you go to file personal income taxes, there is no line for reporting 1099-PATR income or ability to upload the form like you do with other tax documents. Because there is no place to simply report the income and the IRS does not provide clear guidance on how to report the income, co-op members have to use work-arounds to report the income on their 1040 or Schedule C (see Mayer, 2021, for details).[13] Personally, I have spent hours explaining this issue to CPAs I have worked with or trying to figure out how to file myself online, simply to report this income and make sure I am paying the right amount of tax on it. This year, the IRS requested more documentation, so I had to send a note and copy of my 1099-PATR in order to get my taxes processed. It really should not be that hard.

A few more notes on our experience finding lawyers/CPAs, etc.:

1. It can be tricky to find legal service providers or tax professionals who specialize in co-ops so it does take a little time to find the right providers. Start looking and talking to folks as soon as possible, even if you don't think you're ready. We learned so much in the course of those intake calls that would have taken us much longer to track down on our own.[14]

2. We did not have much money to start the business, so we tried to work with free or low-cost legal clinics, so if you are going that route know that you will have to wait longer for when they have availability for new clients.

If we want worker co-ops to scale as a movement and a business model that helps to empower workers and build community wealth, we need more accessible tools to create, grow, and sustain them. Because of these kinds of experiences, co-op development services are currently essential to the start-up of most new worker cooperatives.

Because of all of the roadblocks we encountered, Samara Collective has been partnering with a group of other worker cooperatives and cooperative developers, to create Launch.coop, an online platform for co-op entrepreneurs to get assistance in starting and growing worker co-ops in the US. We plan to leverage the available resources through developers to reach a broader audience, and remove the bottleneck created by the limited access to development services. The project is still in the planning and development phase, but you can visit us at Launch.coop to sign up for updates as we roll things out.

Opportunities for Improving Workplace Conditions

There have also been a lot of things we have learned about how employers can choose to prioritize covering costs for employees. We started covering 100% healthcare costs from the outset of the business. Because of the industry we work in and making strategic choices like working remotely, we were able to keep our overhead expenses low to get off the ground, but we also really prioritized healthcare as one of key business expenses, because we knew that affordable health coverage was one of our non-negotiables in terms of where to spend or cut.

When we had built up some financial reserves, we also started covering the full cost of the deductible for all full-time employees through a Health Reimbursement Arrangement (HRA). Turns out if employers want to they can create an 100% employer-sponsored fund for employees to cover the cost of their deductible or even additional healthcare expenses. I'd never known that was an option until we started researching it for Samara. One of the biggest things I have learned is just how much is left up to the discretion of employers.

In the US, typically regulations around sick time, pay, or health coverage really only give you floor on what the bare minimum requirement is, so much of creating policies that are actually livable or humane is left in the hands of business owners. So, by putting ownership in the hands of employees there is an amazing amount of power and discretion at our fingertips.

It can also be bewildering — since healthcare is offered by employers instead of through a national program in the United States, we have had countless moments where we are having to research things about health coverage and benefits and felt wildly in over our heads. None of us are experts in this, but because the regulations only give you a bare minimum, we are often having to just look around at other organizations' policies and practices for examples of what fair policies look like. Honestly, it can feel like a bit of a free for all (and something that in my opinion really shouldn't be determined at the employer-level …what do we know about healthcare? We're communications professionals, not health-care providers!)

It's a reminder that we are yet again operating with a lot of friction in relation to the larger institutional and cultural context in the US. Since most businesses operate on the logic of profit-maximization as the indicator of success, not the well-being of employees in conjunction with the business' financial performance, most of the time that discretion results in policies that aren't that great for employees, but are good for the finances of an organization. State minimums are also sometimes really the bare minimum, so we are often trying to write policies that go above what is legally required, but that can pose challenges since different states offer widely varying levels of assistance for programs, for example like parental leave. Given that, it can be hard to afford the policies that align with our values, because we have to base the policy on what the business can afford in states that offer the lowest amount of assistance.

Instead of trying to put a bandage on a broken system, as we are so often forced to do — to simply try and stop the bleeding — if you can get through all the hoops to create them, co-ops are a way of creating, at least internally to your organization, a more functional, equitable and democratic space to exist in and work from. That does not replace large-scale movements and organizing to build and shift power, but it can help to build life-rafts while we work towards larger scale change. And IF we can create ways to make co-ops a more accessible business model (right now there are still too many barriers), they could become a larger player in shifting those power dynamics and building a deeper understanding of democracy that could push along a culture shift — but we've got a lot of work to do to make that a reality.

People are not fundamentally narcissistic or selfish, but we do what is incentivized. So, when we remake the container, we remake the behavior.

What we incentivize is what we do.

End-notes

[1] "Bote" is short for "Bote de dinero" which translates to "pool of money" in Spanish. Bilbao dictionary provides a clear definition of how it is used in this context (Sp.): https://diccionario.bilbao.im/i/bote

[2] When possible I will introduce the Basque word for what I am talking about in italics. *Euskera* (Basque) language preservation is something that was hard fought to restore following its suppression under the Franco regime. It feels important to call things by Basque names as much as possible, although as a native English speaker and Spanish speaker during my time there, I will sometimes use Spanish terms as well. When noting a Spanish term I will identify it in parenthesis.

[3] This is a great Twitter thread on "txikiteo" culture (in Spanish): https://twitter.com/sonetska/status/1155536015295209472.

[4] Goicoechea (1984) also talks about how kuadrillas are always embedded within the class structure, since they are based on where you live – and your class determines where you can afford to live – they are often stratified along class lines. And obviously the idea that everyone can put in the same amount for pooling funds assumes that the group members have similar income levels that make that possible.

[5] I lived in the Basque Country and attended public school when I was 12 for a month and a half while my mom, Christina Clamp, conducted field research on the Mondragon Corporation, one of the most well-known examples of worker cooperatives in the world. She first did field research there in 1982 and was adopted by a kuadrilla while she was there. During college, I studied abroad in Barcelona and later returned to live in Mondragón (Arrasate) for eight months to teach English at a machine tool institute nearby. I am by no means an expert on Basque culture or trained as a sociologist or historian. What I offer here are pieces of my experience that I've found to be helpful touchpoints personally for guiding my thinking about what cultural practices and structures that are people-centered look like.

[6] My experiences in Spain were also that of a white, American woman with decent Spanish. Everyone was always giving me the benefit of the doubt and telling me "how great" I was doing with my Spanish. That is not what I heard from my friends who studied in Spain who were of Latin American descent. They frequently felt like they were dismissed or people acted like they couldn't understand their Spanish even though they'd been raised speaking Spanish. It was clear that they were being met with racism and xenophobia that has increased as immigration has grown over the past 20 years in Spain, which posed a significant barrier to entering social groups and establishing friendships during their time there.

[7] There have been recent criticisms of Mondragon however, as the corporation has expanded internationally, and fewer workers outside of the Basque Country are eligible to become members of the co-op. See Bamburg, 2018.

[8] Carl Cederström in Illing (2018) offers a very interesting discussion of how capitalism incentivizes individualism and the impact that has on human behavior: "I think there's a fundamental human desire to feel connected to other people. I also think capitalism has been very successful at presenting human life as an individual pursuit, but that's a lie. Human life is far more complicated than that, and we're all dependent on other people in ways we rarely appreciate. You're right, though. Like any political or economic ideology, capitalism appeals to something real about human nature. And the justification for capitalism has always been enjoyment and satisfaction — and that's a powerful message. Human beings don't have to be narcissistic and ultra-competitive, but if we're thrown into a system that incentivizes these things, it's obvious that we will be."

[9] On the issue of culture as an obstacle, Spicer (2018, p.124) notes: "I did not explicitly ask interviewees about culture or ideology as an obstacle. Culture and ideology was mentioned by many interviewees as a consideration. A debate on role of material *versus* ideological factors in shaping general socioeconomic and political outcomes is beyond the scope of this research, but I explicitly adopted a materialist stance in this study, one affirmed by the interviewees themselves. When I probed interviewees who suggested culture or ideology as an obstacle, in all cases (N = 16 in the US) their listing of "culture" as an

obstacle ultimately manifested as an issue for education and training of potential cooperative participants, often in very concrete and tangible ways."

10 https://www.samaracollective.coop.
11 https://www.law.cornell.edu/uscode/text/26/subtitle-A/chapter-1/subchapter-T.
12 https://www.irs.gov/businesses/small-businesses-self-employed/apply-for-an-employer-identification-number-ein-online.
13 *Worker Co-op Owners: Where to Report Patronage Dividends (1099-PATR) Income on Your Form 1040 for 2019.* https://www.wegnercpas.com/worker-co-op-owners-where-to-report-1099-patr-income-on-your-form-1040/.
14 The US Federation of Worker Cooperative's *Service Provider Directory* is a great place to start looking for support: https://www.usworker.coop/service-provider-directory/.

References

Bamburg, J. (2018, July 11). Mondragon through a critical lens. *Medium.* Retrieved January 4, 2022, from https://medium.com/fifty-by-fifty/mondragon-through-a-critical-lens-b29de8c6049.

Boggs, J. & Boggs, G.L. (2008). *Revolution and Evolution in the Twentieth Century.* Monthly Review Press.

Clamp, C.A. (2003). *The Evolution of Management in the Mondragon Cooperatives.* Retrieved January 4, 2022, from https://community-wealth.org/sites/clone.community-wealth.org/files/downloads/paper-clamp.pdf.

Escobar, L. (2015, October 19). What's the difference between tapas and Pintxos? *Pura Aventura.* Retrieved December 31, 2021, from https://pura-aventura.com/us/travel-stories/whats-the-difference-between-tapas-and-pintxos.

General Laws of Massachusetts (n.d.). *Chapter 157A: EMPLOYEE COOPERATIVE CORPORATIONS.* Retrieved January 4, 2022, from https://malegislature.gov/laws/generallaws/parti/titlexxii/chapter157a.

Goicoechea, E.R. (1984). Cuadrillas en el País Vasco: Identidad local y revitalización étnica. *Revista Española De Investigaciones Sociológicas*, (25), 213–222. https://doi.org/10.5477/cis/reis.135.

Hess, A. (2018). Gastronomic societies in the Basque Country. In J. Glückler, R. Suddaby & R. Lenz (eds.), Knowledge and institutions. *Knowledge and Space*, vol 13. Springer, Cham. https://doi.org/10.1007/978-3-319-75328-7_5.

Illing, S. (2018, Oct 31). A history of happiness explains why capitalism makes us feel empty inside: Swedish researcher Carl Cederström on how corporations redefined happiness and turned hippies into Reagan voters. *Vox.* https://www.vox.com/science-and-health/2018/9/4/17759590/happiness-fantasy-capitalism-culture-carl-cederstrom.

Mayer, B. (2021, June 25). *Worker Co-op Owners: Where to Report Patronage Dividends (1099-PATR) Income on Your Form 1040 for 2019.* Wegner CPAs. Retrieved January 17, 2022, from https://www.wegnercpas.com/worker-co-op-owners-where-to-report-1099-patr-income-on-your-form-1040/

Merriam-Webster (n.d.). Capitalism definition & meaning. Merriam-Webster. Retrieved January 4, 2022, from https://www.merriam-webster.com/dictionary/capitalism.

Pintxos App (2019, July 16). *The Origin of the Zurito.* Pintxos Donostia / San Sebastián. Retrieved December 31, 2021, from https://pintxos.es/en/the-origin-of-the-zurito/.

Prichep, D. (2012, May 14). At Basque cooking clubs, food and fraternity mix heartily. *NPR.* Retrieved December 31, 2021, from https://www.npr.org/sections/thesalt/2012/05/14/152672497/at-basque-cookings-clubs-food-and-fraternity-mix-heartily.

San Sebastian Tourism (n.d.). *Pintxo-Pote.* Retrieved January 4, 2022, from https://www.sansebastianturismoa.eus/en/blog/food-drink/996-pintxo-pote-en.

Spicer, J. (2018). Exceptionally un-American? Why co-operative enterprises struggle in the United States, but scale elsewhere. [Ph.D. Thesis, Massachusetts Institute of Technology] DSpace@MIT. https://dspace.mit.edu/handle/1721.1/120238.

Zallo, R. & Ayuso, A. (2009, January). *The Basque Country: Insight into Its Culture, History, Society and Institutions.* Eusko Jaurlaritzaren Argitalpen Zerbitzu Nagusia Servicio Central de Publicaciones del Gobierno Vasco Donostia-San Sebastián 1 • 01010 Vitoria-Gasteiz. https://www.euskadi.eus/gobierno-vasco/contenidos/informacion/ezagutu_eh/es_eza_eh/adjuntos/eza_en.pdf.

CHAPTER 28

Worker-owned & Unionized Worker-owned Cooperatives: Two Tools to Address Income Inequality

Carmen Huertas-Noble

Introduction

Income inequality[1] is prevalent throughout the globe. In the United States income inequality has reached extremes not seen since the Great Depression.[2] And similar to what occurred in the labor market during the Great Depression, living-wage jobs today have become scarce and wages have steeply declined, resulting in an increasing number of Americans who are unable to provide for themselves and their families.[3]

Even as the US economy starts to rebound, income inequality remains stark.[4] A crisis of wage stagnation and middle class erosion, combined with increased corporate power may even threaten our political system. As a new report from the Commission on Inclusive Prosperity notes, these economic problems threaten to become a serious problem for our democracy:

> The ability of free-market democracies to deliver widely shared increases in prosperity is in question as never before. [F]or the first time since the Great Depression, many industrial democracies are failing to raise living standards and provide social mobility to a large share of their people. Some of those countries that have produced economic growth have done so in a manner that has left most of its citizens no better off.[5]

Although many US businesses have regained healthy profit margins,[6] such profits are still not equitably shared with workers.[7] Instead, profits are disproportionately distributed among CEOs and shareholders.[8] For instance, today's worker to CEO pay ratio is 1:354.[9] This ratio is inequitable but not inevitable.[10]

Despite wide-ranging legal discretion to choose their form of entity and governance structure, the vast majority of businesses choose a governance structure the author will refer to as "traditional corporate governance" – which results in inattention to the interests of most workers, unjust distribution of profits in the form of dividends instead of wages and undemocratic workplaces.[11] Traditional corporate governance operates under the "standard shareholder-oriented model,"[12] a model that provides flexibility for corporations to be guided by the principles of maximizing the wealth of shareholders[13] and prioritizing executive compensation. Workers pay for these priorities, almost always in the form of suppressed wages.

Thus, an important strategy for addressing income inequality more effectively would be to re-examine and institute changes to (or departures from) the traditional corporate model. One promising structural change to the traditional form of business organization is the worker-owned cooperative and its more democratic ownership and governance structure. This article argues that worker-owned cooperatives and unionized worker-owned cooperatives are important alternatives to corporate ownership and governance structures that strongly tend to depress workers' wages.

While worker-owned cooperatives have existed for many years, now is a critical moment to press for widespread expansion of worker-ownership as a tool to stem the surge of income inequality. Recognition of and support for worker-owned cooperatives and union co-ops are gaining traction from diverse quarters. City governments fund worker-owned cooperative expansion and pass legislation to assist worker-owned cooperatives in growing to scale and in achieving sustainability by successfully gaining access to municipal procurement processes.[14] Following the United Nations' Year of the Cooperative, the International Cooperative Alliance has proposed a blueprint for a cooperative decade.[15] Pope Francis has called for an end to the "gig economy."[16] Last, in a list that could include many more examples, New York Mayor Bill DeBlasio specifically has stated that "… worker-owned cooperatives embody the democratic spirit on which our nation was built, offering every worker the right to self-determination and an equal say in how their organization is run."[17]

This growing support reflects a recognition that worker-owned cooperatives and union co-ops offer a critically important alternative to traditional corporate governance. The governance structures of cooperatives mandate equitable distribution of earnings, in the form of distribution of profits based on patronage, and democratic operation of the entity, in the form of one person, one vote.[18] Serving as models of business organizations that counteract severe income inequality, worker-owned cooperatives and union co-ops are enjoying success worldwide,[19] and have garnered increased political support in the United States. The growing interest in cooperative business entities that provide for profit sharing and democratic governance presents a meaningful opportunity for attorneys and law students to engage in transactional social justice lawyering and participate in a movement to expand this progressive form of business organization. It also provides an occasion to reflect upon strategies for teaching community economic development and lawyering skills.

Section I of this article discusses current US income inequality and its impact on workers and their communities. Section II describes the traditional corporation and some of its detrimental impacts, including its contribution to the current economic crises. This section also suggests the need for alternative, more egalitarian forms of business organization. Section III describes worker cooperatives and union coops and argues that such business formations offer better alternatives to traditional business organizations in that they operate to maximize wages and benefits of workers, provide democratic workplaces, demonstrate more responsible corporate behavior, and create a positive impact for communities. Section IV describes how worker-ownership has operated successfully in practice, providing as two examples Mondragon in Spain[20] and Cooperative Home Care Associates[21] in the United States. Section V highlights an initiative taking place in New York City, in which a coalition composed of the author's Community & Economic Development Clinic (CEDC) and community partners secured substantial economic and political support from the New York City government to expand worker-owned cooperatives and union co-ops in the City and to help address the challenge of bringing worker-owned cooperatives to scale.[22] Section VI focuses on CEDC's pedagogical goal of equipping tomorrow's transactional social justice lawyers with expertise in cooperative forms of business organization and skills to counsel clients in creating democratic and participatory decision-making structures. It highlights CEDC's integral role in training legal advisors to cooperatives, garnering governmental support and funding, disseminating public information on cooperative formations, and coalition-building among worker-owners, technical support organizations, educational institutions, and community-based organizations to combat income inequality and its impacts. The article concludes by reflecting upon the lessons learned.

Some Causes & Impacts of Income Inequality

The report by the Commission on Inclusive Prosperity provides an important reminder that income inequality is not just about pay. It is also about how one's pay affects one's standard of living. Income inequality creates a lack of food security, stable shelter, educational opportunities, access to health services, and meaningful life chances. The report explains "[c]ountries with more inequality are also countries with less opportunity for those with low and middle incomes."[23] For the past several decades, the United States has been gripped by a deepening economic crisis in the form of inequitable income distribution, the disappearance of living wage jobs, and the hollowing out of the middle class.[24] Many Americans from all walks of life, not just the poor, have experienced the ill effects of this crisis, much of which may be attributed to the failings of the traditional corporation and its prevailing practices. These ills include, principally, low and stagnant wages that prevent a large proportion of working people in the US[25] from supporting themselves and/or their families and declining social and economic mobility that exacerbates and cements their condition.[26] The specific problem of low wages, when discussed in the context of income inequality, "is often oversimplified" or submerged all together.[27] Economic inequality may be defined as the unequal distribution of income and wealth,"[28] but this framing alone does not capture the most devastating impacts of income inequality in the US. Economic inequality, especially in the context of greatly diminished government programs, often has a cascading effect, resulting in a multitude of injustices that ultimately results in inequality of opportunity and loss of social mobility.[29]

While income inequality in the US has reached levels not seen since the Great Depression,[30] corporate profits have climbed to an all-time 85-year high.[31] At the same time, the real value of wages has stagnated or, in many cases, declined.[32] Wage stagnation is not the result of flat or decreasing productivity.[33] To the contrary, as former Secretary of Labor Robert Reich has noted, wages have stagnated despite substantial increases in productivity; even larger shares of that increased value has been appropriated for corporate profits.[34] Although the economy generates more wealth more efficiently, workers are working longer hours for less pay than their counterparts 30 to 40 years ago.[35]

It cannot be a coincidence that the current trend of wage stagnation is occurring at a time when union membership is at an historic low.[36] Indeed, commentators have noted the direct correlation between union membership and equitable income distribution in the US.[37] When union membership was at its highest, organized labor exercised significant bargaining power, resulting in a more equitable wage distribution, not only within organized industries but also through labor market effects that influenced wage rates throughout the economy.[38] Expanded corporate power (and the increased inequality it has generated) is both cause and effect of the greatly reduced influence unions have in the US, and of their diminishing ability to counteract income inequality. This trend – and the unlikelihood that it will be reversed anytime soon – underscores the need to pursue parallel strategies for changes that advance economic equity, including cooperative forms of enterprise organization, as argued below.

Because a large proportion of the population is experiencing the economic and social struggles associated with structural income inequality, there is an increasing recognition of an urgent need for such changes. Even those more aligned with maintaining the current capitalist structure have expressed misgivings about extreme inequality, recognizing that US capitalism itself depends on rising middle class consumerism for 75% of its GNP[39] and that the current trends threaten this critical source of demand. More generally, and reminiscent of the Great Depression, many people in the US have come to realize that hard work and playing by the rules no longer guarantee economic security or even the ability to make ends meet.[40] In the United States, previously strong linkages between working class jobs and middle class benefits no longer seem to exist and hardworking people still experience poor social mobility.[41]

As income inequality accelerates across occupations and classes, it also correlates with increased percentages of households relying almost exclusively on wages as opposed to the small cohort of wealthy individuals and families with inherited wealth who rely on investment income.[42] This is why the Occupy movement's framing of the 1% *versus* the 99% helped bring together and mobilize a broad coalition that cut across work classifications, professional qualifications, or social beliefs. Stark income inequality is not only threatening the existence of future middle-class sustainability, it also delegitimizes capitalism and democracy for current and future middle-class populations. If necessity is truly the parent of invention, current and seemingly intractable societal inequalities present a unique opportunity to re-examine different corporate structures and re-imagine different possibilities and outcomes stemming from a change in traditional corporate ownership to worker ownership.

The next section discusses the traditional corporation and how its corporate governance structure influences the harmful depression of wages for many of its workers and discusses the need for more democratic forms of business, specifically worker-owned cooperatives and union coops.

Structural Ills of the Traditional Corporate Form & Need for More Egalitarian Forms of Business Organization

Although income inequality, low wages, and wage stagnation undoubtedly flow from a complex of interacting causes, it seems apparent that a significant cause is the traditional corporate structure – with its focus on profit maximization – coupled with the absence of an effective labor-centered counterweight to corporate power. In the US, state laws authorize the formation of business corporations and establish standards and parameters that corporations must abide by when adopting governance structures.[43] These laws impose guidelines on the type of governance structure a corporation may adopt, but allow corporations a great degree of discretion in determining decision- making power, including how and on whose behalf those powers are exercised.[44] Such governance structures, in turn, influence ownership, control, and corporate culture.

Generally in a corporation, ownership is based on capital investment and comes with two main rights: the right to share in profits (usually proportional to shareholders' capital investment) and the right to participate in governance.[45] As noted earlier, a "traditional corporation" is one that is organized under a state's business corporation laws, that adheres to the ownership definition above, and that operates under the Standard Shareholder-oriented Model (hereinafter "SSM").[46] SSM is characterized by four principal features:

- [First, T]he ultimate control over the corporation should rest with the shareholder class; the managers of the corporation should be charged with the obligation to manage the corporation in the interests of its shareholders;

- [Second] other corporate constituencies, such as creditors, employees, suppliers, and customers, should have their interests protected by contractual and regulatory means rather than through participation in corporate governance;

- [Third] noncontrolling shareholders should receive strong protection from exploitation at the hands of controlling shareholders; and

- [Fourth] the market value of the publicly-traded corporation's shares is the principal measure of its shareholders' interests.[47]

The SSM essentially subordinates the interests of all corporate stakeholders who are not shareholders[48] — including workers — to the goal of maximizing shareholder interests. SSM is so embedded in the governance traditional corporation that corporate officers' fiduciary duties are often interpreted by managers to include a duty to minimize costs, even at the expense of workers.[49] Because providing employment at a living wage is not necessarily a priority for a traditional corporation, the labor necessary to produce the corporation's goods or services and carry on its business is frequently viewed as just another component of the costs that should be reduced to the lowest level the market will bear in order to maximize shareholder interests.[50]

Business corporation laws allow, but do not mandate, such a severe approach to labor relations and wage setting. Corporate officers may, consistent with their fiduciary responsibilities, adopt more equitable and enlightened approaches to employee compensation. And government may, through direct regulation or economic policy, encourage or require such choices. A combination of these factors likely explains the interval between the close of World War II and the mid 1970s known as "The Great Compression" – a period marked by broadly shared prosperity and large reductions in income inequality.[51] Tax, trade and labor policies, high union density and a different corporate ethos all counteracted the severe logic of SSM — and workers experienced a far more equitable income distribution.

Today, unfortunately, the landscape looks quite different. Union membership has plummeted, in part as a result of hostile state and federal policies, government has significantly relaxed regulation of corporations and instituted tax policies that disproportionately favor the wealthy, and trade policies have placed domestic workers in competition with highly exploited, low-paid workers from developing nations across the globe. In the new climate, with external constraints removed, the inherent logic of SSM has re-emerged in its severe form, providing incentives for traditional corporations to select the approach of unmitigated profit maximization. This incentive to devalue labor, while always present to some degree, has led to increased corporate profiteering, with many businesses rejecting the notion that the hourly pay of their workers should increase with increased productivity and profitability.[52] Simply stated, pay and productivity – which once moved in tandem – are no longer linked; the idea of shared prosperity holds little, if any, sway in the corporate calculus.[53] The SSM has carried the day and, in the process, contributed mightily to income inequality, wage exploitation and the myriad ills that attend these phenomena.[54]

Prevailing SSM corporate governance practices should be changed to reduce or eliminate incentives that contribute to excessive income inequality and wage exploitation in the United States. Since productivity and profits are increasing while the wage share of workers continues to decrease, it is an opportune time to reassess organizational practices to emphasize wage gains that track productivity gains and to promote more equitable income distribution. Mechanisms should be implemented to help to narrow the gap between productivity and pay and to ensure that a worker today need not work longer and harder for less pay than his or her counterpart from years ago.[55] Admittedly, any such efforts to reform corporate governance and priorities would face severe obstacles. There are, however, a growing number of alternative, democratic business structures that can and do distribute income and wealth in a more sustainable and equitable fashion.[56] Such structures include worker-owned cooperatives and union co-ops.[57] The next section discusses worker-owned cooperatives and union co-ops as significant and transformative alternatives, with equitable governance practices that can stem the tide of income inequality.

Principles & Practices of Cooperative Enterprises

Worker-owned cooperatives and union co-ops represent innovative and viable forms of worker-ownership that are based on principles of democratic governance and equitable distribution of income and wealth.[58] In New York City, worker-owned cooperatives are formed under the Business Corporations Statute, Limited Liability Company Statute and the NY Cooperative Statute.[59] Not all states have cooperative statutes. Even where a state may have a cooperative statute, prospective worker-owners, upon advice of counsel, may choose to form under the state's limited liability company law, the choice of most NYC worker-owned cooperatives because of its flexibility, or the business corporation law. The point is not to put form over substance. Each statute has its own strengths and limitations. Once the needs of the prospective worker-owned cooperative are known, lawyers can counsel prospective worker-owned cooperatives on the options for entity formation that work best for that particular group.

In a worker-owned cooperative each worker has one share[60] and one vote. Such cooperatives are governed by democratic principles of shared governance.[61] Unlike traditional business organization structures, where ownership (including both profit sharing and governance rights) is based primarily on capital investment, ownership in a worker-owned cooperative is based primarily on labor and the democratic principle of one person, one vote.[62] In a worker-owned cooperative, worker-owners share governance responsibilities and profits. Profits are typically distributed equitably based on patronage.[63]

Worker-owned cooperatives have a long history, especially in marginalized communities. It has been observed that throughout history worker-owned cooperatives have tended to develop during severe economic crises.[64] Worker-owned cooperatives "have also been intertwined with workers' movements, nationalist movements, social-religious movements, and political movements,"[65] all seeking to find job security and to avoid exploitation. As noted more fully below, worker-owned cooperatives and union co-ops are based on principles designed to support inclusive governance and equitable sharing of responsibilities and profits.

Worker-owned cooperatives as an alternative model to traditional corporations

The worker-owned cooperative model offers a meaningful alternative to the traditional corporation that is of particular import in the quest to reduce income inequality. The worker-owned cooperative model makes capital subordinate to labor and puts a premium on labor rights. Ownership is primarily based on labor and not solely on purchasing shares. To help ensure capital remains subordinate to labor, shares are also generally kept affordable. The worker-owned cooperative model also tends to keep jobs locally based and keep profits circulating in the community.[66] In addition to keeping most profits in hosting communities, worker-owned cooperatives are also more likely to be environmentally friendly and more attuned to environmental injustice because worker-owners live in or near the very communities where their businesses are located.[67]

A union co-op is a worker-owned cooperative that is unionized.[68] There is an array of reasons for which cooperatives choose to unionize. Cooperatives may unionize in order to acquire clear structures and processes for democratic workplace governance, including handling workplace disputes. They may also join unions in order to take advantage of the unions' resources, in order to improve the cooperatives' sustainability. I will address, first, the advantages with regard to dispute resolution and governance, and then the advantages relating to sustainability.

At first, unionization of worker-owned cooperatives may seem counter-intuitive, primarily because it is perceived that owners would be bargaining against their own interests. However, that assumption implies that the interests of the various owners are always aligned, which is not the case. Conflicts between worker-owners and their selected management can mirror conflicts in other workplaces and conflicts may also arise among worker-owners in non-management roles. In one rarely occurring but conceivable example, individual worker-owners can lose their membership by a vote of a majority of other worker-owners and thus lose their ownership interest. Being part of a union, in this context, can serve as a trusted added layer of protection for worker-owners, offering worker-owned cooperatives an external option of conflict resolution by an organization that is mission aligned and has expertise in conflict resolution.

Worker-owned cooperatives may also elect to unionize for non-governance reasons. These reasons include the possibilities that unions offer to increase the cooperatives' sustainability. Union co-ops can leverage many attractive features of union affiliation: for instance, union purchasing power to secure better benefits packages for worker-owners and union political clout to obtain limited training opportunities[69] to enhance the quality of services or products they provide to the membership. Worker-owned cooperatives also may unionize in order more fully to integrate into larger economic justice movements. In addition, the union emphasis on creating and maintaining solidarity and the structures which unions have formed to achieve solidarity can also help inform/shape the creation of inter-co-operation among cooperatives, which can help worker-owned cooperatives scale up by creating a steady demand and consumer base.

Worker-owned cooperatives as contributors to economic justice movements

The current connection of the worker-owned cooperative movement to economic justice movements, and the diversity of people and groups that are interested in creating such alternatives, represent exciting developments. This resurging interest in expanding worker-owned cooperatives is occurring at a time when various economic justice movements are coming together in a shared struggle to fight for human dignity and rights of workers.[70] Many view worker ownership as a major way to address income inequality. As I will note below, a significant proportion of worker-owned cooperatives are based on the Mondragon Principles. These Principles include payment solidarity, which means "sufficient and fair pay for work as a basic principle of its management."[71]

Participants extend beyond the few expected advocates for these alternatives; the movement supporting these cooperatives is broad and is growing. For example, government officials,[72] educational institutions with leading academics[73] and bankers[74] are joining social and economic justice activists, in advocating for alternatives and are increasingly supporting these alternative models. A strong and growing national movement of both advocates and government officials is creating more worker-owned cooperatives and union cooperatives and bringing them to scale. This development is taking place across the United States. It includes California, where organizations like Prospera[75] partner with low-income Latina women to build and maintain cooperative businesses; Jackson, Mississippi, where recently the late mayor, Chokwe Lumumba, had referred to his economic plan as creating the Mondragón[76] of the South;[77] and Madison, Wisconsin, where worker-owned cooperative advocates were able to secure $5 million over the course of five years to expand worker-owned cooperatives as a key to economic revitalization and social justice.[78] These examples, and others like them, raise the prospect of expanding the proportion of worker-owned cooperatives, possibly helping them stem the growth of income inequality. This would respond to some of the critiques of worker-owned cooperatives noted below.

Critiques of worker-owned cooperatives & the union co-op model
There are two main critiques of cooperatives:[79]

- They do not always reach their transformative potential to create successful democratic workplaces that are an alternative to a capitalist economy.

- They operate at a small scale (partly because they are difficult to capitalize) and scaling up has proven difficult.

As to the first critique, the failure to reach transformative potential to contest capitalism can be addressed through governance strategies such as unionization that put cooperative principles into operation.[80] For example, by creating more union cooperatives, unions can help create and/or bolster solidarity and integrate worker-owned cooperatives into the larger economic justice movement.[81]

The second challenge, to build a successful cooperative movement of sufficient scale to make a real difference, can be addressed by including businesses where capitalization is less of an issue as well as by improving access to capital for businesses that need investment capital. Unlike the very successful Mondragon cooperatives in Spain, which provide, among other benefits, access to financing, the US has no robust network of cooperatives and no real inter-cooperation exists in the form of worker cooperatives doing business with each other as way to increase demand for their products and services and remain sustainable. To address the capitalization issue, the New York City cooperative movement described below is trying to learn from Mondragon and create more worker-owned cooperatives based on the Mondragon model, seeking funding from cities as well as banks that were created to lend to cooperatives.

Scale can also be increased when unions bring additional purchasing power and political clout to obtain contracts that serve to increase demand and revenue for the cooperative businesses. As demand increases, worker-owned cooperatives can also bring on additional worker-owners, moving from relatively small businesses with few worker-owners to more sizeable businesses with greater numbers of worker-owners. Unions also open up slots for job licensing training. For example, with Make the Road New York, the United Steel Workers were instrumental in securing OSHA training slots for Make the Road New York members. These members took the training together to form a worker-owned cooperative that would inspect and ensure building compliance post-Hurricane Sandy.

Below are two examples that address the critiques that cooperatives fail to effect meaningful transformation in the workplace and fail to achieve sufficient scale for such transformation to be widespread.

Successful Examples of Worker-Ownership: Mondragon & CHCA

As the worker-owned cooperative movement grows, advocates are looking to successful examples abroad and at home from which to draw lessons, including what worked, did not work and why, as well as to learn how successful models have overcome the critiques listed above. Two successful examples are Mondragon in Spain and CHCA in the Bronx.

The Mondragon Corporation[82]

Mondragon, the world's largest network of worker-owned industrial cooperatives, is the top Basque region industrial group, ranked 10th in Spain with 80,000 personnel, a presence in 70 countries, and winner of the 2013 *Financial Times* "Boldness in Business" award.[83]

Mondragon's more than 60-year-old mission is to generate wealth for society through business development and job creation under the "one worker, one vote" cooperative framework, where labor is sovereign and capital, while essential, is subordinate to sustainable job creation. Mondragon is an entrepreneurial socioeconomic entity inspired by the Basic Principles founding its Co-operative Experience, which include Open Admission and Neutrality, Democratic Organization, Sovereignty of Labor, Instrumental and Subordinate Nature of Capital, Participatory Management, Wage Solidarity, Inter-cooperation, Social Transformation, Universality of the Cooperative Experience, and Education.[84]

Mondragon was "developed through the spirit and work carried out by José María Arizmendiarrieta, a young priest who in 1941 came to Arrasate-Mondragón, which at the time was living through the painful aftermath of the Spanish civil war in the form of poverty."[85] Father Arizmendiarrieta started to address the issues of poverty by first focusing on health needs and on educational training with the idea that it was first necessary to share knowledge before democratizing power. Father Arizmendiarrieta trained Mondragon's first graduates to create Mondragón's first cooperative, Falgor, based on the 10 Mondragon principles.[86]

All of Mondragon's cooperative enterprises are driven by the following 10 principles:[87]

- **Open Admission:** Open to all who agree to the cooperative principles regardless of age, ethnicity, political orientation, spiritual practice or gender.
- **Democratic Organization:** All workers must be members, with a few exceptions, and the organization is democratically controlled by the workers on the basis of one worker receiving one vote in electing leadership.
- **Sovereignty of Labor:** The cooperatives renounce wage labor and give primacy to workers in distribution of surpluses and attempt to extend the cooperative to all members of society.
- **Instrumental Character of Capital:** Capital is a necessary factor in business and savings, however, return on capital investment or savings is not directly tied to surpluses or losses of the cooperatives.
- **Self-Management:** Cooperation is the manifestation of individual responsibility and collective effort. Clear information on the organization's operations must be available to members in order

to facilitate both the collective effort of participation in management and individual requirements of ongoing skills development for self- management.

- Pay Solidarity: Internally this means the ratio between highest and lowest paid worker cannot exceed 6 to 1. Externally this means that wages should be comparable to prevailing wages in neighboring conventional firms.
- **Group Cooperation:** Individual cooperatives organized in groups, between groups and between Mondragon and other movements.
- **Social Transformation:** Mondragon is an instrument for social transformation.
- **Universal Nature:** The co-ops proclaim their solidarity with all who labor for economic democracy, peace, justice, human dignity, and development.
- **Education:** It is fundamentally important to devote sufficient human and economic resources to cooperative education, professional training, and general education of young people for the future.

The Mondragon model addresses the two main critiques of worker-owned cooperatives. Mondragon has put into effect the transformative tenets expressed in the Principles, and is not just another business structure that replicates the *status quo*. Workers participate in democratic decision-making in businesses that are economically successful. The workers themselves earn living wages. Mondragon also maintains a small CEO to worker pay ratio.

By example, Mondragon has met the critique that cooperatives fail to achieve sufficient scale to put their principles into meaningful practice. Mondragon, while starting out small, has successfully scaled through its unique capitalization strategies, including creating its own bank and creating a network of worker-owned cooperatives that serve to implement its principle of inter-cooperation. By creating its own bank, Mondragon cooperatives were/are able to gain access to loans with non-traditional lending criteria, especially in Mondragon's early stages and by creating different types of worker-cooperatives that exist and operate in a network that purchases good and services from among its network, they were able to help increase and stabilize demand for their products and services.

Cooperative Home Care Associates (CHCA)

CHCA, located in the Bronx, is currently the largest unionized worker-owned cooperative in the US and is very successful. The Community Service Society (CSS) formed CHCA in 1985 as a cooperative under the Business Corporation Law. "CHCA has over 1,600 members and revenues of $40 million."[88]

CHCA works in home health care, an industry that is notorious for exploiting its workers, both in terms of low pay and poor working conditions.[89] CSS founded CHCA in 1985 "on the premise that if workers owned their own company they could maximize wages and benefits, and if workers were better trained and better treated, they'd offer better care for their clients."[90] CHCA exemplifies a business that can be started with little capitalization and grow by leveraging union clout and securing government contracts. This health-care cooperative also provides a good example of unionization's contribution to the transformative potential of worker-owned cooperatives. CHCA focused on industry-wide change.

To that end, CHCA worked on several connected tracks. To raise industry standards, not just for CHCA workers but across the field, CHCA started the worker-run Paraprofessional Health care Institute (PHI) that trains agencies across the country while also fighting policy shifts. (PHI was instrumental in the campaign that recently expanded the Fair Labor Standards Act.)[91]

The union played a major part in securing government contracts, thus strengthening CHCA's continued existence, which in turn raised the worker-owners' earnings. Currently, CHCA worker-owners who labor as home health aides earn approximately $16 an hour with benefits, double the industry standard. CHCA's worker-owners are also guaranteed an average of 36 hours per week – significantly more hours than the 25 to 30 hours that prevail in the industry. Together, guaranteed hours and increased pay promote work-life balance among worker-owners.[92] These increased wage and benefits are made possible, in part, by a relatively equitable income distribution of pay: the CEO earns just 11 times as much as the average worker.

CHCA worker-owners, who are over 90% women,[93] have consistently commented on their improved quality of life. Worker-owners frequently note that participation in CHCA allows them to spend more time with their families and be more present in their children's lives. CHCA worker-owners, many who formerly received public assistance, also note the upward mobility opportunities worker-ownership provides. For example, one worker-owner Zaida Ramos, who was raising her children on public assistance before CHCA, recently celebrated her daughter's college graduation and is also able to partially pay for her son's Catholic school education.[94] Mrs. Ramos not only experienced upward mobility herself but significantly increased the possibility of the same for her children.

Individual worker-owners also note that unionization provides them with additional benefits. For example, prior to unionization, workers tended not to utilize CHCA's grievance procedure. They attribute their reluctance to feelings of workplace vulnerability, despite the fact that they were also owners of the enterprise. A worker-owner who complained about the worker-owner who was responsible for assigning cases, for example, feared that she would thereafter be assigned to unfavorable cases in retribution. After CHCA unionized, the worker-owners felt more comfortable utilizing the grievance procedure and, in fact, did.[95]

An Example of Building on Prior Successes: New York City Worker- & Union-Cooperative Initiative & CUNY School of Law's Community & Economic Development Clinic

Advocates for worker-owned cooperatives in NYC, like advocates in other cities nationwide, are looking to successful models from abroad, like Mondragon, and domestically, like CHCA, to inform their strategies for creating a local cooperative ecosystem. The NYC Worker Cooperative Coalition (The Coalition), of which CUNY School of Law's Community and Economic Development Clinic has been an active and essential member, secured $1.2 million in 2014[96] and $2.1 million in 2015 from the NYC Council to fund worker-owned cooperative expansion.[97]

Community & Economic Development Clinic

Community Economic Development efforts adopt one of three basic approaches, primarily emphasizing either the community empowerment aspect (termed "Ced"), the economic growth aspect ("cEd"), or the institutional development aspect ("ceD").[98] CUNY's CEDC[99] deliberately emphasizes the "community" and "development" aspects of community economic development in its client representation. CEDC's approach is guided by the belief that social justice lawyering is most effective when strategically delivered to help build the power of low-income and marginalized communities. To that end, CEDC uses an empowerment-driven approach in its teaching and representation of clients.[100] CEDC represents both start-up and established organizations that envision and implement vibrant neighborhood institutions and social and economic justice programs.

CEDC[101] has a growing worker-owned cooperative law docket and is part of a number of worker-owned cooperative development initiatives in New York City and across the nation.[102] To promote job creation, CEDC's lawyering strategy extends beyond helping individual small businesses, which is needed and important work in and of itself, to creating more democratized and empowering forms of collective ownership.[103] As the author has noted in a previous article:

> Empowerment driven CED lawyering, in a transactional context, is an emerging approach to progressive lawyering that fosters the collective action and active democratic participation of low-income and working class people to reshape our social, economic and political system.[104]

CEDC is playing a key role with its clients, community partners, and their members in designing an ecosystem in New York City to expand and support the worker-ownership movement. The Clinic's efforts include raising awareness of the worker-owned cooperative model and representing worker-owned cooperative clients in formation and on-going legal issues. This work includes CEDC's role in the New York City Worker Cooperative Coalition (the Coalition).

The Coalition

The Coalition is comprised of organizations and individuals advocating for increased government commitment to and support for worker-owned cooperatives. The Coalition is comprised of individuals, including several CEDC alumni, and community based organizations, including several CEDC organizational clients such as Make the Road New York, New York City Network of Worker Cooperatives, and Green Worker Cooperatives. These members of the Coalition are at the forefront of forming or expanding worker-owned cooperatives and union coops.[105]

The Coalition has accomplished a great deal in 2014 and 2015. In January of 2014, the Coalition produced a report titled *Worker-owned Cooperatives for New York City: A Vision for Addressing Income Inequality*[106] in order to raise awareness of the worker-owned cooperative model and its benefits. The Report outlined the benefits by documenting that worker-ownership leads to living wages, self-governance and determination, asset accumulation, and quality working conditions to a much greater extent than do other forms of business organization.[107] The Report's publication was celebrated with a standing-room only conference, also co-organized and sponsored by the CEDC, entitled "Worker-Owned Cooperatives: Jobs for New York City's Future."[108] The conference included presentations by the author, CEDC alums, CEDC clients, and community partners and was attended by several New York City Council members, including Councilwoman Maria Carmen del Arroyo, the Chairperson of the Committee on Community Development.

Following the Report and conference, Councilwoman Arroyo held a public hearing in February 2014, entitled "Worker-owned Cooperatives – Is this a Model that Can Lift Families out of Poverty?"[109] At the request of the City Council, CEDC clients, community partners, and students and alums presented testimony in support of expanding worker-owned cooperatives in New York City as a tool to reduce poverty. The Coalition collectively organized the order of the testimonies to be as inclusive and comprehensive as possible, ensuring that testimony was provided by worker-owners, academics, technical assistance providers, and community based organizations that incubate worker-owned coops. The hearing was so well attended due to the Coalition's outreach that it required an overflow room.

The CED Clinic and New York City Network of Worker Cooperatives also hosted the first annual worker-owned coop conference in New York City in mid-2014.[110] The conference began with a celebration of securing the $1.2 million and included panels by worker-owners, technical assistance providers, resource allies and academics. The Conference culminated in a plenary that addressed the growing and needed role of government in supporting worker-owned cooperatives. The author moderated a discussion between Councilwoman Arroyo and Assemblyman Carl Heastie, then the Chair of the New York State Assembly's Labor Committee. The conference ended with proclamations from the Mayor, the Public Advocate and the Manhattan Borough President.[111]

In 2015, New York City Council funding for the Coalition to create new worker-owned cooperatives and help support pre-existing worker-owned cooperatives has nearly doubled. In its second year, the Coalition has expanded to include new groups (an intentional decision to ensure greater access) and has secured $2.1 million. Additionally, Councilwoman Helen Rosenthal of the New York City Council successfully introduced legislation, Int. 0423-2014, that requires city agencies to report on their outreach and contracts with worker-cooperatives.[112] Drafted with the assistance of a former student attorney in CEDC, and supported by CEDC's efforts, this legislation is seen as one of the first steps in facilitating worker-owned cooperatives access to the City's procurement process.

Educating Tomorrow's Transactional Lawyers in Establishing Effective Worker-owned Cooperatives & Unionized Cooperatives

This is a critical moment to develop and support the teaching of integrated legal and business skills around worker-ownership, especially in a social justice context. With income inequality reaching a destructive tipping point, new organizational solutions are needed to reverse the trend. As noted above and by various scholars and observers, worker-ownership presents a more balanced approach to entrepreneurship that has many strengths.[113] In addition, this business organization form can improve the lives of people who might otherwise work in exploitative industries that fail to pay legally-mandated wages and maintain substandard working conditions. Finally, and importantly, this structure also gives workers a voice and a vote and distributes equity throughout the enterprise.

Once students recognize these benefits, they often ask, "Why don't more worker-owned cooperatives exist?" In part, the answer is that cooperatives are more prevalent than the public is aware. Although a significant number of cooperative businesses exist, including ACE Hardware stores[114] and Florida's natural orange juice growers,[115] most people are not aware that these businesses operate as cooperatives. Many people and the lawyers advising them are also unacquainted with the nuances of options for entity formation, such as incorporating under worker-owned cooperative statutes, and, in New York, forming as LLCs or B corporations. In addition, many entrepreneurs and workers are not aware of the worker-owned cooperative model in part because the model to date has not been widely publicized or taught in schools.

To address this void, CEDC teaches lawyering for worker-owned cooperative models as part of its empowerment-driven CED practice. CEDC teaches law students the basic tenets of worker-ownership and the challenges that worker-owned cooperatives face in their start- up phases (e.g., capitalization and scaling up). Students also learn how to counsel clients on their options for entity formation, as well as on creating governance structures that will ensure meaningful, democratic, participatory decision-making.

CUNY Law's CEDC is also collaborating with Mondragon's North American Delegation and cooperative incubator, Saiolan, to collaboratively develop a worker-owned cooperative curriculum. CEDC is interested in making the Mondragon educational model available in the US to provide opportunities for students to earn certificates in social economy and cooperative development. To date, CEDC is collaborating with 1 Worker 1 Vote, Saiolan and other CUNY schools, such as Medgar Evers College, to develop curriculum packages and programs to teach organizational practices that support community empowerment. Students will learn the legal, structural, transactional, and community-building skills and perspectives necessary to support worker-owner models that are economically viable and that effectively meet the challenges often associated with these models.

Many leading educational institutions such as MIT and Harvard have already expressed interest in the curriculum being developed. The pedagogical goal of the curriculum is to support people interested in being part of or running a worker-owned cooperative based on Mondragon principles. CEDC is also working with Catholic Scholars for Worker Justice to draft an encyclical for the Pope of the Catholic Church and will present the encyclical in Rome in 2016.

Student lawyering lessons learned in legal work supporting CEDC's participation in the Coalition

As one of the founding members of the Coalition, CEDC has, to date, been working with the Coalition for two years. Through this collaboration, students engage in many traditional lawyering tasks by representing clients in the Coalition that were incubating worker-owned cooperatives. Such tasks include:

- Conducting policy advocacy[116] and formulating and drafting legislation;[117]
- Counseling clients on entity formation options, e.g. a limited liability company or a cooperative under the New York Cooperative Statute and forming the respective entities;[118] and
- Counseling clients regarding governance structures and drafting governance documents,[119] including counseling on the intersection between client governance documents and unionization, particularly the intersection between their governance documents and collective bargaining agreements.

In counseling the CEDC clients in the coalition on entity formation options and setting up the coalition's governance structures, students also learned how to navigate the intersection of labor law and entity formation options, not often taught in an integrated way in law schools.

In addition to the lawyering task above, students helped with:

- Movement-building[120] and creating the Coalition's own governance structure and committees;
- Providing community education not only for clients but elected officials, e.g. providing testimony to City Council;
- Advocating for and securing funding for the Coalition; and
- Serving as co-strategists in the Coalition internally and externally and facilitating meetings and negotiations among members.[121]

One major lesson was for the students to learn to serve in multiple roles, including strategist in support of broad efforts to advance a cause such as worker-owned cooperatives in ways that benefit specific clients and many others.[122]

Applying the skills of integrative & collaborative counseling to an empowerment-driven CED practice

Students in CEDC learned that CEDC's role as both member and counsel to some organizational clients within the coalition required that they exercise a unique combination of legal counseling skills, non-legal strategic advice and problem-solving skills. Perhaps one of the students' most important lessons, in this regard, involved identifying and making explicit that they were not counsel to the coalition, but were counsel to certain organizations within the coalition and identifying and making explicit when their input was based on which role (*e.g.* as lawyer to one of the members or solely as a coalition member not giving legal advice but strategic input). To accomplish this, students learned and used intentional counseling skills of collaborative and integrative lawyering when counseling their organizational clients that were also part of the coalition in forming worker-owned cooperatives.

Collaborative counseling engages the client as a shared decision-maker in every phase of the counseling process and ". . .requires lawyer and client to collaboratively identify: the decisions that need to be made, the people empowered to make those decisions and the process for engaging decision-makers in making and evaluating those decisions. This includes involving the client in the generation of strategies and the development of options to choose from." In this context, students made sure to amplify the organizational client's voice, including the voices of its members, by including them in every step of the decision-making process.[123]

The students also used the integrative counseling approach as part of their coalition work.[124] Integrative counseling requires an advanced appreciation of the multiple roles that a lawyer may play as both member of and lawyer for a coalition. According to Brian Glick and Sheila Forster, integrative counseling is a form of counseling that integrates the lawyers' work in two necessary interconnected ways:

> Lawyers – like their clients – need to integrate flexibly and functionally a broad range of practice areas, skills and roles. And they need to make sure that all of their work is thoroughly integrated into the overall strategy, program and process of the organization so that their lawyering is closely tied to the organization's efforts to build community capacity and power. Each form of integration shapes the other.[125]

Borrowing from the integrative counseling approach, students learned to be intentional about when to contribute and how to make clear whether or not their communications were based on the law and offered as legal advice. In working with the Coalition as a whole, Inclusive Legal Problem Solving Skills, which include robust information gathering, active listening, language reframing, facilitation, problem-solving, and consensus building skills,[126] were also particularly helpful. This was particularly true when the Clinic served as facilitator and consensus builder within the coalition context.

Substantive lessons learned about how best to leverage governmental & institutional support to create & expand sustainable worker-owned cooperatives

The Coalition learned that, in addition to directly funding worker-owned cooperatives and union cooperative incubators, government could play other major roles in helping worker-owned cooperatives establish and sustain themselves. For example, government contracts often provide a stable and continuous demand for services and a source of revenue that can act as a hedge against fluctuations in demand as cooperatives get started. Governments can also support worker-owned cooperatives and union cooperatives by making cooperatives preferred contractors in the city's procurement process.[127] This is somewhat similar to the Cleveland model,[128] which also uses private or educational anchor institutions, as a way to scale up the worker-owned cooperative model by increasing incomes and assets as well by ensuring demand. Cities themselves can serve as needed anchor institutions. Anchor institutions are large service institutions, such as hospitals and universities, that are not easily relocated and are themselves major consumers that can use their purchasing power to create sustained demand for worker cooperatives.

Another way for governments to support scaling up worker-owned cooperatives is to promote and support business conversions.[129] One major target has been businesses owned by baby boomers whose children do not want to take over the family business. These businesses, currently profitable, can be converted to worker-ownership and help further ensure a cooperative's success and have the business sustain a local presence.[130]

Conclusion

Worker-owned cooperatives are countering severe income inequality. They can counter inequality on a larger scale if we create greater strategies for base building, mobilization and bringing the operations of cooperatives to a sustainable scale., These strategies can include government funding and legislative support. Today's stark inequality and the growing interest in cooperative business entities that democratize the workplace and equitably distribute profits present a meaningful opportunity to advocate for the expanding and scaling up worker-owned cooperative models. These conditions also invite lawyers to participate in CED empowerment lawyering that can bring about needed systemic change.

Anchor institutions, whether they be private or public or entire cities, are critical to meet the challenge of making worker-owned cooperatives sustainable in the marketplace. Trying to advocate that governments give worker-owned and union coops preferences in their procurement processes and create more public banks, as in Denver[131] and banks like the National Cooperative Bank would be tremendously helpful. The Mondragon Cooperative's own Bank has recently collaborated with the National Cooperative Bank to think of ways of funding US cooperatives as well as advocating for legislation. And, again, there are a number of states that have cooperative statutes. In some states that do not or recently did not have cooperative statutes, legal services providers are in the course of or recently drafted such legislation.[132] These developments are promising. They mean that there will be a growing role for law students in working with these entities — not just in terms of entity formation options, but also in terms that meld corporate law, transactional law, and labor law, a practice which the author has found to be the most challenging and rewarding.

Again, for law school graduates, there will be more worker-owned cooperatives and union cooperatives that will be their client-base. Law graduates who are interested in this work will need to know the intersection between labor law and transactional law. They will need to have the skills to work with state cooperative statutes and to adapt other corporate structures to incorporate cooperative values, to draft legislation to work with government officials. These new lawyers will be like any other corporate lawyer who goes beyond the basics of the field to become strategists and planners — they will be an integral part of their client's team, just as we already are and will continue to be.[133]

End-notes

1   Economic inequality includes both income and wealth inequality. The difference between the two is important. "Income refers to a flow of money over time [often earned through one's labor]. Wealth is a stock of assets owned at a particular time [and is often not tied to having to work]." Melvin L. Oliver & Thomas M. Shapiro, *Black Wealth/White Wealth 5* (2 ed. 2006). See also Christopher Ingraham, If you thought income inequality was bad, get a load of wealth inequality, *Washington Post, Wonkblog*, May 21, 2015, http://www.washingtonpost.com/news/wonkblog/wp/2015/05/21/the-top-10-of-ameri-cans-own-76-of-the-stuff-and-its-dragging-our-economy-down/. While wealth inequality is greater and even more disproportionately skewed against workers than income inequality, this article focuses on income inequality because as a society we can more immediately address income inequality and bring about desperately needed quality of life changes. In addition, addressing income inequality is an important first stage in any process designed to ultimately address wealth inequality through the purchase of assets. For more details on the wealth and income distribution distinctions see also Lawrence R. Mishel, Josh Bivens & Elise Gould, *The State of Working America 99-100* (12 ed. 2012) [hereinafter Mishel *et al.*, *State of Working America*]; Jesse Bricker, Lisa J. Dettling, Alice Henriques, Joanne W. Hsu, Kevin B. Moore, John Sabelhaus, Jeffrey Thompson & Richard A. Windle, *Changes in US family finances from 2010 to 2013: Evidence from the Survey of Consumer Finances*, 100 *Fed. Res. Bull.* Sept. 2014, at 1, 10, available at http://www.federalreserve.gov/pubs/bulletin/2014/pdf/scf14.pdf.

2   See Drew DeSilver, *US Income Inequality on the Rise for Decades is Now Highest Since 1928*, Pew Research Center/Facttank, (Dec. 5, 2013), http:www.pewresearch.org/fact-tank/2013/12/05/u-s-income- inequality-on-rise-for-decades-is-now-highest-since- 1928/ (last visited Feb. 5, 2016).

3   See David B. Grusky, Marybeth J. Mattingly & Charles Varner, *State of the States: The Poverty and Inequality Report 8* (2015).

4   See Neil Irwin, The benefits of economic expansions are increasingly going to the richest Americans, *New York Times*, Sept. 26, 2014 at B1, available at http://www.nytimes.com/ 2014/09/27/upshot/the-benefits-of-economic-expansions-are-increasingly-going-to-the-richest-americans.html?_r=0&abt=0002&abg=0 (referring to research that shows that over 90 percent of all income growth between 2009 and 2012 went to the 1%).

5   See Lawrence H. Summers & Ed Ball, Center for American Progress, *Report of the Commission on Inclusive Prosperity 1* (2015), available at https://www.americanprogress.org/issues/economy/report/2015/01/15/104266/report-of-the-commission-on-inclusive-prosperity/.

6   Robert B. Reich, *Why the Economy is Still Failing Most Americans* (September 28, 2014) available at http://robertreich.org/post/98668011635 (former Secretary of Labor Robert B. Reich reporting that, as of late 2014, all economic gains since the US recovery began in 2009 have been allocated to the wealthiest 10%). See also Neil Irwin, The benefits of economic expansions are increasingly going to the richest Americans, *New York Times*, Sept. 26, 2014, at B1, available at http://www.nytimes.com/2014/09/27/upshot/the-benefits- of-economic-expansions-are-increasingly-going-to-the-richest-americans.html?_r=0&abt=0002&abg=0.

7   See Summers *et al.*, *supra* note 5 at 40 (explaining that, while worker productivity is increasing, ". . .the incomes of the vast majority of households have not grown alongside their productivity."). Both wage income growth and capital income growth have accrued at the top of the income distribution. "This shift from labor to capital incomes between 1979 and 2007 is significant: The share of personal, market-based income accruing to capital owners rose from 15.0 to 19.7 percent during this time. This 4.7 percentage-point increase came mainly from a 5.3 percentage-point reduction in the share of overall income accounted for by wages and benefits of employees." Mishel *et al.*, *State of Working America, supra* note 1 at 99-100.

8   See Josh Bivens, Elise Gould, Lawrence Mishel & Heidi Shierholz, Econ, Pol'y Inst., *Raising America's Pay: Why It's Our Central Economic Policy Challenge*, Briefing Paper No. 378 (June 4, 2014), available at http://s1.epi.org/files/2014/ raising-americas-pay-report-final.pdf. In their analysis of comprehensive household income including wages, capital gains, employee benefits, government transfers, the authors found that the comprehensive income of top 1% of households saw larger gains between 1979 and 2007 than did the aggregate incomes of bottom 80%. *Id.* at 22. See also Huasheng Gao *et al.*, *A Comparison of CEO Pay in Public and Private US Firms*, 2010 (September), available at

https://www.researchgate.net/profile/Kai_Li5/publication/228239667_Are_
CEOs_in_Public_U.S._Firms_Overpaid_New_Evidence_from_Private_Firms/links/02e7e53304b92d43a7000000.pdf.

9   Sorapop Kiatpongsan & Michael I. Norton, How much (more) should CEOs make? A universal desire for more equal pay, 9 *Persp. Psychol. Sci.* 587 (2014).

10 See, *e.g.,* Thomas Piketty, Capital in the 21st Century, 237-467, 244 (Arthur Goldhammer transl., 2014) (arguing that "...inequality with respect to capital is always greater than inequality with respect to labor" and that the ". . .distribution of capital ownership (and of income from capital) is always more concentrated than the distribution of income from labor."). This article does not argue for an exact equal distribution of income but a more equitable distribution of income based on worker labor and profitability. See also Interview by Lynn Parramore [LP] with Lance Taylor (LT), What Thomas Piketty and Larry Summers don't tell you about income inequality, *Institute for New Economic Thinking Blog* (Feb. 15, 2015) http://ineteconomics.org/ideas-papers/blog/what-thomas-piketty-and-larry-summers-dont-tell-you-about-income-inequality: [LP]: "Your research suggests that it's not just some natural process that's causing more wealth to flow towards the rich. How is it happening?" [LT:] "It remains hard to explain skyrocketing executive pay on purely economic grounds. There is no reason to believe that top managers or other highly paid individuals *circa* 2015 are more or less essential than, say, in 1975 when comparable pay was 10 times lower. The best explanation I can come up with is that a social contract or unwritten law against exorbitant executive income has disappeared in the US. We will only get this contract back by social consensus and/or seriously progressive taxation."

11 See Section II, *infra,* for a further description of traditional corporations and the dominant form of corporate governance in the US.

12 See Henry Hansmann & Reinier Kraakman, Reflections on the end of history for corporate law 1 (August 15, 2011), Yale Law & Economics Research Paper No. 449, reprinted in Convergence of Corporate Governance: Promise & Prospects (Abdul Rasheed and Toru Yoshikawa, eds., Palgrave-MacMillan, 2012), available at SSRN: http://ssrn.com/abstract=2095419 (explaining that ". there is increasing consensus among the relevant actors, around the globe, that what we term the 'standard shareholder- oriented model' ('SSM') of the business corporation is the most attractive social ideal for the organization of large-scale enterprise."). This article does not seek to dispute their argument that corporate governance has converged around the SSM. It does, however, dispute that the SSM is "the most attractive social ideal" for business enterprises. SSM is not the most attractive model because of its gross inequities in the distribution of value generated by productivity gains in recent decades. See Summers *et al., supra* note 5, at 12 ("Corporations have come to function less effectively as providers of large-scale opportunities. Increasingly, their dominant focus has been on maximization of share prices and the compensation of their top employees").

13 Hansmann & Kraakman, *supra* note 12 at 3: "We asserted that the SSM has four principal elements: [and the fourth is] the market value of the publicly-traded corporation's shares is the principal measure of its shareholders' interests."

14 See *infra* at note 112 and accompanying text.

15 The blueprint outlines the International Co-operative Alliance's "2020 Challenge" and came on the heels of the United Nation's Year of the Cooperative.

16 Catholic Scholars for Worker Justice recently requested that the author and her clinic assist with organizing, drafting and presenting an encyclical on worker-owned cooperatives and the importance of unions to Pope Francis in 2016.

17 Office of the Mayor City of New York, Proclamation Declaring June 21st, 2014 "Worker-Owned Cooperative Day," on file with Author.

18 For further detail concerning the governance structures of worker cooperatives, see Section III, *infra.*

19 For interesting articles on international cooperatives see, *e.g.* David F. Ellerman, Harvard Business School, *The Mondragon Cooperative Movement,* Case No. 1-384-270, (1984), http;//www.ellerman.org/Davids-Stuff/The-Firm/Mondragon-HBS-Case.pdf; G. Mitu Gulati, T.M. Thomas Isaac & William A. Klein, When a workers' cooperative works: The case of Kerala Dinesh Beedi, 49 *UCLA L. REV.* 1417, 1427-28 (2002).

20 See Section IVA, *infra,* for more information on Mondragon, one of the largest networks of worker-owned cooperatives in the world. See generally, William Foote Whyte & Kathleen King Whyte, *Making Mondragon: The Growth & Dynamics of the Worker-owned Cooperative Complex* (1991).

21 Cooperative Home Care Associates (CHCA) is the largest unionized cooperative in the US. For a discussion of CHCA, see Section IVB, *infra.*

22 See National Cooperative Business Association CLUSA International (NCBA CLUSA), *New York City Invests $1.2 Million in Worker-owned Cooperatives* (2014), http://www.ncba.coop/ncba-media/press-releases/610-new-york-city-invests-1-2-million-in-worker-cooperatives.

23 Summers *et al., supra* note 5 at 45. In the report, Summers, former US Secretary of the Treasury, and Balls, former Shadow Chancellor of the Exchequer in the British Parliament, further explain that income inequality translates into a multitude of injustices, with perhaps the most disturbing injustice being inequality of life expectancy.

[24]   Between 1979 and 2012, the bottom 90% of wage earners saw real wage growth of 17.1% – largely due to increased working hours, while the top 1% saw real wage growth of 153.6% over the same period, and the top 0.1% saw growth of 337%. Bivens *et al.*, *supra* note 8, 18-20. See also DeSilver, *supra* note 2; Thomas Piketty & Emmanuel Saez, Income inequality in the United States, 1913-1998, 118 *Q. J. ECON.* 1 (2003); Thomas Piketty & Emmanuel Saez, The evolution of top incomes: A historical and international perspective, 96 *Am. Econ. Rev.* 200 (2006); Anthony B. Atkinson, Thomas Piketty & Emmanuel Saez, Top incomes in the long run of history, 49 *J. Econ. Literature* 3 (2011); Thomas W. Volscho & Nathan J. Kelly, The rise of the super-rich: Power, resources, taxes, financial markets, and the dynamics of the top 1 percent, 1949 to 2008, 77 *Am. Soc. Rev.* 679 (2012).

[25]   See Deborah Povich, Brandon Roberts & Mark Mather, *Low-Income Working Families: The Racial/Ethnic Divide, The Working Families Project Policy Brief* 2 (Winter 2014-2015), http://www.workingpoorfamilies.org/wp-content/uploads/2015/03/WPFP-2015-Report_Racial-Ethnic Divide.pdf.

[26]   See City University of New York, Law Review Symposium, The long crisis: Economic inequality in New York City: A conversation between Fahd Ahmed, Tom Angotti, Jennifer Jones Austin, Shawn Blumberg & Robin Steinberg, 18 *CUNY L. REV.* 153, 157 (2014) [hereinafter, CUNY, The long crisis] (stating that. . ."social mobility and upward economic mobility—the phenomena that are said to make vast disparities of income and wealth tolerable in a democracy are on the decline."). See generally Robert B. Reich, Beyond Outrage: What has Gone Wrong with Our Economy and Our Democracy, and How to Fix It (2012).

[27]   See CUNY, The long crisis, *supra* note 26 at 158.

[28]   *Id.*

[29]   *Id.* at 159-160.

[30]   See DeSilver, *supra* note 2.

[31]   Floyd Norris, Corporate profits grow and wages slide, *New York Times*, April 5, 2014, at B3, available at http://www.nytimes.com/2014/04/05/business/economy/corporate-profits- grow-ever-larger-as-slice-of-economy-as-wages-slide.html.

[32]   Robert B. Reich, Higher wages can save America's economy – and Its democracy, *Salon* (September 13, 2013), available at http://www.salon.com/2013/09/03/higher_wages_can_save_americas_economy_and_its_democracy_partner/ (observing that "[e]mployee pay is now down to the smallest share of the economy since the government began collecting wage and salary data 60 years ago; and corporate profits, the largest share").

[33]   *Id.* See also Mishel *et al.*, *The State of Working America*, *supra* note 1 at 7 (explaining that productivity refers to "the ability to produce more goods and services per hour worked ").

[34]   Reich, *supra* note 32; see also Lawrence Mishel, Elise Gould & Josh Bivens, Econ. Pol'y Inst., *Wage Stagnation in Nine Charts* 10, (January 6, 2015), http://s1.epi.org/files/2013/wage-stagnation-in-nine-charts.pdf; see also Elise Gould, Econ. Pol'y Inst., *Why America's Workers Need Faster Wage Growth – and What We can Do about It*, Briefing Paper No. 382, (Aug. 27, 2014), available at http://s4.epi.org/files/ 2014/why-americas-workers-need-faster-wage-growth-final.pdf (observing that, while non-supervisory compensation tracked productivity increases from 1948 to 1979, productivity from 1979 to 2013 has increased approximately eight times faster than has compensation).

[35]   See Econ. Pol'y Inst., The Top 10 Charts of 2014 (December 18, 2014), http://www.epi.org/publication/the-top-10-charts-of-2014 (explaining that, as of 2014, "… there is a growing recognition that the root of rising American inequality is the failure of hourly pay for the vast majority of American workers to keep pace with economy-wide productivity … When hourly pay for the vast majority tracked productivity … the American income distribution was stable and growth broadly shared. Since the late 1970s, [however,] the link between typical workers' pay and productivity has broken down and allowed capital owners (rather than workers) to claim a larger share of income and allowed those at the very top of the pay distribution to claim a larger share of overall wages." See also Bivens *et al.*, *supra* note 8: "Between 1979 and 2007, annual hours worked by bottom fifth working-age households rose by 165 hours, while (inflation-adjusted) average hourly wages of the bottom fifth rose by $0.28. [T]he late 1990s was the only period of sustained wage growth over the last four decades. Outside of this period, wages were either stagnant or fell for low-wage workers. This can be seen by comparing the actual 1979-2007 outcomes with those that would have prevailed had the late 1990s boom not occurred. Without the late 1990s, annual hours of bottom-fifth workers still would have increased, though only by 24 rather than 165 hours. In contrast, hourly wages of the bottom fifth would have actually fallen by $0.57."

[36]   Union membership in the United States has declined markedly since the 1970s: the percentage of the workforce represented by unions in 2011 (13.0%) was less than half that of 1973 (26.7%). See Mishel *et al.*, *The State of Working America*, *supra* note 1, at 268-9.

[37]   Private sector union membership in the United States declined from 34% to 8% for men and from 16% to 6% for women between 1973 and 2007, while wage inequality increased by over 40% during the same period. Bruce Western & Jake Rosenfeld, Unions, norms, and the rise in US wage inequality, 76 *Am. Soc. Rev.* 513 (2011). It is important to note that de-unionization has a disparate impact across demographic groups. Mishel *et al.* calculated a "union wage premium" – differences

in hourly wages between unionized and nonunionized workers (controlled for industry, occupation, region, experience, education, and marital status). They found that the union premiums are especially pronounced for workers of color – especially black and Latino men, as well as for immigrants. See Mishel et al., *The State of Working America, supra* note 1, at 268-9.

[38] At the time, union workers did not face as much competition from the ability of corporations to exploit workers (*e.g.* nominal pay) from the global south and/or face the same extent of the challenges caused by increasing technological advances that replace the need for labor.

[39] See generally, Thomas W. Mitchell, Growing inequality and racial economic gaps, 56 *How. L. J.* 849 (2013); see *Income Inequality in the United States: Testimony before the Joint Economic Committee*, United States Congress, (statement of Robert R. Reich) (January 16, 2014), available at http://www.jec.senate.gov/public/_cache/files/3455c373-7557- 4581-8cd8-34b43b759f53/reich-testimony.pdf.

[40] See Summers et al., *supra* note 5 at 7: "People are no longer confident in the expectation that hard work will be rewarded or have their children live better than they did. Most families find it harder to raise their living standards than they did generations ago, and there are grounds for concern about stagnation in living standards. Those that are in work are working longer for less ..." See generally CUNY, The long crisis, *supra* note 26.

[41] See Miles Corak, Income inequality, equality of opportunity, and intergenerational mobility, 27 *J. Econ. Persp.* 79 (2013) (observing that increased income inequality is associated with less intergenerational mobility).

[42] The top 1% of households by income dramatically increased the share of their income deriving from capital-based sources (including realized capital gains, dividends, and rents), with the average capital income for the top 1% rising 309.3% from 1979 levels by 2007. The top 1% received 65.0% of all capital income in 2007, up from 39.4% in 1979. Over the same period, average capital income declined by 59.2% for the bottom 20% of income households, and the bottom 90% of households received only 14.8% of all capital income – less than half of the 32.2% figure they received in 1979. See Mishel et al., *The State of Working America, supra* note 1, at 96-99.

[43] See 46 *Am. Jur. 2d Corporations* §14 (2015) (stating, "... A corporation acquires its existence and authority to act from the state.") citing *Baldwin County Electric Membership Corp. v. Lee*, 804 So. 2d 1087 (Ala. 2001); *Community Bd. 7 of Borough of Manhattan v. Schaffer*, 84 N.Y.2d 148, 615 N.Y.S.2d 644, 639 N.E.2d 1 (1994); *Worthington City School Dist. Bd. of Edn. v. Franklin Cty. Bd. of Revision*, 85 Ohio St. 3d 156 (1999)); (further noting, "... The general corporation law of the state, in force at the time of the incorporation, is just as much a part of the contract between the corporation and its stock-holders as are any other documents.", citing *Middleburg Training Center, Inc. v. Firestone*, 477 F. Supp. 2d 719 (E.D. Va. 2007) (applying Virginia law).

[44] Sometimes referred to as "corporate constituency statutes," these laws enumerate stakeholders other than shareholders to whom a corporate board of directors may owe a duty. See Lawrence E. Mitchell, A theoretical and practical framework for enforcing corporate constituency statutes, 70 *Tex. L. Rev.* 579, 587-88 (1992); see also *N.Y. Bus. Corp. Law* § 717 (McKinney, 2015).

[45] See Henry Hansmann, When does worker-ownership work? ESOPS, law firms, co-determination and economic democracy, 99 *Yale L. J.* 1749 (1990).

[46] See Hansmann & Kraakman, *supra* note 12 at 1.

[47] *Id.* at 1-2.

[48] *Id.*

[49] See, e.g., *Dodge v. Ford Motor Co.*, 204 Mich. 459, 507 (1919) ("A business corporation is organized and carried on primarily for the profit of the stockholders. The powers of the directors are to be employed for that end. The discretion of directors is to be exercised in the choice of means to attain that end, and does not extend to a change in the end itself, to the reduction of profits, or to the non-distribution of profits among stockholders in order to devote them to other purposes."); ECA, *Local 134 IBEW Joint Pension Trust of Chicago v. JP Morgan Chase Co.*, 553 F.3d 187, 200 (2d Cir. 2009) ("Earning profits for the shareholders is the essence of the duty of loyalty[.]").

[50] Contract is the prevailing method of dealing with labor. As Hansmann & Kraakman state: "Simple contracts, and the basic doctrines of contract law, are inadequate in themselves to govern the long-term relationships between workers and the firms that employ them – relationships that may be afflicted by, among other things, substantial transaction-specific investments and asymmetries of information." Henry Hansmann & Reinier Kraakman, The end of history for corporate law, 89 *Geo. L. J.* 439, 444 (2001).They go on to say that: "In general, contractual devices, whatever their weaknesses, are *(when supplemented by appropriate labor market regulation)* [emphasis added] evidently superior to voting and other collective choice mechanisms in resolving conflicts of interest among and between a corporation's investors and employees." *Id.* at 446. Assuming this statement is true without defending it, current levels of income inequality imply, among other things, a lack of "appropriate labor market regulation." While it is worthwhile to pursue more effective labor market regulation, given the current levels of income inequality it seems prudent to pursue more than one solution to the problem.

51 See Claudia Goldin & Robert A. Margo, The Great Compression: The wage structure in the United States at mid-century, 107 Q. J. Econ. 1 (1992) (coining the term).

52 See Lawrence Mishel & Ross Eisenbrey, Econ. Pol'y Inst., How to Raise Wages: Policies that Work and Policies that Don't, Briefing Paper No. 391 at 7 (March 19, 2014).

53 Id.

54 Patricia Cohen, Counting up hidden costs of low pay, New York Times, April 13, 2015, at B1, available at http://www.nytimes.com/2015/04/13/business/economy/working-but-need ing-public-assistance-anyway.html.

55 Inequality for All (72 Productions, 2013)(a documentary film raising awareness about widening income inequality in the US and approaches needed to reverse this trend). The documentary shows that the cause of widening income inequality is not that workers are not working hard and shows that in fact workers are actually working longer and harder for less. The documentary also suggests ways of addressing income inequality.

56 In addition to worker-owned cooperatives, such alternative business structures include, but are not limited to, social enterprises and benefit corporations. Social enterprises are generally for-profit businesses whose primary purpose is to serve the common good. See generally Social Enterprise Alliance, What's a Social Enterprise? (2014), available at https://www.se-alliance.org/why#whatsasocialenterprise. Benefit corporations (B Corporations) are a subset of social enterprises and are generally structured as for-profit enterprises incorporated under a state's business corporation law. B Corporations, however, include among their purposes the creation of public benefits, such as protecting the environment or providing services to underserved communities. Because B Corporations have purposes beyond profit-maximization, directors are both permitted and required to pursue the public benefit purpose(s) as part of their fiduciary duties to act in the best interests of the corporation. At present, 26 states and the District of Columbia have enacted legislation recognizing the corporate structure of benefit corporations. See Benefit Corporation Information Center, State by State Legislative Status, http://www.benefitcorp.net/state-by-state-legislative-status (last visited Feb. 21, 2015), (also indicating that legislation is pending in an additional eight states).

57 To be sure, there are other forms of employee ownership, e.g., Employee Stock Ownership Plans ("ESOPs"); however, this article focuses on worker-owned cooperatives and union co-ops as more transformative forms of ownership. For a brief discussion of these differences, see Carmen Huertas-Noble, Promoting worker-owned cooperatives as a CED empowerment strategy: A case study of colors and lawyering in support of participatory decision-making and meaningful social change, 17 Clin. L. Rev. 255 (2010) [hereinafter Huertas-Noble, Promoting worker-owned cooperatives].

58 See, generally, Jessica Gordon Nembhard, Cooperatives and wealth accumulation: Preliminary analysis, 92 Am. Econ. Rev. 325 (2002); Peter Molk, The puzzling lack of cooperatives, 88 Tul. L. Rev. 899 (2014).

59 For a detailed discussion of entity formation options for worker-owned cooperatives see Edward W. De Barbieri & Brian Glick, Legal entity options for worker-owned cooperatives, 2 Grassroots Economic Organizing (GEO) Newsletter (2011), available at http:www.geo.coop/node/628.

60 The mechanism of the share only applies to C Corporations and Cooperative corporations. In an LLC worker-owners would have equal membership interest.

61 See generally David Ellerman & Peter Pitegoff, The democratic corporation: The new worker-owned cooperative statute in Massachusetts, 11 N.Y.U. Rev. L. & Soc. Change 441 (1982); Peter Pitegoff, Worker-ownership in Enron's wake – revisiting a community development tactic, 8 J. Small & Emerging Bus. L. 239 (2004); John Pencavel, Luigi Pistaferri & Fabiano Schivardi, Wages, employment, and capital in capitalist and worker-owned firms, 60 Indus. & Lab. Rel. Rev. 23 (2006).

62 New York Cooperative Corporations Law §§ 89(2), 88(2) (2015), http://pub- lic.leginfo.state.ny.us/lawssrch.cgi?NVLWO:

63 Typically, worker-owned cooperatives distribute net income in proportion to each worker-owner's labor contribution; this distribution is called a patronage dividend. See, The ICA Group, Patronage Dividend (2015) http://ica-group.org/patronage-dividend; see generally Melanie Conn, No bosses here: Management in worker cooperatives, 9 J. Bus. Ethics 373 (1990).

64 Gowri J. Krishna, Worker-owned cooperative creation as progressive lawyering? Moving beyond the one-person, one-vote floor, 34 Berkely J. Emp. & Lab. L. 65 (2013)

65 Id. at 114.

66 See Carmen Huertas-Noble, Jessica Rose & Brian Glick, The greening of community and economic development: Dispatches from New York City, 31 W. New Eng. L. Rev. 645 (2009) (explaining that worker-owned cooperatives tend to anchor businesses in the local community in part, because worker-owners are likely to live in the communities in which their businesses are located and are more likely to hire and purchase their goods and services locally. Such owners are also less likely to disinvest during economic down- turns.) See also William H. Simon, The Community Economic Development Movement: Law, Business, & The New Social Policy, 69-72 (2001). Unions can also help in connecting worker-owned cooperatives to larger economic justice movements.

[67] Cooperatives also operate under the principle of concern for community. See Jessica Nembhard, *Collective Courage: A History of African American Cooperative Economic Thought & Practice* (2014); Jessica Nembhard, Principle and strategies for reconstruction: Models of African American community based cooperative economic development, 12 *Harv. J. Afr. Am. Pub. Pol'y* 39, 44 (2006); and Simon, *supra* note 66 at 69-72.

[68] For an example of a union co-op model collaboratively developed by Mondragon USA, the Ohio Employee Ownership Center (OEOC), and United Steelworkers (USW), see Rob Witherell *et al.*, *Sustainable Jobs, Sustainable Communities: The Union Co-op Model* (March 26, 2012), available at http://assets.usw.org/our-union/coops/The-Union-Co- op-Model-March-26-2012.pdf.

[69] For examples, see Section IIIC, *infra*.

[70] For example, the coalition is made up of various individuals and organizations, including the Clinic, the Federation of Protestant Welfare Agencies, the Urban Justice Center, Make the Road New York, etc. which are all active participants in larger economic justice movements.

[71] See Section IVA, *infra*, for a discussion of the Mondragon Principles.

[72] See Cameron Keng, If Apple were a worker-owned cooperative each employee would earn at least 403k, *Forbes* (stating that Prof. Huertas-Noble and 1Worker1Vote have taken their success with promoting worker-owned cooperatives and securing New York City government funding to help spur other communities and governments such as Madison, Wisconsin to make similar pledges of financial support for worker-owned cooperatives) http://www.forbes.com/sites/cameronkeng/2014/12/18if-apple-was-a-worker-coop erative-each-employee-would-earn-at-least-403k/ (Last visited on 7/23/2015).

[73] For a discussion of the involvement of leading educational institutions in developing curricula for training cooperatives, see Section VI, *infra*.

[74] Left Forum, *Union Co-ops: A Powerful Tool in a Broad-Based Movement to End Income Inequality and Create Transformative Economic Justice* (June 1, 2014). Panelists included David Levine, Co-founder and CEO of the American Sustainable Business Council; Michael Peck, Mondragon North American Delegate; Stephen Edel, Green & Equitable Economies Organizer, The Center for Working Families; Carmen Huertas-Noble, CUNY, and Missy Risser, Co-founder, 1 Worker 1 Vote. The audience included Citibank representatives and other bankers, activists and educators. The diversity of the audience was exciting. As one of the author's lawyer colleagues said, "When you get the bankers in the room, then you know you're making progress."

[75] Prospera was formerly known as Women's Action to Gain Economic Security (WAGES).

[76] Mondragon is one of the largest networks of worker-owned cooperatives in the world, and is highly profitable. For further description of the Mondragon Cooperative, see Section IVA, *infra*.

[77] See Malcolm X Grassroot Movement, *The Jackson Plan: A Struggle for Self-Determination, Participatory Democracy, and Economic Justice* (July 2012), https://mxgm.org/the- jackson-plan-a-struggle-for-self-determination-participatory-democracy-and-economic-jus- tice/.

[78] See Keng, *supra* note 72 (stating that the City of Madison has approved a plan to provide $1 million over the course of five years to support worker-owned cooperatives).

[79] See, *e.g.*, Krishna, *supra* note 64 (arguing that the one-person, one vote principle is not enough to make the worker-owned cooperative model transformative). Other critiques, outside the scope of this article, concern cooperatives' ability to compete in the marketplace and the drawbacks of participatory decision-making structures as a tax on workers' time (if governance work is not paid) and inefficiency based on the amount of work that could be accomplished if each person specialized. But see generally Carmen Huertas-Noble, Promoting worker-owned cooperatives, *supra* note 57 (arguing that worker-owned cooperatives promote collaboration and a more communally productive workplace).

[80] See Krishna, *supra* note 64 at 76-77 (noting that some cooperatives "… seem to merely transform labor(ers) into capital(ists) without aggregating worker power"). The applicability of this statement depends on how the cooperative is set up and governed.

[81] This idea is developed further in the discussion of the Community Economic Development Clinic described more fully below. See Section V, *infra*.

[82] Mondragon does not refer to itself as a "model." It speaks of the "Mondragon experience." This recognizes the importance of always needing to improve.

[83] As of 2013, Mondragon had over €34 billion in assets across 103 cooperatives, 122 production plants, 8 foundations, 1 mutual society, 10 support entities and 13 international service companies. See Mondragon Corporation, *Annual Report 2013*, available at http://www.mondragon-corporation.com/eng/about-us/economic-and-financial-indicators/annual-report/.

[84] Interview with Michael Peck, Mondragon's North American Delegate and co-founder of 1Worker1Vote (May 21, 2015) (on file with Author).

[85] See Mondragon Cooperative Corporation, *Mondragon: 1956-2014*, available at http://www.mondragon-corporation.com/wp-content/themes/mondragon/docs/History-MONDRAGON-1956-2014.pdf.

[86] Although Falgor's cooperative recently "failed," its ability to re-employ almost all its worker-owners by retraining them and placing them at other Mondragon cooperatives and the decision by the Mondragon Network's worker-owners to take a 1.5% (?) cut in their salaries illustrate Mondragon's commitment to its individual worker-owners. Despite the attention paid to the owner-members of the cooperative, an important critique that Mondragon faces is that it is a multinational corporation and has many subsidiaries where most or all of the workers are not members.

[87] See Greg MacLeod, *From Mondragón to America: Experiments in Community Economic Development*, 40-41 (1997).

[88] See Krishna, *supra* note 64 at 92 (quoting *American Worker-Owned Cooperative: A Brief History of CHCA*).

[89] Id. at 101 (citing Anne Inserra, Maureen Conway & John Rodat, The Aspen Institute, *Cooperative Home Care Associates: A Case Study of a Sectoral Employment Development Approach*, 18-19 (2002)), available at http://www.aspenwsi.org/resource/ chca/.

[90] Laura Flanders, The kind of jobs that lift you up: Finally, New York City invests in worker co-ops, *YES! magazine*, Fall 2014.

[91] *Id.* at 35.

[92] *Id.*

[93] *Id.*

[94] *Id.* at 34.

[95] Interviews with Michael Elsas, President, Cooperative Home Care Associates (April 29, 2013, and Nov. 4, 2013) and Keith Joseph, Vice President, Service Employees International Union Local 1199 (Sept. 19, 2013).

[96] See Flanders, *supra* note 90 (noting that, at the time of the allocation, this was the largest amount ever allocated by a city in the United States).

[97] New York City Council Finance Division, Latonia McKinney, Acting Director, *Fiscal Year 2015 Adopted Expense Budget Adjustment Summary / Schedule C*, June 25, 2014, 121, available at: http://council.nyc.gov/html/budget/fy15_documents.shtml (last viewed July 1, 2015).

[98] See Huertas-Noble, Promoting worker-owned cooperatives, *supra* note 57 at 257- 261.

[99] CUNY School of Law's Community and Economic Development Clinic ("CEDC") is part of Main Street Legal Services' clinical program, which is ranked 3rd in the nation and 1st in NY.

[100] For informative and interesting articles on CED legal practice, see Brian Glick & Matthew J. Rossman, Neighborhood legal services as house counsel to community-based efforts to achieve economic justice: The East Brooklyn experience, 23 *N.Y.U. Rev. L. & Soc. Change* 105 (1997); Scott L. Cummings, Community economic development as progressive politics: Towards a grassroots movement for economic justice, 54 *Stan. L. Rev.* 399 (2001); Carmen Huertas-Noble, Jessica Rose & Brian Glick, *supra* note 66; Alicia Alvarez, Community development clinics: What does poverty law have to do with them? 34 *Fordham Urb. L. J.* 1269, 1275 (2007); Susan R. Jones, Small business and community economic development: Transactional lawyering for social change and economic justice, 4 *Clin. L. Rev.* 195, 202–07 (1997); Daniel S. Shah, Lawyering for empowerment: Community development and social change, 6 *Clin. L. Rev.* 217, 217–22 (1999); Krishna, *supra* note 64.

[101] CEDC has four main project areas: The Worker-owned Cooperative Law Project, The Nonprofit Legal Support Project, The Labor Law and Organizing Project and the Tenant Law and Organizing Project. For more info on CEDC, see Beryl Blaustone & Carmen Huertas-Noble, Lawyering at the intersection of mediation and community and economic development: Interweaving inclusive legal problem solving skills in the training of effective lawyers, 34 *Wash. U. J. L. & Pol'y* 157 (2010).

[102] CEDC locally represents such organizations such as Make the Road New York, Green Worker-owned cooperatives and 1Worker1Vote. Outside of NYC, CEDC serves as co-counsel with Regional Legal Housing Services of Pennsylvania to represent Pittsburgh's Clean and Green Laundry, which is in the process of becoming a worker-owned cooperative that will most likely be unionized. 1Worker1Vote is also a national nonprofit that helps create union co-ops across the United States.

[103] Additional law clinics that employ a similar strategy are, *e.g.*, Fordham Law's CED Clinic, Hofstra Law's CED Clinic, Brooklyn Law's CED Clinic, and University of Michigan Law's CEDC Clinic.

[104] For an explanation of the different approaches to CED, and an argument for an empowerment driven approach, see Huertas-Noble, Promoting worker-owned cooperatives, *supra* note 57 at 265. See also *id.* at 257-61 for additional articles written by scholars that view CED lawyering as a way to collaborate with and empower clients and communities.

[105] Coalition members include: SCO Family of Services-Center For Family Life, Green Worker Cooperatives, ICA Group, The Working World, Make the Road New York, Urban Upbound, Democracy at Work Institute, NYC Network of Worker Cooperatives, Commonwise Education, Inc., Business Outreach Center Network, Inc., Urban Justice Center, CUNY Law School, Federation of Protestant Welfare Agencies and Third Sector New En- gland. See New York City Council Finance Division, Latonia McKinney, Director, Fiscal Year 2016 Adopted Expense Budget Adjustment Summary / Schedule C, June 26, 2015, 121, available at: http://council.nyc.gov/html/budget/fy16_documents.shtml (last viewed July 1, 2015)

[106] Report is on file with Author.

[107] See, *e.g.,* Saioa Arando *et al.,* Efficiency in employee-owned enterprises: An econometric case study of Mondragon, Institute for the Study of Labor Discussion Paper No. 5711 (May 2011), available at http://ssrn.com/abstract=1849466; http://online-library.wiley.com/journal/10.1111/(ISSN)1467-8292.

[108] The conference was held on January 30, 2014, at the Federation of Protestant Welfare Agencies. For more information on the conference, see John W. Lawrence, *A Call to Develop a Worker Cooperative Sector in New York City: How the City Can Create Jobs and Address Inequality at Its Roots*, available at http://www.geo.coop/story/call-develop-work er-cooperative-sector-new-york-city. This Initiative started with the Federation of Protestant Welfare Agencies convening a group of NYC worker-owned co-ops, worker-owned co-op technical assistance providers and the CEDC to brainstorm how we could create more worker-owned cooperatives in the City and eventually bring them to scale.

[109] See *Oversight – Worker Cooperatives – Is This a Model That Can Lift Families Out of Poverty?* Hearing Before the N.Y.C. Council Committee on Community Development (Feb. 2014) available at http://legistar.council.nyc.gov/Departments.aspx.

[110] The inaugural conference was held on June 21, 2014, at the City University of New York School of Law. More information on the annual conference, now in its third year, is available at http://www.nycworker.coop/conference.

[111] Proclamations on file with author.

[112] nt. 0423-2014 is available at http://nycprogressives.com/2015/02/26/progressives- pass-bill-to-support-worker-co-operatives/.

[113] See generally, Paulette L. Stenzel, The pursuit of equilibrium as the eagle meets the condor: Supporting sustainable development through fair trade, 49 *Am. Bus. L. J.* 557 (2012).

[114] See Press Release, *Ace Hardware Reports First Quarter 2012 Financial Results* (May 11, 2012), available at http://ourcompany.acehardware.com/pdfs/2012Q1pressrelease.pdf (describing Ace Hardware Corporation as the largest retailer-owned hardware cooperative in the industry).

[115] See Citrus World, Inc., *Who We Are* (2014), available at http://www.floridasnatural.com/who-we-are (describing Florida's Natural Growers as one of the largest cooperatives of citrus growers with 1,000 grower-owners).

[116] See Hina Shah, Notes from the field, The role of lawyer in grassroots policy advocacy, 21 *Clin. L. Rev.* 393 (2015).

[117] See *id.* at 407, 408 (citing Chai Rachel Feldblum, The art of legislative lawyering and the six circles theory of advocacy, 34 *McGeorge L. Rev.* 785,805 (2003)). Shah explains that while Feldman focuses on top down, hierarchical models staffed by outside experts, which is antithetical to grassroots campaigns that are often but not always democratic, Feldman "nonetheless provides a useful dissection of the specific skills necessary for an effective advocacy campaign". These skills include the skillset of strategist, lobbyist, legislative lawyer, policy researcher, outreach strategist, and communications director.

[118] See *N.Y. Ltd. Liab. Co. Law § 101 et seq.* (McKinney, 2015) and *N.Y. Coop. Corp Law § 80* (McKinney, 2015). See also De Barbieri & Glick, *supra* note 59.

[119] See Section VIB, *infra,* for a discussion of the various counseling approaches taken, including collaborative counseling and integrative counseling. See also William M. Sullivan, Anne Colby, Judith Welch Wegner, Lloyd Bond & Lee S. Shulman, *Educating Lawyers: Preparation for the Profession of Law* (2007).

[120] See generally Sameer M. Ashar, Law clinics and collective mobilization, 14 *Clin. L. Rev.* 355 (2008).

[121] For comprehensive perspectives on the lawyer's role, see Blaustone & Huertas-Noble, *supra* note 101 at 2; Marjorie M. Shultz & Sheldon Zedeck, Predicting lawyer effectiveness: Broadening the basis for law school admissions decisions, 36 *Law & Soc. Inquiry* 620 (2011); Sullivan *et al., supra* note 119; Sheila R. Foster & Brian Glick, Integrative lawyering: Navigating the political economy of urban redevelopment, 95 *Cal. L. Rev.* 1999 (2007).

[122] This is a key lesson with strong precedent in the civil rights movement, as well as the LGBTQ movement and the early stages of the labor movement.

[123] See Huertas-Noble, Promoting worker-owned cooperatives, *supra* note 57 at 274; see also Ascanio Piomelli, Foucault's approach to power: Its allure and limits for collaborative lawyering, 2004 *Utah L. Rev.* 395, 446-50 (supporting the idea of engaging clients throughout every phase of counseling and lawyers and clients working as partners to determine strategy and implementation and to assess its effectiveness).

[124] See Foster & Glick, *supra* note 121.While CEDC did not represent the coalition as a whole, it did represent some of the coalition members. As lawyers in the coalition, we did provide brief advice when we saw the coalition headed for legal pitfalls.

[125] *Id.* at 2055.

[126] See Blaustone & Huertas-Noble, *supra* note 101.

[127] New York City Small Business Administration, *Selling to Government,* http://ww.nyc.gov/html/sbs/html/procurement/mwbe.shtml (last visited July 1, 2015).

[128] See generally Gar Alperovitz *et al.,* The Cleveland model, *The Nation* (March 1, 2010), available at http://www.thenation.com/article/cleveland-model.

[129] ICA is currently working on business conversions as a main priority. See The ICA Group, *What We Do*, http://ica-group.org/what-we-do/ (last visited July 1, 2015).

[130] *Id.* For more information on conversion, see Ohio Employee Ownership Center, *Small Business Ownership Succession: The Cooperative Solution*, at http://www.oeockent.org/download/cooperatives/1042coopbrochure.pdf.pd; ICA Group, http://ica-group.org/the-conversion-process/.

[131] See Banking on Colorado, *About the Colorado Initiative to Establish a State-owned Bank*, http://bankingoncolorado.org/colorado-initiative/ (last visited July 1, 2015).

[132] See 2015 *Legis. Bill Hist. CA A.B.* 816 available at http://leginfo.legislature.ca.gov/faces/billNavClient.xhtml?bill_id=201520160AB816 (amending California corporations law to recognize worker cooperatives).

[133] See Glick & Rossman, *supra* note 100.

Reprinted from *Clinical Law Review*, Vol. 22, Number 2, 2016.

CHAPTER 29

Financing Worker Cooperatives: Challenges & Opportunities

John Holdsclaw IV

Now is an auspicious time to write the next chapter on the capitalization of worker cooperatives. In grappling to recover from the pandemic's impact, cities and towns are exploring new strategies for economic development, especially in underserved communities. The country is also on the precipice of a record turnover of businesses in the coming decade-plus, putting tens of thousands of more jobs at risk.

Worker cooperatives are also having a moment. A spate of articles in major news outlets champions their ability to improve job quality and create wealth-building opportunities for low- and moderate-income workers and fleshes out an otherwise abstract idea with real people and places. After all, small businesses have long served to anchor their communities, a reality that became even more appreciated during the Covid shutdown.

This chapter is intended as a practical guide to resources enabling the development of a scalable worker cooperative model—with Mondragon as a paradigm—for achieving replicable structural change. Unlike in Spain's vast cooperative network, which is largely funded by its own internal bank (Caja Laboral), worker-owned businesses in the US must navigate a labyrinthine landscape involving decentralized banks and credit unions, venture capital firms, private and public foundations, and cooperative loan funds. According to a study by Project Equity, as of 2017 the estimated collective pool of all cooperative-earmarked capital was an estimated $50 million, with a mere $25,000 targeted specifically at worker cooperatives. That's a pittance compared to the billions funneled into Mondragon's ecosystem (Lingane & McShiras, 2017).

Any discussion about the practical considerations for capitalizing worker cooperatives must address the persistent underpinnings of racial and income inequalities. What's clearly needed is more robust funding, and of a more diverse structure, to truly grow and scale these businesses, primarily through conversions but also by continuing to support start-ups. Technical assistance is a prerequisite to getting capital ready.

Fortunately, radical thinking is leading the way within the cooperative ecosystem. Labor and equity organizations are sounding the alarm and cooperative development and values-aligned financial enterprises are responding.

This chapter will set forth the challenges and opportunities and identify existing capital sources. Because of the lack of a standardized financial model, case studies more aptly demonstrate the different approaches taken by worker cooperatives across industry sectors, regional locations, and stages. Ultimately, they point to the power of patient, risk-tolerant, place-based financing that meets worker cooperatives where they are at, and with flexible terms to promote, rather than obfuscate, short-term success and long-term sustainability.

These stories illustrate as well how worker cooperatives, with appropriate financing, can achieve the overarching mission of employee ownership—enabling economically disadvantaged entrepreneurs to become self-sufficient stakeholders in their own futures, providing a pathway for more minority business owners, and creating wealth for low- and moderate-wage workers.

The Role of Capital in the Worker Cooperative Structure

Having a wide-eyed, realistic grasp of capital needs is paramount to getting a worker co-op off the ground—and for ensuring it remains sustainable over the long term.

As is the case for non-cooperative businesses, the demands for worker cooperative capital can run the gamut according to industry, and like any business spans practically all spheres—be it a barber shop, restaurant, day care provider, web design firm, or construction company, to name but a few.

Start-up financing can include the costs of inventory and equipment, leasing commercial space, working capital for raw materials, and technology infrastructure as well as marketing, fulfilment, and other operating costs. Wages and benefits are of course an important expenditure—worker-owners and employees are the key stakeholders in the democratic structure, as are suppliers and the community members they serve.

Aggregated research based on the US Census Bureau's *Annual Survey of Entrepreneurs* (2020) shows the average start-up costs for businesses range from less than $5,000 for a small service company to well over $1 million for a larger manufacturing or housing cooperative, and with approximately $143,000 being the average capital needs (and a median of just under $29,000) for all surveyed businesses (Wylie, 2020). Financing such a broad spread requires a diverse basket of options that are just not available at conventional institutions.

Financing for growth capital often involves making leasehold improvements or the purchase of real estate, as well as additional inventory and/or equipment and employees. The bulk of worker cooperatives that do not have the means to grow a sizable enough internal capital account (through worker-owner buy-in and other contributions) must rely on outside investment to fund this expansion phase.

Co-op conversions involving the sale of existing businesses from a sole proprietor to employees require a different brand of capital infusion, allowing for the acquisition of the business. These transactions tend to be much larger than for start-ups—often the new business is financing 80% to 100% of the company's market value, mostly through debt, to pay off the selling owner(s).

As the conversion pipeline grows over the coming decade-plus, available capital will also need to grow, preferably patient risk capital that spans debt, equity, and hybrid debt-equity structures. In turn, these higher-capital transactions can capture the attention of larger lenders, where the collateral is the business being sold, or when it involves seller financing.

In either type of worker co-op formation, the structure of ownership is such that each worker-owner purchases one share that imparts one vote, and these shares form the basis of the co-op's democratic control. The buy-in cost varies widely based on the capitalization needs of the co-op and what the worker-owners can afford to pay. Businesses in a high-return sector might be able to price the share higher to cover extra capital investment needs, knowing they will see a strong return on their investment.

For example, shares at Cooperative Home Care Associates (CHCA), a worker-owned health care provider in the Bronx, are priced at $1,000, with a $50 initial buy-in amount; CHCA provides an interest-free loan for the remaining $950 and then takes a weekly deduction until the balance is paid off (Lingane & McShiras, 2017). "For co-ops in a low-return sector, notably many service providers, the benefit of being a worker-owner is not getting some big payout at the end, it's the quality of work, sharing in the control of the business, job security, and other intangibles," says Micha Josephy, Executive Director of Community Fund of New England (CFNE), a community development financial institution (CDFI) that was formed in the mid-1970s in response to the need for financing within the food co-op sector and in the 1980s started to finance worker co-ops, starting with Equal Exchange. In addition, worker-owners are not chosen based on their income but rather their skill set and commitment to the business. In those cases, Josephy tends to see the buy-in share set at a few hundred dollars.

To better grasp the worker co-op conundrum, Josephy contrasts them with a much more familiar form of cooperative: food co-ops, which require hundreds or thousands of community members to step forward and say they are committed to supporting this business, first by buying a share with current money and also by shopping there with future money, because the share is only valuable if they continue to support the business. "Having broad community support is a strong plus in a food co-op loan applicant" (M. Josephy, personal communication, August 6, 2021).

With worker co-ops, there are far fewer owners—the largest might surpass the thousand mark but the bulk has between five and 50 worker-owners. "We are therefore underwriting the worker co-op as a business and certainly the engagement of the worker-owners is critical for us to feel confident it is a shared enterprise and not just one person with a grand idea" (M. Josephy, personal communication, August 6, 2021).

Many food co-ops are also able to raise a significant amount of capital (over $1 million) from their membership, both through equity shares and fundraising campaigns. That significantly reduces the amount of capital they need to get from outside lenders.

For example, when Berkshire Co-op expanded by building a larger grocery store in Great Barrington, Massachusetts, the co-op was able to raise $1.3 million from its members (which includes a deep-pocketed community of second-home owners from New York City and Boston). CFNE then lent $1.25 million and helped pull together other investors (M. Josephy, personal communication, August 6, 2021).

Whereas for the generic worker co-op, the sheer number of people is smaller but also the people in worker co-ops tend to have less wealth, either because of structural systems or personal circumstances. Worker-owners also tend not to seek out other owners with the right skillset and values alignment rather than those who could bring capital to the table. Therefore, it is much harder for worker-owners to invest a significant amount of money in their business. As such worker co-ops are often unable to directly access CFNE programs that are otherwise available to food co-ops and other types of cooperatives.

There is as well a tendency for participants in worker co-ops to be inherently more risk averse. The collective process dictates that the benefit to any one individual is not going to be on par with a sole proprietorship or other hierarchical models. "Many of the worker co-ops we work with are among the most conservative financial businesses out there, even though culturally they would rarely be characterized in that way," says Christine Jennings, Executive Director of Shared Capital Cooperative, a CDFI based in Minneapolis-St. Paul that lends exclusively to cooperatives and is itself a cooperative association. Whether substantiated or not, the low-risk/low-return predisposition among worker-owners can be another obstacle to obtaining financing, though Jennings's approach is to "acknowledge that presumption and work around those natural financially conservative aspects of collective work in creating alternative mechanisms" (C. Jennings, personal communication, August 23, 2021).

II The Barriers to Accessing Capital

Despite the growing recognition of worker cooperatives as catalysts for community development and economic stability, they continue to face a disproportionate difficulty in gaining access to capital. Unlike private entrepreneurial enterprises, collective-minded worker co-ops are usually formed by people in communities with limited financial means, making it that much more difficult for individuals to start new businesses. Potential worker-owners cannot rely on their own savings or credit or turn to friends and family for support during the important start-up phase. Systemic inequalities make it inordinately harder for communities of color to raise the necessary funds, thereby perpetuating the cycle of disenfranchisement.

Instead of self-funding, worker co-ops generally must rely on the two most common types of financing available to any company when it needs to raise capital: equity financing and debt financing. Equity financing places no additional financial burden on the company and helps maintain a low debt-to-equity ratio for accessing debt financing in the future. However, equity investors typically demand a proportionate amount of control in the form of voting shares, which goes against the essence of keeping full control within the worker-owners.

Hence borrowed money is usually what worker co-ops must rely on for start-up and growth—often taking on debt without exposure to or even awareness of the available resources, and sometimes with a deep distrust of institutional lenders. These nascent businesses face a steeper uphill climb before even getting to the starting gate in figuring out how to navigate the commercial financing landscape, only to then meet roadblocks in obtaining access to the same funding that other, non-worker-owned small businesses are entitled to.

Worker cooperatives formed from conversions of existing businesses can bump into similar obstacles, as can later-stage worker cooperatives interested in expanding the business. Even those that boast a proven track record are often turned down for loans and forced to explore alternative avenues.

One example from Shared Capital is a stark illustration of the problem.

Case Study: A1 Design Build in Bellingham, Washington

When the couple-owners of A1 Design Build (https://a1designbuild.coop), which had been operating for over 40 years, were approaching retirement, they approached some of their long-time managers to see if they wanted to buy the business and convert it to a worker cooperative. With "Yes" as the answer, they began a five-year transition process and approached their local bank for a loan to cover the conversion costs.

"It was such an example of an already thriving business and despite having a solid five-year plan and having been in the community for so long, they could not get a bank loan. They came to us, and we were more than happy to work with them, but it is shocking—why would that not have been bankable?! A lot of it has to do with the lack of access to the SBA programs" (C. Jennings, personal communication, August 23, 2021).

Thanks to Shared Capital's underwriting, the business was sold to five of the 18 employees in 2018. According to Jennings, its profitability went through the roof and it doubled in size during the first three years, not because it had been poorly managed or underproductive, but because the literal and figurative ownership inspired the worker-owners to get "super creative" about how they operated, including building out a robust benefits package and making sure people could actually take vacations and time off, providing cross-training to increase employee skill sets, and building out their internal systems to support their team (C. Jennings, personal communication, August 23, 2021).

Debt capital: Conventional vs. SBA loans

Whereas the bulk of US businesses obtain financing through traditional banks or credit unions, these depository institutions are subject to regulatory oversight that prevents them from underwriting riskier loans to worker-owners who are often unable to satisfy the stringent credit history and personal or business collateral requirements. Furthermore, because smaller loans involve the same transaction costs as a large loan, banks have less of an incentive to take on those costs in underwriting smaller loans. The average worker co-op simply doesn't have the borrowing power or needs that banks require.

"We can begrudge the big banks for a lot of things they do, but at the end of the day, even mission-driven banks like NCB that have a real desire to do great work still have to answer to these regulators and prove the deposits in the bank are going to be safe," Jennings says (C. Jennings, personal communication, August 23, 2021).

Worker co-ops have historically been denied access to the $20 to $25 billion annual coffer through the Small Business Administration (SBA) programs, namely the flagship SBA 7(a) loans. These programs are the primary mechanism by which banks and other lenders can offer financial assistance to small businesses because the SBA provides a guarantee for up to 85% of the loan amount in case of default.

Part of the passing of the Main Street Employee Ownership Act (MSEOA) in 2018 was a stipulation by Congress that SBA provide a path for co-ops to apply for SBA 7(a) loans. Yet the SBA failed to change policies that would have allowed for more widespread access. Thus, even though co-ops are now technically eligible, the agency still requires an owner with at least a 20% stake in the business to sign a personal guarantee (usually in the form of a mortgage on their home) for the loan (US Small Business Administration, 2023).

Such a requirement, however, is unreasonable to impose on a cooperative with multiple worker-owners. If there are five worker-owners, it is unreasonable to require all of them to put up their home, or to have just one individual do so on behalf of the cooperative. For most worker co-ops with more than five owners, there is no way to meet the 20% ownership threshold. Even if two or more owners were willing to guarantee the loan, the arrangement undermines the fundamental collective ethos.

R.L. Condra, Senior Vice President of Government Relations for National Cooperative Bank (NCB), has been focusing on this issue on behalf of the cooperative community writ large (of which NCB is a member) for over a decade along with United States Federation of Worker Cooperatives (USFWC) and National Cooperative Business Association CLUSA International (NCBA CLUSA): "The Main Street Act required SBA to listen to its stakeholders and to listen to its counterparts in the public and private sector that don't require a guarantee in coming up with a viable alternative to the personal guarantee. Instead, the agency doubled down on existing requirements" (R.L. Condra, personal communication, September 27, 2021).

In his recent appearance before the House Committee on Small Business, Condra set forth precedent in the private and public sectors: NCB for example has provided loans of more than $2 billion to cooperatives and independent retailers—all without a personal guarantee requirement per its loan policies. The US Department of Agriculture (USDA) does not require a personal guarantee for loans to cooperatives, though because that agency has a rural constituency, the mostly urban worker cooperative start-ups are exempt. The SBA itself does not require personal guarantees for loans to Employee Stock Ownership Plans (ESOPs) that have a similar structure as worker cooperatives.

Congress also removed the personal guarantee requirement in the CARES Act for Economic Impact Disaster Loans (EIDL) and Paycheck Protection Program (PPP) business loans. As a result, over 2,500 cooperatives (of all types) received Covid relief loans totaling $1.2 billion in funding that saved over 93,000 jobs. Yet the same cooperative businesses that received Covid relief funding are not able to access the SBA's existing loan programs.

Rather than remove the personal guarantee, SBA set forth two paths for worker cooperatives to apply for SBA 7(a) loans without having to provide a personal guarantee: in the case of a conversion whereby the original owner could guarantee the loan until it is repaid; and by setting up a separate entity with enough assets to guarantee the loan. But most often the owner is looking to retire and may not be willing or able to support the business for the loan term; and the "entity guarantee" option, which is nowhere stated on the loan application, is left to lenders to figure out. The meaning of "entity" is nowhere defined, leaving that at question—it could be a foundation or an investor or some other form of capital that could secure the loan, but that would require a worker co-op to find such an entity to secure a loan. "It's an empty solution for them because as a federal agency with tons of rules and regulations, they have not applied any such guidelines to indicate how a cooperative can satisfy the entity guarantee requirement" (R.L. Condra, personal communication, September 27, 2021).

Thus far there has only been one entity guarantee transaction approved by SBA. In 2020, NCB worked with the Fredericksburg Food Co-op to capitalize a guarantor by raising $1.7 million in loans and grants and setting aside another $150,000 in cash collateral. (Because nowhere is the entity guarantee provided for on the application, NCB had to write it in the margins.) While that achievement could provide a model for other cooperatives in wealthier communities, it is not a replicable or viable solution for the communities most in need—or for the majority of worker cooperatives that already struggle to come up with collateral.

The consensus within the cooperative community is that the solution is for SBA to remove the personal guarantee requirement altogether, although history is not on their side. That said, if it did, Condra indicates NCB would take a stronger look at underwriting loans to worker cooperatives, offering as an example a day care center that approached NCB to underwrite the conversion to a worker cooperative, with what he saw as three factors in its favor: "They had a track record of being a successful business; they were providing an essential service to the community, and the conversion would be saving 50 jobs. But we weren't able to do that deal without the SBA loan guarantee, it presented too much of a risk and would take years to make it work. That's just one of hundreds of examples of how a worker co-op could be a good fit for an SBA loan but not without the bank having the guarantee by SBA."

Venture capital

Many small businesses turn to venture capitalists and angel investors for equity rather than taking on debt—especially when the business cannot afford the debt they are being offered or cannot qualify based on the lack of sufficient credit or capitalization.

Although venture capital firms are known for making higher-risk investments than a bank, the expectation is that they will receive a higher return on their investment. Worker co-ops in general present neither the earnings potential nor growth curve that venture capitalists require. Only 31% of worker cooperatives have annual revenues over $1 million, and the average annual profit margin for a worker cooperative is 6.4% (Democracy at Work Institute, *n.d.*).

Venture capitalists also demand control over the company in the form of a controlling seat on the board, a prospect that is anathema to the one-member, one-vote worker co-op ownership structure—and thus can be a poison pill from the start. What's more, venture capital firms often require an exit strategy, usually by selling off the business, when the purpose of worker cooperatives is to provide long-term employment to present and future members.

At least one proposed solution is to have private equity firms exit their shares to a worker-owned business, an especially palatable option for selling off socially responsible businesses and/or by social impact private investors interested in continuing to support the community served by the business going forward. Indeed, impact investing is being proposed as a key mechanism for meeting the capital needs in scaling worker co-op conversions. The Global Impact Investing Network (GIIN) defines impact investments as "investments made with the intention to generate positive, measurable social and environmental impact alongside a financial return" (Global Impact Investing Network, 2022).

Public & Private Grants

Although a limited number of grants are available directly to worker co-ops most grants, including government grants around the area of workforce development, require the co-op to partner with a fiscal sponsor in the community with mission overlap or a partner in the co-op movement that is looking to work in the same sector. That prospect might not be feasible for an unknown business that is seeking start-up capital and lacks the community network. To date, grants have not played a significant role in conversions, though that is likely to change as more businesses transition to worker cooperatives.

In Josephy's experience, CFNE and other CDFIs have faced difficulty in accessing conventional grant dollars available to the small business sector because co-ops are often seen as too niche or marginal, though he has been able to partner with smaller foundations from values-aligned private institutions, including National Cooperative Bank.

Even if more grant dollars were available to worker co-ops, the amounts are generally not enough to fund other than pre-launch or early development stage needs and/or ongoing technical assistance on their own or to do more than serve as supplemental dollars to debt and equity investments.

III Emerging Opportunities for Capital Access

Not content to stand by to see whether SBA programs become available, cooperative entities and other equitable organizations are working to disrupt the dominant economic system by promoting alternative pathways to building more worker-controlled enterprises and more equitably distributing wealth and power.

"It's an interesting time to engage in a conversation around capitalizing worker cooperatives because the field is very much in flux," Josephy says (M. Josephy, personal communication, August 6, 2021). He is seeing a shift away from historical debt financing to a real commitment to recognizing the full spectrum of capital that worker co-ops need and finding solutions for providing equity financing that would not change control by the workers as well as revenue-based financing like other more unconventional, nuanced types of financing that in many cases will help start-ups much better than conventional or even CDFI debt. Considered a hybrid of debt and equity, revenue-based financing allows businesses to raise capital by pledging a set percentage of future revenue, with no-interest-bearing payments that vary based on profits and without any exchange of ownership.

The impact of Covid on small business closures and unemployment has also put economic inequity in sharper relief given communities of color and low-income communities were disproportionately affected and by overmuch. For a bright-side indicator, CFNE raised more money from investors during the pandemic (for fiscal year 2020) than in any year prior, which Josephy sees as a direct result of the crisis. "It mobilized people to think about the importance of small businesses generally and co-ops specifically and to find ways to support them even though they couldn't access their goods or services because of the shutdown" (M. Josephy, personal communication, August 6, 2021).

Covid's call for a reckoning, in conjunction with the "silver tsunami" of baby boomers approaching retirement, is propelling a movement within the cooperative community writ large toward promoting co-op conversions to scale the worker-owned model and help repair impacted communities.

"As people think about what happened during the health and economic crisis and how they want to rebuild the economy so it is more sustainable and equitable and racially just, co-ops are rising to the top as a solution," says Alison Powers, Cooperative & Community Initiatives Manager at Capital Impact Partners (CIP). "Hopefully as an ecosystem, we can catapult co-ops to the next level and not have them be the best-kept secret anymore, which is not what you want to be in community development" (A. Powers, personal communication, October 20, 2021).

Some of this work is being channeled through advocating for legislative changes, but most efforts are happening within the private sector and at the grassroots level.

Legislative levers

Proposed changes to SBA programs

Bills have gone to Congress that would effectuate changes to SBA loan programs beyond mere mandates and open lending to worker co-ops by banks, credit unions, and other intermediaries.

A new bill introduced in May 2021 by US Senator John Hickenlooper of Colorado (where co-ops are commonplace) would more clearly do what the MSEOA aspired to do but with more directive language.

In effect, The Capital for Cooperatives Act would require SBA to change regulations on loan guarantees made to co-ops to ensure that risk is adequately mitigated, without requiring a personal or entity guarantee from borrowers.

SSBCI funding

Advocates are framing the reauthorization of the State Small Business Credit Initiative (SSBCI) under the American Rescue Act to catalyze employee-owned businesses to help narrow gender and racial wealth and income gaps, and to create a public-private partnership to broaden awareness around employee ownership. More broadly, when designed for scale, the SSBCI could be yet another vehicle for promoting employee-ownership transitions.

The SSBCI allocates $10 million in funding for small business financing programs, including capital access programs, loan participations, loan guarantees, collateral support, and venture equity programs. It also provides for critical technical assistance to small businesses applying for SSBCI and other government programs (US Department of Treasury, 2023).

In response to a request for information, the Democracy at Work Institute (DAWI) and the Employee Ownership Expansion Network (EOX) sent letters to the Treasury Department to encourage implementation of support for state employee ownership centers and to dedicate a small portion of funds to technical assistance and education alongside patient capital, to help businesses sell to their employees in conversions.

Specific recommendations included mandating a percentage of a state's allocated SSBCI funds be set aside for lending and technical assistance; pairing funding for technical assistance with equity-like capital to support employees to purchase shares; and working through the CDFI Fund and prioritizing CDFIs with conversion lending experience and expertise (McKinley, 2021).

The conclusion by DAWI and EOX was that "employee ownership has the potential to benefit economically distressed communities and disadvantaged small businesses and should be a well-supported part of the SSBCI toolbox."

State credit union legislative policies

The worker cooperative community has long lamented the lack of funding available from credit unions, which are themselves non-profit cooperatives that are owned by their members, due to federal and state regulations. But at least one credit union has shown how these institutions can make a deep impact in scaling worker co-ops.

The mission of Vermont State Employees Credit Union (VSECU), a values-based financial cooperative open to everyone who lives or works in Vermont, is "to inspire a movement that brings people together to empower the possibilities for greater financial, environmental, and social prosperity" (https://www.vsecu.com).

Through its Co-Op Capital program, VSECU supports the development of cooperatives with long-term capital investment. It can do this because of a Vermont statute allowing state-chartered credit unions to invest directly into other credit unions and cooperatives both inside and outside of Vermont. Specifically, 8 V.S.A. § 32104 (2005) enables credit unions to invest equity of up to 10% of their shares, deposits, and surplus into cooperatives, without counting against the 12.25% member business lending cap.

According to CreditUnions.com, a leading research site for the credit union industry, since the program's launch in 2016, VESCU has supported the cooperative sector through traditional products as well as direct investments ($148,000 to date), generally in the form of non-voting preferred stock (Harrison, *n.d.*). It has also partnered with other lenders outside of Vermont, including CDFIs such as the Cooperative Fund of New England (CFNE) and LEAF of Boston (VESCU invested $20,000 in the Wellspring Harvest co-op discussed later in this chapter) to expand its reach beyond state borders.

Although similar legislation exists in seven other states, including Arkansas, Illinois, Kentucky, Montana, Nevada, New Jersey, and New Mexico, Vermont is the only one in which a credit union has acted on the allowance. Therefore, advocates are trying to build awareness among credit unions in those other states—and to lobby other state legislatures and Congress to broaden the range of credit unions that are legally permitted to make such investments.

It's worth noting that VSECU was made aware of the statute by the director of the Vermont Employee Ownership Center, proving how these centers can be instrumental in scaling worker co-ops at the capital level (Harrison, *n.d.*).

Leveraging the expertise of CDFIs

From the time it was first established by the US Department of Treasury in 1994, the CDFI Fund's mission has been to "expand economic opportunity for underserved people and communities by supporting the growth and capacity of a national network of community development lenders, investors, and financial service providers" (US Dept. of Treasury CDFI Fund, *n.d.*).

Through various awards programs, the CDFI Fund supports Community Development Financial Institutions (CDFIs), which can then leverage the resources awarded to them by the CDFI Fund to draw in new or increased sources of private funding consisting of low-interest loans, grants, and donations.

Since its inception, the CDFI Fund has awarded $1.8 billion to CDFIs and certified Community Development Entities (CDEs), which act as intermediaries for the provision of financial tools and counselling in low-income communities (US Dept. of Treasury CDFI Fund, *n.d.*).

There are currently more than 1,000 CDFIs—made up of mission-driven banks, credit unions, microloan funds, and venture capital providers—across the country, each one playing an enormous role in addressing the systemic bias that exists in the communities that they serve.

Importantly, a few CDFIs, such as CFNE, Shared Capital, and LEAF Fund, lend extensively to cooperatives (including worker co-ops). Among these, efforts are underway to increase the worker co-ops in their respective portfolios. In 2021, CFNE's loan portfolio was 39% worker co-ops and 37% food co-ops. More notable, is that 77% of CFNE's newly approved loans went to worker co-ops when the previous four years averaged 28%. "I am sure that 77% will prove to be a pandemic-related outlier, but it is indicative of the growth in uptake of worker co-ops as solutions to community challenges" stated Josephy (M. Josephy, personal communication, August 6, 2021).

At Shared Capital, worker co-ops represent about 60% of total loan volume, up from 15% just eight years ago. According to Jennings, the average loan amount at that time was $50,000 but that has also increased significantly over time (C. Jennings, personal communication, August 23, 2021).

The Working World is a non-profit loan fund providing investment capital exclusively to the worker cooperative sector as opposed to other types of businesses. What makes Working World different is that they position themselves as venture capitalists that supports their radical social mission through non-extractive financing, defined by community wealth community Seed Commons as financing that is never harmful to the borrower. By this definition, borrowers are not required to make interest or principal repayments until they are able to cover operating costs.

Other CDFIs are now pivoting toward funding cooperatives. Notably, as part of the Employee Ownerships Initiative, the Washington Area Community Investment Fund (Wacif) is returning to its roots as a cooperative lender, having transitioned over the years to small business lending. Wacif's mission is to promote equity and economic opportunity in underserved neighborhoods in the Washington, D.C. region. Bryant credits the knowledge-sharing nature of the CDFI nature, especially Shared Capital and CFNE, which have been helping CDFIs like Wacif learn the differences between traditional lending and cooperative lending and how to structure the loans—and with partnering on the capital stack Wacif can offer, as it has a relatively low maximum loan amount of $250,000.

At the other extreme, Capital Impact Partners, created in 1978 as part of the National Consumer Cooperative Bank Act, supports food, worker and housing co-ops in historically marginalized communities and communities of color. With a minimum loan amount of $1 million (and a maximum of $8 million), CIP is positioned between smaller CDFIs and lenders like NCB (A. Powers, personal communication, October 20, 2021). "Our strategy is focused on bridging the racial wealth gap and supporting co-ops that create services, affordable housing, and quality jobs in their communities," Powers says (A. Powers, personal communication, October 20, 2021).

Place-based patient financing

Collectively these CDFIs are part of a collaborative force that brings together diverse private and public sector investors to create lasting economic opportunity and more resilient communities using patient financing that values relationships over investment returns, and with flexible terms that meet the specific needs of each business. Rather than collateralization, this so-called character-based lending model revolves around place-based community building and integrated capital or closed-loop investing.

In Josephy's estimation, "One of the superpowers of the co-op-oriented CDFIs is to effectively aggregate investment from a lot of individuals to allow everyday people to participate" by setting a low entry point for investments starting at $1,000. The CDFIs then aggregate those individual contributions and invest them in a large portfolio of many different co-ops, thereby spreading the risk. "The responsibility of underwriting is centered among people who have experience doing that, but it's a way for the community to support the development of community cooperatives" (M. Josephy, personal communication, August 6, 2021).

Another advantage afforded by CDFIs is that because they are not subject to depository institution regulations, they can make loans that would otherwise not be bankable—instead, they are beholden to their board and in the case of a cooperative-formed CDFI like CFNE, their cooperative members.

Case Study: A Yard & a Half Landscaping Co-op in Waltham, Massachusetts

Founded in 1988, A Yard & A Half Landscaping was ranked in the top 15% of landscaping companies and the top 3% of all women-owned companies by annual sales nationwide in 2013, at which time the owner decided to retire. A group of employees took her up on the offer of buying her out, subsequently forming as a for-profit worker-owned cooperative (after initial hesitation and hands-on training and education) "to preserve and continue to develop a locally-owned, safe, just, and democratic workplace in an industry where workers often face exploitation, wage theft, and hazardous working conditions. Participation in the cooperative is a financial and career investment for members, not just a job...We also share in the profits of our labor, allowing us to reinvest in our own local economy, communities, and families" (A Yard & A Half, *n.d.*).

Josephy reports that seven years post-conversion, the company had growing internal capital accounts, higher wages (from $15.63 to an average of $19.29 per hour), and an increase in annual revenue, from $2 million to over $3 million. Membership was at 50%, including longtime employees from the Latinx community. Allocated owner equity had soared from $70,000 to approximately $330,000 (M. Josephy, personal communication, August 6, 2021)

New employees become eligible for membership after two seasons of employment and must be proposed by a current worker-owner and then approved by a majority vote. Candidates agree to purchase one share of voting common stock, which does not appreciate or depreciate, and to pay 50% of the buy-in upon acceptance. The balance of the share may be paid by payroll deductions.

"CFNE's loan was the single most significant factor in our coop's ability to purchase our company from the retiring owner, preserving our jobs and company culture" (M. Josephy, personal communication, August 6, 2021).

If at any point the business is not hitting its projections, the staff can sit down with the worker-owners and renegotiate the terms of the repayment. That flexibility has allowed Jennings's team at Shared Capital to postpone repayment to allow a start-up business to increase their sales, and to quickly pause payments during COVID by creating an emergency loan program that offered up to three months of deferred payments. Of the 68% of businesses (including worker co-ops) that took advantage of the program, only three (out of 100) businesses failed to return to regular payments right away. Once the federal funds kicked in, Shared Capital shifted to helping businesses access those because it didn't qualify as a PPP lender (based on total loan volume).

"Through that flexibility and the additional hands-on technical assistance we can provide, CDFIs can have deeper engagement than traditional banks can have," Jennings says. "We can patiently wait for projects to pay off, and there were some that were questionable at certain points in the loan term. But because we were able to stick by **their side** and do what they needed us to do, they were able to pay us back 100% and prove successful over time" (C. Jennings, personal communication, August 23, 2021).

Collaborative, cross-platform financing
With their ability to devote additional time and energy towards each transaction, CDFIs are in a unique position to be able to aggregate funding on behalf of their community co-ops, pulling from a broad basket of values-aligned financiers.

Creative collaboration is often what is needed to get larger deals done, often by pooling the resources of two or more CDFIs together. As in the following two case studies, Shared Capital often serves as the instigator and facilitator on behalf of the other lenders. "We couldn't lend $1 million on our own," Jennings says. "So, we all share the risk and get to spread our capital further, and there are advantages to furthering our mission as well" (C. Jennings, personal communication, August 23, 2021).

Case Study: Cooperative Home Care Associates (CHCA)

Founded in the Bronx in 1985, Cooperative Home Care Associates (CHCA) is a nationally recognized worker-owned cooperative in the US with more than 2,000 employees, about 1,300 of which are worker-owners, primarily women of color and immigrant women (Cooperative Home Care Associates, *n.d.*)

Its mission—to deliver quality care through quality jobs—is achieved through providing gold-standard training; offering full-time hours, competitive wages, and worker ownership; and integrating peer mentoring, financial literacy training, and supervision that effectively balances coaching, support, and accountability. CHCA generates almost $65 million in annual revenue and has been profitable for nearly every year in operation (Welch, 2016).

At one point, a major shift in their funding source for state reimbursements left them with a $2 million payroll gap because they had to continue to pay their employees while waiting to get reimbursed. Shared Capital worked together with CFNE and four other CDFIs—a large one that put up $1 million and the rest covering the other $1 million. Rather than having to close on five separate loans, there were only two, saving CHCA on those transactional costs (and paperwork). Shared Capital serviced the collective loan on behalf of all four lenders and handled the back-office part of dealing with those other lenders, which it has done on many occasions.

Shared Capital and other CDFIs collaborate as well with depository institutions, such as for the expansion described in the Bike Hub Co-op case study below whereby NCB provided a real estate loan and Shared Capital provided financing for additional capital needs exceeding the amount that NCB could underwrite due to regulatory requirements. "That combination is useful in allowing us to provide the gap financing alongside a bank or credit union" (C. Jennings, personal communication, August 23, 2021).

The Hub Bike story is yet another example of how the personal guarantee poses a hardship to even proven worker-owned businesses in need of growth capital.

Case Study: Hub Bike Co-op in Minneapolis, Minnesota

The Hub Bike Co-op is a worker-owned bike repair and retail shop on a mission: "As a cooperatively-owned business, we seek to enrich community rather than extract from it. We have programs and policies in place to make sure that The Hub is a contributing member of the urban landscape. The Hub is firmly committed to donating labor, money, and merchandise to support various community initiatives throughout the year. We dedicate a portion of our profits to supporting the cycling community, the community at large, and our environment" (Hub Bike Co-op, *n.d.*).

When it was forming in 2002 and needed upfront cash flow to cover the costs of inventory, the worker-owners went looking for a loan from one of the local banks. "Even though that inventory could have acted as collateral on the loan, the banks didn't understand the co-op model," Jennings says (C. Jennings, personal communication, August 23, 2021).

Turns out the co-op was profitable from the beginning, a rarity for a business of any kind. It has since expanded to three locations in the Twin Cities and some 14 years later was able to purchase one of the buildings through joint financing by NCB and Shared Capital—but only after being turned down by a local bank, which required personal guarantees along with a mortgage despite the fact the business had been operating out of the building for years, and despite it being in a target redevelopment area.

The worker-owners were prepared to do the deal with the bank, albeit with some anxiety, and even lined up an internal agreement setting forth who would be responsible for putting up the required collateral. "But that distorted the internal financial arrangements and didn't sit well," Jennings says. "When we found out that was the only offer they had been able to get, we said we'd love to continue to work with them but a bank can offer you a lower interest rate, and it was a great deal for a bank" (C. Jennings, personal communication, August 23, 2021).

Therefore, Shared Capital approached NCB and based on the long relationship and history of solid financial performance, NCB was able to underwrite the loan without personal guarantees for the purchase of the building.

Recognizing that one-off, case-by-case efforts like the above are not scalable, Jennings points to the need for effective, replicable models—credit unions, for instance, have demonstrated creative ways to share resources—in tapping into shared pools more quickly and efficiently (C. Jennings, personal communication, August 23, 2021).

Loan funds as catalysts for further capital

Capital Impact Partners (CIP) launched the Co-op Innovation Award in 2015, starting with a grant of $50,000, to encourage growth and development of co-ops in communities of color and historically disinvested communities and identify early-stage projects with the potential for replication. The award is also intended to showcase promising co-op models, attract other grant dollars, and initiate policy change and public interest. "As CIP has grown and the average loan size has gotten bigger, we have wanted to find ways to support smaller mission-aligned initiatives and the Co-op Innovation Award was one way to do that," Powers says (A. Powers, personal communication, October 20, 2021).

In 2020, NCB became a co-sponsor of the award, providing an additional $50,000 grant; in 2022 the pot grew to $170,000, thanks to additional sponsorships. "We would love to grow the pot by including funding by other entities that are even outside the co-op world because it's not just about co-ops, it's about racial equity and wealth building" (A. Powers, personal communication, October 20, 2021).

Powers sees CIP not only as a funder but as the one to tell the story of the specific projects and how they are tools of change within their communities and in stabilizing economies. "So, it's been an exciting program over the years" (A. Powers, personal communication, October 20, 2021).

Over the life of the award, 17 grantees have used their combined $515,000 in award money to leverage more than $6.3 million of additional funding from foundations, investment, and government (A. Powers, personal communication, October 20, 2021). "This shows that small investments in the worker co-op space can go a long way and having that seed capital that's first in the door can be catalytic. Chi Fresh and Drivers Cooperatives, both former recipients, are perfect examples of that" (A. Powers, personal communication, October 20, 2021).

Case Study: ChiFresh Kitchen in Chicago, Illinois

ChiFresh Kitchen was founded by formerly incarcerated people of color as a women- and minority-owned worker cooperative in April 2020 to deliver freshly cooked, healthy, and delicious food that's rooted in the culture of the people being served. It is "part of a collaboration of urban farms, food operators, worker centers, policy advocates, and other community organizations led by people of color on the South and West Sides of Chicago, who are coming together to promote food sovereignty, racial justice, and equitable food access in the City" (ChiFresh Kitchen, *n.d.*).

After pushing the launch date up by a month in response to Covid and its disproportionate impact on communities of color and lower-income residents, the five-member co-op went from delivering a planned 50 meals per week to 500 meals per day in the very first week, including to larger facilities. For many people, this was the only meal of the day. In a video produced by Shared Capital (2021), founder Kimberly Britt said, "it wasn't a matter of whether we could deliver them, it was that we had to get it done. That's the type of attitude we brought to the kitchen—everyone was determined." *(Note: This is the first of many Shared Capital's Shared Stories series.)*

ChiFresh was one of three recipients of the 2020 Co-op Innovation Award, receiving a one-year $50,000 grant. The two other grantees included The Bronx Cooperative Development Initiative, a community-led economic development organization focused on building an equitable, democratic economy that creates shared wealth and ownership for people of color with low incomes; and Atlanta-based The Guild, which is focused on building community wealth through real estate, entrepreneurship programs, and access to capital, creating equitable and sustainable communities by addressing the root causes of economic inequality.

According to Powers, when ChiFresh applied to the grant program, the business was still in the ideation phase—they had received neither grants nor investments. "It was a group of justice-involved women who were looking to get back into the mainstream economy and to access a good job." She says she will never forget when she called them with the news: "Camille Kerr, a consultant who put together a team of advisors in the kitchen with all the worker-owners, put me on speakerphone and there was all this cheering, and it was such a happy moment. But that $50,000 investment, which is not huge, validated the project" (A. Powers, personal communication, October 20, 2021).

Since then, ChiFresh has been able to raise enough money to buy a 6,000 square foot building through a $350,000 loan from Shared Capital, a mere seven months after launching. The purpose of the facility, besides being more conducive to handling the substantial meal preparation, is to run a retail store in the front and a potential catering operation—all to provide employment to other formerly incarcerated people, who can become worker-owners after a certain period of employment.

Case Study: The Drivers Cooperative in New York City

Launched in May 2021, The Drivers Cooperative is a worker-owned company whose mission is "to end exploitative conditions in the for-hire vehicle industry through system change—putting drivers in the driver's seat of the platform economy" (The Drivers Cooperative, *n.d.* a). It has since grown to include over 3,000 driver-members and a proprietary ride-hailing app, Co-op Ride.

Similar to ChiFresh Kitchen, The Drivers Cooperative was in the very early stage when the person behind the idea applied for and won, a $25,000 grant as part of the Fifth Annual Co-op Innovation Award in May 2019.

That person was Erik Forman, then Education Director with the Independent Drivers Guild (IDG), a union that represented more than 85,000 for-hire vehicle drivers across the city, 90% of whom were immigrant workers. The purpose of the grant was to launch a purchasing cooperative that would reduce expenses for drivers and help its drivers find more financial stability in a highly competitive industry by providing more take-home pay. IDG also envisioned creating a rideshare app to compete with Uber and Lyft. The grant funded research into what impact worker-owned co-ops could have on drivers and a workshop to inform drivers of what a worker co-op could look like.

As quoted in Capital Impact Partner's press release (2019) announcing the recipients, Forman described the award as "pioneer[ing] a new union-cooperative strategy to turn the gig economy into a launching pad for the new economy. In the for-hire vehicle industry, workers spend around half of their income on the tools that they need to do their jobs. Developing worker and consumer cooperatives to source these key inputs has the potential to elevate the earnings and transform the lives of thousands of immigrant workers and workers of color in New York City, and eventually around the world."

The next step was for Forman to form the actual co-op (IDG was the official grant recipient) and eventually collaborated with Ken Lewis, a Black car driver, and Alissa Orlando, former head of operations for Uber's business in East Africa, in launching The Drivers Cooperative. They continue to lead the company, and drivers can serve on the board.

According to its website (The Drivers Cooperative, *n.d.* b), member-drivers earn 8% to 10% more on each trip than Uber and Lyft drivers, and all profits go back to drivers as dividends based on how much labor they contributed. The Drivers Cooperative takes a 15% commission for operating costs, which will go toward driver onboarding, licensing, customer service, engineering, and so on.

At least one source (Toussaint, 2021) reports that The Drivers Cooperative has secured more than $350,000 (that was in July 2021), including $200,000 from Shared Capital and other loans from LEAF Fund and Start.coop, plus grants from the Workers Lab and the Emergent Fund. It also raised $25,000 in donations from the crowdfunding platform Ioby and as of April 2022 (when the campaign was last funded) it had reached $1,625,191 from 1,184 investors of a $2,500,000 goal through a DPO on WeFunder (https://wefunder.com/driverscoop/); the non-voting shares generate a 2.5% return until investors recoup 2.5 times their initial investment, which starts at $100.

The co-op has also received support from the Lower East Side People's Federal Credit Union in helping drivers refinance their car loans to lower rates, an example of the cooperative's purchasing power that tangibly accrues to worker-owners. National Cooperative Bank also provided a $50,000 grant in 2021 to the cooperative.

Powers is happy to trace The Drivers Cooperative's roots to the Co-op Innovation Award. "After launching the ride-share app, it quickly grew to capture over 30,000 rider accounts (including US Representative Alexandria Ocasio Cortez, or AOC) and the co-op has been able to raise investments to grow into other geographies. That's the whole idea behind the award" (A. Powers, personal communication, October 20, 2021).

CDFIs and racial equity

Created to supply the tools enabling economically disadvantaged individuals to become self-sufficient stakeholders in their own future, CDFIs can provide solutions for minority-owned small businesses that are often unable to access capital and investments from traditional lenders. CDFIs have done that for years, serving those communities and businesses left outside the economic mainstream. And while SBA's Paycheck Protection Program (PPP) played a tremendous role in keeping small businesses afloat during the pandemic, many minority-owned small businesses were unable to secure those loans for their long-term sustainability.

The foundation for that sustainability, however, can come from the CDFI Coalition's advocacy for the $1 billion for the CDFI Fund proposed in the House of Representatives-passed HEROES Act, allowing CDFIs to provide loans beyond the Payroll Protection Program (PPP).[1]

Over the past decade, minority-owned businesses accounted for more than 50% of the nearly two million new businesses and created nearly five million new jobs. More than four million minority-owned companies generate close to $700 billion in annual sales. Yet great disparities persist—though minorities make up 32% of the population, minority business ownership represents only 18%. And while the number of minority-owned firms has grown by 35%, their average revenue dropped by 16% (even before Covid-19). Ensuring that all small businesses have access to capital and technical assistance is a top priority and one that the Senate Committee on Small Business and Entrepreneurship is charged with spearheading. "Diversity is one of the nation's greatest strengths, and diverse small-business ownership is essential to our nation's continued economic success and growth" (US Committee on Small Business & Entrepreneurship, n.d.).

Further evidence that minority-owned businesses continue to face systemic inequities disproportionately affecting access to capital: citing a survey by the US Department of Commerce, Wacif reports that minority firms are less likely to receive loans than white-owned businesses, and when loans are approved, the loan amounts are lower and interest rates are higher—hence the study also found a hesitancy among minority firms to even apply for loans (Wacif, n.d., The Need & the Opportunity section, para 2).

Zooming in on specific regions helps put the inequity in sharper relief. According to the same webpage (Wacif, n.d., The Need & the Opportunity section, para 3), the National Capital District, comprising Washington, D.C., Maryland, and Virginia (WMV), is one of the most diverse metropolitan areas in the country, and yet white-owned businesses are valued at least three times higher than businesses owned by people of color.

CDFIs' excellent track record providing access to capital for underserved and underbanked communities makes them the ideal resources to aid those communities. However, a need for improvement still exists in inclusivity and diversity. That was the thesis of a breakout panel during the 2019 CDFI Coalition Institute, focused on understanding unconscious bias. This panel was a follow-up session to a 2018 Institute plenary panel sponsored by the W.K. Kellogg Foundation on Fostering Racial Equity in the CDFI Field.

The clear call to action was this: CDFIs must now begin to look at their work through a racial equity lens to ensure that they are making an impact in all communities. Essential to carrying out the mission of CDFIs is the creation of a diverse pipeline of young leaders who can become the next level of leaders of the industry, so the industry reflects the communities it serves. Moreover, there is a competitive business advantage for organizations that understand, embrace, and champion racial equity.

Picking up the gauntlet, CFNE launched a strategic plan in 2021 with the primary goal of addressing the racial equity gap. A key component of that plan was the development of the co-op launch loan (funded by a sizable grant) to specifically address the fact that many low-wealth communities, particularly Black and brown communities, are often foreclosed on a major path to accessing the initial investment to start a new business.

The loan enabled CFNE to offer even more flexible options than before. In place of collateral or a formal business plan, the only prerequisite was the existence of at least some solid pieces—perhaps the worker-owners had vast experience in the industry or have been running an informal co-op out of someone's basement but now need to do a business plan to formalize the business.

When initial demand for the product fell short of expectations, Josephy grasped the need for an ecosystem to promote awareness and the development of co-ops in the first place for there to be a pipeline for new financial products. (The ecosystem idea is explored in further detail in the following pages.)

Remarking on that specific experience and the evolution of CDFIs in general, Josephy sees the lack of a broad education around the possibility of worker co-op ownerships as the first barrier to entry. Then the need for technical assistance by business development services follows on the heels of that. Without those two foundational supports, even the most favorable financial products will not help mitigate the racial equity gap.

"As a predominately white financial institution, whether due to a history of mistrust between communities of color and banking in general, CFNE is not always going to be the best ambassador of the co-op sector," Josephy says (M. Josephy, personal communication, August 6, 2021). "The challenge then is how can we partner and direct resources to the community members, who really are going to be the best ambassadors, and build those partnerships out. That's where we see our efforts being focused over the next two years" (M. Josephy, personal communication, August 6, 2021).

Jennings too sees the worker co-op model as being a core component of Shared Capital's work in communities of color. Historically, around 80% of loan volume has supported a combination of women, low-wage earners, and people of color. But in 2020, over 40% went specifically to fund Black and Latinx co-ops, and that is on the rise. "We are very proud of that 80% figure and want to continue to grow all facets of that group. For 2021, the BIPOC percentage is even higher, well above the 42% of 2020 and that is through a lot of intentional outreach and collaboration" (C. Jennings, personal communication, August 23, 2021).

Part of that uptick is attributed to the efforts of community-based organizations "that don't come out of co-op development, but which now recognize co-op development as one of the strategies that could build a more inclusive economy and address their mission work and adopt that work" (C. Jennings, personal communication, August 23, 2021).

One example is Nexus Community Partners, a longstanding community development organization with deep roots in BIPOC communities within the Twin Cities. "Of a variety of projects they have put together, an outstanding fellowship program called North Star Black Cooperative Fellowship allows a cohort of Black leaders in the community to come together and build out their cooperative vision" (C. Jennings, personal communication, August 23, 2021). According to its website, the six-month fellowship teaches Black cooperative economic history, analyses and rethinks capitalism, and supports and networks new black co-op enterprises and their leaders, including by providing access to financing opportunities (Nexus, *n.d.*).

Such efforts are lending a propitious racial equity emphasis to the worker co-op narrative.

The inclusive economy: Building a cooperative growth ecosystem

The purpose of establishing a cooperative ecosystem as a means of scaling worker cooperatives and fostering an inclusive economy has been percolating for at least a decade, but with more urgency considering the pandemic and the perpetuation of income inequality and discrimination within communities of color and lower-income populations.

Underlying the ecosystem model is a finding that one-third of today's worker cooperatives were built in partnership with cooperative development organizations or other community-based organizations, with those organizations providing critical access to outside capital or technical assistance programs (Kerr, 2015). These "high touch" cooperative development organizations exist in many different guises, from incubators and accelerators to private organizations that serve to connect the dots between worker cooperatives and providers of technical assistance, business consultancy, and capital financing, and with civic and philanthropic entities being spokes in the community-support wheel.

The ecosystem framework

The ecosystem concept and framework were effectively formalized in a ground-breaking report entitled *The Cooperative Growth Ecosystem: Inclusive Economic Development in Action* (Hoover & Abell, 2016), a year-long joint project of Project Equity and the Democracy at Work Institute (DAWI) that was funded by Citi Community Development.

As it pertains to the topic of this chapter, one of four "high-level elements" identified as being an Essential Element—without which neither impact nor scale can be achieved—was financial capital. The other three pillars are member skills and capacity, technical assistance, and the aforementioned growth-oriented co-op developers, each an important asset in obtaining the necessary capital and therefore areas in need of deeper financial investment, such as through grants or investments that are earmarked for worker cooperative education and technical assistance.

Achieving sustainability, the fifth and final phase of the purposeful ecosystem's development requires all stakeholders—worker cooperatives, co-op developers, capital providers, and advocacy partners—to be working together in close collaboration at a systems-level such that "entrepreneurs are forming worker cooperatives as a matter of course" (Hoover & Abell, 2016, p.26).

While not prescriptive, the report does draw recommendations based on the best practices, patterns, and other learnings of the five cooperative-friendly cities that were studied. One finding is that a primary cause of worker co-op failure is an over-reliance on debt as opposed to equity investment. Another "key insight" is that capital providers do not have sufficient deal flow to deploy the debt capital they are willing to provide—echoing Josephy's own experience with the CFNE launch loan.

Two proposed solutions to the above challenges include:

- Providing worker co-ops with enough values-aligned equity investment;
- Funding technical assistance and co-op development services that can help worker co-ops start, grow, and scale.

The latter speaks to the resounding refrain calling for broader education and exposure to the worker co-op model as a preliminary step to broader acceptance and application of the model.

Like Josephy, Jennings sees the need for exposure to worker co-ops as being important for propagating the idea—these unorthodox businesses don't just happen in isolation. "Fundamentally, it's hard to come up with the idea without having seen it, so if you haven't had the opportunity to visit a worker co-op, or your community doesn't have any worker co-ops, or even if it does but they are not promoting themselves as such, how would you even know this model? You might come up with some other version of getting a better work environment, or a more horizontal structure, but you still might not come up with a worker co-op unless you've had the fortune to come across one" (C. Jennings, personal communication, August 23, 2021).

As ever, success stories are the best form of outreach. The Project Equity/DAWI report highlighted the journey of Opportunity Threads (https://www.opportunitythreads.com), a worker-owned textile mill in North Carolina with a largely immigrant workforce and a multi-pronged, ecosystemic tale that enabled it to grow from a three-person group to a company with more than 20 workers that generated over $700,000 in revenue within six years. The local ecosystem comprised start-up funding from values-aligned funders, loans from a community-based loan fund, and the help of local technical assistance providers. Additional support was provided by a credit union in helping the worker-owners establish a special company account that they can borrow against to build credit and secure mortgages.

It may come as no surprise that New York City was one of the city-subjects of the report, as it has a rich history of employee-owned businesses along with a deep divide among racial and income demographics. Among other best practices, NYC shows how municipalities make a significant impact in expanding the worker cooperative by buttressing efforts already underway in the private sector. (Government bureaucracies may not be the most potent instigators of change, but at least in NYC they prove to be ardent accomplices.)

In 2015, Mayor Bill de Blasio and the NYC Council launched the Worker Cooperative Business Development Initiative (WCBDI) "to strengthen the existing ecosystem of cooperative developers in NYC, promote the creation of new cooperatives, and grow existing cooperatives" (NYC Department of Small Business Services, n.d.), emphasis on "ecosystem."

In its first year, the initiative funneled $1.2 million to 10 partner organizations to help propel the creation of both new worker cooperatives and co-op conversions. By 2019, funding had more than doubled and 142 new co-ops, including worker-owned businesses, had been created.

In 2020, WCBDI partners received a total of $3.6 million in the fiscal year 2020 (NYC Small Business Services, 2021). Those partners include numerous community organizations across the five boroughs that provide financing as well as technical assistance, education, and training, and cooperative development guidance, namely (among others): The Working World, DAWI, ICA Group, The, CUNY School of Law's Community & Economic Development (CED) Clinic, and New York City Network of Worker Cooperatives (NYC NOWC).

Another partner, Green Worker Cooperatives (https://www.greenwork.coop), is an incubator in the South Bronx that helps to grow eco-friendly businesses through its free (city-funded) five-month Co-op Academy (Green Workers Cooperatives, n.d. b).

One such business is Uptown Village Cooperative (https://www.uptownvillage.coop), "a multicultural community of maternal childbirth professionals (*aka doulas*) supporting gentle birth and postpartum, breastfeeding, and reproductive health justice in Upper Manhattan and the Bronx" (Uptown Village Cooperative, n.d.).

After the two founding members completed the training at Green Worker Cooperative in 2015, they worked with the Business Outreach Center (BOC) Network South Bronx business incubator, realizing an increase in revenue, adding another worker-owner (all three members are women of color), and, in 2018, receiving patient financing from The Working World, which they did not have to repay until the business was profitable. Plans include building a birthing center in the Bronx, requiring additional growth capital—and thereby bringing the financing discussion full circle.

The ultimate call to action of the 58-page report—which should be mandated reading for anyone with a vested interest in promoting an inclusive economy—for the essential financing element is the cultivation of a diverse funding ecosystem that provides short-term cash flow, such as for start-ups and conversions, paired with impact, mission-aligned investment to support long-term growth and sustainability. Equally essential is funding co-op development organizations as providers of technical assistance and business acumen. Effectively CDFIs and other loan funds can provide debt or revenue-based capital in the form of loans, while values-aligned private investors can provide equity capital that preserves the principles of worker-owned and -controlled businesses.

The "silver tsunami:" Scaling worker cooperatives through conversions

Ahead of the approaching "silver tsunami" of retiring business owners, local and national equitable and cooperative organizations are exploring ways to radically scale the co-op sector *via* conversions. The statistics are staggering: More than half of all privately held businesses are owned by those 55 and older. That equates to approximately 2.9 million baby boomer-owned businesses ranging in value from under $300,000 to over $10 million and representing a total of $6.5 trillion in revenues, and which employ over 32 million people with a $1.3 trillion payroll (Project Equity, 2021). As owners reach retirement, these businesses are projected to be shuttered or sold off in the next decade—many sooner than expected because of the devastating economic impact of Covid-19, which disproportionately impacted communities of color and low-wage (often frontline) workers.

Citing the above statistics by Project Equity in a paper entitled *Opportunity Knocking: Impact Capital As The Transformative Agent To Take Employee Ownership To Scale*, the members of Fifty by Fifty, an initiative of The Democracy Collaborative, propose that "impact investors and other capital providers could be the agents to give this crisis a silver lining by catalyzing employee ownership buyouts at scale" as opposed to allowing those businesses to fall into the hands of private equity and corporations (Rose *et al.*, 2021).

Given the estimated $68 trillion transfer of baby boomer wealth on the horizon, even major investment firms are launching impact programs to attract socially responsible investors (*aka* millennials). The demand for greater values-aligned investment opportunities is therefore on the rise.

Emerging impact private equity funds are poised to bridge the current gap between low-return impact investing offered by CDFIs, microfinance, and other fixed-return loan funds, and the high-risk, high-return investing by venture capital firms.

According to the Fifty by Fifty report (Rose *et al.*, 2021, p.43): "Employee ownership today presents an unprecedented opportunity for visionary and catalytic investors to step forward and enjoy attractive returns while paving a new path for others to follow. The time has come to share ownership more broadly through ESOPs and worker cooperatives. Impact capital, organized to provide the proverbial knock on the door, is the agent that can take this vital process to scale."

Indeed, a projected $650 million could be deployed for co-op conversion annually through over a dozen employee-ownership-oriented funds, including the following identified in the paper:

- The Fund for Employee Ownership, launched in 2018 by Evergreen Cooperatives of Cleveland, is used to acquire businesses and exit some or all firms into the Evergreen Cooperative network of worker-owned companies (Evergreen Cooperatives, *n.d.*).

- The Business Legacy Fund, launched by Co-op Cincy, a Cincinnati co-op developer, in partnership with Seed Commons, is modelled on the pioneering Evergreen Cooperative model and Fund for Employee Ownership in Cleveland in financing business acquisitions (in Southwest Ohio) and converting them to worker ownership. It is one of many regional funds that are responding to the needs of their immediate communities (Co-op Cincy, *n.d.*).

- The Accelerate Employee Ownership Fund is a non-profit collaborative initiative by Project Equity and Shared Capital Cooperative (with a $5M seed investment from the Quality Jobs Fund) to finance employee ownership conversions in 10 regions across the country (Project Equity, *n.d.* a). Since its inception, the fund has financed multiple transitions to cooperative ownership, including Cal Solar, a solar installer in rural Grass Valley, CA, and Happy Earth Cleaning, a Minneapolis green cleaning company.

- The industry-focused Fund for Jobs Worth Owning was developed by Massachusetts-based ICA Group (discussed later in this chapter) to create opportunities for low-income workers in the childcare and home health care industries (ICA Group, n.d. b).

- The Working World Fund by The Working World seeks to benefit low-income workers and people of color through converting firms to employee ownership. Since 2012, $17 million has been raised and deployed. The fund has also been working with the New York City's Office of the Mayor and City Council to raise capital to reach a sustainable capacity of $30 million (The Working World, *n.d.*).

Among other private impact investment firms noted in the paper, Chicago-based Torana Group is dedicated to ownership transitions that benefit women and people of color in middle-market firms using a range of structures, including employee-owned trusts. The firm prepares deal-specific investment opportunities (capitalized at up to $25 million) and partners with select family businesses on the transactions (Torana Group, *n.d.*).

A blueprint for conversions

Cooperative lenders are being encouraged to work with these organizations to access a market of vetted businesses ranging in value from under $300,000 to over $10 million. Clearly, within the co-op sector, conversions of established businesses present a greater financing opportunity than start-up ventures as higher dollar and lower risk transactions (Project Equity, *n.d.* b).

"We are only now beginning to see worker co-op conversions that are of the size and magnitude that fits into the lending that we do," says Ian Wiesner, of Capital Impact Partners (CIP), which just closed on its first conversion loan at the end of 2020. That deal, profiled in the Ward lumber case study below, involved seller financing, where the seller takes the note on the purchase price and is paid back over time, and is a common occurrence in being favorable to the borrower and the lender. "As a lender, it's not just about having consistency in cash flow. That seller's note keeps the owner involved at the management level, so there's both a financial and operational aspect to it" (I. Wiesner, personal communication, October 22, 2021).

Case Study: Ward Lumber in Jay, New York

When the owner of Ward Lumber—a fourth-generation, 130-year-old business with over 40 employees—began planning for the company's future (his daughters were not interested in continuing the family business), he offered to sell it to his long-time employees rather than a regional conglomerate. "That business had stabilized the community and jobs, and if it had closed it would have had a huge ripple effect on the workers, the families, the supply chain, and beyond," says CIP's Powers (A. Powers, personal communication, October 20, 2021).

Ward's flexible succession plan and successful buyout have become a model for worker co-op conversions—besides creating 40 new business owners, the conversion shows how invested employees can carry the legacy in a time when family transitions are less common.

The conversion also shows just how much collaboration is often needed to pull off these transitions: training, business plan development, and grant writing assistance was provided by the SUNY Canton Small Business Development Center (SBDC) at Clinton Community College (CCC) and the Co-op Development Institute, a USDA-funded rural development center; financing came from CFNE and Capital Impact Partners and a $250,000 grant from Empire State Development (ESD) was awarded through New York State's Regional Economic Development Council initiative.

Rather than having to deal with three different funders, CFNE managed the process from start to finish. "That's something CDFIs bring to the table—they have the patience and flexibility for these types of deals, which are challenging and do take a lot of time. It's a testament to this co-op ecosystem of lenders that these deals can get done and people are willing to work together and to share knowledge," Powers says (A. Powers, personal communication, October 20, 2021).

Wiesner agrees that Ward's is a good example of the ecosystem at work and Capital Impact Partner's role within that: By doing smaller deals, **CFNE** and Shared Capital get the momentum started, and then CIP can come in as that next step for slightly larger transactions that those CDFIs cannot do on their own. But CIP is relying on their expertise and can be a late-stage participant knowing that the necessary due diligence has been done. "These types of conversions will create opportunities for ever-larger transactions for lenders like NCB to underwrite and, ultimately, even mission-agnostic lenders will invest in the model based on a steady track record of deals. That's the trajectory" (I. Wiesner, personal communication, October 22, 2021).

That said, the time frame for these transitions is not scalable: CFNE and the other partners worked with Jay Ward for years before reaching the point of bringing in CIP, and then it took another year to close after that.

"That will happen as larger financial institutions do this, and as larger businesses show interest in conversions," Wiesner says (I. Wiesner, personal communication, October 22, 2021).

Certainly, the existence of replicable models by institutions that are deeply familiar with the worker cooperative structure will prove much more efficient to the funding entities and, resultantly, those efficiencies of scale will translate to more favorable and affordable funding to worker-owners as would having a blueprint for the conversion process.

Non-extractive risk-tolerant capital

Co-op-oriented CDFIs and co-op developers are starting to look at outside investments in a way that offers sustainable but not extractive returns to the investors and that maintains control with the workers. As opposed to extractive financing, the result and goal of non-extractive investing is to provide businesses with access to capital rather than to deprive them of that capital through high, often usurious returns.

Non-extractive loan funds

One CDFI is leading the charge: The Working World's non-extractive loans typically only recover repayments from profits of the project that is being financed. For a start-up, repayments would not begin until the business was sustainable and able to cover operating costs and wages. Rather than collateral or personal guarantee, the only security is whatever asset that's purchased with the loan, such as a piece of equipment. Repaid funds are reintegrated into its locally based revolving loan fund to continually feed further investment opportunities in underserved communities.

Besides serving New York City, The Working World can refer worker co-ops to other resources through its membership in Seed Commons, a national network of non-extractive loan funds whose mission is "taking guidance from the grassroots and sharing capital and resources to support local cooperative businesses… [in] building the infrastructure necessary for a truly just, democratic and sustainable new economy" (Seed Commons, n.d.).

Another Seed Commons member is profiled below.

Case Study: Black Farmer Fund (BFF)

The Black Farmer Fund (BFF) is an emerging community investment fund that invests in Black food systems entrepreneurs in New York State with the stated purpose of creating a means for community members to access non-extractive, patient capital that recognized the historical discrimination of lending and banking that informs the racial disparities present in our agricultural system today.

The fund serves Black farmers, vendors, food distributors, caterers, restaurant owners, composters, and other food business actors as well as social impact investors by providing a means to support and strengthen the economic infrastructure of Black food businesses and build community power through a reparative capital framework. The fund is the brainchild of two Black farmer-activists who met at a conference in 2017 and shared their frustrations about the lack of financial assistance available for Black farmers. In 2020 they launched a year-long pilot program with 12 Black food businesses in different stages and holding various roles in the food system.

According to its 2021 *Annual Report* (Black Farmer Fund, 2022), BFF successfully raised a $1 million Pilot Fund from individuals and institutions and distributed $457,000 in grants and low-interest loans to Black food businesses, with repayment terms geared towards the specific needs of the selected food business. Another $194,000 in sub-grantmaking went to four organizations in the BFF ecosystem.

At CFNE, Josephy is engaged in a research project to identify the issues involved in getting equity to co-ops in exploring equity or revenue-based products for its product line. Part of that process is reaching out to socially minded venture capital firms and equity investors who have expressed an interest in investing in co-ops. "When we were on a call with some of these investors, the big message was they are not seeing the deal flow or pipeline, whereas community developers are seeing the pipeline but not the equity opportunities. So, we need to make stronger connections between those two groups" (M. Josephy, personal communication, August 6, 2021).

One issue might be that in equity lending, where the risk is higher, investment firms need to understand the industry sector—whether that's housing, agriculture, or construction.

"That said, there are some industries with concentrations of co-ops and so we should be able to find for example food manufacturing equity investors who can support the Real Pickles of the world, and same for driver co-ops and home health care co-ops" (M. Josephy, personal communication, August 6, 2021). See the Real Pickles story below.

Case Study: Real Pickles

Real Pickles, which has been producing 100% organic, naturally fermented, and raw plant-based food since 2001, is committed to promoting human and ecological health by providing people with delicious, nourishing food and by working toward a regional, organic food system (Real Pickles, 2022).

In its second season, Real Pickles began operating out of the Western Massachusetts Food Processing Center in Greenfield, a business incubator kitchen created to boost the local agricultural economy by providing a venue for making value-added foods with local farm ingredients.

In 2009, it relocated to a century-old industrial building in Greenfield, requiring significant renovations for improved energy efficiency and to become a certified organic food-production facility. The purchase and other project costs were made possible by two community loan funds—Franklin County Community Development Corporation and Equity Trust—along with financing from a local community bank.

By 2013, the founding entrepreneurs wanted to stay as members of the business but to share the benefits and responsibilities of ownership with their employees, both to retain a strong workforce and to preserve its social mission for the long term. At the time it was operating as a sole proprietorship with two owners (a husband-and-wife team) and had annual sales of $581,000.

The co-op and the owners agreed upon a sale price of $523,795, which included $400,000 of goodwill, based on a five-year sales and marketing plan developed by the founding worker-owners that showed reasonable assurance that the debt would be repaid (Project Equity, *n.d.* c).

To help fund the conversion to a worker cooperative, Real Pickles launched a "community investment campaign," raising $500,000 in stock in Massachusetts and Vermont (in compliance with Massachusetts state law) and attracting 80 investors in just eight weeks. Stock purchases ranged from $2,500 from individual investors to a $25,000 investment from a local food cooperative and a $50,000 investment from a local foundation (Real Pickles, 2013).

CFNE provided a five-year, interest-only $69,000 loan secured by a second position on all business assets. The first position was held by a small local bank's $150,000 line of credit. In addition, each of the five worker-owners contributed $6,000 towards the purchase of a voting share, for a total of $749,000 towards the purchase of the business and working capital. After this initial funding, CFNE provided Real Pickles with a more sizable loan for expansion.

IV: Existing Resources

Technical assistance: Getting capital-ready

Before a worker cooperative can obtain any method of outside financing, the owners must formulate a solid business plan, which can be daunting for a first-time entrepreneur or start-up business in the early stages of development. It can be equally challenging for employees who are seeking to purchase the business from the owner as part of a cooperative conversion.

"Financial projections are critical, as is making sure the assumptions embedded in those projections are realistic," Jennings says. "It's about demonstrating how even if your pie-in-the-sky plan doesn't pan out, you will still be earning enough to cover the loan payment" (C. Jennings, personal communication, August 23, 2021).

Much of Shared Capital's training is about emphasizing the lenders' need for certainty. "Many borrowers do not understand why they cannot obtain financing from the big banks, but it's about proving the capacity to repay," Jennings says. "Banks are not in the business of taking any risks and we CDFIs are only slightly more in the business of taking risks. What we can do is be a lot more patient and creative and flexible in how we finance, not because we are willing to take on more risk but because we have ways to mitigate it that banks just don't have" (C. Jennings, personal communication, August 23, 2021).

Some "high-touch" lenders like The Working World, another CDFI, are staffed to provide the necessary technical assistance to help worker co-ops get loan-ready, whether they are borrowing from them or preparing to take the business plan to a bank or other lender.

All CDFIs are part of a network of cooperative support organizations that can provide the necessary education and resources to help worker cooperatives meet the business plan prerequisite, often by connecting them to professionals and consultants within their direct community.

The USDA, for example, funds a network of over 35 Rural Cooperative Development Centers (RCDCs) across the country through annual grants, and rural food and worker cooperatives are eligible for development programs such as the Value-Added Producer Grant Program and the Business and Industry Loan Guarantee Program. (NCB is a major supporter of the grant program in conjunction with CooperationWorks!, the association that disperses the funds for the network centers.)

But the USDA's constituency is centered in rural areas, which have populations of 50,000 or less, and tend to be overwhelmingly white. That perhaps indiscriminate bias ignores urban areas, where communities of color are largely found, and where most worker cooperatives exist. (On the bright side, in certain areas such as Minnesota and Washington state, once-rural areas that now touch city centers are making the centers more accessible to the urban demographic. Covid recovery money is also creating opportunities for some RCDCs to increase their work in urban areas.)

Through the Minority Business Development Agency (MBDA), the US Department of Commerce invests in a national network of MBDA business and specialty centers located in areas with the largest concentration of minority populations that offer customized business development and industry-focused services to provide small and medium-sized firms with greater access to capital, contracts, and markets.

One such MBDA center was launched in 2021 by Wacif. Jennifer Bryant, Program Manager, Community Wealth Building Initiatives for Wacif, who was brought on in 2019 to lead the Employee Ownership Initiative, said The Greater Washington Center for Employee Ownership (GWCEO) was intended to address gaps in the local ecosystem around advisory support for people who want to start, grow, or convert a business to employee ownership. As the first center to be launched by a CDFI, providing access to capital is a chief ingredient. It is also one of only two centers in the country (along with the North Carolina Employee Ownership Center, or NCEOC, launched in 2019) with an explicit racial equity focus. "That's a core component of the center and given the demographics of our region, we are always thinking of ways to be inclusive of Black and Latinx owners" (J. Bryant, personal communication, September 12, 2021).

Bryant says another primary focus area of all Employee Ownership Centers is co-op conversions. "We are dealing with business owners for whom their business is their largest asset. Wacif is especially poised to help raise the visibility of conversions in the National Capital District" (J. Bryant, personal communication, September 12, 2021).

Wacif also supports early-stage and pre-start-up businesses through programming and grant funding. "Whereas New England has many established cooperatives, the co-ops in the Capital District region are nascent or early stage, so getting them ready to access capital was identified as a significant need," Bryant says (J. Bryant, personal communication, September 12, 2021). To date, the D.C. Co-op Impact Grant has distributed $80,000 to businesses. That grant was in partnership with Capital Impact Partners, another CDFI that is based in Arlington, Virginia.

As an example of tapping into the expertise of the cooperative ecosystem, Bryant points to the paradigm established by the Workers to Owners Collaborative, a national network of CDFIs and cooperative development organizations that support conversions to employee ownership under the leadership of DAWI. Specifically, she says Wacif's work at its Employee Ownership Center is built on the Collaborative's five-stage process (J. Bryant, personal communication, September 12, 2021).

Those five stages include (Becoming Employee Owned, *n.d.*):

- **Explore:** Key stakeholders learn about employee ownership and decide whether it is worth pursuing.
- **Assess:** Experienced professionals evaluate the feasibility of transition based on the value of business and its organizational structure.
- **Structure:** An employee transition team establishes sale terms and organizational/leadership changes.
- **Execute:** Legal, financial, and organizational details are finalized and enacted (purchase agreements signed, loans drawn, boards formed).
- **Support:** Ongoing training addresses leadership, organizational, and operational gaps; roles for board, management, and members are established.

Before launching the Greater Washington Center for Employee Ownership, Wacif launched The Enterprising Women of Color District, Maryland, Virginia (DMV) Business Center to foster and support a small business ecosystem for women of color in the National Capital Region through financial capital, business advisory services, and networking support. It is one of four such specialty MBDA centers in the country. "We are doing cross-programming among these centers to help businesses, including training them in how to obtain the necessary certification to access valuable government contracts" (J. Bryant, personal communication, September 12, 2021).

Two other urban examples of public-private worker cooperative support systems include:

- The Massachusetts Center for Employee Ownership.
- The Cooperative Development Institute.

The Massachusetts Center for Employee Ownership (MassCEO), created by an act of the Massachusetts Legislature in 2017, advocates for employee ownership through education and outreach to business owners across the Commonwealth (MassCEO, *n.d.*).

It is administered by ICA Group, a mission-driven non-profit organized as a worker cooperative and dedicated to bringing strategic analysis and industry-focused supports to the worker-ownership sector. Since 1977, ICA has launched dozens of worker-owned cooperatives and social enterprises, helped dozens of companies convert to worker ownership, and created and preserved over 10,000 jobs (ICA Group, *n.d.* a). In 2015, ICA Group began work with the NYC's Department of Small Business Services to fight income inequality across the five boroughs as part WCBDI (introduced previously in this chapter).

Launched in 2008 by a working group of Cleveland-based private and public institutions (including the Cleveland Foundation, the Ohio Employee Ownership Center, the City of Cleveland, and the city's major hospitals and universities), the Evergreen Cooperative Initiative had an ambitious goal: "to create an economic breakthrough in Cleveland" in an inclusive way, namely by catalyzing new employee-owned businesses. Partially modelled on the Mondragon network, Evergreen Cooperatives seeks to develop worker-owned businesses that pay living wages while also building a regional supply chain for its anchor institutions, a model that has drawn national and even global attention (Evergreen Cooperatives, *n.d.*).

In 2018, Evergreen Cooperatives and the Democracy Collaborative launched the Fund for Employee Ownership to support conversions of businesses to co-ops and thereby stem job loss and loss of wealth in target communities (Heller, 2018).

Private cooperative development entities are also serving as critical conduits. Through its Co-op Clinic, the US Federation of Worker Coops (USFWC) connects potential worker-owners with a network of technical assistance providers for additional support with getting loan ready as well as a model of connecting potential worker-owners with worker co-op "peer advisors" who have been through the process of applying for loans and can share their experience.

The Cooperative Development Institute (CDI), a regional non-profit founded in 1994 by co-op leaders in the Northeast, provides direct technical assistance for co-ops of all kinds and at all stages of development throughout. Through its Business Ownership Solutions (BOS), CDI works with business owners and their employees to explore conversion to a worker-owned model, whether as a succession plan or as a growth strategy (Cooperative Development Institute, *n.d.*).

CooperationWorks! (CW), part of the Cooperative Development Network, provides pre-development and ongoing training for worker-owned and other cooperatives through webinars and a rigorous three-week training program aimed at cooperative developers but ostensibly open to entrepreneurs interested in launching or converting to a cooperative model.

What's evident is that all these different tentacles wrap around the worker cooperative community to provide critical support for start-ups and conversions—and serve as resources and models for an ever-expanding network of place-based technical assistance providers.

Incubators and accelerators

One of the directives of the ecosystem report was to encourage worker cooperative development organizations to go beyond investing in the "basic supports for shared entrepreneurship to more coordinated, high-investment incubation and conversion models." Hence, incubators and accelerators are gaining ground, with numerous ones sprouting in urban centers. These grassroots organizations offer intensive training boot camps to actively pollinate co-ops in their communities.

For example, Start.coop is a Boston-based accelerator of cooperatives and shared ownership businesses whose mission is to combat income- and race-based inequality by growing the cooperative pipeline and strengthening the cooperative ecosystem. Its rigorous accelerator program is designed to provide cooperative entrepreneurs with the necessary supports and connect them with capital sources (Start.coop, *n.d.*).

Start.coop created the Equitable Economy Fund to provide capital that can accelerate cooperatively owned and shared ownership companies, while also providing a financial return to investors. Each investment buys a diversified portfolio of multiple businesses. It goes beyond mere financing by identifying entrepreneurs to participate in its 16-week virtual accelerator program; upon completion, each team receives a $10,000 investment, and "high-performing" graduates are eligible to apply for follow-on funding of up to $50,000 from the Equitable Economy Fund. Start.coop assists cooperatives in securing additional financing from individual and institutional investors, co-op loan programs, and philanthropy (Equitable Economy Fund, *n.d.*).

Worker-owned entrepreneurs who received funding from Start.coop include Baltimore-based Obran, which bills itself as a "worker-cooperative conglomerate" in that it leverages its portfolio of small- to medium-sized businesses and real estate on behalf of its worker-owners. Founded in 2019, "Obran's work is built to serve those closest to the problem of economic and social oppression" (Obran, *n.d.*).

Other examples include:

- Money Positive (https://www.moneypositive.com), a Start.coop alumni, is a worker-owned financial planning service in Texas focused on democratizing financial planning and building long-term financial health. The company's proprietary software platform allows its financial planners "to help clients build intuitive budgets and personalized strategies for their savings, debts, and investments at a fraction of the price of traditional financial planning services" (National Cooperative Business Association CLUSA, *n.d.*).

- Green Worker Cooperatives (GWC) is an incubator in the South Bronx that helps to grow eco-friendly businesses through its free (city-funded) five-month Co-op Academy (Green Worker Cooperatives, *n.d.* a).

- Co-op Cincy, an incubator that aims to create a collaborative network of family-sustaining, worker-owned businesses in Greater Cincinnati and Southwest Ohio, launched two projects— Become Worker Owned and the Business Legacy Fund—to help owners transition their business to worker-ownership. Financing from the fund (in partnership with Seed Commons) is accompanied by technical assistance to ensure a successful transition (Become Worker Owned, *n.d.*)

- In addition to providing non-extractive financing for start-ups, existing businesses, and ownership transitions, the Detroit Community Wealth Fund (DCWF) runs a free 10-week incubator program as well as ongoing workshops—all intended to support Black business ownership and community wealth building (Detroit Community Wealth Fund, *n.d.*).

Grants and awards

Industry incubators and accelerators offer competitive funds, as do many universities and trade associations. Due to their social benefit in creating opportunities for jobs and wealth in underserved communities, some worker co-ops have succeeded in raising equity through contributions and grants. Start-up worker co-ops in particular have been able to leverage grants and donations to fund outside technical assistance (TA) support, which is often critical to complete the initial feasibility assessment. Foundation money can also be used to bring other types of lenders to the table.

Conclusion

Since their inception in the Riegle Community Development Regulatory Improvement Act of 1994 (P.L. 103-325) to promote economic development in distressed urban and rural communities, CDFIs have grown from a concept into a movement into an entire industry. Their unique positions within communities made them financial first responders during the pandemic, and since 2020, they have received tremendous Congressional support and the Federal Government dollars to further advance their mission. While CDFI primary sectors were consumer, residential real estate and small business loans, they have ventured into the health care, food security, renewable energy, and cooperative sectors to meet the needs of those they serve.

Today, there are nearly 1,400 Certified CDFIs headquartered in all 50 states, the District of Columbia, Guam, and Puerto Rico, with combined assets of more than $160 billion. Incubated at strategic partner National Cooperative Bank, Rochdale Capital is an emerging CDFI that entered the industry in late 2021. Rochdale Capital believes that ownership is the foundation to vibrant communities; the mission is centered on community ownership, equity, diversity and inclusion. As CDFIs compete for precious public funding, Rochdale will spend an enormous amount of time seeking alternate funding from foundations, mainstream banks, and other investors.

With the growing need for alternative funding and increased Congressional appropriations, I am hopeful that the CDFI industry reverts to being a movement. The need is too great in under-resourced communities; minority- and women-owned businesses deserve equitable access to capital that will provide them the opportunity to build, close the racial wealth gap, and create racial economic justice across the United States, and the world.

End-notes

[1] In September 2021, Wacif CEO Harold Pettigrew, Jr. was appointed by President Biden to serve on the CDFI Fund Community Development Advisory Board, which consists of 24 members, including the Secretary of the Departments of Agriculture, Commerce, Housing and Urban Development, Interior, Treasury, and the Administrator of the Small Business Administrator, and nine private citizens. (Wacif, 2021)

References

8 V.S.A. § 32104 (2005). https://legislature.vermont.gov/statutes/section/08/222/32104 .

A Yard & A Half (n.d.). *About Us.* http://www.ayardandahalf.com/.

Become Worker Owned (n.d.). *About Us.* https://www.becomeworkerowned.org/about-us.

Becoming Employee Owned (n.d.). *What are the Stages of a Transition to Employee Ownership for a Small Business?* http://becomingemployeeowned.org/learn/explore/stages-2/.

Black Farmer Fund (2022). *Annual Report 2021.* https://www.blackfarmerfund.org/annualreport21.

Capital Impact Partners (2019, May 7). For the Fifth Co-op Innovation Award, Capital Impact Partners and The Workers Lab collaborate to support immigrant communities [Press release]. https://www.capitalimpact.org/capital-impact-announces-fifth-coop-innovation-award/.

ChiFresh Kitchen (n.d.). *Feeding Our Community Together.* https://www.chifreshkitchen.com/.

Co-op Cincy (n.d.). *Business Legacy Fund.* https://coopcincy.org/transition-initiative.

Co-op incubator, Detroit Community Wealth Fund (n.d.). https://www.detroitcommunitywealth.org/new-page.

Cooperation Works! (n.d.). *Trainings.* https://cooperationworks.coop/trainings/.

Cooperative Development Institute (n.d.). *Programs/Business Ownership Solutions.* https://cdi.coop/our-work/programs/.

Cooperative Home Care Associates (n.d.). *About Us.* https://www.chca.org/about.

Democracy at Work Institute (n.d.). *What is a Worker Cooperative?* https://institute.coop/what-worker-cooperative.

Detroit Community Wealth Fund (n.d.). https://www.detroitcommunitywealth.org/new-page.

Equitable Economy Fund (n.d.). *About.* https://www.equitablefund.net/about.

Evergreen Cooperatives (n.d.). *About Us: A Nationally Watched Initiative in Grassroots Economic Development/Our Partners.* https://www.evgoh.com/about-us.

Evergreen Cooperatives of Cleveland (n.d.). *The Fund For Employee Ownership.* https://www.evgoh.com/tfeo.

Global Impact Investing Network (2022). *What You Need to Know About Impact Investing.* https://thegiin.org/impact-investing/need-to-know.

Green Worker Cooperatives (n.d. a). https://www.greenworker.coop.

Green Worker Cooperatives (n.d. b). *Co-op Academy – NYC.* Retrieved September 27, 2022, https://www.greenworker.coop/coopacademy.

Harrison, E.C. (n.d.). *Local Cooperatives Thrive with VSECU, CreditUnions.com.* Retrieved September 27, 2022, from https://www.creditunions.com/articles/local-cooperatives-thrive-with-vsecu/#ixzz7A8KSvjZ.

Heller, J. (2018, November 27). One of America's poorest cities has a radical plan to remake itself. *Huffington Post.* https://www.huffpost.com/entry/cleveland-ohio-poorest-cities-regeneration_n_5bf2e9d5e4b0f32bd58c137.

Hoover, M. & Abell, H. (2016, January 29). *The Cooperative Growth Ecosystem: Inclusive Economic Development in Action.* Project Equity and Democracy at Work Institute. https://institute.coop/sites/default/files/resources/Ecosystem%20Report.pdf.

Hub Bike Co-op (*n.d.*). *Our Mission: "All Types of Bikes For All Types of People."* https://www.thehubbikecoop.org/articles/our-mission-pg296.htm.

ICA Group (*n.d.* a). *National Reach section.* https://icagroup.org/.

ICA Group (*n.d.* b). *Fund for Jobs Worth Owning.* https://icagroup.org/jobsworthowning/.

Kerr, C. (2015, April 28). *Investing in Worker Ownership.* Democracy at Work Institute. https://institute.coop/sites/default/files/resources/DAWI%20-%20Investing%20in%20Worker%20Ownership.pdf.

Lingane, A. & McShiras, A. (2017). *Addressing the Risk Capital Gap for Worker Coop Conversions.* Project Equity: https://project-equity.org/wp-content/uploads/2017/04/Addressing-the-Risk-Capital-Gap-for-Worker-Coop-Conversions_Strategies-for-the-Field_Project-Equity.pdf.

Lingane, A. & McShiras, A. (2017). *The Original Community Investment A Guide to Worker Coop Conversion Investments.* Project Equity: https://www.project-equity.org/wp-content/uploads/2017/04/The-Original-Community-Investment_A-Guide-to-Worker-Coop-Conversion-Investments_Project-Equity.pdf.

MassCEO (*n.d.*). *About MassCEO.* https://massceo.org/.

McKinley, J. (2021, June 17). *The Democracy at Work Institute, EOX urge support for employee.* Democracy at Work Institute. https://institute.coop/news/democracy-work-institute-eox-urge-support-employee-ownership-treasury-program.

National Cooperative Business Association CLUSA [NCBA CLUSA] (*n.d.*). *Lews Weil* [Money Positive founder profile]. https://ncbaclusa.coop/lewis-weil/.

Nexus Community Partners (*n.d.*). *North Star Black Cooperative Fellowship.* https://www.nexuscp.org/our-work/north-star-black-cooperative-fellowship/.

NYC Department of Small Business Services (*n.d.*). *Worker Cooperative Business Development Initiative.* City of New York. https://www.nyc.gov/nycbusiness/article/worker-cooperatives.

NYC Small Business Services (2021). *Working Together: A Report on the Sixth Year of the Worker Cooperative Business Development Initiative (WCBDI)* [Annual report]. https://www1.nyc.gov/assets/sbs/downloads/pdf/about/reports/worker_coop_report_fy20.pdf.

Obran (*n.d.*). *A Cooperative Corporation.* https://obran.org/cooperative.

Project Equity (2021). *Small Business Closure Crisis.* https://project-equity.org/communities/small-business-closure-crisis/.

Project Equity (*n.d.* a). *Accelerate Employee Ownership.* https://project-equity.org/accelerate-employee-ownership/.

Project Equity (*n.d.* b). *Financing FAQs.* https://project-equity.org/financing-faqs/.

Project Equity (*n.d.* c). *Real Pickles Financing.* https://project-equity.org/financing/real-pickles-deal-structure/.

Real Pickles (2013, May). *Community Investment Campaign.* https://realpickles.com/invest/.

Real Pickles (2022, August 5). *Our Mission.* https://realpickles.com/our-mission/.

Rose, J., Kelly, M., Stranahan, S., Camou, M. & Kahn, K. (2021, January). *Opportunity Knocking: Impact Capital As The Transformative Agent To Take Employee Ownership To Scale.* https://www.fiftybyfifty.org/2020/12/opportunity-knocking/.

Seed Commons (*n.d.*). *About Seed Commons.* https://seedcommons.org/about-seed-commons/.

Shared Capital Cooperative (2021, October 2021). Shared stories by Shared Capital - ChiFresh Kitchen [Video]. *YouTube.* https://www.youtube.com/watch?v=oQKrJxpE2WM.

Start.coop (*n.d.*). *About/Our Approach.* https://www.start.coop/about.

The Drivers Cooperative (*n.d.* a). *Our Mission.* https://drivers.coop/about-us.

The Drivers Cooperative (*n.d.* b). *Drive with Us section.* https://drivers.coop.

The Working World (*n.d.*). *The Working World Fund.* https://www.theworkingworld.org/us/.

Torana Group (*n.d.*). *Essential Owners Fund.* https://www.toranagroup.com/.

Toussaint, K. (2021, July 15). How The Drivers Cooperative built a worker-owned alternative to Uber and Lyft. *Fast Company.* https://www.fastcompany.com/90651242/how-the-drivers-cooperative-built-a-worker-owned-alternative-to-uber-and-lyft.

Uptown Village Cooperative (*n.d.*). *Home page.* https://www.uptownvillage.coop/.

US Census Bureau (2020, November 17). *Annual Survey of Entrepreneurs.* https://www.census.gov/data/developers/data-sets/ase.html.

US Committee on Small Business & Entrepreneurship (*n.d.*). *Minority Entrepreneurs.* https://www.sbc.senate.gov/public/index.cfm/minorityentrepreneurs.

US Department of Treasury (2023, February 4). State Small Business Credit Initiative. https://home.treasury.gov/policy-issues/small-business-programs/state-small-business-credit-initiative-ssbci.

US Dept. of Treasury CDFI Fund (n.d.). *CDFI Program Benefits*. https://www.cdfifund.gov/programs-training/programs/cdfi-program.

US Small Business Administration (2023, February 1). *Types of 7(a) Loans*. https://www.sba.gov/partners/lenders/7a-loan-program/types-7a-loans.

Wacif (2021, September 16). *President Biden appoints Harold Pettigrew, Jr. to join Community Development Advisory Board* [Press release]. https://wacif.org/president-biden-appoints-harold-pettigrew-jr-to-join-community-development-advisory-board/.

Wacif (n.d.). *The Need & the Opportunity*. Enterprising Women of Color DMV Business Center. https://ewoc.wacif.org/about/.

WeFunder (n.d.). *The Drivers Cooperative* [Fund campaign]. https://wefunder.com/driverscoop/.

Welch, B. (2016, October 31). *Simply the Best: CHCA's Employee-Ownership Model*. B The Change. https://bthechange.com/bryan-welch-simply-the-best-9a507258d7ee.

Wylie, M. (2020, January 15). *How Much it Costs to Start a Business in Every Industry*. https://www.lendingtree.com/business/startup-costs-by-industry/.

CHAPTER 30

Reflection: Building the New Mutualism

Sara Horowitz

The way to reorganize the billions of dollars spent to confront climate change, to redistribute wealth to the working and middle class, to restore solidarity in our communities and to enable more of us to live our lives with equanimity is a "what is old is new" frame called mutualism.

Mutualism is a breakthrough workaround providing a stark contrast to the current, "same-old-same-old" that is now rehashed in the "*blah blah* sphere" of social media, think tanks, podcasts, and foundation and corporate board rooms.

Mutualism is hiding in plain sight. It's been with us for centuries. Every culture has a way to build solidarity and organize its wealth collectively, such as unions, cooperatives, and immigrant lending circles.

Enslaved people formed benevolent burial societies and banks. Those institutions went on to be the building blocks of the civil rights movement. Rural electric cooperatives serve our myriad rural communities with affordable energy. Garment-worker unions in the 1920s in the United States created the remittance system that immigrants use today to send money to their families in their home countries. Those same unions also created affordable housing models that are still relied on.

Mutualism provides communities with the capacity and know-how to actually run social-purpose institutions and create distributed networks that propagate easily.

Yet mutualism has been pushed out of the picture by both the left and the right, by foundations and philanthropy, and by government and the for-profit sector.

We can change all that by getting clarity about what mutualism is, building upon its re-emergence, and then being part of the new mutualist wave.

Three Principles of the Mutualist Sector
All mutualist organizations share these three essential characteristics:

- **Principle 1: Mutualists are formed into solidaristic communities.** Each has boundaries based on solidarity. In unions, workers come together to bargain against a specific employer. In cooperatives, members produce, group purchase, or market together. The members of mutual-aid groups are typically neighbors located in the same geographic area. In faith communities, adherents share a common belief system passed down generationally within families.

- **Principle 2: Mutualist entities have a shared economic mechanism.** This means that the community typically has an economic model like dues, service, fees, paid events, time banks, bartering, or lending circles. This economic mechanism enables the community to pool its own revenue, to control that revenue, and to recycle it back within the community.

- **Principle 3: Mutualists create institutions with a long-term focus.** Through mutualist institutions, members can pass down wisdom from generation to generation. As humans, we live one life, but institutions are vessels to hold insight, ideas, values, and lessons beyond one person's lifetime to reach future generations.

Reclaiming the Mutualist Sector

The economy is a three-lane highway of government, the private sector, and the mutualist sector.

But in the last 40 years, and now as we confront climate change, the mutual lane has become the highway's shoulder, and the highway looks as if it only has two lanes: one for the private sector and one for the government.

As climate change becomes our top priority and the push to build the next era's infrastructure begins, we have a chance of a lifetime to redirect government climate-change expenditures and restore mutualists to their proper third lane.

To do this, we need to start with a guarantee that a certain percentage of government contracts must be performed by the mutualist sector.

This will help create new anchor economic systems upon which local communities can build. Mutualists will generate new mutualist markets, create additional private-sector jobs, and catalyze new markets for a more prosperous middle of the economy.

If we don't develop a policy agenda for restoring the mutualist third lane, we will see the same play we've been watching for the last 40 years play out again. Here's the basic plot:

- **Scene 1:** We rely on mutualists to immediately respond to climate-driven natural disasters (for instance). They organize food pantries, get people critical medication, take care of pets, comfort one another and create mutual aid networks. In short order, they pioneer innovative solutions within their communities and have mapped their mutualist networks.

- **Scene 2:** FEMA and other government agencies come in and, after thanking the local community profusely, they begin to outsource all activity away from local mutualist groups. The majority of these services go to the for-profit sector.

- **Scene 3:** Venture capital and private equity are not stupid, and see what a great deal this can be — especially given the enormity of effort needed to address climate change. They see huge returns for businesses to address climate change and build new infrastructure. In the last 40 years, investors and industry have written the rules they need to get fabulously wealthy from these investments.

The result of this three-act play repeating over and over again is a massive, scaled-up uniformity with a series of lower-paying jobs done by workers who are often moved across the country by giant placement agencies. These huge contracts fail to ask local people to give of their talent and their knowledge of how their communities work. Mutualists build all this local infrastructure with their hearts and souls, only to watch "experts" swoop in and swoop out without their input or consent. And these big contractors don't share their returns on investments!

Sadly, many of today's titans of industry have gone one step further to create massive greenwashing strategies, misusing impact investing, ESG-SDG criteria, and other social-purpose business designations that let them continue to drive income inequality and ensure that their workforces aren't unionized. Think of Starbucks' fight against unionization.

In popular discourse and culture, they've gotten into the mutualists' lane, and have declared themselves the change agents, the drivers of impact, the real "good guys."

But the climate just gets worse, income inequality has only increased, and two generations have been deprived of the lessons of the mutualists whose social movements — civil rights, unions and cooperatives — have transformed our economy, our society, and ourselves.

Culture and history matter. The next generation needs to learn anew about mutualist strategies for their own survival, and for their children's.

We need to take back our lane.

Public policy and think-tankers need to evolve their frame. They are stuck in a binary two-lane-highway mindset that only offers them a choice between free markets and centralized government. New thinkers need to reclaim the lost mutualist tradition in their fresh analysis of public policy.

The Three Point Plan to Rebuild a Robust Mutualist Sector

1. Grow a new mutualist capital market

Think what this could look like after climate change drives the next natural disaster. Communities could have mature mutual-aid networks, with community members rehearsed in getting food, medicine, and childcare to those who need it immediately. Yes, it needs coordinated local institutions, along with mayors and local leaders with foresight, vision, and humanity. This is all possible because faith groups, unions, cooperatives, and mutual aid groups are already on the ground across the country.

Where to begin?

- **Start seeding the field** with RFP and fellowship programs to build small mutualist groups with community support — and local members who can pass the hat and get involved. Foundations and governments need to make this requirement the first phase of their funding as well. Like startups, most will fail, but it's the group that starts to grow and demonstrates a likelihood of success that will need follow-on funding.

- **Build a pipeline for mutualists to begin the growth process.** Small mutualist organizations can tap into funding by showing that there is a community need for their work, that they have a strategy to solve the problem, and that they have some nascent leadership. The start-up world has a great model in Y Combinator, and in social-entrepreneur fellowships such as Ashoka and Echoing Green. This model helps develop the pipeline, and demonstrates the intermediary strategy needed to build the pipeline over time.

- **Grow current mutualists.** They are already experienced in building communities and revenue, and have the ability to grow if capital markets are organized properly. But they can't solve the next era's challenges without active support and protection as a sector. Even though the mutualist sector must grow to meet our rapidly expanding survival needs, they already run hospitals, insurance companies, credit unions, union pension funds, rural electrical co-ops, and mutual-aid organizations in virtually every city and town. Their economic reach is already in the trillions of dollars right now!

- **Build these new capital markets into law and the Constitution.** For instance the Mondragon Cooperatives in the Basque region of Spain established a 10% return (pre-tax from profits) to support the Mondragon cooperative community ecosystem. This capital rule was incorporated into Basque co-op law and integrated into the national law of Spain.

Italian cooperatives also have a form of capital called "indivisible reserves" that enable real growth over time. Indivisible reserves are an innovative capital tool embedded in the Italian Constitution. Each cooperative returns 3% of revenue back to cooperatives' capital funds. Each new cooperative is eligible to get start-up funding from this capital pool, which sits on their balance sheet. The result is a capital market created for new cooperative formation, and each successful cooperative must "pay it forward" to keep the sector vibrant.

2. Next role of government: Safeguard the mutualist lane

The first order of business for the government at all levels is to make sure it does not do the job of the mutualists. In the three-lane highway of economic activity, the government needs to stay out of the mutualist lane. The government's role is NOT to provide the service, but to build up the mutualists to do the job. Governments must deploy strategies for creating a mutualist market similar to the Italian model.

Next, we need to move away from the idea that the government should "outsource" its functions to the nonprofit sector as a way to trim government. Instead, government contracts need to go to the mutualist sector so it can do its job of rebuilding democracy by providing for the needs of their communities.

In this model, mutualists get paid market rates for the services they render, and can use any margin to invest back into their organizations on R&D, developing seasoned staff, and starting more complex mutualist enterprises over time.

Governments spend whether they are right or left wing. Natural disasters happen and climate-change disasters will only be increasing. Government dollars already go to education, health care, maintaining land, hospitals, technology, veterans affairs, subsidizing key industries — the list goes on and on.

The point is, one key way for governments to support and rebuild the mutualist sector is to make sure that the mutualist sector is included in procurement and other programs so they can bid and win those projects.

A lot of this is happening at the margins, almost willy-nilly. The tax code is already deployed to provide the nonprofit sector, ESOPs, unions, and rural electric cooperatives with preferred treatment. Instead of this scattershot approach, the IRS, and antitrust and state insurance regulations, need to be readjusted and strengthened to see this as a whole mutualist sector.

3. Mutualists & local communities have to advocate for themselves

Mutualists must devise a Mutualist Index to gauge how effective governments are at the local, regional, and national level in increasing the number of cooperatives, community gardens, urban farms, mutual-aid societies, credit unions, mutual insurance companies, collective wellness centers, unionized workplaces, rural electric cooperatives — to name a few — in their area.

The next political leaders will learn how to "map mutualism" because this will be their political base. Since so much of this is happening at the local level, here's a Mutualist Mayor's to-do list:

1. Start a small local mutualist fellowship program to identify potential change agents in your area.

2. Provide building space, empty land, or zoning preference for mutualists to gather and to help communities.

3. Grow municipal and rural technology assistance to build local infrastructure where users can control their data.

4. Pioneer the rollout of the Mutualist Index to measure the growth of mutualists so we can evaluate what in government builds mutualism and what does not.

Mutualism will Transform Us by Changing Our Culture

The best way to see this transformation is to imagine a "Mutualist Day." Our daily lives will not be just living to work. Instead the idea of "living" will be about experiencing mutualist ecosystems to enable you to be the whole person you want to be.

This turning toward mutualism requires a profound change within ourselves. While condemning hyperindividualism within capitalism may now be fashionable, we need to go deeper. The change is probably so deep that it's in our brain chemistry. We are all trained to be so individualist that our first impulse is to critique from our own vantage point. In fact, we are a nation of "critique-ers."

Instead, we must behaviorally switch our brains to becoming "builders." We need to see that we first have to recognize what our individual needs are — and be free to be honest with ourselves. Then, we need to see who else is working together already and join them. If no one, then YOU need to be what Bill Drayton of Ashoka calls a change agent in an EACH [Everyone A CHangemaker] world.

What is completely lost in our hyperindividualist economy is the very thing that people need — a way to be less lonely and anxious. People's isolation and fear diminishes when they are asked to help others as peers, by being a part of organizations together. Mutualists create systems by bringing people together regularly to decide on what they should do and how they should run.

To heal ourselves and to build democracy, "We the Mutualists" need to engage people into shared economic and political institutions where our fates are bound up together. We build our collective institutions to provide the services we need, and have a vested interest in making them successful. In the context of our shared destinies we also understand our differences.

This is how we begin our strong pivot toward mutualism — with small, practical tasks that ask us to help ourselves, our neighbors, our co-workers. These kinds of actions have been carried out from generation to generation before us all, and are what make us feel human, cared for, and loved. These are the building blocks of every successful social movement in our country's history — and the building blocks of our democracy.

Virtually Convening the Contributors: A Round Table Discussion

Christina Clamp & Michael Peck

As we neared the end of this project, we asked ourselves how to bring this book to closure in a way that is meaningful to you the reader, and that brings the contributors together as a community. What follows is a summary and a transcript of a virtual gathering of most of the contributors, who were asked to provide a short summary of their key points to share with the group.

Martin Lowery served as the respondent at the end of the presentations, and identified four general areas or themes that emerged over the course of the conversation, all representing different facets of the co-op movement's opportunity in the coming months and years:

- The nature of the cooperative movement's positioning in the United States.
- The value of clarity on cooperative identity.
- The importance and opportunity of leveraging the power of networks.
- The need to focus more attention on worker-ownership.

Martin's full summary of the conversation follows the transcript below.

Contributor Introductions

Brian Corbin: My name is Brian Corbin. I'm an Executive Vice President for Catholic Charities USA. I'm the chief lobbyist for Catholic Charities in the nation's capital in public policy and statutory work. For 27 years, I ran Catholic Charities in Youngstown, Ohio, which was totally decapitalized by the industrial revolution of the 1970s. And at that time I helped build several cooperatives and community-development corporations, and fell by accident into Michael Peck's orbit, who used to come visit when I was teaching an MBA program at a local university. Mondragon was always one of my case studies. I've had the great pleasure of contributing an article with Michael and our friendship has grown as a result. I'm in Washington, D.C.

Jason Spicer: I'm Jason Spicer. At this time I'm just outside of Chapel Hill, North Carolina, visiting my mother for her birthday, but I'm based in Toronto, Canada, and now teach a graduate urban-planning program at the University of Toronto. My work primarily centers on alternative enterprise structures, like cooperative and related business models, and their potential to help us achieve both sustainability and equity. It was my pleasure to be invited to be involved in this project.

Rebecca Lurie: I'm Rebecca Lurie, currently at the City University of New York as an adjunct faculty at the School of Labor and Urban Studies, where I founded a project called Community and Worker Ownership Project. We also recently launched a certificate program in cooperative economics. I'm also on the Union Co-op Council Executive Committee and the Board of Democracy at Work Institute.

Mary Hoyer: Hi, I'm Mary Hoyer in Amherst, Massachusetts. I'm thrilled to be here today. Rebecca Lurie and I worked together on a chapter on the conjunction between labor unions in Mondragon. We both serve on the Union Co-ops Council of the US Federation of Worker Co-ops. Our chapter deals with the lengthy history of worker co-ops and co-ops in general with the labor movement. We talk about the efforts made by Mondragon to connect to the United States *via* Michael Peck in the late 1900s and early 21st century — the outcome of which was the Mondragon-US Steelworkers Agreement — and then go on to talk about the Union Co-ops Council of the US Federation of Worker Co-ops, and a number of local projects across the country, including in Cincinnati and Northern California. There are many, many union co-op projects.

Esteban Kelly: Hi, my name's Esteban and I am the executive director for the US Federation of Worker Co-ops, and I'm on the Democracy at Work Institute Board with Rebecca Lurie, and also Doug O'Brien's board with the National Cooperative Business Association. I'm a worker, owner, and founder of several different kinds of cooperatives. I'm based in Philadelphia and we'll talk about my chapter in a moment.

Doug O'Brien: Hello everybody. I'm the CEO of the National Cooperative Business Association CLUSA International. Indeed, Esteban is first vice chair of our board and Martin [Lowery] is a former chair of the board. NCBA CLUSA has a mission of promoting, defending, and advocating for cooperatives. That's been our mission for 106 years. Our vision, which is about six years old, just recently recommitted to by the board, is to ensure that more people can use cooperatives to build an inclusive economy. So I'm really, really glad to be part of this project and with all of you today.

Chris Cooper: I'm director of the Ohio Employee Ownership Center at Kent State University. We've been around for a lot of years and I've been around a lot too, getting a little grayer, but it's good to see a lot of folks that I haven't talked to in a while.

Dan Swinney: I'm the founder and now the director for strategic initiatives for Chicago's Manufacturing Renaissance. We've been around for about 40 years. I came out of the labor movement, the steelworkers, and have been focused on the link between manufacturing, community development, and economic democracy. I think we're now at a period where system change is a mainstream issue. The Mondragon example is fundamental as part of a new vision of development that has to be more comprehensive than just a democratic structure. We can provide a real alternative to neoliberal thinking and right-wing populism. That's how we should be framing our discussion in a very broad way, in a way that's expansive and inclusive of a variety of models, with the co-op model and the Mondragon model being one of the most pristine components of that vision.

Ana Aguirre: I'm from the Basque Country of Spain. I'm not originally from Mondragón but I work as close as you can get to Mondragón. I graduated from the first-generation entrepreneurship program class of Mondragón University, and I'm co-founder and a worker-owner at our own co-op that has been operating for 10 years now. I was asked to be part of this book, and I was quite taken aback at the beginning, feeling that I'm not at the level of what this book needs. So I gave both Christina and Michael a very bad editor's headache at the beginning and now here we are.

Jésus María Herrasti: Hello. I worked in Mondragon for many, many years, more than 48 years. Beginning as a student and then engineer, I had the opportunity to know José María Arizmendiarrieta when I was very young, maybe 14 years old. And over time I had the opportunity to be chairman, and general managers of different companies. I was the chairman of the Mondragon Congress and first president of Mondragon International. I retired and am happy to come to share my experiences with you.

April de Simone: Good morning, everyone. I'm a principal at Trahan Architects, co-founding partner of a platform called Designing from Democracy, and really looking at how we expand this concept of inclusive economies within the built environment, not only through a design medium, but really merging design mediums into the spatial practice of how cooperatives show up in a multiplicity of communities. I have the pleasure and honor of working with Michael Peck and Sandra McCardell on the board of the American Sustainable Business Network. Ana Aguirre, great to see you again. I'm really excited about pushing something out that captures all of our voices, and being in fellowship with each of you around how cooperative models can also be a vessel to close the racial wealth gap and inequities and disparities across this country, and am looking forward to learning more.

Sandra McCardell: Good morning, everybody. I have a company called Current-C Energy Systems, Inc. that started working on systemic sustainability when this subject was even less accepted than it is now. I transitioned to developing a cooperative development organization in New Mexico focusing on the most socially and economically vulnerable among us, now with next generation leadership. As all of you know, you can't get cooperatives out of your system, so I've also started another one which is the A to Z Hemp Cooperative. What I'm working on now is at the intersection of sustainability, marginalized communities, trades programs, building affordable housing, developing our local economy, and focusing on hemp products. So it's in some ways related to our book chapter as the next stage and I'm excited to be here.

Terry Lewis: I started out in cooperatives because I was born in one, the summer community I grew up in, and it changed my life and taught me a very great deal. And then when I was in law school, as a member of a housing cooperative, I really began to understand what cooperatives were as opposed to just the center of communities. I became the president of the National Association of Housing Cooperatives, served there for eight years, eventually became a lawyer, and eventually went to work for the National Cooperative Bank. Served on the board of NCBA and was the chair of the Cooperative Development Foundation. I'm now semi-retired. I returned to Detroit, the city I grew up in, at the moment in which it was exiting bankruptcy. I had the opportunity to give something back to that city by becoming part of the

Center for Community Based Enterprise, which develops and promotes worker co-ops. So having been in housing co-ops, and then representing the broad spectrum of cooperatives while I was in D.C., now I am a worker co-op person in my semi-retirement.

Kristen Barker: Ellen and I work together. We're co-founders of Co-op Cincy and 1worker1vote, and very excited to be here today.

Ellen Vera : I'm Ellen Vera, co-founder of Co-op Cincy and also super excited to be here today.

Caitlin Gianniny: I'm one of the co-founders of Samara Collective, that's a communications-consulting worker co-op. I'm also Chris Clamp's daughter, so I came into co-ops also because I was introduced at a very, very young age. I actually lived in the Basque Country for six weeks when I was 12. My mom was doing research back then interviewing folks at Mondragon. I think I might have sat in on one of those interviews and then I actually went back after college and was teaching English in Spain for eight months and lived in Mondragón while I was there.

Kevin O'Brien: All you really need to know is that you guys are all my heroes, so I'm just glad to be here today. I'm the founder manager of Worx Printing Cooperative, and I think I have a slide later that can explain.

Sara Horowitz: I started the Freelancers Union, but I do feel for the purposes of this conversation that I'd have to say my co-op, Bonafides, comes from my grandmother who lived in Amalgamated Co-op housing for about 40 years. And I visited her many times and regularly. I would say that out of the Freelancers Union, we had a social-purpose model that really was a cousin to the co-op model in many ways. And both got me thinking about this idea of mutualism, a phrase obviously I did not coin, but to see the connections between unions, co-ops, mutual aid, and the faith community, and to start building a network … We have a lot of shared ways of seeing the world, and a bunch of people on this call are part of the Mutualist Society. We're having our first congress to see how we will bridge across our movements, which so many of us already are doing. So it's networks of networks and networks and networks.

Julian Manley: I'm from England, employed in Preston at the University of Central Lancaster. I've been working with this thing called the Preston Model, which is a cooperative ecosystem since round about 2011. I think it's fair to say that I'm one of the founders who brought the Mondragon experience into the Preston Model. I've written about that in a couple of books and some articles, but I'm also interested in bridging academic work and actual real life work. I'm the founder-member and the first chair of the Preston Cooperative Development Network, founder-member of the Preston Cooperative Education Centre — a union co-op, and also founder-member of the cooperative New Social, which is a digital platform that aims to network cooperative-minded people principally around Preston, but later branching out all over the UK, Europe, the United States, and so on.

Christina Clamp: My chapter talks a little bit about some of my experiences with the Basque and Mondragon culture and how it relates to my work now in co-ops. As Terry modelled it, I first got interested in cooperatives because I had a professor in college who introduced me to the way that agricultural cooperatives were making a huge difference for farmers in the northwest of Georgia. I visited a chicken processing co-op, and then that professor took us up to the Tennessee Valley Authority where I came to appreciate that co-ops were an important part of how they got started. Since then I've been for almost 42 years at Southern New

Hampshire University, where I was originally hired as a co-op specialist. As Terry can tell you, I've benefited from multiple experiences, in part through my board work with different groups across different co-op sectors. I have done capacity building for community development credit unions, and I've worked with the worker co-ops from the early years when we were really just trying to get our feet on the ground with groups like the Association for Workplace Democracy. I did a program at Boston College that was on social economy and social policy with Severyn Bruyn, who was part of the founding board for the ICA Group when it got started. Michael will want me to mention that my dissertation was actually on the Mondragon cooperatives, so I had the good fortune of meeting three of the five co-founders of Mondragon's first worker coop, ULGOR, who were with Mondragon when I first visited in 1982. I had the opportunity to interview 50 people within co-op management of the group at the time. I got to see a lot of different group experiences during a time of recession, serving as a lifelong inspiration for me.

The Conversation

Michael Peck: What we're trying to achieve through our collective book is create a literary "roadmap portal" to the immediate cooperative and mutualist future. We use the phrase "seeing around corners and peering over horizons," to position not just where the movement has been, but where we think and hope it's going, and to show there's all these different models out there that can be connected based on shared, aligned values, and produce incredible, transforming economic results changing the whole game and flattening all extractive curves. Our core model is Mondragon. We have so many different examples from so many different countries and sectors in the book that hopefully it'll serve its intended purpose.

Caitlin Gianniny: My chapter kicks off talking about the tradition in the Basque Country, when meeting up with your friends in a public setting on a weekly basis. There's usually a set of bars that you'll go to, and the way that people tend to pay for things at the bars is when you get there, everybody puts in the same amount of money, which is called *"bote."* And so one person has the money for everybody for the night, and that way at each bar you don't have to be like, "Who paid for what?" There's your pay-in at the beginning, you can get drinks, go to all the different bars, and at the end of the night, if there's money left over, you could either split it up or just keep it for next week. Most of the time in my experience, we kept it for next week. But I love this story because for anybody who's familiar with co-ops, right at its base level, there's a buy-in, there's a sharing of resources that actually facilitates people having this experience together and that is different than if people were individually on their own. I feel like it's a great example of cooperative principles in a cultural norm. As an American I was very much like, wow, this makes things so simple. It's so efficient and makes it more fun to not have to be parsing out money on a case by case basis.

My chapter then goes into how some of those norms run counter to dominant culture and economic systems in the USA, and I draw on some of the research from one of our fellow authors here, Jason Spicer. Then, the second half of the chapter really goes into just starting up a worker cooperative. I have worked with a lot of unions, a lot of grassroots groups, or nonprofits that are doing advocacy work. But unfortunately, as in-house staff, a lot of times it felt like there was a misalignment between the work that we were doing, like the campaigns we were working on, and then the internal practices for staff. So that was really one of the core reasons we founded Samara Collective: to create a place where we could do the work that we wanted to be doing and have more control over staff conditions. That's continued to be a core guiding principle in how we operate as an organization.

The final part of the chapter goes into just some of the structural challenges we ran into starting up a co-op. We came in with a lot of resources, but we still encountered challenges. You have all the normal small-business hoops, and then there's just a lot more hoops after that in starting as a worker co-op. I tell a story about trying to incorporate our business in Massachusetts, which has a cooperative statute. We had to go to the office three times before we could get someone who could actually answer our questions. We tried to get the forms off the website for incorporation, and it turns out that they don't even have the form for co-ops on the website reflecting the legislation that was updated. That changed the form for all businesses except for co-ops. So there's all these weird little ins and outs where people have the information, but it's kept hidden as institutional knowledge and the process is not simple without having to go talk to a bunch of people and gather all this information.

I see cooperatives as a really amazing tool for building more equitable workplaces. But I think we have a lot of work to do to make the entry process into founding co-ops more accessible. One of the things that Samara has been working on with a few other worker co-ops and co-op developers is a project to launch a web portal to help guide people through that startup process. We've been talking with the folks at the US Federation of Worker Cooperatives about it as well, to try and help with that kind of bar to entry.

Placing where we place value

Cooperatives, cultural norms, and challenges co-ops face in the United States

- **Cooperative principles can show up in simple cultural norms** like how we share a drink with friends
- **Cooperative principles run counter to the dominant culture and economic system in the United States**, presenting some unique challenges for co-ops
- **Co-founded a communications consulting worker cooperative after seeing the ways in which advocacy organizations do not always align their internal staff practices with the issues they fight for externally** (like many co-ops ...founded after some kind of marginalization)
- **Even with a lot of resources, we ran into a number of structural challenges**. Co-op founders face all of the normal startup challenges, plus additional hoops unique to co-ops.

Esteban Kelly: I was really concerned about movement building and ecosystem development, and making sure that with all of our interest in Mondragon, we're really applying the right lessons for the vision in the US of what it is we're trying to build. So I kept my chapter at this global level, looking at the idea of the ecosystem itself, which of course is really central to how they've developed their cooperatives.

My interview-chapter is how a lot of this was about us reverse-engineering an ecosystem model, and how that translated here into lenders and business leagues or activists and coalitions and policy frameworks. Then I spent the majority of my interview-chapter on the "table," the metaphor that Mondragon uses, and breaking down these legs of the table around education, R&D, finance, and social services. I mentioned the Democracy at Work Institute, and its purpose around education, research, and development — if we're actually trying to advance and build out this national cooperative ecosystem and resource for local co-op development. I mentioned some of the other groups who contribute to that and do a bit of an assessment about how we aren't as robust as we could be, that there's more opportunity for innovation, and building institutions that can more robustly support cooperative development, and R&D expansion, franchising, and some of the things that have been part of Mondragon's success.

There's public-policy work with existing, public government agencies, whether they're local or federal, and then work to do with capital itself, and building mechanisms for distributing finance, and an ecosystem of cooperative professionals who are able to underwrite and finance and look at these investment portfolios. The piece on social services is where I feel we are weakest in the US, we don't really do a good job and that a lot of that is because the ecosystem in the US is very much focused on the development of the enterprise itself. That's what's grant-funded; those are the kinds of metrics and deliverables that even government supports. Only by having things like a worker co-op federation can we start to establish worker benefits, so that once you create a cooperative, it can actually thrive and resource the workers to have good jobs. There still is no national retirement program for worker owners. And what do you do when there's conflict among the workers? What do you do about health coverage and things like that?

I conclude on, yeah: Let's bring this actually back to what Father Arizmendiarrieta was doing, which was not necessarily about, you know, some grandiose business innovation or global contestation with capitalist firms, but was really focusing on that community and what people needed, and really rooting in the values, in the solidarity there, and doing an assessment of the social and political, and economic landscape. That's what we should be doing if we're looking at the opportunities to scale worker ownership and build the field. Tech innovation, good jobs — the industries around food, healthcare, childcare, just essential industries that we know are poised or really well positioned to take root and to find support and partnership from social movements or from government allies.

Sara Horowitz: I've been thinking about what are the underlying principles that unite unions and co-ops and faith communities and mutual aid networks and some social-entrepreneurial endeavors? It really seems like there are these three principles that we all share.

One is that we all are formed around solid communities where we're "boundaried;" there's a community of people that we work with, and that's distinct from the public square, the commons. They're both great — this isn't "one is better than the other," though I think that sometimes we get confused. But we mutualists all tend to be around solidaristic communities.

Second is that we all have an economic mechanism that can be dues, that can be services, but it can also be currency. It can all be exchanges of time.

And the third is that we all have a long-term focus. We all want to pass wisdom from generation to generation.

That is, to me, helpful, because once you start to think about those three principles, you can walk into almost any environment and say: "Oh my God, this is mutualist." The task at hand to me for the next 12 months is that we have to get some clarity about what we're about. Because I think there's been tremendous confusion in some ways — not really with this group, I think the cooperative model has such deep understanding of itself — but so many others don't. And the world has sort of gotten confusing, with impact investing and B Corps — they're wonderful things, but our economy is a three-lane highway: there is the for-profit sector, the government sector, and the mutualist sector. I think what has happened is a lot of the for-profit sector has started to bleed into our sector. And so you see these odd things where corporate leaders are seemingly being the good guys around certain things, but you don't see them supporting unionization. You don't see them developing cooperatives. Their models are completely extractive.

We have this whole opportunity, especially around climate change, really thinking about racial inequality, about how government is spending its money through procurement, and that we need to start to really realign these pipelines of money. So yes, it's so hard to start and organize a union or start a co-op, but if there were money flows that really were better organized, we would actually be in such a better position.

I'll just close with this: I make a little joke to myself, which is, I "rail against scale." And it's not that I think scale is bad, but really for biodiversity, and for the type of scale that comes from local communities, building and reflecting who their community is and keeping their resources together, developing their know-how.

Ana Aguirre: My summary is a little shorter because I wrote from a very personal perspective. What I did was share our experience creating a worker cooperative working around co-ops in Mondragón, and my understanding of how Mondragon created an undergraduate degree that allows people to challenge the co-ops as we understand them, even inside a group, and start new co-ops, and learn by doing. I shared a little bit on the entrepreneurship unit of the University of Mondragon. I was the first generation; I was also a team coach there, and my company is mostly from that first generation. I wanted to share with you some of the keys for using the creation of team companies as tools for learning, and for [building] cooperative habits. I think Jésus María can also share with you that a lot of the people graduating from Mondragon University don't necessarily know a lot about cooperatives.

Almost every circle I go into is different. How to do co-ops is different, and the way that we understand co-ops, or want to make them tools for development for the future, is different to what we saw 60 years ago.

Doug O'Brien: I have the great pleasure of actually doing an interview with Chris and Michael on a number of key topics surrounding the wonderful chapters and the wonderful work that this cohort is doing. It was a mixture of an examination of some contemporary issues and dynamics that the cooperative movement and in particular the worker cooperative movement, finds itself today — and then reaching back into some history of how, from the US context in particular, a number of the sectors came to scale. The farmer cooperatives, credit unions, rural electrics in particular.

Talking about this, I went a little bit deep into the serial co-entrepreneur, Murray Lincoln, who was kind of a force of nature in the middle of the century, leveraging farmer cooperatives into many other different types of cooperatives. We talked about the opportunity and the challenges around the rise of big data and artificial intelligence and technology. We talked about social services, cooperatives, and opportunities there. We talked about the potential for what we generally call federated cooperatives, shared-services cooperatives, and others to help accelerate scale for worker cooperatives. And then about the ocean or the water that I swim in, advocacy. We talked about the policy environment here in the United States and the opportunities and some of the distinctions in the cultural and the political environment the United States presents to the worker-cooperative movement.

Imanol Olaskoaga: My chapter on innovation describes the changes made when the Erreka co-op in Basque Country was faced with a very hard situation. We started noticing that we were uninvited guests in a situation where our product was not selling any more. We were producing screws, industrial screws, the most simple product in our value chain. When the wind turbine sector stumbled on hard times, we suffered very, very hard, because we were just producing a commodity, a product that was not valued in the market, the most mature and with the lowest margins. So, with a team of four and with team support, we changed our product by adding a sensor to offer more value to the supply chain. This was very difficult, but combining market insights, product knowledge, and using technology from our group's research and technical facilities, we were able to increase value, add new services, and turn a commodity product into one with advanced digital as well as structural capacity. We were very proud to be able to achieve this change and my chapter speaks to it.

Michael Peck: **Chapter 1** is titled, "Cooperative Capitalism at the Coalface," and it's intended to set the stage for what follows. In a world where the invasion of Ukraine by Russia changed the global climate-security and energy-security dynamic, threatening the Glasgow, Egypt, and soon Montreal summits' climate advances the world was already haltingly committing to, it's time to go back to the models that work for the most vulnerable, to find out: How do we find our way forward?

Starting in the US Appalachian region, where many of us, including Doug, Kristen, Ellen, and others are focused, the world has taken notice that even the relatively small percentage of coal miners operating now in the US — somewhere less than 63,000 in 2022, and much less than what used to be — represent coal-industry interests that still drive what happens to climate in the US for a number of social, economic, cultural, and political reasons. We took the phrase "coalface" — which is basically in the mining days, where the seams were exploited, and the coalface collier was the person who really knew how to detect those seams, and organized the teams underground in those always dangerous mines to capture the coal and get it above ground.

The chapter looks briefly at what's happened from the industrial revolution to today, and uses a sociocultural lens to look at how we create systems that can transform processes, products, and ecosystems into something that's so much better, where stakeholders hold equity and democratically govern.

Our directly related campaign — to value human and social capital assets as resources to honor and nurture — had a nice breakthrough in early November 2022 which Ibon Zugasti and I describe in more detail in our joint **Chapter 5**. It's only one small toehold in the hazardous climb up the socioeconomic-equality and climate-resiliency/zero-emissions mountains, but the goal of the Sabbath serving mankind instead of the trickle-down opposite is well worth the pain.

We will not be able to claim success until the coalface is transformed because the current price to survive, paid involuntarily by too many communities left behind — combined with the imperial tax costs imposed by Musk-like "Robber Barons" — are equally too steep for "humanity at work and life" to afford. We've harvested the grim results of those policies and projects in the US, and even though we sidestepped a disaster during the 2020 midterm elections in the US, it just means we have to do it all over again in 2024.

Jason Spicer: My chapter is entitled "What's in a Name? Conceptual Frameworks for a Cooperative World." And the point of the chapter is, as Sarah was saying before, some attempts to "co-op wash" traditional corporations' actions, which are problematic. But there are a host of other alternative enterprise models, which operate in conjunction and in parallel around the world that sometimes are regrouped along with cooperatives under different framing names, which I explore in the chapter: community wealth, alternative enterprises, the social and solidarity economy. We get these frames as a way to knit together broader families of enterprises trying to accomplish shared goals.

What's In a Name? Conceptual Frameworks for a Co-operative World
Jason S. Spicer, PhD

- Reviews **differences/consequences of competing framing/naming** conventions simultaneously exist to describe inter-related alternative economic models.
- **Frames**: alternative, diverse, and community economies (ADCE); commons/commoning; community wealth and control; collectivist/democratic organizations and alternative enterprises; economic democracy; the social and solidarity economy (SSE/ESS); post-capitalism; and degrowth.
- Systematic review suggests **commons/community or social and solidarity economy names may have greatest unifying potential**.
- Affirms **no frame has been systematically applied** to help us collectively organize, or to understand and measure when we should use one alternative business model instead of another.

What's the difference? Does it matter that there are these different names? These are the questions that I'm wrestling with in this chapter, which offers a systematic review of academic and applied literature to identify some of the differences between these approaches — and which reflect different linguistic and national focus, academic-disciplinary focus, different factors of production in economics lingo, land, labor and capital, as well as different topics whether it's about addressing climate change, whether it's addressing internal governance and mission drifts.

And the point I conclude with is that some of these frameworks and framing names appear to be narrower than others, and have less potential to perhaps act as an overarching unifying framework for us all. The two that I come out of my analysis as having the most promise to be an overarching frame for everyone to use are those that use some form of the root word, 'commons', or community, or commoning and then the social and solidarity economy. If we're in a world of a contest of economic ideas, and we're fighting to attract eyeballs of rising generations to our ideas, I do think there is a potential value to having a big frame that we can all get behind. So those were two that I thought had the most potential as unifying frames.

And then, I also draw some conclusions on how we could move this research, that we're all doing, to answer some unanswered questions about the potential for these models to achieve their goals.

Sandra McCardell: I'll attempt to give this chapter a little bit of justice and listening to other people present I am gobsmacked by the vision that you all put together in trying to create this book and how many angles and incredible people you have pulled together to do it. So thank you for the honor of being included in this grouping.

Our chapter is based on a submission that we made for grant funding, with some others who are on this call, and one of the videos that is used as an introduction states that the promise of liberty, equity and justice for all has not been achieved. This initiative was to try to find ways to do that. There were many methodologies that we used, but they all focused on melding racial equity and workplace democracy.

Starting with the goal of racial equity through racial healing and the methodology through collaboration, there were three phases: developing relationships, mapping the situation on the ground, and then co-defining collaborative or cooperative projects. So the piece, I think, speaks most clearly to what others have talked about, which is that any path forward needs to be co-defined and whoever is involved in the group needs to work together on it. Then the other piece is that communities carry the projects forward. There were three geographic communities who were part of this initiative, and they carry it forward; and we who helped pull the pieces together stepped away. Some of the things that we were trying to do is to document the work throughout the communities — on paper, through recordings, and through films — that the communities themselves would do, documenting in ways that would resonate in the future.

Investing in ownership, of course, was a key, and then using supportive webs — mentors and investors. Having the communities at the center, and then allies of various types who would enable their vision to move forward with everybody advocating for transformation.

The key was to center the communities, and everything surrounded those communities. They were the reason for all of us to exist. That's the lens through which everything else passed.

Jésus María Herrasti: I am very pleased to be listening to you, but I think my presentation is a little bit different, because I am focusing on how important the big principles and the big values are, and at the same time how do we improve the ability to develop these values as practice for the future and for today. What I talk about as Mondragon begins after [the Spanish Civil War] and a tremendous crisis in society, and how José María Arizmendiarrieta decides to be very ambitious. He believes he has to develop a new kind of society where things like war will not be possible in the future. And then he thinks his college institute will have to deal necessarily with issues like education, work, and health, because these are very important to develop a new kind of society where the possibilities for all the people will be more or less equal.

Previously, the main tools for this kind of change were education and work, but not common work conditions. However, the possibility of work where the worker could participate as an owner and could decide everything became important. One of the main reasons for the war was this kind of divided society, where the poor are very poor and the rich are very rich forever. And the only way was to change how the people could work and also how the people could develop their life in better ways. And José María creates a new model based from the very beginning on work participation. At that time, one of the possible legal formulas to do this was a co-op, and José María began founding companies with these people. Fortunately over time we were able to develop a corporation where these kinds of values house approximately 81,000 people in different companies, yes, but very important, competitive companies globally representing many businesses.

Numbers are very important, but after the civil war we developed a kind of remuneration that is more equal in closing the gap between the people who earn more money or less money, and we developed a society reflecting this change. These linkages between company and society create the most equal community in our province, probably in Spain. And clearly this change that we make in our companies means they do not close when facing harder times. Instead, these values compel us to change our companies and society through better practices and these bigger values. Our first bylaws come from the social doctrine of the church, because José María was a priest. He saw very clearly, and we see very clearly, that we are based on the important and very difficult Christian legacy to put into practice the principle that defines work as the fundamental dimension of human assistance.

This social dignity to work relationship means we must increase the social dimension of work, which is superior to any production factor and participation of the work in property ownership and so on. All these principles enter directly into our founding bylaws. We develop these principles into practices and participation in our organization.

For example, what kinds of decisions a manager can make and what decisions are made by the co-op board; how the people can participate in everything; and how do we combine management and participation when you are a worker, you are a member, and you are an owner — these are very, very important considerations. How we develop a culture to fulfil these principles in the face of constant change means that we always need to invent and try new models and new ideas. As I try to explain, the relationship between big principles and how we develop the practice is ever more fundamental and necessary.

Chris Clamp: I took on the task of referring back to a report (*Mondragon History, 1956-2019.* mondragon-corporation.com/en/history/) that was prepared by the Young Foundation that Ibon Zugasti had shared with Michael and Michael shared with me. This report was looking at the ways in which Mondragon is a model of best practices in social innovation. The report identified seven principles that they thought were really important.

First was shared values. Second is the networked organizational model that works from the ground up based on those values, and ongoing commitment to social means and ends that guide working practice: democratic and egalitarian governance and ecosystems of intra- and inter-cooperation and success, grounded in disruptive business ideas, profit sharing and member mobilization. Last is the internal development of complementary institutions serving the wider mission and commitment to the sovereignty of labor.

What I tried to do in reflecting on those principles was what I had seen when I first visited Mondragon in 1982 and in subsequent visits. And so in developing the chapter, what I focused on is the way that Mondragon's bank, Caja Laboral, which now does business as Laboral Kutxa, played an important role in the growth of the Mondragon Cooperative Corporation (MCC). And just to highlight some of the key elements of this — when you look at the period up till 1991, in the course of 37 years, the bank was able to nurture significant growth in the Mondragon cooperatives: 45% of the cooperatives were created with support from the bank. Employment increased from 4,211 in 1965 to over 22,860 in 1990. And, of course, we know how much it's increased since then. Subsequently, MCC created and provided the ecosystem — they talk about it as the "table," meaning that for institutional leadership and the sectoral groups to advance and to be successful it was largely because they supported each other in the process of doing business. I ended the chapter with an interview with Julio Gallastegui, who's been a long term friend of mine and is a former general manager of Laboral Kutxa. He very kindly affirmed the points that I'd made about how Mondragon and Laboral Kutxa had worked closely together in the early years up through 1991. What I knew from talking with Don José María Ormaetxea, Caja Laboral's founding CEO, is that the bank was under a lot of pressure from the Central Bank to change its practices to essentially become a commercial bank rather than a development bank. And because of what they had been through in the 1980s with the recession, they saw that by building strong sectoral groups, the Mondragon group as a whole would be able to be more sustainable and prosper. These are the key elements of the chapter that I contributed.

Brian Corbin: To prepare this chapter, Michael got dragged through moral theology, which is my training, and he did OK. He's moral and that's a good thing. But what we did together is have a conversation about what Father José María Arizmendiarrieta would have seen in 1941 in terms of moral theology, but dragged it to the future, to now, and how those concepts have deepened and actually gotten more systematized in Catholic moral framework.

But more importantly, how Pope Francis specifically is directly aiming a lot of conversations to what is a popular movement, asking what does a popular movement entail ethically and meeting with what's called the World Convening of Popular Movements. The first one was in Bolivia. Then one in Rome. I went to the one in Modesto, California, myself. Pope Francis is saying it's about low-income people, people in the margins, people in the dumpsters, people in the dump heaps, people doing little things on the side that have been perceived as abandoned and not important, and what he calls disposable; but it's the voice of those who are just disposable that need to be in the center of the table, and you build your economy around that and your structures to include and to do that. So, Michael and I had a two-year conversation between a moral theologian and a social thinker, and tried to come up with a way to invest in that exchange. But I do want to tell you, Michael passed Moral Theology 101. So that's really great. So Michael, I don't know if you want to add anything to that.

Michael Peck: No, Brian, I just followed your lead and thank you so much for everything you taught me in cooperating on this chapter.

Julian Manley: My chapter is about the development of the Preston model and in particular how the Preston model takes its inspiration from Mondragon. In 2011, the traditional form of investing in a city, inward investment, the neoliberal way of working, collapsed in Preston. And when that happened we were left with a complete void, and in order to fill that void we tried to take different ideas from different places, basically anything that would work.

We were facing austerity in the UK. We're still facing austerity; there's crisis, hopelessness, and we just needed some kind of inspiration. Since I'd done previously some consultancy work with Mondragon — this was before I went to Preston — I decided to start developing a relationship with Mondragon. We brought in Mikel Lezamiz, of Otalora, who was responsible for international dissemination of the Mondragon project to Preston. And from that moment we understood, as a couple of people have mentioned, that the cooperative ecosystem drives the Mondragon table with its four pillars (education, financial, research and development, and retail/social services), and this became our inspiration for developing the Preston ecosystem.

So, importantly, the work in Preston, because of its inspiration from Mondragon, is really all about networking. The system in Mondragon works because the cooperatives work inter-cooperatively. That's a fundamental aspect of the work in Mondragon, and it's one of the things I think that is lacking in many cooperative developments around the world, where there's a lot of emphasis on cooperative governance within single cooperatives, but there's less thinking about how each cooperative can help each other to progress. So as a result of that we developed this Preston Cooperative Development Network, which was very loosely based on the Mondragon Cooperative Corporation. Of course, you know, I have to mention a *caveat* here, and that is that we are not pretending that in Preston we are anywhere near or anywhere like Mondragon. When we say we want to be like you, what we mean is we want to be like you in terms of principles, inspirations, ideas, not in terms of the actual kinds of cooperatives that are developed.

So, in Mondragon, of course, we've got a fantastic collection of industrial cooperatives, and it's unlikely that in Preston we'd have many industrial cooperatives. "Inspired by Mondragon" means "inspired by the principles and values and the networking ecosystem that Mondragon has developed." I think it's important to bear that in mind. We developed the Preston Cooperative Development Network to try and build a cooperative network of intercooperation in Preston. Little by little we've been trying to emphasize the importance of social value as opposed to economic or financial value. That's been a great difficulty because of course we are living in an extreme-neoliberal society, where money is everything.

So, to try and understand a system that works to generate wealth — because the Preston model is about generating local wealth and retaining local wealth — the word wealth itself needs to include social capital and social value, as well as financial value.

That is an ongoing concept that we're constantly developing, and taking our inspiration from Mondragon, where the cooperatives put money back into the community as part of their community project. Also in Preston, we're trying to work as hard as we can to interact and focus on worker-owned cooperatives as opposed to all the other kinds of cooperatives that exist. In the UK that's actually quite a challenge because worker-owned cooperatives are few and far between. We met quite a bit of opposition in our emphasis on worker-owned cooperatives. But again, taking our inspiration from Mondragon, it's only through worker-owned cooperatives that you truly get the sense of autonomy and empowerment for the workers. We're very keen on that because it's about empowerment, it's about democracy as well, workplace democracy, so that each worker has an equal say in leading the project.

That the worker-owned cooperatives idea is inspired and sustained by Mondragon, as well as by communities, is important. The social fabric in Mondragon is not just about the cooperatives and the work. When someone works in Mondragon, they take the principles and values of Mondragon back into the community, they take them back into the family, into the church, and so on. It's important to understand that we're not just talking about work, we're talking about how work becomes community.

We've tried to develop a Preston-meets-Mondragon series of talks and lectures. We're developing relationships in Mondragon. We have fairly frequent visits by different people from Mondragon to Preston, and recently we've gone to Mondragon as well. We're trying to develop a relationship with Mondragon as well so that we get a living example of what Mondragon means. Once again, as people have mentioned before, the theory is great but the practice has got to go along with the theory. There's nothing like having real-life people from Mondragon come to Preston and tell us about their experiences, and vice versa. We've been developing the idea of the union co-op, greatly inspired by Michael Peck, because the idea is that we are inspired by Mondragon, but we're not Mondragon.

I'm very grateful to Michael for inspiring us, because in the UK, just as in the US, workplace democracy, worker democracy is really related to the tradition of trade unions. We want to build the tradition of the trade unions into the cooperative system in ways that we've been learning from Michael. We're introducing that in different ways through the education system. We've developed the Preston Cooperative Education Centre, because as has been mentioned before, education is an absolute key and pillar of maintaining the Mondragon system. We intend education to be key and a pillar to sustaining the system in Preston. The social value that I mentioned before, the idea that social value is as important or even more important as financial or economic value, can only come through to people, can only be communicated to people through constant work in education and training, exactly as happens in Mondragon. Our Preston Cooperative Education Centre is precisely a union co-op, and it's the first union co-op in the UK. We like to feel that we are walking our talk in that way.

Finally, I talk about the bank and it's being mentioned just now, Laboral Kutxa, as fundamental to the development of Mondragon — not so important in that sense now, but in the very beginnings it was fundamental. We've begun and we are two-thirds of the way through the process of creating the Northwest Mutual Cooperative Bank, which will serve precisely to fund future cooperatives exactly the same way as Caja Laboral did in Mondragon years ago, and as they continue to do as Laboral Kutxa.

So in a nutshell, that's what the chapter's about. It's about Preston and it's about how Preston tries to create its own ecosystem, largely inspired by Mondragon, but attempting to make it part of what's special in particular about Preston in the UK.

Dan Swinney: First of all, I think that manufacturing is central to the success and significance of Mondragon. I actually think to focus on manufacturing is as important as the issue of democratic structure. That's one of my general principles. And second, I think that the Mondragon model needs to be part of a larger vision of society, not just a third way, and that we have to be part of a vision that really contends in total with the neoliberal as well as the right-wing populist visions and development that are emerging.

My background was certainly as an activist in the 1960s, and I spent 13 years as a machinist and a union leader and union organizer. Then my company closed as did 3,000 other companies in the 1980s in Chicago and then 60,000 around the country. I founded Manufacturing Renaissance, and we've gone through several names to try to understand what was going on in manufacturing, and was the decline in manufacturing inevitable, or were there problems that could be solved?

Probably after 20 years of being sort of the SWAT team on plant closings and looking at individual companies that are in crisis, we of course saw some companies that should have closed, a small percentage, but in large part every publicly traded company, every large company we looked at was being forced into closing by Wall Street, and by management decisions looking at the highest return in the shortest amount of time, which many times led to the cannibalization of the company itself. In manufacturing, 90% of manufacturing companies have less than 100 employees. We found that to be a major issue. In those small companies in Illinois that are privately held, they're typically owned by men, 99% of them are owned by whites. We found that a large number of those owners also come from the baby boom generation which means Mother Nature is wreaking generational havoc starting with that generation. It means, for example in Chicago alone, there's probably 1,000 companies available for sale in the next 10 years.

The ability to intervene and engage with those companies to me is central to both retaining and building a sustainable society, and also offers the opportunity for better, proven models like Mondragon to take hold. Central to that is we're an organization that focuses on serving the social aspect of manufacturing, the impact on community, on labor. A major part of our view is that once you see there's this huge crisis in manufacturing as a required foundation for a society, the solution lies in changing ownership structures in those companies. A lot of our work has been focused on how the social movement has to go from just being focused on redistribution of wealth — which is the tradition of the labor movement and community-based organizations, Saul Alinsky and so on — and has to embrace an amending model which affirms that, yes, you have to continue to fight for fair redistribution of wealth and working conditions, but you also have to begin to step in and drive the *creation* of wealth and step up into questions of management of finance and so on and so forth.

To us, the Mondragon model offered a perspective of how you can compete within a market economy with different values that are focused on sustainable development and are restorative socially, economically, and environmentally. A lot of our work is how to shape the public to embrace and engage and be ready or not to retain our industrial base. With that goal in mind, the logic of the model is central, critical, and we think the model itself has to be taken to a different paradigm of development, and taken to scale through the political process. So, in the last year or two that we were with a group of other organizations, we submitted a bill to Congress called, HR 5124, which merges the issue of promoting manufacturing with the issue of inclusion in manufacturing, which means, in our bill, there's $20 million set aside for employee ownership, but also education, all the various components that make economic democracy possible. That's the thrust of the comments in my chapter given that actually my first experience with Mondragon was seeing the BBC documentary in 1980. Once you saw that movie, you were committed to the process no matter how long it took, no matter where you went, that was something you were going to follow. Mondragon represents that to me.

Mary Hoyer & Rebecca Lurie: Thank you everybody. My name is Rebecca Lurie. Mary gave a good overview in her introduction.
We both are on the executive committee of the Union Co-op Council. We're trying to tell the story of the labor movement's involvement with co-ops inspired by Mondragon over the years. What I really wanted to add is this incredible gratitude as I'm sort of at the end of the list of speakers, hearing how wonderful all these chapters are and what a great book it will be as we teach co-ops at the university. Yesterday there was a conference in New York on teaching economic democracy that some of us attended, to talk about what we teach, and it was inspired by some of the same things that inspired everybody else here. I think that this will help to anchor this hard thread of the history of the labor movement with co-ops, and many of those people who are part of that history-making are in the room today. I'll save time and share that, and thank you, Chris and Michael, for your vision to put this together.

LABOR UNIONS AND WORKER CO-OPS: DEMOCRATIZING THE ECONOMY

by Mary Hoyer, Ed.D., and Rebecca Lurie, M.S.

This chapter discusses Mondragon's influence on labor in the U.S. and includes:
- the need for innovative solutions in the current elite-oriented economy to work, wealth sharing, and social support.
- frictions between labor organizing and worker-owned enterprise, as well as the natural and obvious congruences.
- history of mutual efforts on the part of unions and cooperatives.
- Mondragon's connections to the U.S. during the first decade of the 21st century.
- the United Steelworkers/Mondragon Union Co-ops Model, 1worker:1vote, Co-op Cincy.
- The emergence in 2007 of the Union Co-op Council of the U.S. Federation of Worker Co-ops.
- local developments around the country,
- tools for unions and developers working in this arena.
- How collaboration between labor unions and worker co-ops can contribute significantly to the creation of a democratized economy.

Kristen Barker: Thank you. I also want to echo this. I want to echo Rebecca's comments and I'm really excited to read the book. It's been fun to hear about the chapters. Our chapter, Ellen's and mine, is focused on bringing the Mondragon International and the United Steelworkers agreement to life. We start the chapter, again, as so many of us have stated, that Mondragon is our guiding light. For us it's because there's such a proven model really moving the needle on things like unemployment and poverty and inequality. That's what we want to see everywhere.
   Like-minded people highlighted this interconnected network, where the co-ops support each other for their long-term resilience. We think that's such a beautiful part of their deep success, along with their focus on education, and their 10 principles, and then their reinforcing structures. We talk about these sorts of things, including their social council which, when that idea comes to life in that historic Mondragon International and United Steelworkers Agreement, it comes together as a union co-op agreement. The social council becomes the Union Committee. We were excited to bring that to life in 2011. We talk about what we had and what we didn't have: we had lots of passion and purpose and grit and determination;

we did not have at that time access to funds, or much time, or many other things. Lots of people say they won't get started for not having access to those things. We highlight how those things are unnecessary.

Then we talk about our key lessons. From our early years it's been really tough. We had hoped it would be much easier. The importance of the team, how critical the team is in bringing co-ops to life, how important co-op culture is, as well as building business literacy. Having that access to financial capital, ultimately being connected to the Seed Commons, has really been a game changer for us in terms of getting capital into our co-ops and growing that movement, as well as having all sorts of allies, mentors, and community connections.

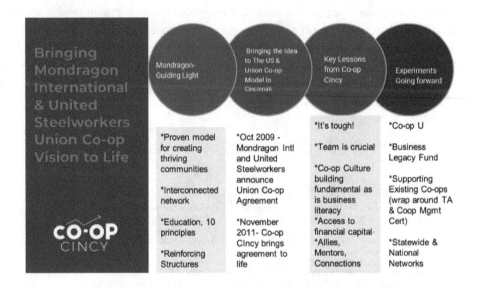

Then we highlight our experiments going forward, because while our context is 100% different than Mondragon, the Basque region is roughly the same size as the greater Cincinnati area, and thus we want to have 80,000 workers in worker owned co-ops and Democratic ESOPs in 50 years, by 2072. We talk about our four strategies and experiments through Co-op U, through our Business Legacy Fund and helping existing business owners transition to worker-owned co-ops through supporting our existing co-op network, which currently has 14 co-ops in it. That's our wraparound technical assistance and our co-op management certificate with Xavier University. Then, being parts of national networks and international networks and state networks because we're always so much more powerful together than we are apart.

Kevin O'Brien: I'm always the guy who shows up with pictures to a word party, so I apologize. I think the only thing I really felt like I could contribute today, being a sidebar to Rebecca's and Mary's chapter, is just about our small union co-op in Massachusetts and the dumb luck we found ourselves in when we partnered with a company who specializes in the US Democratic-politics merchandising industry, and they've introduced us to so many incredible partners. We've found partners on our own who all become clients. Right now we kind of feel like we're watching a storm of economic justice forming. And we feel like we're in the eye of it because when we look out we see the political candidates who use us for their merchandise, and political parties who use us.

We have all of the left-leaning political parties who are using us and then nonprofits, a small grouping of them, also the labor unions, and importantly the progressive labor unions, the newer labor unions that are forming, and all of the wonderful cooperative-development institutions. They're both our partners and our clients. Ultimately, I just want to figure out how to use our position to raise awareness about worker cooperatives with the politicians who control the purse strings, and figure out ways to make them more aware of worker cooperatives and all the socioeconomic benefits. If there's anybody who wants to help me work on that, I would greatly appreciate your inputs.

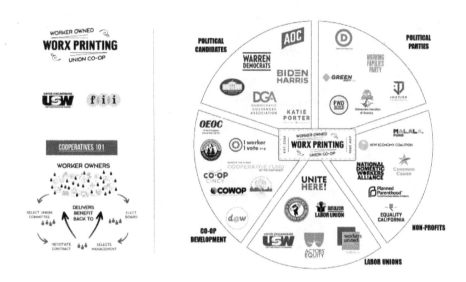

I also want to throw in a plug for Co-op Cincy — next Monday, we're going to be doing worker-ownership training with our new owners, and we're going to be using this wonderful book that they published and gave to the world. So thank you Co-op Cincy and thank all of you for doing this work. It makes us feel less lonely when we're toiling behind our printing presses and it's just great to be a part of this call and this community.

Terry Lewis: I will tell you that I cannot wait to read this book, having listened to all of you. I really mean it. So, I'm going to talk about my chapter and I'm going to talk about the city of Detroit in the context of the creation of an organization to build worker ownership, technical assistance, building cooperatives, creating a network. The context in which we're working is the city of Detroit, and it's a very specific context. My chapter talks about Detroit, its decline, its drastically fallen population, its being the largest municipal bankruptcy filing in the history of the US, huge amounts of residential and commercial property abandonment, and especially a highly distressed population. That's the context in which C2BE, the Center for Community Based Enterprise, operates. I talk about the organization itself, the ideas and its history and how it evolved and its challenges. Its mission is to build a sustainable, more equitable and inclusive living-wage local economy by developing a cooperating network of worker-owned businesses and increasing the number of worker owners.

You can see and feel the vision of Mondragon in that mission statement, right? We tend to say internally we're building Mondragon in Detroit — our version. We start out with a different notion, a not cookie-cutter notion of what a community-based enterprise is. We're not wedded to a specific cooperative, or cooperative form. We require a sustainable business or business idea involving the collaboration of multiple individuals through worker ownership or some other form of collective ownership. The enterprise must be rooted in the community. It has to pay living wages and be willing to participate in a network of similar enterprises. The notion of just work, and by that I mean not "just working," but "justice working," which adds an expression of social justice. Then the notion of a network accommodating a society different from Mondragon in structure and culture.

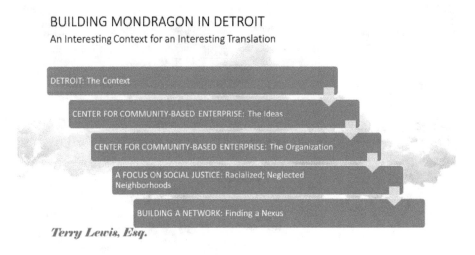

BUILDING MONDRAGON IN DETROIT
An Interesting Context for an Interesting Translation

DETROIT: The Context

CENTER FOR COMMUNITY-BASED ENTERPRISE: The Ideas

CENTER FOR COMMUNITY-BASED ENTERPRISE: The Organization

A FOCUS ON SOCIAL JUSTICE: Racialized; Neglected Neighborhoods

BUILDING A NETWORK: Finding a Nexus

Terry Lewis, Esq.

C2BE was founded in 2007 by an ESOP lawyer, Deborah Groban Olson, and three of its first five staff members were lawyers. We have a real legal focus, but C2BE got its first funding to do education within the surrounding community, mostly in Detroit. Then we got substantially more grant-based funding to implement the creation of C2BE's community based-enterprises. Our original focus was on community based start-ups, which anybody who has done a community-based start-up, or anybody who has done a co-op start-up knows, is the hardest work there is, and I'm grateful that there are a bunch of chapters that deal with exactly that.

We looked at shifting our focus to add fee-based activity, and to build a balance between start-ups and conversions, and to build relationships with other economic-development organizations and local governments. We did not have to recreate the wheel in order to serve our clients whom we regard as our partners. We call them project partners, and we do not engage with anybody who is not willing to engage with us. Partner-clients have to have a driver within their organization. They have to be committed to making this happen. We've added fiscal-agency support for community organizations, but in addition to building strict worker-owned enterprises, we have also continued to foster community-owned enterprises, art-creating enterprises, and also a little bit in the way of service cooperatives. We have a wheelhouse that's relatively large. I focus on a lot of the lessons learned in terms of developing crispness of operations, scaling, and branding. I want to address specifically the focus on social justice that C2BE has expressly added to what it sees itself as being, because the city of Detroit and other neglected communities within the state of Michigan are focuses of social injustice.

In Detroit we have a highly racialized city. Its population is 89.5% black. It is the blackest major city in the country. It is full of neglected neighborhoods. There has been an exodus of population, a decline. From 1950 to now, we have lost two-thirds of our population, and that means vacant land and vacant properties. We have an inadequate public transportation system. We have huge unemployment well above the state's, and Michigan's is a little higher than the national average. We have an inadequate public school system and we have an extractive notion of economic development being carried on within the city of Detroit and the Detroit metro area, and in Michigan at large. I think a lot of other people have addressed that notion and why it's not good enough. So I'm grateful for those other chapters.

Finally, I want to talk about building a network, because building a network in Detroit is really, really, really, really, really different from building a network in Mondragon. It's my understanding that the church created a nexus right for its network, and that all of the cooperatives were industrial cooperatives and they shared an outline in terms of their structure and their function.

Well, that's not what's going on with C2BE. That's not what's going on in the city of Detroit. That's not what's going on in the US, but I'm just focusing on what we do. We have three potential nexuses.

First, by industry: when C2BE thought about creating its network, it thought about having nodes that were by industry. We have a developing fabrics industry in the city of Detroit, sewing and fabric creation. It's a nice part of what is happening in Detroit, and a lot of our original project partners were focused on that specific thing. But we have a bunch of other things, artist cooperatives, service cooperatives, a bunch of other ways of looking at their coming together as a community-based enterprise.

Second, there's also the notion of a neighborhood in Detroit as a nexus for cooperative-network building. We have some very vibrant community organizations in the city. We have some very high-functioning communities in Detroit, and we partner with them to be nexus of potential co-op network foci, right?

Third, we have the notion of providing shared services to those cooperative community-based enterprises (CBEs) that we create.

We'll probably end up using some combination of all of these three things to build a network. But that's where we're going, that's what we're doing. There's a lot of movement between ideas, operationalization practicum in what we're doing, and how to scale, and how we are currently facing and using the notion of the "silver tsunami" that is the loss of ownership of small, independent enterprises to achieve funding from various municipal and county organizations to do succession planning and conversion.

Martin Lowery: Thank you. Well, first of all this has been very enjoyable and enlightening. There is no way that I can concisely summarize or synopsize what's been said. So I have two thoughts in concluding today, and then of course we'll talk further. I'm hearing four levels of conversation, and they go from the macro to the very micro.

Overall, I think everyone's saying that looking to Mondragon is inspirational and not simply something to copy. And at the same time, I'm hearing that there are aspects of Mondragon history and Mondragon today that are very much transferable into the US environment. But generally what we're looking at is the inspiration of the Mondragon story.

At the macro level, at the broadest level, there's specific interest in how the cooperative model can overcome neoliberalism and right-wing populism. And I believe, Dan, it was you who talked about the idea that this may be the time in the US for systemic change, and that the cooperative approach certainly has great potential in that regard. And you can look at Julian's presentation and recognize that's actually happening with the Preston Model. So there is precedent there that says we could very seriously embrace the idea that the cooperative model, and I'll talk in more detail about specific interrelationships there, and what's needed in the US to move beyond the neoliberal culture.

In particular, I like the comment about right-wing populism because it is a major threat, as we know, and has to be overcome. When you look at the red and blue map, there's a great deal to do in rural areas, in urban areas of course, but a really great deal to do in rural areas. I think we know that historically the cooperative model has been very, very useful in rural communities, starting with agriculture.

I'm also hearing at this broadest level that we need a new vision for development, and to quote Jésus María, if we look at Mondragon — that was a vision for a new kind of society. And that's really what I'm hearing from a number of folks now. That is a very broad hope or vision for the future. As Michael said, we're trying to move not a long-term, 40-year vision, but more of — what is the next greatest thing that we see in terms of the use of cooperatives in the US economy? So that's tier one, the highest tier.

The second level, I think, comes in particular from Sarah and Jason, and Brian also, on moral values. The idea that we need to really focus on what is the big unifying frame that brings us all together. Sarah's idea is mutual solidarity. Jason's idea is more along the lines of the commons or community. But they do come together in that sense of people recognizing that they can meet their needs through relationships that are trustworthy, honest, and beneficial to them personally, but also to the community at large. And then if you add into that segment Brian's comments about moral values, the moral theologian speaking, there's no doubt in my mind that when you look at the cooperative values, they really do have a sense of morality about them. We treat with human beings, and of course, "HUMANITY @ WORK & LIFE" is the working title of the book, and that fits very nicely.

Then the third level, getting into more of the "Where are we going with all of this?" I was hearing cooperation among cooperatives, and as Terry just said, networking beyond simply cooperative networks into a sense of what we understand can be accomplished through community networks and networks of communities. We're working independently of this discussion on the whole Principle 6 cooperation among cooperatives, what can be done there.

And there's a lot of learning that's going on, and much of it is in the context of what Terry said, you really have to work hard to understand what the value proposition is when you're talking with another entity, whether it's a cooperative or not. So I think that there's a great deal to be looked at.

And Kevin, my goodness, the client base with Worx that you presented in that graphic really shows a fascinating potential for the worker-cooperative movement in thinking about a client base that is driven by a desire to work with an organization that has a basic value system associated with the work that's being done.

And then we get to what I would call the practical level that is focusing specifically on worker-owned cooperatives. I think that's going be a very important point to be made to the readers — that, yes, this is about cooperatives in general and the future of cooperatives in the US and the world, but it's the worker-cooperative movement, the worker-ownership part, that is really driving the whole discussion and that has to do with the nature of work and its relationship to community. The question of workplace democracy, the role of trade unions in workplace democracy, and how that relates to cooperatives.

Esteban had a very interesting notion of a national retirement program for worker cooperatives. This kind of brings us both to a network of networks, as well as to scale. I notice that there is some difference of opinion about the value, the importance of scale, and the negativity in some sense about scaling too much and losing that community, as a central notion in this practical area.

I've got to say, I'm really, really impressed with what Dan is saying about the future of manufacturing and the industrial base in the United States. I think this can be emphasized from the point of view as he's saying, of the fact that we're going to see significant turnover of the baby boomers. The question is, can you establish a system that really does allow for a serious approach to gaining recognition, that worker ownership of manufacturing plants that will otherwise go to a vendor capitalist or venture capitalist is the way to maintain workplace democracy.

I think that pretty much covers the four levels. I know I've missed a number of things that have been said in each of the presentations, but I would say that unless there was a lot of pushback on it, that the synopsis at the end could very well work off of those four levels:

- The broadest sense of "Can we make a difference in creating a different kind of society, equal justice for all?"
- The idea that we as cooperators need to be clear on terminology and a sense of *who we are* that can reverberate in multiple communities.
- The level of cooperation among cooperatives, as well as broader networking that creates an outreach potential that we may not feel that we have today.
- And then the great practical ideas as to how we move the worker cooperative movement to a much higher level of impact in the world.

And let me stop there. Would anyone like to respond or comment?

Michael Peck: Martin, I've had the honor of being associated with you for almost 20 years and every time you speak, I learn something. This was a great summary and a really important and helpful frame, but also right in line with your in-person intervention in the atrium of the United Steelworkers headquarters building in Pittsburgh, March 26, 2012, when you, representing the highest echelons of the US cooperative community, spoke out publicly in support of the USW-Mondragon International USA-OEOC union-coop template launch and again made us feel proud and inspired (youtube.com/watch?v=N_TSwRKZ6KU). We will always be deep-down grateful for this legacy, partnered with your expressed vision today, that neither we nor history will ever forget. We're so grateful that you could share time with us and contribute.

And in that "**HUMANITY @ WORK & LIFE**" context, I would like to thank everybody who participated for all your incredible ideas and contributions, collaboration, solidarity, friendship and living, lived values. You have no idea how important it is in doing something like this to receive such support and outreach from the "everybody-ness" of aligned community.

Julian just finished writing a great book on the Preston Model last year and so he knows from firsthand experience what it takes ,and so do many others who have put together incredible initiatives, probably everybody on this call. The final point for me is that **HUMANITY @ WORK & LIFE** is truly a global endeavor. Of our 36 current collaborators, 26 are from the United States, including both co-editors, and the remaining 11 are from the UK, Germany, South Korea, Canada, and Spain's Basque Country, and that includes five associated with Mondragon. Lately we have made major strides in Asia and will focus in 2023 on Latin America-Caribbean and Africa. So, 36 collaborators from six countries on three continents and this living, inclusive book is just getting started.

Christina Clamp: We are dedicating the book to Chuck Snyder of NCB who introduced me to Michael Peck with this kind of a collaboration in mind. We thank Kevin O'Brien for masterminding the book cover art in collaboration with Co-op Cincy. This has been such an amazing and interesting two hours to have to shepherd where my multitasking skills were definitely put to the test and to the limit, but it's been a real pleasure working with all of you right from the get-go.

Julian Manley: Thanks much, thank you everyone, and thank you for your time. Thank you, Chris and Michael, you are the most fantastic experts in Mondragon, and you're the most humble people around. The one thing you forget to say is to thank yourselves.

Martin Lowery's Conclusions Post-Session

Throughout this excellent collection of essays, there is inspiration to be found in the history and current successes of Mondragon. Much can be learned from the Mondragon experience in expanding the cooperative ecosystem in the United States. None of the authors is arguing to imitate the exact model, but all would agree that there are many lessons to be learned by studying and reflecting upon the Mondragon experience.

Reading these essays from the perspective of the immediate future of cooperatives in the US, there is a consistent focus on at least four major areas:

- **Cooperative positioning in the US economy:** Cooperatives have a unique opportunity in coming years to represent a significant option to the dominant neoliberal tradition. With a laser focus on a new vision of community development and with a commitment to an inclusive and equitable society, US cooperatives can replicate the goal of Mondragon's founder — not to defeat capitalism, but rather to fully serve the economic and social needs of communities through the cooperative model.

- **Clarity on cooperative identity:** The cooperative movement must embrace a consistent, unifying framework that can be clearly communicated and can be the foundation of new cooperative education opportunities. This will likely revolve around mutual solidarity and commitment to community and can be derived from the Mondragon values and the internationally accepted cooperative values of mutual self-help, self-responsibility, democracy, equality, equity, and solidarity, as well as the ethical values of honesty, openness, social responsibility, and caring for others. The key will be to find a common vocabulary that clearly describes the unique, value-based nature of cooperative enterprise.

- **Leveraging the power of networks:** Many cooperatives in the US today are focused primarily on the management of their enterprises. Greater impact can be achieved by cooperation among cooperatives both within and across sectors as well as by developing new relationships with community-based organizations, especially those committed to expanding the social and solidarity economy.

- **Focusing greater attention on worker-ownership:** Workplace democracy is a growing imperative throughout the US today and represents a critical dimension in achieving a truly inclusive economy. Worker-owned cooperatives will play a central role in this discussion, particularly as they choose to affiliate with trade unions and the labor movement in general. Examples abound, as highlighted in these essays; and a great opportunity lies ahead for dramatic growth in worker-owned cooperatives, particularly through the mutually-beneficial acquisition and conversion of existing small and medium-sized businesses, as well as the opportunity to sustain large manufacturing enterprises. The preservation of the US industrial base through the conversion of manufacturing facilities to worker ownership holds significant potential in this regard.

With a roadmap for success now firmly in hand, the authors and editors are to be congratulated for initiating what promises to be a wide-ranging discussion among educators and students, cooperatives and cooperators, public officials and social agencies on the critical role of cooperatives — and worker-owned cooperatives in particular — in the creation of an inclusive US and global economy with liberty, equity, and justice for all.

November 11, 2022, 10:00-12:00 EST, recorded live, hosted by Christina Clamp